GUARDIANS
OF THE GALAXY

WRITERS
DAN ABNETT & ANDY LANNING

PENCILERS
PAUL PELLETIER (#1-7), BRAD WALKER (#8-10) & WES CRAIG (#11-12)

with CARLOS MAGNO (#9)

INKERS
RICK MAGYAR (#1-7), VICTOR OLAZABA (#8-10) & WES CRAIG (#11-12)

with JACK PURCELL (#9), LIVESAY (#10) & RODNEY RAMOS (#10-11)

COLORISTS
NATHAN FAIRBAIRN (#1-3), GURU-eFX (#4-6) & WIL QUINTANA (#7-12)

with BRUNO HANG (#9)

LETTERERS
VC'S JOE CARAMAGNA

COVER ART
CLINT LANGLEY (#1-10), DAVID YARDIN & BRUNO HANG (#11)
and PAUL RENAUD (#12)

ASSISTANT EDITORS
LAUREN SANKOVITCH, LAUREN HENRY & MICHAEL HORWITZ

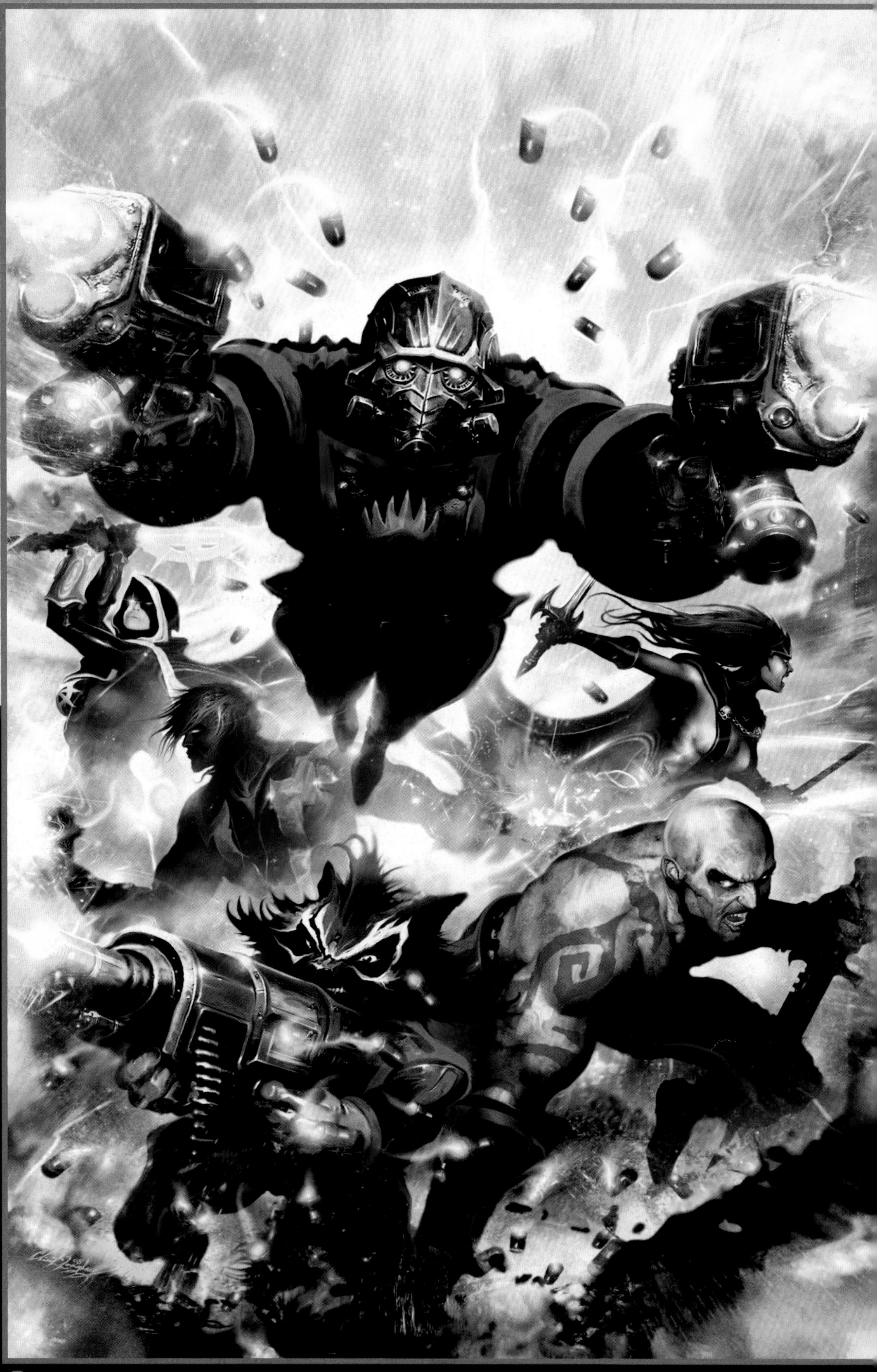

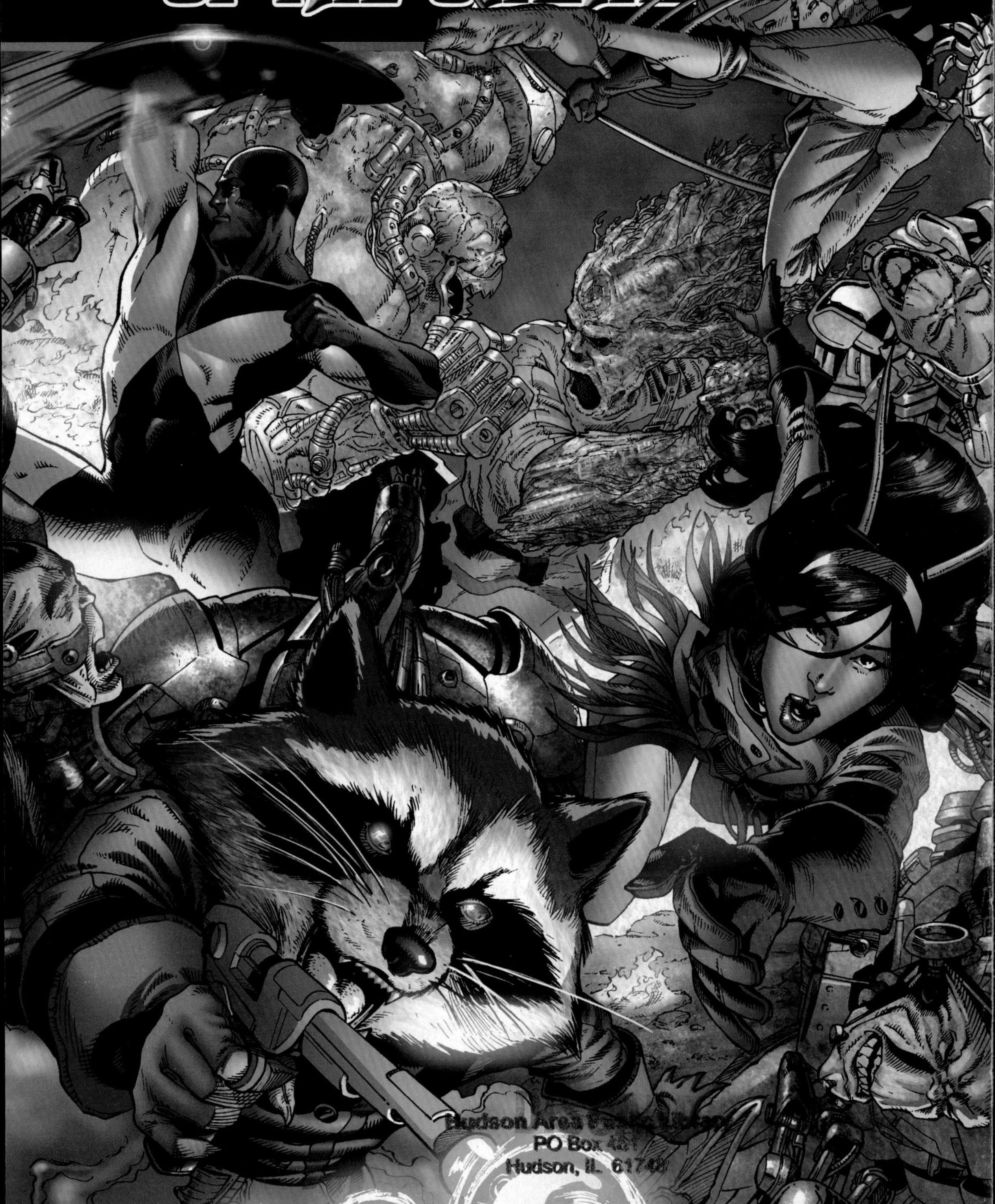

BY ABNETT & LANNING

COVER ARTIST: Clint Langley

LAYOUT: Jeph York
BOOK DESIGNER: Nelson Ribeiro

COLLECTION EDITOR: Mark D. Beazley
DIGITAL TRAFFIC COORDINATOR: Joe Hochstein
ASSOCIATE MANAGING EDITOR: Alex Starbuck
EDITOR, SPECIAL PROJECTS: Jennifer Grünwald
SENIOR EDITOR, SPECIAL PROJECTS: Jeff Youngquist
SVP PRINT, SALES & MARKETING: David Gabriel

EDITOR IN CHIEF: Axel Alonso
CHIEF CREATIVE OFFICER: Joe Quesada
PUBLISHER: Dan Buckley
EXECUTIVE PRODUCER: Alan Fine

GUARDIANS OF THE GALAXY BY ABNETT & LANNING: THE COMPLETE COLLECTION VOL. 1. Contains material originally published in magazine form as GUARDIANS OF THE GALAXY #1-12. Second printing 2014. ISE 978-0-7851-9064-6. Published by MARVEL WORLDWIDE, INC., a subsidiary of MARVEL ENTERTAINMENT, LLC. OFFICE OF PUBLICATION: 135 West 50th Street, New York, NY 10020. Copyright © 2008, 2009 and 20 Marvel Characters, Inc. All rights reserved. All characters featured in this issue and the distinctive names and likenesses thereof, and all related indicia are trademarks of Marvel Characters, Inc. No similarity between a of the names, characters, persons, and/or institutions in this magazine with those of any living or dead person or institution is intended, and any such similarity which may exist is purely coincidental. **Printed in Cana** ALAN FINE, EVP - Office of the President, Marvel Worldwide, Inc. and EVP & CMO Marvel Characters B.V.; DAN BUCKLEY, Publisher & President - Print, Animation & Digital Divisions; JOE QUESADA, Chief Creative Offic TOM BREVOORT, SVP of Publishing; DAVID BOGART, SVP of Operations & Procurement, Publishing; C.B. CEBULSKI, SVP of Creator & Content Development; DAVID GABRIEL, SVP Print, Sales & Marketing; JIM O'KEE VP of Operations & Logistics; DAN CARR, Executive Director of Publishing Technology; SUSAN CRESPI, Editorial Operations Manager; ALEX MORALES, Publishing Operations Manager; STAN LEE, Chairman Emeritus. information regarding advertising in Marvel Comics or on Marvel.com, please contact Niza Disla, Director of Marvel Partnerships, at ndisla@marvel.com. For Marvel subscription inquiries, please call 800-217-91 **Manufactured between 7/30/2014 and 9/1/14 by SOLISCO PRINTERS, SCOTT, QC, CANADA.**

1 0 9 8 7 6 5 4 3 2

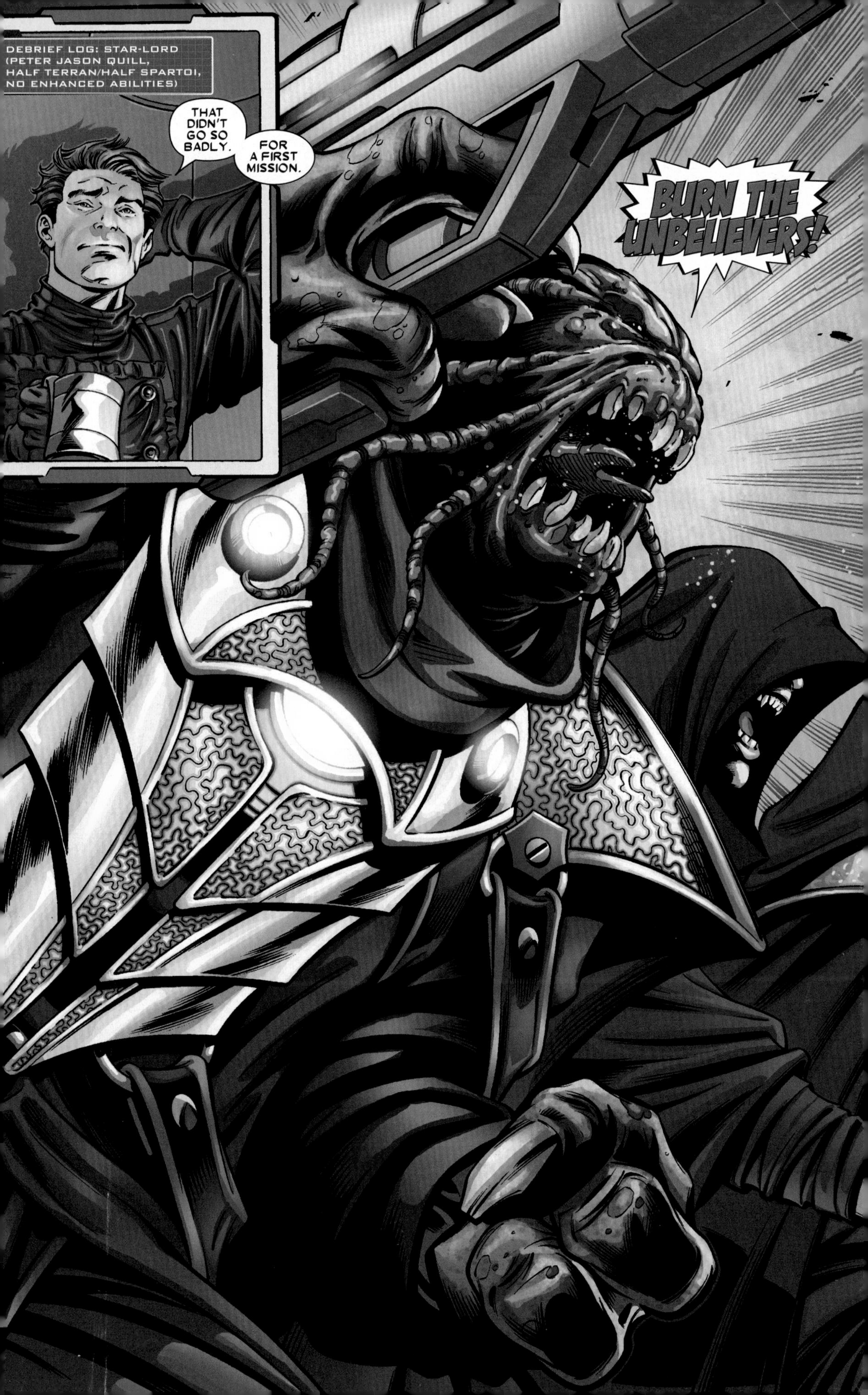

DEBRIEF LOG: STAR-LORD (PETER JASON QUILL, HALF TERRAN/HALF SPARTOI, NO ENHANCED ABILITIES)
THAT DIDN'T GO SO BADLY.
FOR A FIRST MISSION.
BURN THE UNBELIEVERS!

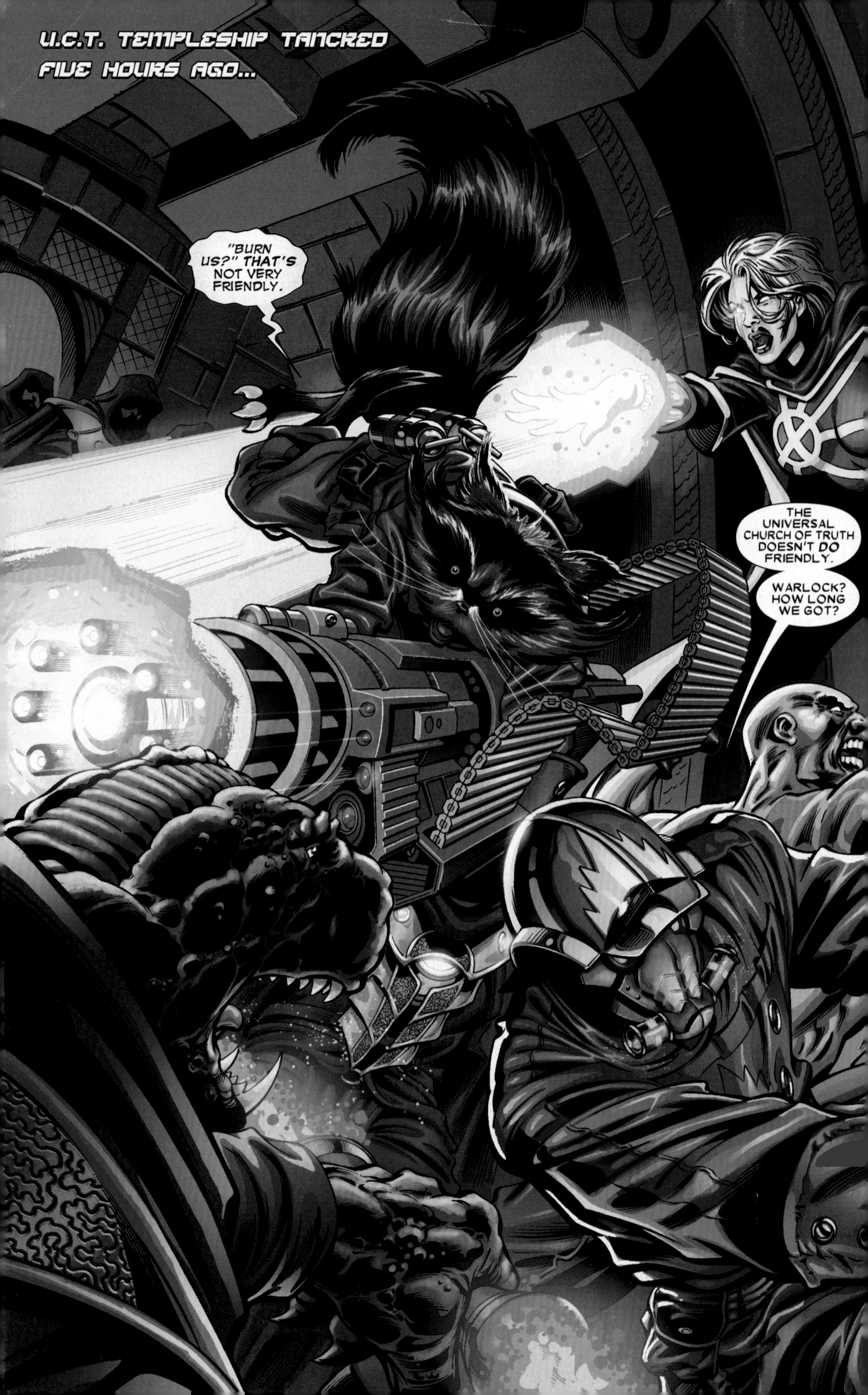
U.C.T. TEMPLESHIP TANCRED
FIVE HOURS AGO...
"BURN US?" THAT'S NOT VERY FRIENDLY.
THE UNIVERSAL CHURCH OF TRUTH DOESN'T DO FRIENDLY.
WARLOCK? HOW LONG WE GOT?

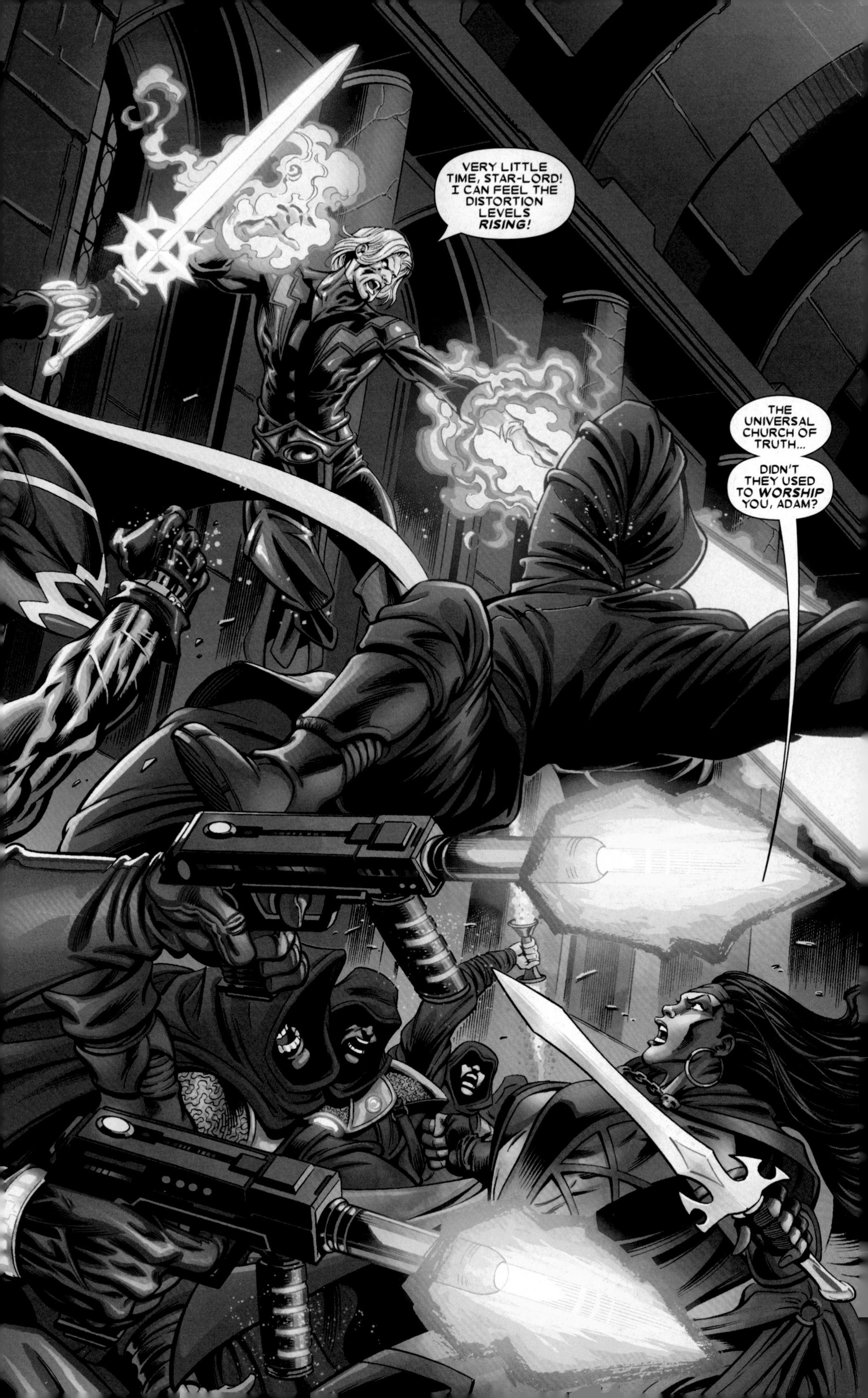
VERY LITTLE TIME, STAR-LORD! I CAN FEEL THE DISTORTION LEVELS RISING!
THE UNIVERSAL CHURCH OF TRUTH...
DIDN'T THEY USED TO WORSHIP YOU, ADAM?

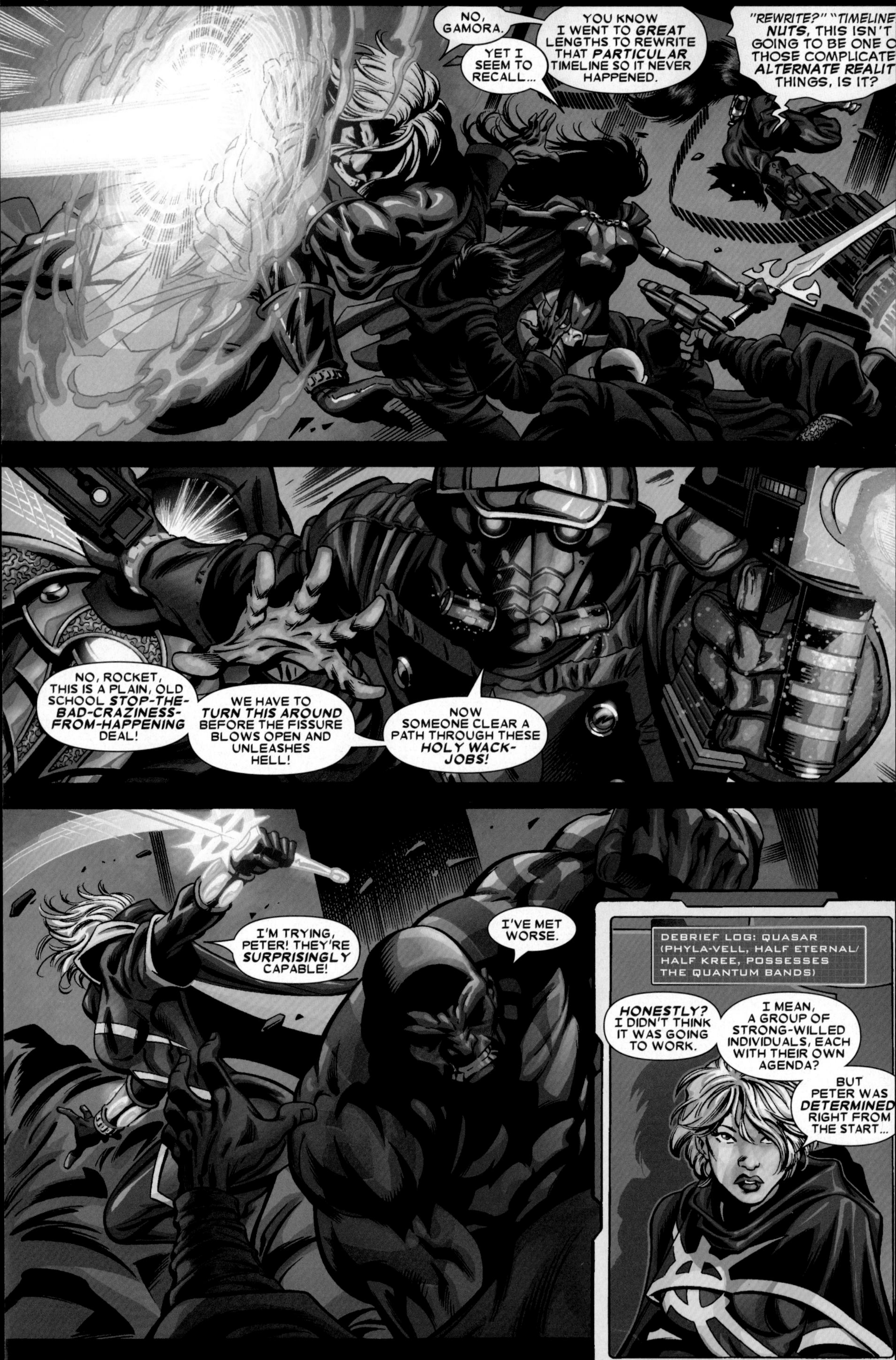
NO, GAMORA.
YET I SEEM TO RECALL...
YOU KNOW I WENT TO GREAT LENGTHS TO REWRITE THAT PARTICULAR TIMELINE SO IT NEVER HAPPENED.
"REWRITE?" "TIMELINE NUTS, THIS ISN'T GOING TO BE ONE O THOSE COMPLICATE ALTERNATE REALIT THINGS, IS IT?
NO, ROCKET, THIS IS A PLAIN, OLD SCHOOL STOP-THE-BAD-CRAZINESS-FROM-HAPPENING DEAL!
WE HAVE TO TURN THIS AROUND BEFORE THE FISSURE BLOWS OPEN AND UNLEASHES HELL!
NOW SOMEONE CLEAR A PATH THROUGH THESE HOLY WACK-JOBS!
I'M TRYING, PETER! THEY'RE SURPRISINGLY CAPABLE!
I'VE MET WORSE.
DEBRIEF LOG: QUASAR (PHYLA-VELL, HALF ETERNAL/ HALF KREE, POSSESSES THE QUANTUM BANDS)
HONESTLY? I DIDN'T THINK IT WAS GOING TO WORK.
I MEAN, A GROUP OF STRONG-WILLED INDIVIDUALS, EACH WITH THEIR OWN AGENDA?
BUT PETER WAS DETERMINED RIGHT FROM THE START...

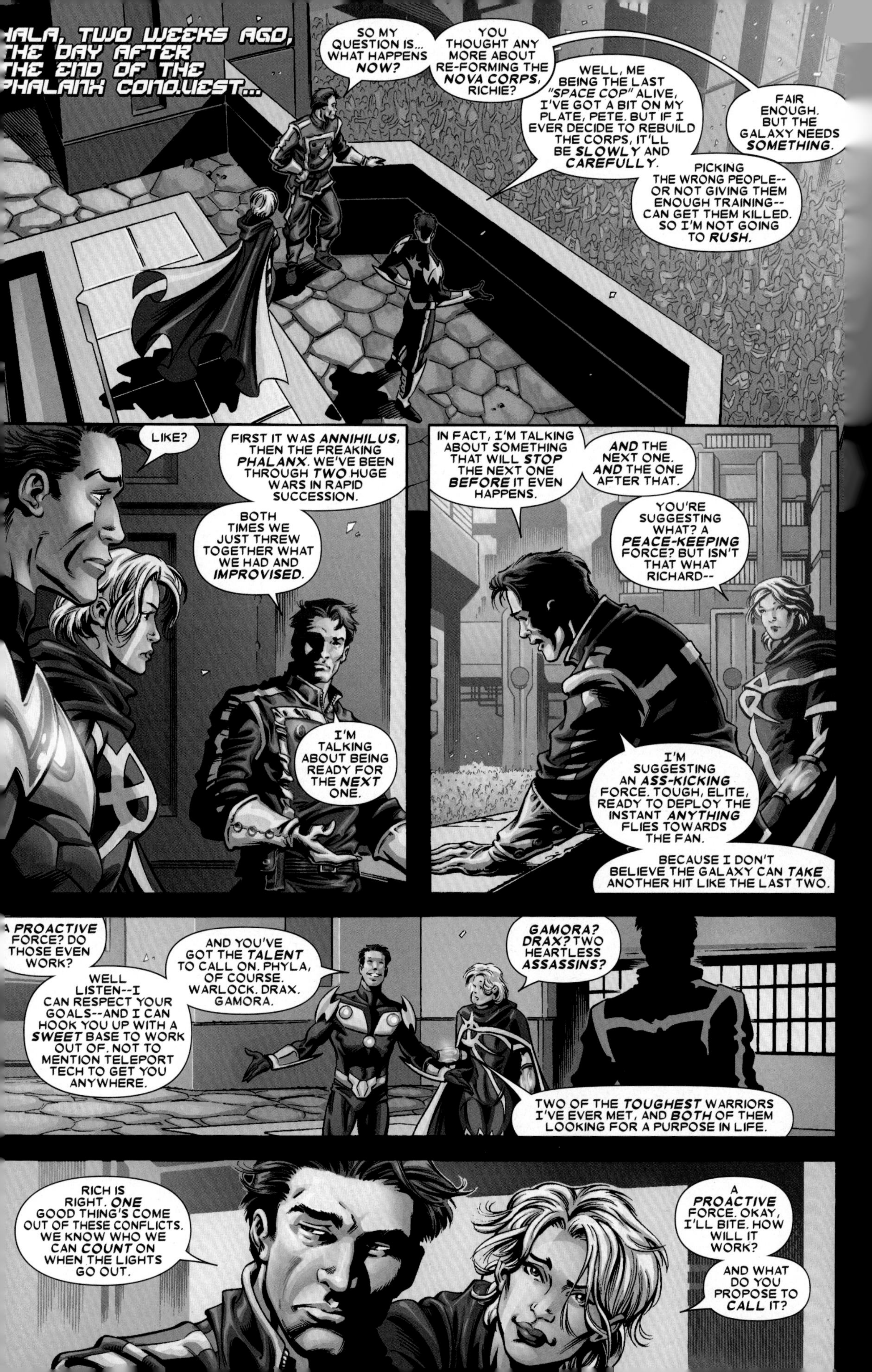
HALA, TWO WEEKS AGO, THE DAY AFTER THE END OF THE PHALANX CONQUEST...
SO MY QUESTION IS... WHAT HAPPENS NOW?
YOU THOUGHT ANY MORE ABOUT RE-FORMING THE NOVA CORPS, RICHIE?
WELL, ME BEING THE LAST "SPACE COP" ALIVE, I'VE GOT A BIT ON MY PLATE, PETE. BUT IF I EVER DECIDE TO REBUILD THE CORPS, IT'LL BE SLOWLY AND CAREFULLY.
FAIR ENOUGH. BUT THE GALAXY NEEDS SOMETHING.
PICKING THE WRONG PEOPLE--OR NOT GIVING THEM ENOUGH TRAINING--CAN GET THEM KILLED. SO I'M NOT GOING TO RUSH.
LIKE?
FIRST IT WAS ANNIHILUS, THEN THE FREAKING PHALANX. WE'VE BEEN THROUGH TWO HUGE WARS IN RAPID SUCCESSION.
BOTH TIMES WE JUST THREW TOGETHER WHAT WE HAD AND IMPROVISED.
I'M TALKING ABOUT BEING READY FOR THE NEXT ONE.
IN FACT, I'M TALKING ABOUT SOMETHING THAT WILL STOP THE NEXT ONE BEFORE IT EVEN HAPPENS.
AND THE NEXT ONE. AND THE ONE AFTER THAT.
YOU'RE SUGGESTING WHAT? A PEACE-KEEPING FORCE? BUT ISN'T THAT WHAT RICHARD--
I'M SUGGESTING AN ASS-KICKING FORCE. TOUGH, ELITE, READY TO DEPLOY THE INSTANT ANYTHING FLIES TOWARDS THE FAN.
BECAUSE I DON'T BELIEVE THE GALAXY CAN TAKE ANOTHER HIT LIKE THE LAST TWO.
A PROACTIVE FORCE? DO THOSE EVEN WORK?
WELL LISTEN--I CAN RESPECT YOUR GOALS--AND I CAN HOOK YOU UP WITH A SWEET BASE TO WORK OUT OF. NOT TO MENTION TELEPORT TECH TO GET YOU ANYWHERE.
AND YOU'VE GOT THE TALENT TO CALL ON. PHYLA, OF COURSE. WARLOCK. DRAX. GAMORA.
GAMORA? DRAX? TWO HEARTLESS ASSASSINS?
TWO OF THE TOUGHEST WARRIORS I'VE EVER MET, AND BOTH OF THEM LOOKING FOR A PURPOSE IN LIFE.
RICH IS RIGHT. ONE GOOD THING'S COME OUT OF THESE CONFLICTS. WE KNOW WHO WE CAN COUNT ON WHEN THE LIGHTS GO OUT.
A PROACTIVE FORCE. OKAY, I'LL BITE. HOW WILL IT WORK?
AND WHAT DO YOU PROPOSE TO CALL IT?

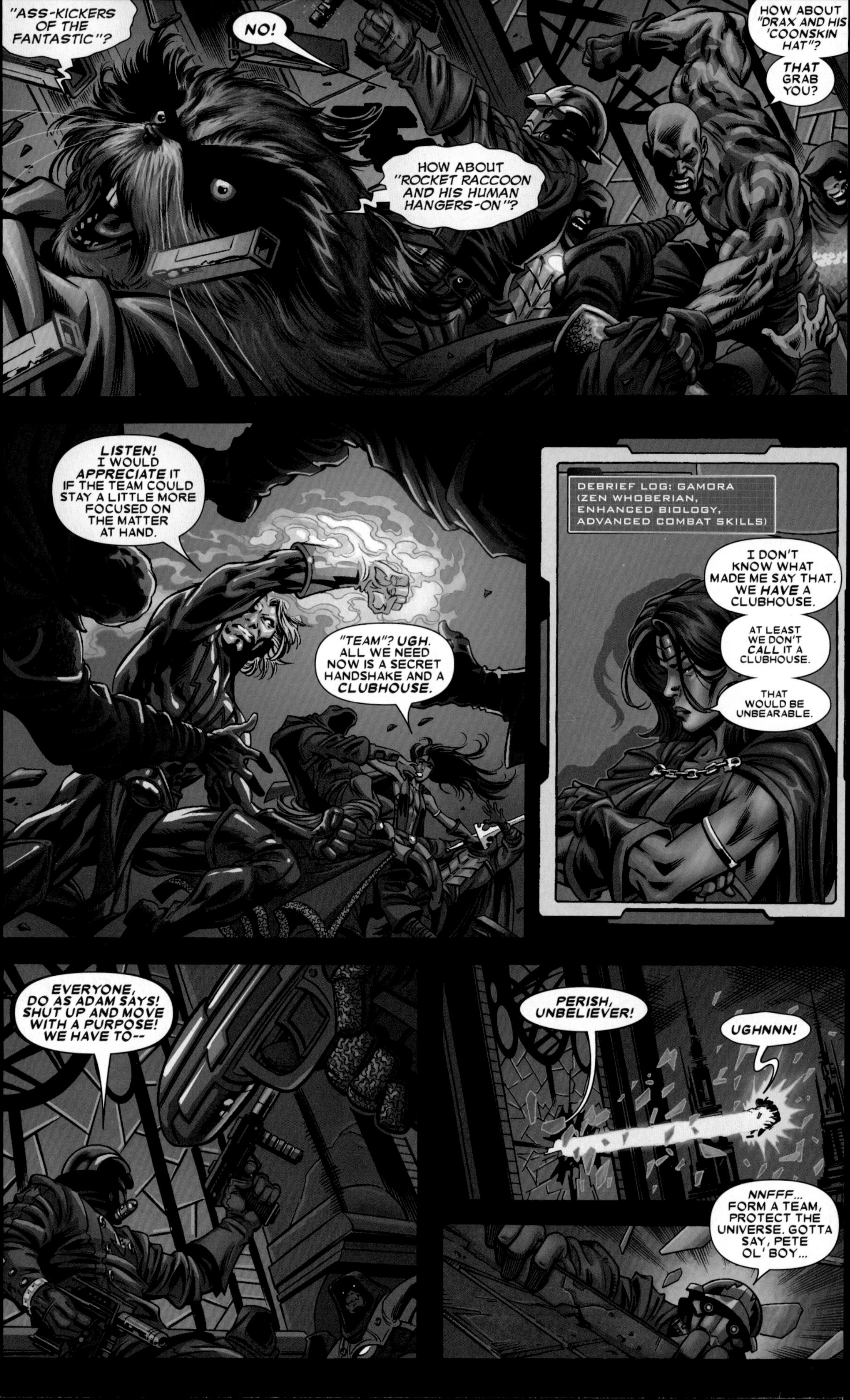
"ASS-KICKERS OF THE FANTASTIC"?
NO!
HOW ABOUT "DRAX AND HIS 'COONSKIN HAT'"?
THAT GRAB YOU?
HOW ABOUT "ROCKET RACCOON AND HIS HUMAN HANGERS-ON"?
LISTEN! I WOULD APPRECIATE IT IF THE TEAM COULD STAY A LITTLE MORE FOCUSED ON THE MATTER AT HAND.
"TEAM"? UGH. ALL WE NEED NOW IS A SECRET HANDSHAKE AND A CLUBHOUSE.
DEBRIEF LOG: GAMORA (ZEN WHOBERIAN, ENHANCED BIOLOGY, ADVANCED COMBAT SKILLS)
I DON'T KNOW WHAT MADE ME SAY THAT. WE HAVE A CLUBHOUSE.
AT LEAST WE DON'T CALL IT A CLUBHOUSE.
THAT WOULD BE UNBEARABLE.
EVERYONE, DO AS ADAM SAYS! SHUT UP AND MOVE WITH A PURPOSE! WE HAVE TO--
PERISH, UNBELIEVER!
UGHNNN!
NNFFF... FORM A TEAM, PROTECT THE UNIVERSE. GOTTA SAY, PETE OL' BOY...

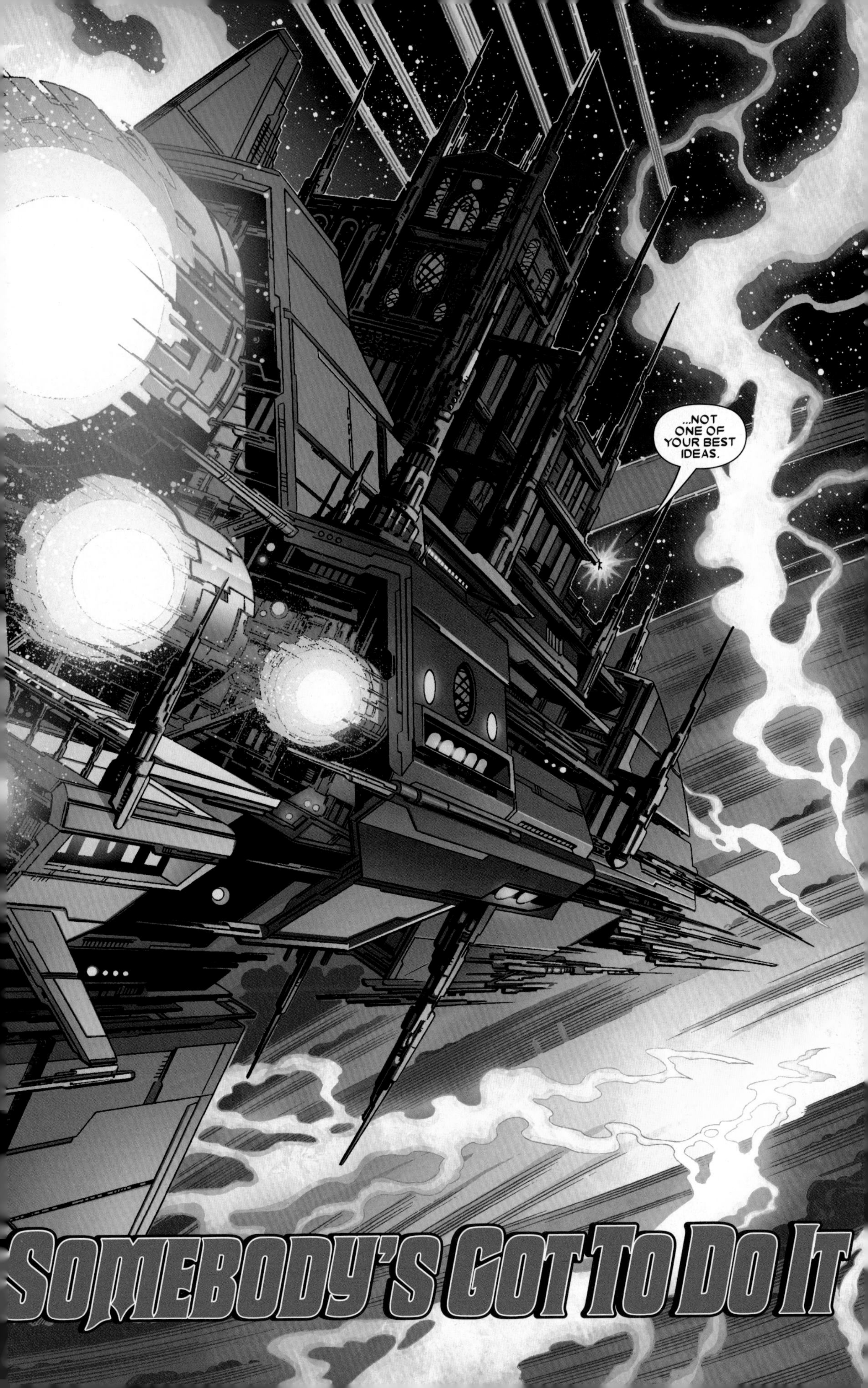

...NOT ONE OF YOUR BEST IDEAS.
SOMEBODY'S GOT TO DO IT

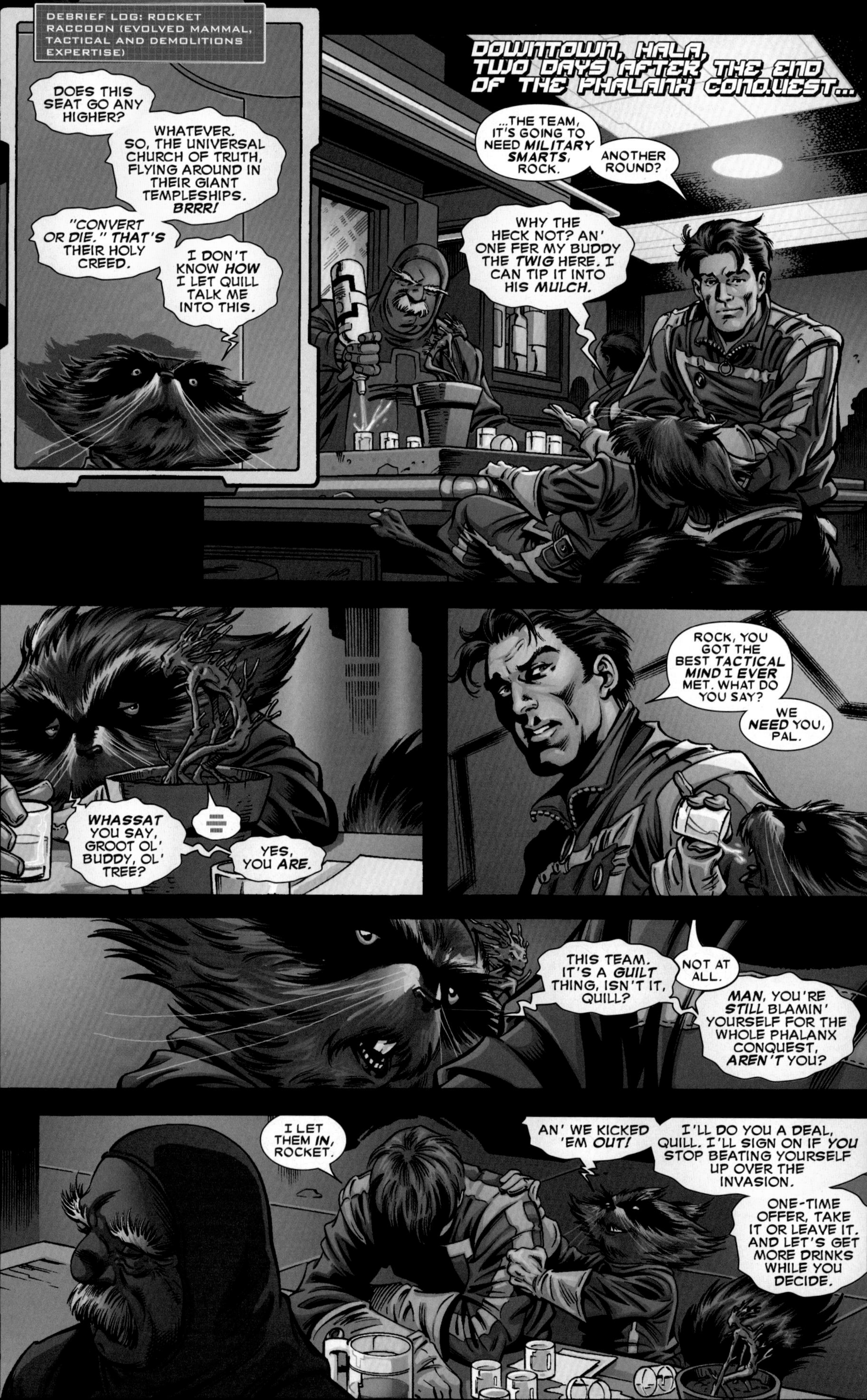
DEBRIEF LOG: ROCKET RACCOON (EVOLVED MAMMAL, TACTICAL AND DEMOLITIONS EXPERTISE)
DOES THIS SEAT GO ANY HIGHER?
WHATEVER. SO, THE UNIVERSAL CHURCH OF TRUTH, FLYING AROUND IN THEIR GIANT TEMPLESHIPS. BRRR!
"CONVERT OR DIE." THAT'S THEIR HOLY CREED.
I DON'T KNOW HOW I LET QUILL TALK ME INTO THIS.
DOWNTOWN, HALA, TWO DAYS AFTER THE END OF THE PHALANX CONQUEST...
...THE TEAM, IT'S GOING TO NEED MILITARY SMARTS, ROCK.
ANOTHER ROUND?
WHY THE HECK NOT? AN' ONE FER MY BUDDY THE TWIG HERE. I CAN TIP IT INTO HIS MULCH.
WHASSAT YOU SAY, GROOT OL' BUDDY, OL' TREE?
YES, YOU ARE.
ROCK, YOU GOT THE BEST TACTICAL MIND I EVER MET. WHAT DO YOU SAY?
WE NEED YOU, PAL.
THIS TEAM. IT'S A GUILT THING, ISN'T IT, QUILL?
NOT AT ALL.
MAN, YOU'RE STILL BLAMIN' YOURSELF FOR THE WHOLE PHALANX CONQUEST, AREN'T YOU?
I LET THEM IN, ROCKET.
AN' WE KICKED 'EM OUT!
I'LL DO YOU A DEAL, QUILL. I'LL SIGN ON IF YOU STOP BEATING YOURSELF UP OVER THE INVASION.
ONE-TIME OFFER, TAKE IT OR LEAVE IT. AND LET'S GET MORE DRINKS WHILE YOU DECIDE.

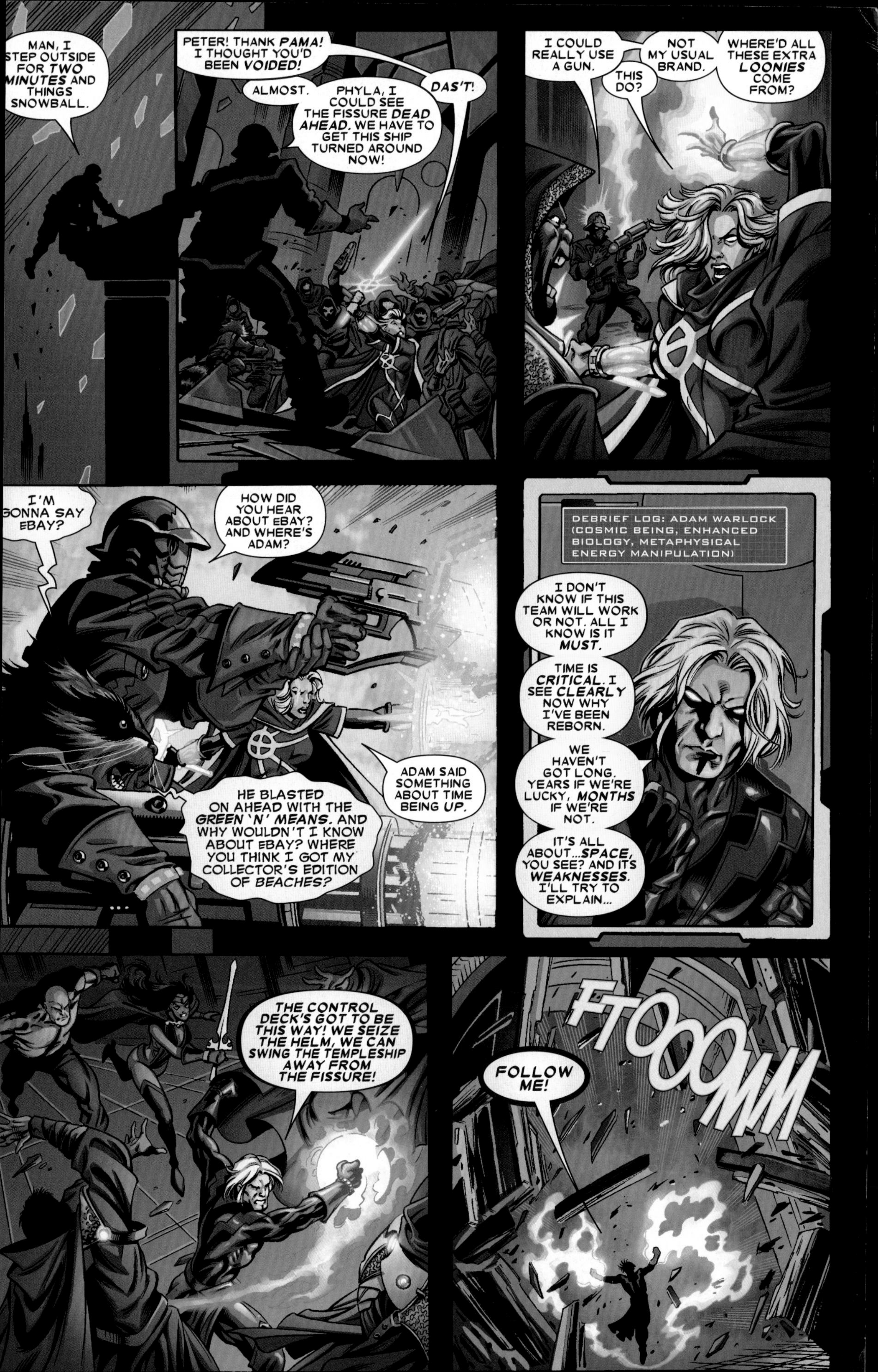

MAN, I STEP OUTSIDE FOR TWO MINUTES AND THINGS SNOWBALL.
PETER! THANK PAMA! I THOUGHT YOU'D BEEN VOIDED!
ALMOST.
PHYLA, I COULD SEE THE FISSURE DEAD AHEAD. WE HAVE TO GET THIS SHIP TURNED AROUND NOW!
DAS'T!
I COULD REALLY USE A GUN.
THIS DO?
NOT MY USUAL BRAND.
WHERE'D ALL THESE EXTRA LOONIES COME FROM?
I'M GONNA SAY EBAY?
HOW DID YOU HEAR ABOUT EBAY? AND WHERE'S ADAM?
ADAM SAID SOMETHING ABOUT TIME BEING UP.
HE BLASTED ON AHEAD WITH THE GREEN 'N' MEANS. AND WHY WOULDN'T I KNOW ABOUT EBAY? WHERE YOU THINK I GOT MY COLLECTOR'S EDITION OF BEACHES?
DEBRIEF LOG: ADAM WARLOCK (COSMIC BEING, ENHANCED BIOLOGY, METAPHYSICAL ENERGY MANIPULATION)
I DON'T KNOW IF THIS TEAM WILL WORK OR NOT. ALL I KNOW IS IT MUST.
TIME IS CRITICAL. I SEE CLEARLY NOW WHY I'VE BEEN REBORN.
WE HAVEN'T GOT LONG. YEARS IF WE'RE LUCKY, MONTHS IF WE'RE NOT.
IT'S ALL ABOUT...SPACE, YOU SEE? AND ITS WEAKNESSES. I'LL TRY TO EXPLAIN...
THE CONTROL DECK'S GOT TO BE THIS WAY! WE SEIZE THE HELM, WE CAN SWING THE TEMPLESHIP AWAY FROM THE FISSURE!
FTOOOMM
FOLLOW ME!

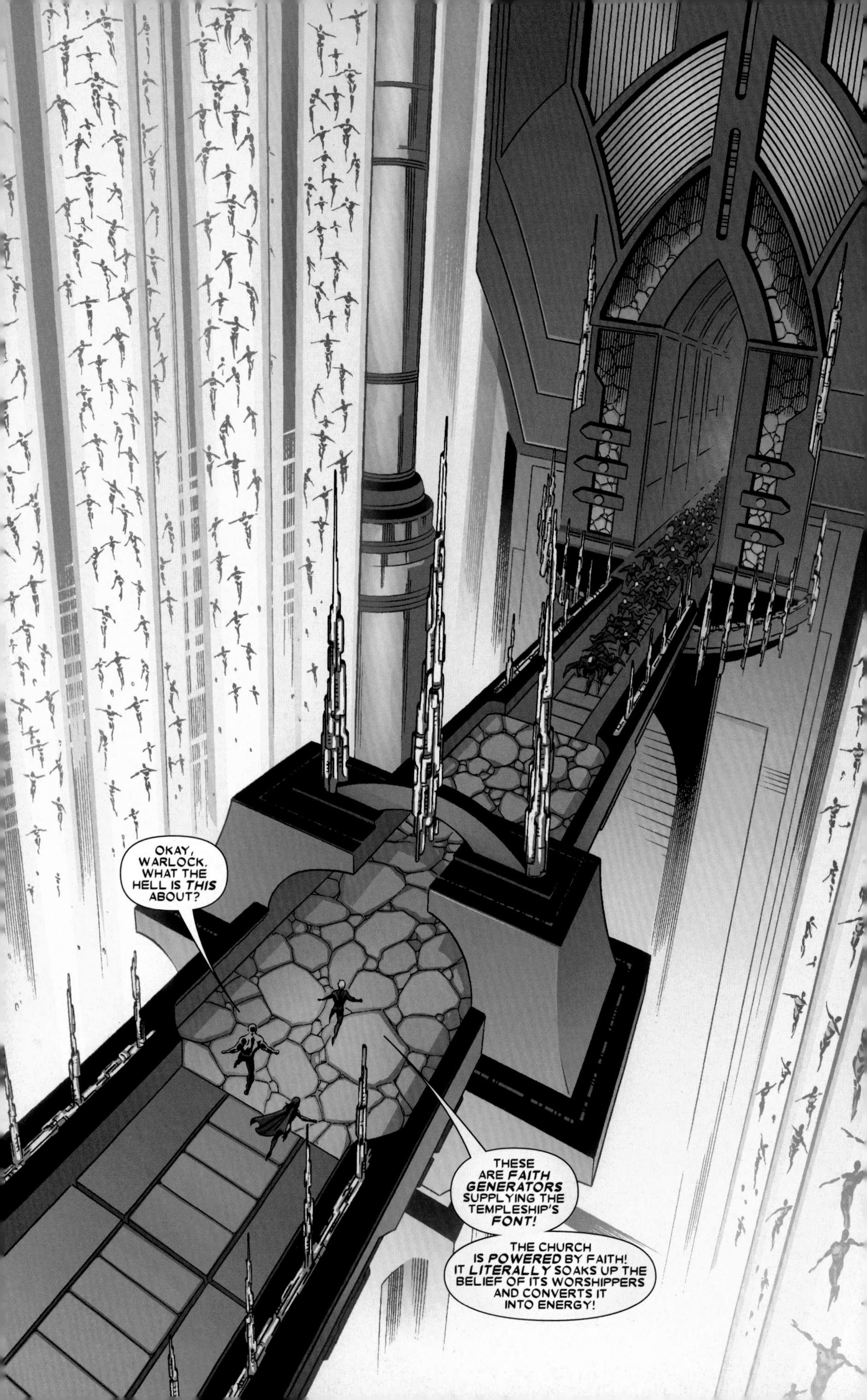
OKAY, WARLOCK. WHAT THE HELL IS *THIS* ABOUT?
THESE ARE *FAITH GENERATORS* SUPPLYING THE TEMPLESHIP'S *FONT!*
THE CHURCH IS *POWERED* BY FAITH! IT *LITERALLY* SOAKS UP THE BELIEF OF ITS WORSHIPPERS AND CONVERTS IT INTO ENERGY!

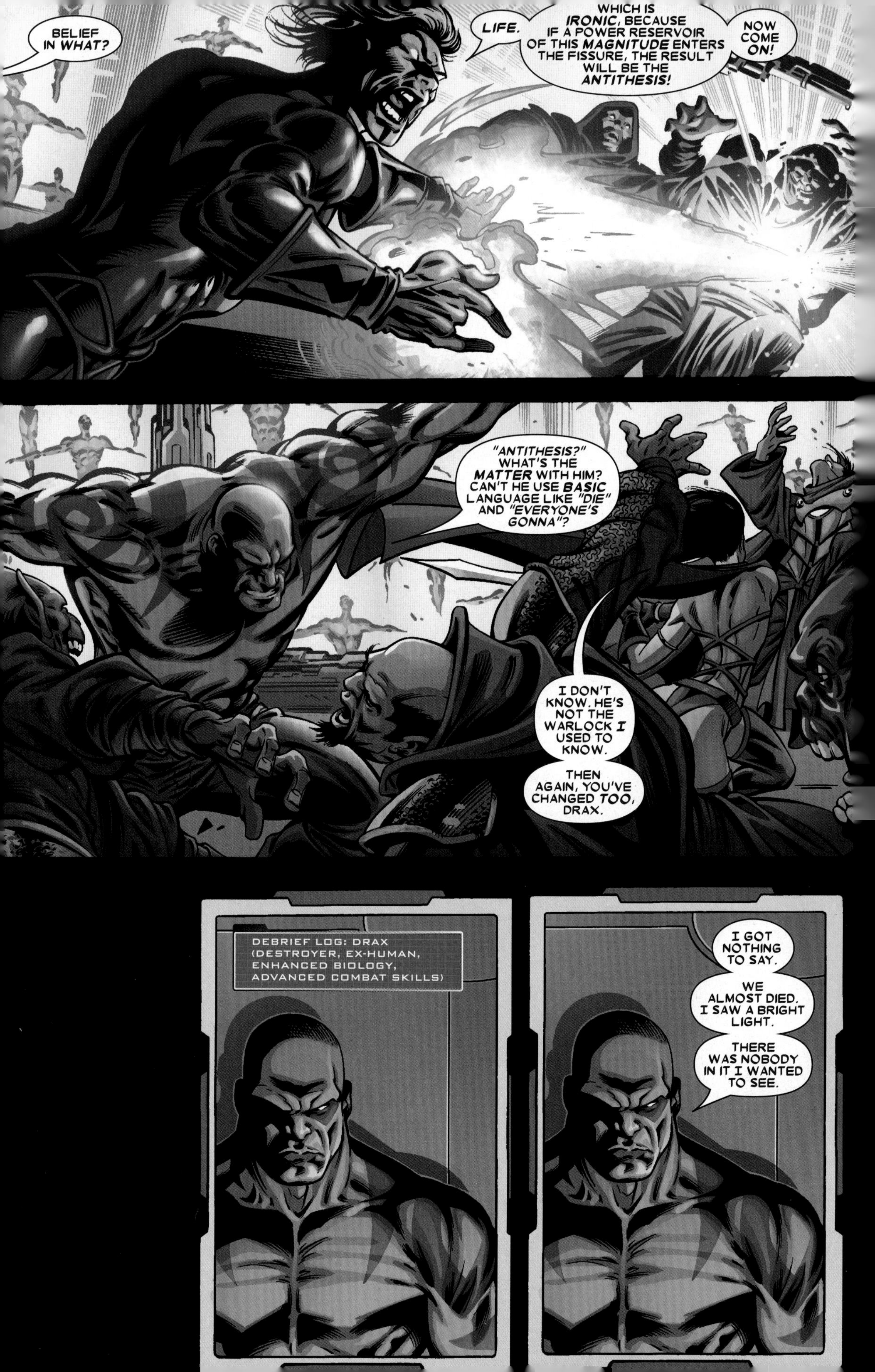
BELIEF IN WHAT?
LIFE.
WHICH IS IRONIC, BECAUSE IF A POWER RESERVOIR OF THIS MAGNITUDE ENTERS THE FISSURE, THE RESULT WILL BE THE ANTITHESIS!
NOW COME ON!
"ANTITHESIS?" WHAT'S THE MATTER WITH HIM? CAN'T HE USE BASIC LANGUAGE LIKE "DIE" AND "EVERYONE'S GONNA"?
I DON'T KNOW. HE'S NOT THE WARLOCK I USED TO KNOW.
THEN AGAIN, YOU'VE CHANGED TOO, DRAX.
DEBRIEF LOG: DRAX (DESTROYER, EX-HUMAN, ENHANCED BIOLOGY, ADVANCED COMBAT SKILLS)
I GOT NOTHING TO SAY.
WE ALMOST DIED. I SAW A BRIGHT LIGHT.
THERE WAS NOBODY IN IT I WANTED TO SEE.

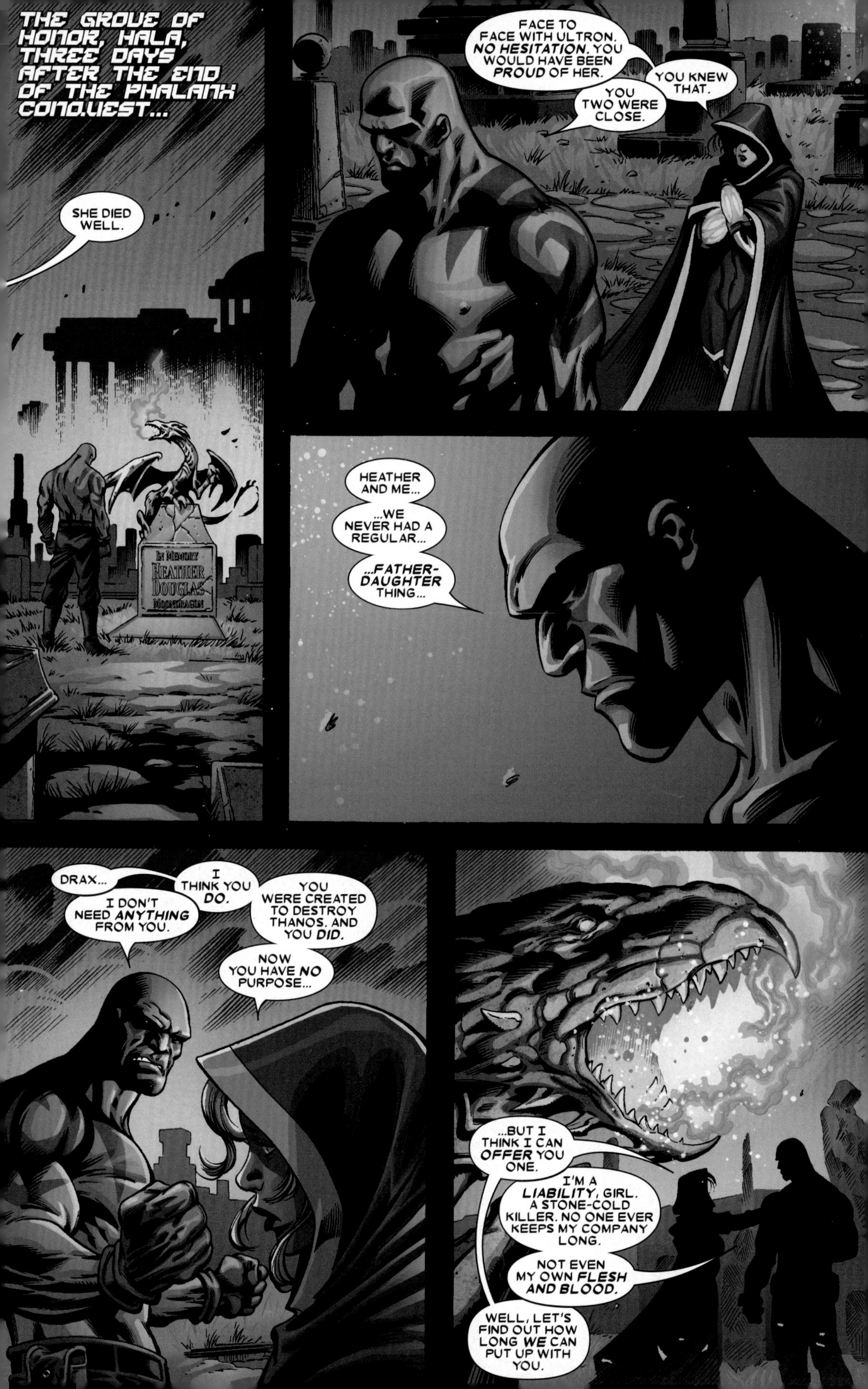
THE GROVE OF HONOR, HALA, THREE DAYS AFTER THE END OF THE PHALANX CONQUEST...
SHE DIED WELL.
IN MEMORY HEATHER DOUGLAS MOONDRAGON
FACE TO FACE WITH ULTRON. NO HESITATION. YOU WOULD HAVE BEEN PROUD OF HER.
YOU TWO WERE CLOSE.
YOU KNEW THAT.
HEATHER AND ME...
...WE NEVER HAD A REGULAR...
...FATHER-DAUGHTER THING...
DRAX...
I DON'T NEED ANYTHING FROM YOU.
I THINK YOU DO.
YOU WERE CREATED TO DESTROY THANOS. AND YOU DID.
NOW YOU HAVE NO PURPOSE...
...BUT I THINK I CAN OFFER YOU ONE.
I'M A LIABILITY, GIRL. A STONE-COLD KILLER. NO ONE EVER KEEPS MY COMPANY LONG.
NOT EVEN MY OWN FLESH AND BLOOD.
WELL, LET'S FIND OUT HOW LONG WE CAN PUT UP WITH YOU.

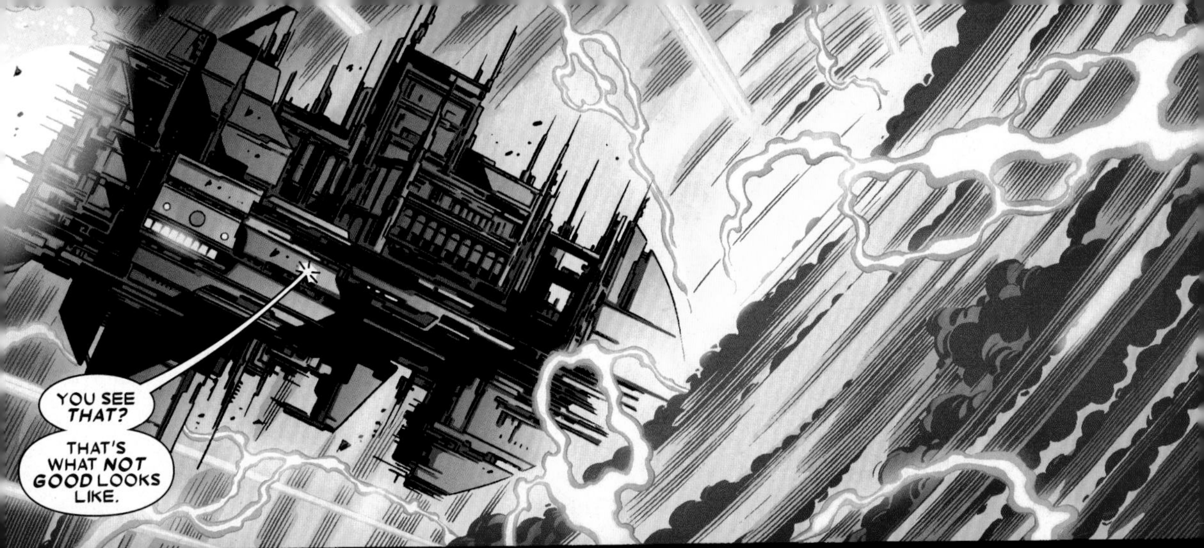
YOU SEE THAT?
THAT'S WHAT NOT GOOD LOOKS LIKE.

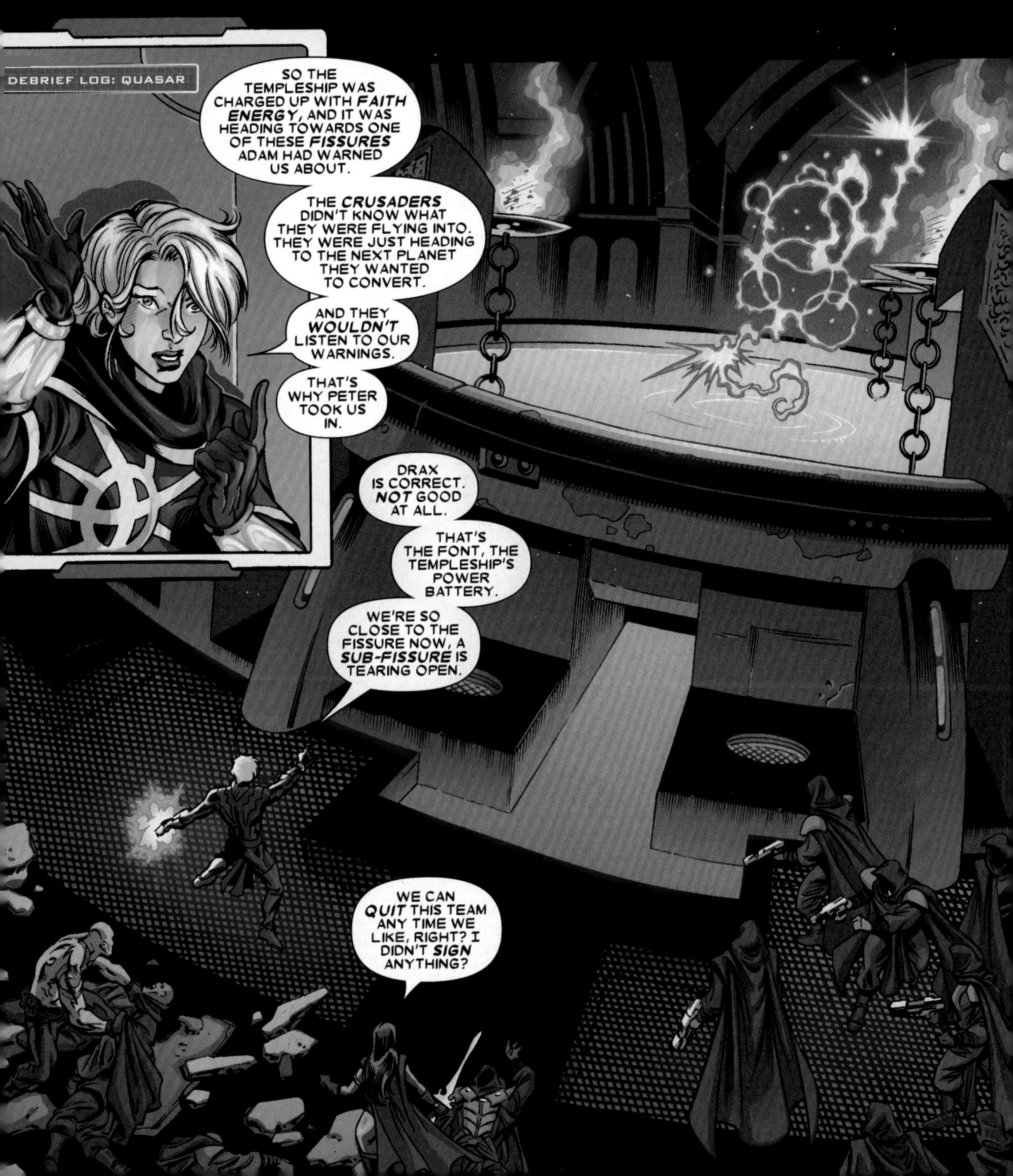
DEBRIEF LOG: QUASAR
SO THE TEMPLESHIP WAS CHARGED UP WITH FAITH ENERGY, AND IT WAS HEADING TOWARDS ONE OF THESE FISSURES ADAM HAD WARNED US ABOUT.
THE CRUSADERS DIDN'T KNOW WHAT THEY WERE FLYING INTO. THEY WERE JUST HEADING TO THE NEXT PLANET THEY WANTED TO CONVERT.
AND THEY WOULDN'T LISTEN TO OUR WARNINGS.
THAT'S WHY PETER TOOK US IN.
DRAX IS CORRECT. NOT GOOD AT ALL.
THAT'S THE FONT, THE TEMPLESHIP'S POWER BATTERY.
WE'RE SO CLOSE TO THE FISSURE NOW, A SUB-FISSURE IS TEARING OPEN.
WE CAN QUIT THIS TEAM ANY TIME WE LIKE, RIGHT? I DIDN'T SIGN ANYTHING?

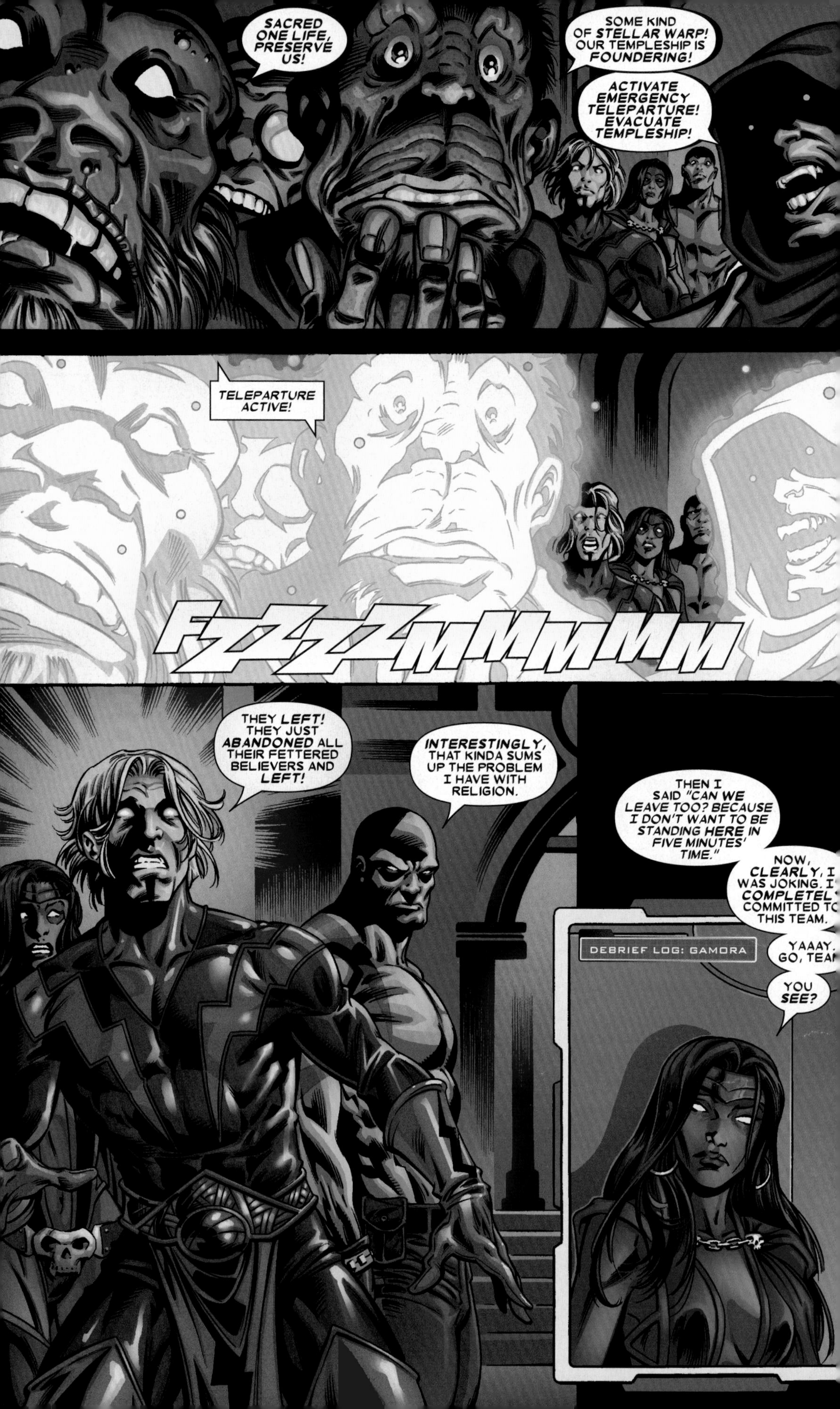
SACRED ONE LIFE, PRESERVE US!
SOME KIND OF STELLAR WARP! OUR TEMPLESHIP IS FOUNDERING!
ACTIVATE EMERGENCY TELEPARTURE! EVACUATE TEMPLESHIP!
TELEPARTURE ACTIVE!
FZZZMMMMMM
THEY LEFT! THEY JUST ABANDONED ALL THEIR FETTERED BELIEVERS AND LEFT!
INTERESTINGLY, THAT KINDA SUMS UP THE PROBLEM I HAVE WITH RELIGION.
THEN I SAID "CAN WE LEAVE TOO? BECAUSE I DON'T WANT TO BE STANDING HERE IN FIVE MINUTES' TIME."
NOW, CLEARLY, I WAS JOKING. I' COMPLETEL COMMITTED TO THIS TEAM.
DEBRIEF LOG: GAMORA
YAAAY. GO, TEAM
YOU SEE?

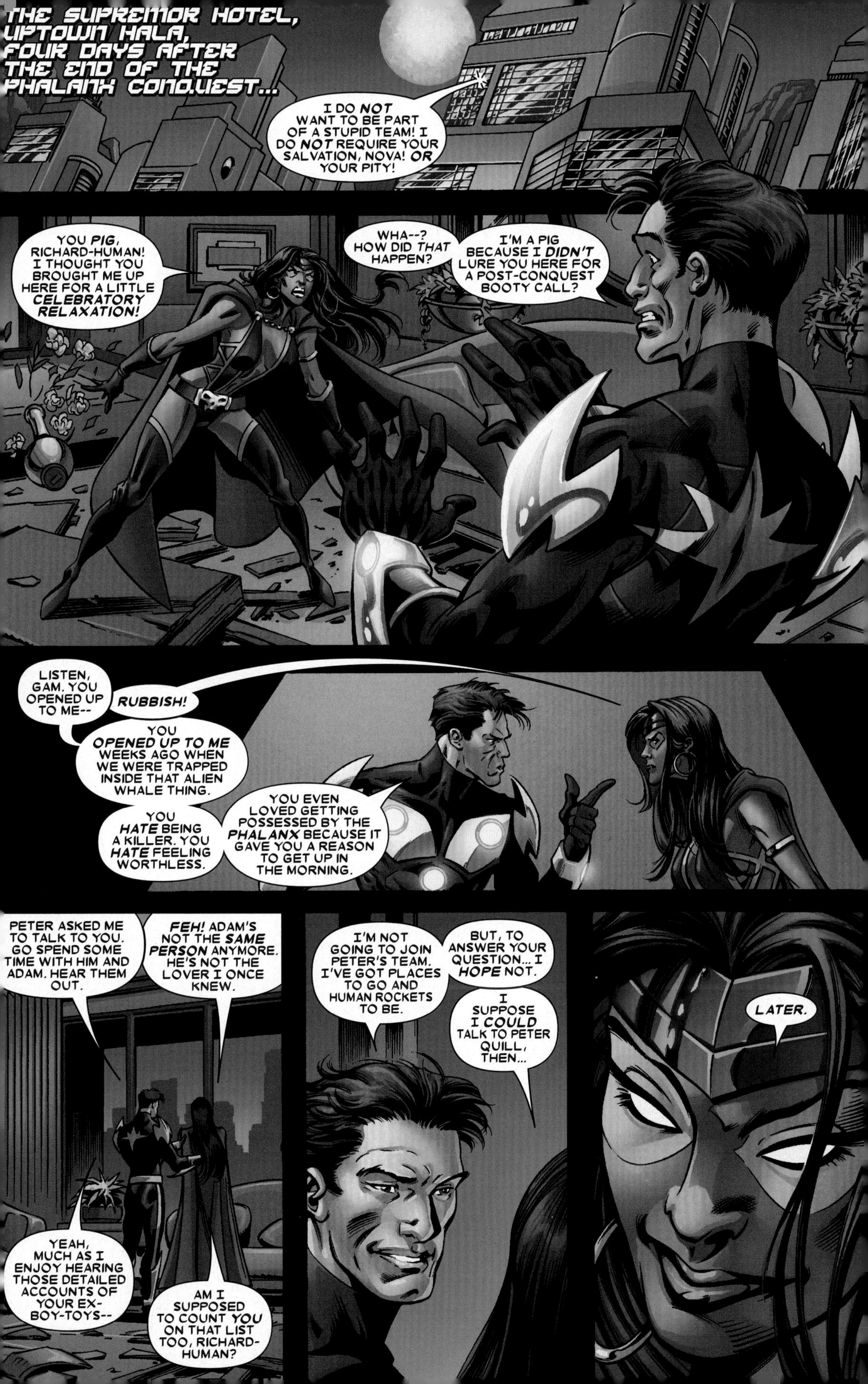
THE SUPREMOR HOTEL, UPTOWN HALA, FOUR DAYS AFTER THE END OF THE PHALANX CONQUEST...
I DO NOT WANT TO BE PART OF A STUPID TEAM! I DO NOT REQUIRE YOUR SALVATION, NOVA! OR YOUR PITY!
YOU PIG, RICHARD-HUMAN! I THOUGHT YOU BROUGHT ME UP HERE FOR A LITTLE CELEBRATORY RELAXATION!
WHA--? HOW DID THAT HAPPEN?
I'M A PIG BECAUSE I DIDN'T LURE YOU HERE FOR A POST-CONQUEST BOOTY CALL?
LISTEN, GAM. YOU OPENED UP TO ME--
RUBBISH!
YOU OPENED UP TO ME WEEKS AGO WHEN WE WERE TRAPPED INSIDE THAT ALIEN WHALE THING.
YOU HATE BEING A KILLER. YOU HATE FEELING WORTHLESS.
YOU EVEN LOVED GETTING POSSESSED BY THE PHALANX BECAUSE IT GAVE YOU A REASON TO GET UP IN THE MORNING.
PETER ASKED ME TO TALK TO YOU. GO SPEND SOME TIME WITH HIM AND ADAM. HEAR THEM OUT.
FEH! ADAM'S NOT THE SAME PERSON ANYMORE. HE'S NOT THE LOVER I ONCE KNEW.
YEAH, MUCH AS I ENJOY HEARING THOSE DETAILED ACCOUNTS OF YOUR EX-BOY-TOYS--
AM I SUPPOSED TO COUNT YOU ON THAT LIST TOO, RICHARD-HUMAN?
I'M NOT GOING TO JOIN PETER'S TEAM. I'VE GOT PLACES TO GO AND HUMAN ROCKETS TO BE.
BUT, TO ANSWER YOUR QUESTION... I HOPE NOT.
I SUPPOSE I COULD TALK TO PETER QUILL, THEN...
LATER.

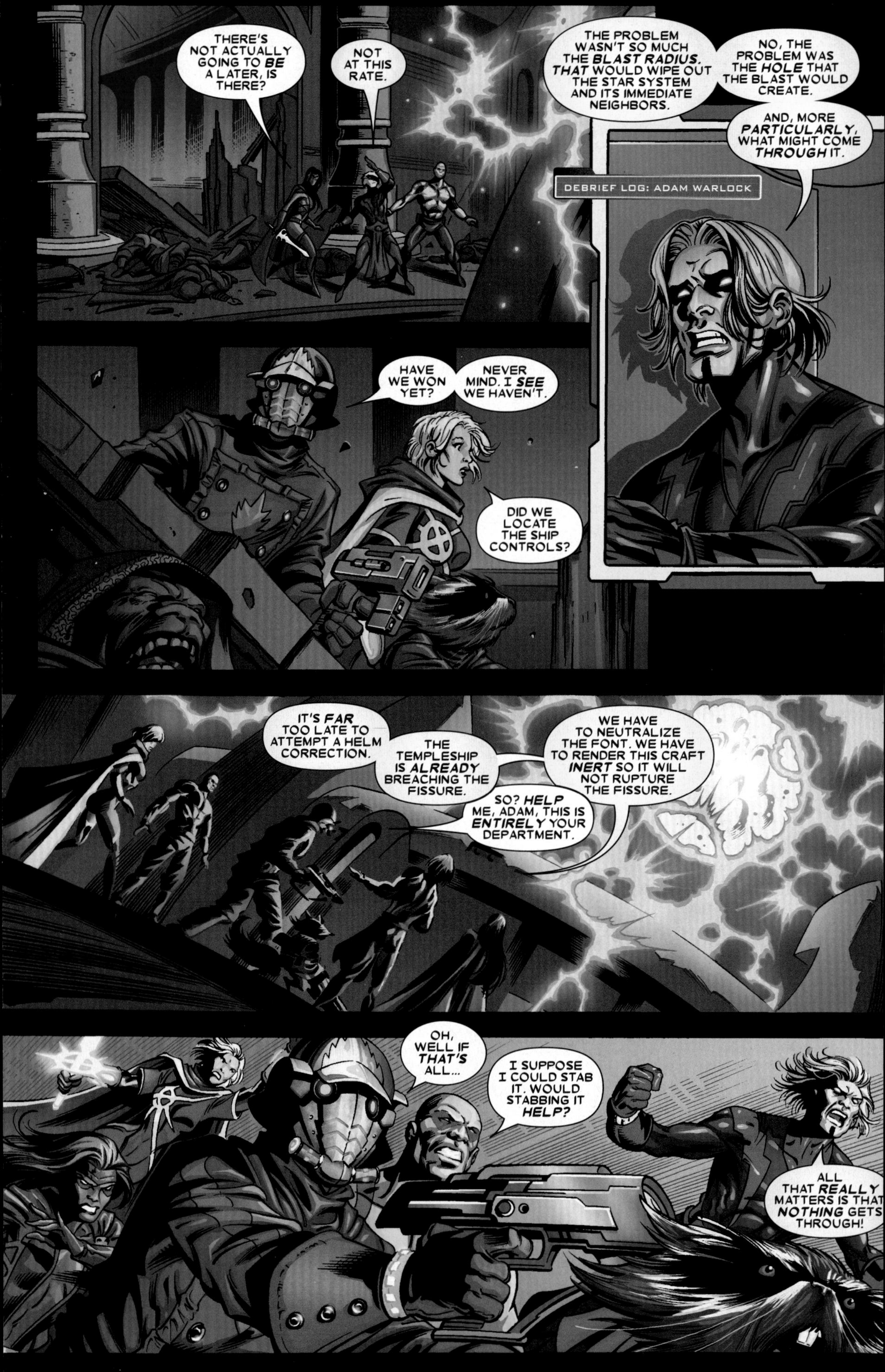
THERE'S NOT ACTUALLY GOING TO BE A LATER, IS THERE?
NOT AT THIS RATE.
THE PROBLEM WASN'T SO MUCH THE BLAST RADIUS. THAT WOULD WIPE OUT THE STAR SYSTEM AND ITS IMMEDIATE NEIGHBORS.
NO, THE PROBLEM WAS THE HOLE THAT THE BLAST WOULD CREATE.
AND, MORE PARTICULARLY, WHAT MIGHT COME THROUGH IT.
DEBRIEF LOG: ADAM WARLOCK
HAVE WE WON YET?
NEVER MIND. I SEE WE HAVEN'T.
DID WE LOCATE THE SHIP CONTROLS?
IT'S FAR TOO LATE TO ATTEMPT A HELM CORRECTION.
THE TEMPLESHIP IS ALREADY BREACHING THE FISSURE.
WE HAVE TO NEUTRALIZE THE FONT. WE HAVE TO RENDER THIS CRAFT INERT SO IT WILL NOT RUPTURE THE FISSURE.
SO? HELP ME, ADAM, THIS IS ENTIRELY YOUR DEPARTMENT.
OH, WELL IF THAT'S ALL...
I SUPPOSE I COULD STAB IT. WOULD STABBING IT HELP?
ALL THAT REALLY MATTERS IS THAT NOTHING GETS THROUGH!

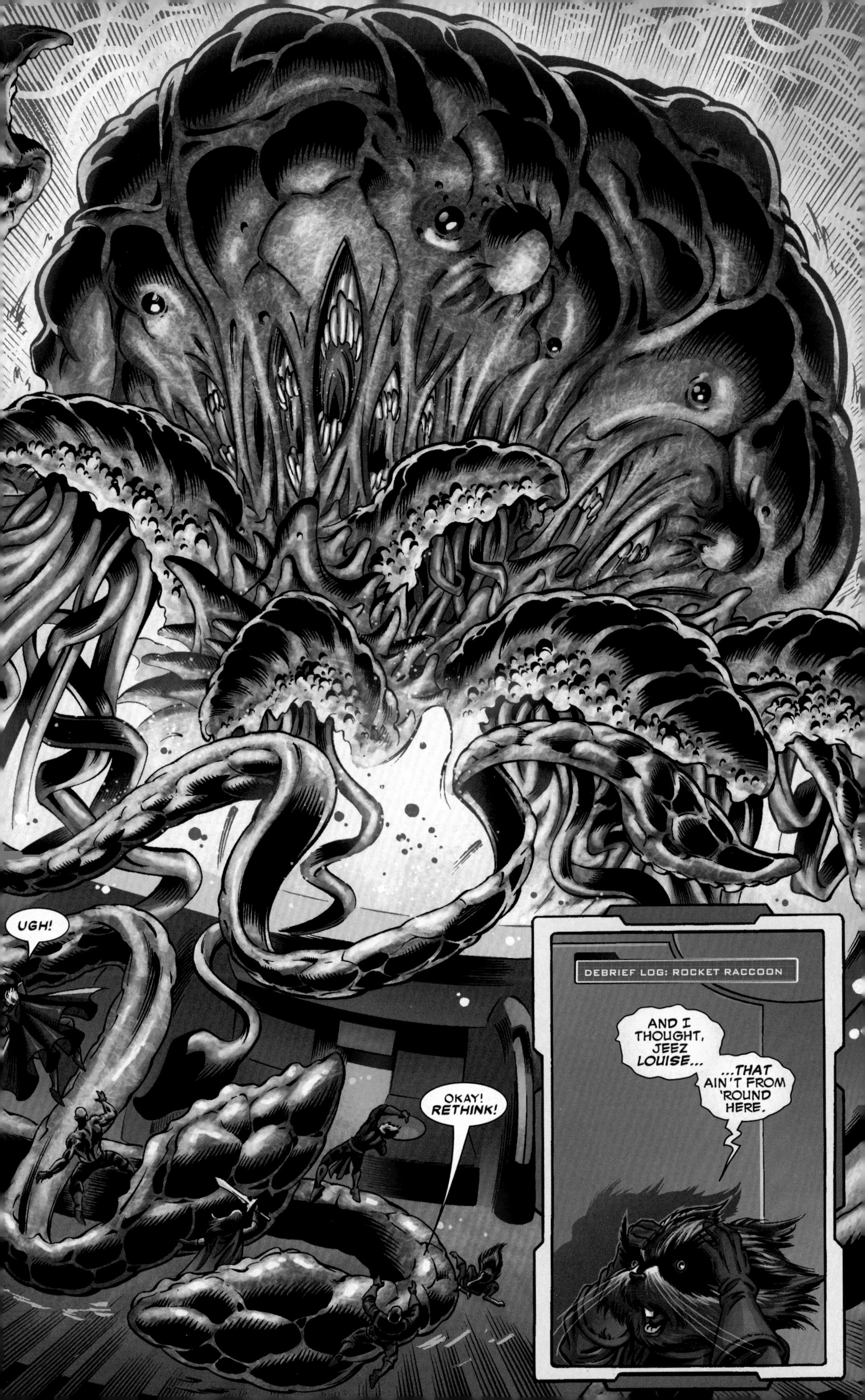
UGH!
OKAY! RETHINK!
DEBRIEF LOG: ROCKET RACCOON
AND I THOUGHT, JEEZ LOUISE...
...THAT AIN'T FROM 'ROUND HERE.

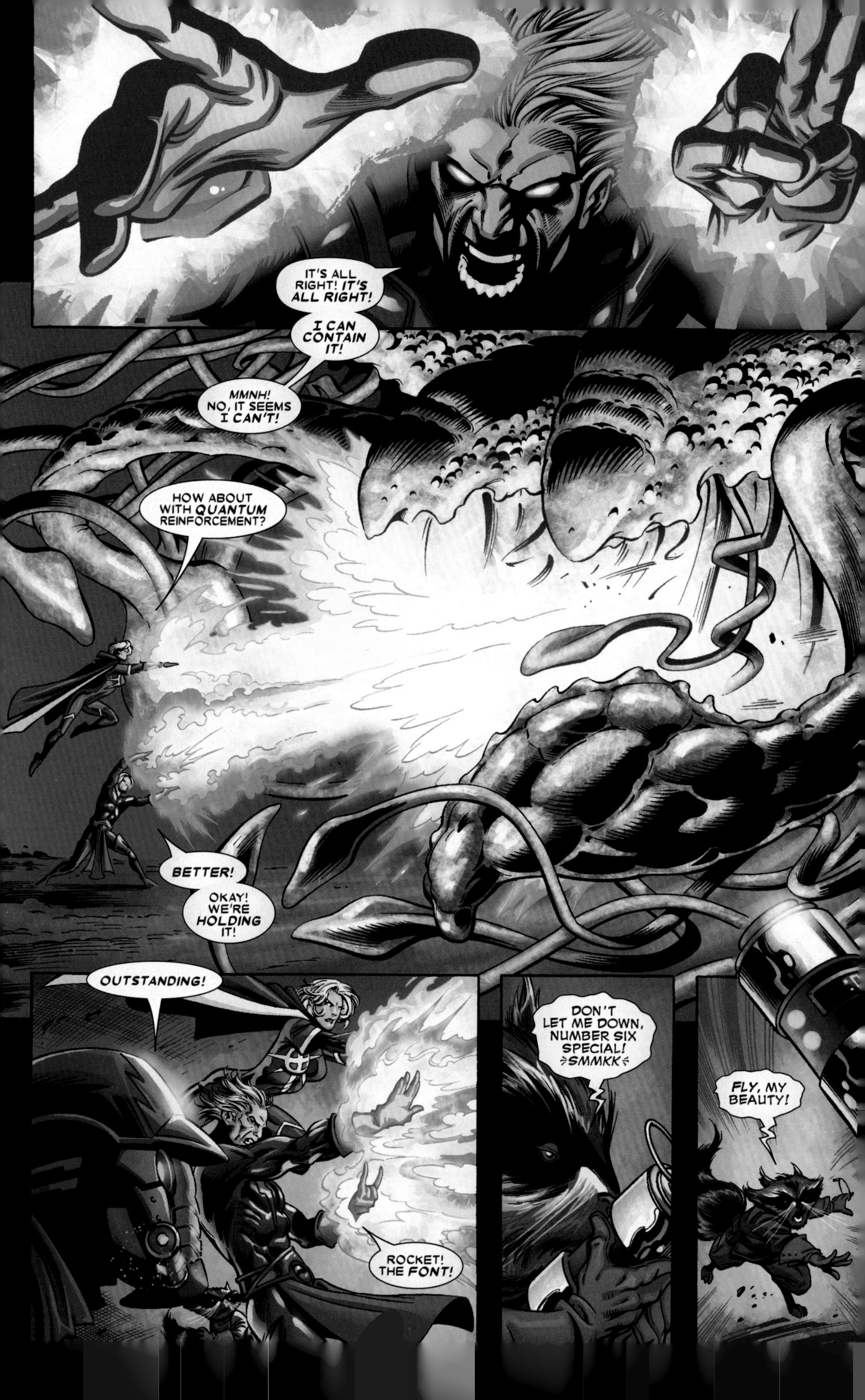
IT'S ALL RIGHT! IT'S ALL RIGHT!
I CAN CONTAIN IT!
MMNH! NO, IT SEEMS I CAN'T!
HOW ABOUT WITH QUANTUM REINFORCEMENT?
BETTER!
OKAY! WE'RE HOLDING IT!
OUTSTANDING!
ROCKET! THE FONT!
DON'T LET ME DOWN, NUMBER SIX SPECIAL! SMMKK
FLY, MY BEAUTY!

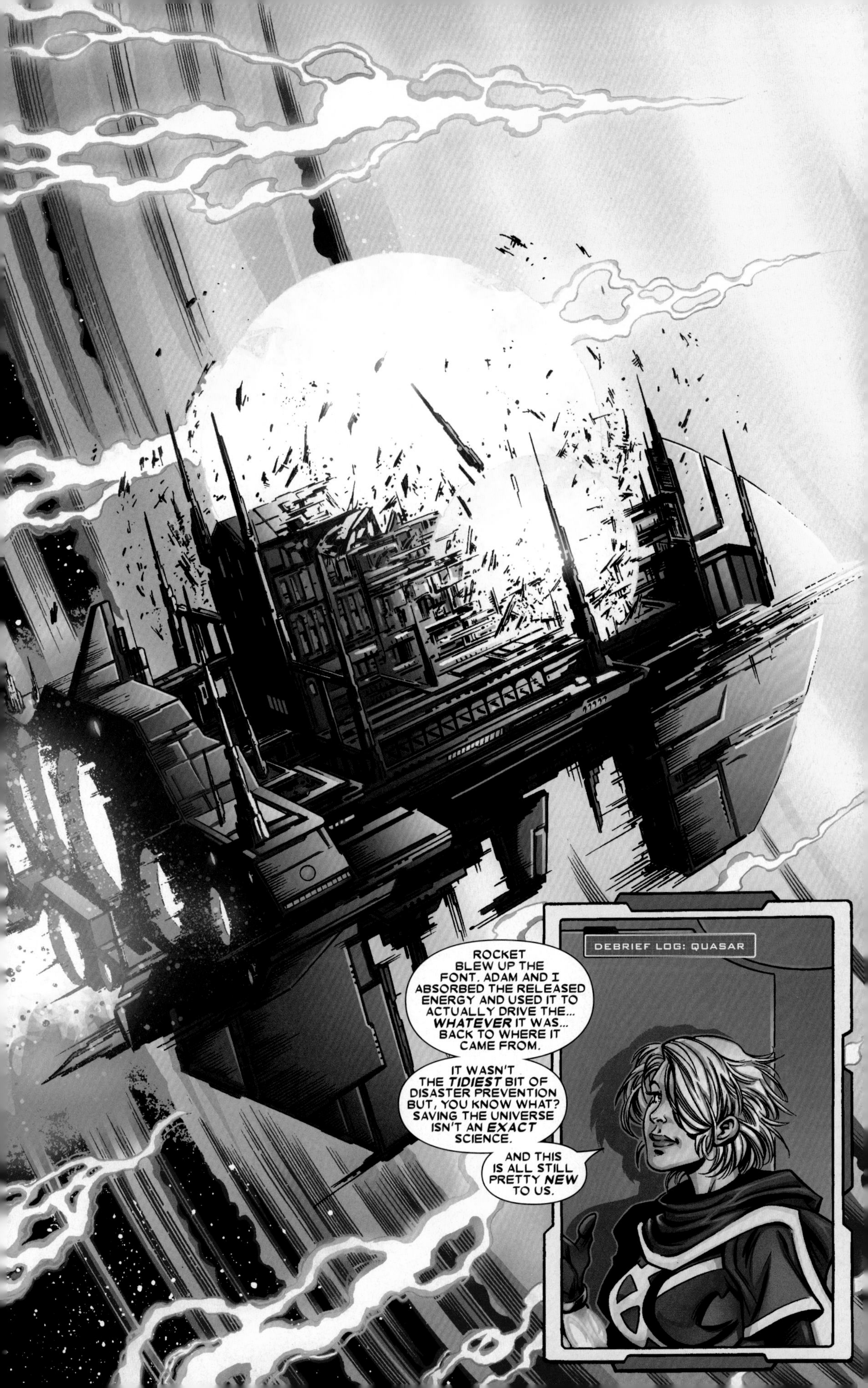
DEBRIEF LOG: QUASAR
ROCKET BLEW UP THE FONT. ADAM AND I ABSORBED THE RELEASED ENERGY AND USED IT TO ACTUALLY DRIVE THE... *WHATEVER* IT WAS... BACK TO WHERE IT CAME FROM.
IT WASN'T THE *TIDIEST* BIT OF DISASTER PREVENTION BUT, YOU KNOW WHAT? SAVING THE UNIVERSE ISN'T AN *EXACT* SCIENCE.
AND THIS IS ALL STILL PRETTY *NEW* TO US.

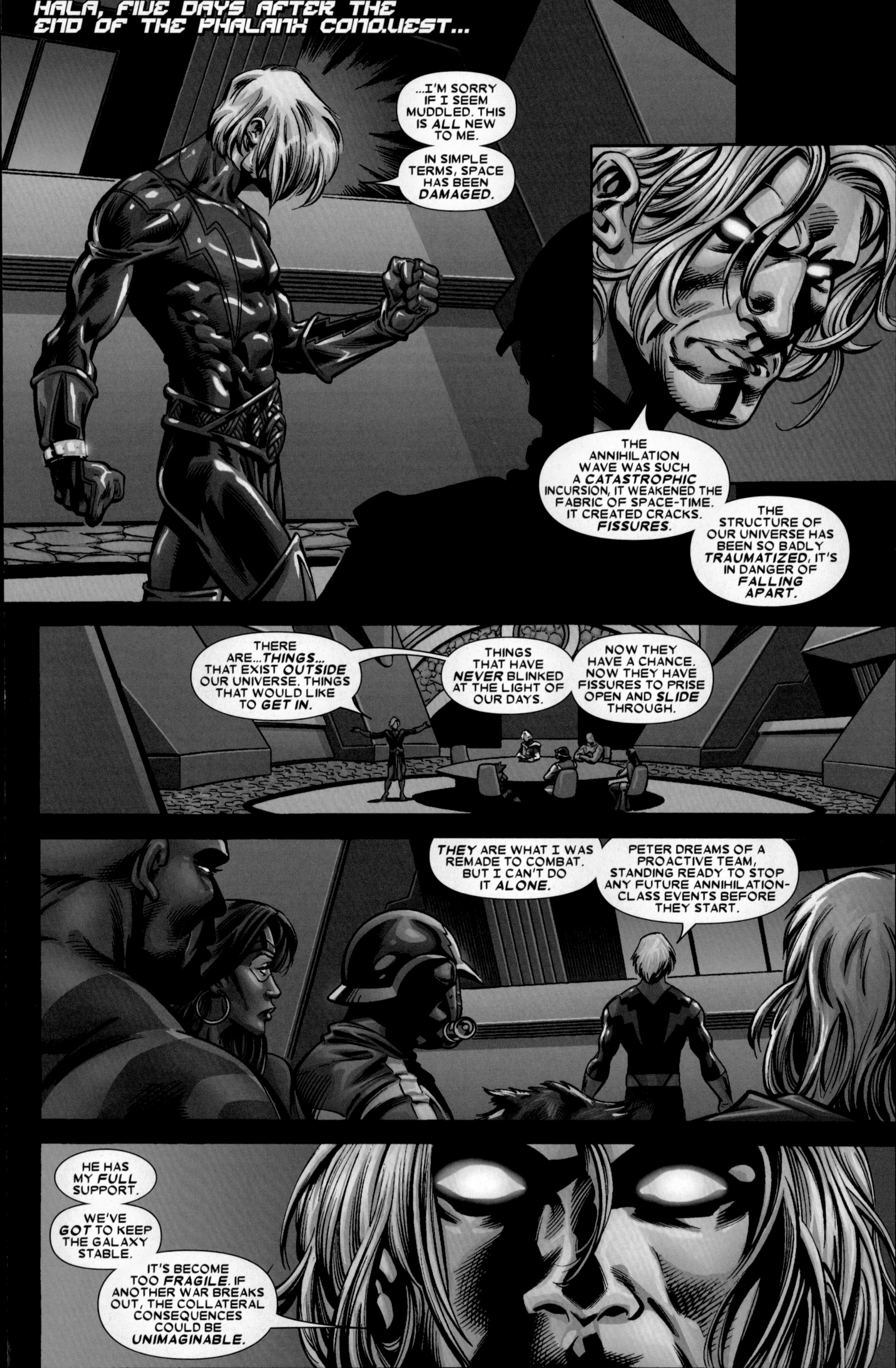
HALA, FIVE DAYS AFTER THE END OF THE PHALANX CONQUEST...
...I'M SORRY IF I SEEM MUDDLED. THIS IS ALL NEW TO ME.
IN SIMPLE TERMS, SPACE HAS BEEN DAMAGED.
THE ANNIHILATION WAVE WAS SUCH A CATASTROPHIC INCURSION, IT WEAKENED THE FABRIC OF SPACE-TIME. IT CREATED CRACKS. FISSURES.
THE STRUCTURE OF OUR UNIVERSE HAS BEEN SO BADLY TRAUMATIZED, IT'S IN DANGER OF FALLING APART.
THERE ARE...THINGS... THAT EXIST OUTSIDE OUR UNIVERSE. THINGS THAT WOULD LIKE TO GET IN.
THINGS THAT HAVE NEVER BLINKED AT THE LIGHT OF OUR DAYS.
NOW THEY HAVE A CHANCE. NOW THEY HAVE FISSURES TO PRISE OPEN AND SLIDE THROUGH.
THEY ARE WHAT I WAS REMADE TO COMBAT. BUT I CAN'T DO IT ALONE.
PETER DREAMS OF A PROACTIVE TEAM, STANDING READY TO STOP ANY FUTURE ANNIHILATION-CLASS EVENTS BEFORE THEY START.
HE HAS MY FULL SUPPORT.
WE'VE GOT TO KEEP THE GALAXY STABLE.
IT'S BECOME TOO FRAGILE. IF ANOTHER WAR BREAKS OUT, THE COLLATERAL CONSEQUENCES COULD BE UNIMAGINABLE.

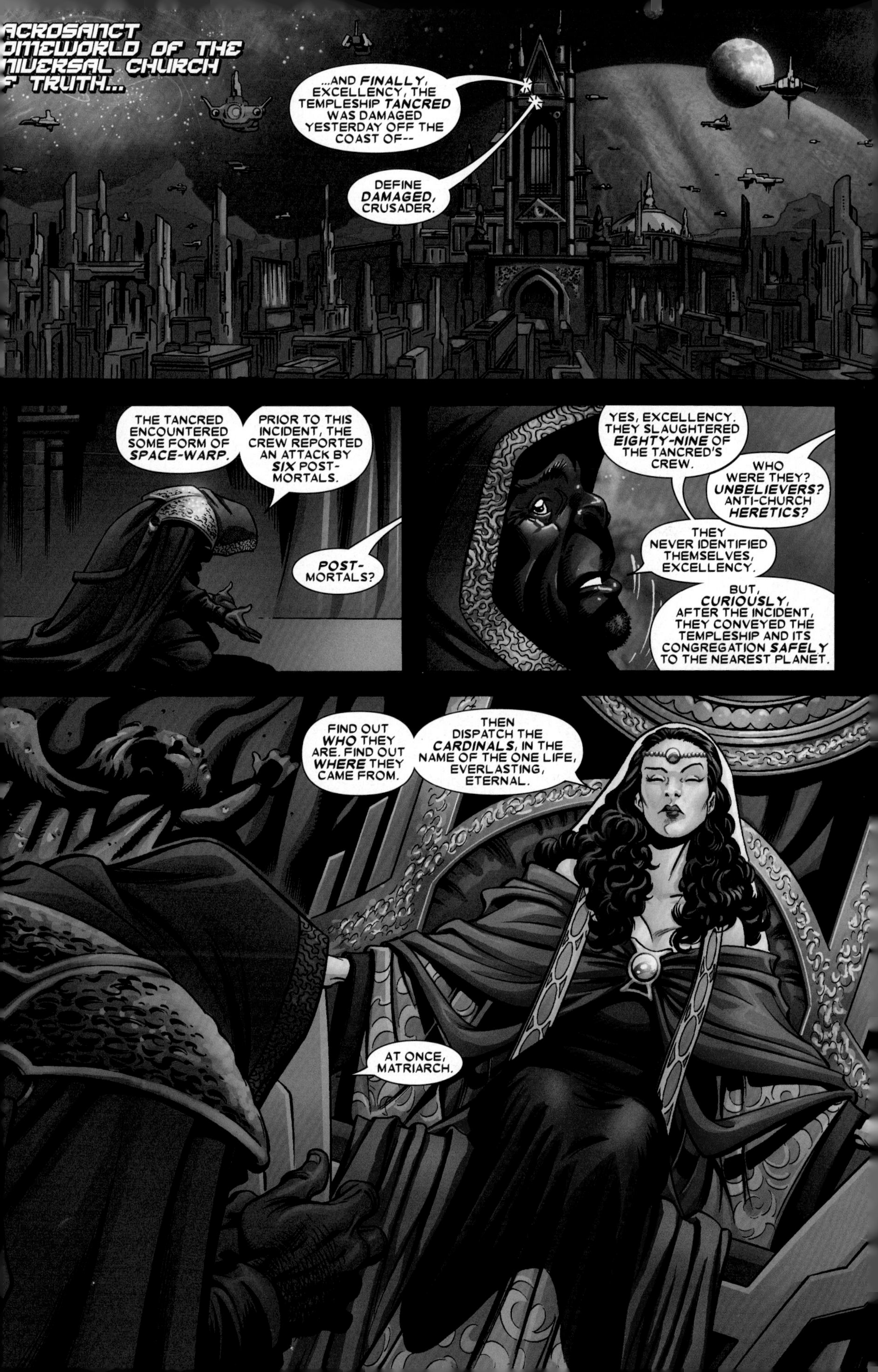
ACROSANCT
OMEWORLD OF THE
NIVERSAL CHURCH
TRUTH...
...AND FINALLY, EXCELLENCY, THE TEMPLESHIP TANCRED WAS DAMAGED YESTERDAY OFF THE COAST OF--
DEFINE DAMAGED, CRUSADER.
THE TANCRED ENCOUNTERED SOME FORM OF SPACE-WARP.
PRIOR TO THIS INCIDENT, THE CREW REPORTED AN ATTACK BY SIX POST-MORTALS.
POST-MORTALS?
YES, EXCELLENCY. THEY SLAUGHTERED EIGHTY-NINE OF THE TANCRED'S CREW.
WHO WERE THEY? UNBELIEVERS? ANTI-CHURCH HERETICS?
THEY NEVER IDENTIFIED THEMSELVES, EXCELLENCY.
BUT, CURIOUSLY, AFTER THE INCIDENT, THEY CONVEYED THE TEMPLESHIP AND ITS CONGREGATION SAFELY TO THE NEAREST PLANET.
FIND OUT WHO THEY ARE. FIND OUT WHERE THEY CAME FROM.
THEN DISPATCH THE CARDINALS, IN THE NAME OF THE ONE LIFE, EVERLASTING, ETERNAL.
AT ONCE, MATRIARCH.

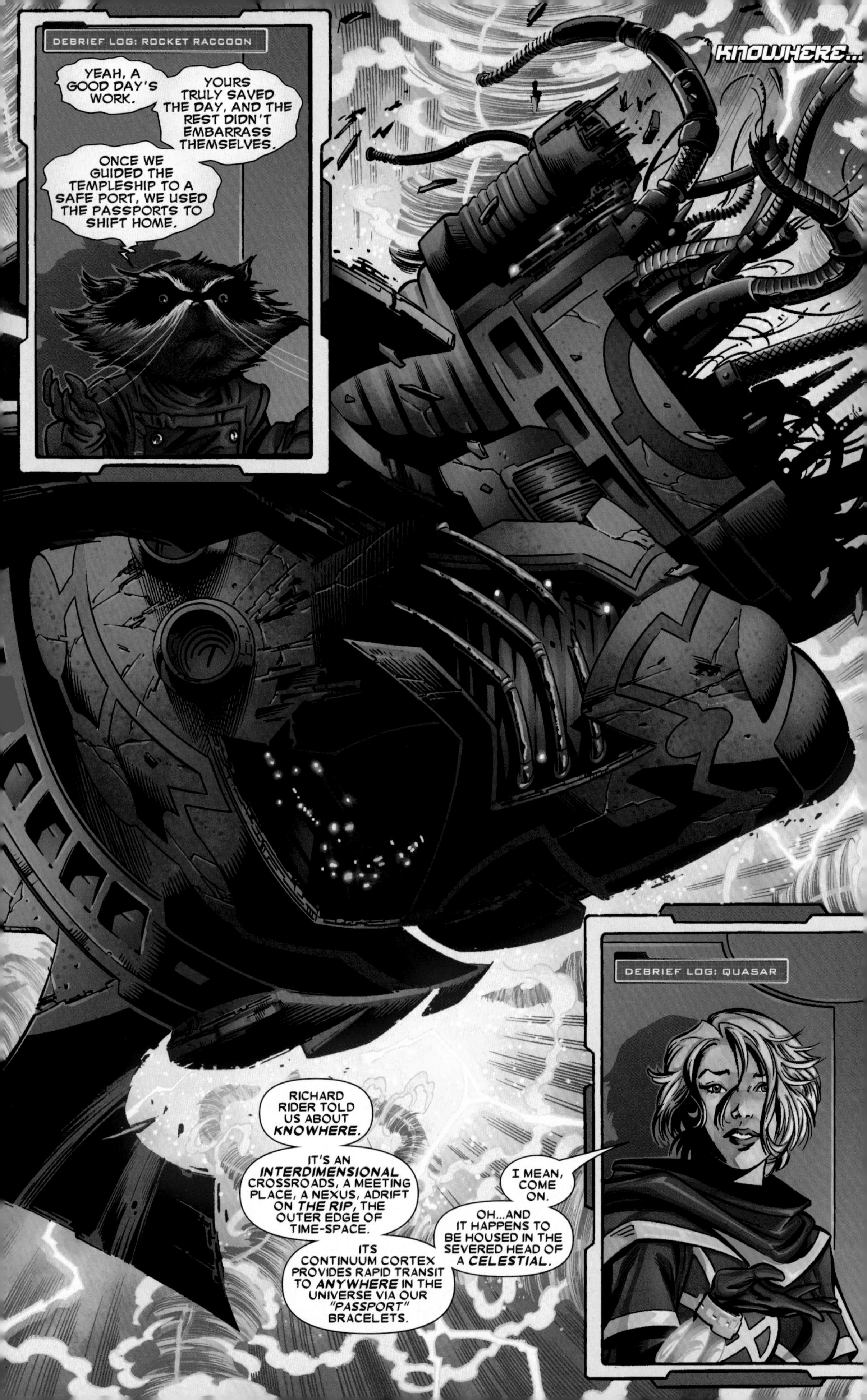
KNOWHERE...
DEBRIEF LOG: ROCKET RACCOON
YEAH, A GOOD DAY'S WORK.
YOURS TRULY SAVED THE DAY, AND THE REST DIDN'T EMBARRASS THEMSELVES.
ONCE WE GUIDED THE TEMPLESHIP TO A SAFE PORT, WE USED THE PASSPORTS TO SHIFT HOME.
DEBRIEF LOG: QUASAR
RICHARD RIDER TOLD US ABOUT KNOWHERE.
IT'S AN INTERDIMENSIONAL CROSSROADS, A MEETING PLACE, A NEXUS, ADRIFT ON THE RIP, THE OUTER EDGE OF TIME-SPACE.
ITS CONTINUUM CORTEX PROVIDES RAPID TRANSIT TO ANYWHERE IN THE UNIVERSE VIA OUR "PASSPORT" BRACELETS.
I MEAN, COME ON.
OH...AND IT HAPPENS TO BE HOUSED IN THE SEVERED HEAD OF A CELESTIAL.

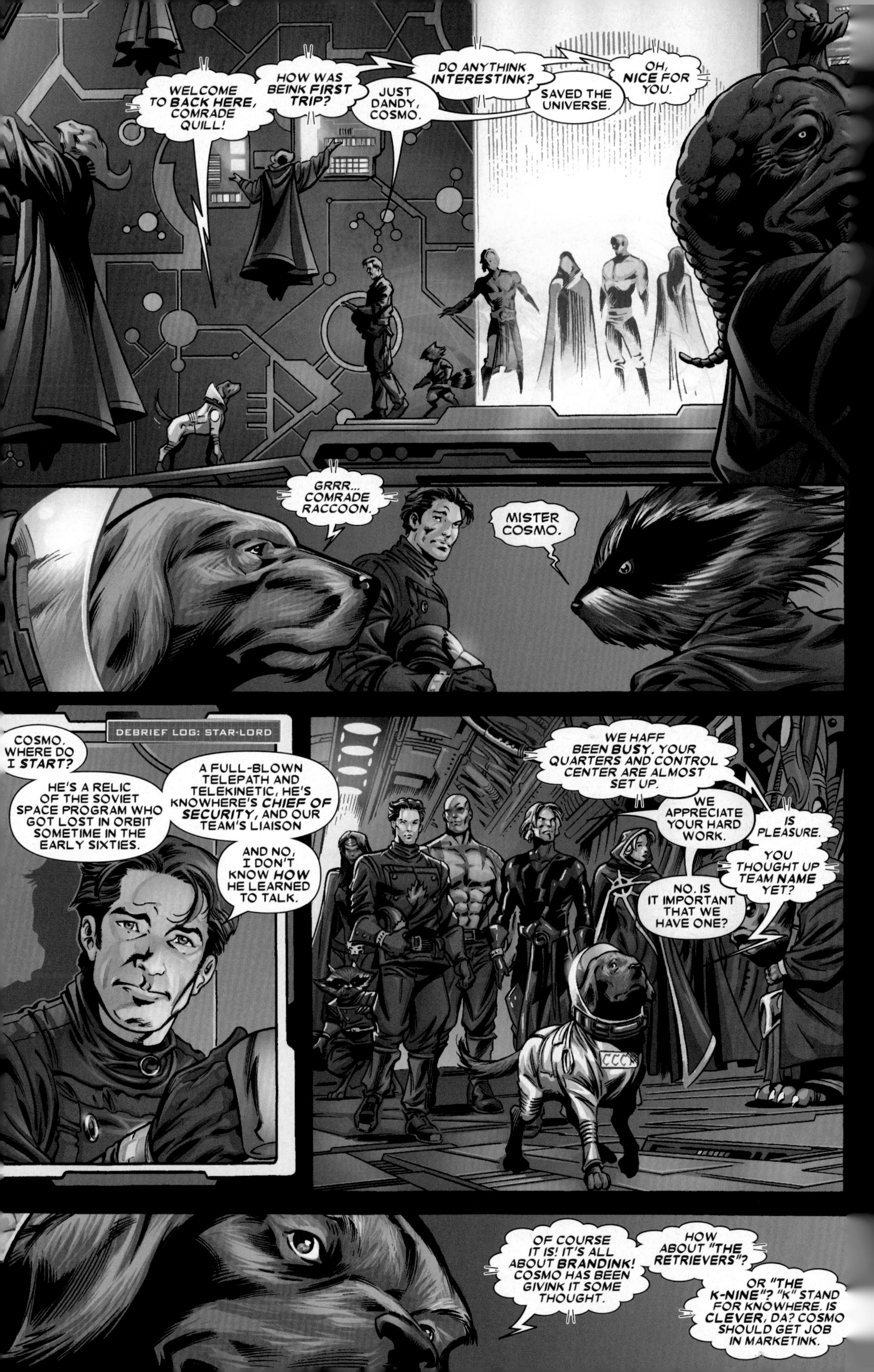
WELCOME TO BACK HERE, COMRADE QUILL!
HOW WAS BEINK FIRST TRIP?
JUST DANDY, COSMO.
DO ANYTHINK INTERESTINK?
SAVED THE UNIVERSE.
OH, NICE FOR YOU.
GRRR... COMRADE RACCOON.
MISTER COSMO.
DEBRIEF LOG: STAR-LORD
COSMO. WHERE DO I START?
HE'S A RELIC OF THE SOVIET SPACE PROGRAM WHO GOT LOST IN ORBIT SOMETIME IN THE EARLY SIXTIES.
A FULL-BLOWN TELEPATH AND TELEKINETIC, HE'S KNOWHERE'S CHIEF OF SECURITY, AND OUR TEAM'S LIAISON
AND NO, I DON'T KNOW HOW HE LEARNED TO TALK.
WE HAFF BEEN BUSY. YOUR QUARTERS AND CONTROL CENTER ARE ALMOST SET UP.
WE APPRECIATE YOUR HARD WORK.
IS PLEASURE.
YOU THOUGHT UP TEAM NAME YET?
NO. IS IT IMPORTANT THAT WE HAVE ONE?
OF COURSE IT IS! IT'S ALL ABOUT BRANDINK! COSMO HAS BEEN GIVINK IT SOME THOUGHT.
HOW ABOUT "THE RETRIEVERS"?
OR "THE K-NINE"? "K" STAND FOR KNOWHERE. IS CLEVER, DA? COSMO SHOULD GET JOB IN MARKETINK.

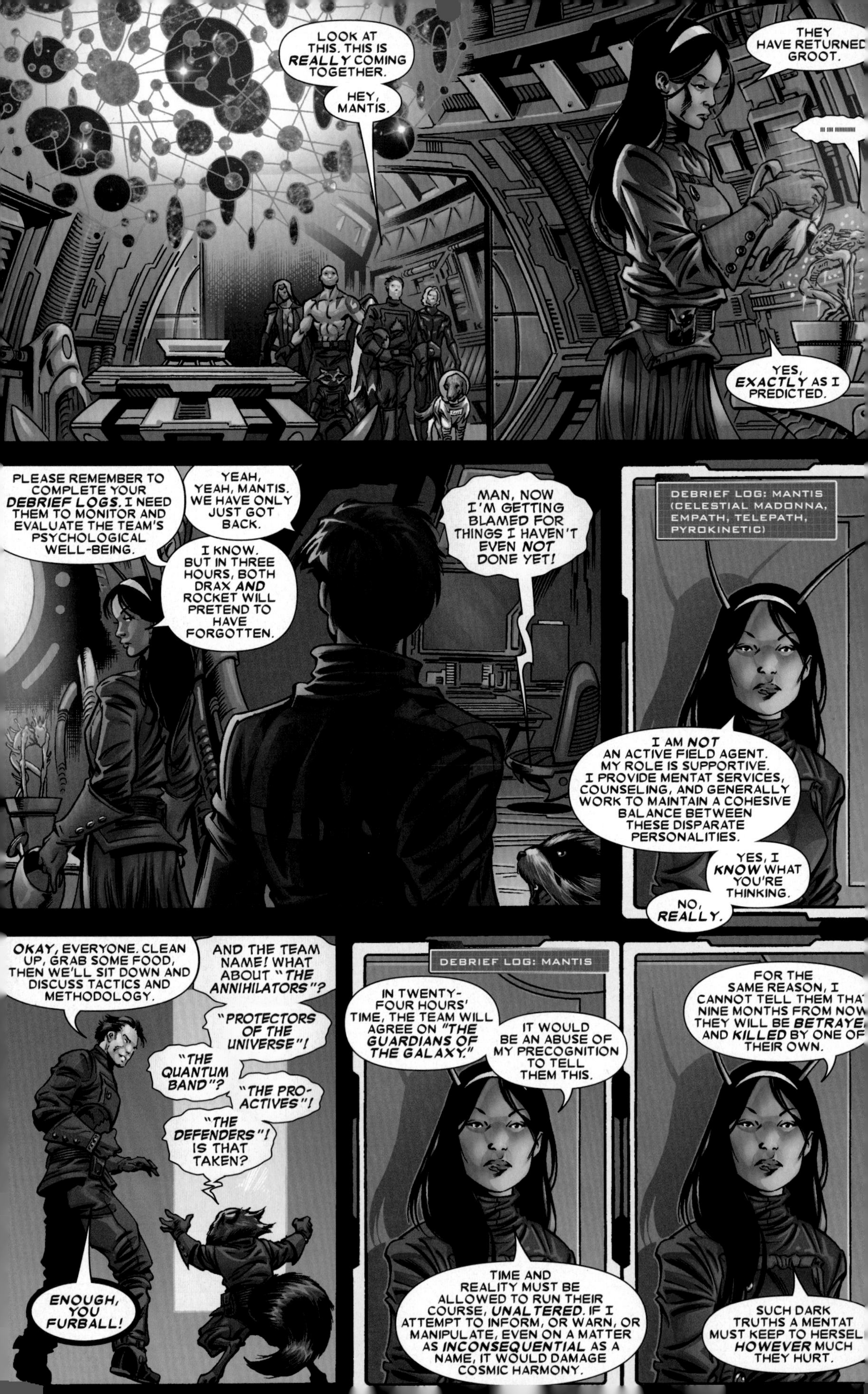

LOOK AT THIS. THIS IS REALLY COMING TOGETHER.
HEY, MANTIS.
THEY HAVE RETURNED GROOT.
YES, EXACTLY AS I PREDICTED.
PLEASE REMEMBER TO COMPLETE YOUR DEBRIEF LOGS. I NEED THEM TO MONITOR AND EVALUATE THE TEAM'S PSYCHOLOGICAL WELL-BEING.
YEAH, YEAH, MANTIS. WE HAVE ONLY JUST GOT BACK.
I KNOW. BUT IN THREE HOURS, BOTH DRAX AND ROCKET WILL PRETEND TO HAVE FORGOTTEN.
MAN, NOW I'M GETTING BLAMED FOR THINGS I HAVEN'T EVEN NOT DONE YET!
DEBRIEF LOG: MANTIS (CELESTIAL MADONNA, EMPATH, TELEPATH, PYROKINETIC)
I AM NOT AN ACTIVE FIELD AGENT. MY ROLE IS SUPPORTIVE. I PROVIDE MENTAT SERVICES, COUNSELING, AND GENERALLY WORK TO MAINTAIN A COHESIVE BALANCE BETWEEN THESE DISPARATE PERSONALITIES.
YES, I KNOW WHAT YOU'RE THINKING.
NO, REALLY.
OKAY, EVERYONE. CLEAN UP, GRAB SOME FOOD, THEN WE'LL SIT DOWN AND DISCUSS TACTICS AND METHODOLOGY.
AND THE TEAM NAME! WHAT ABOUT "THE ANNIHILATORS"?
"PROTECTORS OF THE UNIVERSE"!
"THE QUANTUM BAND"?
"THE PRO-ACTIVES"!
"THE DEFENDERS"! IS THAT TAKEN?
ENOUGH, YOU FURBALL!
DEBRIEF LOG: MANTIS
IN TWENTY-FOUR HOURS' TIME, THE TEAM WILL AGREE ON "THE GUARDIANS OF THE GALAXY."
IT WOULD BE AN ABUSE OF MY PRECOGNITION TO TELL THEM THIS.
TIME AND REALITY MUST BE ALLOWED TO RUN THEIR COURSE, UNALTERED. IF I ATTEMPT TO INFORM, OR WARN, OR MANIPULATE, EVEN ON A MATTER AS INCONSEQUENTIAL AS A NAME, IT WOULD DAMAGE COSMIC HARMONY.
FOR THE SAME REASON, I CANNOT TELL THEM THA NINE MONTHS FROM NOW THEY WILL BE BETRAYE AND KILLED BY ONE OF THEIR OWN.
SUCH DARK TRUTHS A MENTAT MUST KEEP TO HERSEL HOWEVER MUCH THEY HURT.

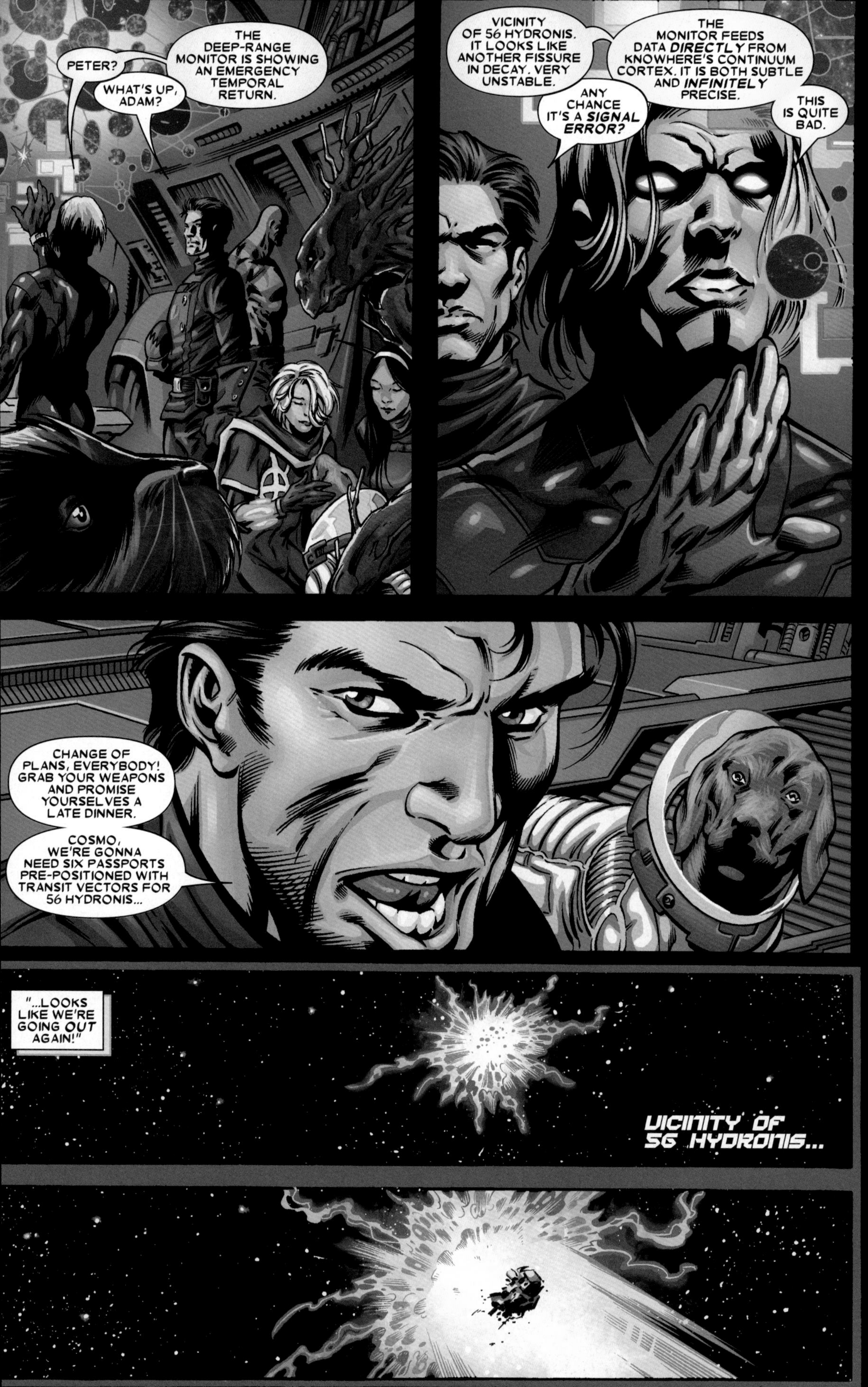
PETER?
THE DEEP-RANGE MONITOR IS SHOWING AN EMERGENCY TEMPORAL RETURN.
WHAT'S UP, ADAM?
VICINITY OF 56 HYDRONIS. IT LOOKS LIKE ANOTHER FISSURE IN DECAY. VERY UNSTABLE.
ANY CHANCE IT'S A SIGNAL ERROR?
THE MONITOR FEEDS DATA DIRECTLY FROM KNOWHERE'S CONTINUUM CORTEX. IT IS BOTH SUBTLE AND INFINITELY PRECISE.
THIS IS QUITE BAD.
CHANGE OF PLANS, EVERYBODY! GRAB YOUR WEAPONS AND PROMISE YOURSELVES A LATE DINNER.
COSMO, WE'RE GONNA NEED SIX PASSPORTS PRE-POSITIONED WITH TRANSIT VECTORS FOR 56 HYDRONIS...
"...LOOKS LIKE WE'RE GOING OUT AGAIN!"
VICINITY OF 56 HYDRONIS...

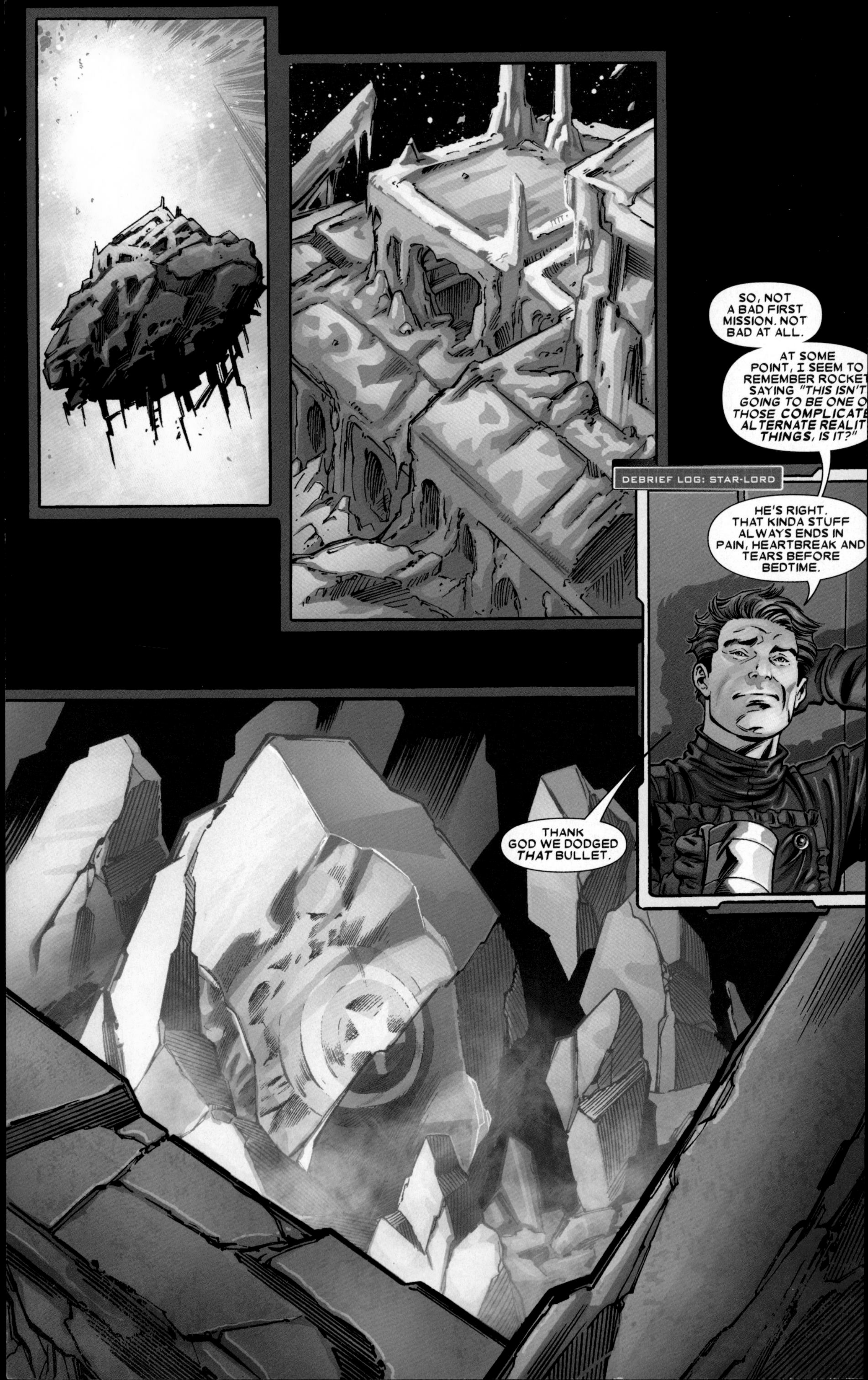
SO, NOT A BAD FIRST MISSION. NOT BAD AT ALL.
AT SOME POINT, I SEEM TO REMEMBER ROCKET SAYING "THIS ISN'T GOING TO BE ONE OF THOSE COMPLICATED ALTERNATE REALITY THINGS, IS IT?"
DEBRIEF LOG: STAR-LORD
HE'S RIGHT. THAT KINDA STUFF ALWAYS ENDS IN PAIN, HEARTBREAK AND TEARS BEFORE BEDTIME.
THANK GOD WE DODGED *THAT* BULLET.

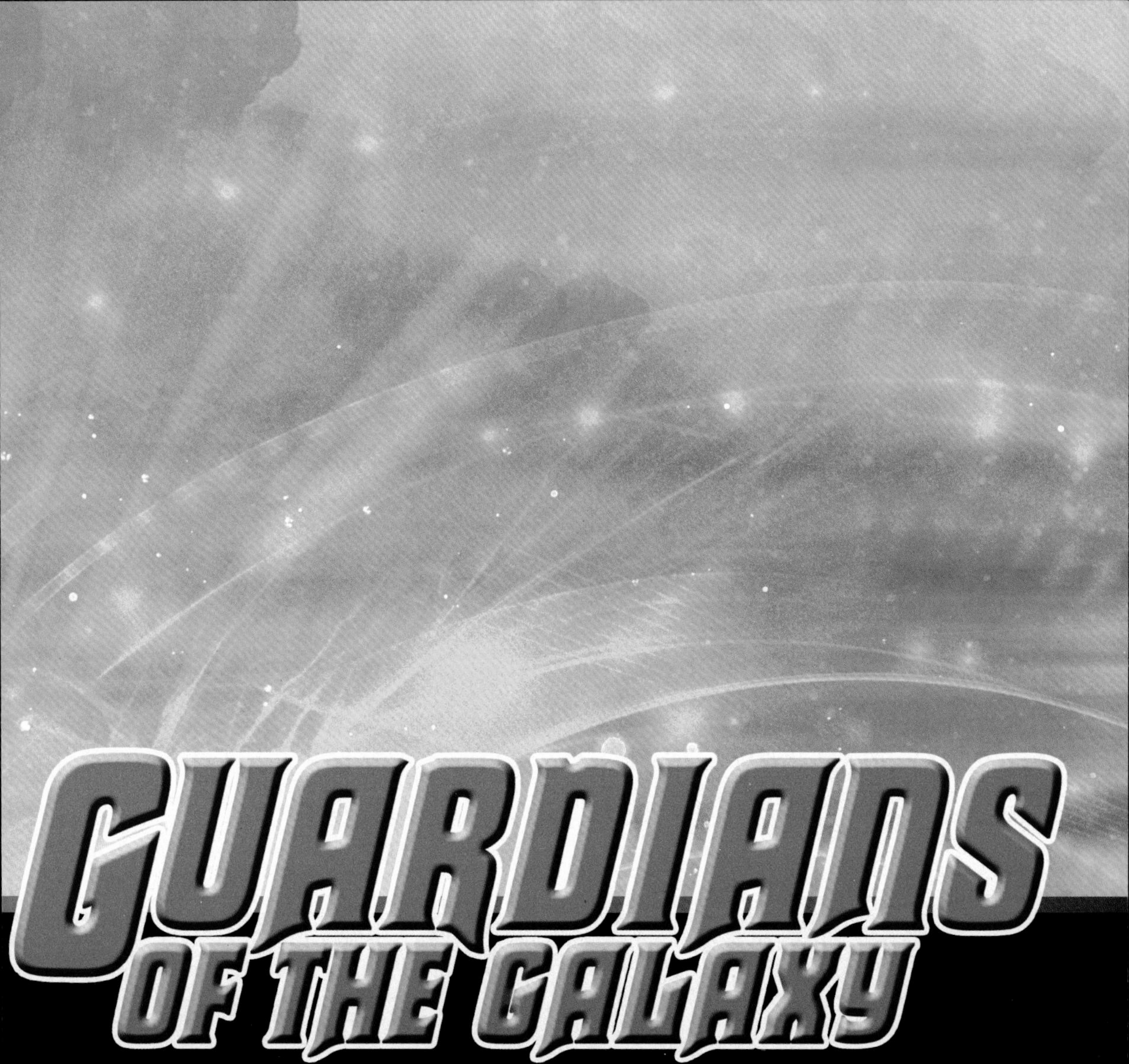
GUARDIANS
OF THE GALAXY

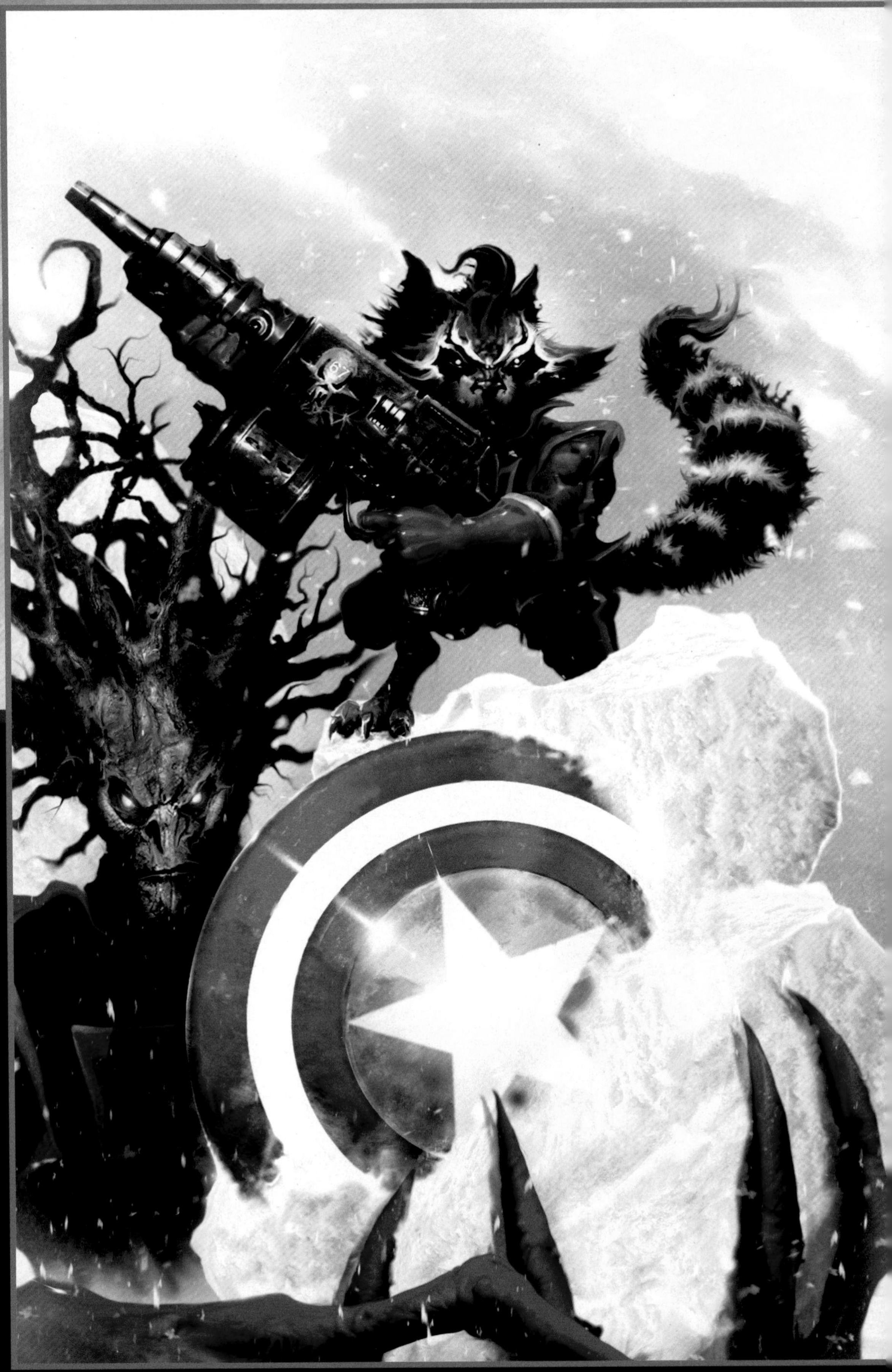

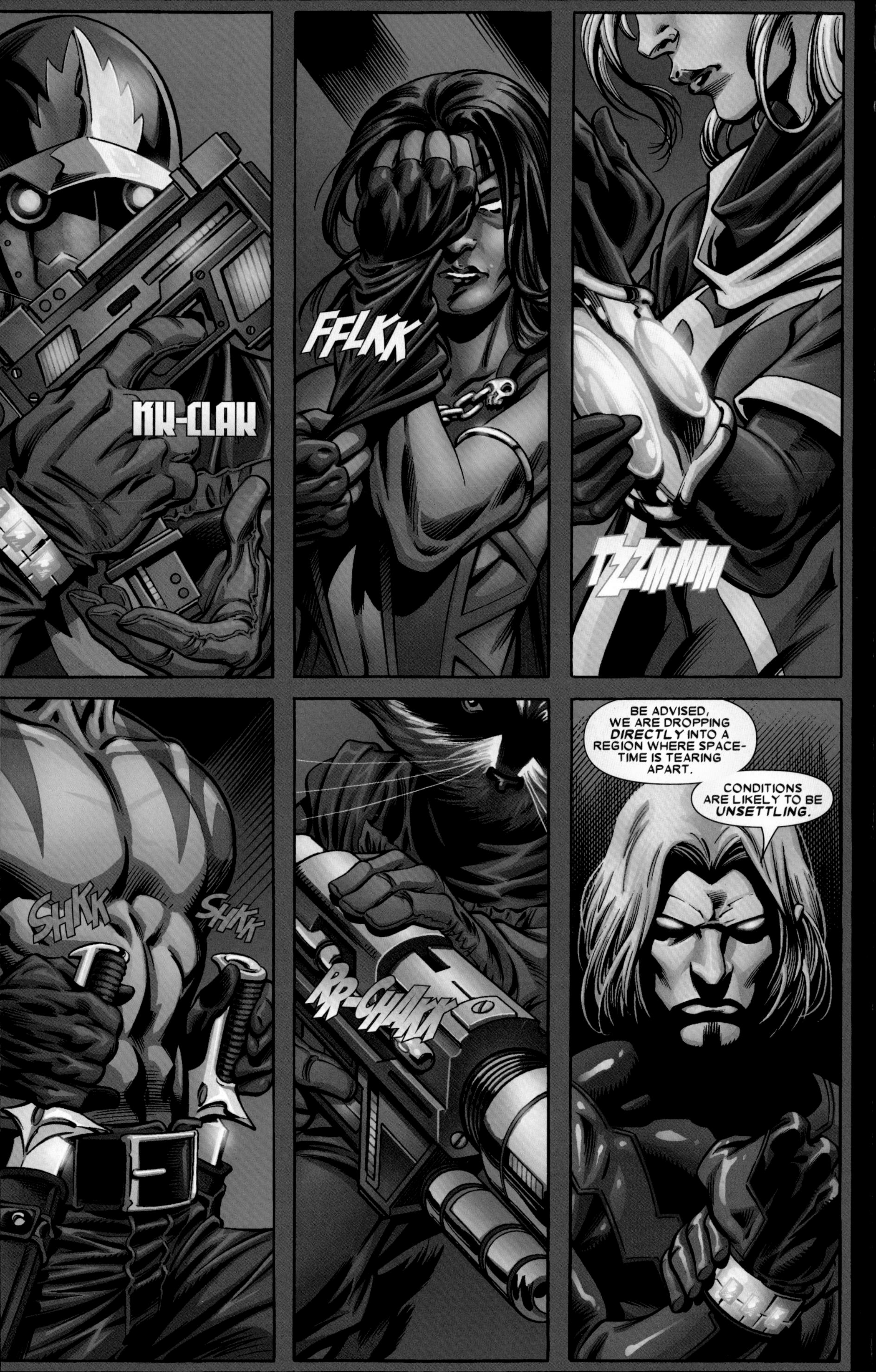
KR-CLAK
FFLKK
TZZMMM
SHKK
SHKK
RR-CHAKK
BE ADVISED, WE ARE DROPPING *DIRECTLY* INTO A REGION WHERE SPACE-TIME IS TEARING APART.
CONDITIONS ARE LIKELY TO BE *UNSETTLING.*

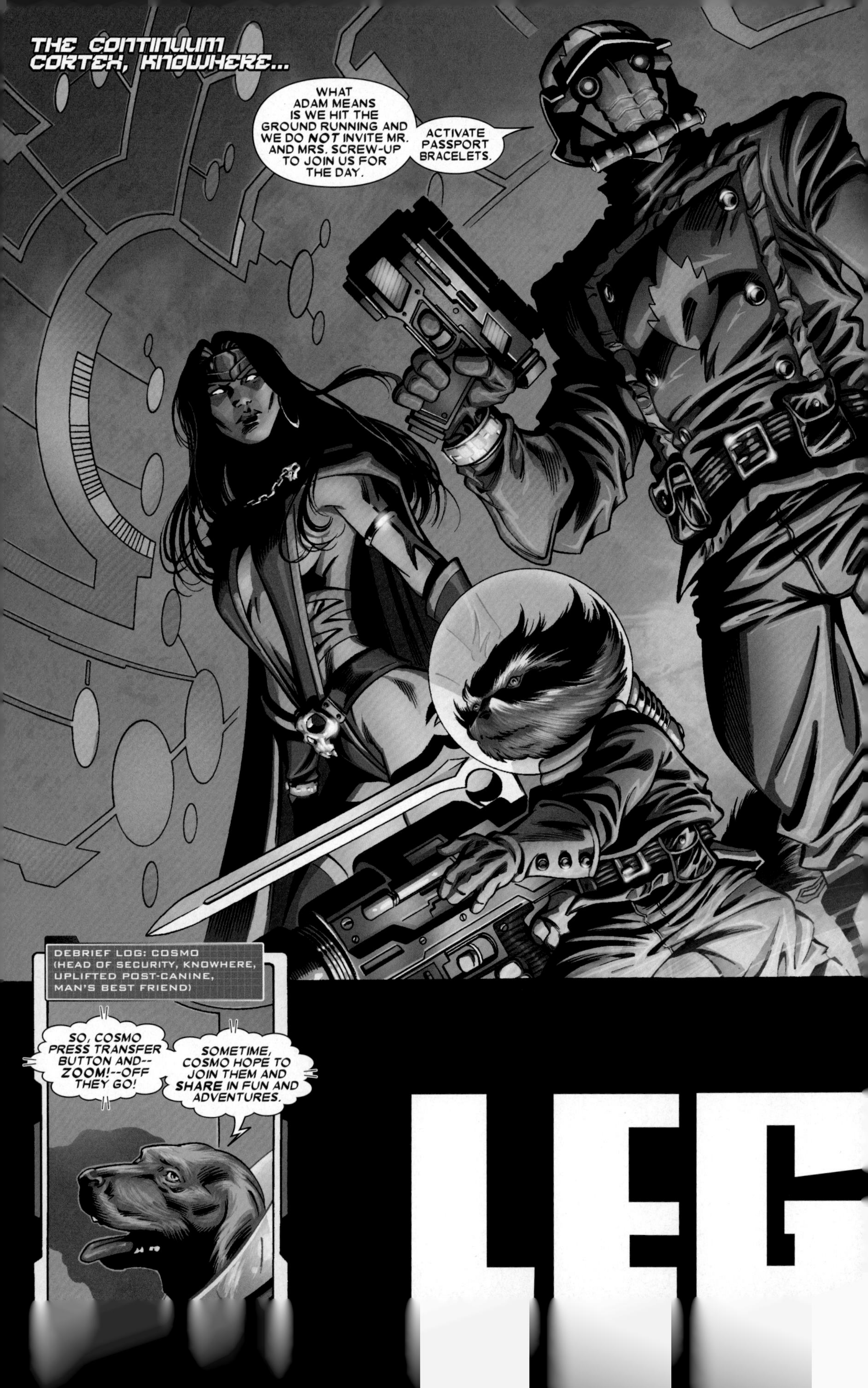
THE CONTINUUM CORTEX, KNOWHERE...
WHAT ADAM MEANS IS WE HIT THE GROUND RUNNING AND WE DO NOT INVITE MR. AND MRS. SCREW-UP TO JOIN US FOR THE DAY.
ACTIVATE PASSPORT BRACELETS.
DEBRIEF LOG: COSMO (HEAD OF SECURITY, KNOWHERE, UPLIFTED POST-CANINE, MAN'S BEST FRIEND)
SO, COSMO PRESS TRANSFER BUTTON AND--ZOOM!--OFF THEY GO!
SOMETIME, COSMO HOPE TO JOIN THEM AND SHARE IN FUN AND ADVENTURES.
LEG

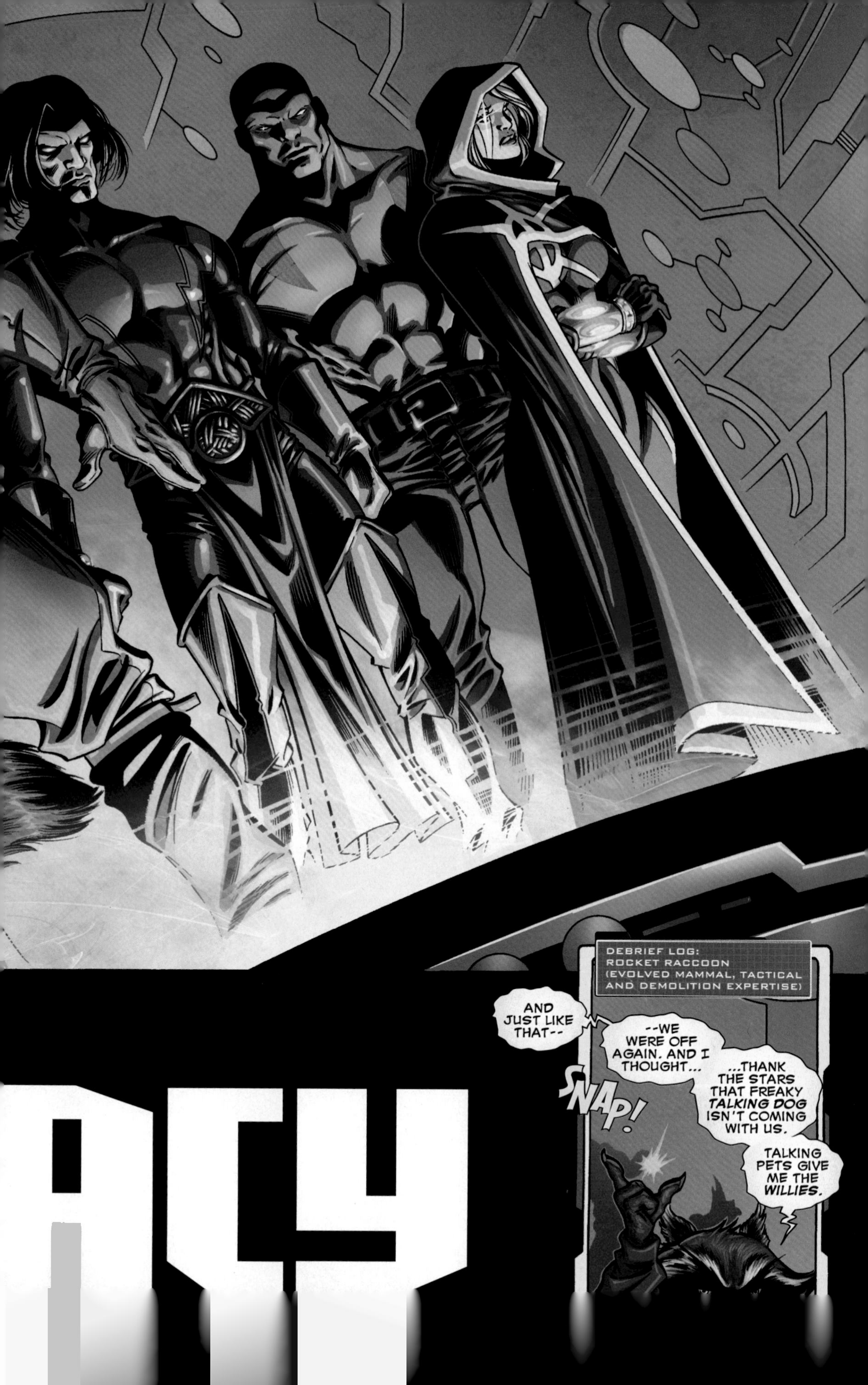
ACY
DEBRIEF LOG: ROCKET RACCOON (EVOLVED MAMMAL, TACTICAL AND DEMOLITION EXPERTISE)
AND JUST LIKE THAT--
--WE WERE OFF AGAIN. AND I THOUGHT...
SNAP!
...THANK THE STARS THAT FREAKY *TALKING DOG* ISN'T COMING WITH US.
TALKING PETS GIVE ME THE *WILLIES*.

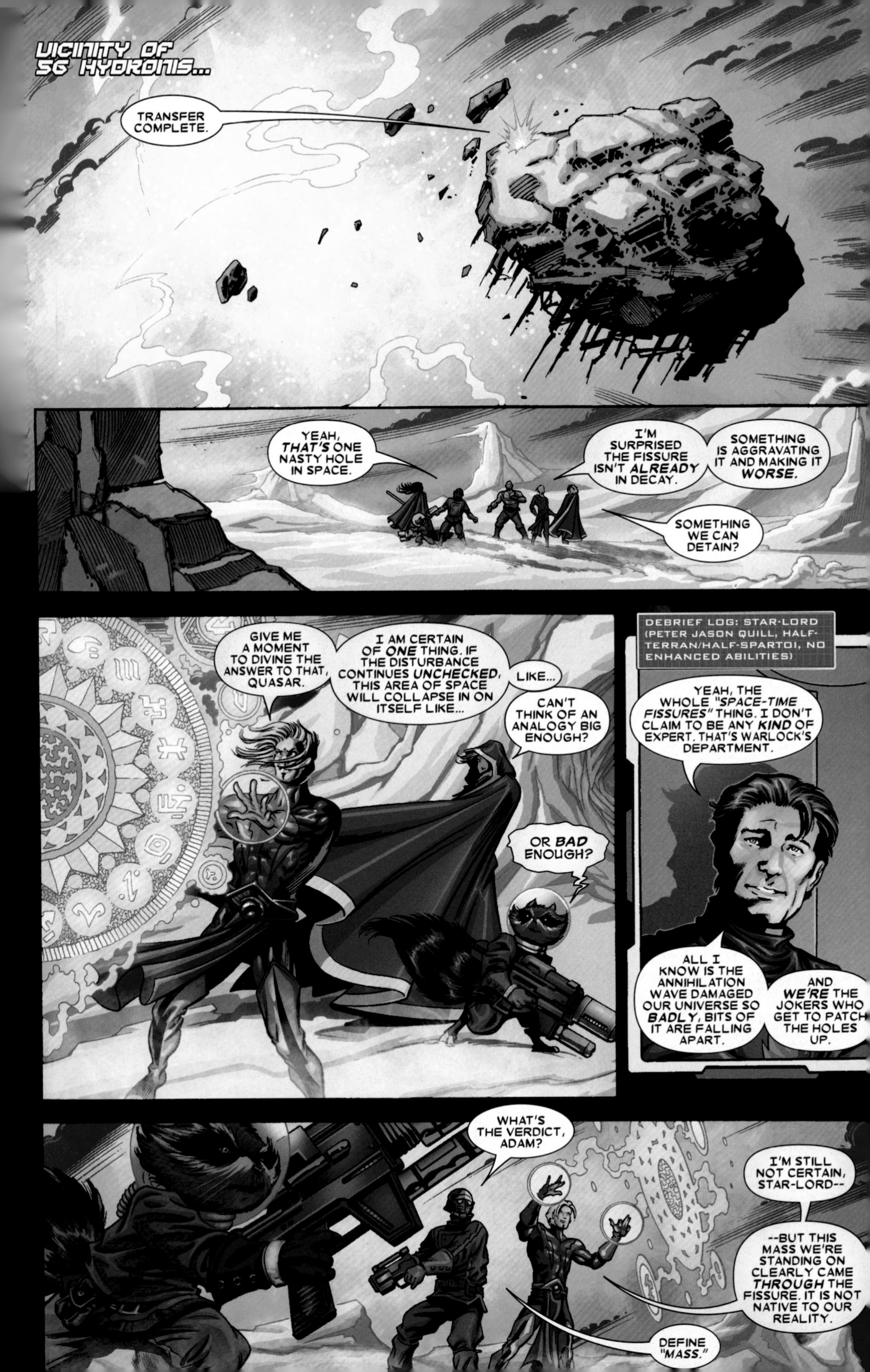
VICINITY OF 56 HYDRONIS...
TRANSFER COMPLETE.
YEAH, THAT'S ONE NASTY HOLE IN SPACE.
I'M SURPRISED THE FISSURE ISN'T ALREADY IN DECAY.
SOMETHING IS AGGRAVATING IT AND MAKING IT WORSE.
SOMETHING WE CAN DETAIN?
GIVE ME A MOMENT TO DIVINE THE ANSWER TO THAT, QUASAR.
I AM CERTAIN OF ONE THING. IF THE DISTURBANCE CONTINUES UNCHECKED, THIS AREA OF SPACE WILL COLLAPSE IN ON ITSELF LIKE...
LIKE...
CAN'T THINK OF AN ANALOGY BIG ENOUGH?
OR BAD ENOUGH?
DEBRIEF LOG: STAR-LORD (PETER JASON QUILL, HALF-TERRAN/HALF-SPARTOI, NO ENHANCED ABILITIES)
YEAH, THE WHOLE "SPACE-TIME FISSURES" THING. I DON'T CLAIM TO BE ANY KIND OF EXPERT. THAT'S WARLOCK'S DEPARTMENT.
ALL I KNOW IS THE ANNIHILATION WAVE DAMAGED OUR UNIVERSE SO BADLY, BITS OF IT ARE FALLING APART.
AND WE'RE THE JOKERS WHO GET TO PATCH THE HOLES UP.
WHAT'S THE VERDICT, ADAM?
I'M STILL NOT CERTAIN, STAR-LORD--
--BUT THIS MASS WE'RE STANDING ON CLEARLY CAME THROUGH THE FISSURE. IT IS NOT NATIVE TO OUR REALITY.
DEFINE "MASS."

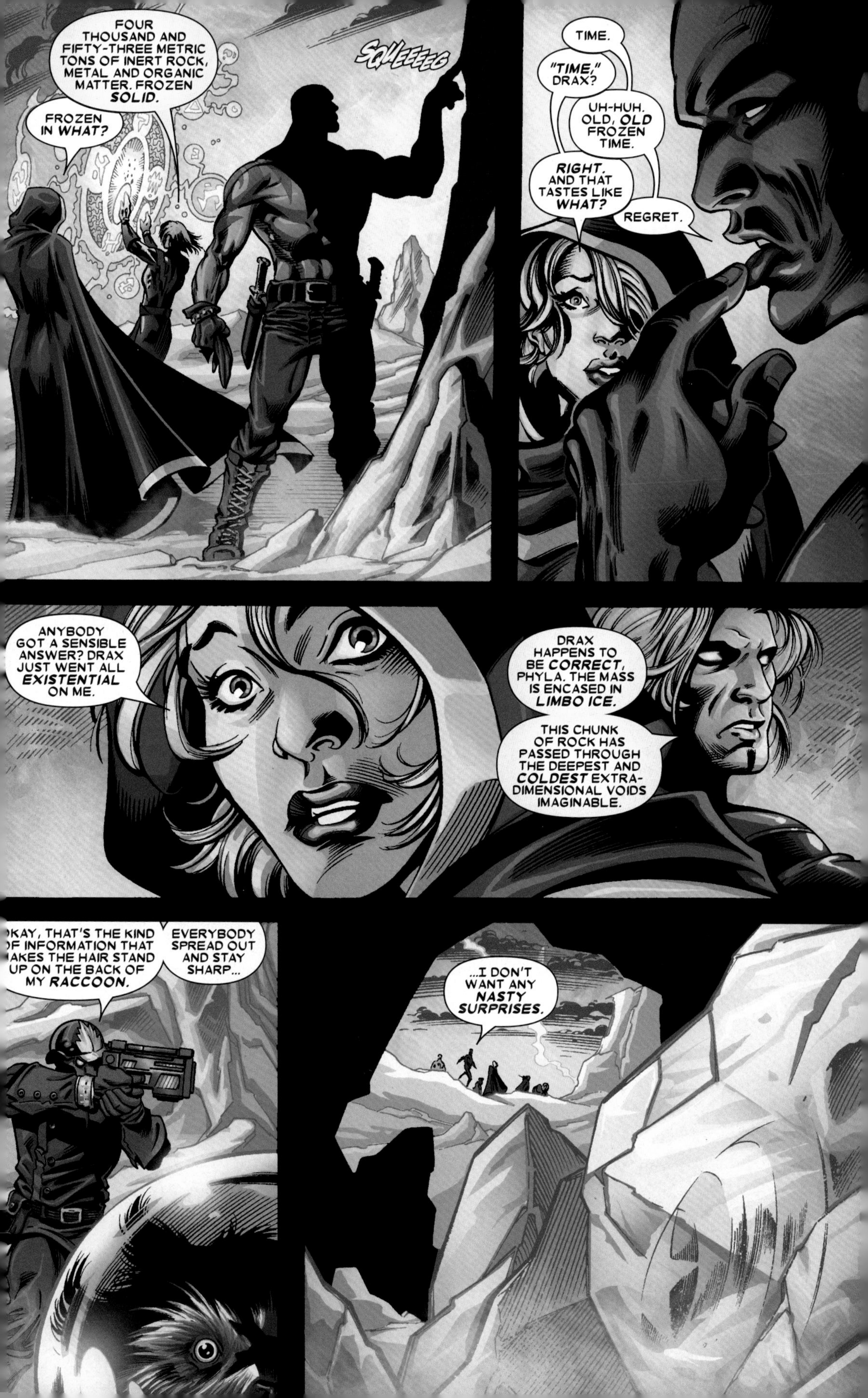
FOUR THOUSAND AND FIFTY-THREE METRIC TONS OF INERT ROCK, METAL AND ORGANIC MATTER. FROZEN SOLID.
FROZEN IN WHAT?
SQUEEEEG
TIME.
"TIME," DRAX?
UH-HUH. OLD, OLD FROZEN TIME.
RIGHT. AND THAT TASTES LIKE WHAT?
REGRET.
ANYBODY GOT A SENSIBLE ANSWER? DRAX JUST WENT ALL EXISTENTIAL ON ME.
DRAX HAPPENS TO BE CORRECT, PHYLA. THE MASS IS ENCASED IN LIMBO ICE.
THIS CHUNK OF ROCK HAS PASSED THROUGH THE DEEPEST AND COLDEST EXTRA-DIMENSIONAL VOIDS IMAGINABLE.
KAY, THAT'S THE KIND F INFORMATION THAT AKES THE HAIR STAND UP ON THE BACK OF MY RACCOON.
EVERYBODY SPREAD OUT AND STAY SHARP...
...I DON'T WANT ANY NASTY SURPRISES.

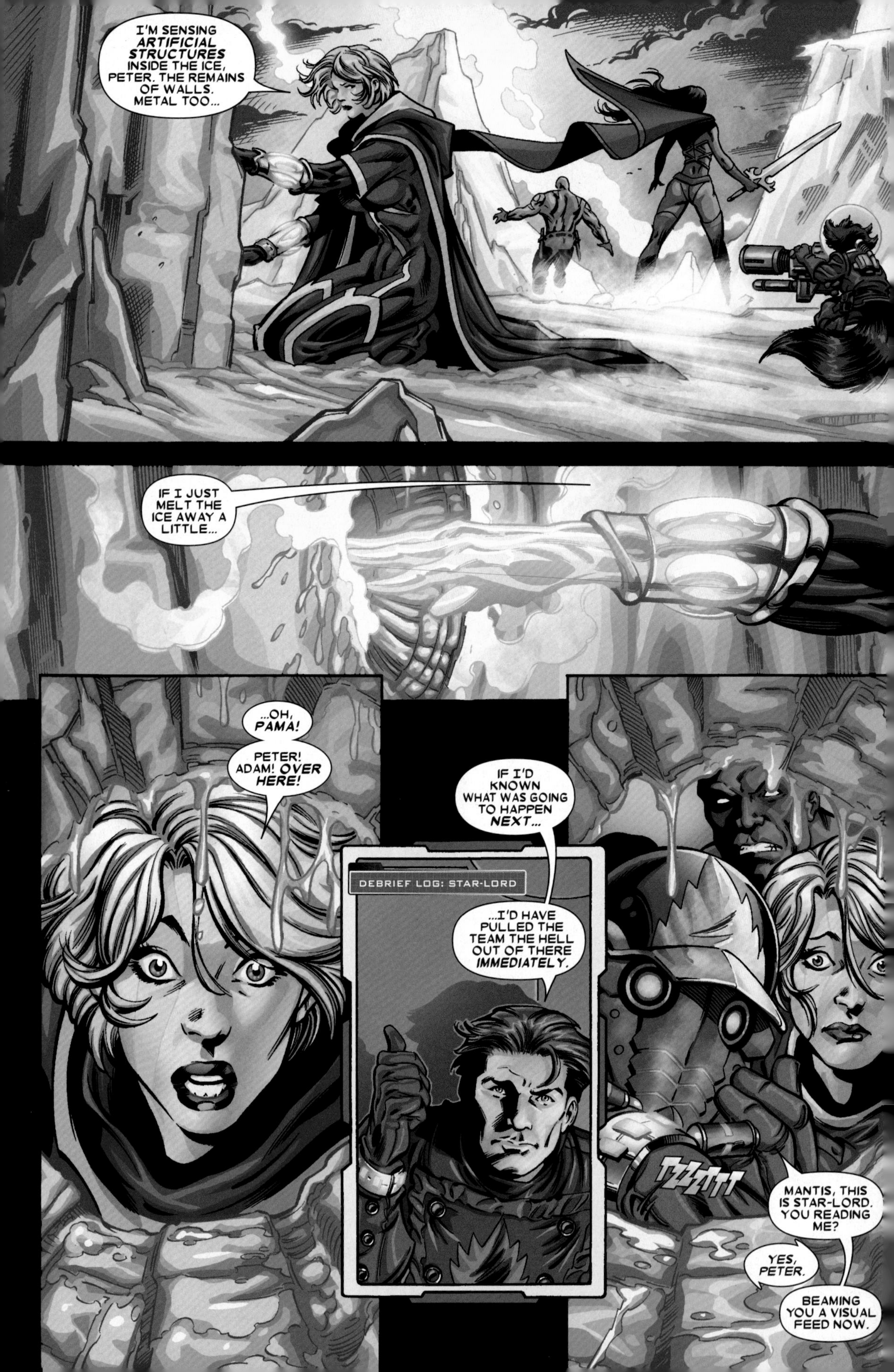
I'M SENSING ARTIFICIAL STRUCTURES INSIDE THE ICE, PETER. THE REMAINS OF WALLS. METAL TOO...
IF I JUST MELT THE ICE AWAY A LITTLE...
...OH, PAMA!
PETER! ADAM! OVER HERE!
IF I'D KNOWN WHAT WAS GOING TO HAPPEN NEXT...
DEBRIEF LOG: STAR-LORD
...I'D HAVE PULLED THE TEAM THE HELL OUT OF THERE IMMEDIATELY.
TZZZTTT
MANTIS, THIS IS STAR-LORD. YOU READING ME?
YES, PETER.
BEAMING YOU A VISUAL FEED NOW.

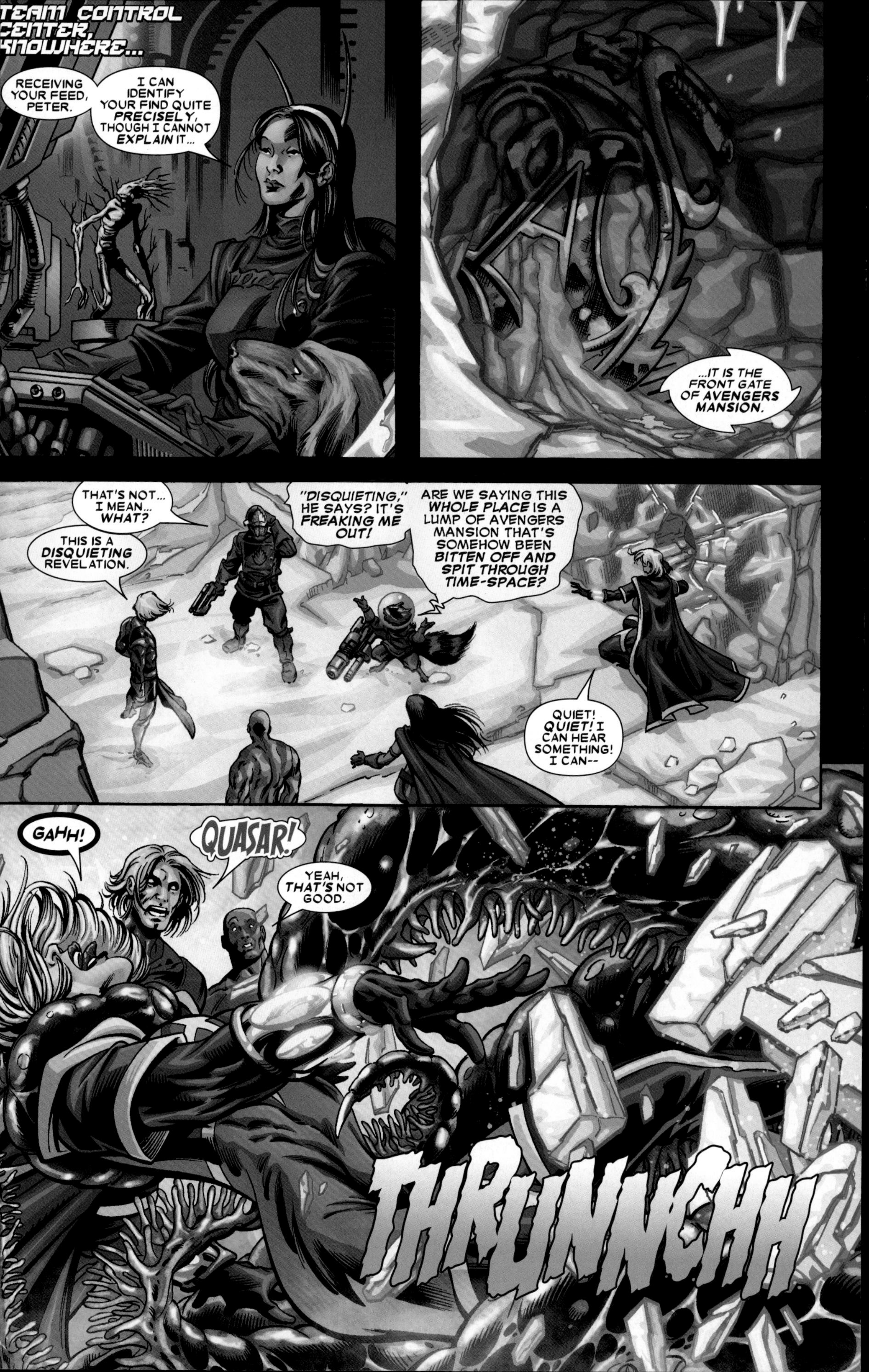
TEAM CONTROL CENTER, KNOWHERE...
RECEIVING YOUR FEED, PETER.
I CAN IDENTIFY YOUR FIND QUITE PRECISELY, THOUGH I CANNOT EXPLAIN IT...
...IT IS THE FRONT GATE OF AVENGERS MANSION.
THAT'S NOT... I MEAN... WHAT?
THIS IS A DISQUIETING REVELATION.
"DISQUIETING," HE SAYS? IT'S FREAKING ME OUT!
ARE WE SAYING THIS WHOLE PLACE IS A LUMP OF AVENGERS MANSION THAT'S SOMEHOW BEEN BITTEN OFF AND SPIT THROUGH TIME-SPACE?
QUIET! QUIET! I CAN HEAR SOMETHING! I CAN--
GAHH!
QUASAR!
YEAH, THAT'S NOT GOOD.
THRUNNCHH!

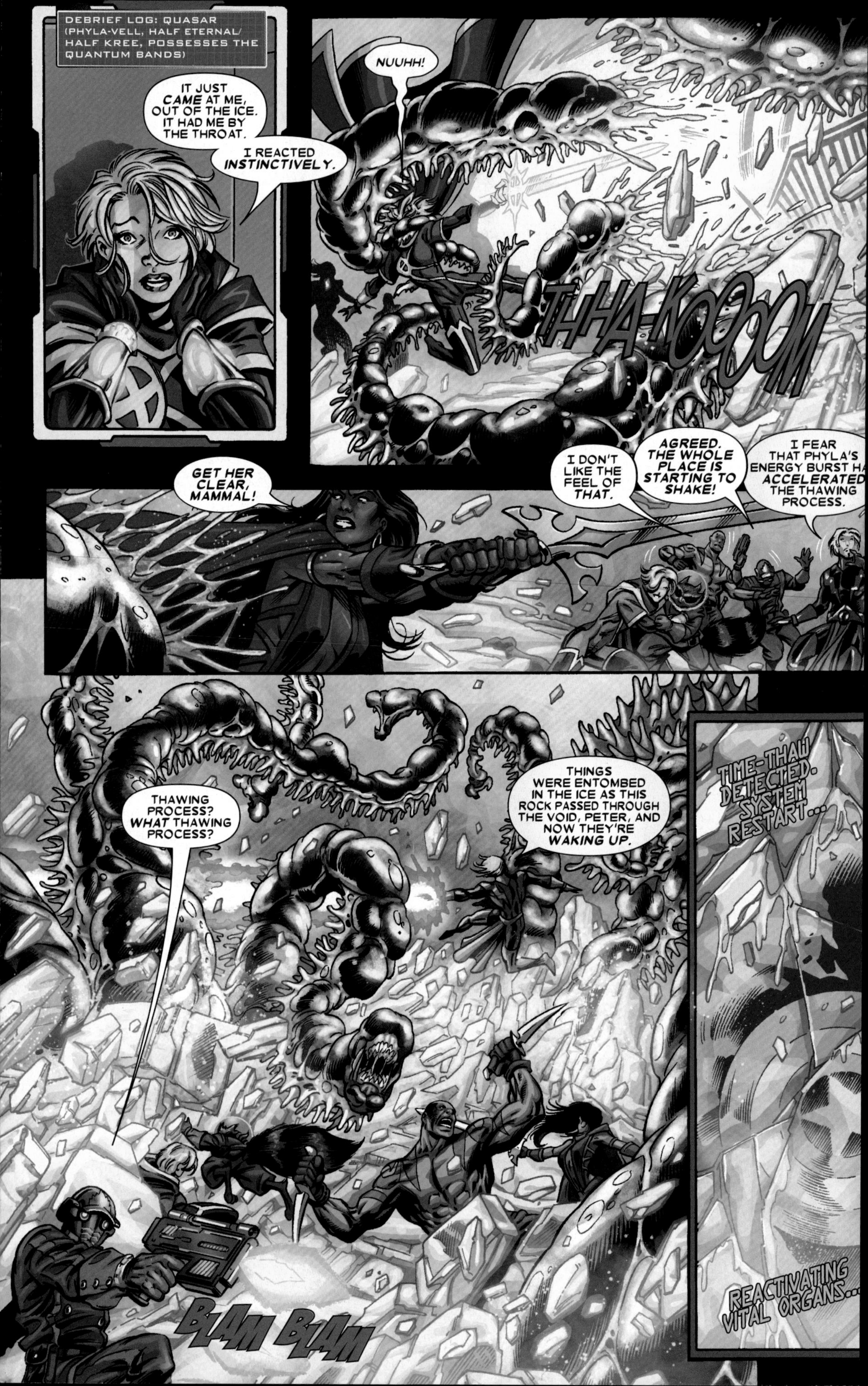

DEBRIEF LOG: QUASAR (PHYLA-VELL, HALF ETERNAL/ HALF KREE, POSSESSES THE QUANTUM BANDS)
IT JUST CAME AT ME, OUT OF THE ICE. IT HAD ME BY THE THROAT.
I REACTED INSTINCTIVELY.
NUUHH!
THHA-KOOOOM
GET HER CLEAR, MAMMAL!
I DON'T LIKE THE FEEL OF THAT.
AGREED. THE WHOLE PLACE IS STARTING TO SHAKE!
I FEAR THAT PHYLA'S ENERGY BURST HA ACCELERATED THE THAWING PROCESS.
THAWING PROCESS? WHAT THAWING PROCESS?
THINGS WERE ENTOMBED IN THE ICE AS THIS ROCK PASSED THROUGH THE VOID, PETER, AND NOW THEY'RE WAKING UP.
BLAM BLAM
TIME-THAW DETECTED. SYSTEM RESTART...
REACTIVATING VITAL ORGANS...

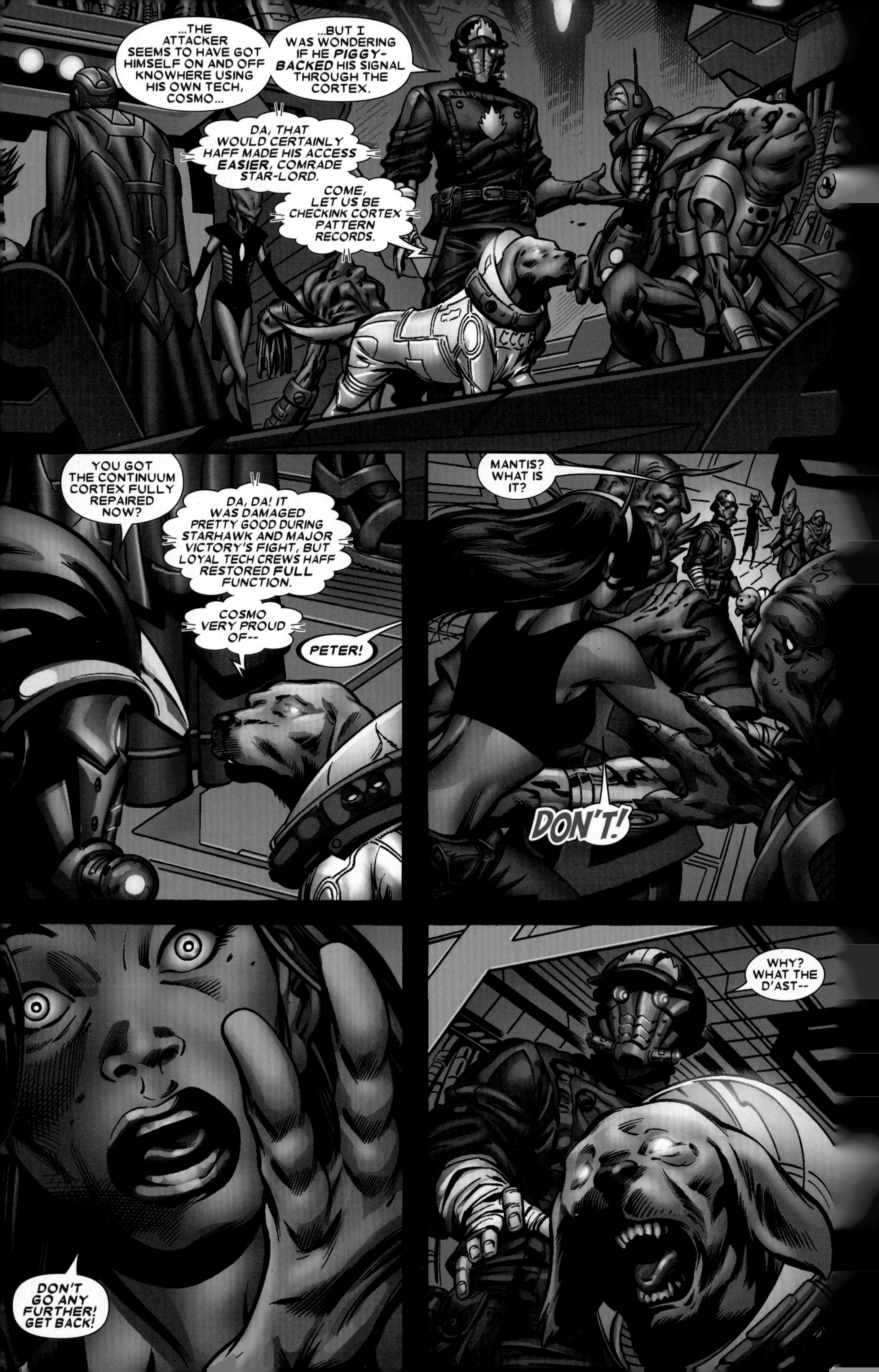

...THE ATTACKER SEEMS TO HAVE GOT HIMSELF ON AND OFF KNOWHERE USING HIS OWN TECH, COSMO...
...BUT I WAS WONDERING IF HE PIGGY-BACKED HIS SIGNAL THROUGH THE CORTEX.
DA, THAT WOULD CERTAINLY HAFF MADE HIS ACCESS EASIER, COMRADE STAR-LORD.
COME, LET US BE CHECKINK CORTEX PATTERN RECORDS.
YOU GOT THE CONTINUUM CORTEX FULLY REPAIRED NOW?
DA, DA! IT WAS DAMAGED PRETTY GOOD DURING STARHAWK AND MAJOR VICTORY'S FIGHT, BUT LOYAL TECH CREWS HAFF RESTORED FULL FUNCTION.
COSMO VERY PROUD OF--
PETER!
MANTIS? WHAT IS IT?
DON'T!
DON'T GO ANY FURTHER! GET BACK!
WHY? WHAT THE D'AST--

DAMAGES

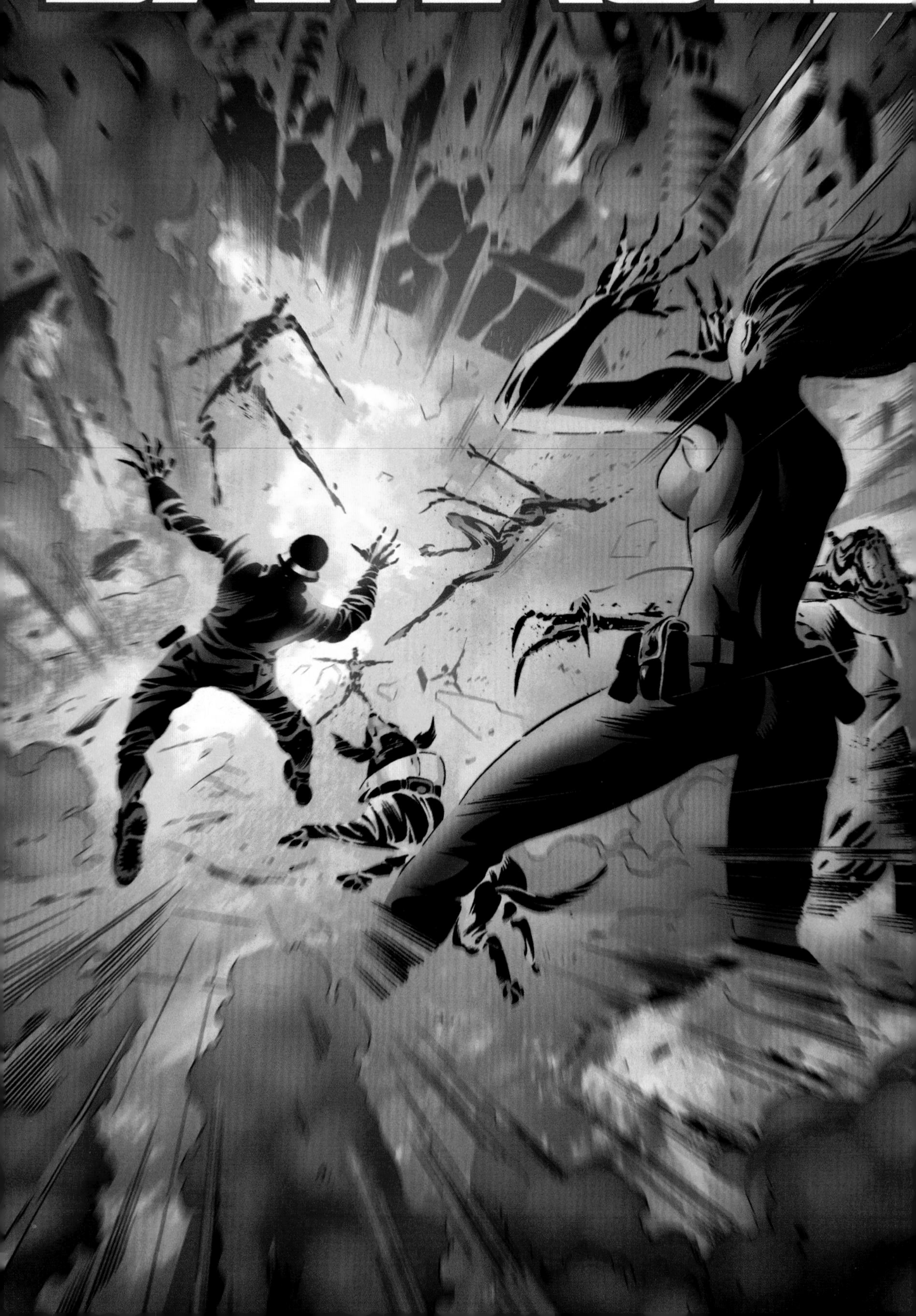

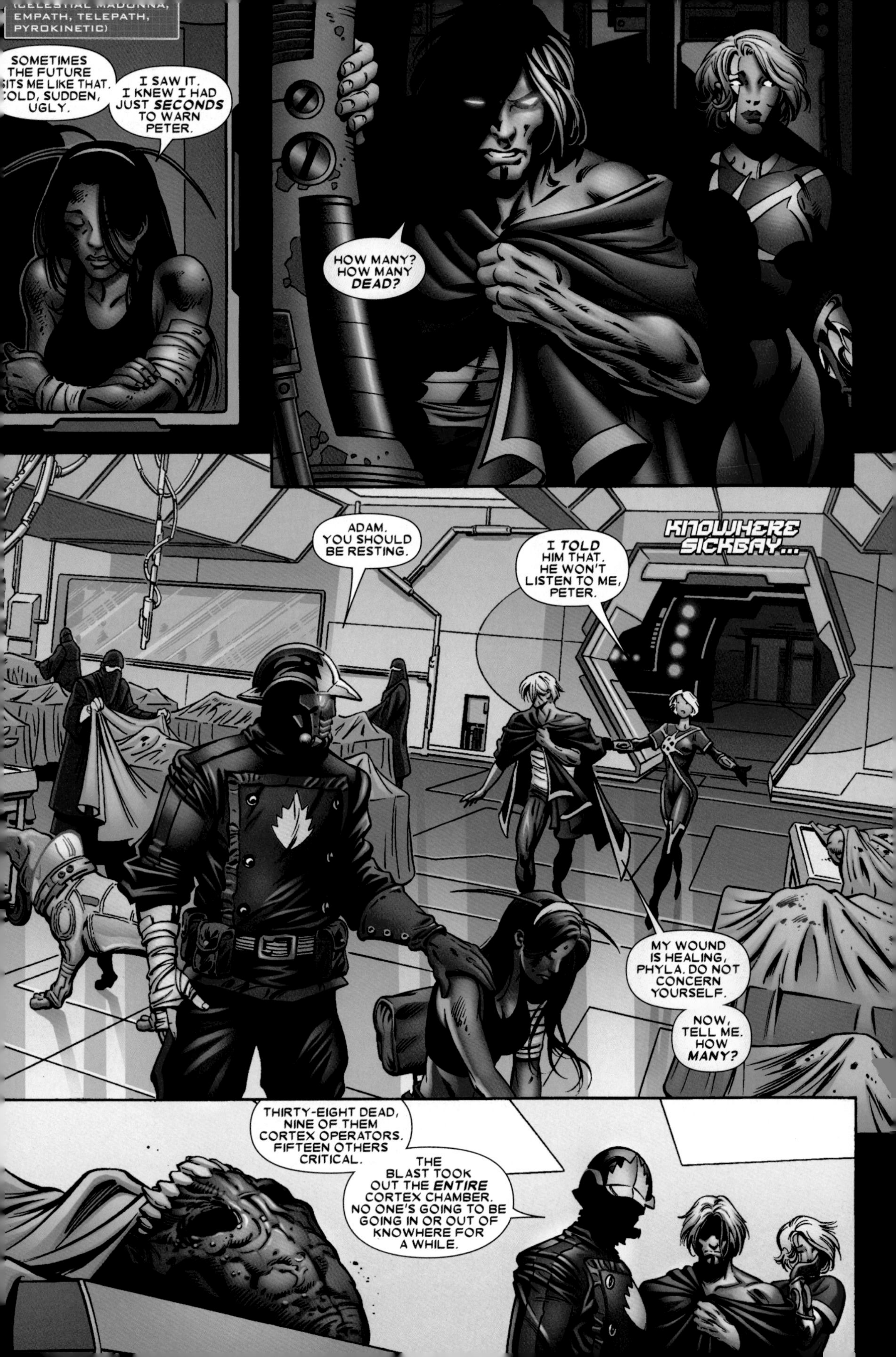
EMPATH, TELEPATH, PYROKINETIC)
SOMETIMES THE FUTURE HITS ME LIKE THAT. COLD, SUDDEN, UGLY.
I SAW IT. I KNEW I HAD JUST SECONDS TO WARN PETER.
HOW MANY? HOW MANY DEAD?
KNOWHERE SICKBAY...
ADAM. YOU SHOULD BE RESTING.
I TOLD HIM THAT. HE WON'T LISTEN TO ME, PETER.
MY WOUND IS HEALING, PHYLA. DO NOT CONCERN YOURSELF.
NOW, TELL ME. HOW MANY?
THIRTY-EIGHT DEAD, NINE OF THEM CORTEX OPERATORS. FIFTEEN OTHERS CRITICAL.
THE BLAST TOOK OUT THE ENTIRE CORTEX CHAMBER. NO ONE'S GOING TO BE GOING IN OR OUT OF KNOWHERE FOR A WHILE.

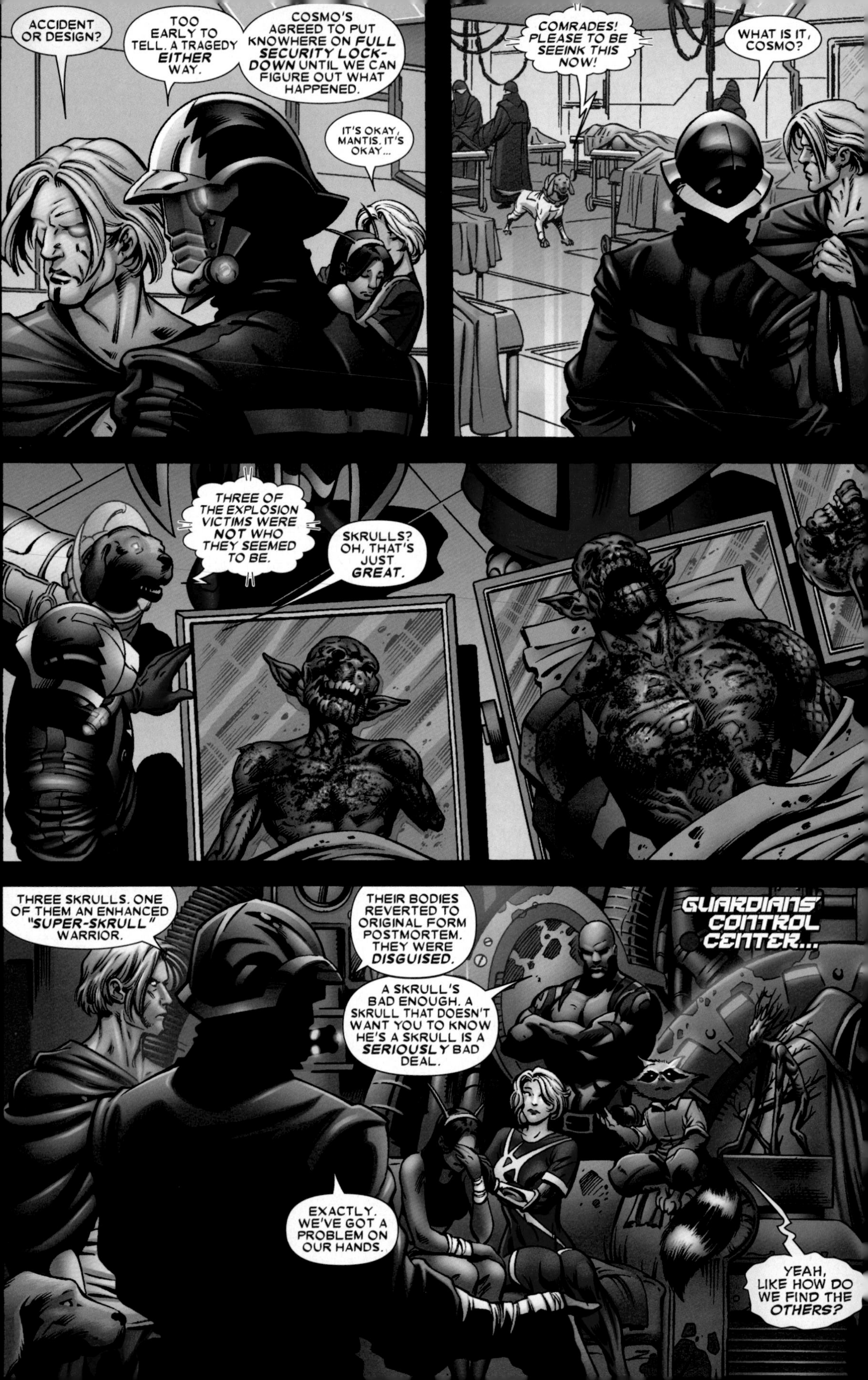
ACCIDENT OR DESIGN?
TOO EARLY TO TELL. A TRAGEDY EITHER WAY.
COSMO'S AGREED TO PUT KNOWHERE ON FULL SECURITY LOCK-DOWN UNTIL WE CAN FIGURE OUT WHAT HAPPENED.
IT'S OKAY, MANTIS. IT'S OKAY...
COMRADES! PLEASE TO BE SEEINK THIS NOW!
WHAT IS IT, COSMO?
THREE OF THE EXPLOSION VICTIMS WERE NOT WHO THEY SEEMED TO BE.
SKRULLS? OH, THAT'S JUST GREAT.
GUARDIANS' CONTROL CENTER...
THREE SKRULLS. ONE OF THEM AN ENHANCED "SUPER-SKRULL" WARRIOR.
THEIR BODIES REVERTED TO ORIGINAL FORM POSTMORTEM. THEY WERE DISGUISED.
A SKRULL'S BAD ENOUGH. A SKRULL THAT DOESN'T WANT YOU TO KNOW HE'S A SKRULL IS A SERIOUSLY BAD DEAL.
EXACTLY. WE'VE GOT A PROBLEM ON OUR HANDS.
YEAH, LIKE HOW DO WE FIND THE OTHERS?

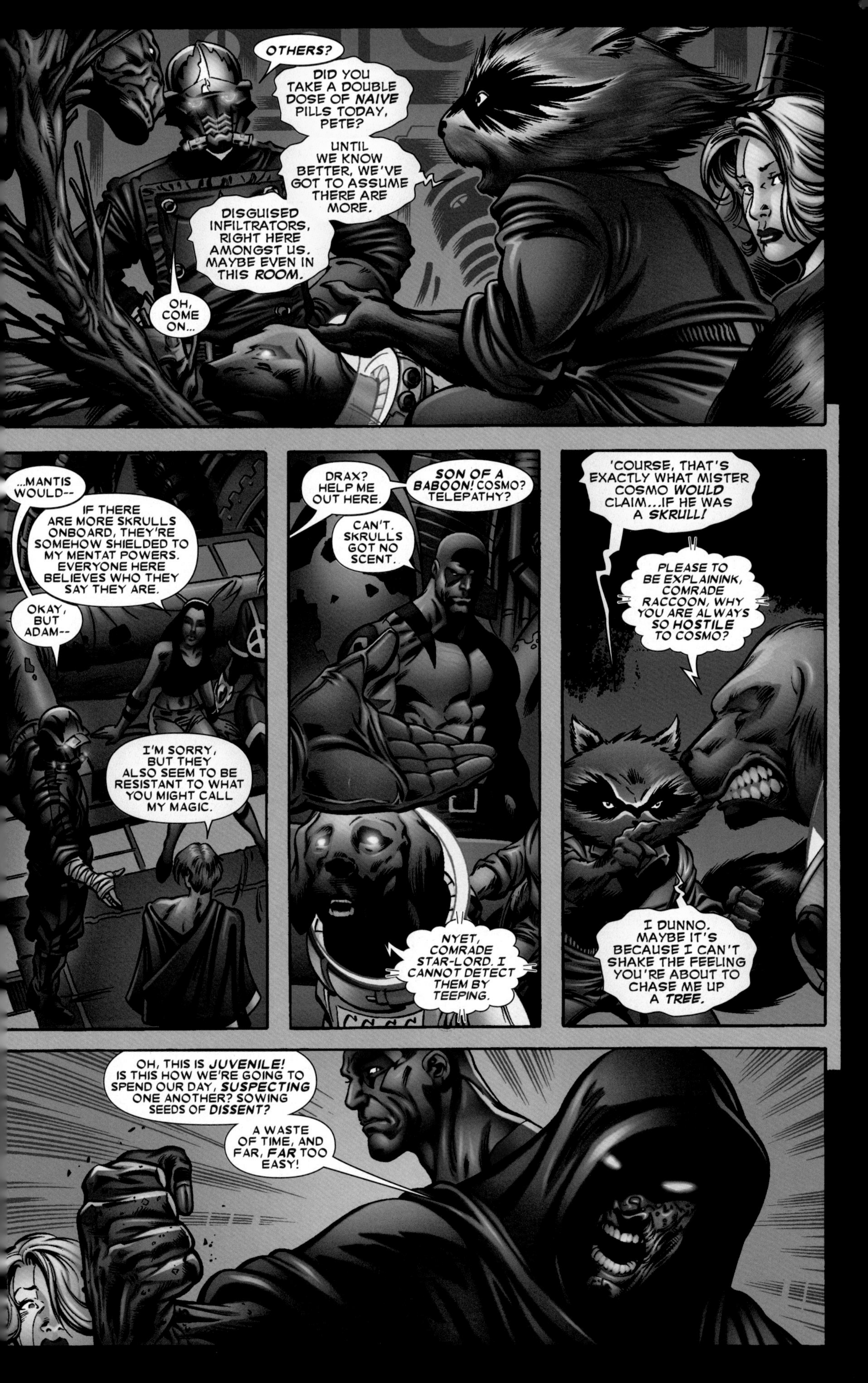
OTHERS?
DID YOU TAKE A DOUBLE DOSE OF NAIVE PILLS TODAY, PETE?
UNTIL WE KNOW BETTER, WE'VE GOT TO ASSUME THERE ARE MORE.
DISGUISED INFILTRATORS, RIGHT HERE AMONGST US. MAYBE EVEN IN THIS ROOM.
OH, COME ON...
...MANTIS WOULD--
IF THERE ARE MORE SKRULLS ONBOARD, THEY'RE SOMEHOW SHIELDED TO MY MENTAT POWERS. EVERYONE HERE BELIEVES WHO THEY SAY THEY ARE.
OKAY, BUT ADAM--
I'M SORRY, BUT THEY ALSO SEEM TO BE RESISTANT TO WHAT YOU MIGHT CALL MY MAGIC.
DRAX? HELP ME OUT HERE.
SON OF A BABOON! COSMO? TELEPATHY?
CAN'T. SKRULLS GOT NO SCENT.
NYET, COMRADE STAR-LORD. I CANNOT DETECT THEM BY TEEPING.
'COURSE, THAT'S EXACTLY WHAT MISTER COSMO WOULD CLAIM...IF HE WAS A SKRULL!
PLEASE TO BE EXPLAININK, COMRADE RACCOON, WHY YOU ARE ALWAYS SO HOSTILE TO COSMO?
I DUNNO. MAYBE IT'S BECAUSE I CAN'T SHAKE THE FEELING YOU'RE ABOUT TO CHASE ME UP A TREE.
OH, THIS IS JUVENILE! IS THIS HOW WE'RE GOING TO SPEND OUR DAY, SUSPECTING ONE ANOTHER? SOWING SEEDS OF DISSENT?
A WASTE OF TIME, AND FAR, FAR TOO EASY!

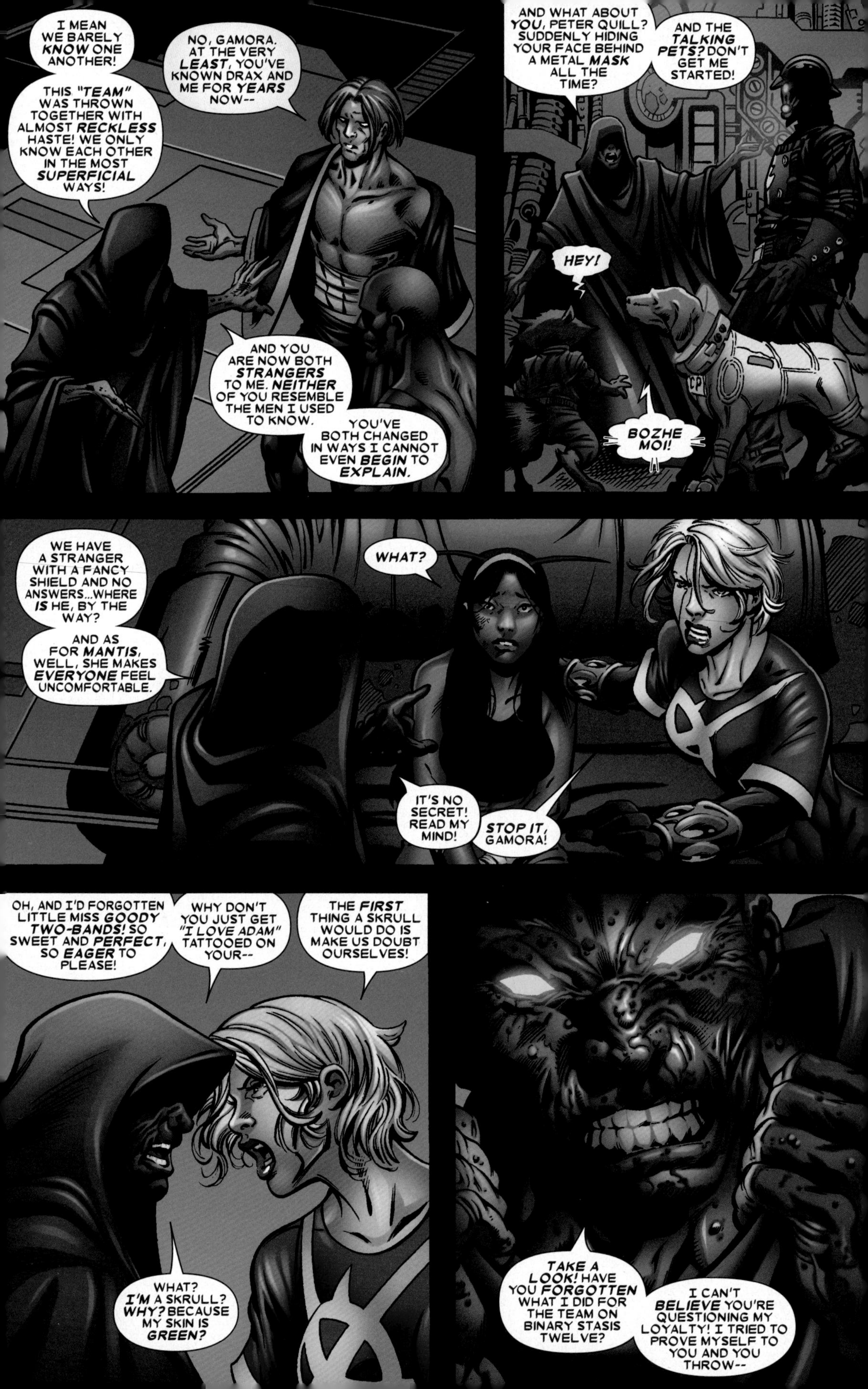
I MEAN WE BARELY KNOW ONE ANOTHER!
THIS "TEAM" WAS THROWN TOGETHER WITH ALMOST RECKLESS HASTE! WE ONLY KNOW EACH OTHER IN THE MOST SUPERFICIAL WAYS!
NO, GAMORA. AT THE VERY LEAST, YOU'VE KNOWN DRAX AND ME FOR YEARS NOW--
AND YOU ARE NOW BOTH STRANGERS TO ME. NEITHER OF YOU RESEMBLE THE MEN I USED TO KNOW.
YOU'VE BOTH CHANGED IN WAYS I CANNOT EVEN BEGIN TO EXPLAIN.
AND WHAT ABOUT YOU, PETER QUILL? SUDDENLY HIDING YOUR FACE BEHIND A METAL MASK ALL THE TIME?
AND THE TALKING PETS? DON'T GET ME STARTED!
HEY!
BOZHE MOI!
CP
WE HAVE A STRANGER WITH A FANCY SHIELD AND NO ANSWERS...WHERE IS HE, BY THE WAY?
AND AS FOR MANTIS, WELL, SHE MAKES EVERYONE FEEL UNCOMFORTABLE.
WHAT?
IT'S NO SECRET! READ MY MIND!
STOP IT, GAMORA!
OH, AND I'D FORGOTTEN LITTLE MISS GOODY TWO-BANDS! SO SWEET AND PERFECT, SO EAGER TO PLEASE!
WHY DON'T YOU JUST GET "I LOVE ADAM" TATTOOED ON YOUR--
THE FIRST THING A SKRULL WOULD DO IS MAKE US DOUBT OURSELVES!
WHAT? I'M A SKRULL? WHY? BECAUSE MY SKIN IS GREEN?
TAKE A LOOK! HAVE YOU FORGOTTEN WHAT I DID FOR THE TEAM ON BINARY STASIS TWELVE?
I CAN'T BELIEVE YOU'RE QUESTIONING MY LOYALTY! I TRIED TO PROVE MYSELF TO YOU AND YOU THROW--

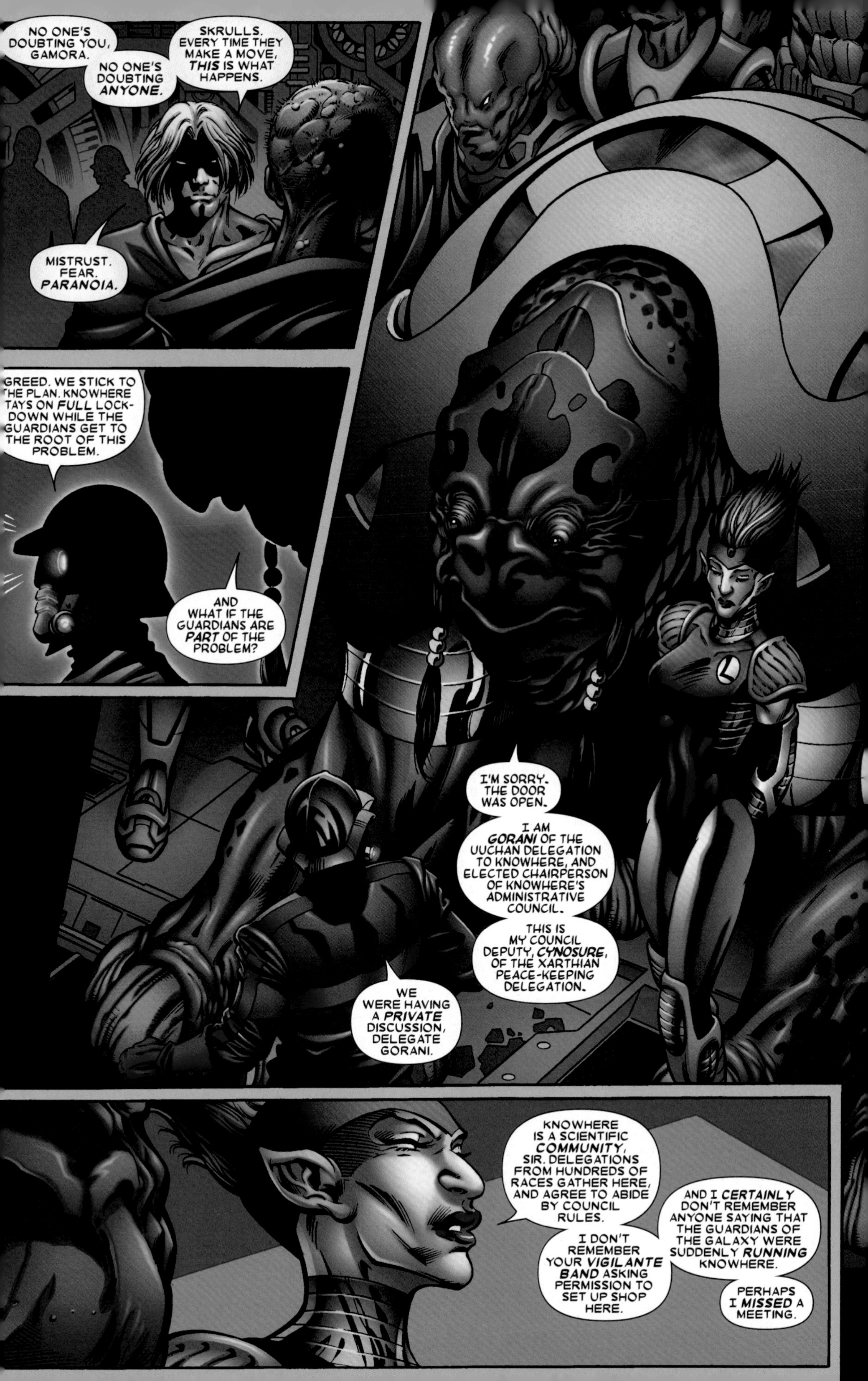
NO ONE'S DOUBTING YOU, GAMORA.
NO ONE'S DOUBTING ANYONE.
SKRULLS. EVERY TIME THEY MAKE A MOVE, THIS IS WHAT HAPPENS.
MISTRUST. FEAR. PARANOIA.
GREED. WE STICK TO THE PLAN. KNOWHERE TAYS ON FULL LOCK-DOWN WHILE THE GUARDIANS GET TO THE ROOT OF THIS PROBLEM.
AND WHAT IF THE GUARDIANS ARE PART OF THE PROBLEM?
I'M SORRY. THE DOOR WAS OPEN.
I AM GORANI OF THE UUCHAN DELEGATION TO KNOWHERE, AND ELECTED CHAIRPERSON OF KNOWHERE'S ADMINISTRATIVE COUNCIL.
THIS IS MY COUNCIL DEPUTY, CYNOSURE, OF THE XARTHIAN PEACE-KEEPING DELEGATION.
WE WERE HAVING A PRIVATE DISCUSSION, DELEGATE GORANI.
KNOWHERE IS A SCIENTIFIC COMMUNITY, SIR. DELEGATIONS FROM HUNDREDS OF RACES GATHER HERE, AND AGREE TO ABIDE BY COUNCIL RULES.
I DON'T REMEMBER YOUR VIGILANTE BAND ASKING PERMISSION TO SET UP SHOP HERE.
AND I CERTAINLY DON'T REMEMBER ANYONE SAYING THAT THE GUARDIANS OF THE GALAXY WERE SUDDENLY RUNNING KNOWHERE.
PERHAPS I MISSED A MEETING.

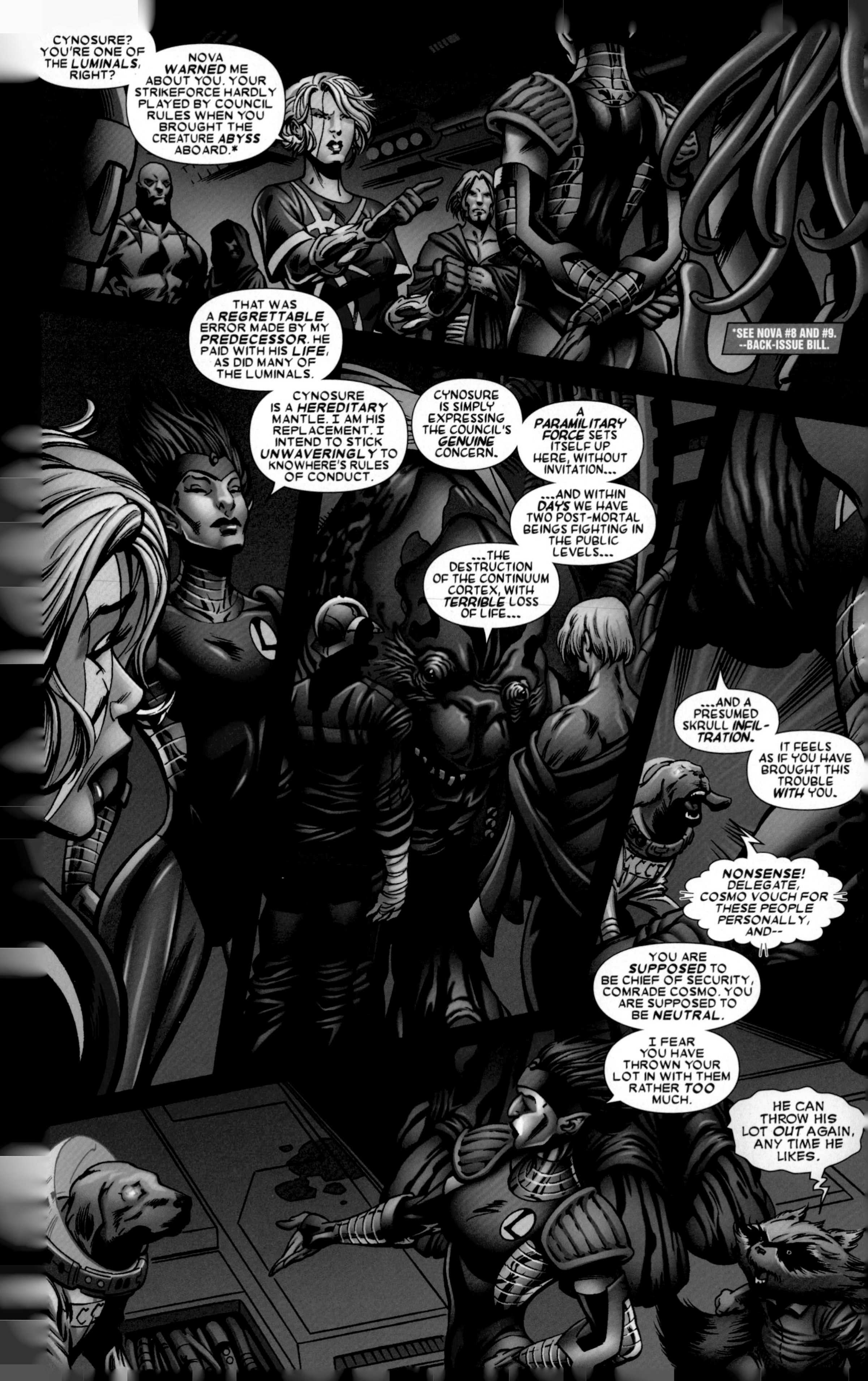
CYNOSURE? YOU'RE ONE OF THE LUMINALS, RIGHT?
NOVA WARNED ME ABOUT YOU. YOUR STRIKEFORCE HARDLY PLAYED BY COUNCIL RULES WHEN YOU BROUGHT THE CREATURE ABYSS ABOARD.*
*SEE NOVA #8 AND #9. --BACK-ISSUE BILL.
THAT WAS A REGRETTABLE ERROR MADE BY MY PREDECESSOR. HE PAID WITH HIS LIFE, AS DID MANY OF THE LUMINALS.
CYNOSURE IS A HEREDITARY MANTLE. I AM HIS REPLACEMENT. I INTEND TO STICK UNWAVERINGLY TO KNOWHERE'S RULES OF CONDUCT.
CYNOSURE IS SIMPLY EXPRESSING THE COUNCIL'S GENUINE CONCERN.
A PARAMILITARY FORCE SETS ITSELF UP HERE, WITHOUT INVITATION...
...AND WITHIN DAYS WE HAVE TWO POST-MORTAL BEINGS FIGHTING IN THE PUBLIC LEVELS...
...THE DESTRUCTION OF THE CONTINUUM CORTEX, WITH TERRIBLE LOSS OF LIFE...
...AND A PRESUMED SKRULL INFILTRATION.
IT FEELS AS IF YOU HAVE BROUGHT THIS TROUBLE WITH YOU.
NONSENSE! DELEGATE, COSMO VOUCH FOR THESE PEOPLE PERSONALLY, AND--
YOU ARE SUPPOSED TO BE CHIEF OF SECURITY, COMRADE COSMO. YOU ARE SUPPOSED TO BE NEUTRAL.
I FEAR YOU HAVE THROWN YOUR LOT IN WITH THEM RATHER TOO MUCH.
HE CAN THROW HIS LOT OUT AGAIN, ANY TIME HE LIKES.

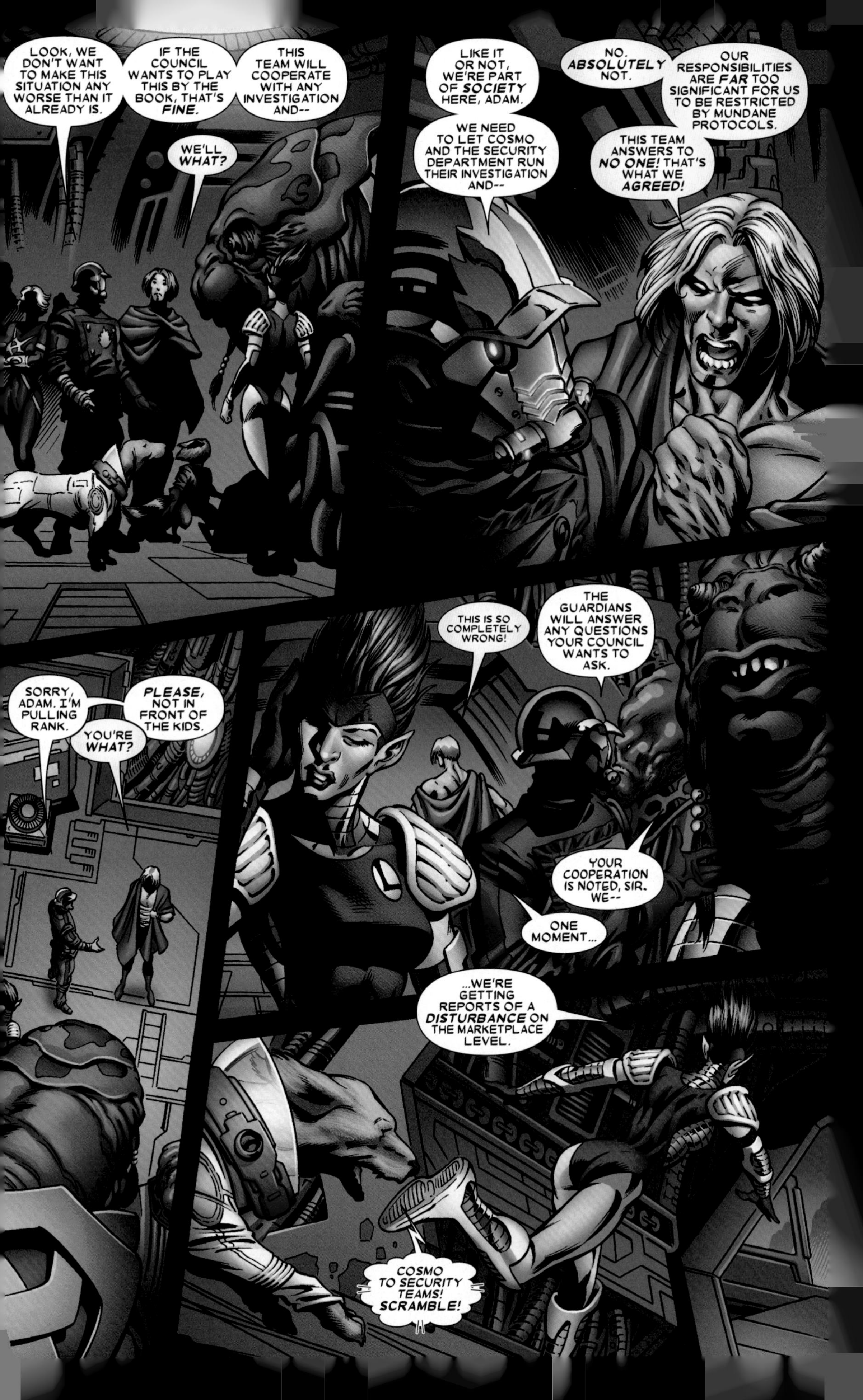
LOOK, WE DON'T WANT TO MAKE THIS SITUATION ANY WORSE THAN IT ALREADY IS.
IF THE COUNCIL WANTS TO PLAY THIS BY THE BOOK, THAT'S FINE.
THIS TEAM WILL COOPERATE WITH ANY INVESTIGATION AND--
WE'LL WHAT?
LIKE IT OR NOT, WE'RE PART OF SOCIETY HERE, ADAM.
WE NEED TO LET COSMO AND THE SECURITY DEPARTMENT RUN THEIR INVESTIGATION AND--
NO. ABSOLUTELY NOT.
OUR RESPONSIBILITIES ARE FAR TOO SIGNIFICANT FOR US TO BE RESTRICTED BY MUNDANE PROTOCOLS.
THIS TEAM ANSWERS TO NO ONE! THAT'S WHAT WE AGREED!
SORRY, ADAM. I'M PULLING RANK.
YOU'RE WHAT?
PLEASE, NOT IN FRONT OF THE KIDS.
THIS IS SO COMPLETELY WRONG!
THE GUARDIANS WILL ANSWER ANY QUESTIONS YOUR COUNCIL WANTS TO ASK.
YOUR COOPERATION IS NOTED, SIR. WE--
ONE MOMENT...
...WE'RE GETTING REPORTS OF A DISTURBANCE ON THE MARKETPLACE LEVEL.
COSMO TO SECURITY TEAMS! SCRAMBLE!

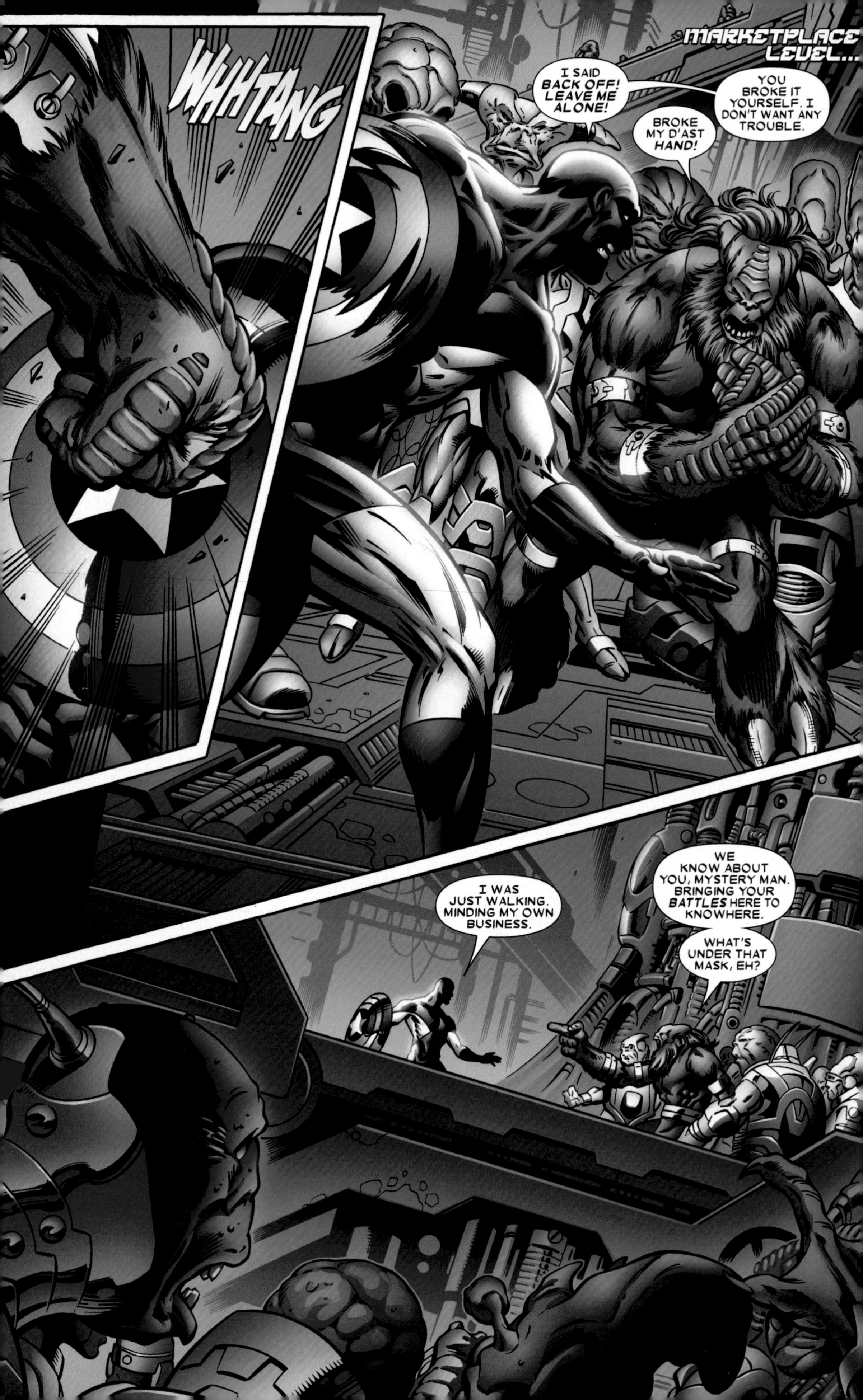
WHHTANG
MARKETPLACE LEVEL...
I SAID BACK OFF! LEAVE ME ALONE!
YOU BROKE IT YOURSELF. I DON'T WANT ANY TROUBLE.
BROKE MY D'AST HAND!
I WAS JUST WALKING. MINDING MY OWN BUSINESS.
WE KNOW ABOUT YOU, MYSTERY MAN. BRINGING YOUR BATTLES HERE TO KNOWHERE.
WHAT'S UNDER THAT MASK, EH?

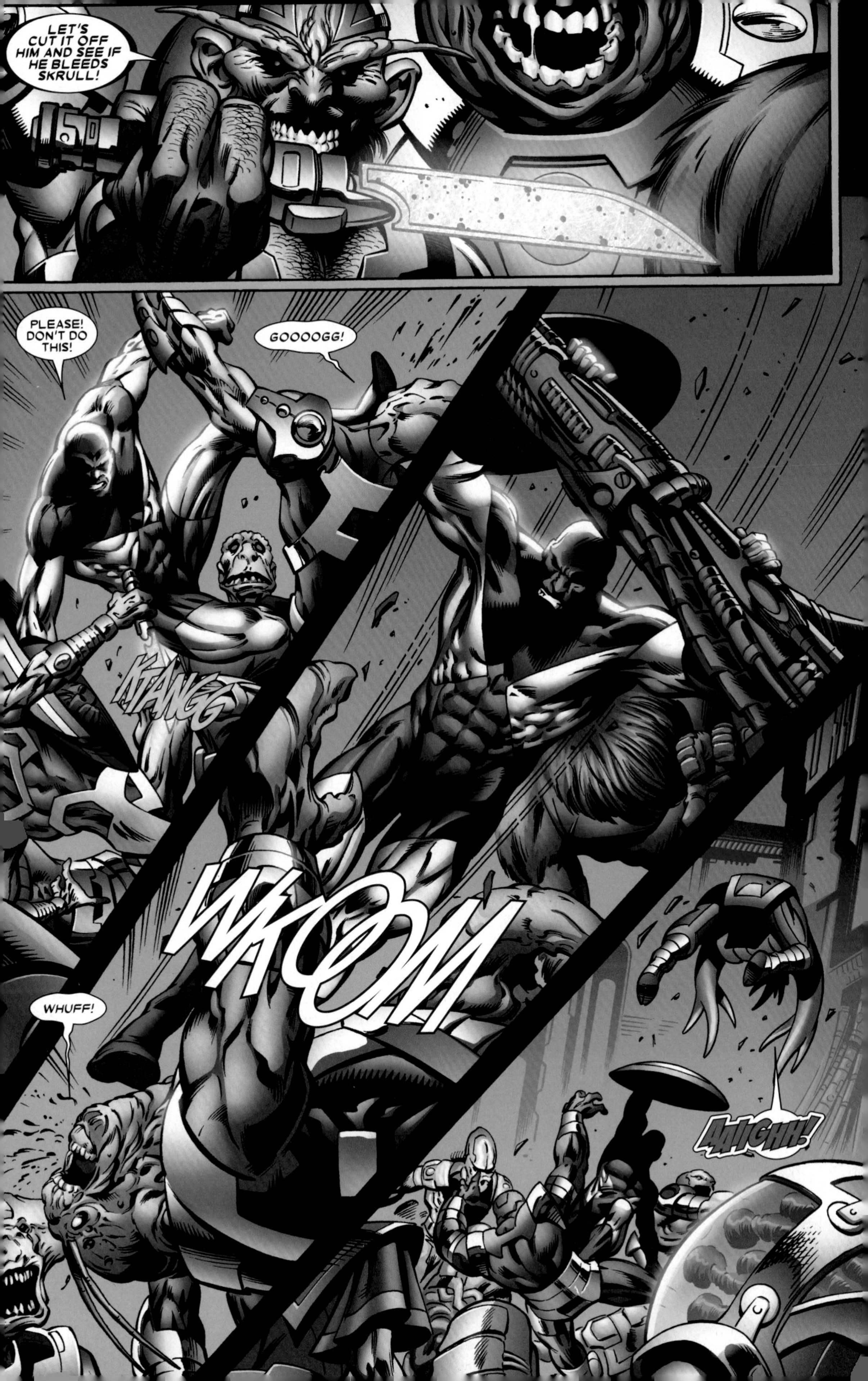
LET'S CUT IT OFF HIM AND SEE IF HE BLEEDS SKRULL!
PLEASE! DON'T DO THIS!
GOOOOGG!
KTANGG
WKOOM
WHUFF!
AAIIGHH!

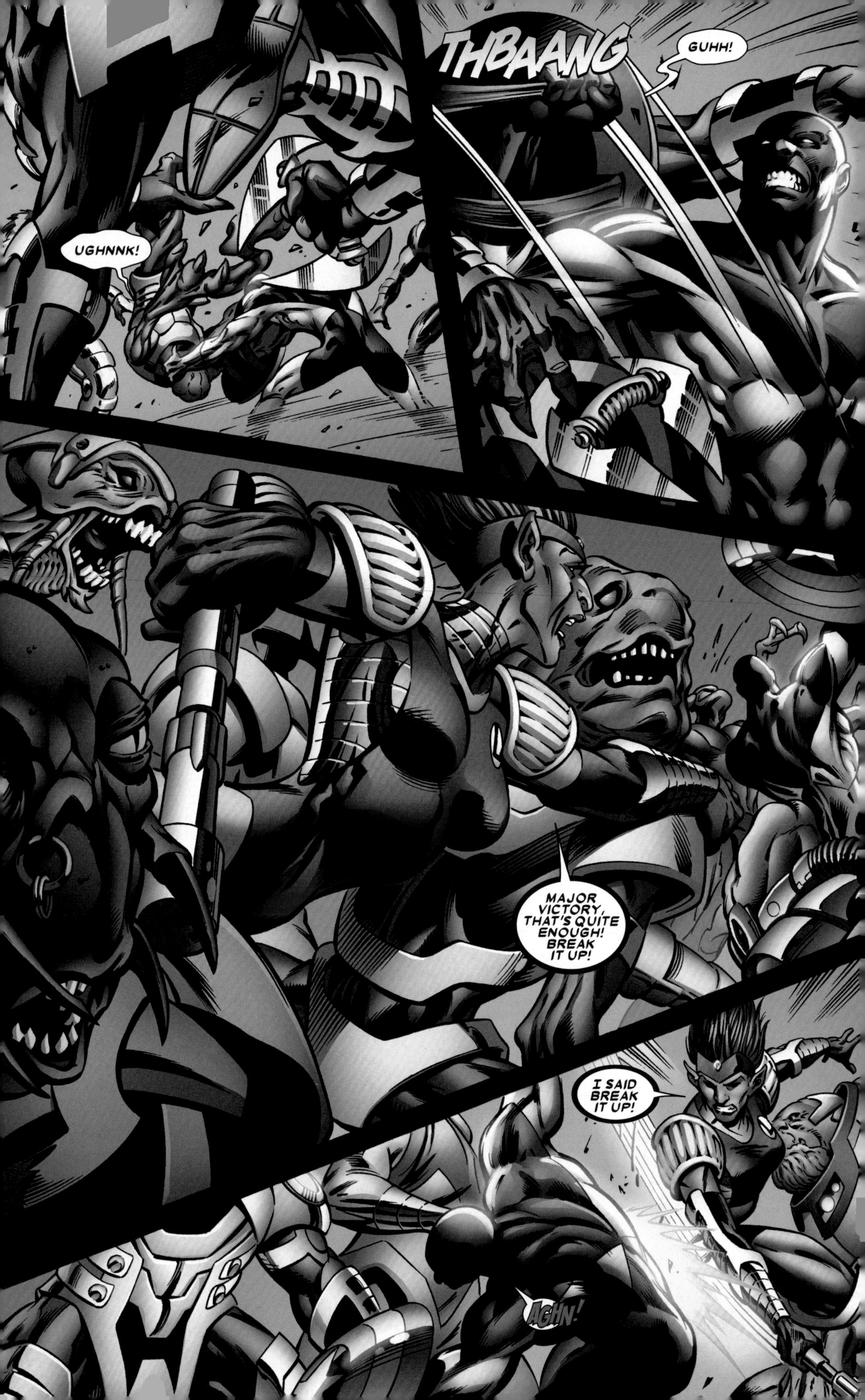

UGHNNK!
THBAANG
GUHH!
MAJOR VICTORY, THAT'S QUITE ENOUGH! BREAK IT UP!
I SAID BREAK IT UP!
AGHN!

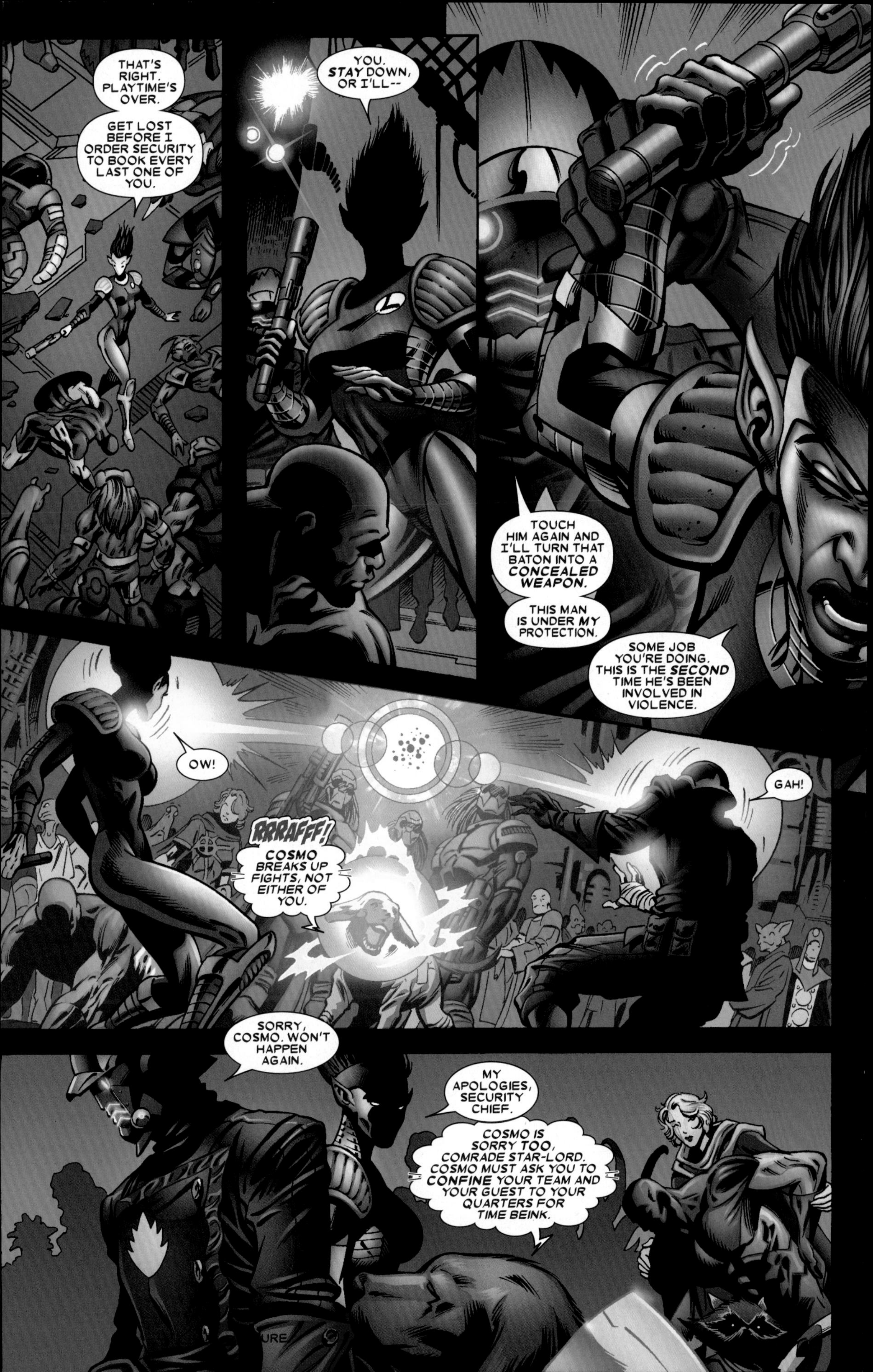
THAT'S RIGHT. PLAYTIME'S OVER.
GET LOST BEFORE I ORDER SECURITY TO BOOK EVERY LAST ONE OF YOU.
YOU. STAY DOWN, OR I'LL--
TOUCH HIM AGAIN AND I'LL TURN THAT BATON INTO A CONCEALED WEAPON.
THIS MAN IS UNDER MY PROTECTION.
SOME JOB YOU'RE DOING. THIS IS THE SECOND TIME HE'S BEEN INVOLVED IN VIOLENCE.
OW!
GAH!
RRRAFFF!
COSMO BREAKS UP FIGHTS, NOT EITHER OF YOU.
SORRY, COSMO. WON'T HAPPEN AGAIN.
MY APOLOGIES, SECURITY CHIEF.
COSMO IS SORRY TOO, COMRADE STAR-LORD. COSMO MUST ASK YOU TO CONFINE YOUR TEAM AND YOUR GUEST TO YOUR QUARTERS FOR TIME BEINK.

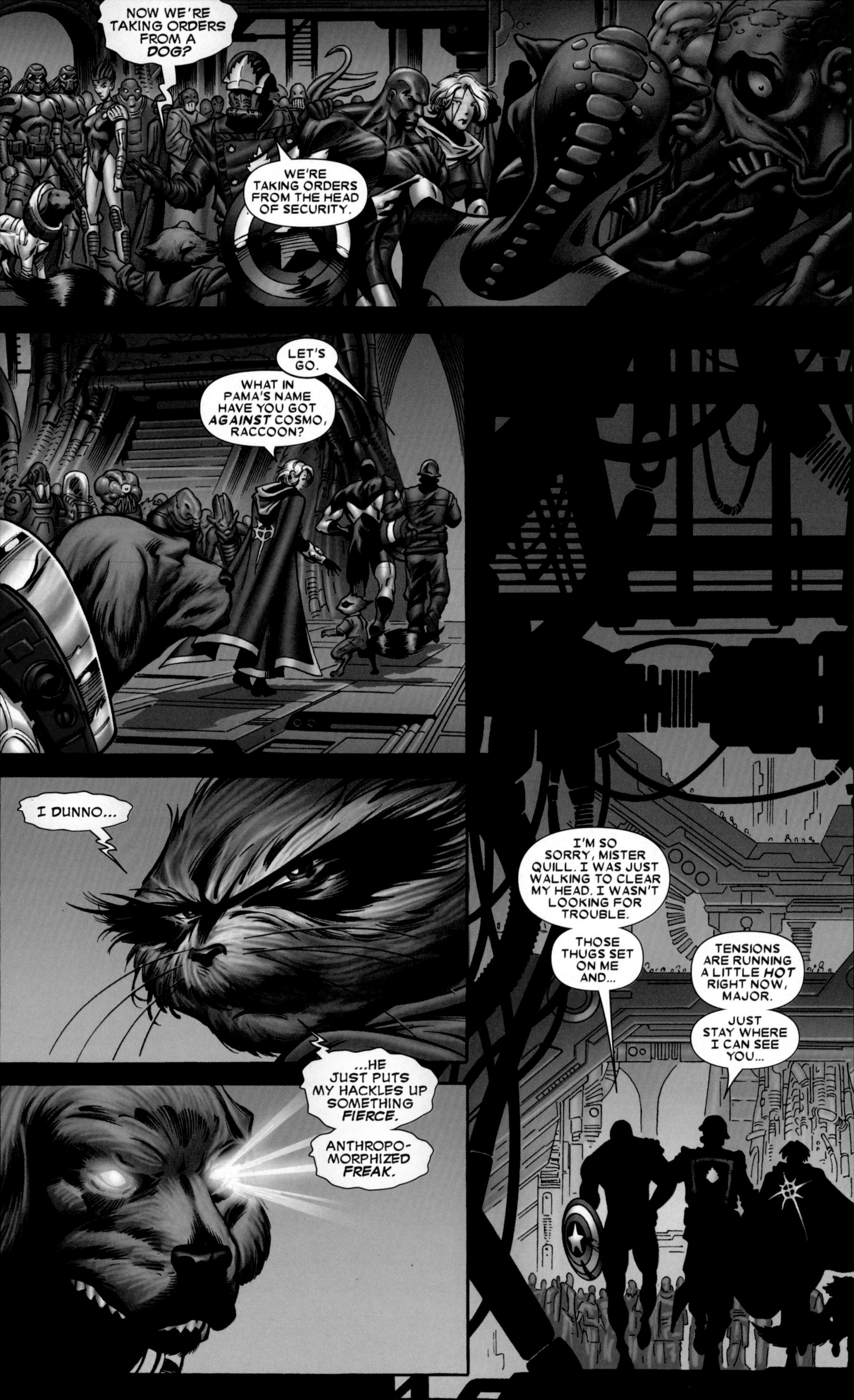
NOW WE'RE TAKING ORDERS FROM A *DOG?*
WE'RE TAKING ORDERS FROM THE HEAD OF SECURITY.
LET'S GO.
WHAT IN PAMA'S NAME HAVE YOU GOT *AGAINST* COSMO, RACCOON?
I DUNNO...
...HE JUST PUTS MY HACKLES UP SOMETHING *FIERCE.*
ANTHROPO-MORPHIZED *FREAK.*
I'M SO SORRY, MISTER QUILL. I WAS JUST WALKING TO CLEAR MY HEAD. I WASN'T LOOKING FOR TROUBLE.
THOSE THUGS SET ON ME AND...
TENSIONS ARE RUNNING A LITTLE *HOT* RIGHT NOW, MAJOR.
JUST STAY WHERE I CAN SEE YOU...

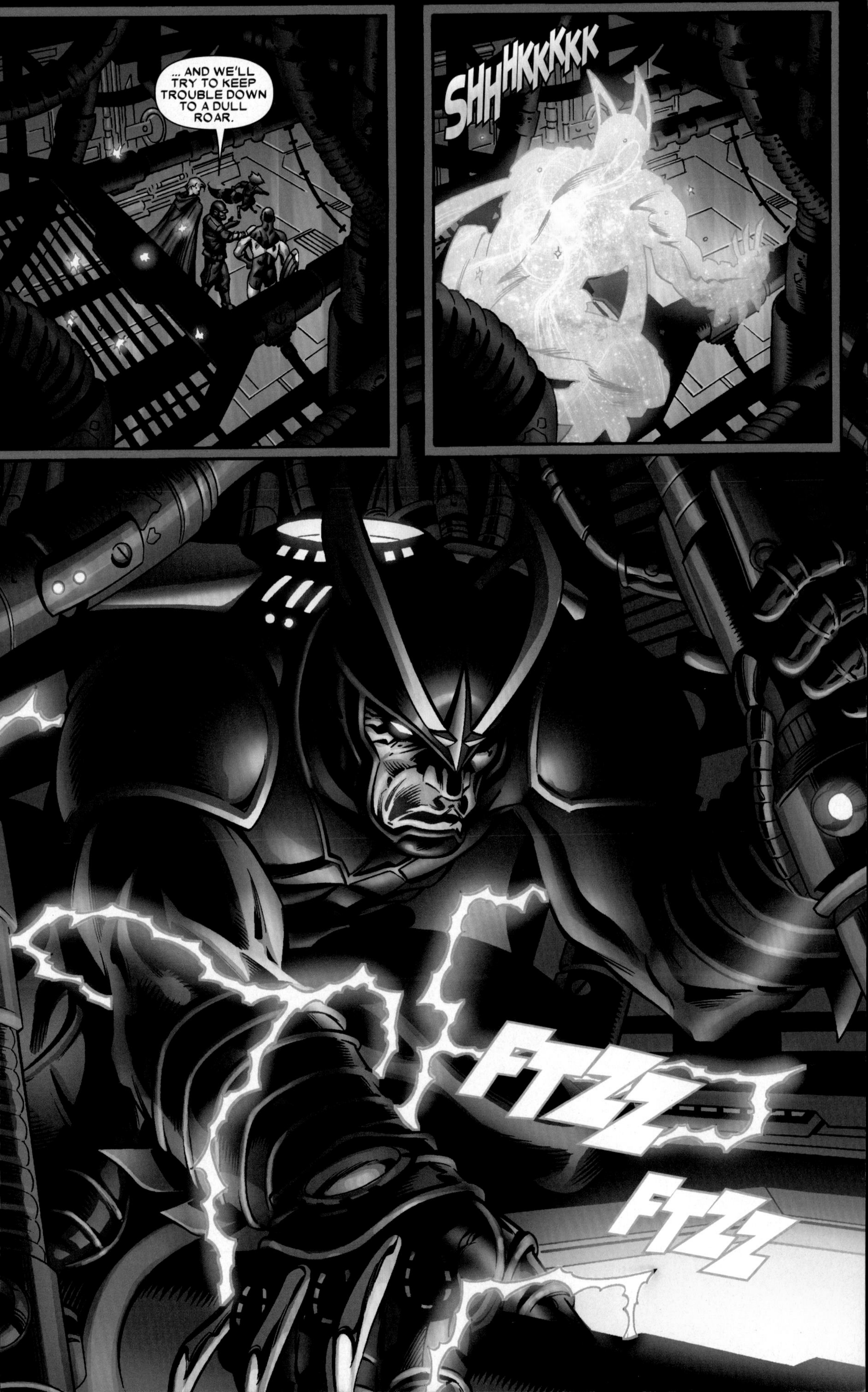
... AND WE'LL TRY TO KEEP TROUBLE DOWN TO A DULL ROAR.
SHHHKKKKK
FTZZ
FTZZ

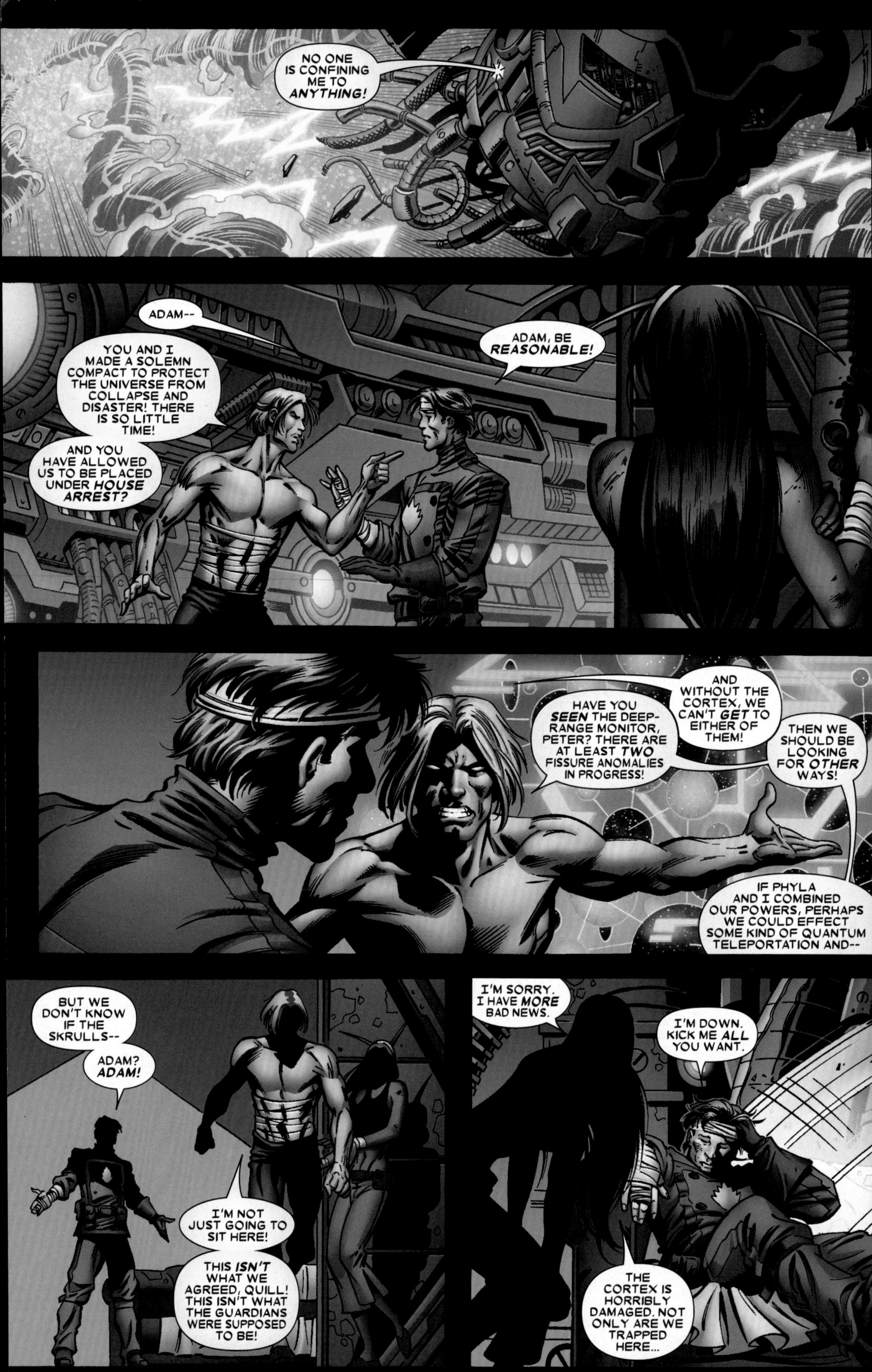
NO ONE IS CONFINING ME TO ANYTHING!
ADAM--
YOU AND I MADE A SOLEMN COMPACT TO PROTECT THE UNIVERSE FROM COLLAPSE AND DISASTER! THERE IS SO LITTLE TIME!
AND YOU HAVE ALLOWED US TO BE PLACED UNDER HOUSE ARREST?
ADAM, BE REASONABLE!
HAVE YOU SEEN THE DEEP-RANGE MONITOR, PETER? THERE ARE AT LEAST TWO FISSURE ANOMALIES IN PROGRESS!
AND WITHOUT THE CORTEX, WE CAN'T GET TO EITHER OF THEM!
THEN WE SHOULD BE LOOKING FOR OTHER WAYS!
IF PHYLA AND I COMBINED OUR POWERS, PERHAPS WE COULD EFFECT SOME KIND OF QUANTUM TELEPORTATION AND--
BUT WE DON'T KNOW IF THE SKRULLS--
ADAM? ADAM!
I'M NOT JUST GOING TO SIT HERE!
THIS ISN'T WHAT WE AGREED, QUILL! THIS ISN'T WHAT THE GUARDIANS WERE SUPPOSED TO BE!
I'M SORRY. I HAVE MORE BAD NEWS.
I'M DOWN. KICK ME ALL YOU WANT.
THE CORTEX IS HORRIBLY DAMAGED. NOT ONLY ARE WE TRAPPED HERE...

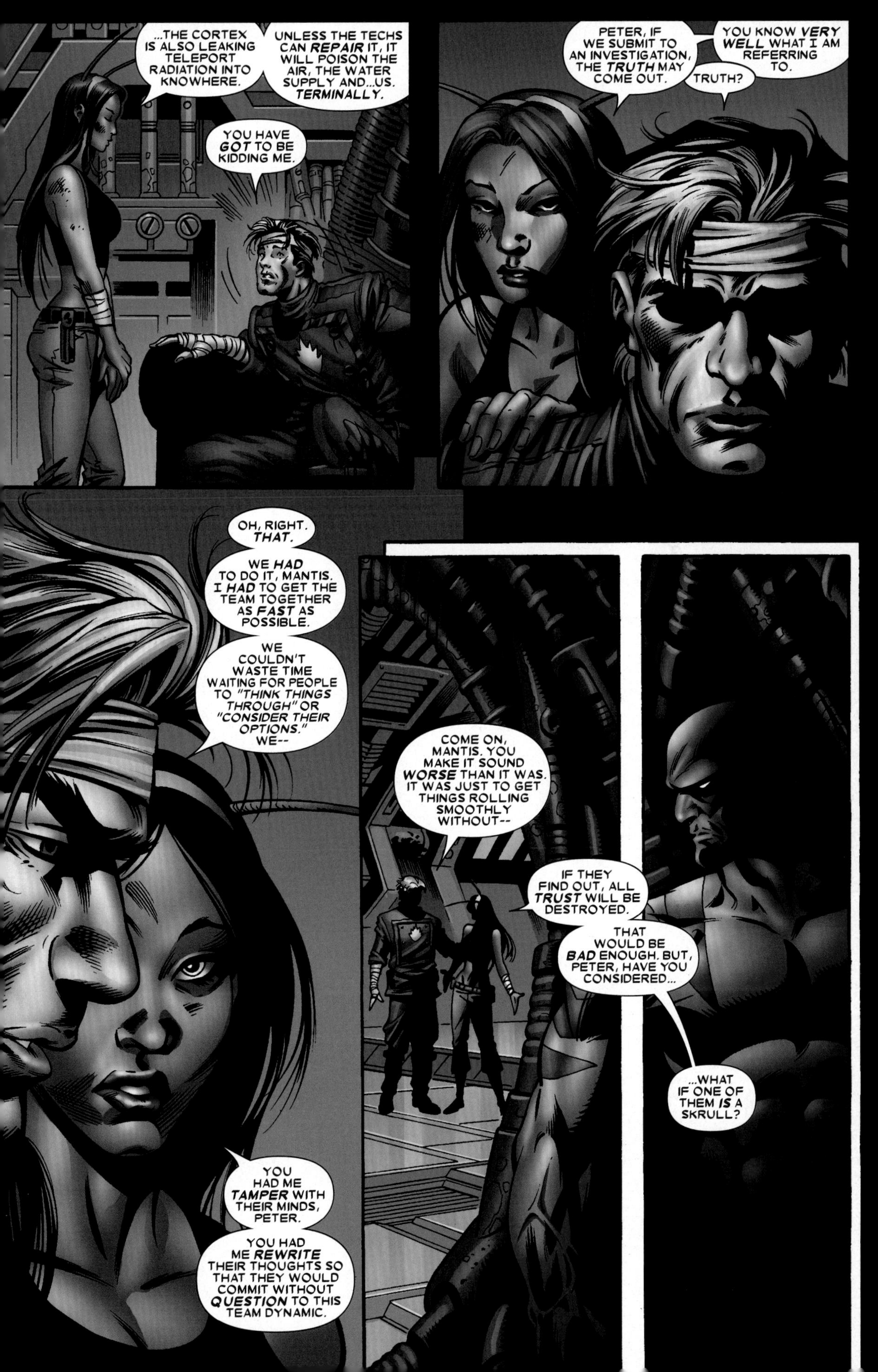
...THE CORTEX IS ALSO LEAKING TELEPORT RADIATION INTO KNOWHERE.
UNLESS THE TECHS CAN REPAIR IT, IT WILL POISON THE AIR, THE WATER SUPPLY AND...US. TERMINALLY.
YOU HAVE GOT TO BE KIDDING ME.
PETER, IF WE SUBMIT TO AN INVESTIGATION, THE TRUTH MAY COME OUT.
TRUTH?
YOU KNOW VERY WELL WHAT I AM REFERRING TO.
OH, RIGHT. THAT.
WE HAD TO DO IT, MANTIS. I HAD TO GET THE TEAM TOGETHER AS FAST AS POSSIBLE.
WE COULDN'T WASTE TIME WAITING FOR PEOPLE TO "THINK THINGS THROUGH" OR "CONSIDER THEIR OPTIONS." WE--
YOU HAD ME TAMPER WITH THEIR MINDS, PETER.
YOU HAD ME REWRITE THEIR THOUGHTS SO THAT THEY WOULD COMMIT WITHOUT QUESTION TO THIS TEAM DYNAMIC.
COME ON, MANTIS. YOU MAKE IT SOUND WORSE THAN IT WAS. IT WAS JUST TO GET THINGS ROLLING SMOOTHLY WITHOUT--
IF THEY FIND OUT, ALL TRUST WILL BE DESTROYED.
THAT WOULD BE BAD ENOUGH. BUT, PETER, HAVE YOU CONSIDERED...
...WHAT IF ONE OF THEM IS A SKRULL?

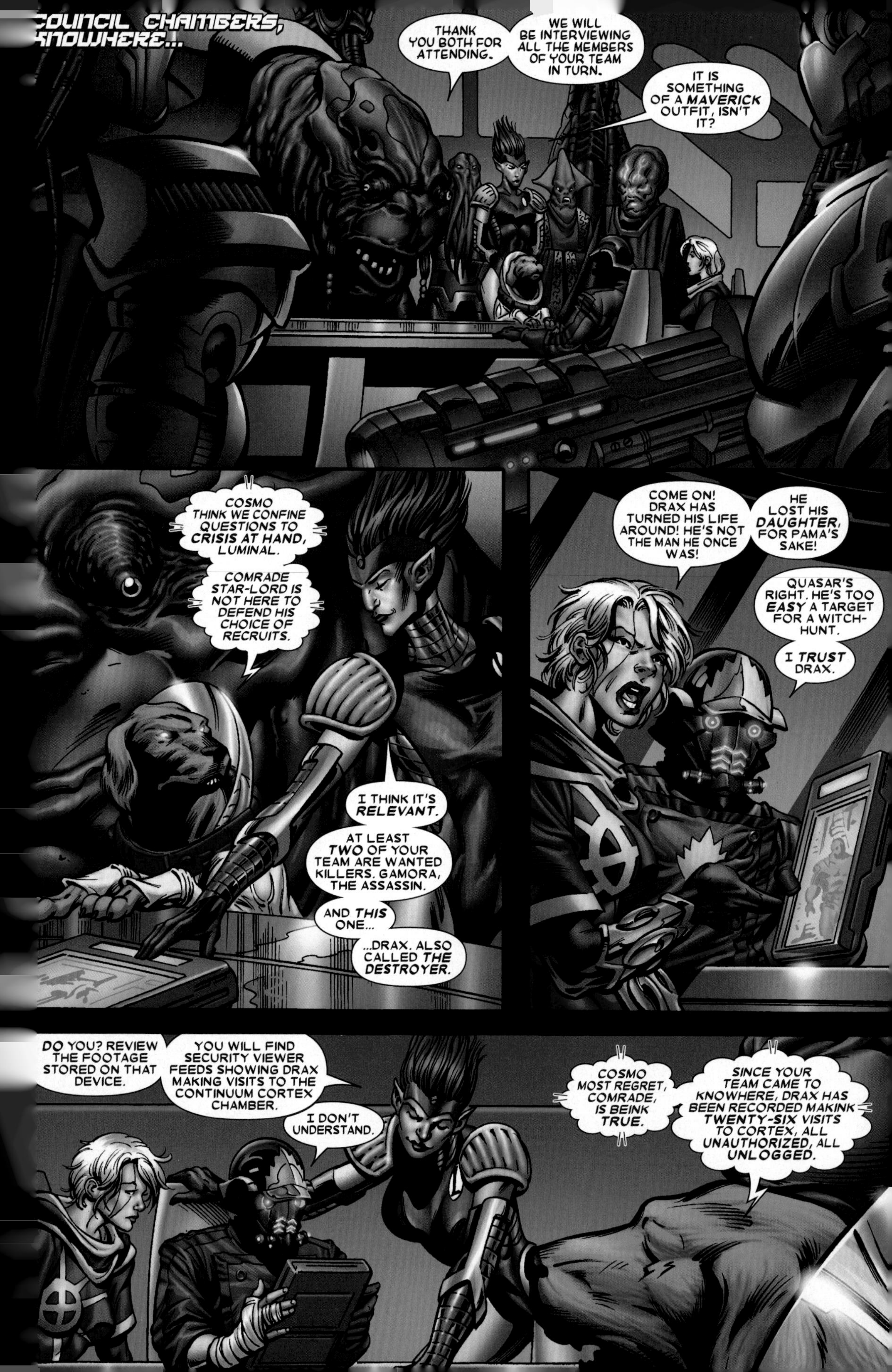
COUNCIL CHAMBERS, KNOWHERE...
THANK YOU BOTH FOR ATTENDING.
WE WILL BE INTERVIEWING ALL THE MEMBERS OF YOUR TEAM IN TURN.
IT IS SOMETHING OF A MAVERICK OUTFIT, ISN'T IT?
COSMO THINK WE CONFINE QUESTIONS TO CRISIS AT HAND, LUMINAL.
COMRADE STAR-LORD IS NOT HERE TO DEFEND HIS CHOICE OF RECRUITS.
I THINK IT'S RELEVANT.
AT LEAST TWO OF YOUR TEAM ARE WANTED KILLERS. GAMORA, THE ASSASSIN.
AND THIS ONE...
...DRAX. ALSO CALLED THE DESTROYER.
COME ON! DRAX HAS TURNED HIS LIFE AROUND! HE'S NOT THE MAN HE ONCE WAS!
HE LOST HIS DAUGHTER, FOR PAMA'S SAKE!
QUASAR'S RIGHT. HE'S TOO EASY A TARGET FOR A WITCH-HUNT.
I TRUST DRAX.
DO YOU? REVIEW THE FOOTAGE STORED ON THAT DEVICE.
YOU WILL FIND SECURITY VIEWER FEEDS SHOWING DRAX MAKING VISITS TO THE CONTINUUM CORTEX CHAMBER.
I DON'T UNDERSTAND.
COSMO MOST REGRET, COMRADE, IS BEINK TRUE.
SINCE YOUR TEAM CAME TO KNOWHERE, DRAX HAS BEEN RECORDED MAKINK TWENTY-SIX VISITS TO CORTEX, ALL UNAUTHORIZED, ALL UNLOGGED.

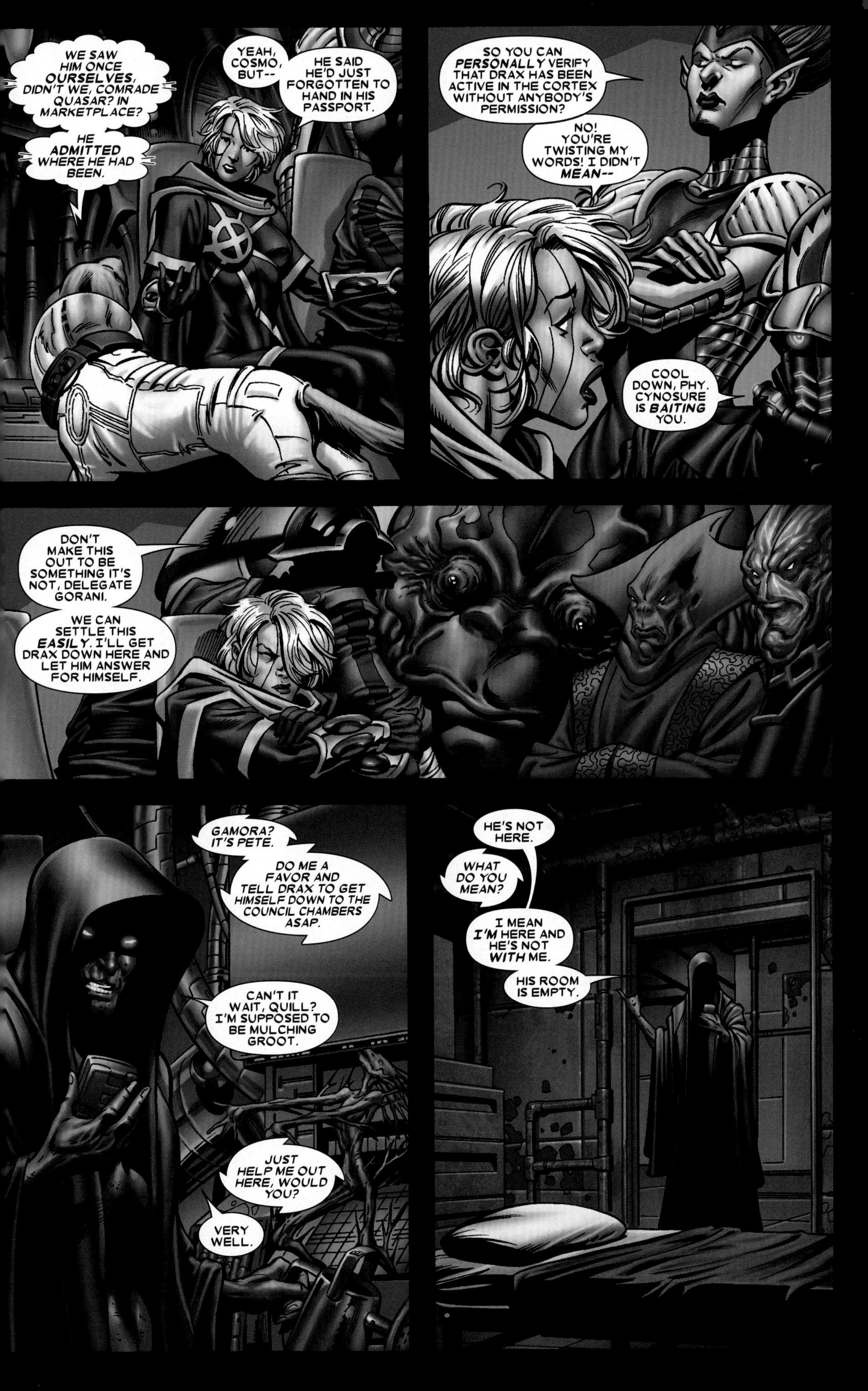
WE SAW HIM ONCE *OURSELVES*, DIDN'T WE, COMRADE QUASAR? IN MARKETPLACE?
HE *ADMITTED* WHERE HE HAD BEEN.
YEAH, COSMO, BUT--
HE SAID HE'D JUST FORGOTTEN TO HAND IN HIS PASSPORT.
SO YOU CAN *PERSONALLY* VERIFY THAT DRAX HAS BEEN ACTIVE IN THE CORTEX WITHOUT ANYBODY'S PERMISSION?
NO! YOU'RE TWISTING MY WORDS! I DIDN'T *MEAN*--
COOL DOWN, PHY. CYNOSURE IS *BAITING* YOU.
DON'T MAKE THIS OUT TO BE SOMETHING IT'S NOT, DELEGATE GORANI.
WE CAN SETTLE THIS *EASILY*. I'LL GET DRAX DOWN HERE AND LET HIM ANSWER FOR HIMSELF.
GAMORA? IT'S PETE.
DO ME A FAVOR AND TELL DRAX TO GET HIMSELF DOWN TO THE COUNCIL CHAMBERS ASAP.
CAN'T IT WAIT, QUILL? I'M SUPPOSED TO BE MULCHING GROOT.
JUST HELP ME OUT HERE, WOULD YOU?
VERY WELL.
HE'S NOT HERE.
WHAT DO YOU MEAN?
I MEAN *I'M* HERE AND HE'S NOT *WITH* ME.
HIS ROOM IS EMPTY.

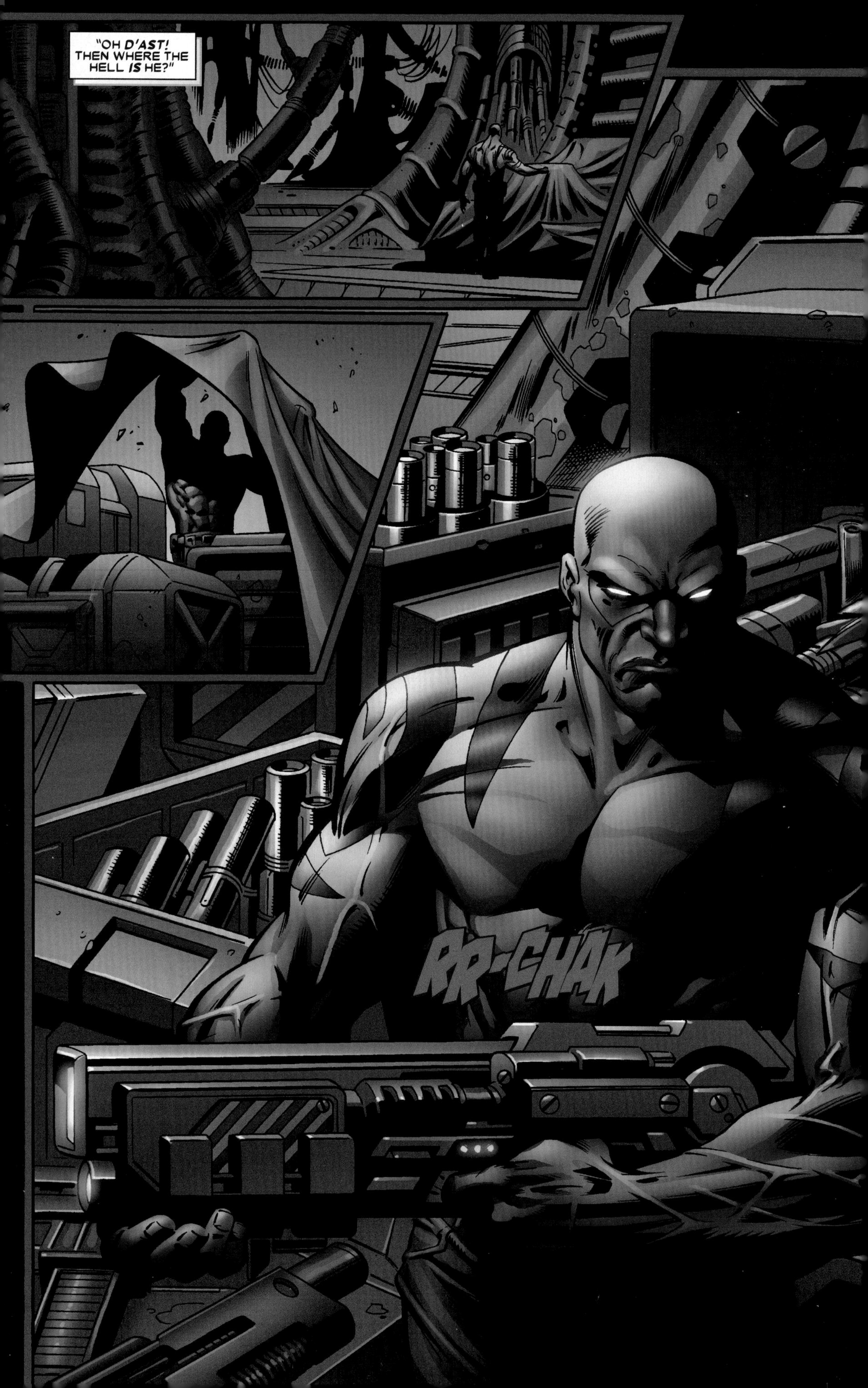
"OH D'AST! THEN WHERE THE HELL IS HE?"
RR-CHAK

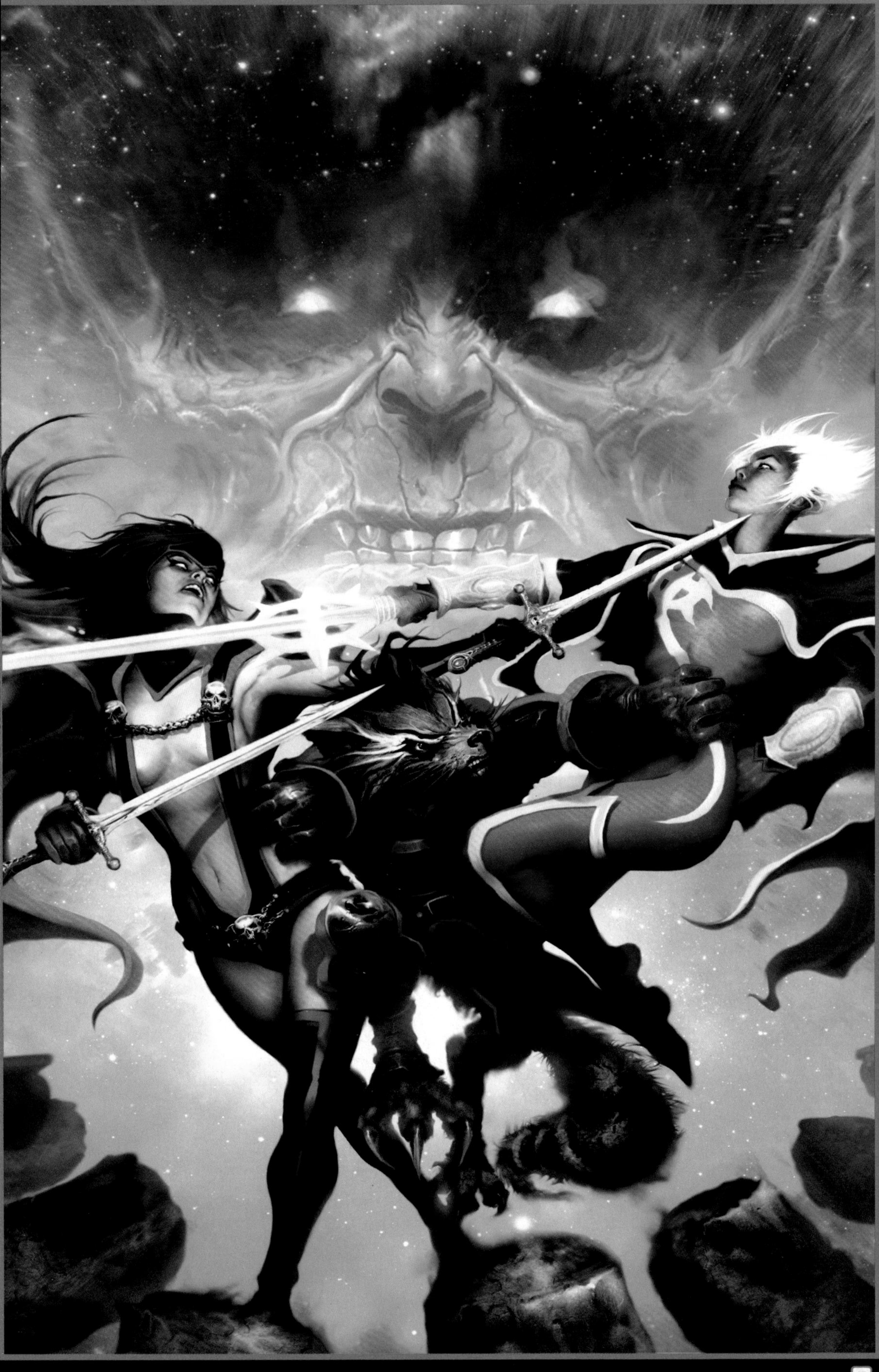

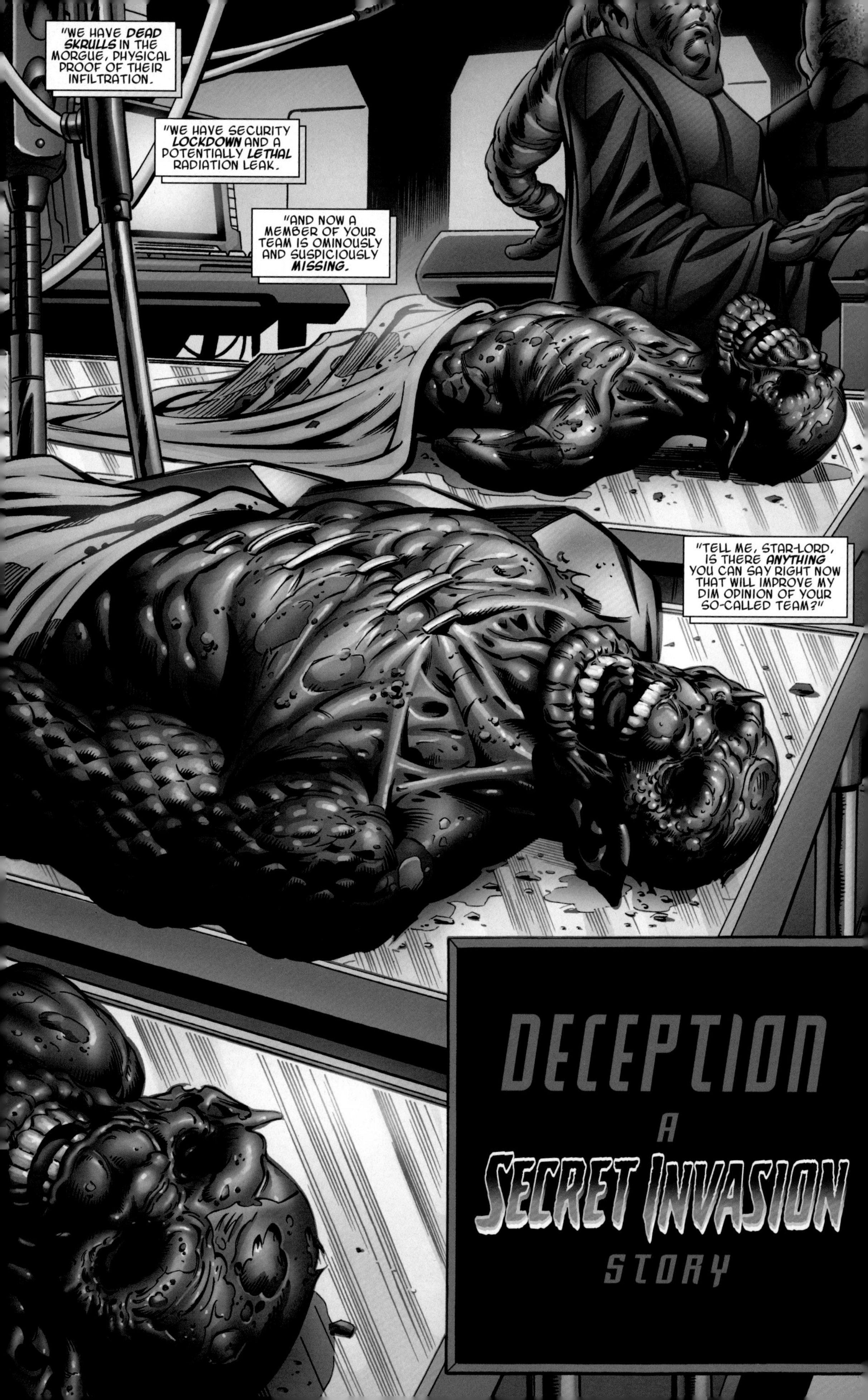
"WE HAVE DEAD SKRULLS IN THE MORGUE, PHYSICAL PROOF OF THEIR INFILTRATION.
"WE HAVE SECURITY LOCKDOWN AND A POTENTIALLY LETHAL RADIATION LEAK.
"AND NOW A MEMBER OF YOUR TEAM IS OMINOUSLY AND SUSPICIOUSLY MISSING.
"TELL ME, STAR-LORD, IS THERE ANYTHING YOU CAN SAY RIGHT NOW THAT WILL IMPROVE MY DIM OPINION OF YOUR SO-CALLED TEAM?"
DECEPTION
A SECRET INVASION STORY

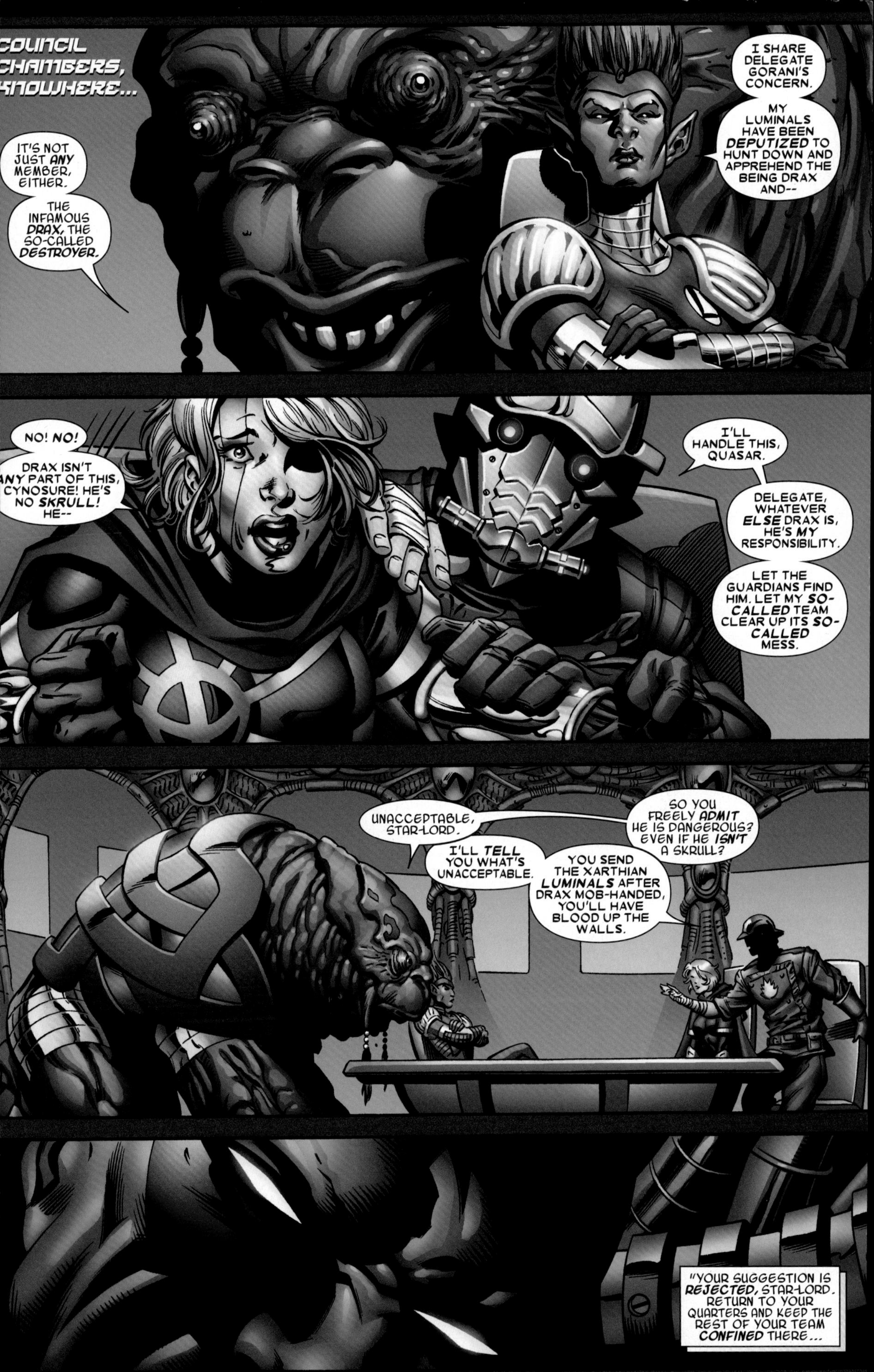
COUNCIL CHAMBERS, KNOWHERE...
IT'S NOT JUST ANY MEMBER, EITHER.
THE INFAMOUS DRAX, THE SO-CALLED DESTROYER.
I SHARE DELEGATE GORANI'S CONCERN.
MY LUMINALS HAVE BEEN DEPUTIZED TO HUNT DOWN AND APPREHEND THE BEING DRAX AND--
NO! NO!
DRAX ISN'T ANY PART OF THIS, CYNOSURE! HE'S NO SKRULL! HE--
I'LL HANDLE THIS, QUASAR.
DELEGATE, WHATEVER ELSE DRAX IS, HE'S MY RESPONSIBILITY.
LET THE GUARDIANS FIND HIM. LET MY SO-CALLED TEAM CLEAR UP ITS SO-CALLED MESS.
UNACCEPTABLE, STAR-LORD.
I'LL TELL YOU WHAT'S UNACCEPTABLE.
YOU SEND THE XARTHIAN LUMINALS AFTER DRAX MOB-HANDED, YOU'LL HAVE BLOOD UP THE WALLS.
SO YOU FREELY ADMIT HE IS DANGEROUS? EVEN IF HE ISN'T A SKRULL?
"YOUR SUGGESTION IS REJECTED, STAR-LORD. RETURN TO YOUR QUARTERS AND KEEP THE REST OF YOUR TEAM CONFINED THERE...

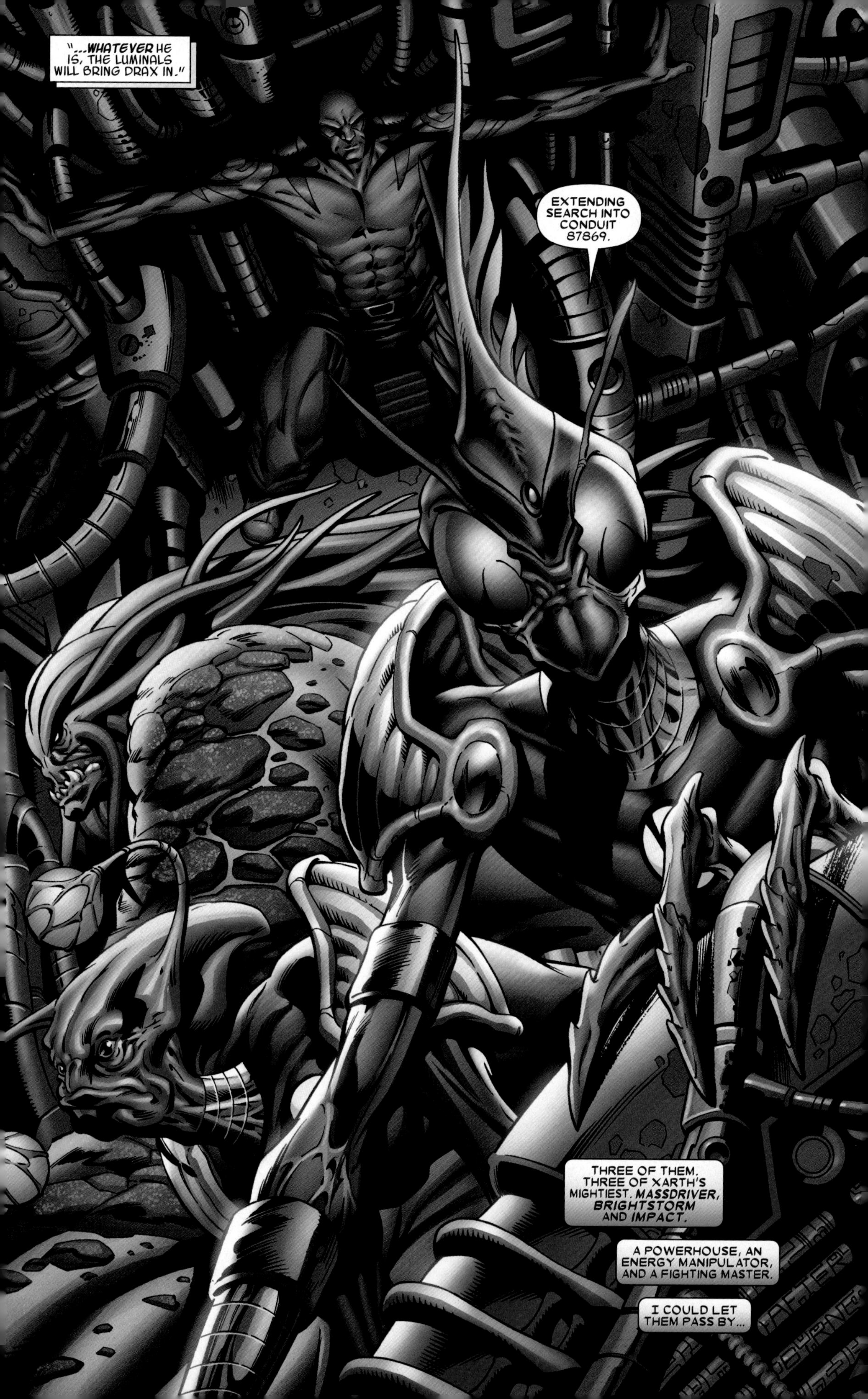
"...WHATEVER HE IS, THE LUMINALS WILL BRING DRAX IN."
EXTENDING SEARCH INTO CONDUIT 87869.
THREE OF THEM. THREE OF XARTH'S MIGHTIEST. MASSDRIVER, BRIGHTSTORM AND IMPACT.
A POWERHOUSE, AN ENERGY MANIPULATOR, AND A FIGHTING MASTER.
I COULD LET THEM PASS BY...

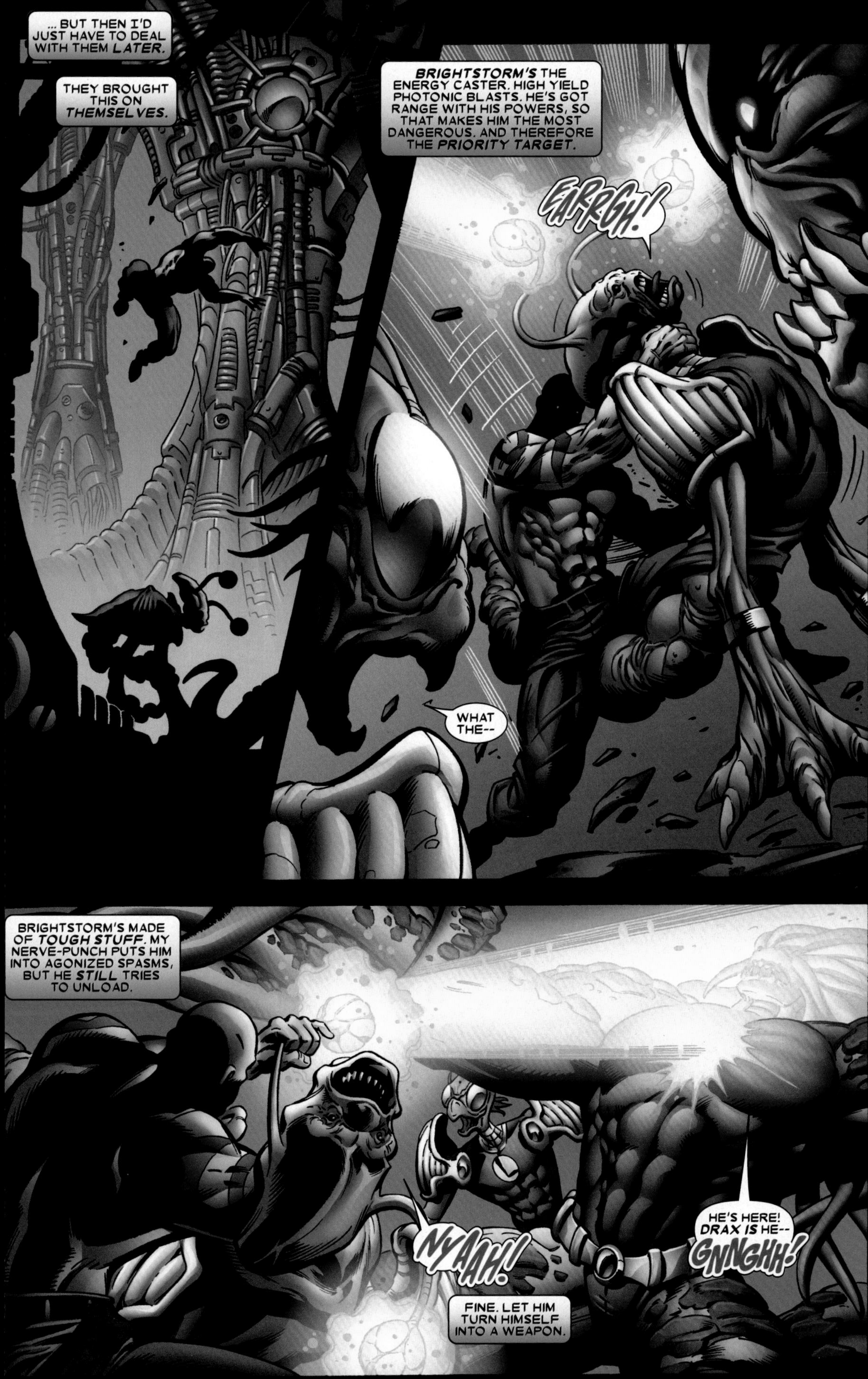
... BUT THEN I'D JUST HAVE TO DEAL WITH THEM *LATER*.
THEY BROUGHT THIS ON *THEMSELVES*.
BRIGHTSTORM'S THE ENERGY CASTER. HIGH YIELD PHOTONIC BLASTS. HE'S GOT RANGE WITH HIS POWERS, SO THAT MAKES HIM THE MOST DANGEROUS. AND THEREFORE THE *PRIORITY TARGET*.
EARRGH!
WHAT THE--
BRIGHTSTORM'S MADE OF *TOUGH STUFF*. MY NERVE-PUNCH PUTS HIM INTO AGONIZED SPASMS, BUT HE *STILL* TRIES TO UNLOAD.
NYAAH!
HE'S HERE! DRAX *IS* HE--
GNNGHH!
FINE. LET HIM TURN HIMSELF INTO A WEAPON.

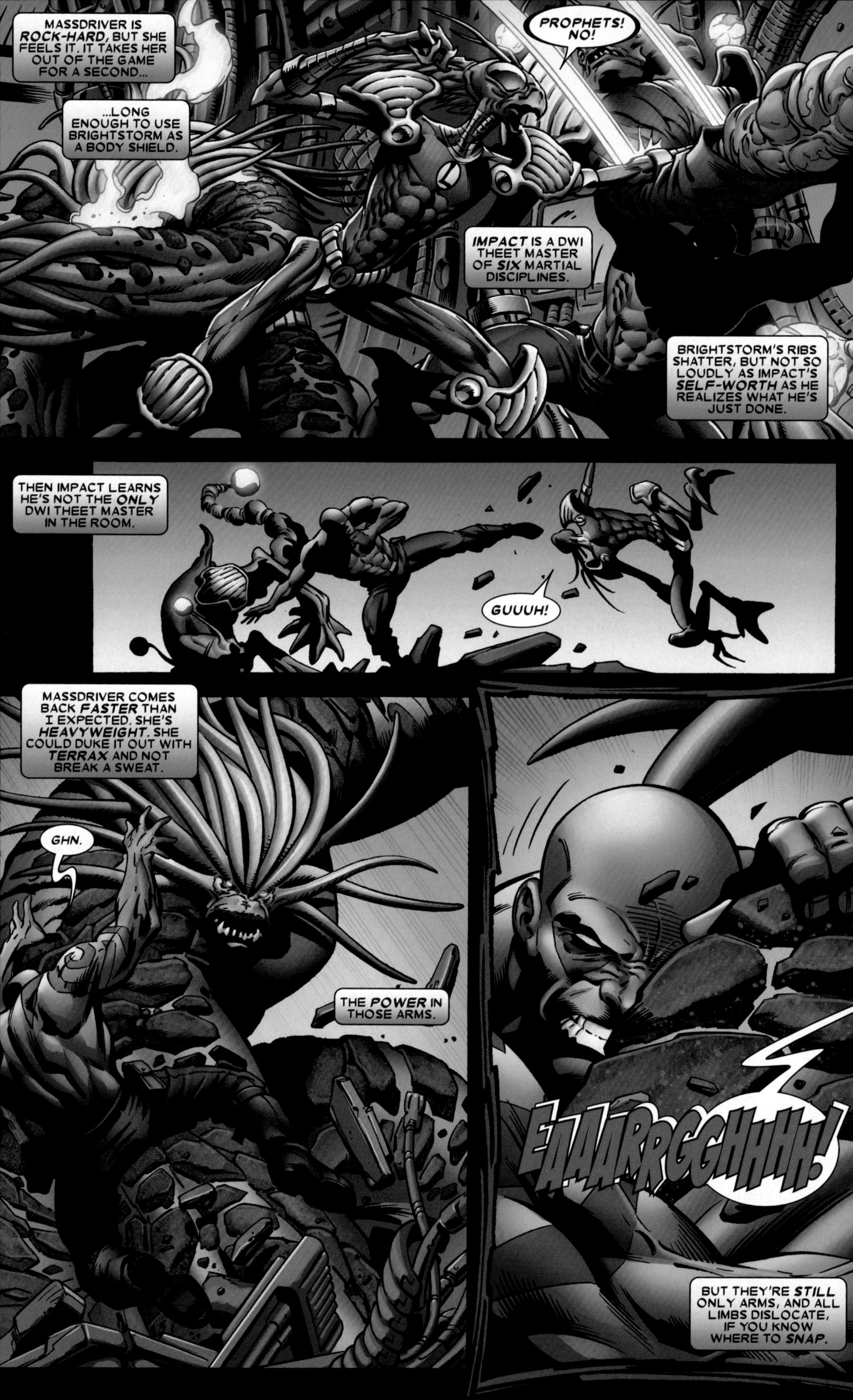
MASSDRIVER IS ROCK-HARD, BUT SHE FEELS IT. IT TAKES HER OUT OF THE GAME FOR A SECOND...
...LONG ENOUGH TO USE BRIGHTSTORM AS A BODY SHIELD.
PROPHETS! NO!
IMPACT IS A DWI THEET MASTER OF SIX MARTIAL DISCIPLINES.
BRIGHTSTORM'S RIBS SHATTER, BUT NOT SO LOUDLY AS IMPACT'S SELF-WORTH AS HE REALIZES WHAT HE'S JUST DONE.
THEN IMPACT LEARNS HE'S NOT THE ONLY DWI THEET MASTER IN THE ROOM.
GUUUH!
MASSDRIVER COMES BACK FASTER THAN I EXPECTED. SHE'S HEAVYWEIGHT. SHE COULD DUKE IT OUT WITH TERRAX AND NOT BREAK A SWEAT.
GHN.
THE POWER IN THOSE ARMS.
EAAARRGGHHHH!
BUT THEY'RE STILL ONLY ARMS, AND ALL LIMBS DISLOCATE, IF YOU KNOW WHERE TO SNAP.

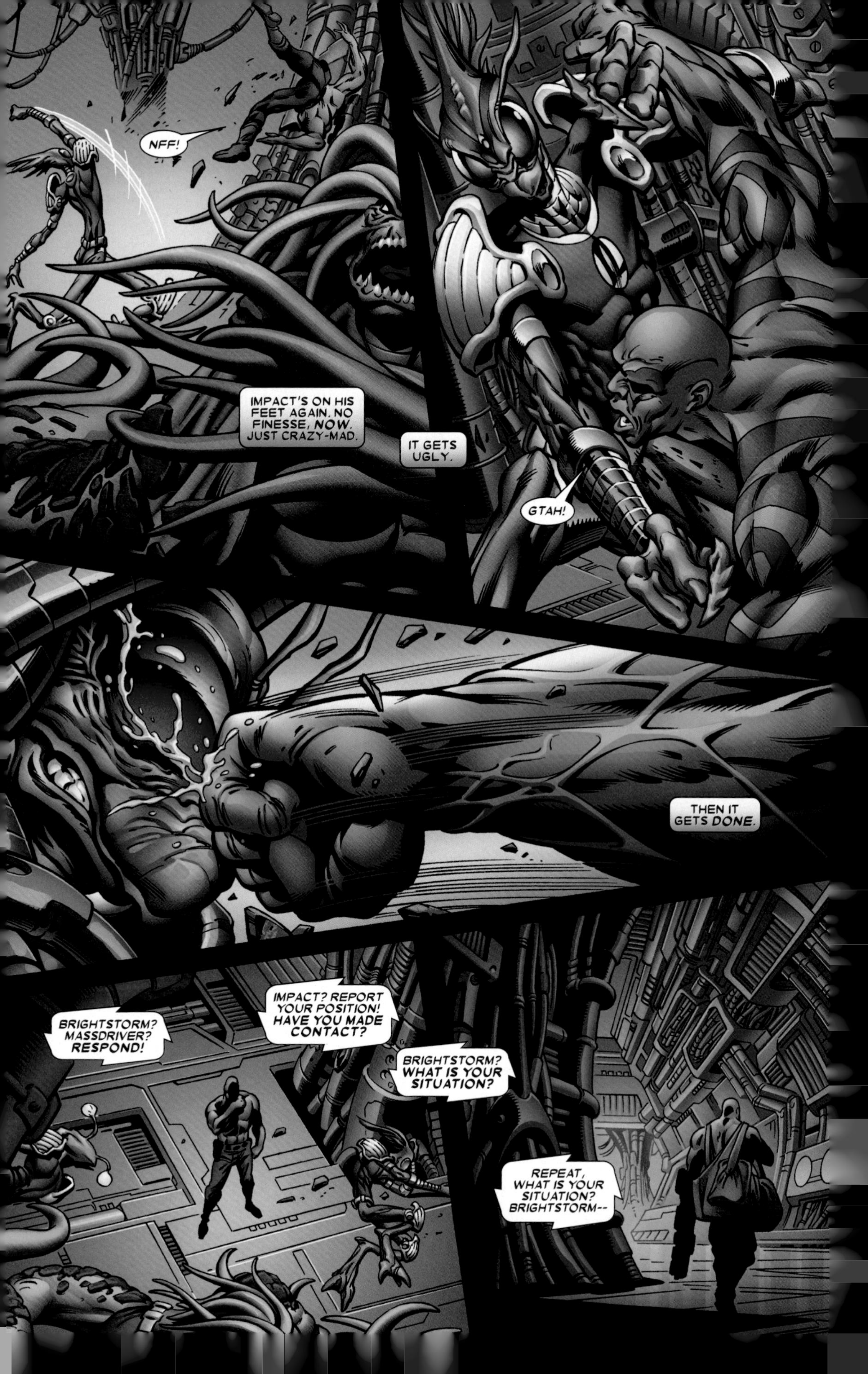
NFF!
IMPACT'S ON HIS FEET AGAIN. NO FINESSE, NOW. JUST CRAZY-MAD.
IT GETS UGLY.
GTAH!
THEN IT GETS DONE.
BRIGHTSTORM? MASSDRIVER? RESPOND!
IMPACT? REPORT YOUR POSITION! HAVE YOU MADE CONTACT?
BRIGHTSTORM? WHAT IS YOUR SITUATION?
REPEAT, WHAT IS YOUR SITUATION? BRIGHTSTORM--

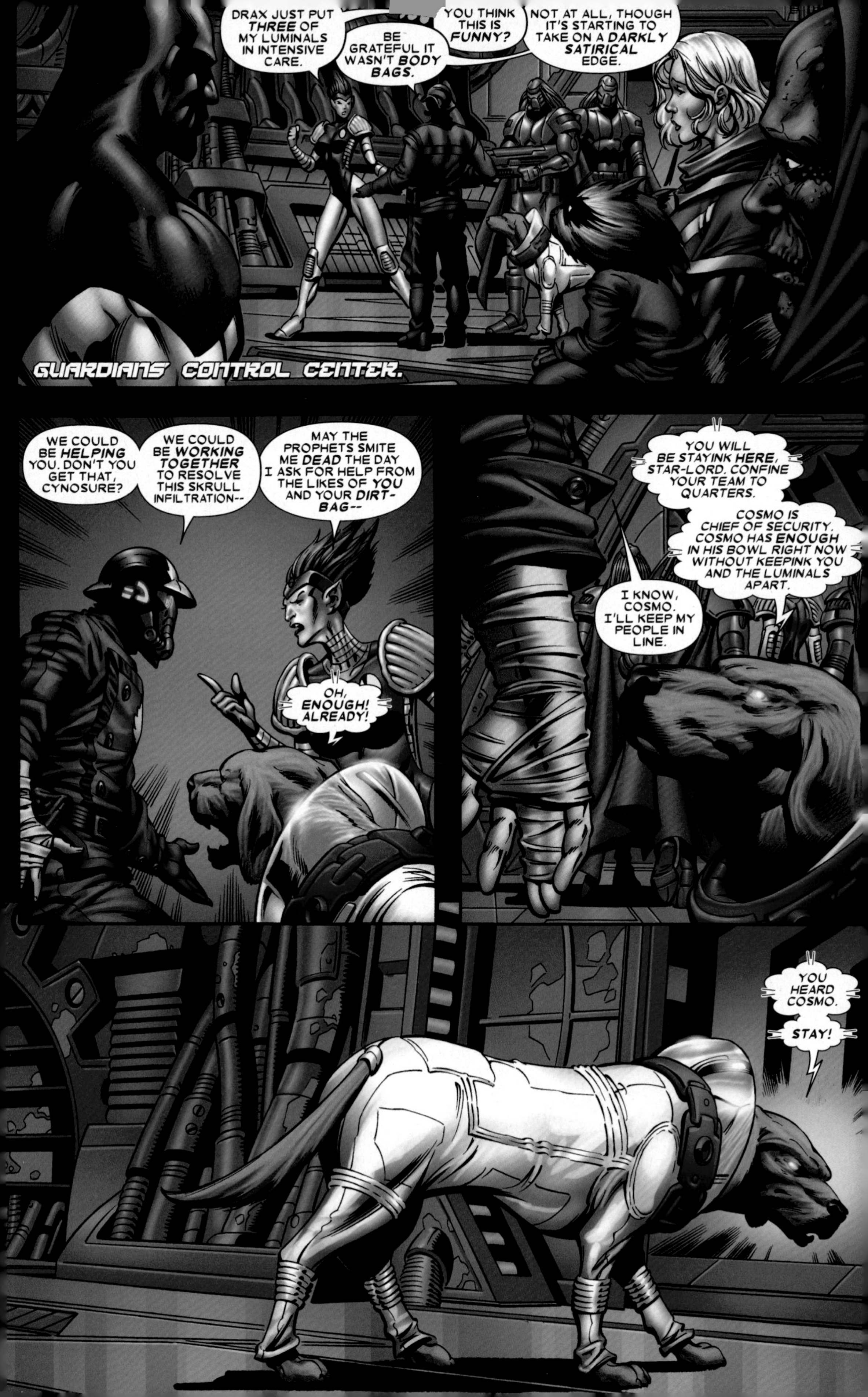
DRAX JUST PUT THREE OF MY LUMINALS IN INTENSIVE CARE.
BE GRATEFUL IT WASN'T BODY BAGS.
YOU THINK THIS IS FUNNY?
NOT AT ALL, THOUGH IT'S STARTING TO TAKE ON A DARKLY SATIRICAL EDGE.
GUARDIANS' CONTROL CENTER.
WE COULD BE HELPING YOU. DON'T YOU GET THAT, CYNOSURE?
WE COULD BE WORKING TOGETHER TO RESOLVE THIS SKRULL INFILTRATION--
MAY THE PROPHETS SMITE ME DEAD THE DAY I ASK FOR HELP FROM THE LIKES OF YOU AND YOUR DIRT-BAG--
OH, ENOUGH! ALREADY!
YOU WILL BE STAYINK HERE, STAR-LORD. CONFINE YOUR TEAM TO QUARTERS.
COSMO IS CHIEF OF SECURITY. COSMO HAS ENOUGH IN HIS BOWL RIGHT NOW WITHOUT KEEPINK YOU AND THE LUMINALS APART.
I KNOW, COSMO. I'LL KEEP MY PEOPLE IN LINE.
YOU HEARD COSMO.
STAY!

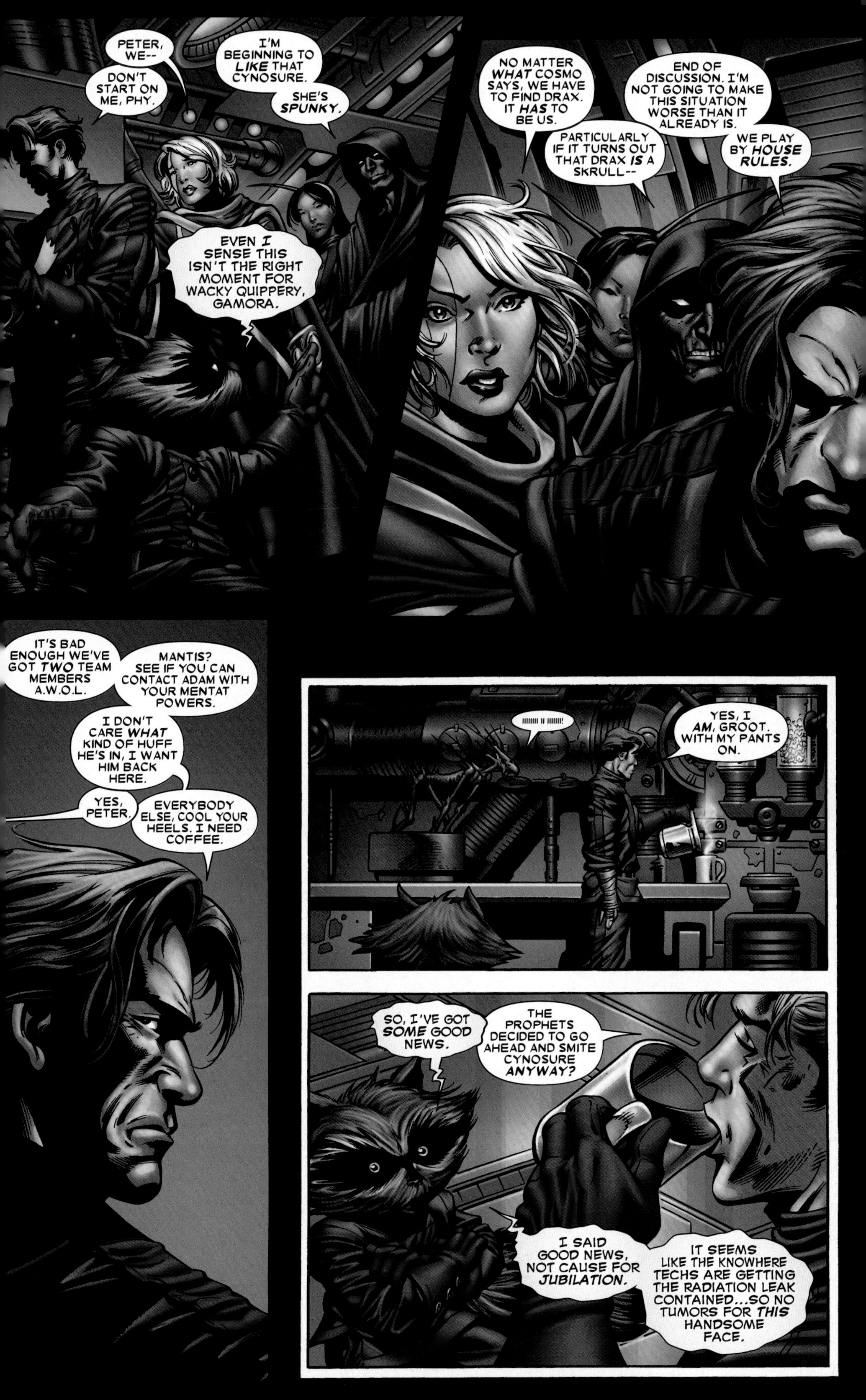
PETER, WE--
DON'T START ON ME, PHY.
I'M BEGINNING TO LIKE THAT CYNOSURE.
SHE'S SPUNKY.
EVEN I SENSE THIS ISN'T THE RIGHT MOMENT FOR WACKY QUIPPERY, GAMORA.
NO MATTER WHAT COSMO SAYS, WE HAVE TO FIND DRAX. IT HAS TO BE US.
PARTICULARLY IF IT TURNS OUT THAT DRAX IS A SKRULL--
END OF DISCUSSION. I'M NOT GOING TO MAKE THIS SITUATION WORSE THAN IT ALREADY IS.
WE PLAY BY HOUSE RULES.
IT'S BAD ENOUGH WE'VE GOT TWO TEAM MEMBERS A.W.O.L.
MANTIS? SEE IF YOU CAN CONTACT ADAM WITH YOUR MENTAT POWERS.
I DON'T CARE WHAT KIND OF HUFF HE'S IN, I WANT HIM BACK HERE.
YES, PETER.
EVERYBODY ELSE, COOL YOUR HEELS. I NEED COFFEE.
YES, I AM, GROOT. WITH MY PANTS ON.
SO, I'VE GOT SOME GOOD NEWS.
THE PROPHETS DECIDED TO GO AHEAD AND SMITE CYNOSURE ANYWAY?
I SAID GOOD NEWS, NOT CAUSE FOR JUBILATION.
IT SEEMS LIKE THE KNOWHERE TECHS ARE GETTING THE RADIATION LEAK CONTAINED...SO NO TUMORS FOR THIS HANDSOME FACE.

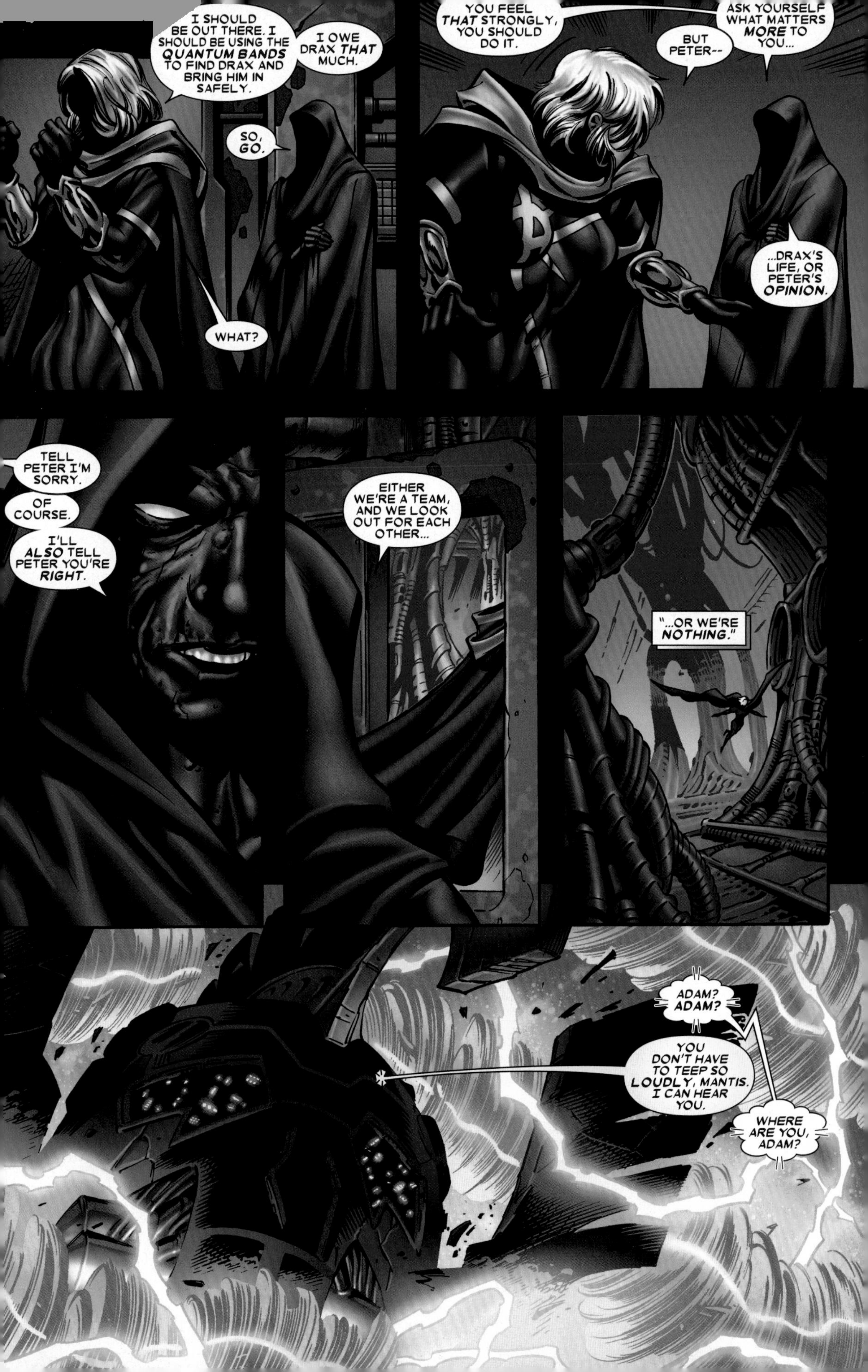
I SHOULD BE OUT THERE. I SHOULD BE USING THE QUANTUM BANDS TO FIND DRAX AND BRING HIM IN SAFELY.
I OWE DRAX THAT MUCH.
SO, GO.
WHAT?
YOU FEEL THAT STRONGLY, YOU SHOULD DO IT.
BUT PETER--
ASK YOURSELF WHAT MATTERS MORE TO YOU...
...DRAX'S LIFE, OR PETER'S OPINION.
TELL PETER I'M SORRY.
OF COURSE.
I'LL ALSO TELL PETER YOU'RE RIGHT.
EITHER WE'RE A TEAM, AND WE LOOK OUT FOR EACH OTHER...
"...OR WE'RE NOTHING."
ADAM? ADAM?
YOU DON'T HAVE TO TEEP SO LOUDLY, MANTIS. I CAN HEAR YOU.
WHERE ARE YOU, ADAM?

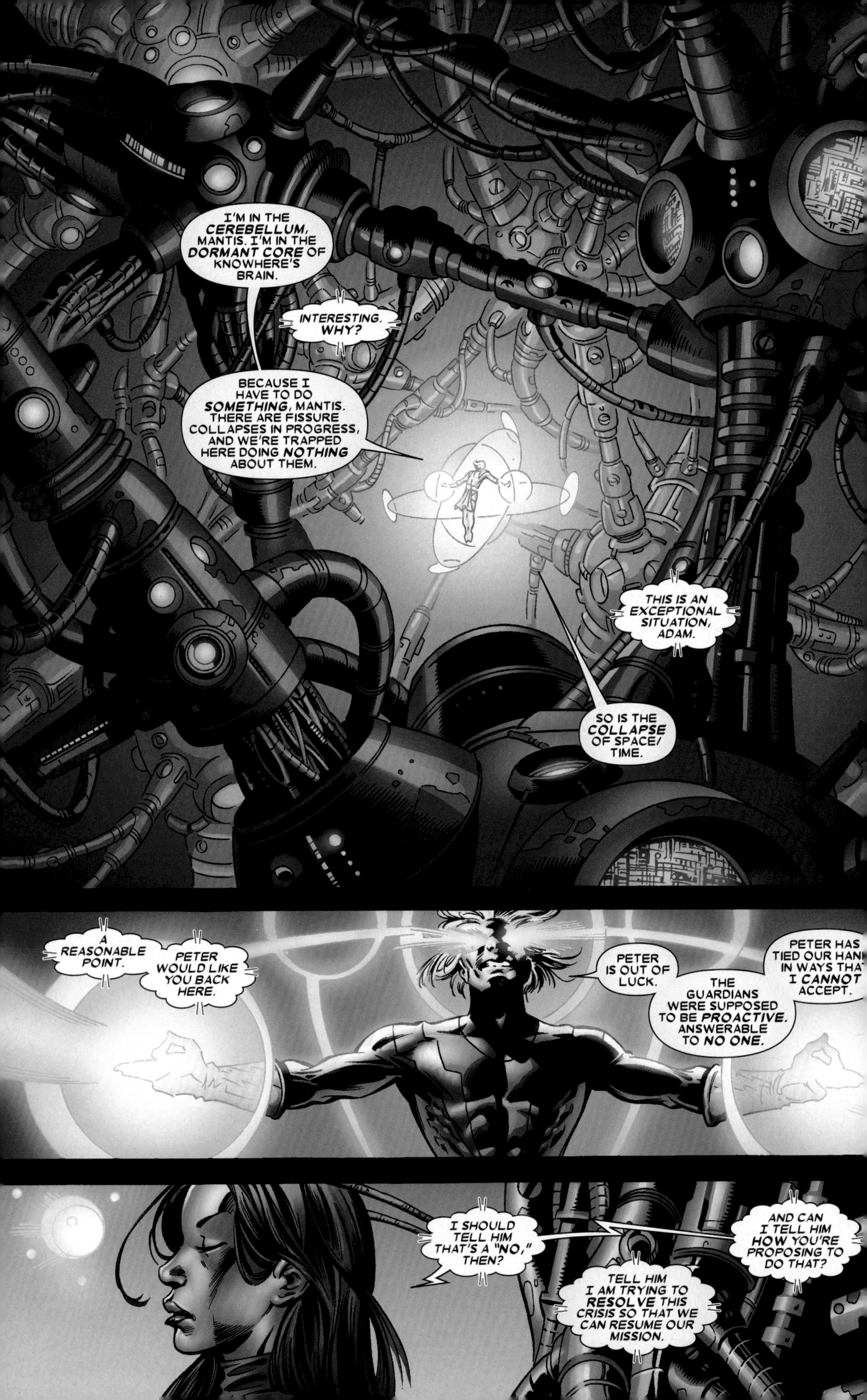
I'M IN THE CEREBELLUM, MANTIS. I'M IN THE DORMANT CORE OF KNOWHERE'S BRAIN.
INTERESTING. WHY?
BECAUSE I HAVE TO DO SOMETHING, MANTIS. THERE ARE FISSURE COLLAPSES IN PROGRESS, AND WE'RE TRAPPED HERE DOING NOTHING ABOUT THEM.
THIS IS AN EXCEPTIONAL SITUATION, ADAM.
SO IS THE COLLAPSE OF SPACE/TIME.
A REASONABLE POINT.
PETER WOULD LIKE YOU BACK HERE.
PETER IS OUT OF LUCK.
THE GUARDIANS WERE SUPPOSED TO BE PROACTIVE. ANSWERABLE TO NO ONE.
PETER HAS TIED OUR HAN IN WAYS THA I CANNOT ACCEPT.
I SHOULD TELL HIM THAT'S A "NO," THEN?
TELL HIM I AM TRYING TO RESOLVE THIS CRISIS SO THAT WE CAN RESUME OUR MISSION.
AND CAN I TELL HIM HOW YOU'RE PROPOSING TO DO THAT?

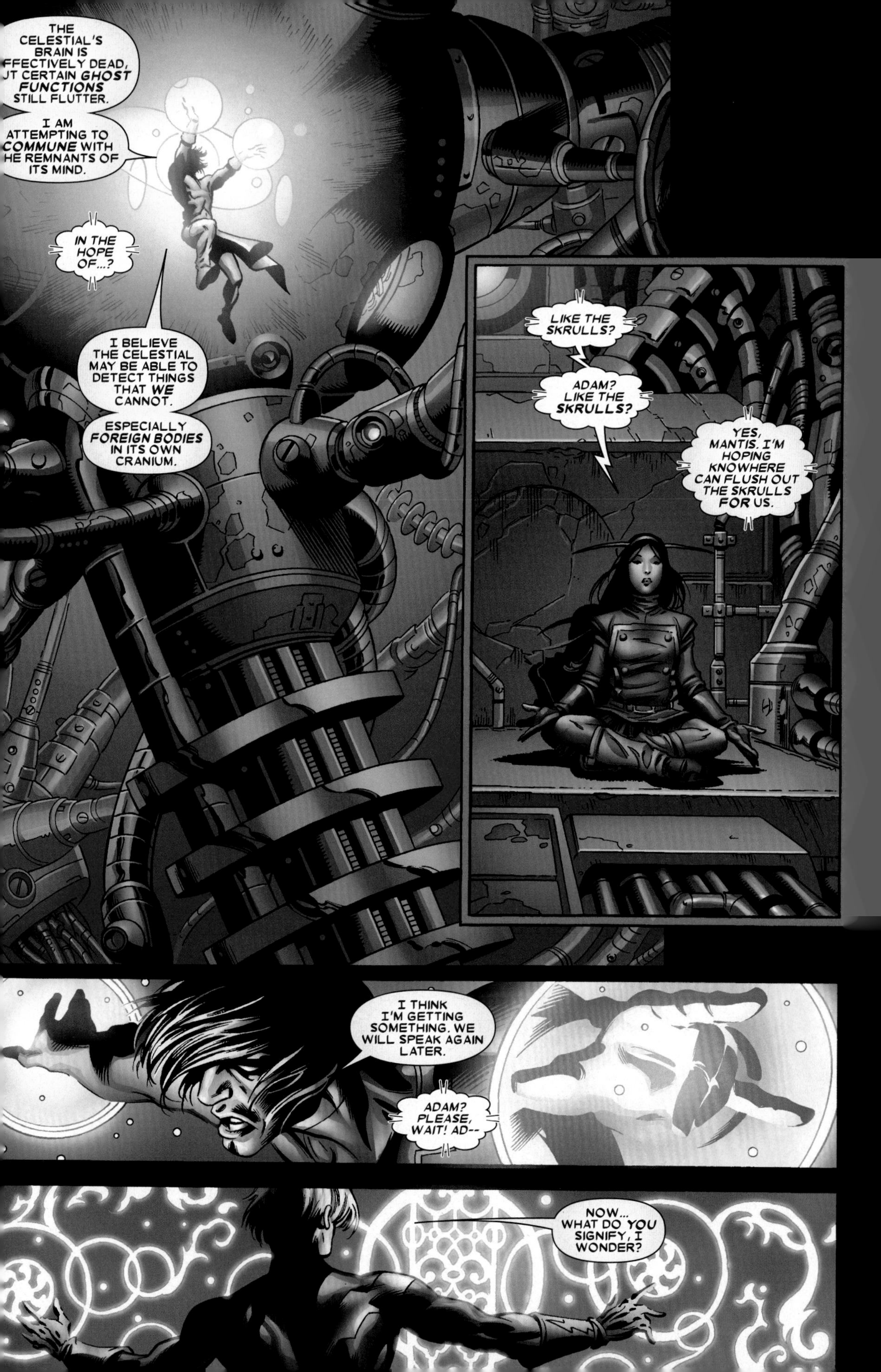
THE CELESTIAL'S BRAIN IS FFECTIVELY DEAD, JT CERTAIN GHOST FUNCTIONS STILL FLUTTER.
I AM ATTEMPTING TO COMMUNE WITH HE REMNANTS OF ITS MIND.
IN THE HOPE OF...?
I BELIEVE THE CELESTIAL MAY BE ABLE TO DETECT THINGS THAT WE CANNOT.
ESPECIALLY FOREIGN BODIES IN ITS OWN CRANIUM.
LIKE THE SKRULLS?
ADAM? LIKE THE SKRULLS?
YES, MANTIS. I'M HOPING KNOWHERE CAN FLUSH OUT THE SKRULLS FOR US.
I THINK I'M GETTING SOMETHING. WE WILL SPEAK AGAIN LATER.
ADAM? PLEASE, WAIT! AD--
NOW... WHAT DO YOU SIGNIFY, I WONDER?

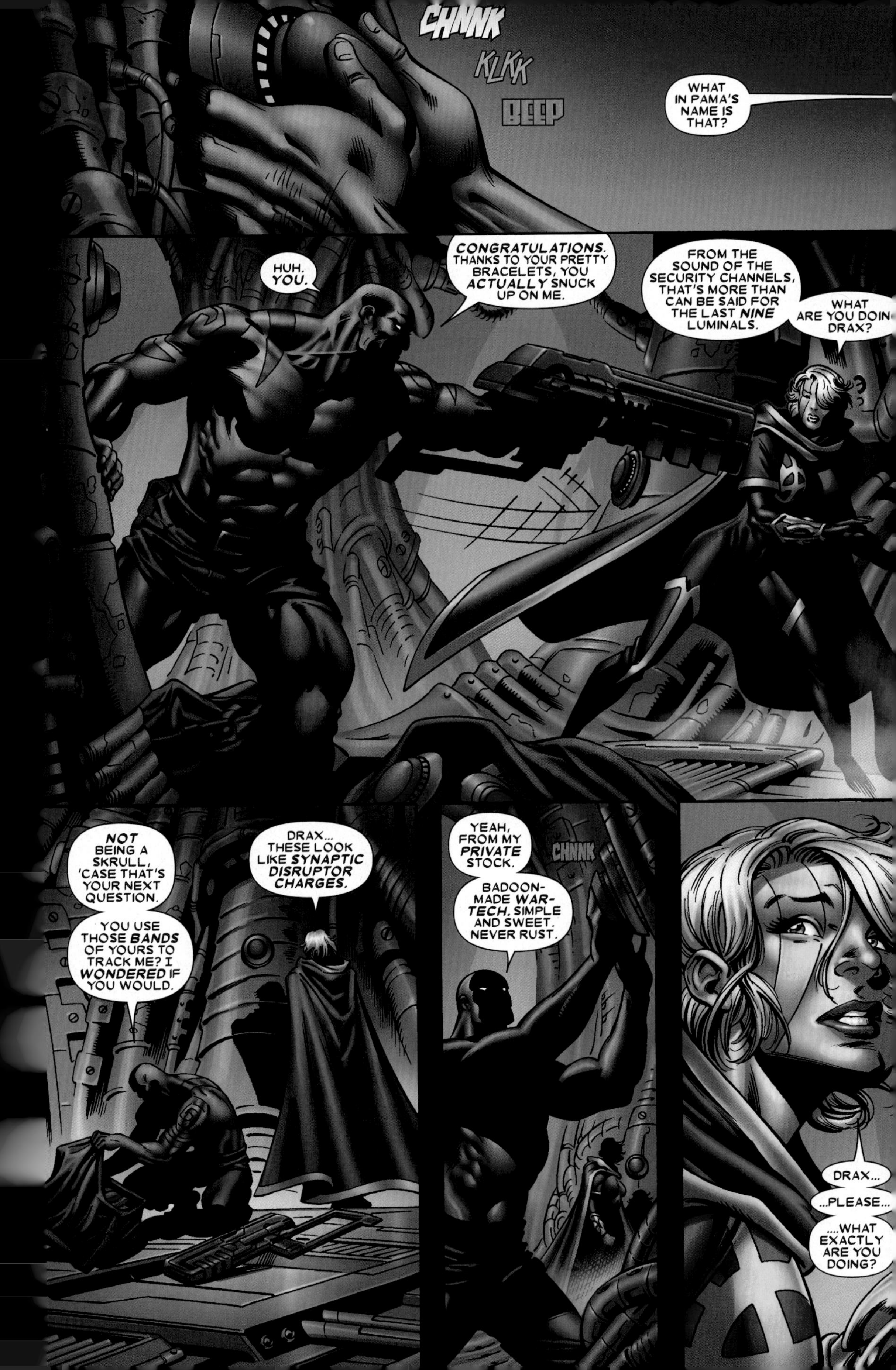
CHNNK
KLKK
BEEP
WHAT IN PAMA'S NAME IS THAT?
HUH. YOU.
CONGRATULATIONS. THANKS TO YOUR PRETTY BRACELETS, YOU ACTUALLY SNUCK UP ON ME.
FROM THE SOUND OF THE SECURITY CHANNELS, THAT'S MORE THAN CAN BE SAID FOR THE LAST NINE LUMINALS.
WHAT ARE YOU DOIN DRAX?
NOT BEING A SKRULL, 'CASE THAT'S YOUR NEXT QUESTION.
YOU USE THOSE BANDS OF YOURS TO TRACK ME? I WONDERED IF YOU WOULD.
DRAX... THESE LOOK LIKE SYNAPTIC DISRUPTOR CHARGES.
YEAH, FROM MY PRIVATE STOCK.
CHNNK
BADOON-MADE WAR-TECH. SIMPLE AND SWEET. NEVER RUST.
DRAX...
...PLEASE...
....WHAT EXACTLY ARE YOU DOING?

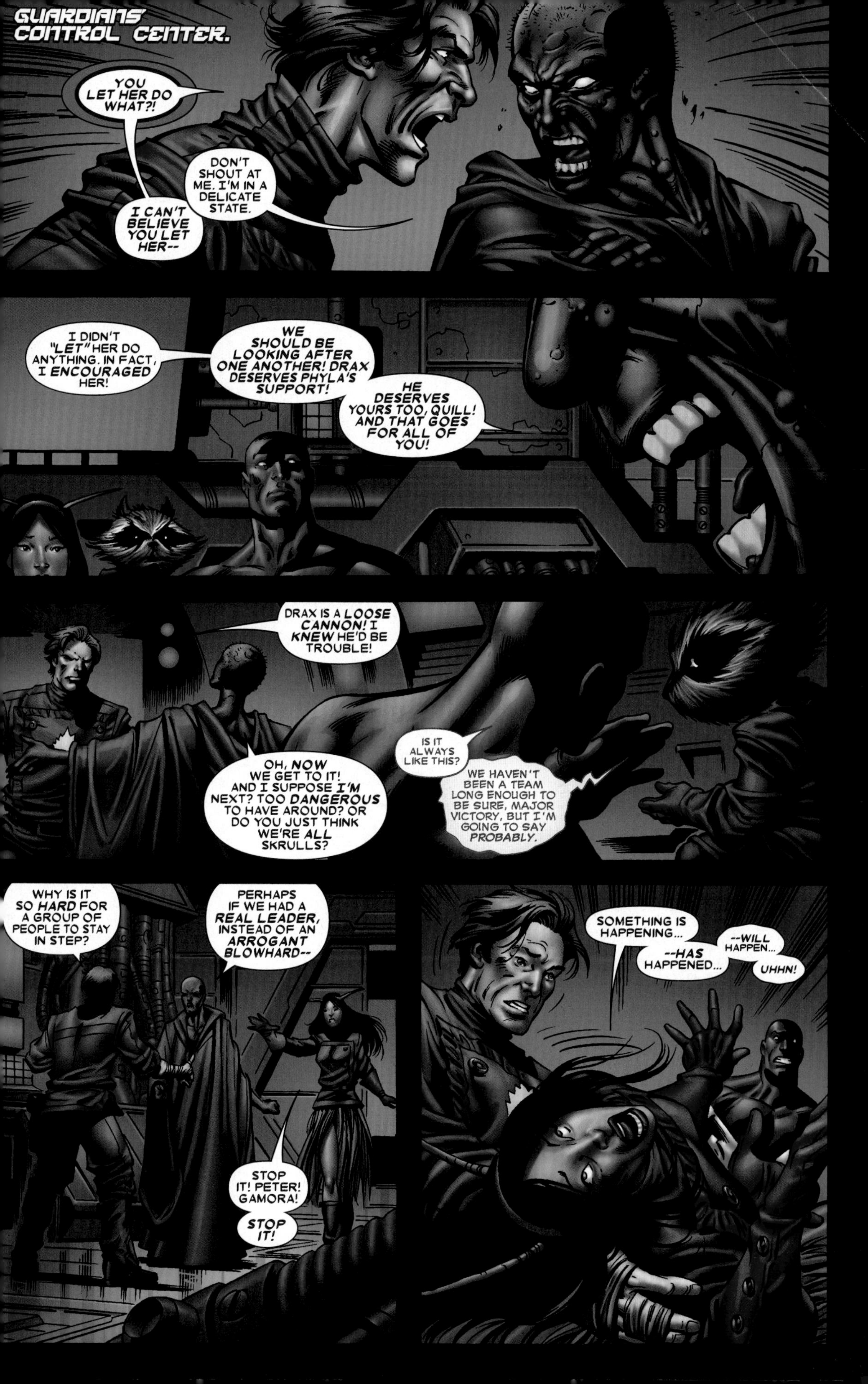
GUARDIANS' CONTROL CENTER.
YOU LET HER DO WHAT?!
DON'T SHOUT AT ME. I'M IN A DELICATE STATE.
I CAN'T BELIEVE YOU LET HER--
I DIDN'T "LET" HER DO ANYTHING. IN FACT, I ENCOURAGED HER!
WE SHOULD BE LOOKING AFTER ONE ANOTHER! DRAX DESERVES PHYLA'S SUPPORT!
HE DESERVES YOURS TOO, QUILL! AND THAT GOES FOR ALL OF YOU!
DRAX IS A LOOSE CANNON! I KNEW HE'D BE TROUBLE!
OH, NOW WE GET TO IT! AND I SUPPOSE I'M NEXT? TOO DANGEROUS TO HAVE AROUND? OR DO YOU JUST THINK WE'RE ALL SKRULLS?
IS IT ALWAYS LIKE THIS?
WE HAVEN'T BEEN A TEAM LONG ENOUGH TO BE SURE, MAJOR VICTORY, BUT I'M GOING TO SAY PROBABLY.
WHY IS IT SO HARD FOR A GROUP OF PEOPLE TO STAY IN STEP?
PERHAPS IF WE HAD A REAL LEADER, INSTEAD OF AN ARROGANT BLOWHARD--
STOP IT! PETER! GAMORA!
STOP IT!
SOMETHING IS HAPPENING...
--HAS HAPPENED...
--WILL HAPPEN...
UHHN!

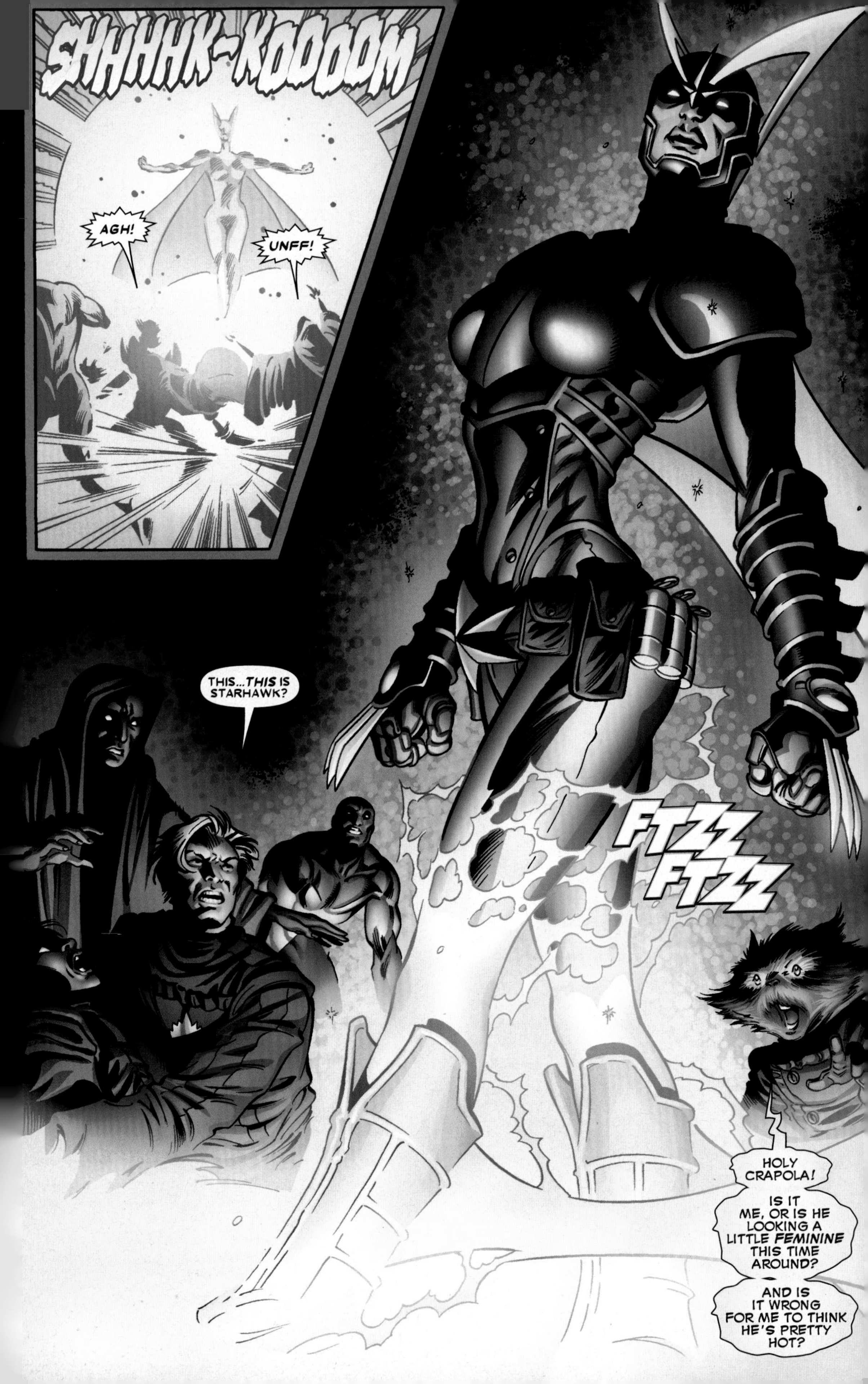
SHHHHK-KOOOOM
AGH!
UNFF!
THIS...THIS IS STARHAWK?
FTZZ FTZZ
HOLY CRAPOLA!
IS IT ME, OR IS HE LOOKING A LITTLE FEMININE THIS TIME AROUND?
AND IS IT WRONG FOR ME TO THINK HE'S PRETTY HOT?

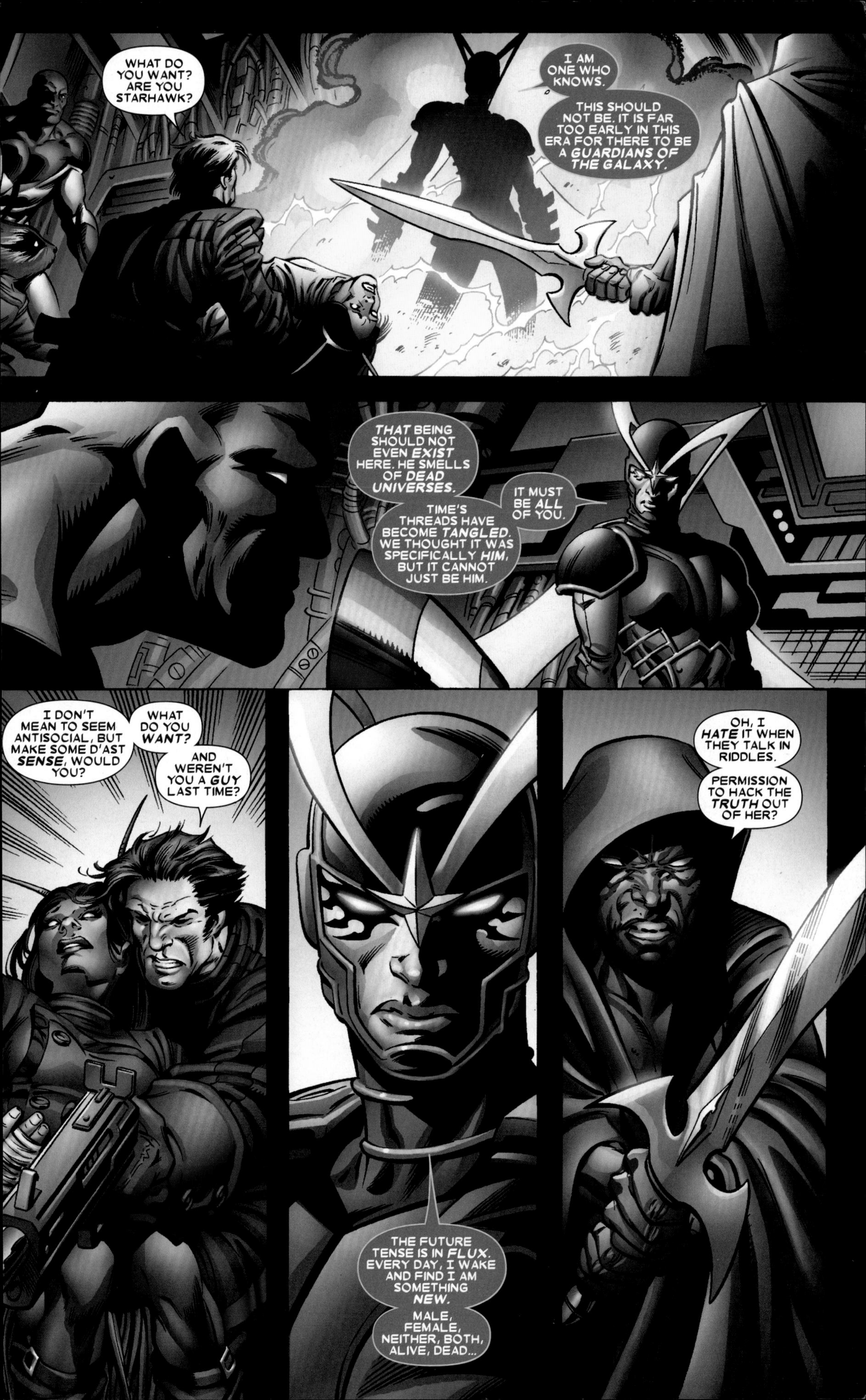
WHAT DO YOU WANT? ARE YOU STARHAWK?
I AM ONE WHO KNOWS.
THIS SHOULD NOT BE. IT IS FAR TOO EARLY IN THIS ERA FOR THERE TO BE A GUARDIANS OF THE GALAXY.
THAT BEING SHOULD NOT EVEN EXIST HERE. HE SMELLS OF DEAD UNIVERSES.
TIME'S THREADS HAVE BECOME TANGLED. WE THOUGHT IT WAS SPECIFICALLY HIM, BUT IT CANNOT JUST BE HIM.
IT MUST BE ALL OF YOU.
I DON'T MEAN TO SEEM ANTISOCIAL, BUT MAKE SOME D'AST SENSE, WOULD YOU?
WHAT DO YOU WANT?
AND WEREN'T YOU A GUY LAST TIME?
THE FUTURE TENSE IS IN FLUX. EVERY DAY, I WAKE AND FIND I AM SOMETHING NEW.
MALE, FEMALE, NEITHER, BOTH, ALIVE, DEAD...
OH, I HATE IT WHEN THEY TALK IN RIDDLES.
PERMISSION TO HACK THE TRUTH OUT OF HER?

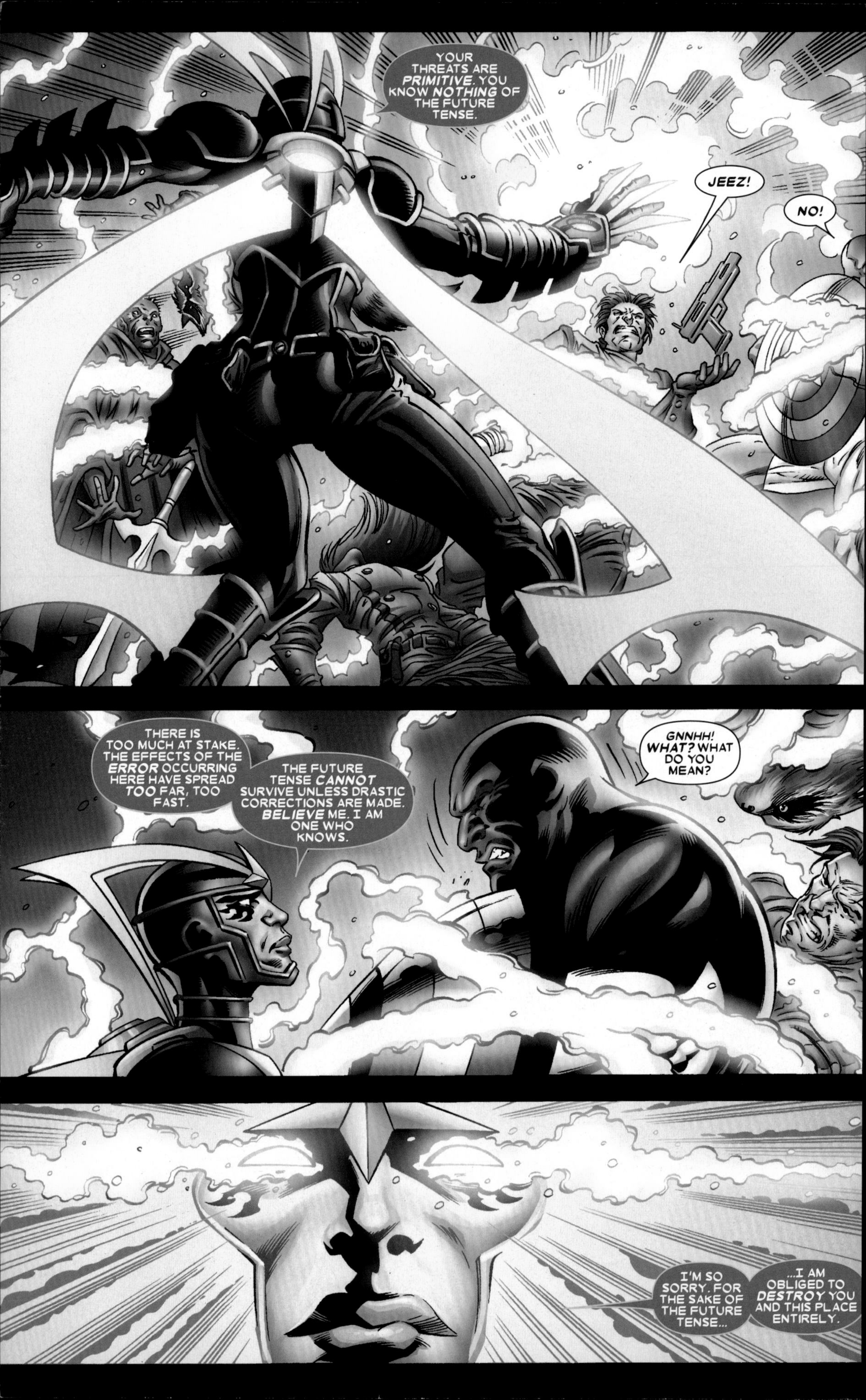
YOUR THREATS ARE PRIMITIVE. YOU KNOW NOTHING OF THE FUTURE TENSE.
JEEZ!
NO!
THERE IS TOO MUCH AT STAKE. THE EFFECTS OF THE ERROR OCCURRING HERE HAVE SPREAD TOO FAR, TOO FAST.
THE FUTURE TENSE CANNOT SURVIVE UNLESS DRASTIC CORRECTIONS ARE MADE. BELIEVE ME. I AM ONE WHO KNOWS.
GNNHH! WHAT? WHAT DO YOU MEAN?
I'M SO SORRY. FOR THE SAKE OF THE FUTURE TENSE...
...I AM OBLIGED TO DESTROY YOU AND THIS PLACE ENTIRELY.

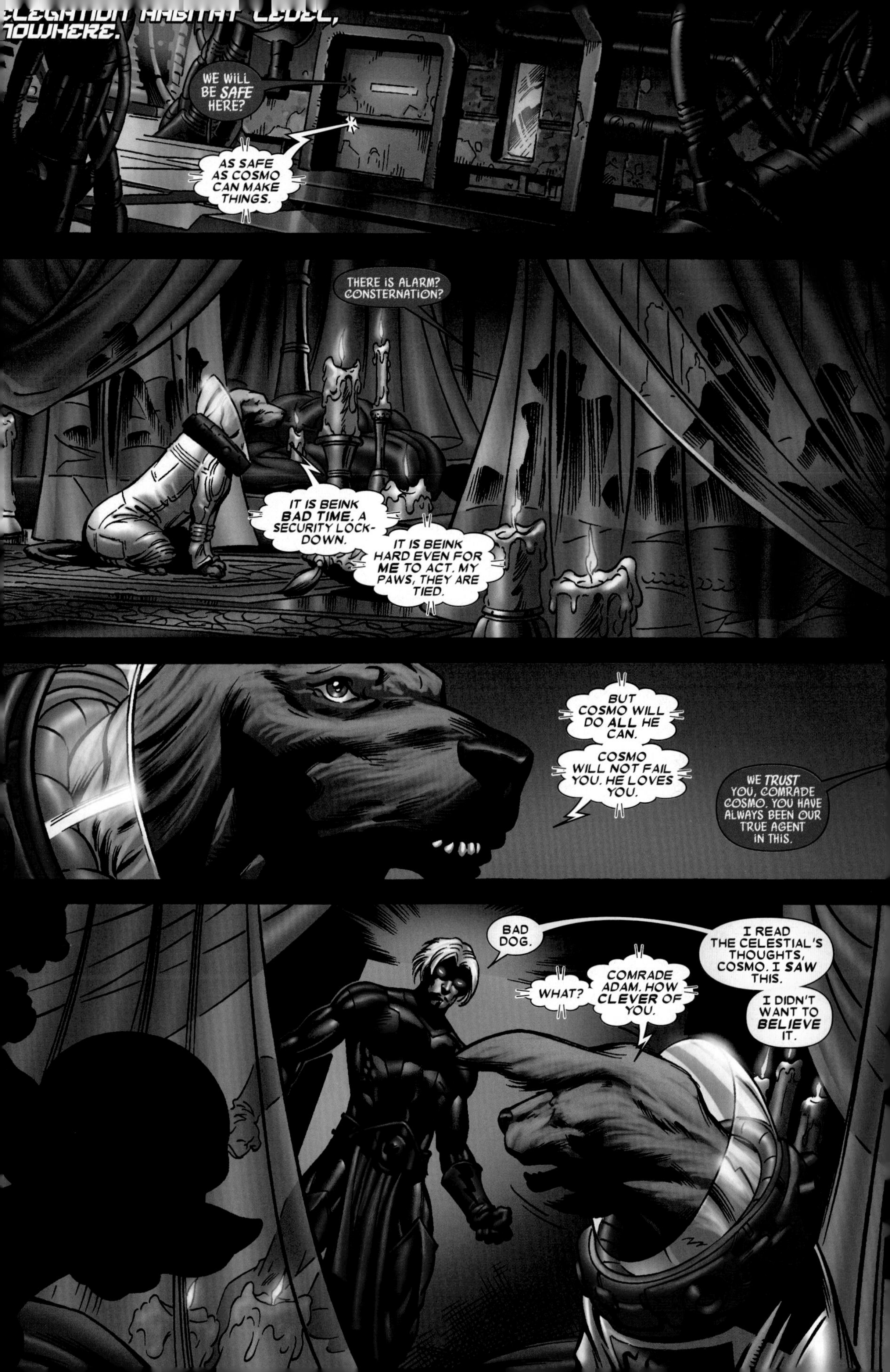
LEGATION HABITAT LEVEL,
NOWHERE.
WE WILL BE SAFE HERE?
AS SAFE AS COSMO CAN MAKE THINGS.
THERE IS ALARM? CONSTERNATION?
IT IS BEINK BAD TIME. A SECURITY LOCK-DOWN.
IT IS BEINK HARD EVEN FOR ME TO ACT. MY PAWS, THEY ARE TIED.
BUT COSMO WILL DO ALL HE CAN.
COSMO WILL NOT FAIL YOU. HE LOVES YOU.
WE TRUST YOU, COMRADE COSMO. YOU HAVE ALWAYS BEEN OUR TRUE AGENT IN THIS.
BAD DOG.
I READ THE CELESTIAL'S THOUGHTS, COSMO. I SAW THIS.
I DIDN'T WANT TO BELIEVE IT.
WHAT?
COMRADE ADAM. HOW CLEVER OF YOU.

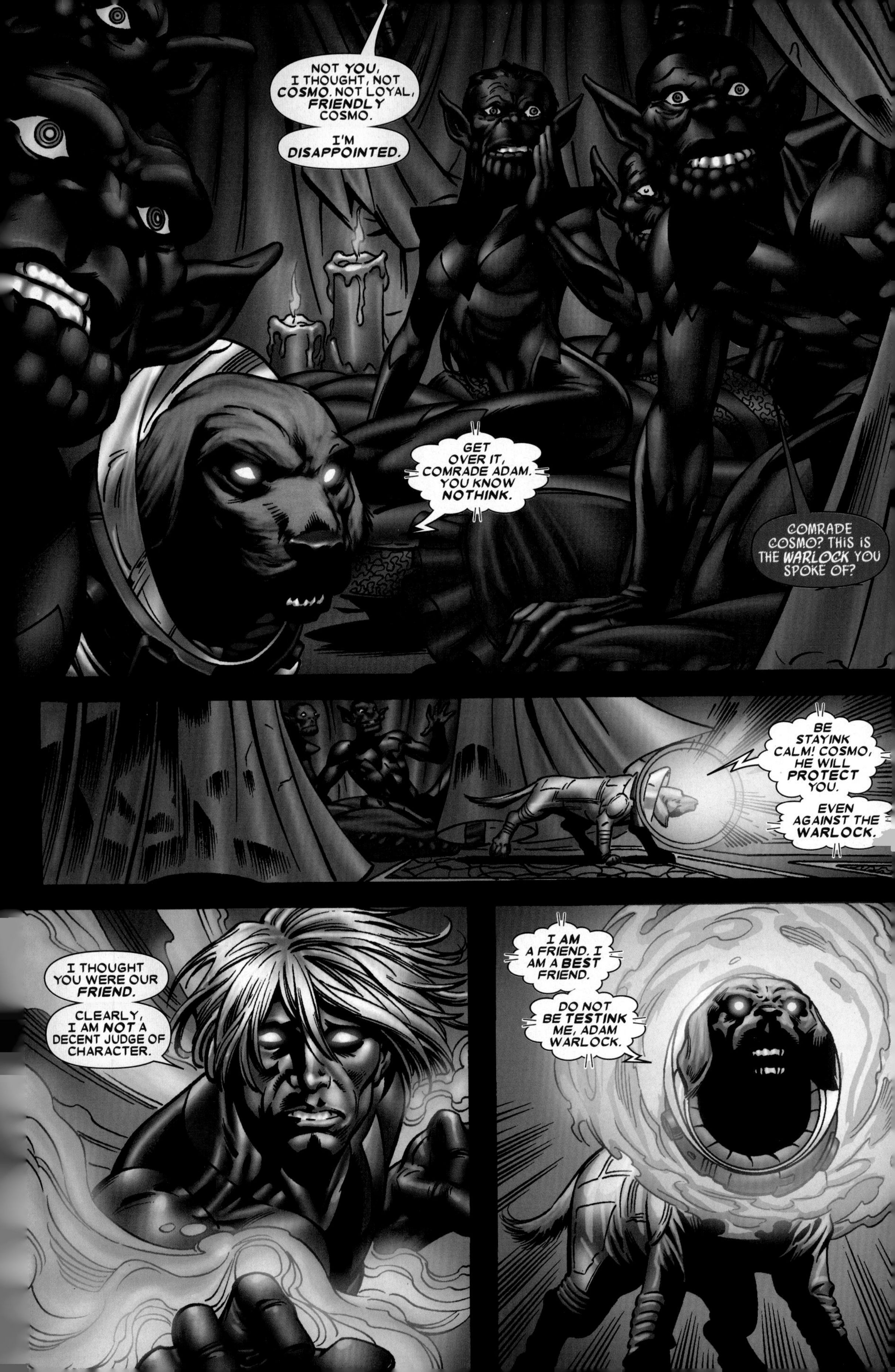
NOT YOU, I THOUGHT, NOT COSMO. NOT LOYAL, FRIENDLY COSMO.
I'M DISAPPOINTED.
GET OVER IT, COMRADE ADAM. YOU KNOW NOTHINK.
COMRADE COSMO? THIS IS THE WARLOCK YOU SPOKE OF?
BE STAYINK CALM! COSMO, HE WILL PROTECT YOU.
EVEN AGAINST THE WARLOCK.
I THOUGHT YOU WERE OUR FRIEND.
CLEARLY, I AM NOT A DECENT JUDGE OF CHARACTER.
I AM A FRIEND. I AM A BEST FRIEND.
DO NOT BE TESTINK ME, ADAM WARLOCK.

DAMAGES

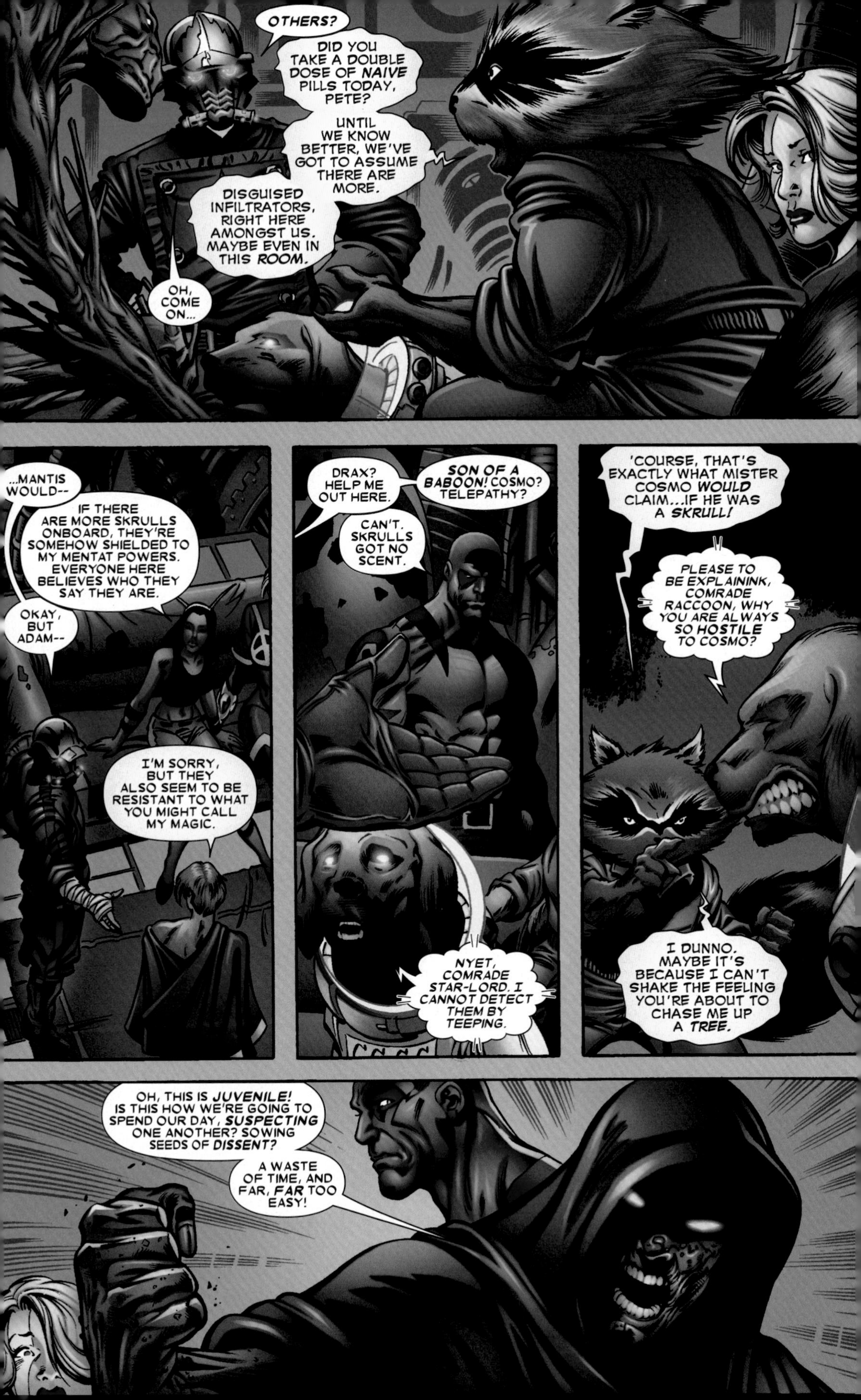

OTHERS?
DID YOU TAKE A DOUBLE DOSE OF NAIVE PILLS TODAY, PETE?
UNTIL WE KNOW BETTER, WE'VE GOT TO ASSUME THERE ARE MORE.
DISGUISED INFILTRATORS, RIGHT HERE AMONGST US. MAYBE EVEN IN THIS ROOM.
OH, COME ON...
...MANTIS WOULD--
IF THERE ARE MORE SKRULLS ONBOARD, THEY'RE SOMEHOW SHIELDED TO MY MENTAT POWERS. EVERYONE HERE BELIEVES WHO THEY SAY THEY ARE.
OKAY, BUT ADAM--
I'M SORRY, BUT THEY ALSO SEEM TO BE RESISTANT TO WHAT YOU MIGHT CALL MY MAGIC.
DRAX? HELP ME OUT HERE.
SON OF A BABOON! COSMO? TELEPATHY?
CAN'T. SKRULLS GOT NO SCENT.
NYET, COMRADE STAR-LORD. I CANNOT DETECT THEM BY TEEPING.
'COURSE, THAT'S EXACTLY WHAT MISTER COSMO WOULD CLAIM...IF HE WAS A SKRULL!
PLEASE TO BE EXPLAININK, COMRADE RACCOON, WHY YOU ARE ALWAYS SO HOSTILE TO COSMO?
I DUNNO. MAYBE IT'S BECAUSE I CAN'T SHAKE THE FEELING YOU'RE ABOUT TO CHASE ME UP A TREE.
OH, THIS IS JUVENILE! IS THIS HOW WE'RE GOING TO SPEND OUR DAY, SUSPECTING ONE ANOTHER? SOWING SEEDS OF DISSENT?
A WASTE OF TIME, AND FAR, FAR TOO EASY!

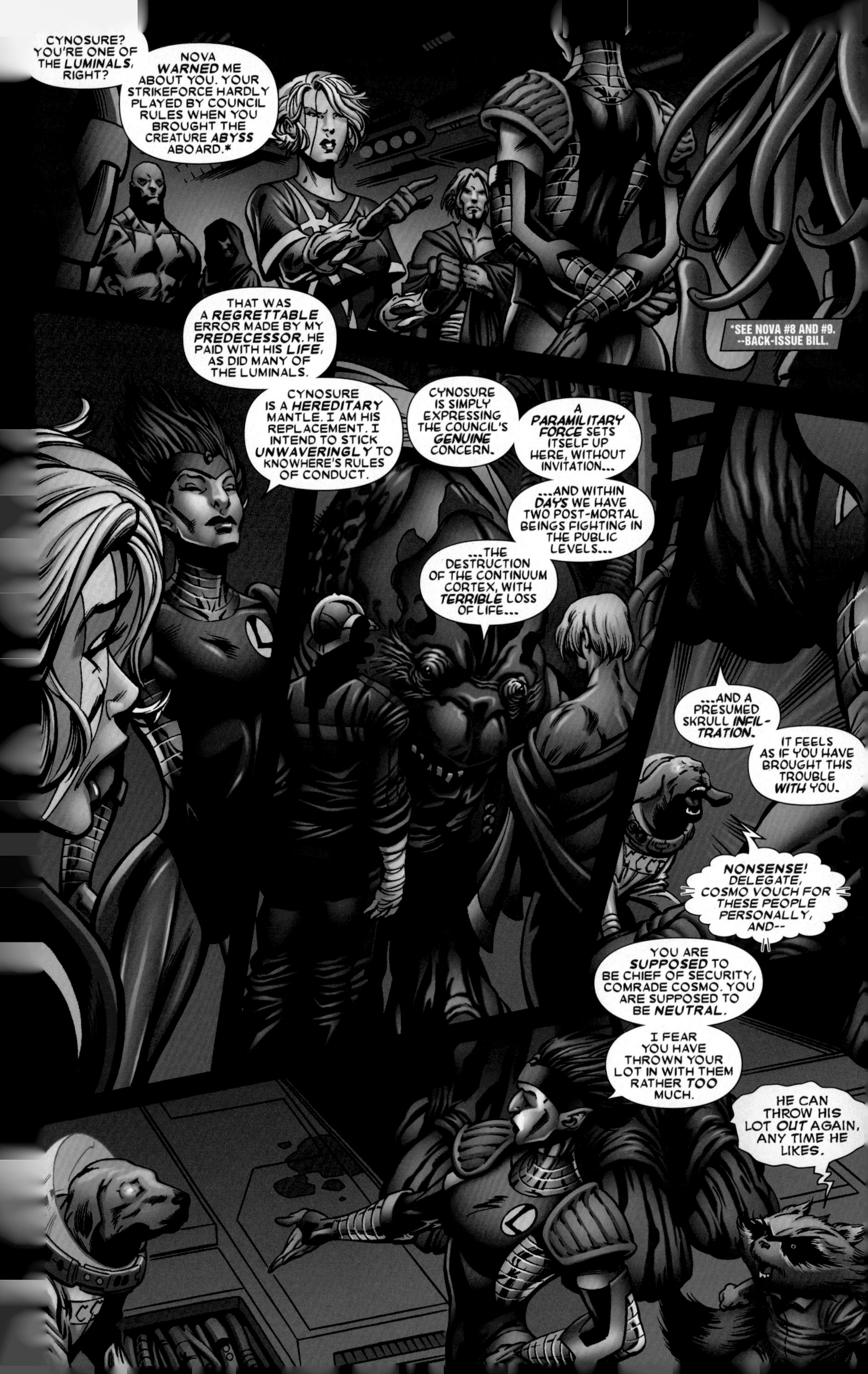
CYNOSURE? YOU'RE ONE OF THE LUMINALS, RIGHT?
NOVA WARNED ME ABOUT YOU. YOUR STRIKEFORCE HARDLY PLAYED BY COUNCIL RULES WHEN YOU BROUGHT THE CREATURE ABYSS ABOARD.*
*SEE NOVA #8 AND #9. --BACK-ISSUE BILL.
THAT WAS A REGRETTABLE ERROR MADE BY MY PREDECESSOR. HE PAID WITH HIS LIFE, AS DID MANY OF THE LUMINALS.
CYNOSURE IS A HEREDITARY MANTLE. I AM HIS REPLACEMENT. I INTEND TO STICK UNWAVERINGLY TO KNOWHERE'S RULES OF CONDUCT.
CYNOSURE IS SIMPLY EXPRESSING THE COUNCIL'S GENUINE CONCERN.
A PARAMILITARY FORCE SETS ITSELF UP HERE, WITHOUT INVITATION...
...AND WITHIN DAYS WE HAVE TWO POST-MORTAL BEINGS FIGHTING IN THE PUBLIC LEVELS...
...THE DESTRUCTION OF THE CONTINUUM CORTEX, WITH TERRIBLE LOSS OF LIFE...
...AND A PRESUMED SKRULL INFILTRATION.
IT FEELS AS IF YOU HAVE BROUGHT THIS TROUBLE WITH YOU.
NONSENSE! DELEGATE, COSMO VOUCH FOR THESE PEOPLE PERSONALLY, AND--
YOU ARE SUPPOSED TO BE CHIEF OF SECURITY, COMRADE COSMO. YOU ARE SUPPOSED TO BE NEUTRAL.
I FEAR YOU HAVE THROWN YOUR LOT IN WITH THEM RATHER TOO MUCH.
HE CAN THROW HIS LOT OUT AGAIN, ANY TIME HE LIKES.

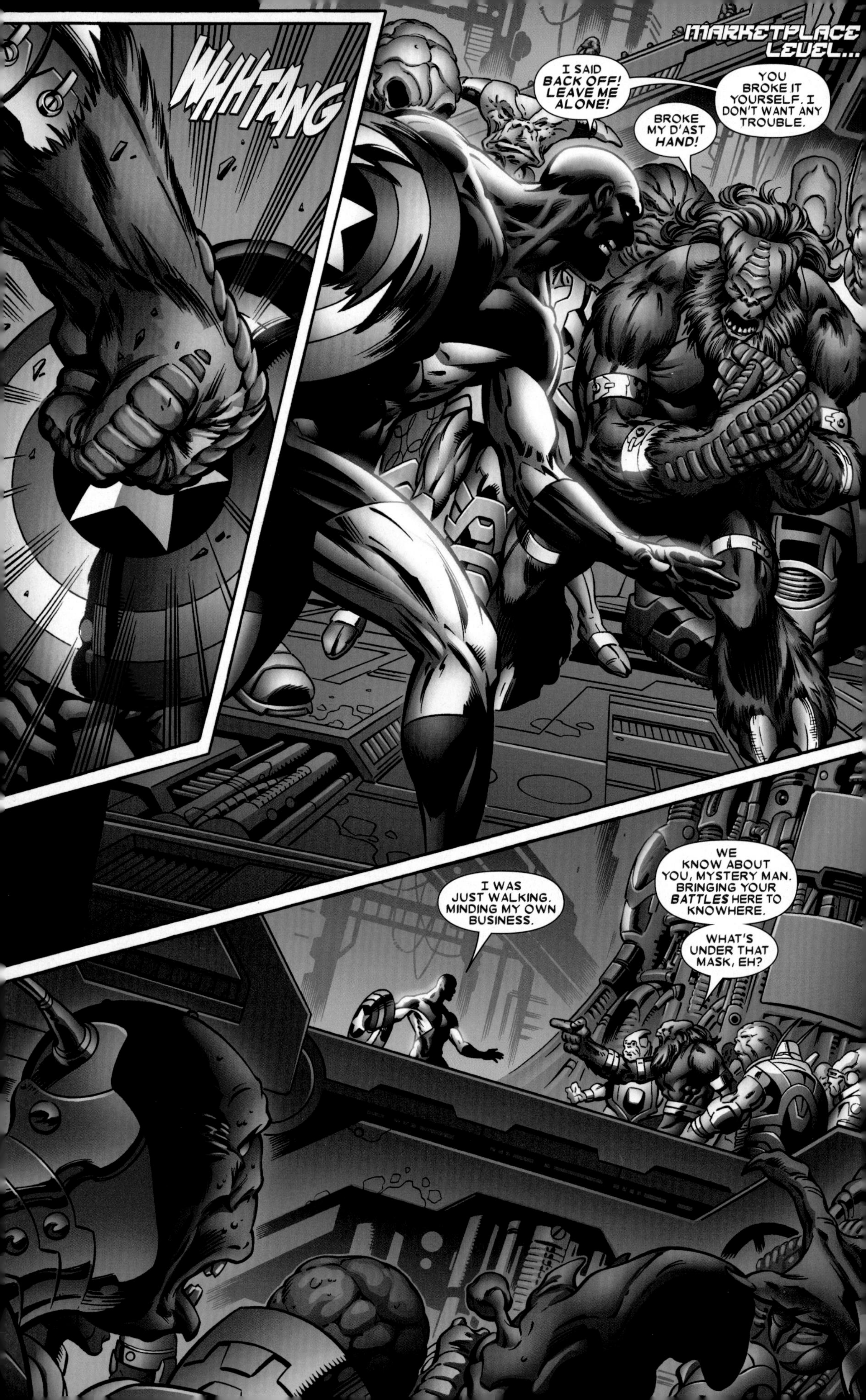
MARKETPLACE LEVEL...
WHHTANG
I SAID BACK OFF! LEAVE ME ALONE!
BROKE MY D'AST HAND!
YOU BROKE IT YOURSELF. I DON'T WANT ANY TROUBLE.
WE KNOW ABOUT YOU, MYSTERY MAN. BRINGING YOUR BATTLES HERE TO KNOWHERE.
I WAS JUST WALKING. MINDING MY OWN BUSINESS.
WHAT'S UNDER THAT MASK, EH?

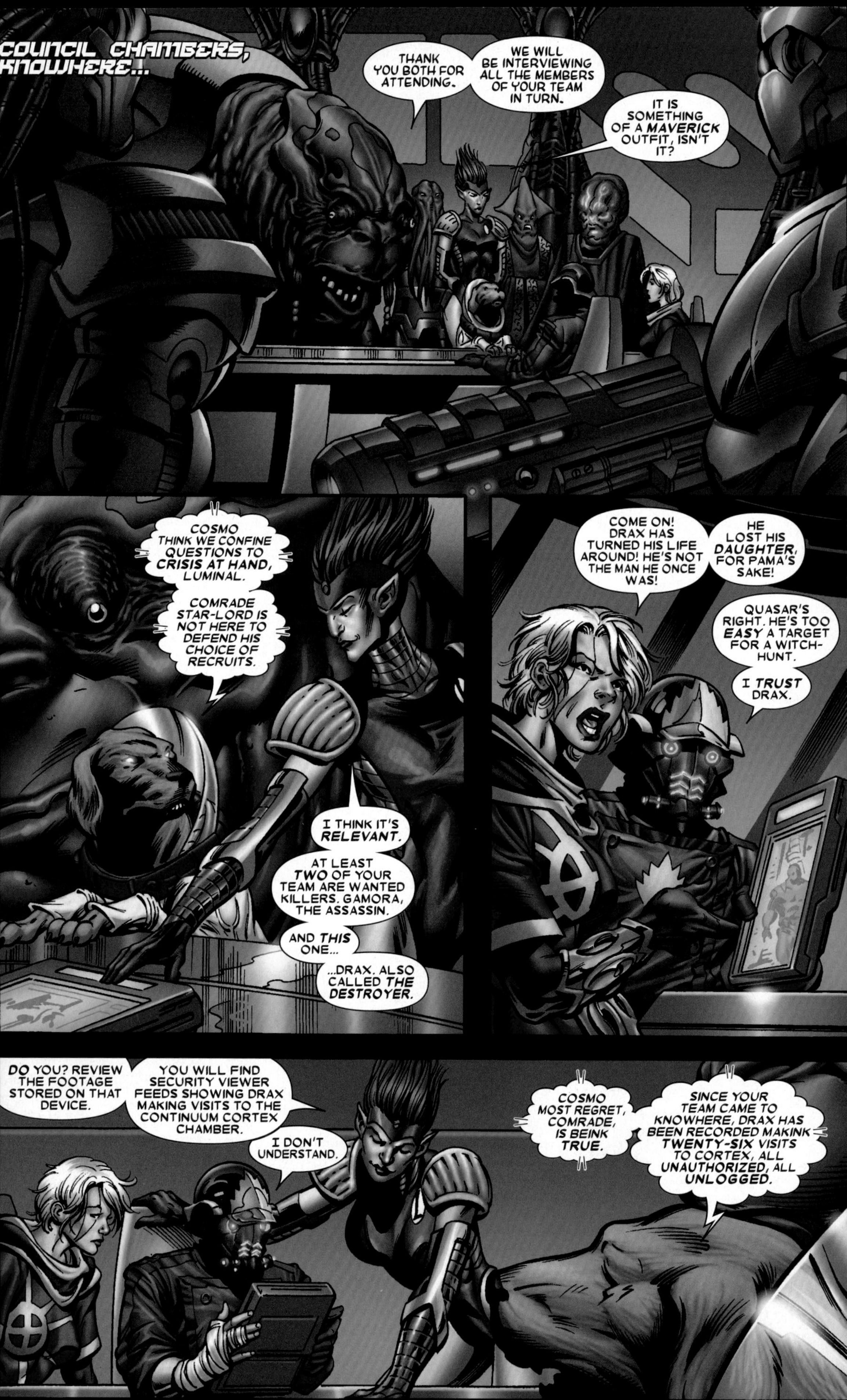

COUNCIL CHAMBERS, KNOWHERE...
THANK YOU BOTH FOR ATTENDING.
WE WILL BE INTERVIEWING ALL THE MEMBERS OF YOUR TEAM IN TURN.
IT IS SOMETHING OF A MAVERICK OUTFIT, ISN'T IT?
COSMO THINK WE CONFINE QUESTIONS TO CRISIS AT HAND, LUMINAL.
COMRADE STAR-LORD IS NOT HERE TO DEFEND HIS CHOICE OF RECRUITS.
I THINK IT'S RELEVANT.
AT LEAST TWO OF YOUR TEAM ARE WANTED KILLERS. GAMORA, THE ASSASSIN.
AND THIS ONE...
...DRAX. ALSO CALLED THE DESTROYER.
COME ON! DRAX HAS TURNED HIS LIFE AROUND! HE'S NOT THE MAN HE ONCE WAS!
HE LOST HIS DAUGHTER, FOR PAMA'S SAKE!
QUASAR'S RIGHT. HE'S TOO EASY A TARGET FOR A WITCH-HUNT.
I TRUST DRAX.
DO YOU? REVIEW THE FOOTAGE STORED ON THAT DEVICE.
YOU WILL FIND SECURITY VIEWER FEEDS SHOWING DRAX MAKING VISITS TO THE CONTINUUM CORTEX CHAMBER.
I DON'T UNDERSTAND.
COSMO MOST REGRET, COMRADE, IS BEINK TRUE.
SINCE YOUR TEAM CAME TO KNOWHERE, DRAX HAS BEEN RECORDED MAKINK TWENTY-SIX VISITS TO CORTEX, ALL UNAUTHORIZED, ALL UNLOGGED.

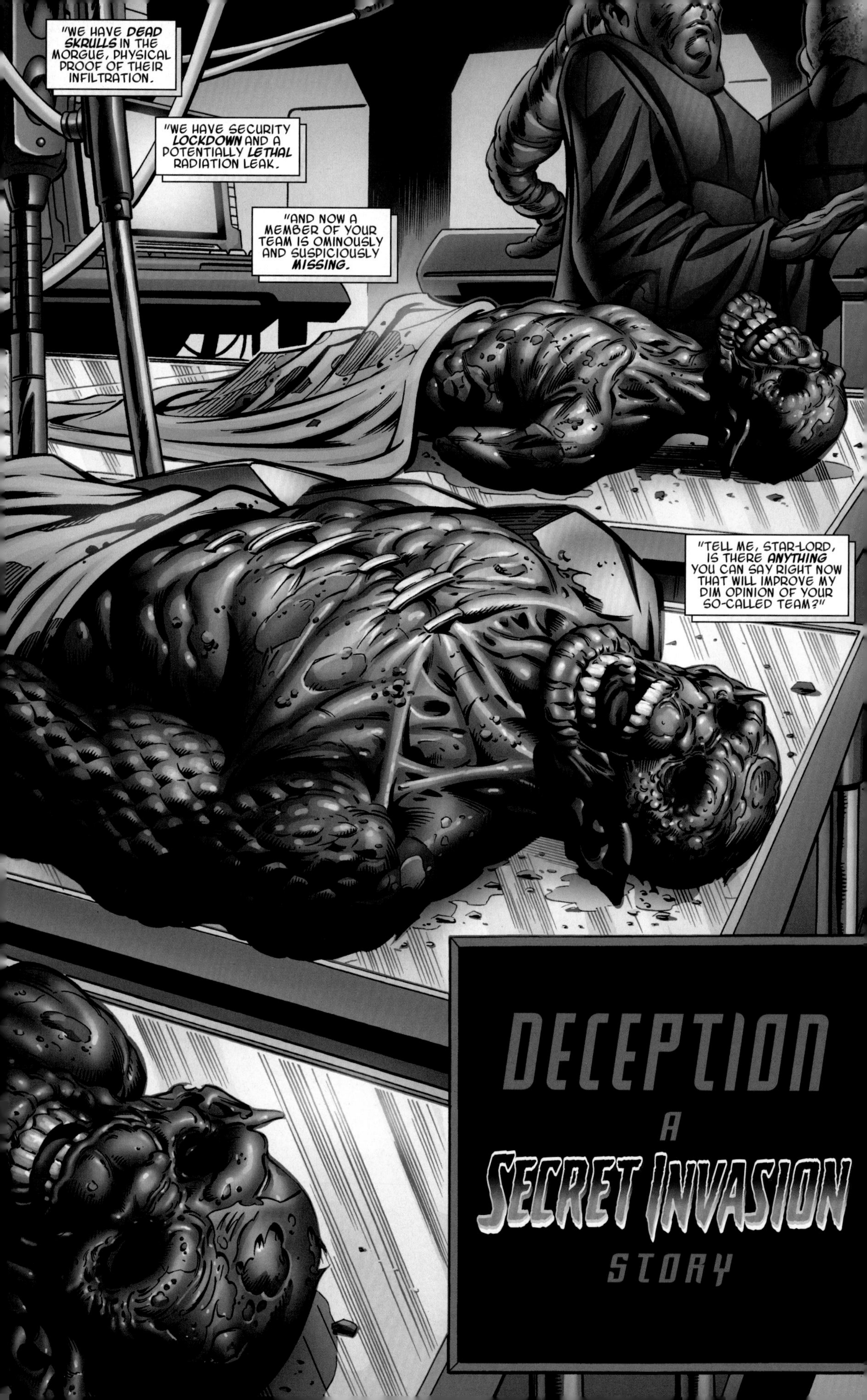
"WE HAVE DEAD SKRULLS IN THE MORGUE, PHYSICAL PROOF OF THEIR INFILTRATION.
"WE HAVE SECURITY LOCKDOWN AND A POTENTIALLY LETHAL RADIATION LEAK.
"AND NOW A MEMBER OF YOUR TEAM IS OMINOUSLY AND SUSPICIOUSLY MISSING.
"TELL ME, STAR-LORD, IS THERE ANYTHING YOU CAN SAY RIGHT NOW THAT WILL IMPROVE MY DIM OPINION OF YOUR SO-CALLED TEAM?"
DECEPTION
A SECRET INVASION STORY

GUARDIANS' CONTROL CENTER.

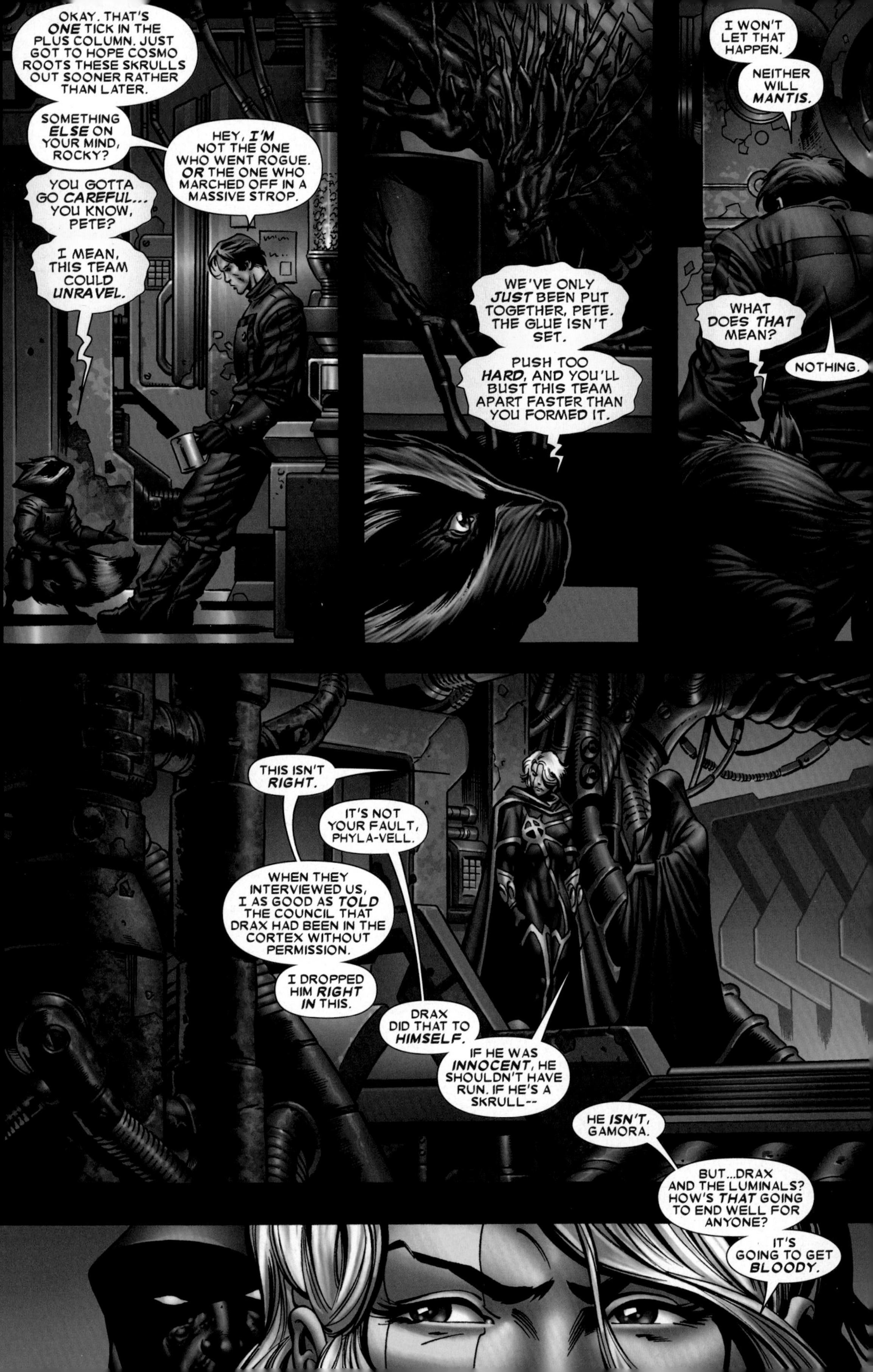
OKAY. THAT'S ONE TICK IN THE PLUS COLUMN. JUST GOT TO HOPE COSMO ROOTS THESE SKRULLS OUT SOONER RATHER THAN LATER.
SOMETHING ELSE ON YOUR MIND, ROCKY?
HEY, I'M NOT THE ONE WHO WENT ROGUE. OR THE ONE WHO MARCHED OFF IN A MASSIVE STROP.
YOU GOTTA GO CAREFUL... YOU KNOW, PETE?
I MEAN, THIS TEAM COULD UNRAVEL.
WE'VE ONLY JUST BEEN PUT TOGETHER, PETE. THE GLUE ISN'T SET.
PUSH TOO HARD, AND YOU'LL BUST THIS TEAM APART FASTER THAN YOU FORMED IT.
I WON'T LET THAT HAPPEN.
NEITHER WILL MANTIS.
WHAT DOES THAT MEAN?
NOTHING.
THIS ISN'T RIGHT.
IT'S NOT YOUR FAULT, PHYLA-VELL.
WHEN THEY INTERVIEWED US, I AS GOOD AS TOLD THE COUNCIL THAT DRAX HAD BEEN IN THE CORTEX WITHOUT PERMISSION.
I DROPPED HIM RIGHT IN THIS.
DRAX DID THAT TO HIMSELF.
IF HE WAS INNOCENT, HE SHOULDN'T HAVE RUN. IF HE'S A SKRULL--
HE ISN'T, GAMORA.
BUT...DRAX AND THE LUMINALS? HOW'S THAT GOING TO END WELL FOR ANYONE?
IT'S GOING TO GET BLOODY.

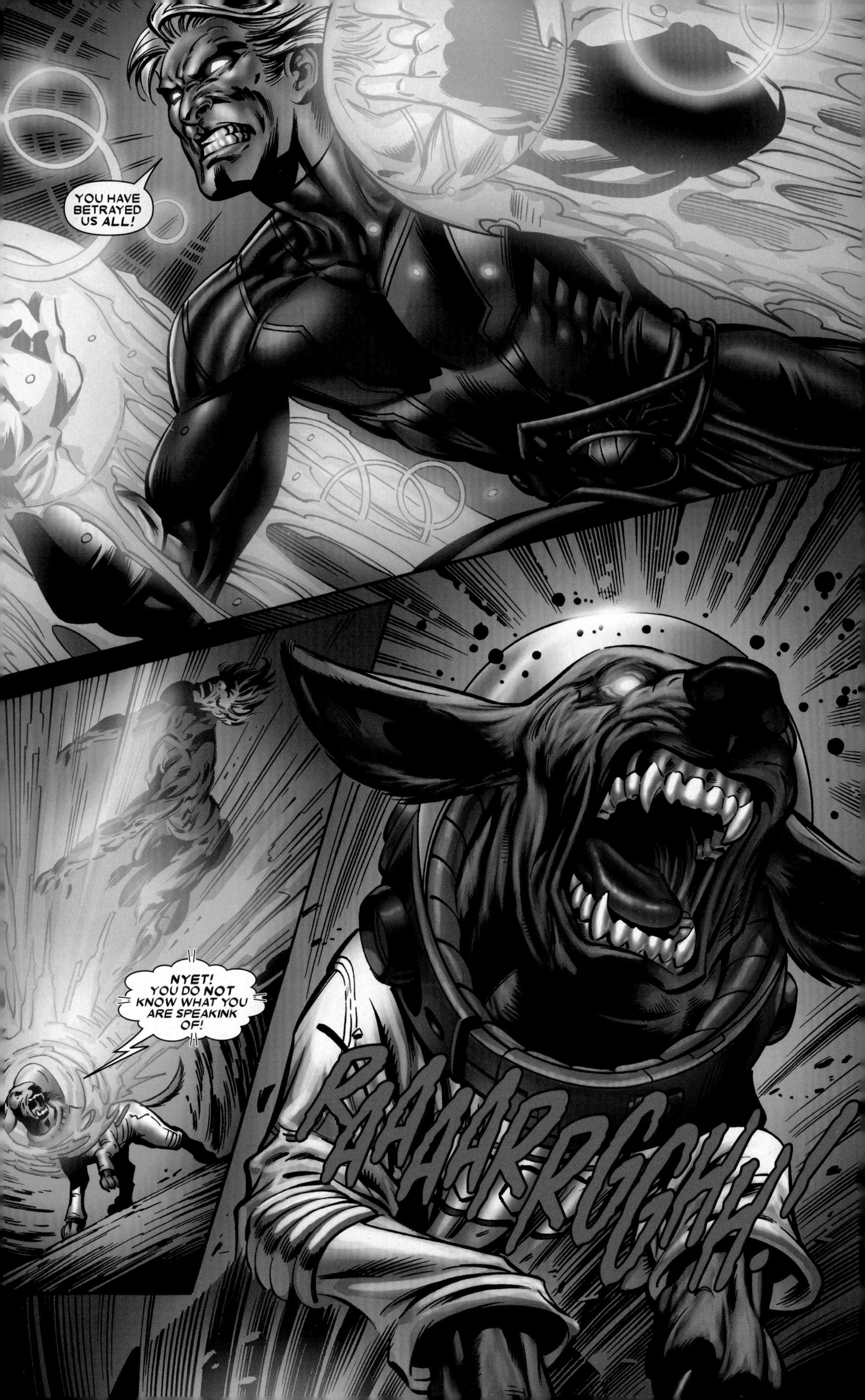
YOU HAVE BETRAYED US ALL!
NYET! YOU DO NOT KNOW WHAT YOU ARE SPEAKINK OF!
RAAAARRGGHH!

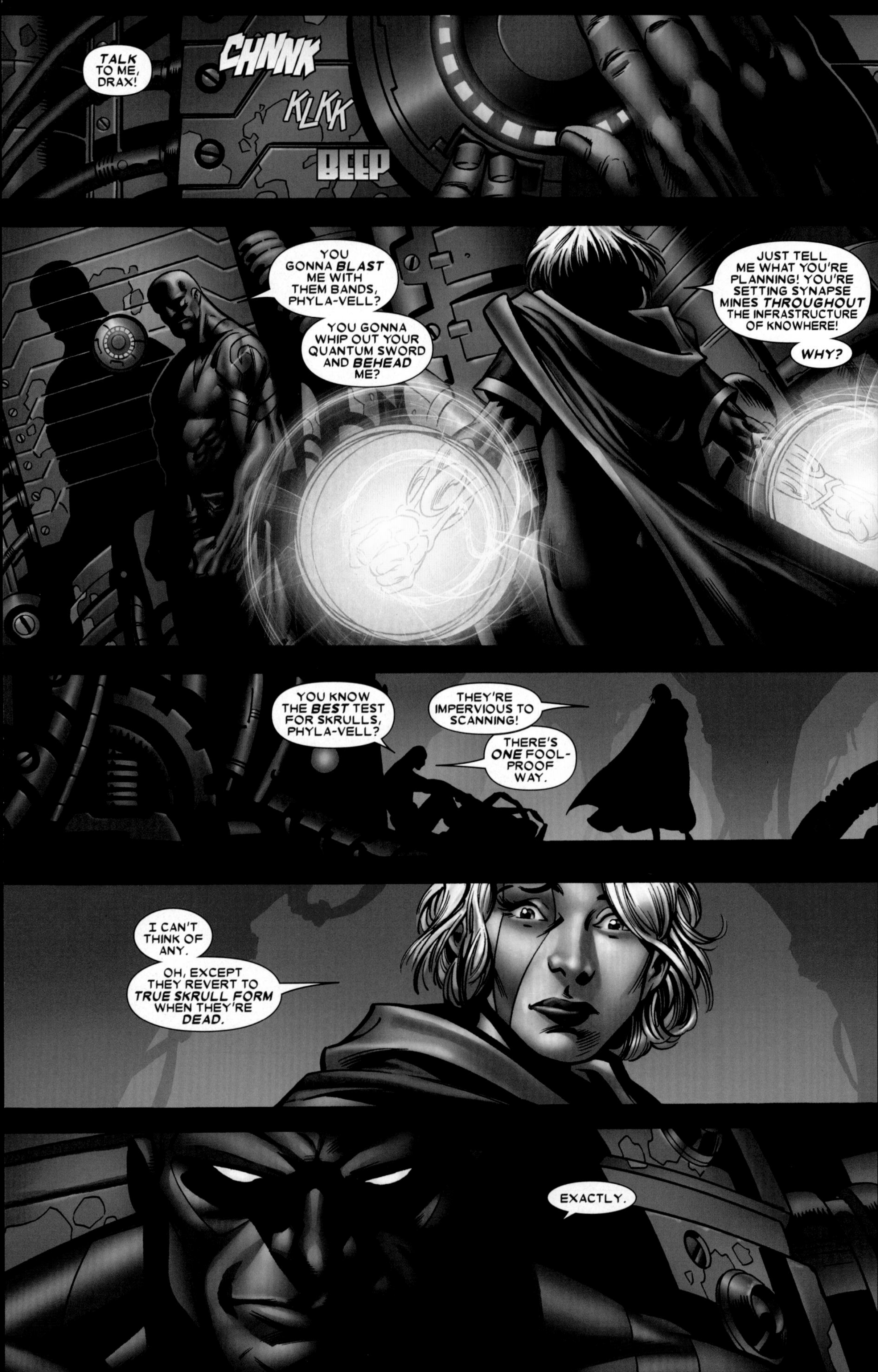
TALK TO ME, DRAX!
CHNNK
KLKK
BEEP
YOU GONNA BLAST ME WITH THEM BANDS, PHYLA-VELL?
YOU GONNA WHIP OUT YOUR QUANTUM SWORD AND BEHEAD ME?
JUST TELL ME WHAT YOU'RE PLANNING! YOU'RE SETTING SYNAPSE MINES THROUGHOUT THE INFRASTRUCTURE OF KNOWHERE!
WHY?
YOU KNOW THE BEST TEST FOR SKRULLS, PHYLA-VELL?
THEY'RE IMPERVIOUS TO SCANNING!
THERE'S ONE FOOL-PROOF WAY.
I CAN'T THINK OF ANY.
OH, EXCEPT THEY REVERT TO TRUE SKRULL FORM WHEN THEY'RE DEAD.
EXACTLY.

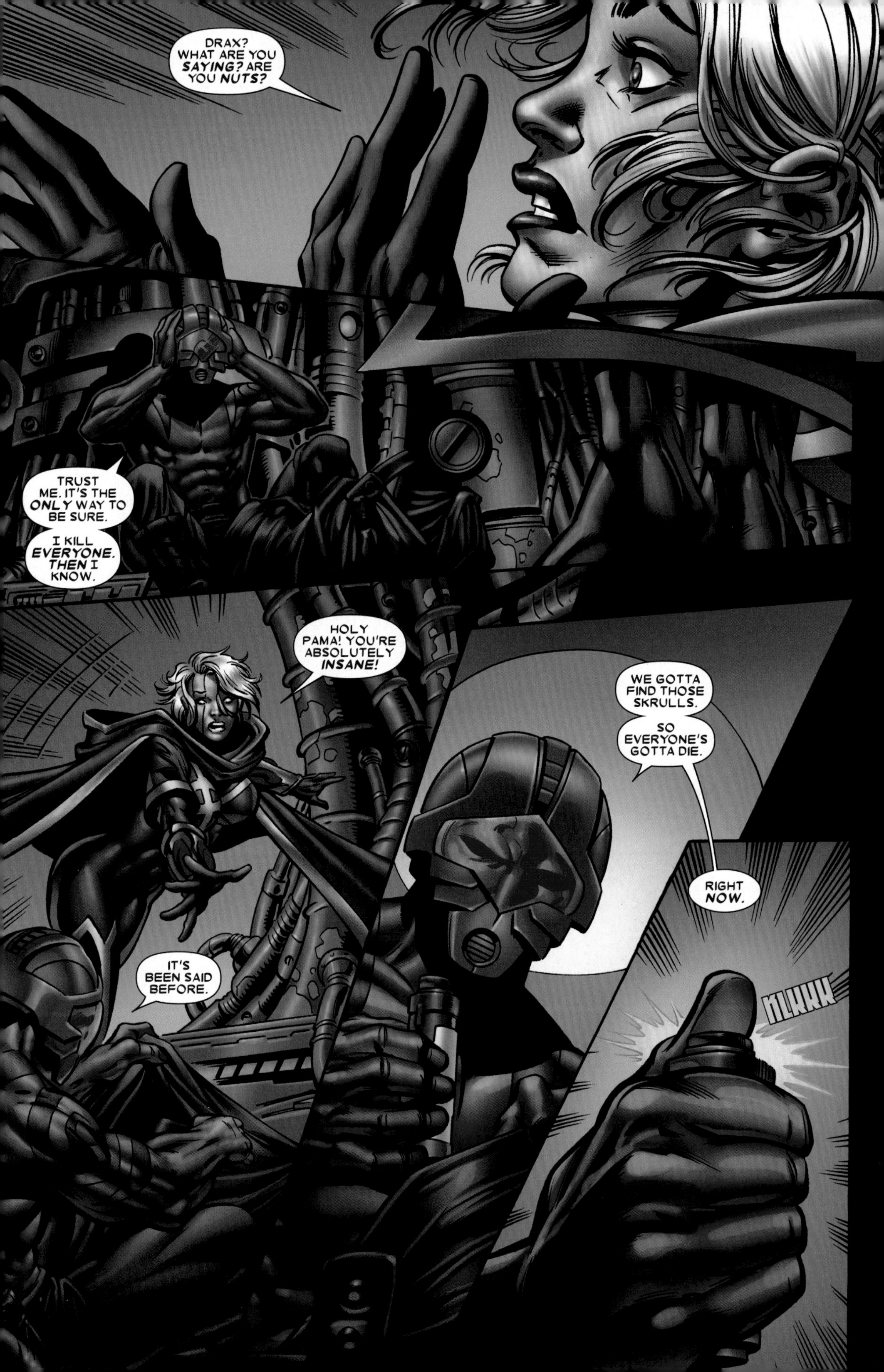
DRAX? WHAT ARE YOU SAYING? ARE YOU NUTS?
TRUST ME. IT'S THE ONLY WAY TO BE SURE.
I KILL EVERYONE. THEN I KNOW.
HOLY PAMA! YOU'RE ABSOLUTELY INSANE!
IT'S BEEN SAID BEFORE.
WE GOTTA FIND THOSE SKRULLS.
SO EVERYONE'S GOTTA DIE.
RIGHT NOW.
KLIKK

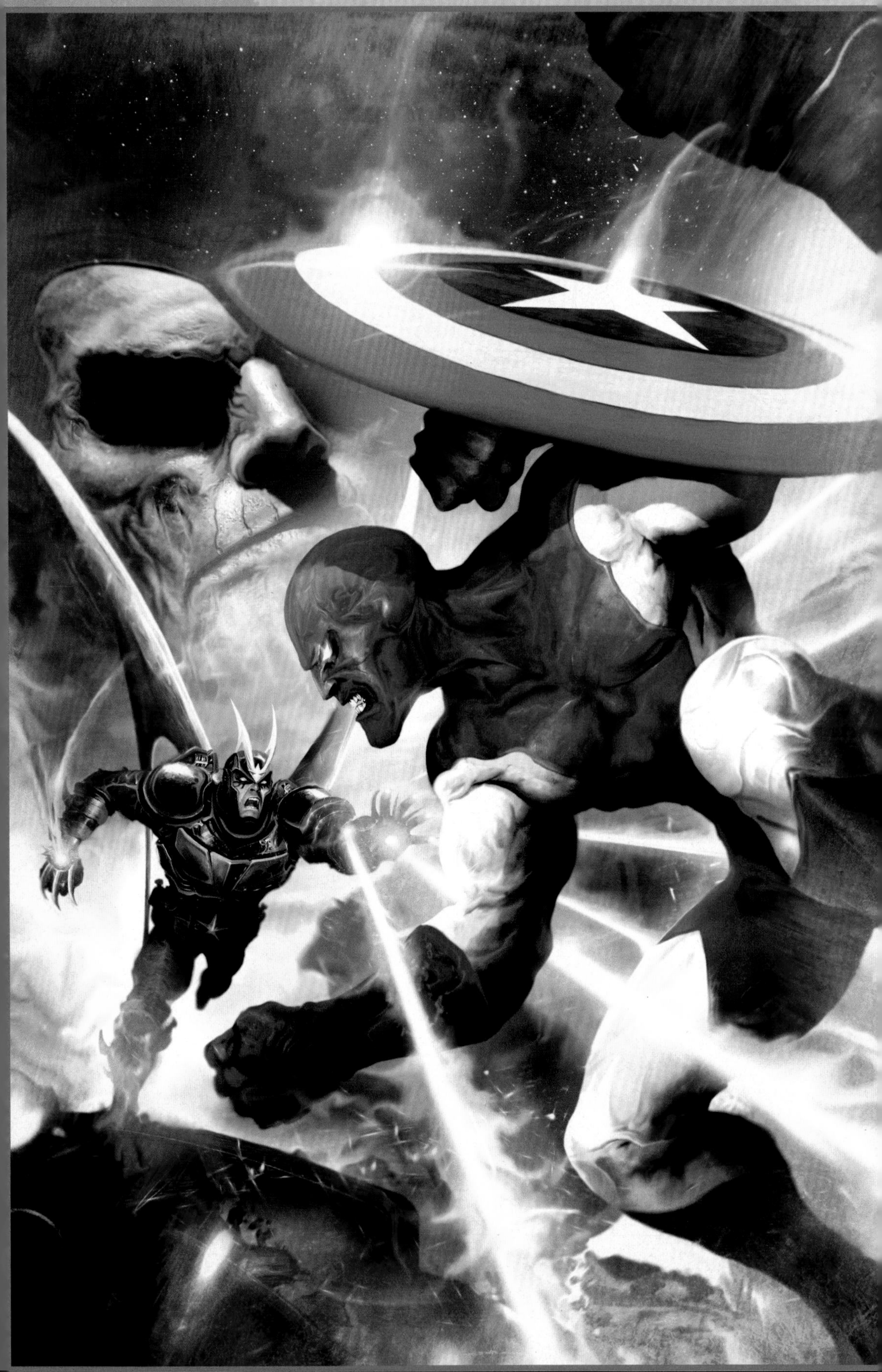

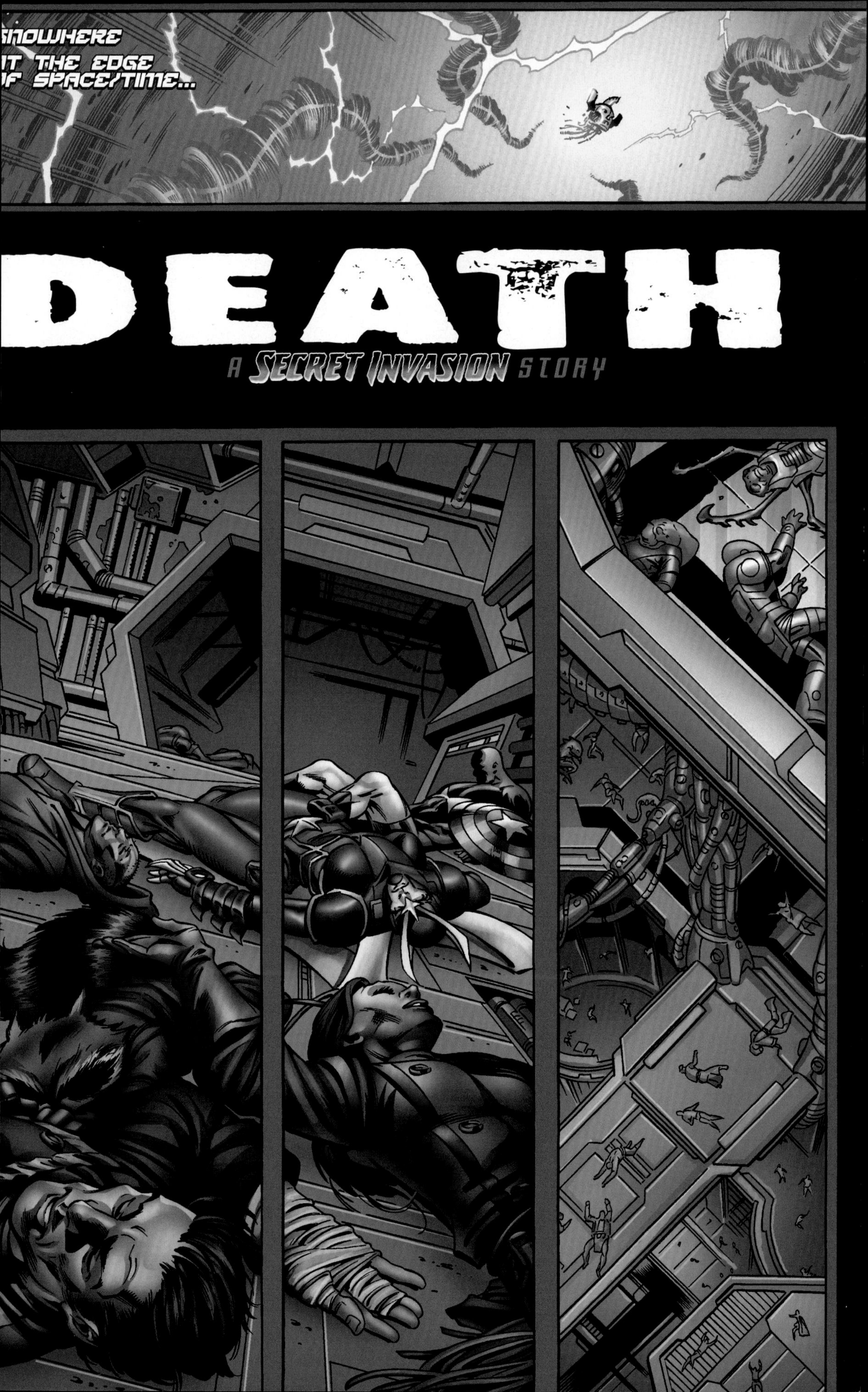
NOWHERE
T THE EDGE
F SPACE/TIME...
DEATH
A SECRET INVASION STORY

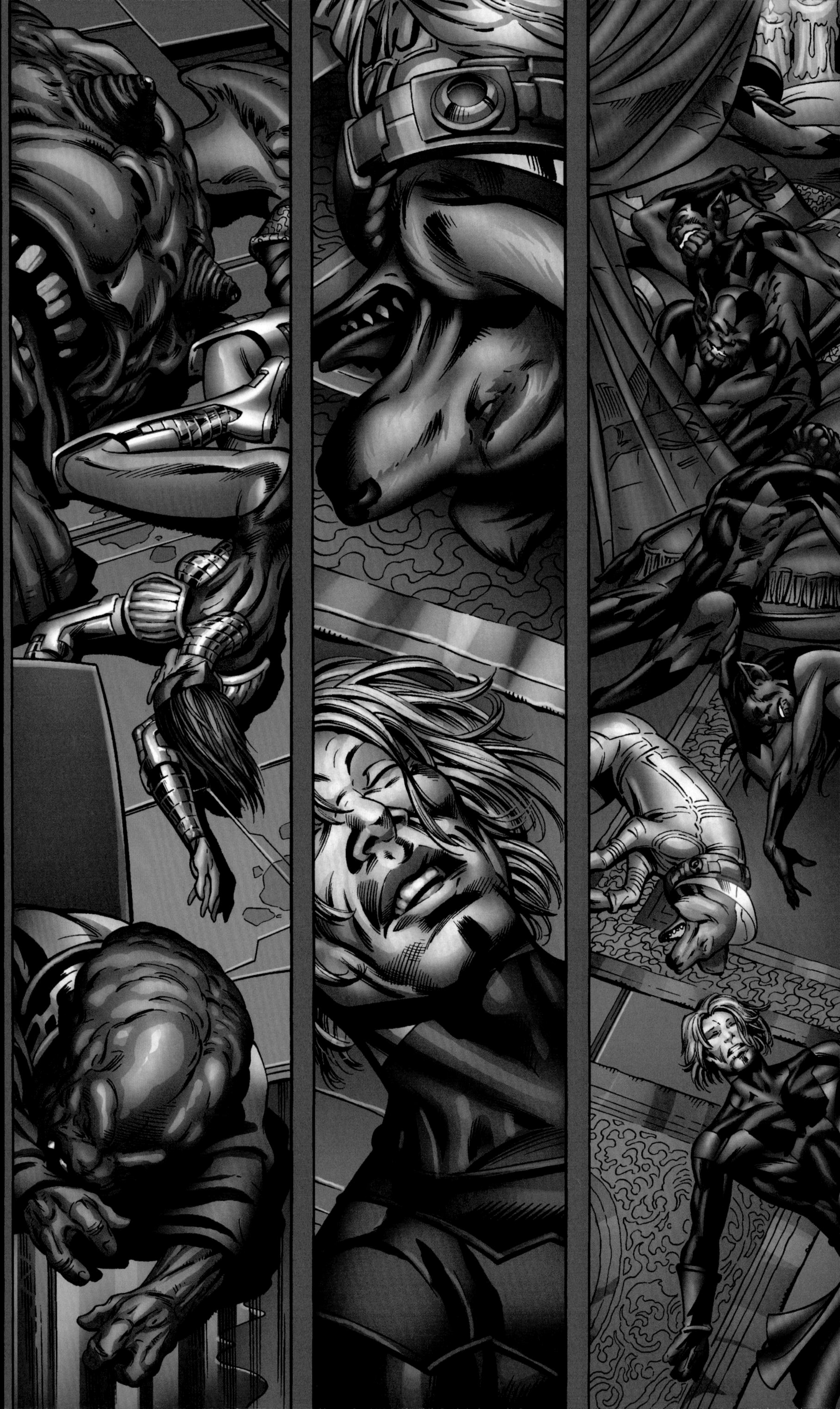

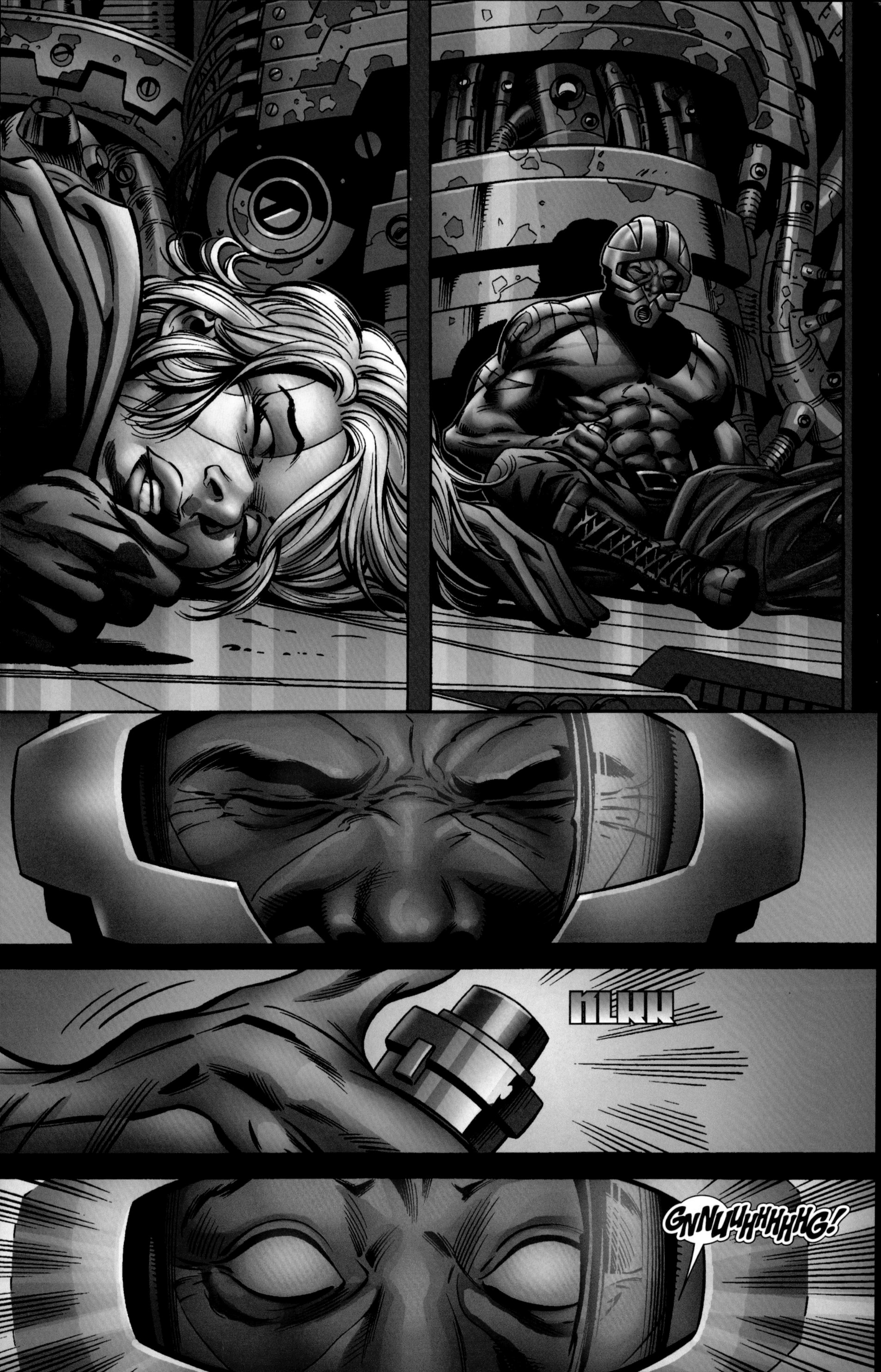
KLKK
GNNUUHHHHHG!

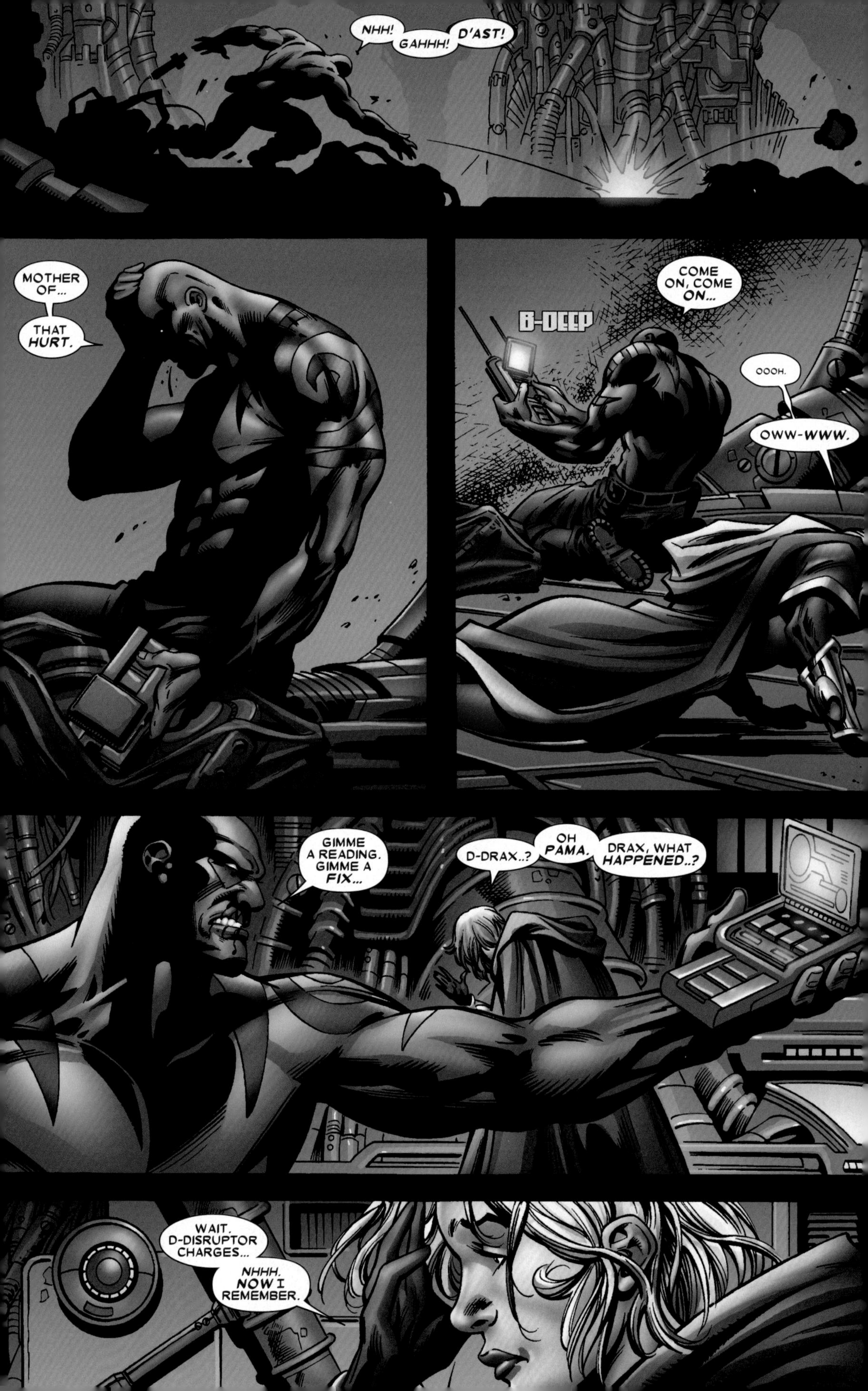
NHH!
GAHHH!
D'AST!
MOTHER OF...
THAT HURT.
B-DEEP
COME ON, COME ON...
OOOH.
OWW-WWW.
GIMME A READING. GIMME A FIX...
D-DRAX..?
OH PAMA.
DRAX, WHAT HAPPENED..?
WAIT. D-DISRUPTOR CHARGES...
NHHH. NOW I REMEMBER.

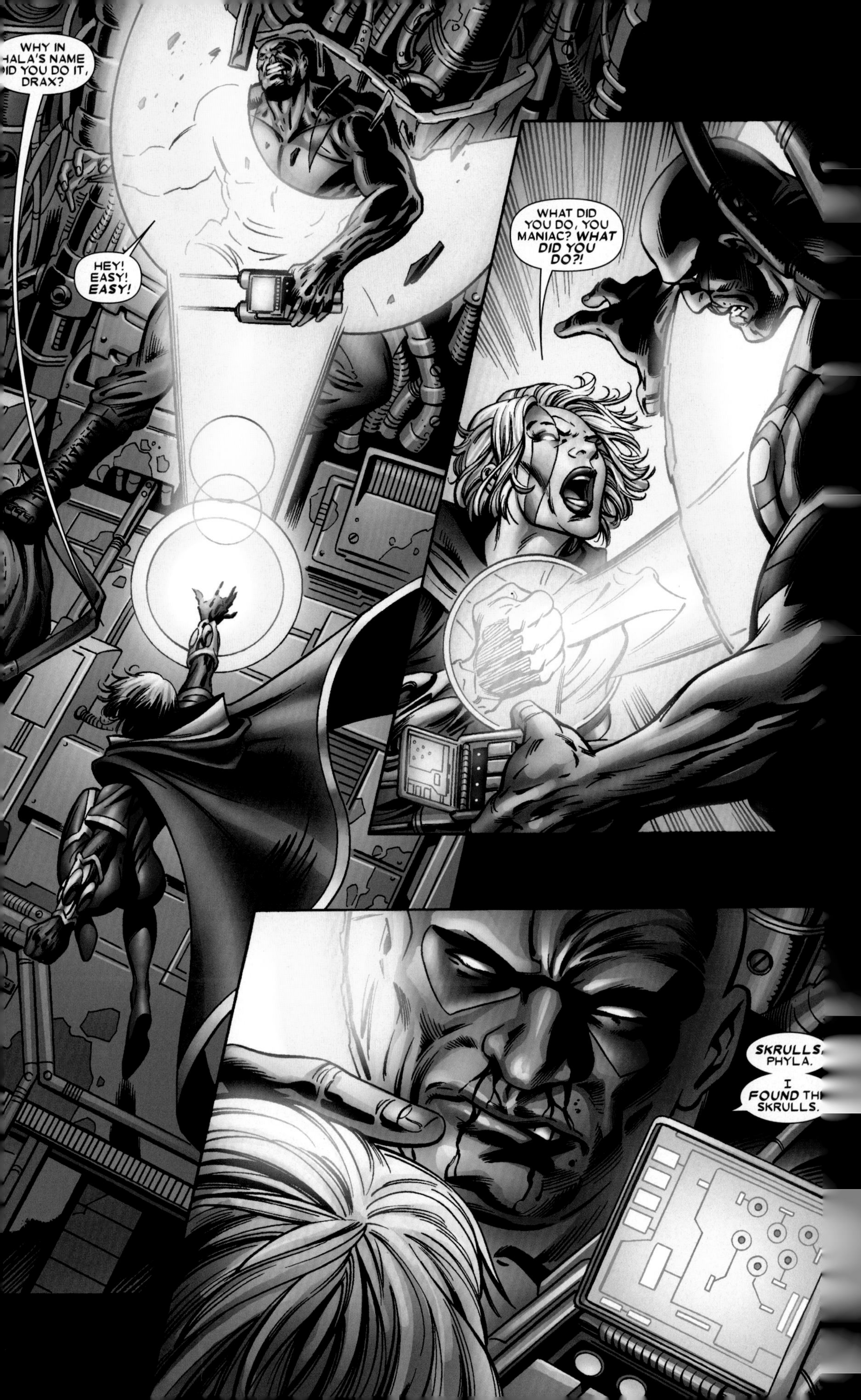

WHY IN HALA'S NAME ID YOU DO IT, DRAX?
HEY! EASY! *EASY!*
WHAT DID YOU DO, YOU MANIAC? *WHAT DID YOU DO?!*
SKRULLS PHYLA.
I *FOUND* TH SKRULLS.

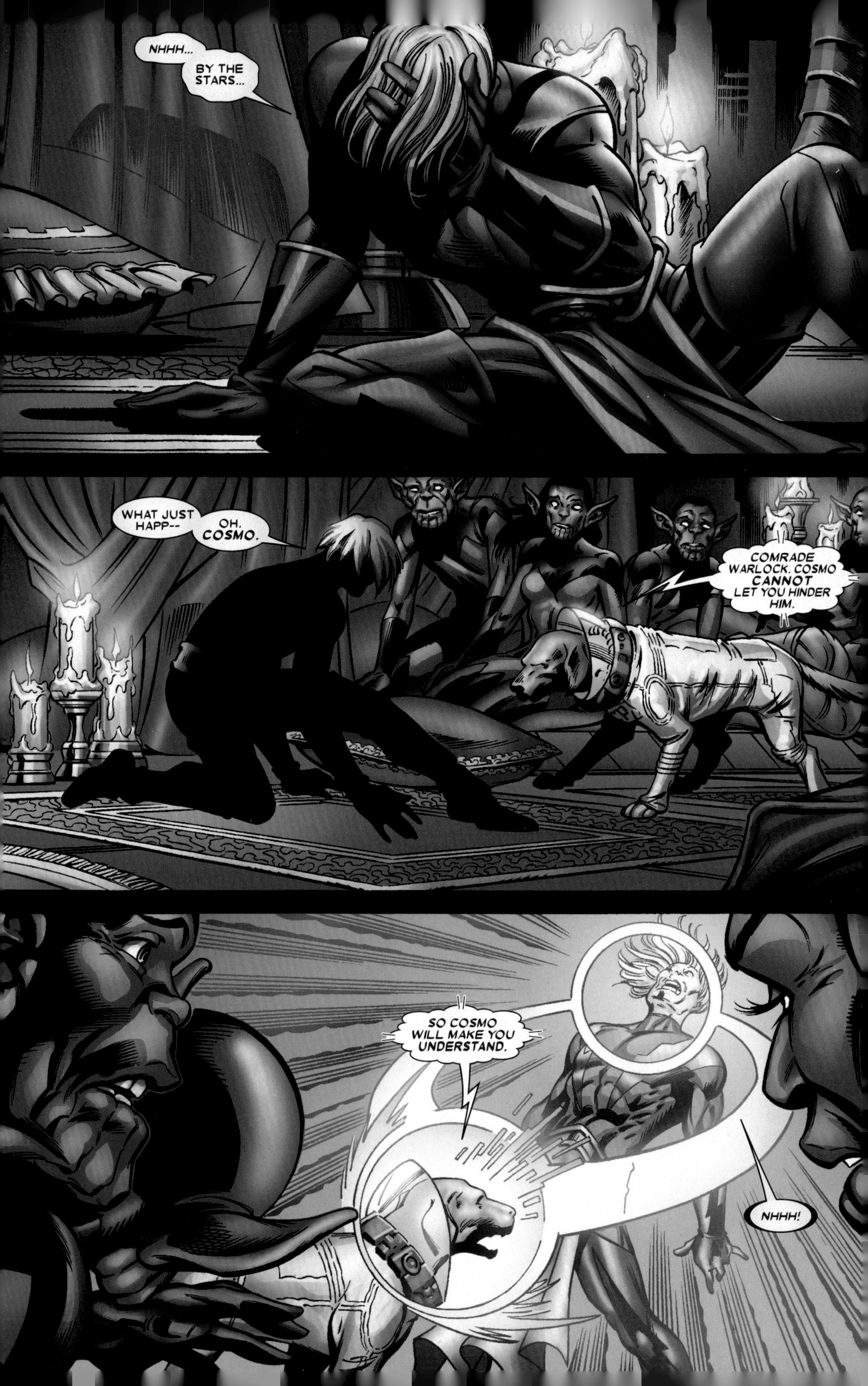
NHHH... BY THE STARS...
WHAT JUST HAPP--
OH. COSMO.
COMRADE WARLOCK. COSMO CANNOT LET YOU HINDER HIM.
SO COSMO WILL MAKE YOU UNDERSTAND.
NHHH!

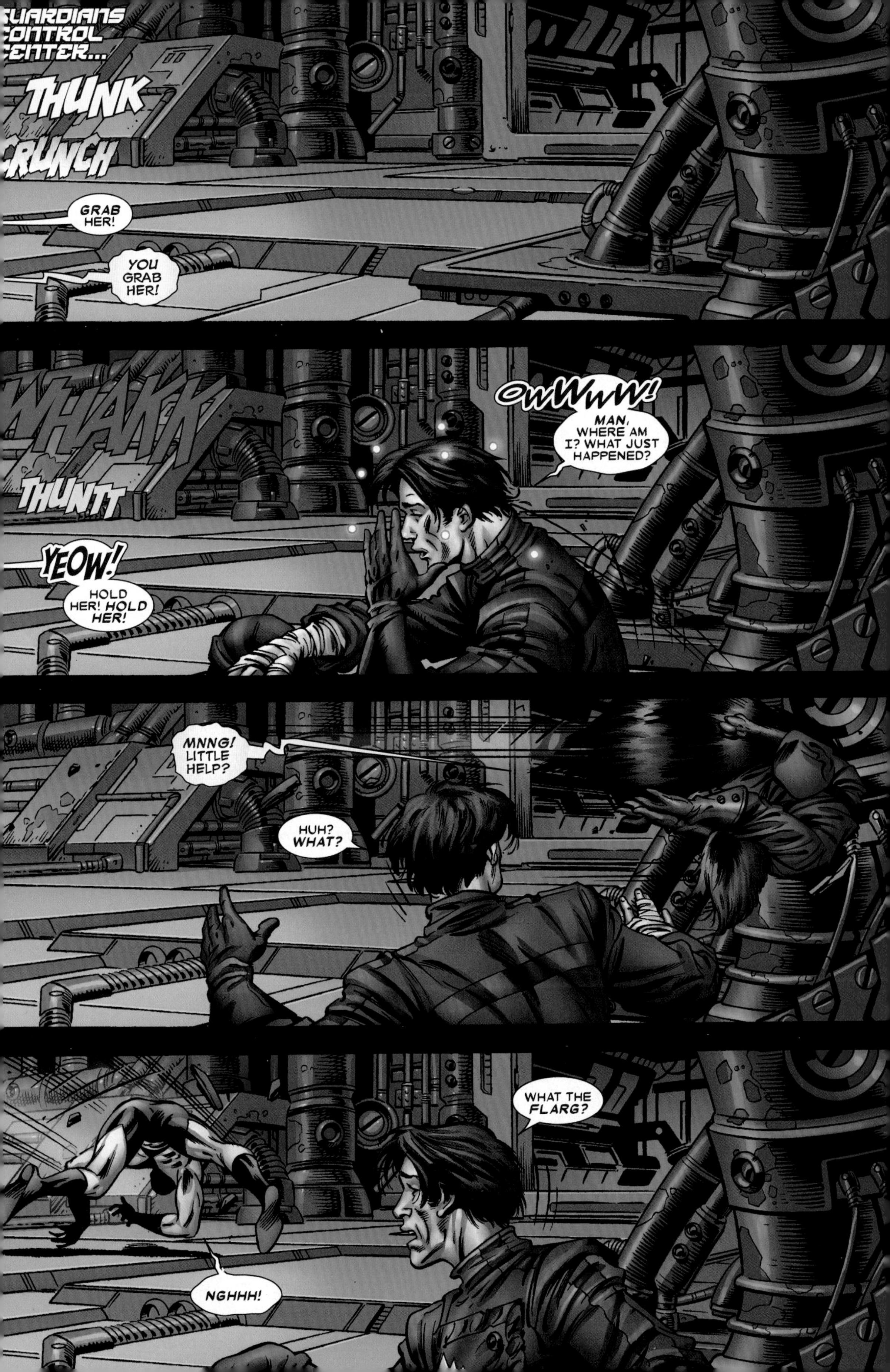

UARDIANS CONTROL CENTER...
THUNK
CRUNCH
GRAB HER!
YOU GRAB HER!
WHAKK
THUNTT
YEOW!
HOLD HER! HOLD HER!
OWWWW!
MAN, WHERE AM I? WHAT JUST HAPPENED?
MNNG! LITTLE HELP?
HUH? WHAT?
WHAT THE FLARG?
NGHHH!

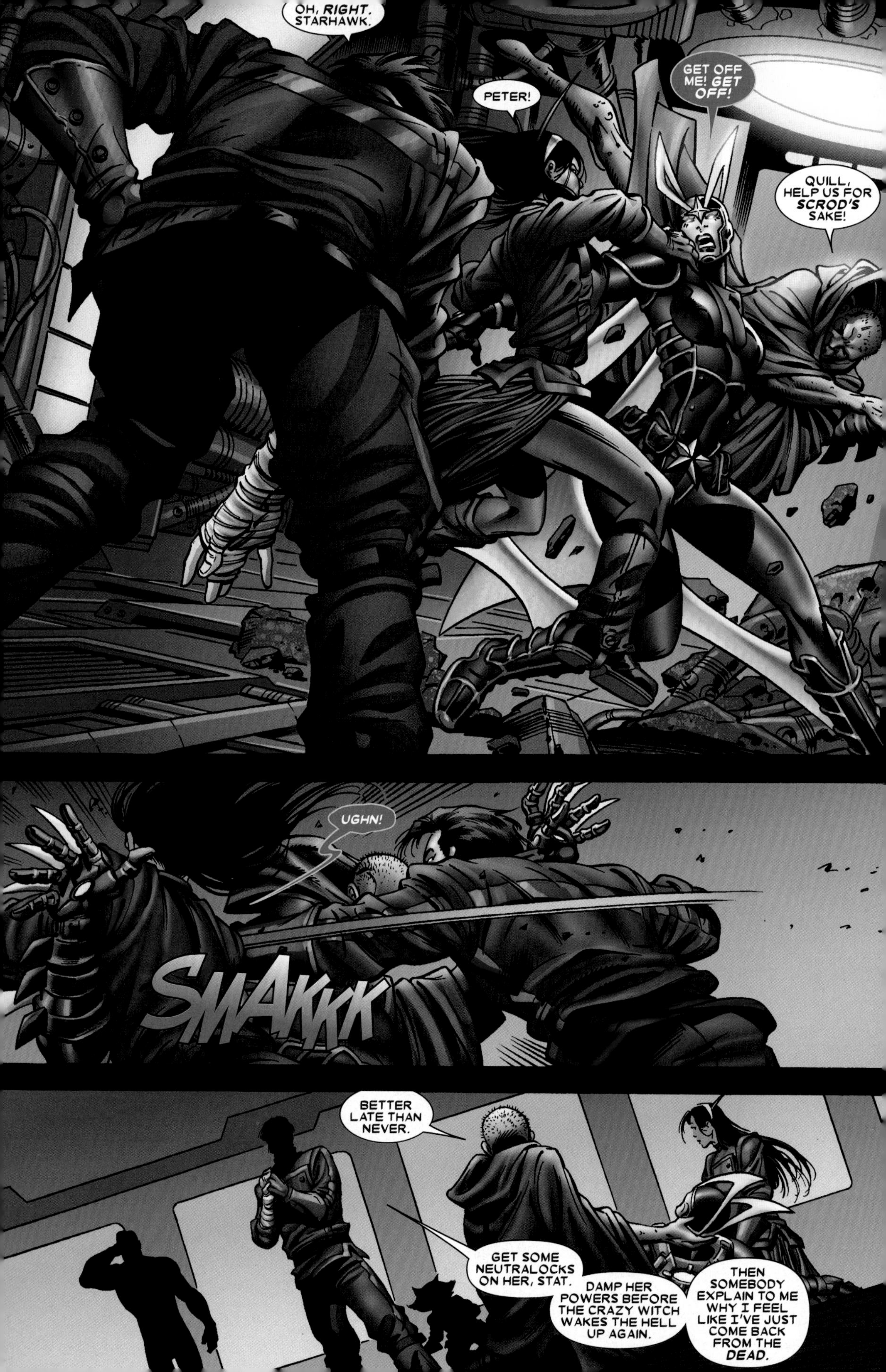
OH, RIGHT. STARHAWK.
PETER!
GET OFF ME! GET OFF!
QUILL, HELP US FOR SCROD'S SAKE!
UGHN!
SNAKKK
BETTER LATE THAN NEVER.
GET SOME NEUTRALOCKS ON HER, STAT.
DAMP HER POWERS BEFORE THE CRAZY WITCH WAKES THE HELL UP AGAIN.
THEN SOMEBODY EXPLAIN TO ME WHY I FEEL LIKE I'VE JUST COME BACK FROM THE DEAD.

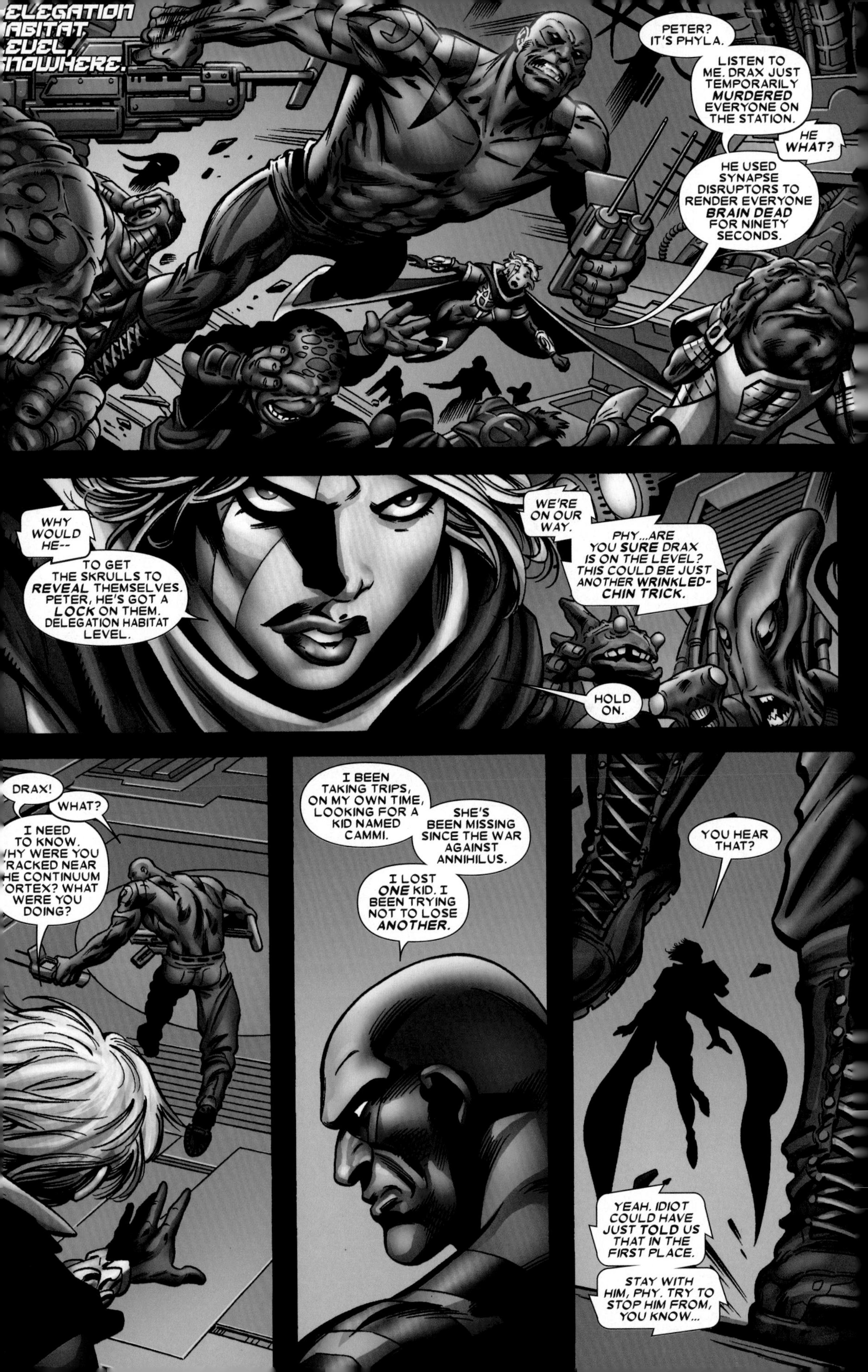
ELEGATION
ABITAT
EVEL,
NOWHERE.
PETER? IT'S PHYLA.
LISTEN TO ME. DRAX JUST TEMPORARILY MURDERED EVERYONE ON THE STATION.
HE WHAT?
HE USED SYNAPSE DISRUPTORS TO RENDER EVERYONE BRAIN DEAD FOR NINETY SECONDS.
WHY WOULD HE--
TO GET THE SKRULLS TO REVEAL THEMSELVES. PETER, HE'S GOT A LOCK ON THEM. DELEGATION HABITAT LEVEL.
WE'RE ON OUR WAY.
PHY...ARE YOU SURE DRAX IS ON THE LEVEL? THIS COULD BE JUST ANOTHER WRINKLED-CHIN TRICK.
HOLD ON.
DRAX!
WHAT?
I NEED TO KNOW. HY WERE YOU RACKED NEAR HE CONTINUUM ORTEX? WHAT WERE YOU DOING?
I BEEN TAKING TRIPS, ON MY OWN TIME, LOOKING FOR A KID NAMED CAMMI.
SHE'S BEEN MISSING SINCE THE WAR AGAINST ANNIHILUS.
I LOST ONE KID. I BEEN TRYING NOT TO LOSE ANOTHER.
YOU HEAR THAT?
YEAH. IDIOT COULD HAVE JUST TOLD US THAT IN THE FIRST PLACE.
STAY WITH HIM, PHY. TRY TO STOP HIM FROM, YOU KNOW...

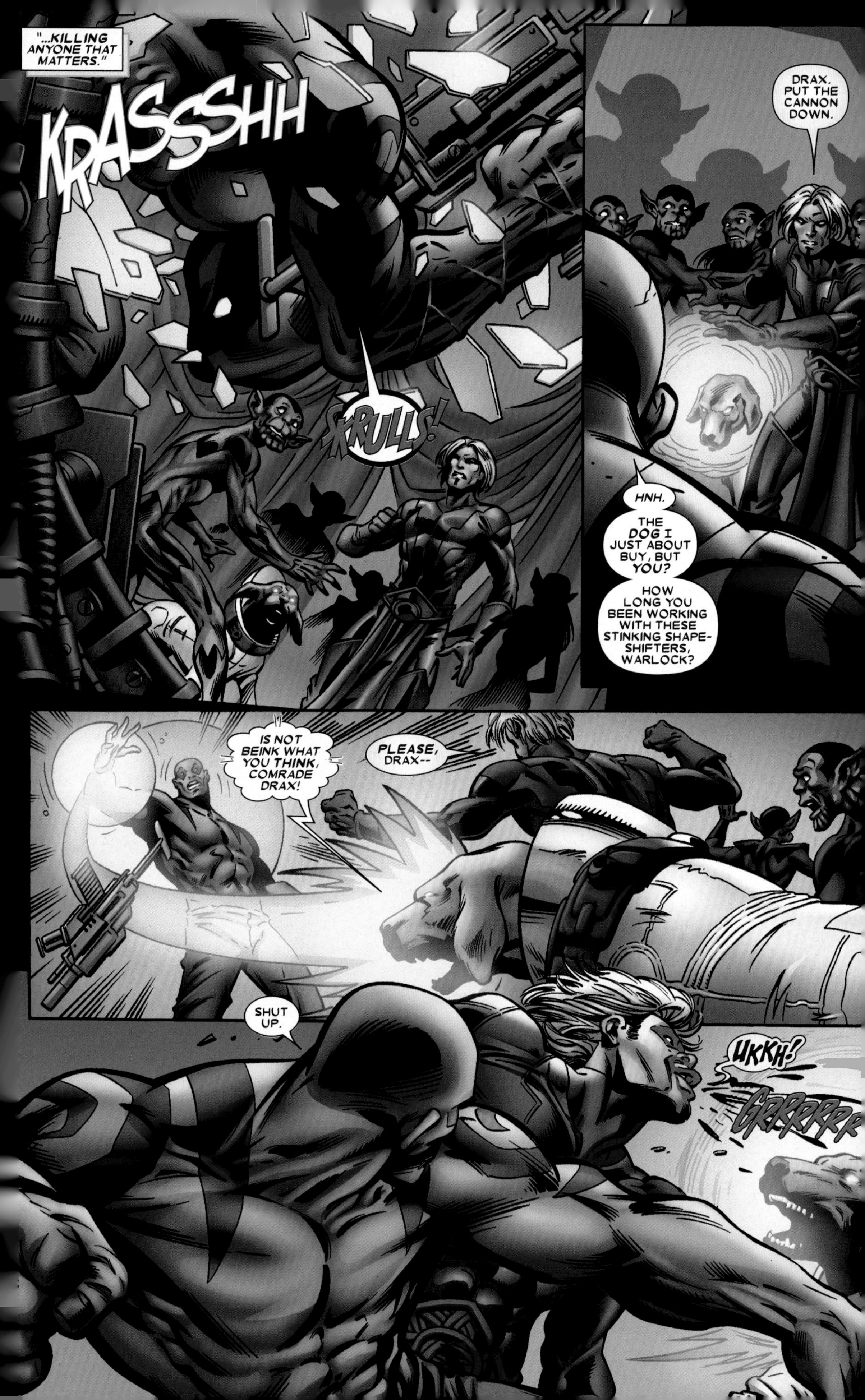
"...KILLING ANYONE THAT MATTERS."
KRASSSHH
SKRULLS!
DRAX. PUT THE CANNON DOWN.
HNH.
THE DOG I JUST ABOUT BUY, BUT YOU?
HOW LONG YOU BEEN WORKING WITH THESE STINKING SHAPE-SHIFTERS, WARLOCK?
IS NOT BEINK WHAT YOU THINK, COMRADE DRAX!
PLEASE, DRAX--
SHUT UP.
UKKH!
GRRRRRR

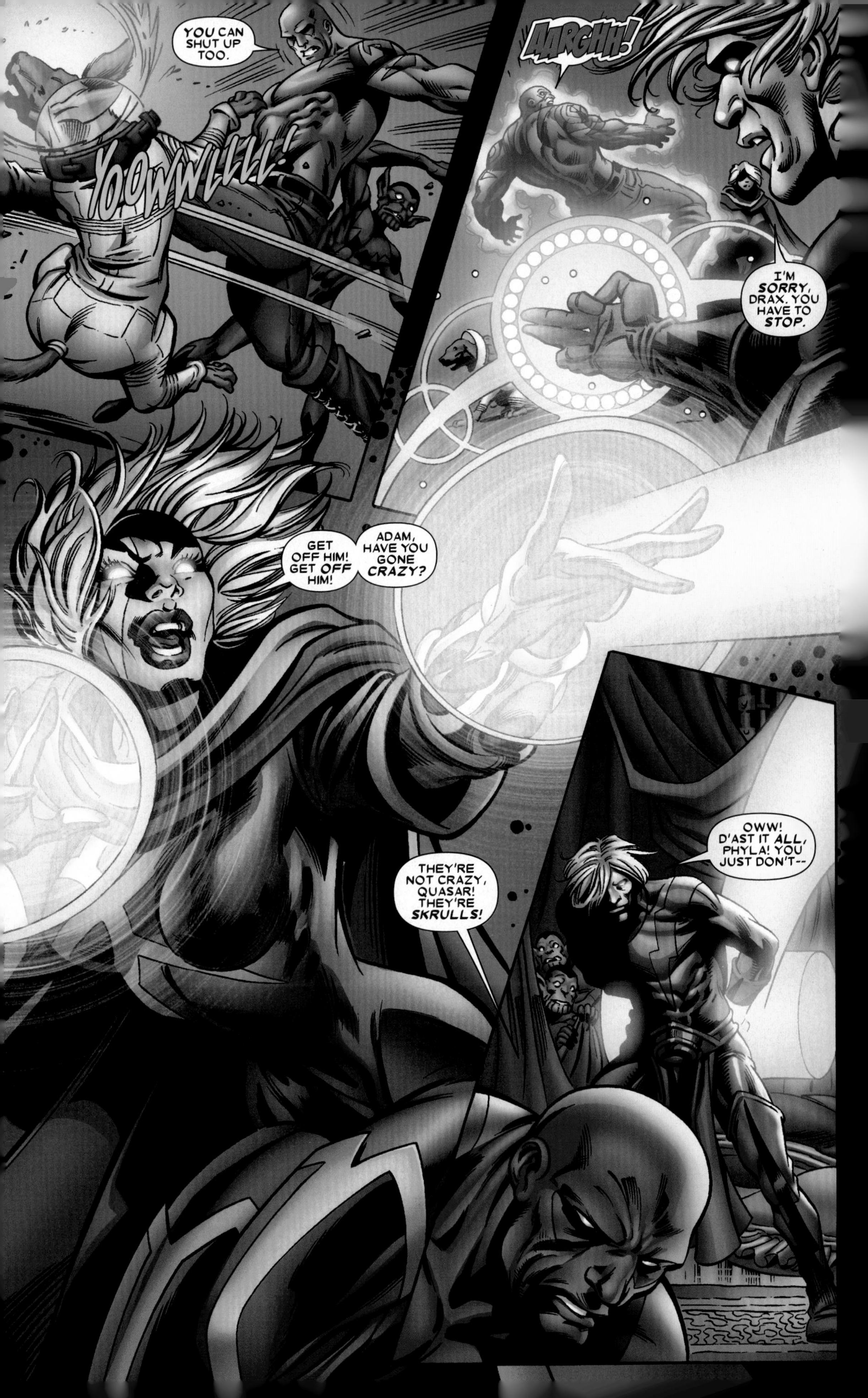
YOU CAN SHUT UP TOO.
YOOWWLLLL!
AARGHH!
I'M SORRY, DRAX. YOU HAVE TO STOP.
GET OFF HIM! GET OFF HIM!
ADAM, HAVE YOU GONE CRAZY?
OWW! D'AST IT ALL, PHYLA! YOU JUST DON'T--
THEY'RE NOT CRAZY, QUASAR! THEY'RE SKRULLS!

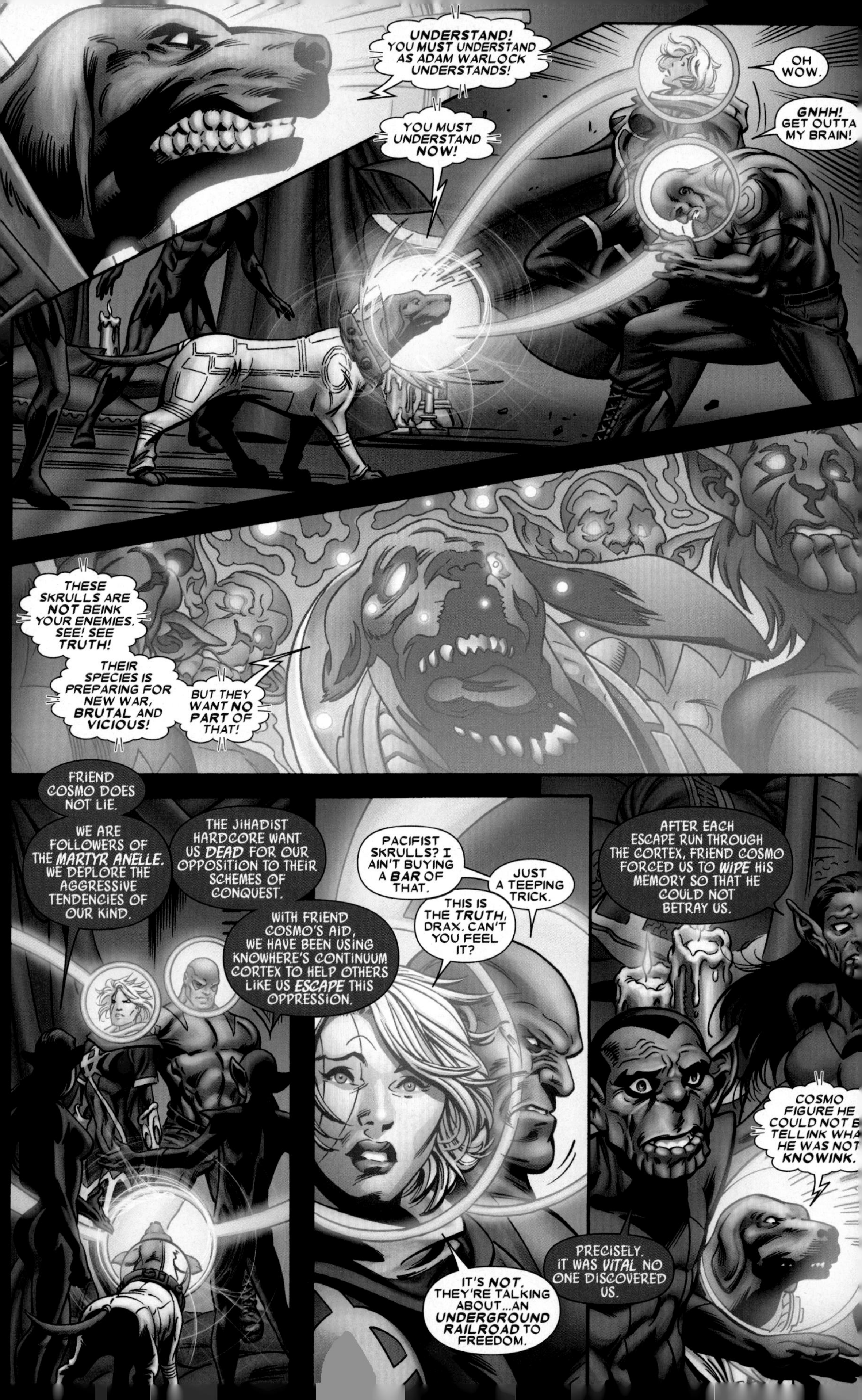
UNDERSTAND! YOU MUST UNDERSTAND AS ADAM WARLOCK UNDERSTANDS!
YOU MUST UNDERSTAND NOW!
OH WOW.
GNHH! GET OUTTA MY BRAIN!
THESE SKRULLS ARE NOT BEINK YOUR ENEMIES. SEE! SEE TRUTH!
THEIR SPECIES IS PREPARING FOR NEW WAR, BRUTAL AND VICIOUS!
BUT THEY WANT NO PART OF THAT!
FRIEND COSMO DOES NOT LIE.
WE ARE FOLLOWERS OF THE MARTYR ANELLE. WE DEPLORE THE AGGRESSIVE TENDENCIES OF OUR KIND.
THE JIHADIST HARDCORE WANT US DEAD FOR OUR OPPOSITION TO THEIR SCHEMES OF CONQUEST.
WITH FRIEND COSMO'S AID, WE HAVE BEEN USING KNOWHERE'S CONTINUUM CORTEX TO HELP OTHERS LIKE US ESCAPE THIS OPPRESSION.
PACIFIST SKRULLS? I AIN'T BUYING A BAR OF THAT.
JUST A TEEPING TRICK.
THIS IS THE TRUTH, DRAX. CAN'T YOU FEEL IT?
IT'S NOT. THEY'RE TALKING ABOUT...AN UNDERGROUND RAILROAD TO FREEDOM.
AFTER EACH ESCAPE RUN THROUGH THE CORTEX, FRIEND COSMO FORCED US TO WIPE HIS MEMORY SO THAT HE COULD NOT BETRAY US.
PRECISELY. IT WAS VITAL NO ONE DISCOVERED US.
COSMO FIGURE HE COULD NOT B TELLINK WHA HE WAS NOT KNOWINK.

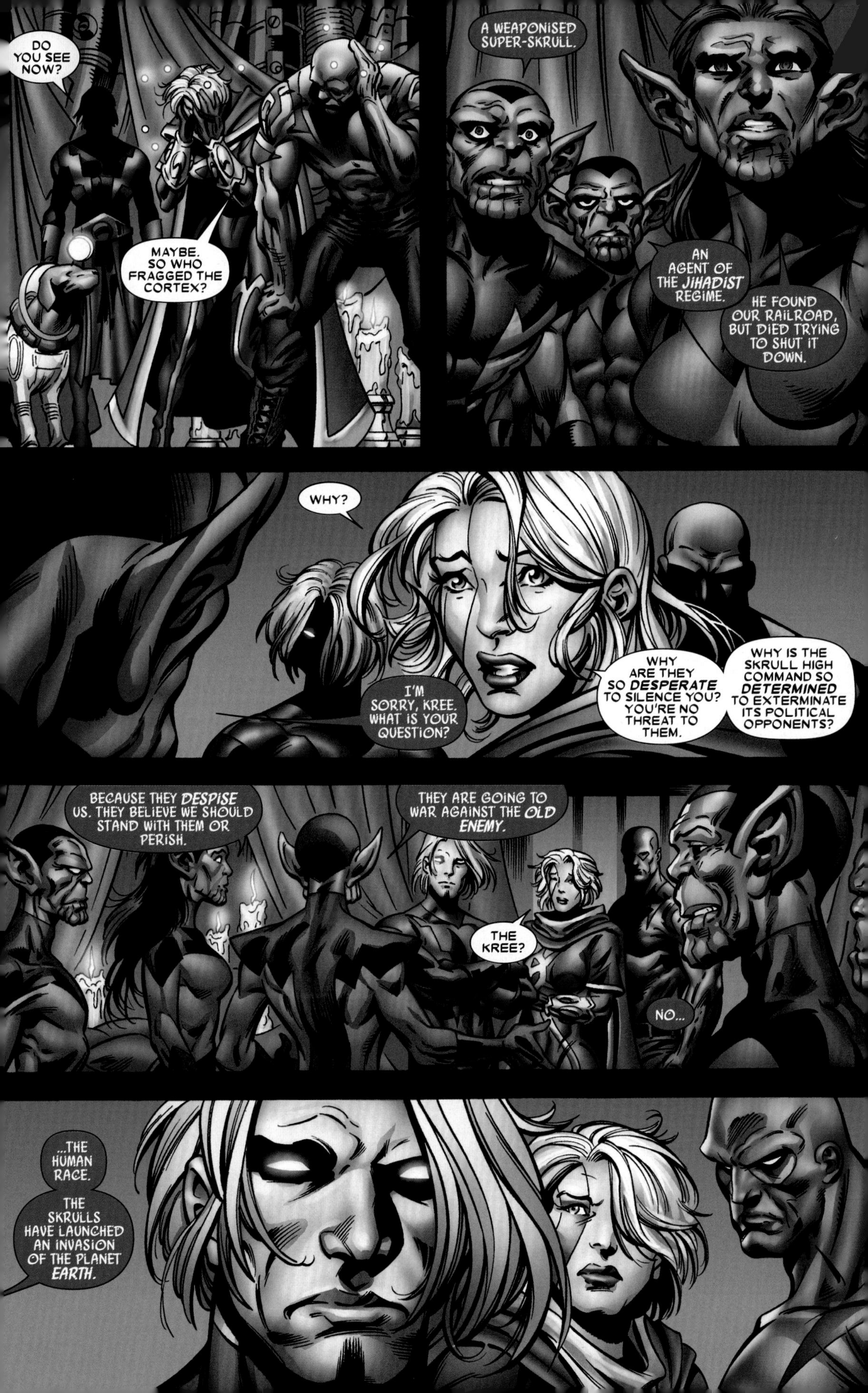
DO YOU SEE NOW?
MAYBE. SO WHO FRAGGED THE CORTEX?
A WEAPONISED SUPER-SKRULL.
AN AGENT OF THE *JIHADIST* REGIME.
HE FOUND OUR RAILROAD, BUT DIED TRYING TO SHUT IT DOWN.
WHY?
I'M SORRY, KREE. WHAT IS YOUR QUESTION?
WHY ARE THEY SO *DESPERATE* TO SILENCE YOU? YOU'RE NO THREAT TO THEM.
WHY IS THE SKRULL HIGH COMMAND SO *DETERMINED* TO EXTERMINATE ITS POLITICAL OPPONENTS?
BECAUSE THEY *DESPISE* US. THEY BELIEVE WE SHOULD STAND WITH THEM OR PERISH.
THEY ARE GOING TO WAR AGAINST THE *OLD ENEMY*.
THE KREE?
NO...
...THE HUMAN RACE.
THE SKRULLS HAVE LAUNCHED AN INVASION OF THE PLANET *EARTH*.

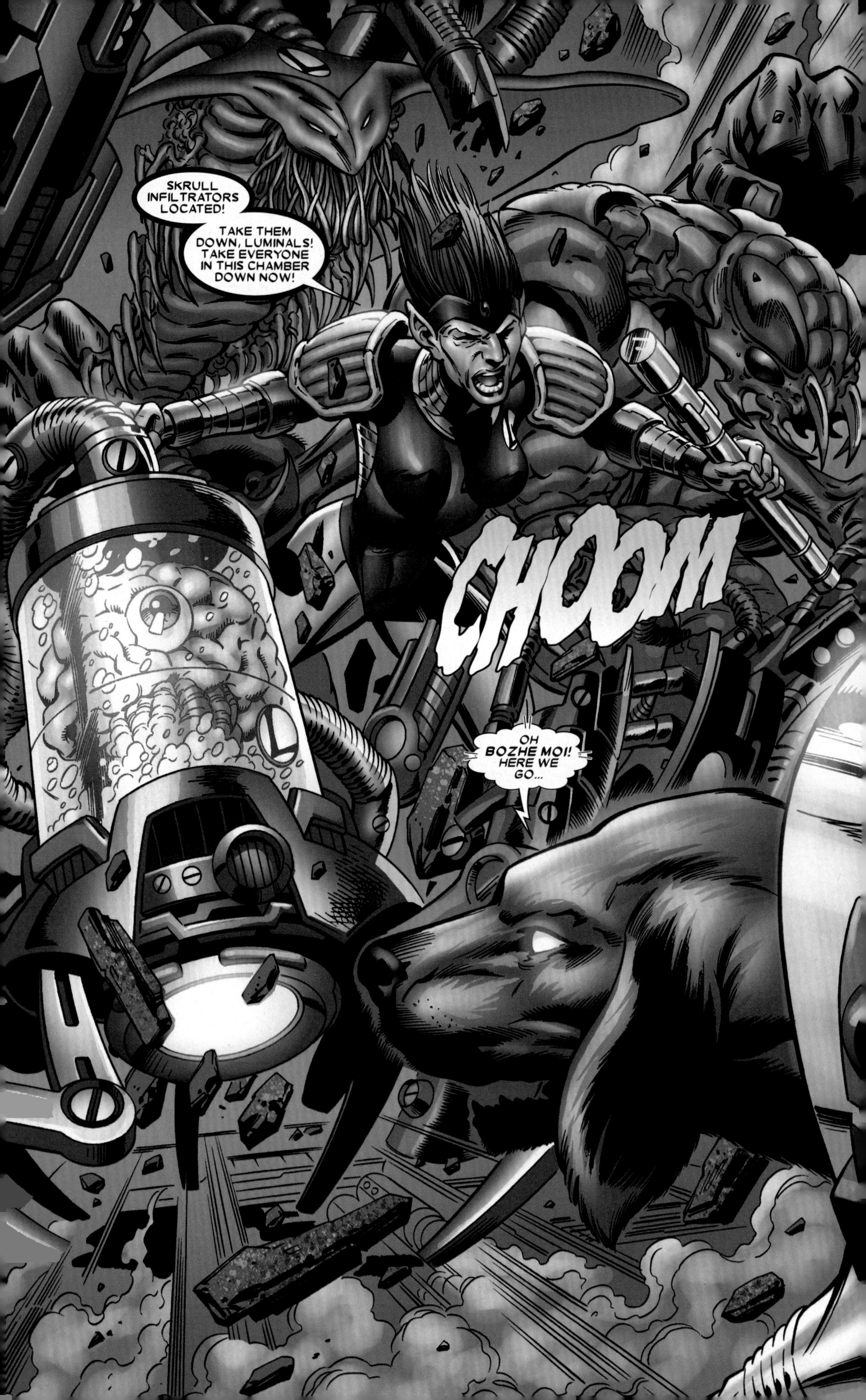
SKRULL INFILTRATORS LOCATED!
TAKE THEM DOWN, LUMINALS! TAKE EVERYONE IN THIS CHAMBER DOWN NOW!
CHOOM
OH BOZHE MOI! HERE WE GO...

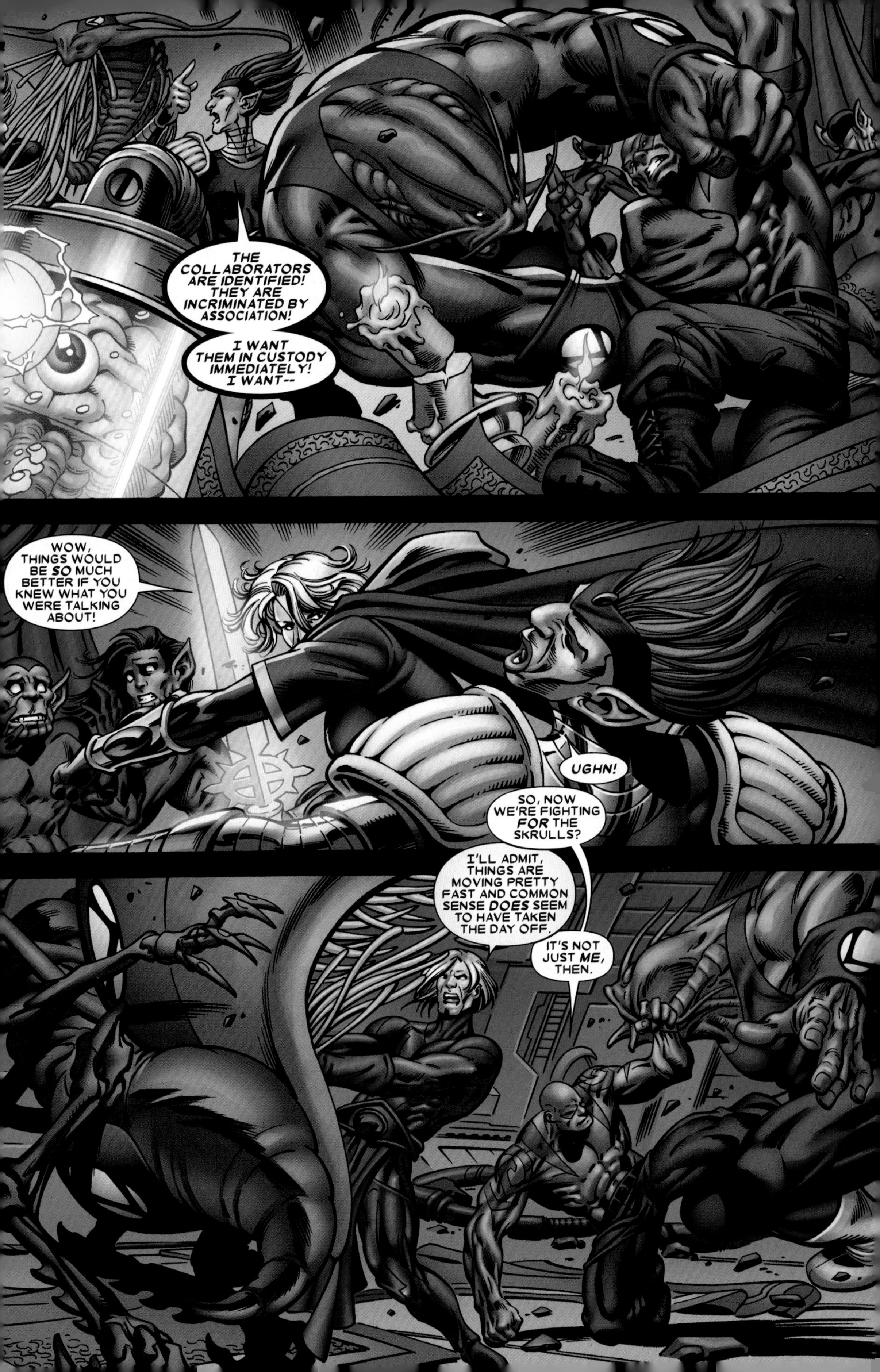
THE COLLABORATORS ARE IDENTIFIED! THEY ARE INCRIMINATED BY ASSOCIATION!
I WANT THEM IN CUSTODY IMMEDIATELY! I WANT--
WOW, THINGS WOULD BE SO MUCH BETTER IF YOU KNEW WHAT YOU WERE TALKING ABOUT!
UGHN!
SO, NOW WE'RE FIGHTING FOR THE SKRULLS?
I'LL ADMIT, THINGS ARE MOVING PRETTY FAST AND COMMON SENSE DOES SEEM TO HAVE TAKEN THE DAY OFF.
IT'S NOT JUST ME, THEN.

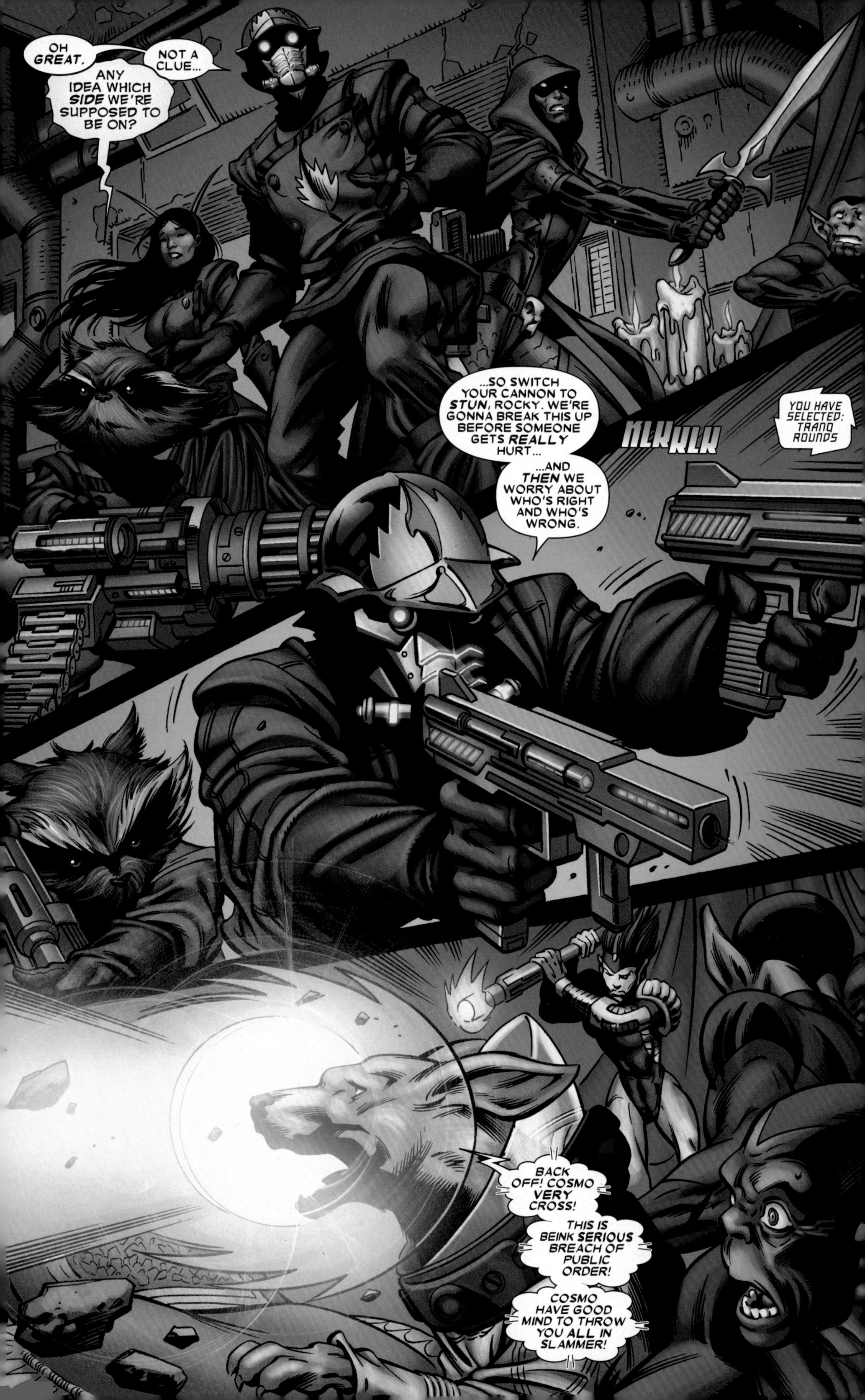
OH GREAT.
NOT A CLUE...
ANY IDEA WHICH SIDE WE'RE SUPPOSED TO BE ON?
...SO SWITCH YOUR CANNON TO STUN, ROCKY. WE'RE GONNA BREAK THIS UP BEFORE SOMEONE GETS REALLY HURT...
...AND THEN WE WORRY ABOUT WHO'S RIGHT AND WHO'S WRONG.
KLKKLK
YOU HAVE SELECTED: TRANQ ROUNDS
BACK OFF! COSMO VERY CROSS!
THIS IS BEINK SERIOUS BREACH OF PUBLIC ORDER!
COSMO HAVE GOOD MIND TO THROW YOU ALL IN SLAMMER!

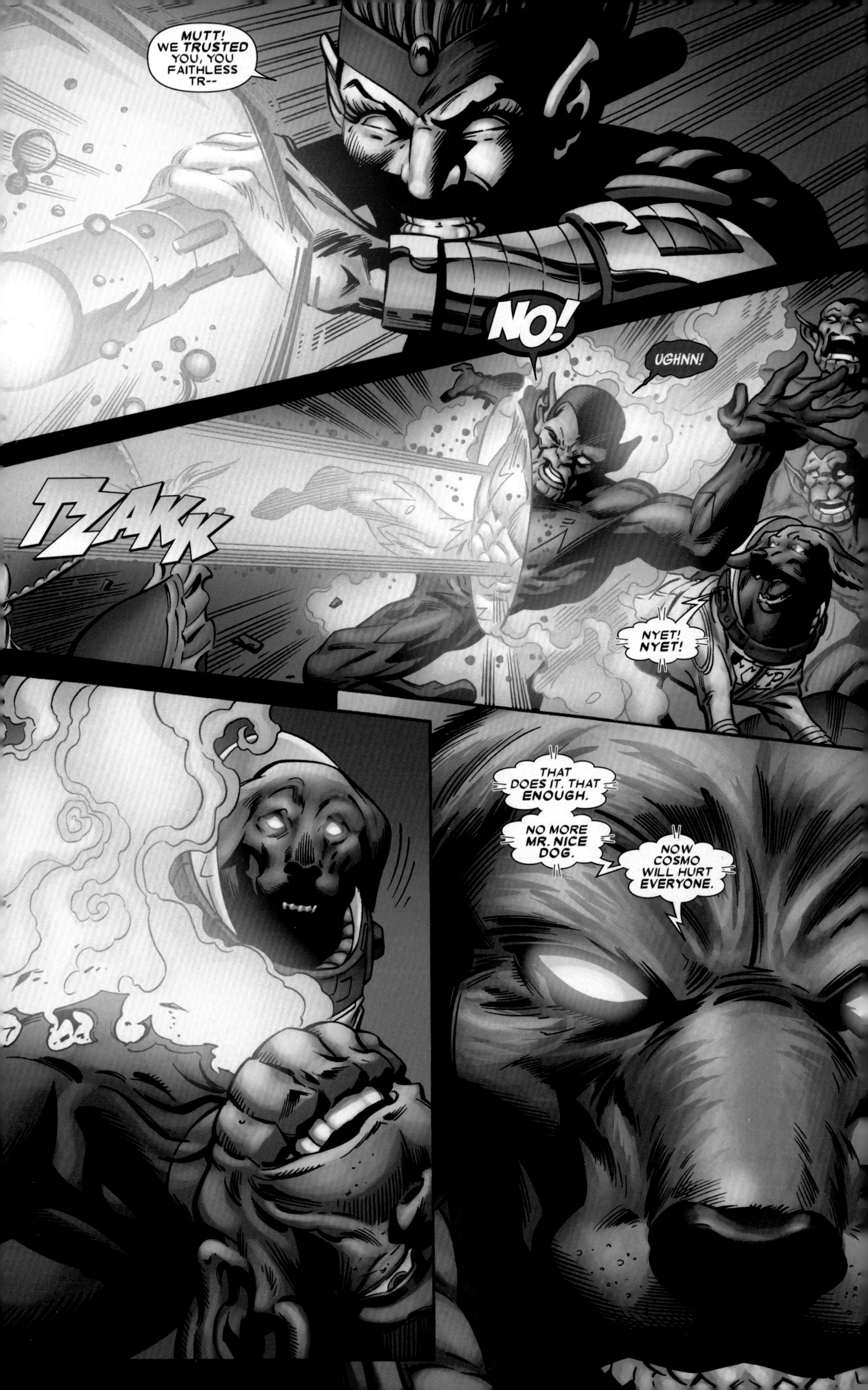
MUTT! WE TRUSTED YOU, YOU FAITHLESS TR--
NO!
UGHNN!
TZAKK
NYET! NYET!
THAT DOES IT. THAT ENOUGH.
NO MORE MR. NICE DOG.
NOW COSMO WILL HURT EVERYONE.

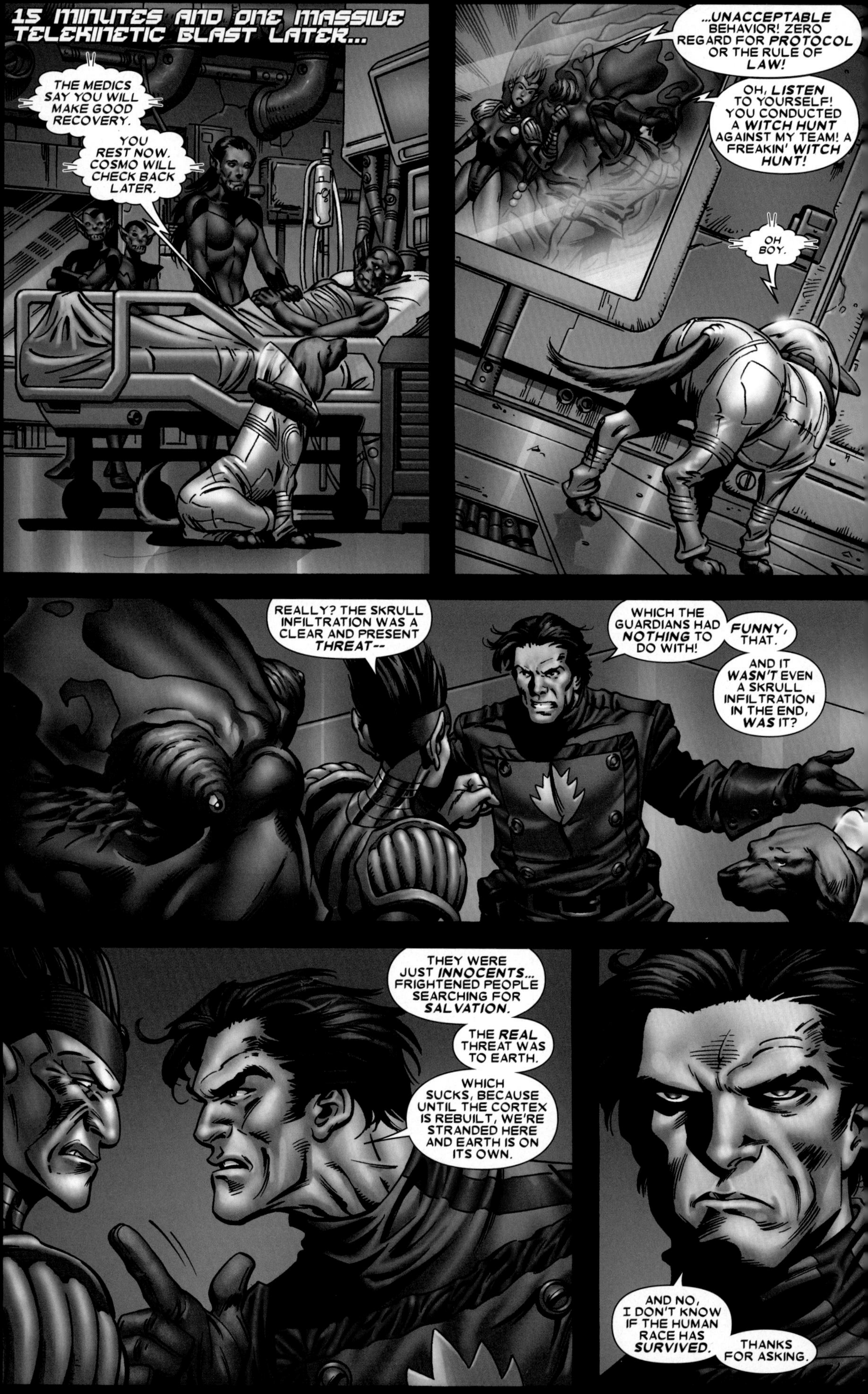
15 MINUTES AND ONE MASSIVE TELEKINETIC BLAST LATER...
THE MEDICS SAY YOU WILL MAKE GOOD RECOVERY.
YOU REST NOW. COSMO WILL CHECK BACK LATER.
...UNACCEPTABLE BEHAVIOR! ZERO REGARD FOR PROTOCOL OR THE RULE OF LAW!
OH, LISTEN TO YOURSELF! YOU CONDUCTED A WITCH HUNT AGAINST MY TEAM! A FREAKIN' WITCH HUNT!
OH BOY.
REALLY? THE SKRULL INFILTRATION WAS A CLEAR AND PRESENT THREAT--
WHICH THE GUARDIANS HAD NOTHING TO DO WITH!
FUNNY, THAT.
AND IT WASN'T EVEN A SKRULL INFILTRATION IN THE END, WAS IT?
THEY WERE JUST INNOCENTS... FRIGHTENED PEOPLE SEARCHING FOR SALVATION.
THE REAL THREAT WAS TO EARTH.
WHICH SUCKS, BECAUSE UNTIL THE CORTEX IS REBUILT, WE'RE STRANDED HERE AND EARTH IS ON ITS OWN.
AND NO, I DON'T KNOW IF THE HUMAN RACE HAS SURVIVED.
THANKS FOR ASKING.

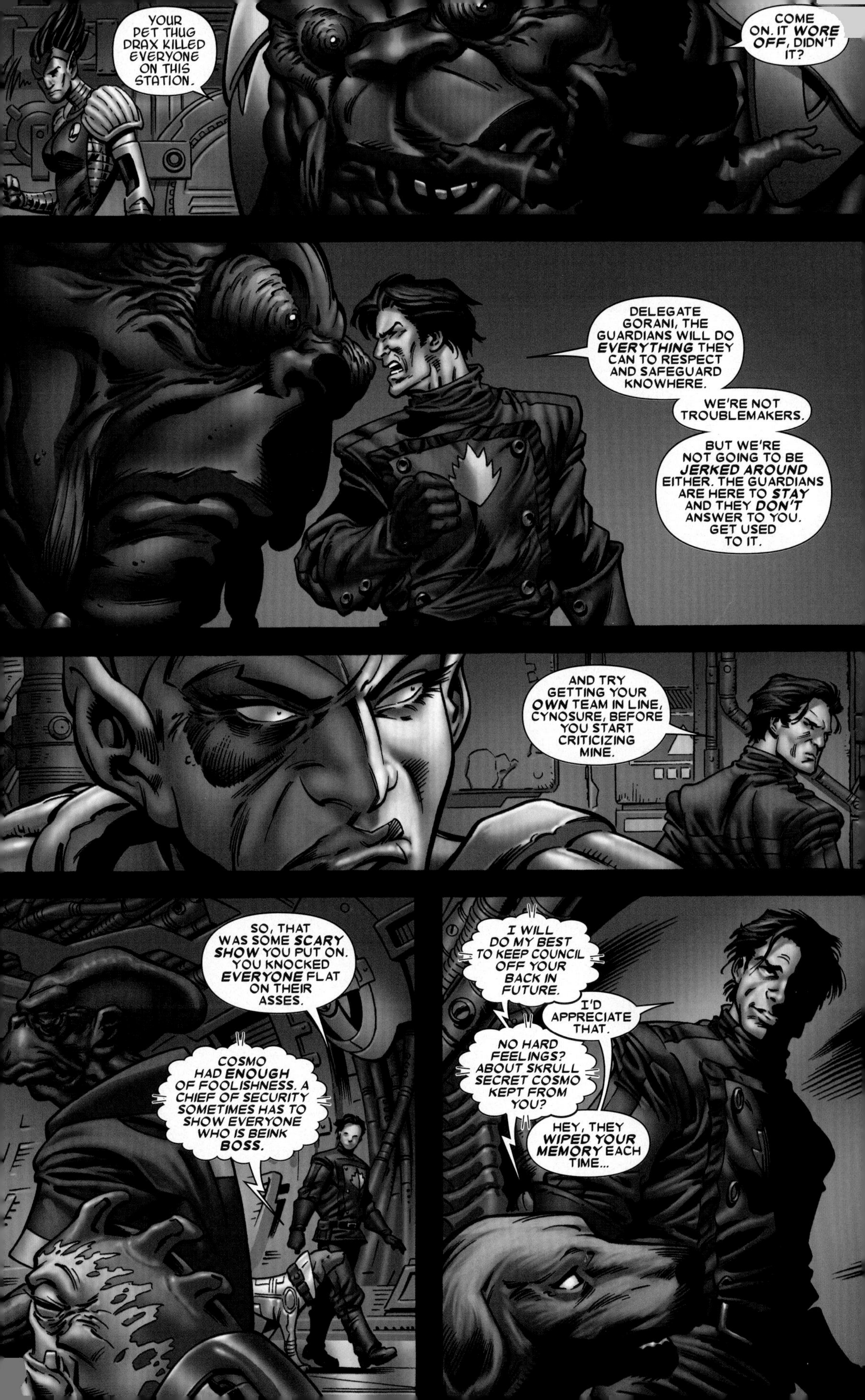
YOUR PET THUG DRAX KILLED EVERYONE ON THIS STATION.
COME ON. IT WORE OFF, DIDN'T IT?
DELEGATE GORANI, THE GUARDIANS WILL DO EVERYTHING THEY CAN TO RESPECT AND SAFEGUARD KNOWHERE.
WE'RE NOT TROUBLEMAKERS.
BUT WE'RE NOT GOING TO BE JERKED AROUND EITHER. THE GUARDIANS ARE HERE TO STAY AND THEY DON'T ANSWER TO YOU. GET USED TO IT.
AND TRY GETTING YOUR OWN TEAM IN LINE, CYNOSURE, BEFORE YOU START CRITICIZING MINE.
SO, THAT WAS SOME SCARY SHOW YOU PUT ON. YOU KNOCKED EVERYONE FLAT ON THEIR ASSES.
COSMO HAD ENOUGH OF FOOLISHNESS. A CHIEF OF SECURITY SOMETIMES HAS TO SHOW EVERYONE WHO IS BEINK BOSS.
I WILL DO MY BEST TO KEEP COUNCIL OFF YOUR BACK IN FUTURE.
I'D APPRECIATE THAT.
NO HARD FEELINGS? ABOUT SKRULL SECRET COSMO KEPT FROM YOU?
HEY, THEY WIPED YOUR MEMORY EACH TIME...

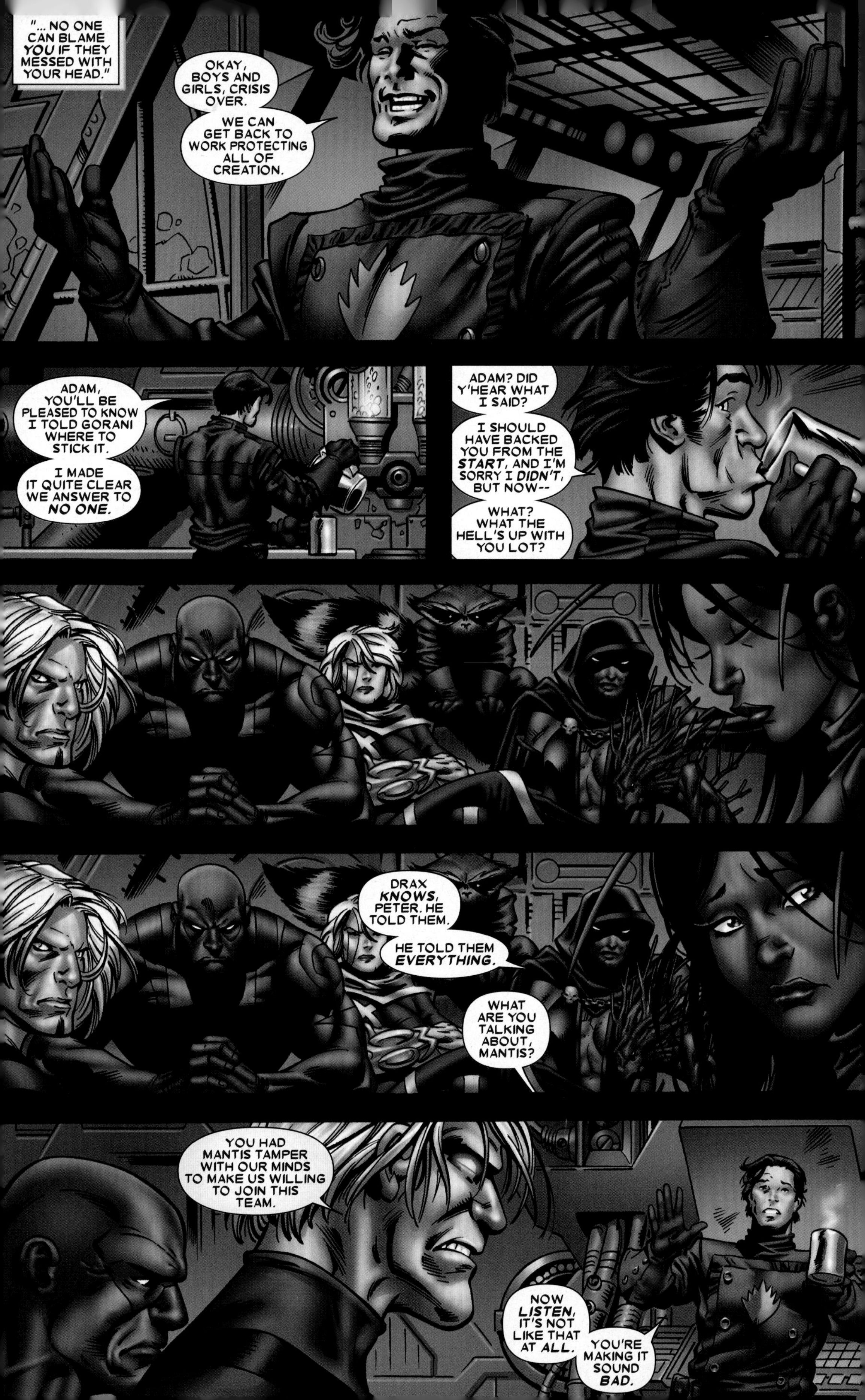
"... NO ONE CAN BLAME YOU IF THEY MESSED WITH YOUR HEAD."
OKAY, BOYS AND GIRLS, CRISIS OVER.
WE CAN GET BACK TO WORK PROTECTING ALL OF CREATION.
ADAM, YOU'LL BE PLEASED TO KNOW I TOLD GORANI WHERE TO STICK IT.
I MADE IT QUITE CLEAR WE ANSWER TO NO ONE.
ADAM? DID Y'HEAR WHAT I SAID?
I SHOULD HAVE BACKED YOU FROM THE START, AND I'M SORRY I DIDN'T, BUT NOW--
WHAT? WHAT THE HELL'S UP WITH YOU LOT?
DRAX KNOWS, PETER. HE TOLD THEM.
HE TOLD THEM EVERYTHING.
WHAT ARE YOU TALKING ABOUT, MANTIS?
YOU HAD MANTIS TAMPER WITH OUR MINDS TO MAKE US WILLING TO JOIN THIS TEAM.
NOW LISTEN, IT'S NOT LIKE THAT AT ALL.
YOU'RE MAKING IT SOUND BAD.

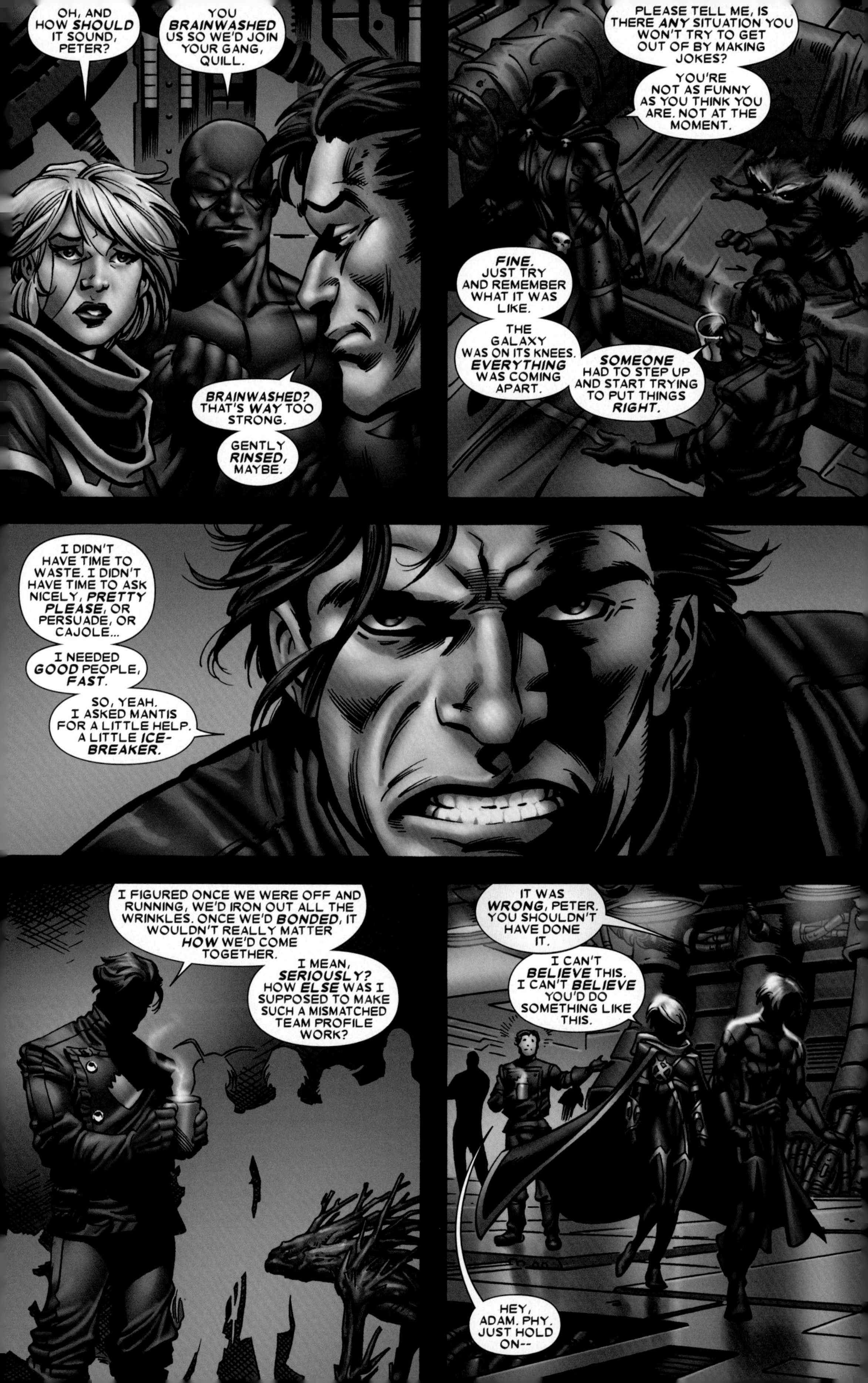

OH, AND HOW SHOULD IT SOUND, PETER?
YOU BRAINWASHED US SO WE'D JOIN YOUR GANG, QUILL.
BRAINWASHED? THAT'S WAY TOO STRONG.
GENTLY RINSED, MAYBE.
PLEASE TELL ME, IS THERE ANY SITUATION YOU WON'T TRY TO GET OUT OF BY MAKING JOKES?
YOU'RE NOT AS FUNNY AS YOU THINK YOU ARE. NOT AT THE MOMENT.
FINE. JUST TRY AND REMEMBER WHAT IT WAS LIKE.
THE GALAXY WAS ON ITS KNEES. EVERYTHING WAS COMING APART.
SOMEONE HAD TO STEP UP AND START TRYING TO PUT THINGS RIGHT.
I DIDN'T HAVE TIME TO WASTE. I DIDN'T HAVE TIME TO ASK NICELY, PRETTY PLEASE, OR PERSUADE, OR CAJOLE...
I NEEDED GOOD PEOPLE, FAST.
SO, YEAH. I ASKED MANTIS FOR A LITTLE HELP. A LITTLE ICE-BREAKER.
I FIGURED ONCE WE WERE OFF AND RUNNING, WE'D IRON OUT ALL THE WRINKLES. ONCE WE'D BONDED, IT WOULDN'T REALLY MATTER HOW WE'D COME TOGETHER.
I MEAN, SERIOUSLY? HOW ELSE WAS I SUPPOSED TO MAKE SUCH A MISMATCHED TEAM PROFILE WORK?
IT WAS WRONG, PETER. YOU SHOULDN'T HAVE DONE IT.
I CAN'T BELIEVE THIS. I CAN'T BELIEVE YOU'D DO SOMETHING LIKE THIS.
HEY, ADAM. PHY. JUST HOLD ON--

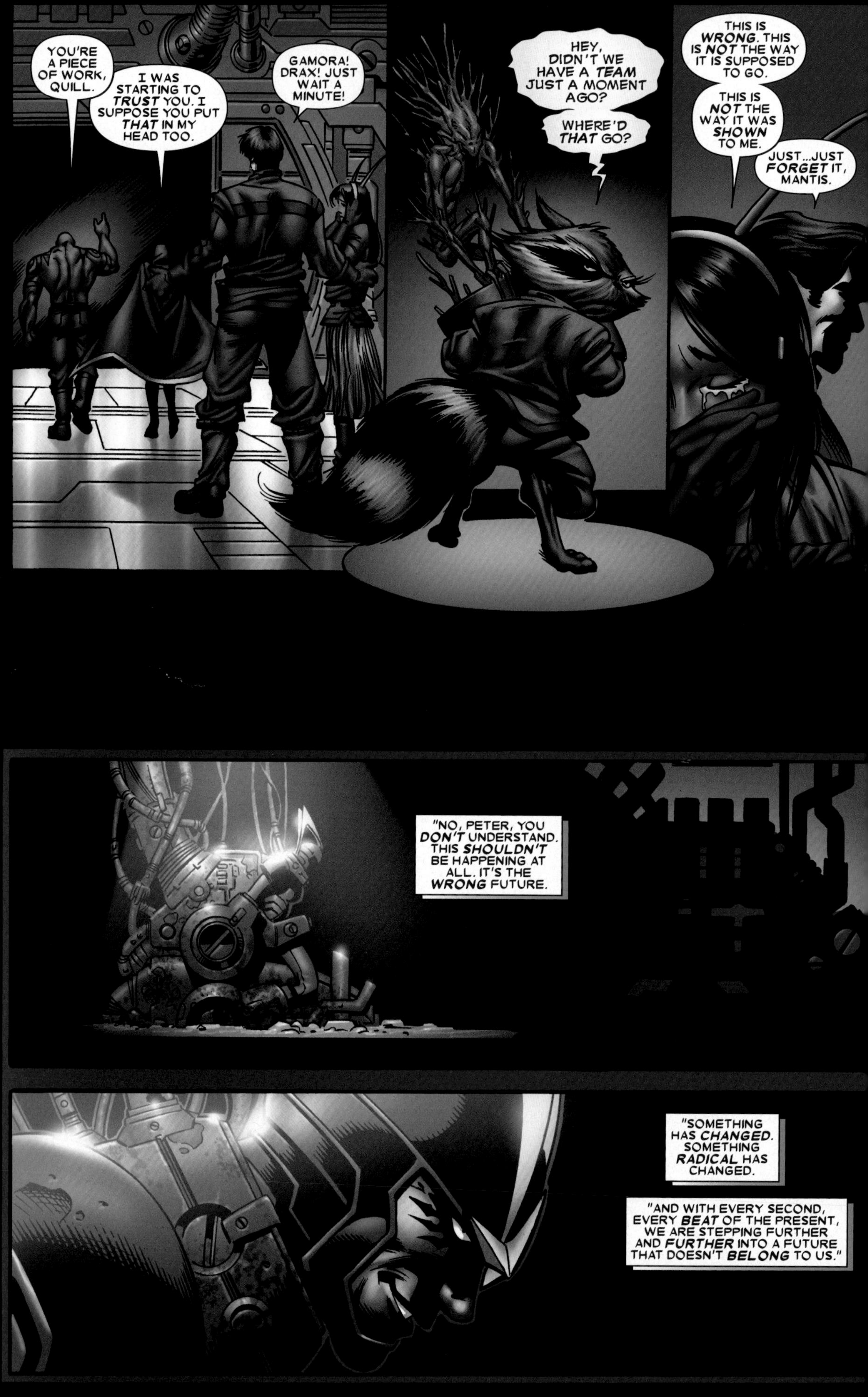
YOU'RE A PIECE OF WORK, QUILL.
I WAS STARTING TO TRUST YOU. I SUPPOSE YOU PUT THAT IN MY HEAD TOO.
GAMORA! DRAX! JUST WAIT A MINUTE!
HEY, DIDN'T WE HAVE A TEAM JUST A MOMENT AGO?
WHERE'D THAT GO?
THIS IS WRONG. THIS IS NOT THE WAY IT IS SUPPOSED TO GO.
THIS IS NOT THE WAY IT WAS SHOWN TO ME.
JUST...JUST FORGET IT, MANTIS.
"NO, PETER, YOU DON'T UNDERSTAND. THIS SHOULDN'T BE HAPPENING AT ALL. IT'S THE WRONG FUTURE.
"SOMETHING HAS CHANGED. SOMETHING RADICAL HAS CHANGED.
"AND WITH EVERY SECOND, EVERY BEAT OF THE PRESENT, WE ARE STEPPING FURTHER AND FURTHER INTO A FUTURE THAT DOESN'T BELONG TO US."

GUARDIANS
OF THE GALAXY

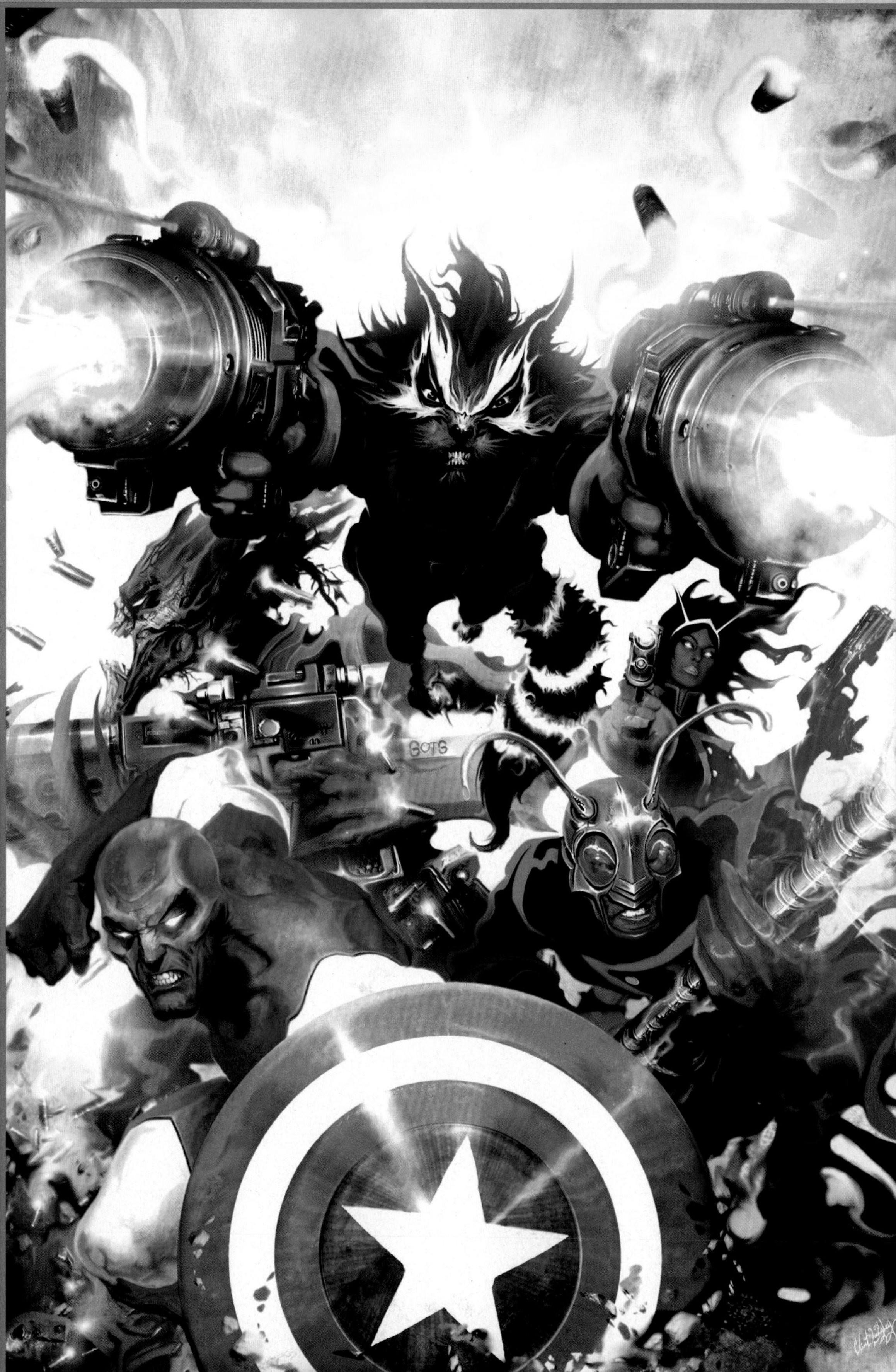
GOTG

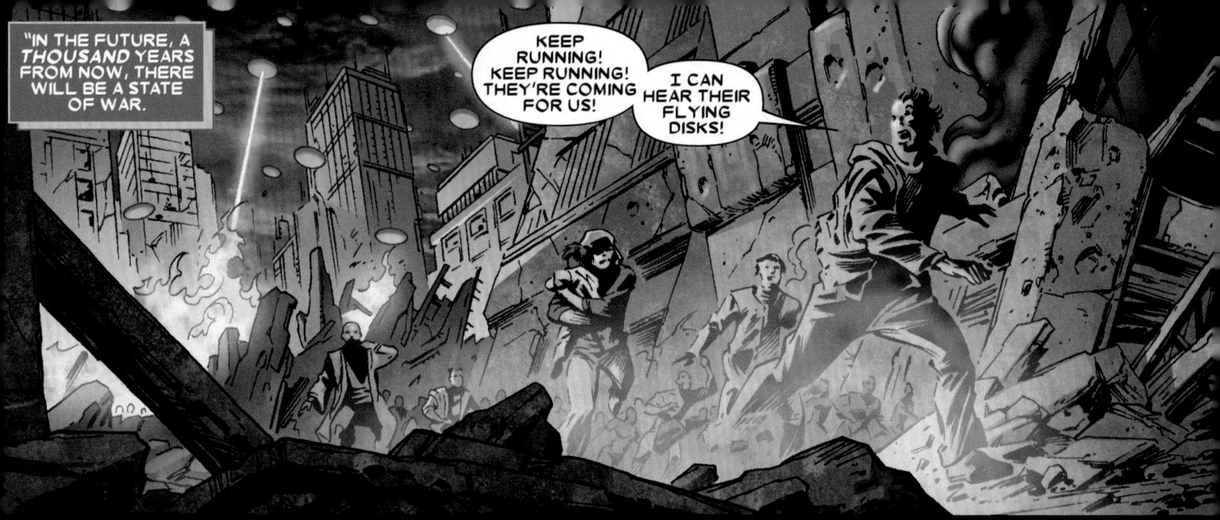
"IN THE FUTURE, A THOUSAND YEARS FROM NOW, THERE WILL BE A STATE OF WAR.
KEEP RUNNING! KEEP RUNNING! THEY'RE COMING FOR US!
I CAN HEAR THEIR FLYING DISKS!

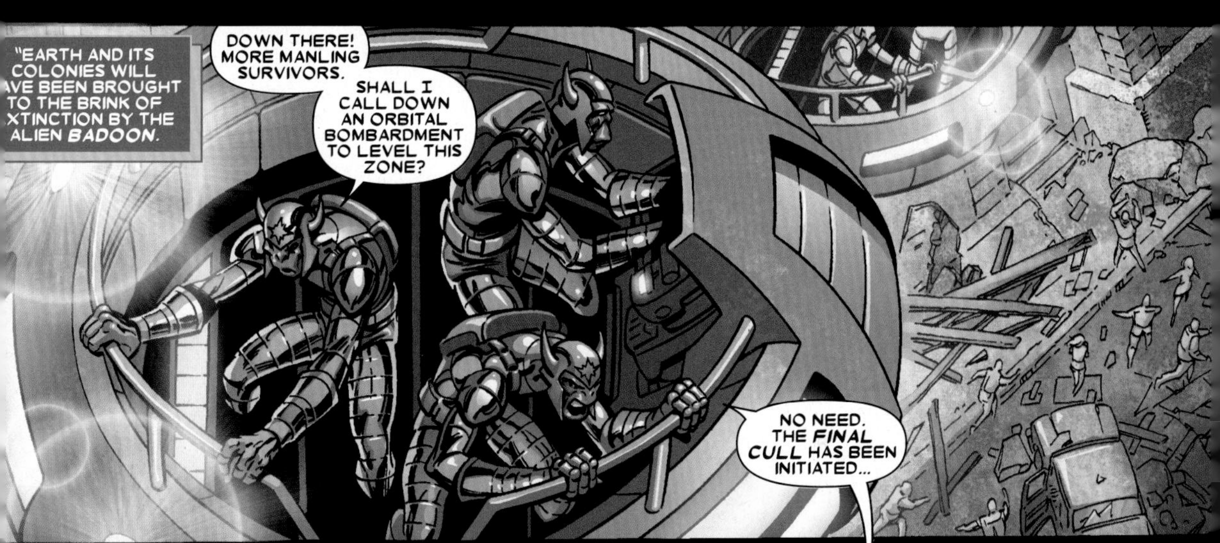
"EARTH AND ITS COLONIES WILL AVE BEEN BROUGHT TO THE BRINK OF XTINCTION BY THE ALIEN BADOON.
DOWN THERE! MORE MANLING SURVIVORS.
SHALL I CALL DOWN AN ORBITAL BOMBARDMENT TO LEVEL THIS ZONE?
NO NEED. THE FINAL CULL HAS BEEN INITIATED...

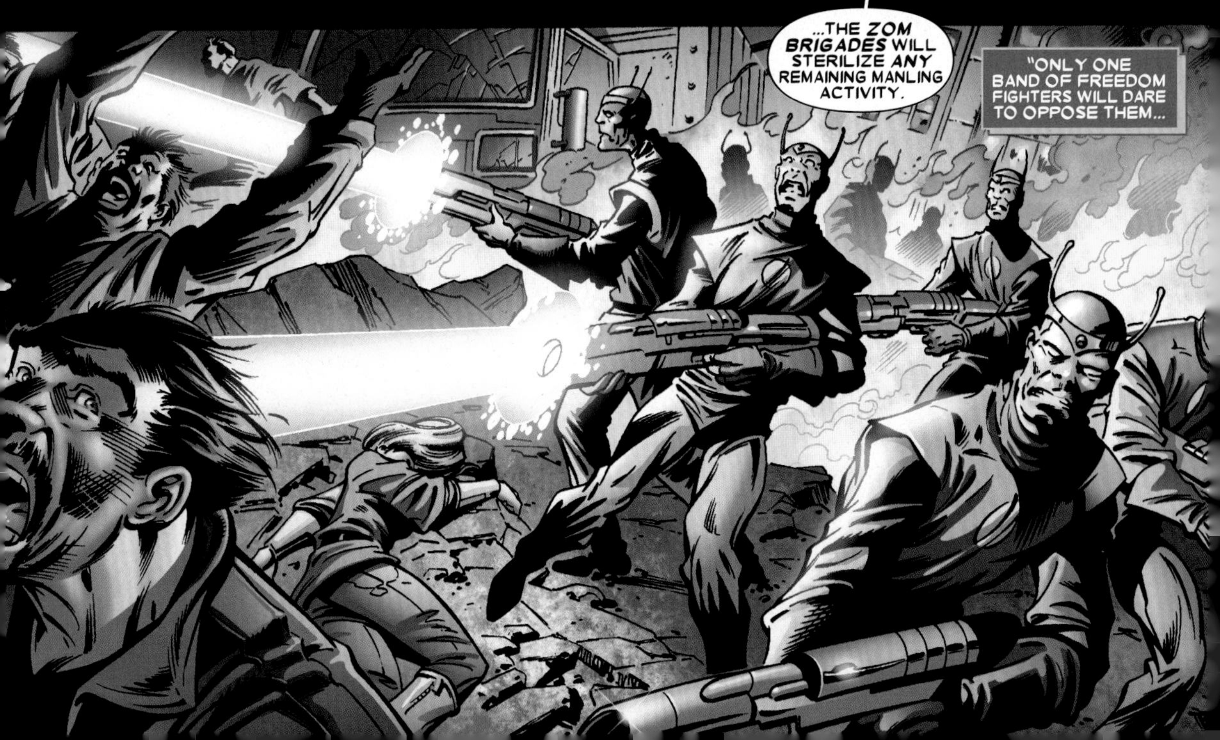
...THE ZOM BRIGADES WILL STERILIZE ANY REMAINING MANLING ACTIVITY.
"ONLY ONE BAND OF FREEDOM FIGHTERS WILL DARE TO OPPOSE THEM...

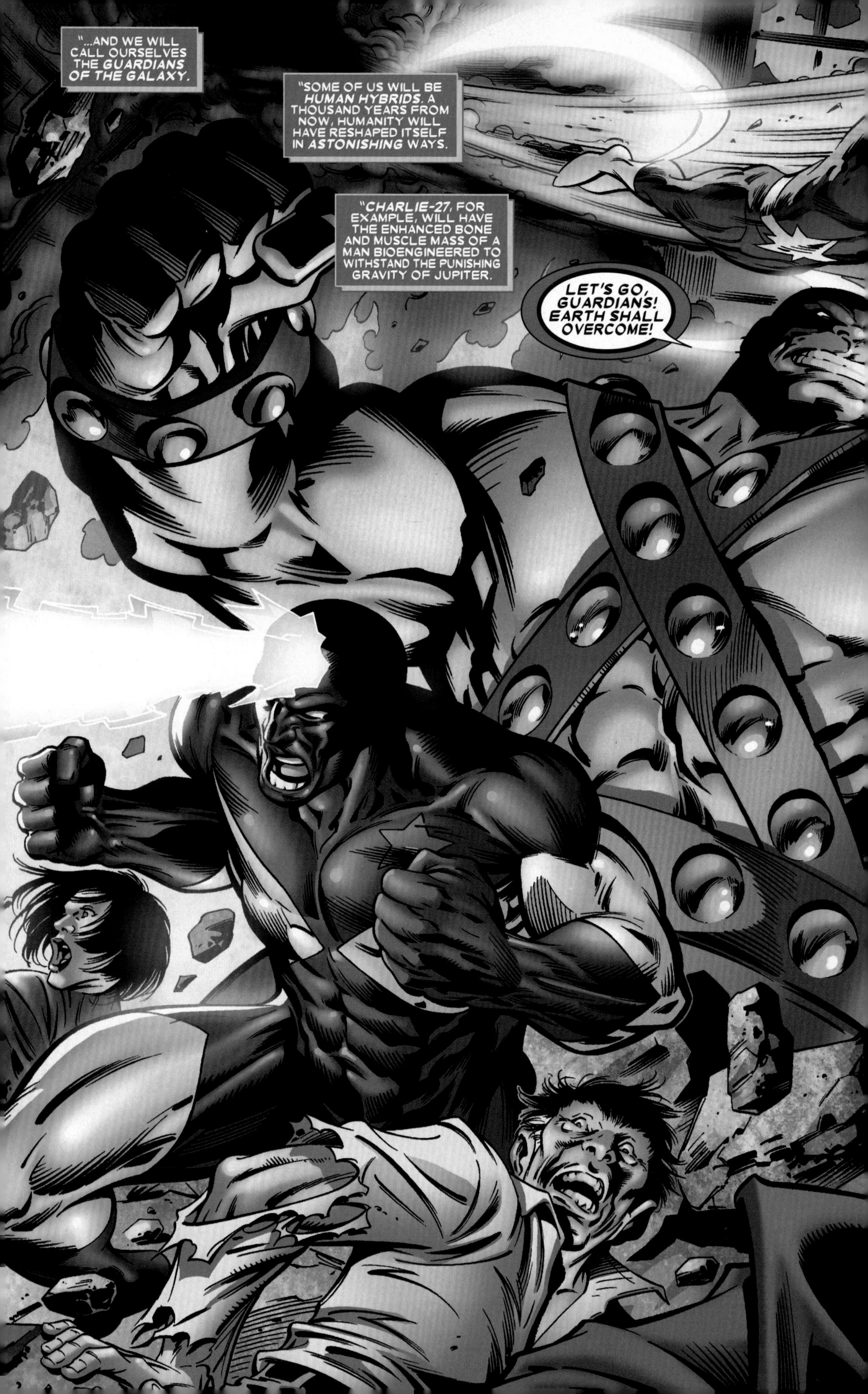
"...AND WE WILL CALL OURSELVES THE *GUARDIANS OF THE GALAXY*.
"SOME OF US WILL BE *HUMAN HYBRIDS*. A THOUSAND YEARS FROM NOW, HUMANITY WILL HAVE RESHAPED ITSELF IN *ASTONISHING* WAYS.
"*CHARLIE-27*, FOR EXAMPLE, WILL HAVE THE ENHANCED BONE AND MUSCLE MASS OF A MAN BIOENGINEERED TO WITHSTAND THE PUNISHING GRAVITY OF JUPITER.
LET'S GO, GUARDIANS! EARTH SHALL OVERCOME!

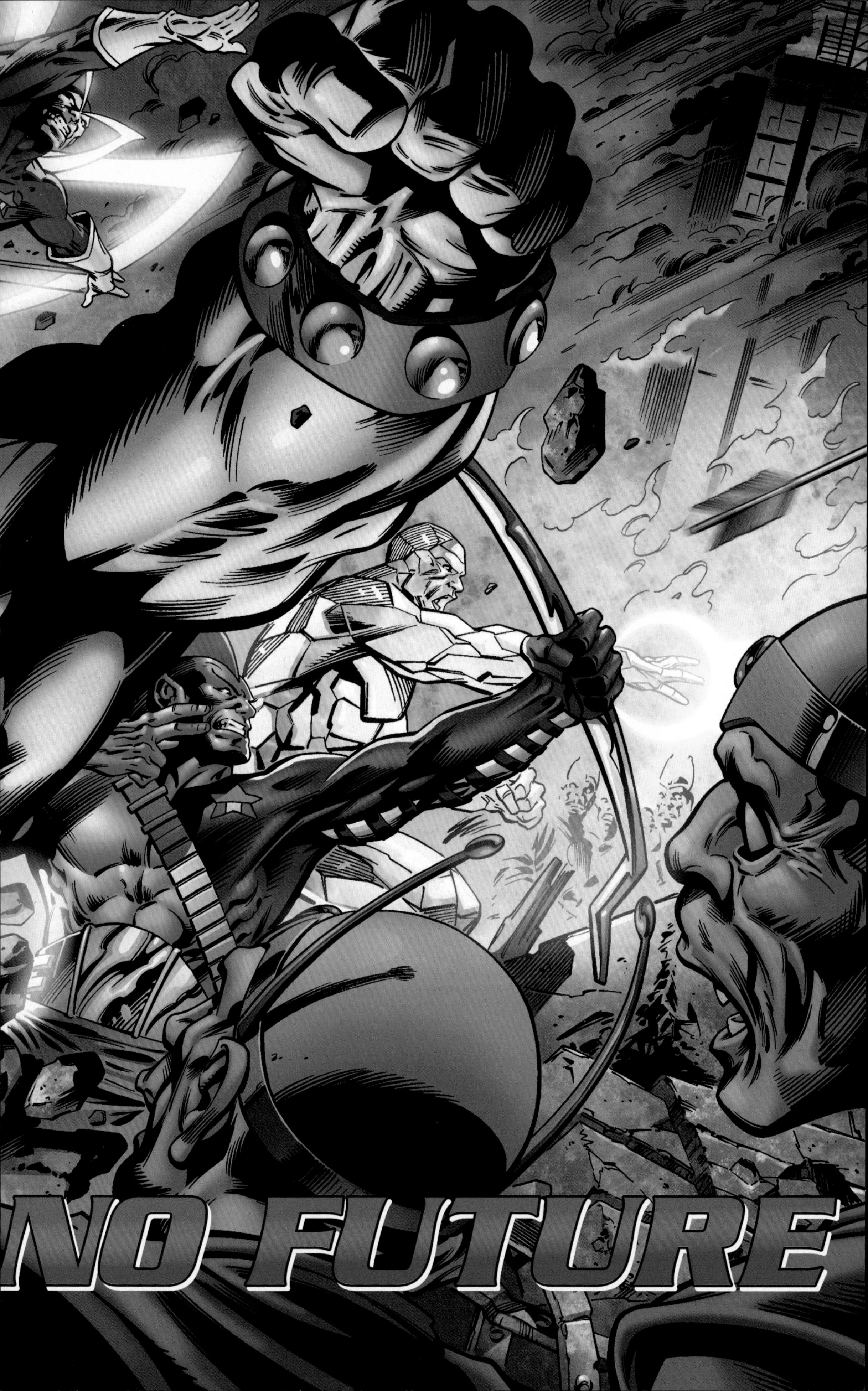
NO FUTURE

GUARDIANS OF THE GALAXY

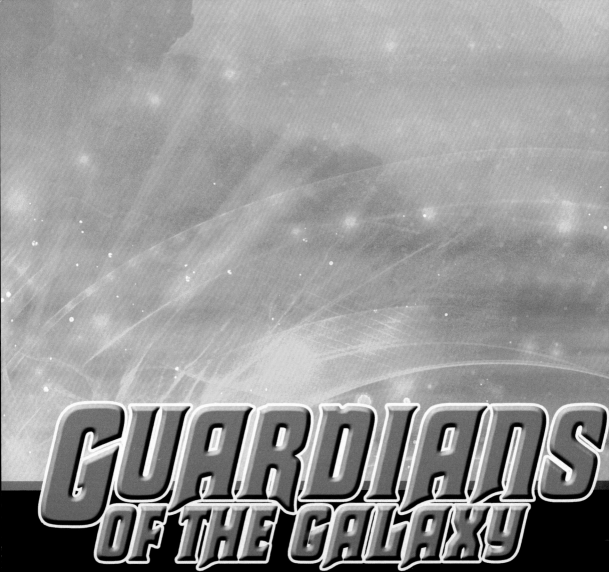

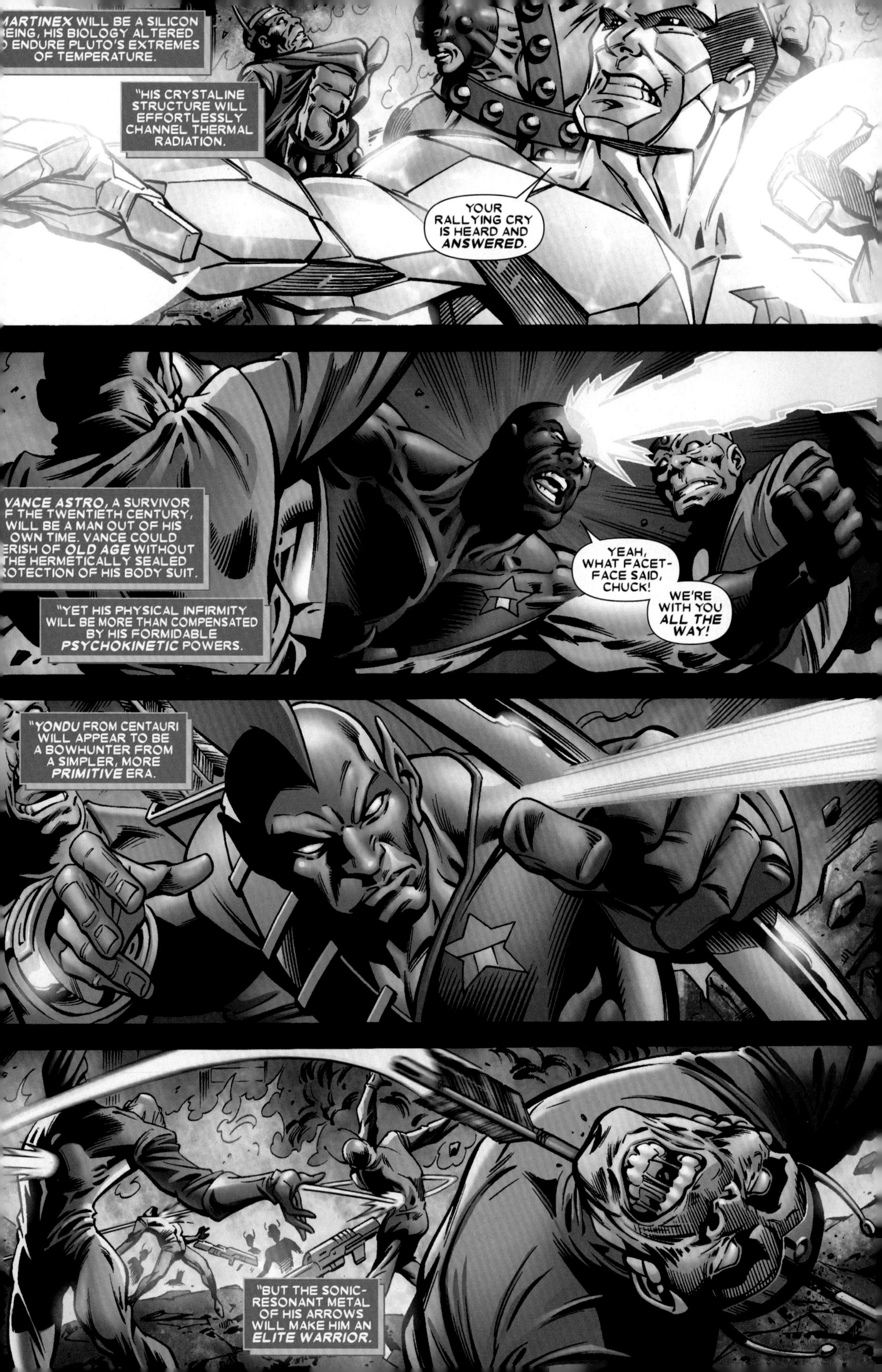
MARTINEX WILL BE A SILICON BEING, HIS BIOLOGY ALTERED TO ENDURE PLUTO'S EXTREMES OF TEMPERATURE.
"HIS CRYSTALINE STRUCTURE WILL EFFORTLESSLY CHANNEL THERMAL RADIATION.
YOUR RALLYING CRY IS HEARD AND ANSWERED.
VANCE ASTRO, A SURVIVOR OF THE TWENTIETH CENTURY, WILL BE A MAN OUT OF HIS OWN TIME. VANCE COULD PERISH OF OLD AGE WITHOUT THE HERMETICALLY SEALED PROTECTION OF HIS BODY SUIT.
"YET HIS PHYSICAL INFIRMITY WILL BE MORE THAN COMPENSATED BY HIS FORMIDABLE PSYCHOKINETIC POWERS.
YEAH, WHAT FACET-FACE SAID, CHUCK!
WE'RE WITH YOU ALL THE WAY!
"YONDU FROM CENTAURI WILL APPEAR TO BE A BOWHUNTER FROM A SIMPLER, MORE PRIMITIVE ERA.
"BUT THE SONIC-RESONANT METAL OF HIS ARROWS WILL MAKE HIM AN ELITE WARRIOR.

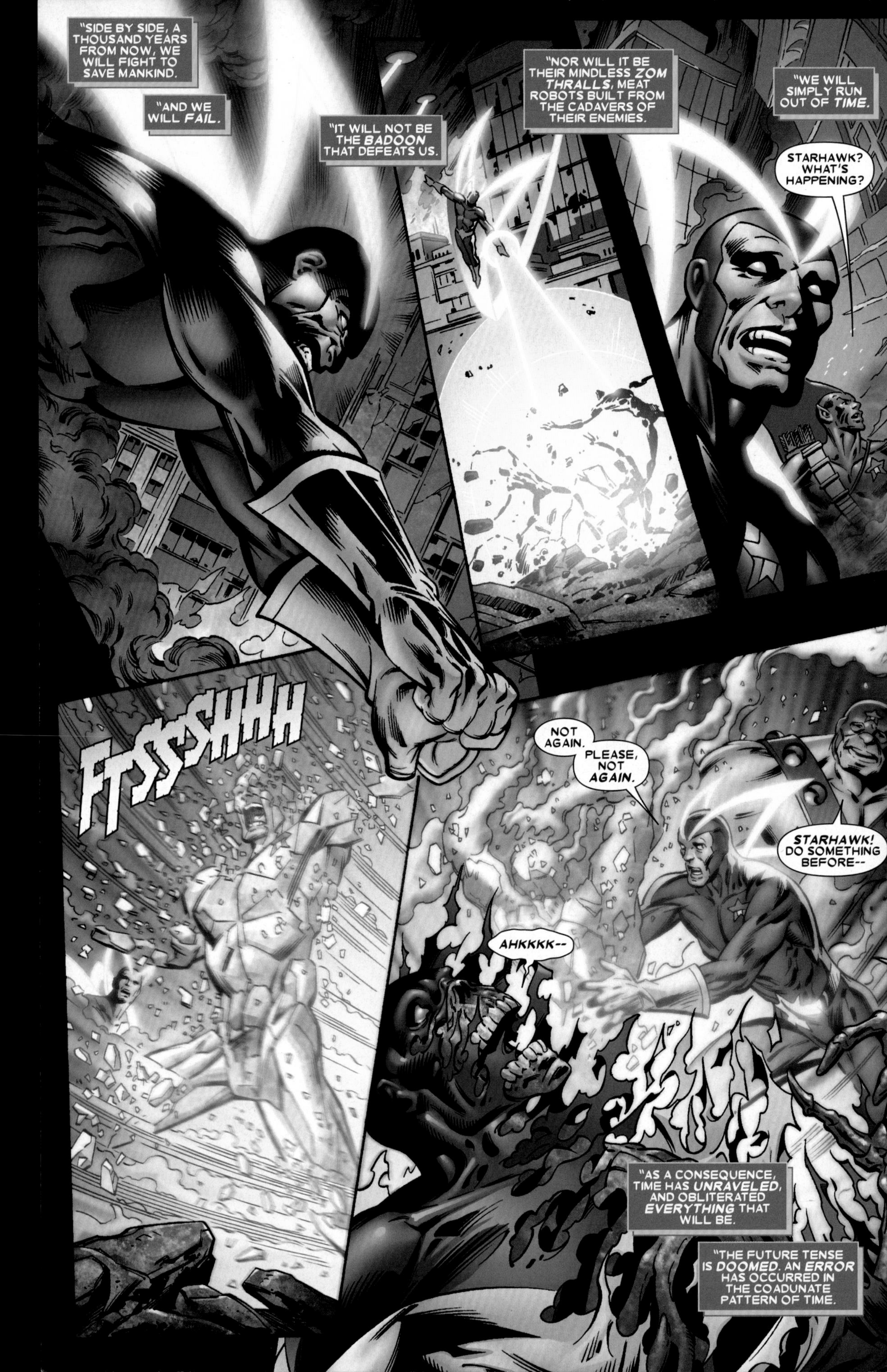
"SIDE BY SIDE, A THOUSAND YEARS FROM NOW, WE WILL FIGHT TO SAVE MANKIND.
"AND WE WILL FAIL.
"IT WILL NOT BE THE BADOON THAT DEFEATS US.
"NOR WILL IT BE THEIR MINDLESS ZOM THRALLS, MEAT ROBOTS BUILT FROM THE CADAVERS OF THEIR ENEMIES.
"WE WILL SIMPLY RUN OUT OF TIME.
STARHAWK? WHAT'S HAPPENING?
FTSSSHHH
NOT AGAIN. PLEASE, NOT AGAIN.
STARHAWK! DO SOMETHING BEFORE--
AHKKKK--
"AS A CONSEQUENCE, TIME HAS UNRAVELED, AND OBLITERATED EVERYTHING THAT WILL BE.
"THE FUTURE TENSE IS DOOMED. AN ERROR HAS OCCURRED IN THE COADUNATE PATTERN OF TIME.

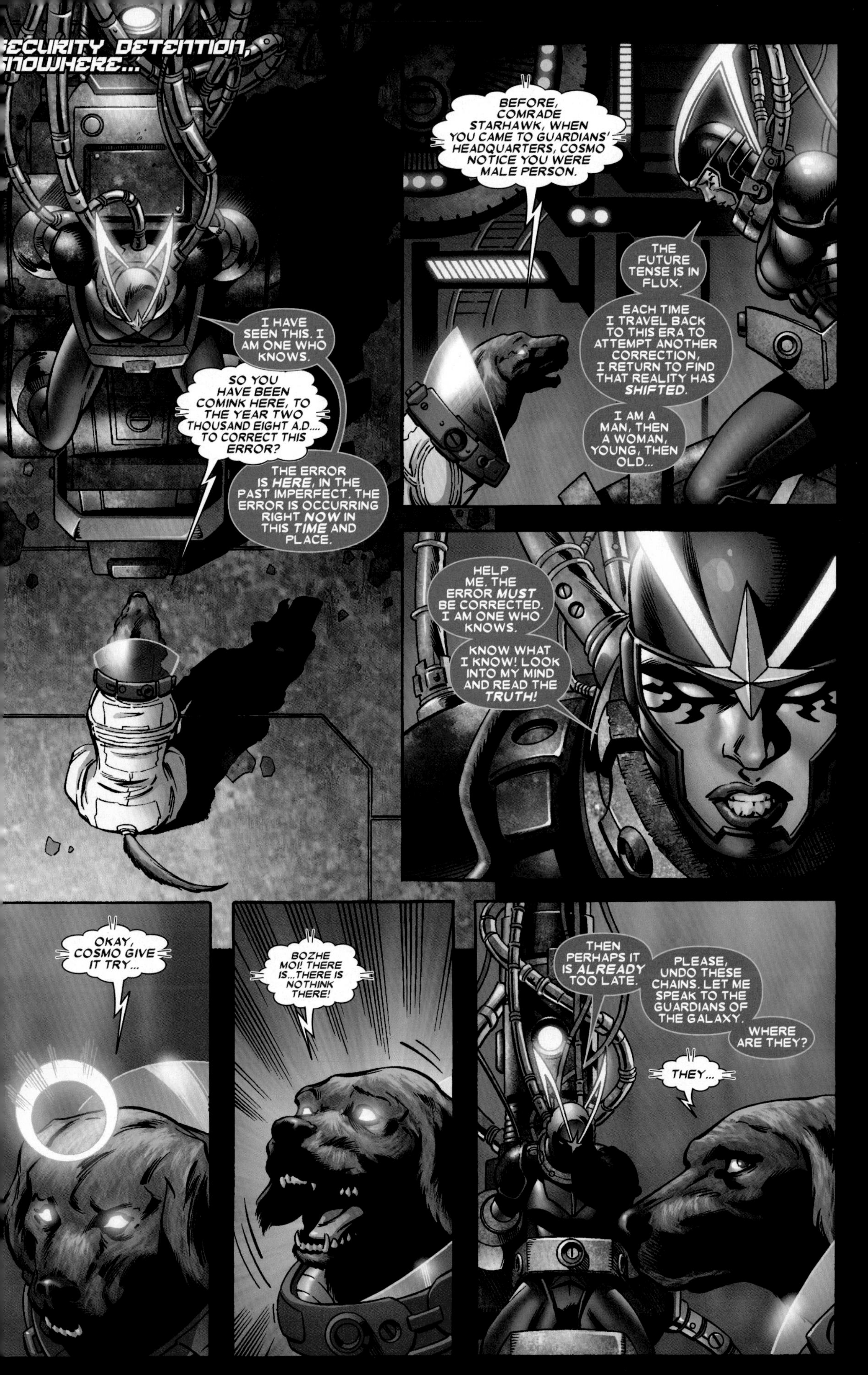
SECURITY DETENTION, KNOWHERE...
I HAVE SEEN THIS. I AM ONE WHO KNOWS.
SO YOU HAVE BEEN COMINK HERE, TO THE YEAR TWO THOUSAND EIGHT A.D.... TO CORRECT THIS ERROR?
THE ERROR IS HERE, IN THE PAST IMPERFECT. THE ERROR IS OCCURRING RIGHT NOW IN THIS TIME AND PLACE.
BEFORE, COMRADE STARHAWK, WHEN YOU CAME TO GUARDIANS' HEADQUARTERS, COSMO NOTICE YOU WERE MALE PERSON.
THE FUTURE TENSE IS IN FLUX.
EACH TIME I TRAVEL BACK TO THIS ERA TO ATTEMPT ANOTHER CORRECTION, I RETURN TO FIND THAT REALITY HAS SHIFTED.
I AM A MAN, THEN A WOMAN, YOUNG, THEN OLD...
HELP ME. THE ERROR MUST BE CORRECTED. I AM ONE WHO KNOWS.
KNOW WHAT I KNOW! LOOK INTO MY MIND AND READ THE TRUTH!
OKAY, COSMO GIVE IT TRY...
BOZHE MOI! THERE IS...THERE IS NOTHINK THERE!
THEN PERHAPS IT IS ALREADY TOO LATE.
PLEASE, UNDO THESE CHAINS. LET ME SPEAK TO THE GUARDIANS OF THE GALAXY.
WHERE ARE THEY?
THEY...

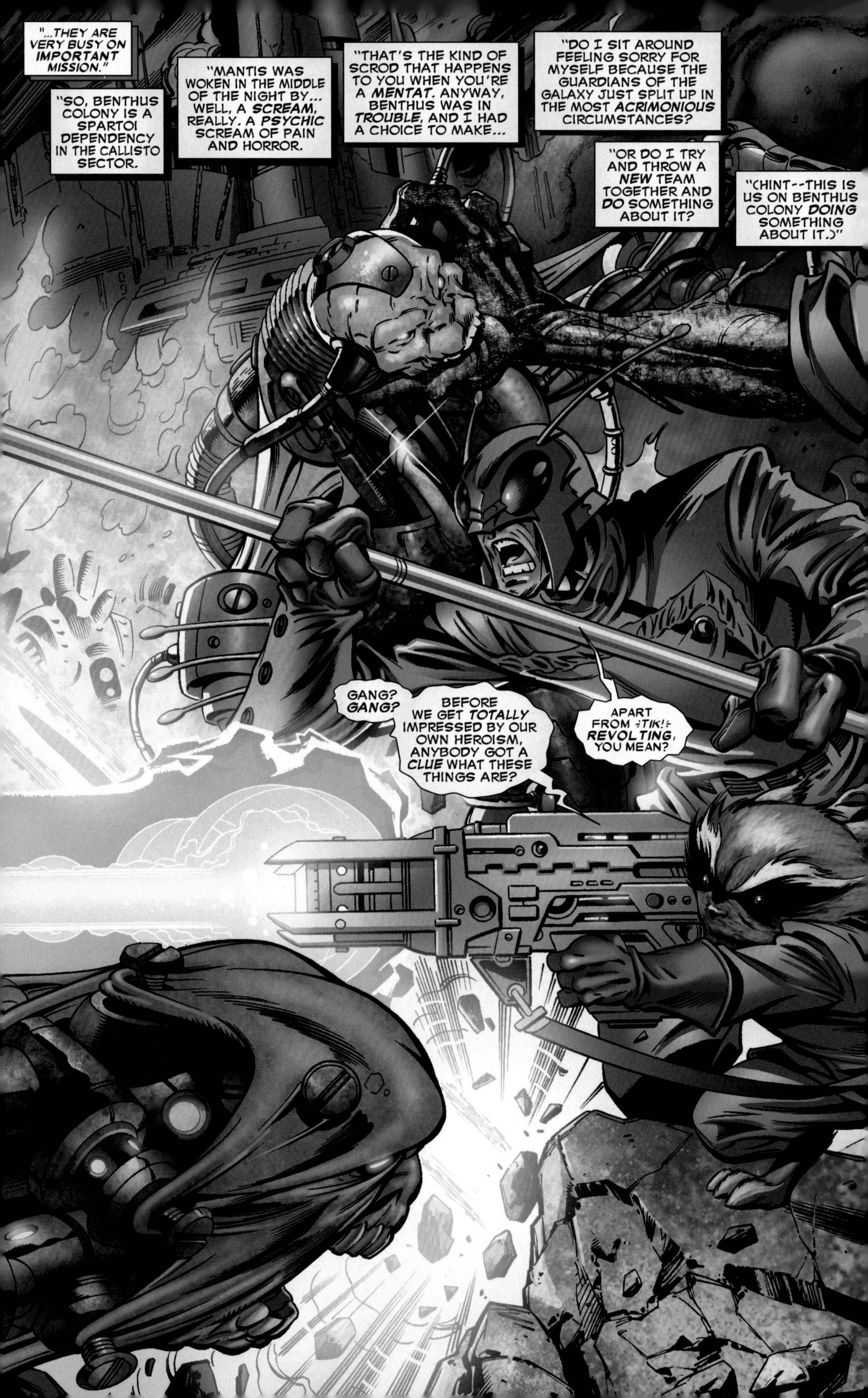
"...THEY ARE VERY BUSY ON IMPORTANT MISSION."
"SO, BENTHUS COLONY IS A SPARTOI DEPENDENCY IN THE CALLISTO SECTOR.
"MANTIS WAS WOKEN IN THE MIDDLE OF THE NIGHT BY... WELL, A SCREAM, REALLY. A PSYCHIC SCREAM OF PAIN AND HORROR.
"THAT'S THE KIND OF SCROD THAT HAPPENS TO YOU WHEN YOU'RE A MENTAT. ANYWAY, BENTHUS WAS IN TROUBLE, AND I HAD A CHOICE TO MAKE...
"DO I SIT AROUND FEELING SORRY FOR MYSELF BECAUSE THE GUARDIANS OF THE GALAXY JUST SPLIT UP IN THE MOST ACRIMONIOUS CIRCUMSTANCES?
"OR DO I TRY AND THROW A NEW TEAM TOGETHER AND DO SOMETHING ABOUT IT?
"(HINT--THIS IS US ON BENTHUS COLONY DOING SOMETHING ABOUT IT.)"
GANG? GANG?
BEFORE WE GET TOTALLY IMPRESSED BY OUR OWN HEROISM, ANYBODY GOT A CLUE WHAT THESE THINGS ARE?
APART FROM ‡TIK!‡ REVOLTING, YOU MEAN?

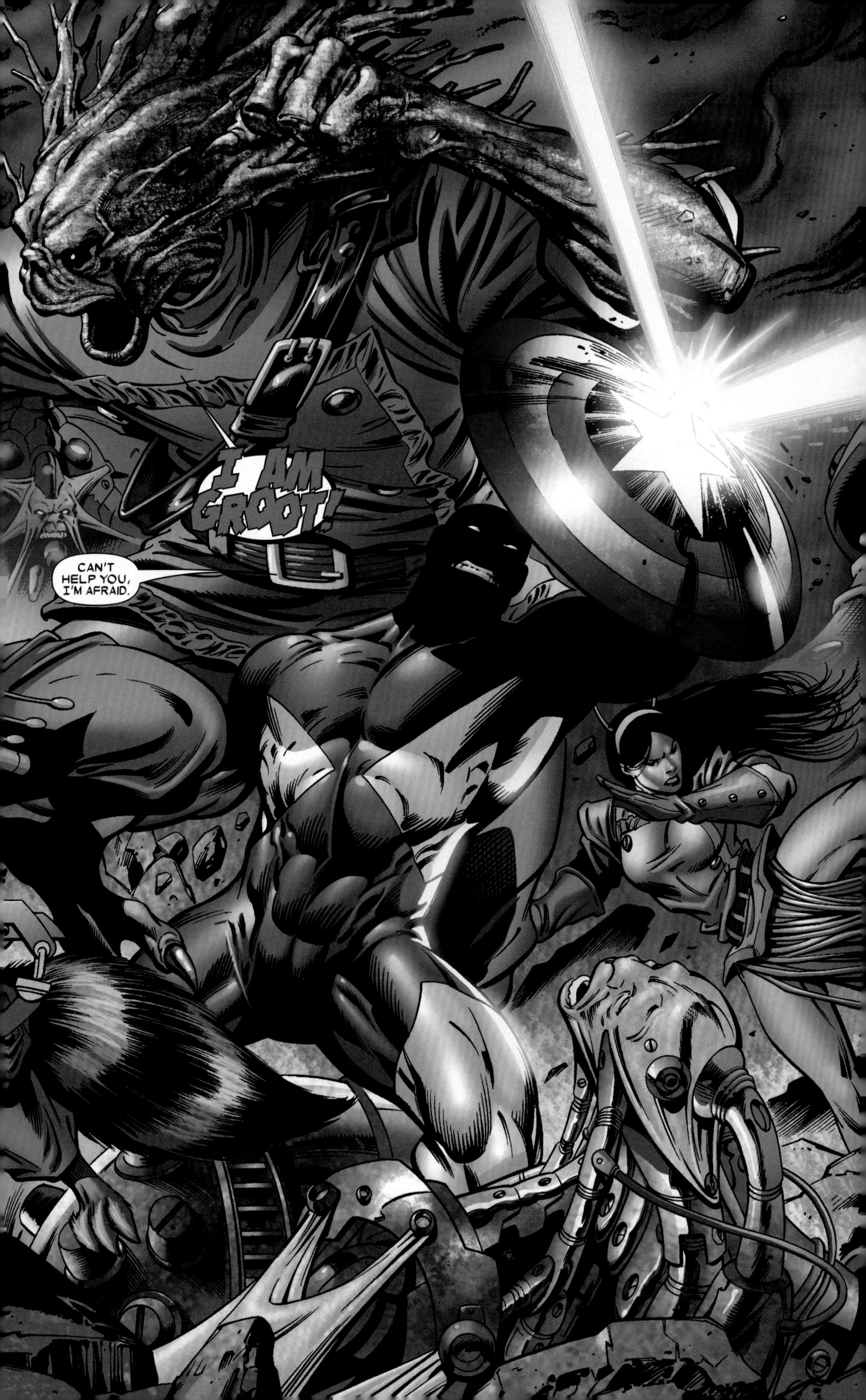
I AM GROOT!
CAN'T HELP YOU, I'M AFRAID.

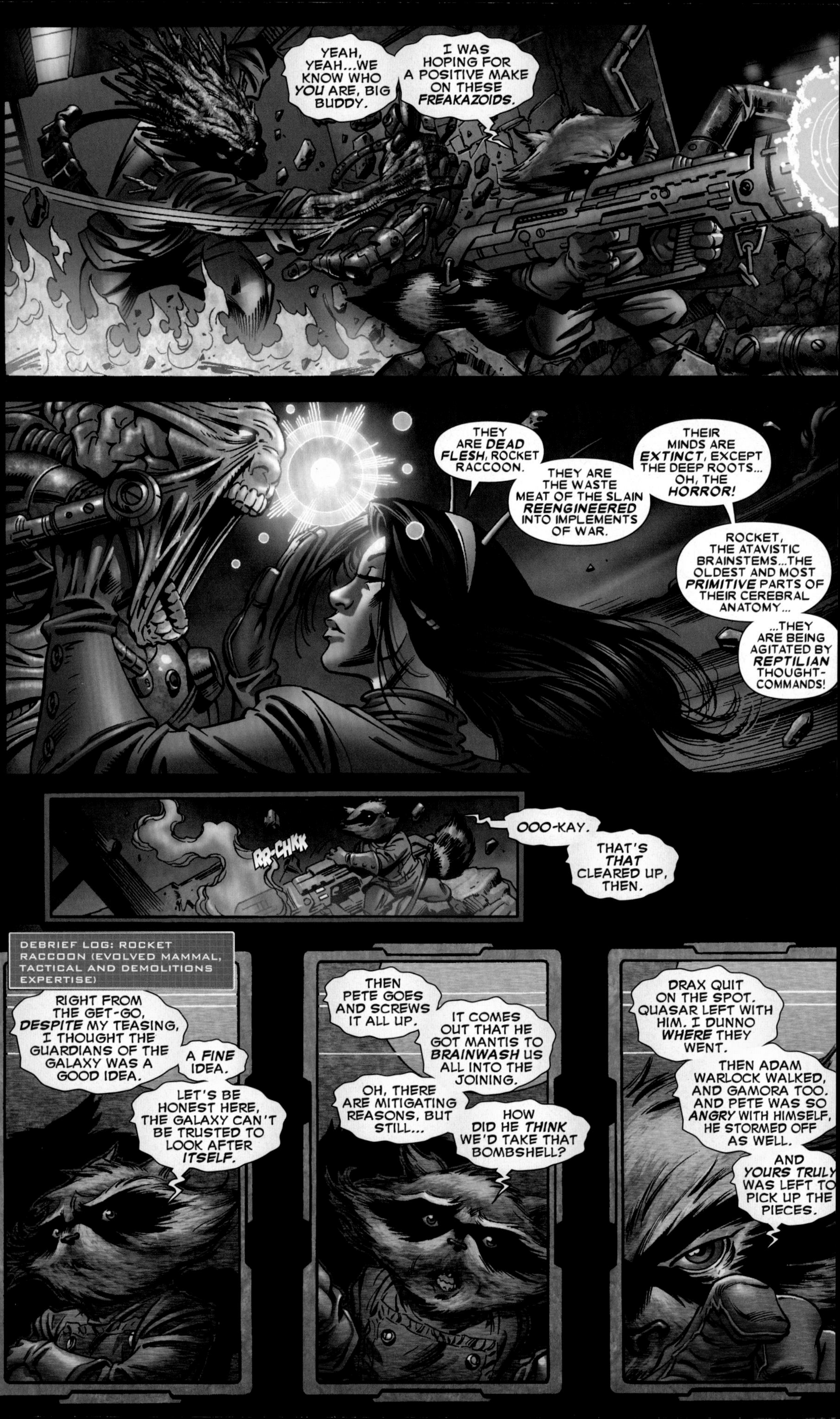
YEAH, YEAH...WE KNOW WHO YOU ARE, BIG BUDDY.
I WAS HOPING FOR A POSITIVE MAKE ON THESE FREAKAZOIDS.
THEY ARE DEAD FLESH, ROCKET RACCOON.
THEY ARE THE WASTE MEAT OF THE SLAIN REENGINEERED INTO IMPLEMENTS OF WAR.
THEIR MINDS ARE EXTINCT, EXCEPT THE DEEP ROOTS... OH, THE HORROR!
ROCKET, THE ATAVISTIC BRAINSTEMS...THE OLDEST AND MOST PRIMITIVE PARTS OF THEIR CEREBRAL ANATOMY...
...THEY ARE BEING AGITATED BY REPTILIAN THOUGHT-COMMANDS!
RR-CHKK
OOO-KAY.
THAT'S THAT CLEARED UP, THEN.
DEBRIEF LOG: ROCKET RACCOON (EVOLVED MAMMAL, TACTICAL AND DEMOLITIONS EXPERTISE)
RIGHT FROM THE GET-GO, DESPITE MY TEASING, I THOUGHT THE GUARDIANS OF THE GALAXY WAS A GOOD IDEA.
A FINE IDEA.
LET'S BE HONEST HERE, THE GALAXY CAN'T BE TRUSTED TO LOOK AFTER ITSELF.
THEN PETE GOES AND SCREWS IT ALL UP.
IT COMES OUT THAT HE GOT MANTIS TO BRAINWASH US ALL INTO THE JOINING.
OH, THERE ARE MITIGATING REASONS, BUT STILL...
HOW DID HE THINK WE'D TAKE THAT BOMBSHELL?
DRAX QUIT ON THE SPOT. QUASAR LEFT WITH HIM. I DUNNO WHERE THEY WENT.
THEN ADAM WARLOCK WALKED, AND GAMORA TOO. AND PETE WAS SO ANGRY WITH HIMSELF, HE STORMED OFF AS WELL.
AND YOURS TRULY WAS LEFT TO PICK UP THE PIECES.

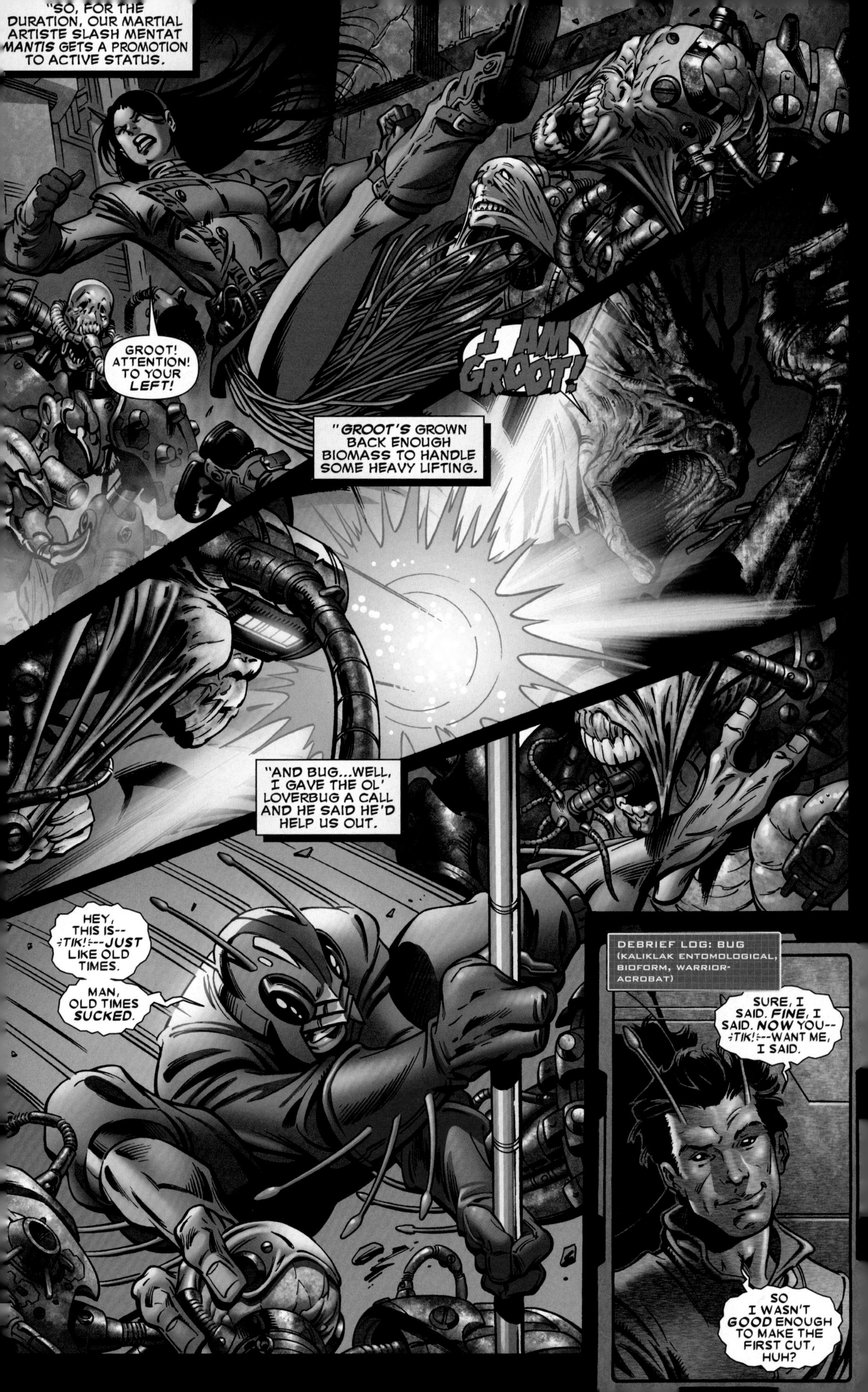
"SO, FOR THE DURATION, OUR MARTIAL ARTISTE SLASH MENTAT *MANTIS* GETS A PROMOTION TO ACTIVE STATUS.
GROOT! ATTENTION! TO YOUR *LEFT!*
I AM GROOT!
"*GROOT'S* GROWN BACK ENOUGH BIOMASS TO HANDLE SOME HEAVY LIFTING.
"AND BUG...WELL, I GAVE THE OL' LOVERBUG A CALL AND HE SAID HE'D HELP US OUT.
HEY, THIS IS-- ‡TIK!‡--*JUST* LIKE OLD TIMES.
MAN, OLD TIMES *SUCKED*.
DEBRIEF LOG: BUG (KALIKLAK ENTOMOLOGICAL, BIOFORM, WARRIOR-ACROBAT)
SURE, I SAID. *FINE*, I SAID. *NOW* YOU-- ‡TIK!‡--WANT ME, I SAID.
SO I WASN'T *GOOD* ENOUGH TO MAKE THE FIRST CUT, HUH?

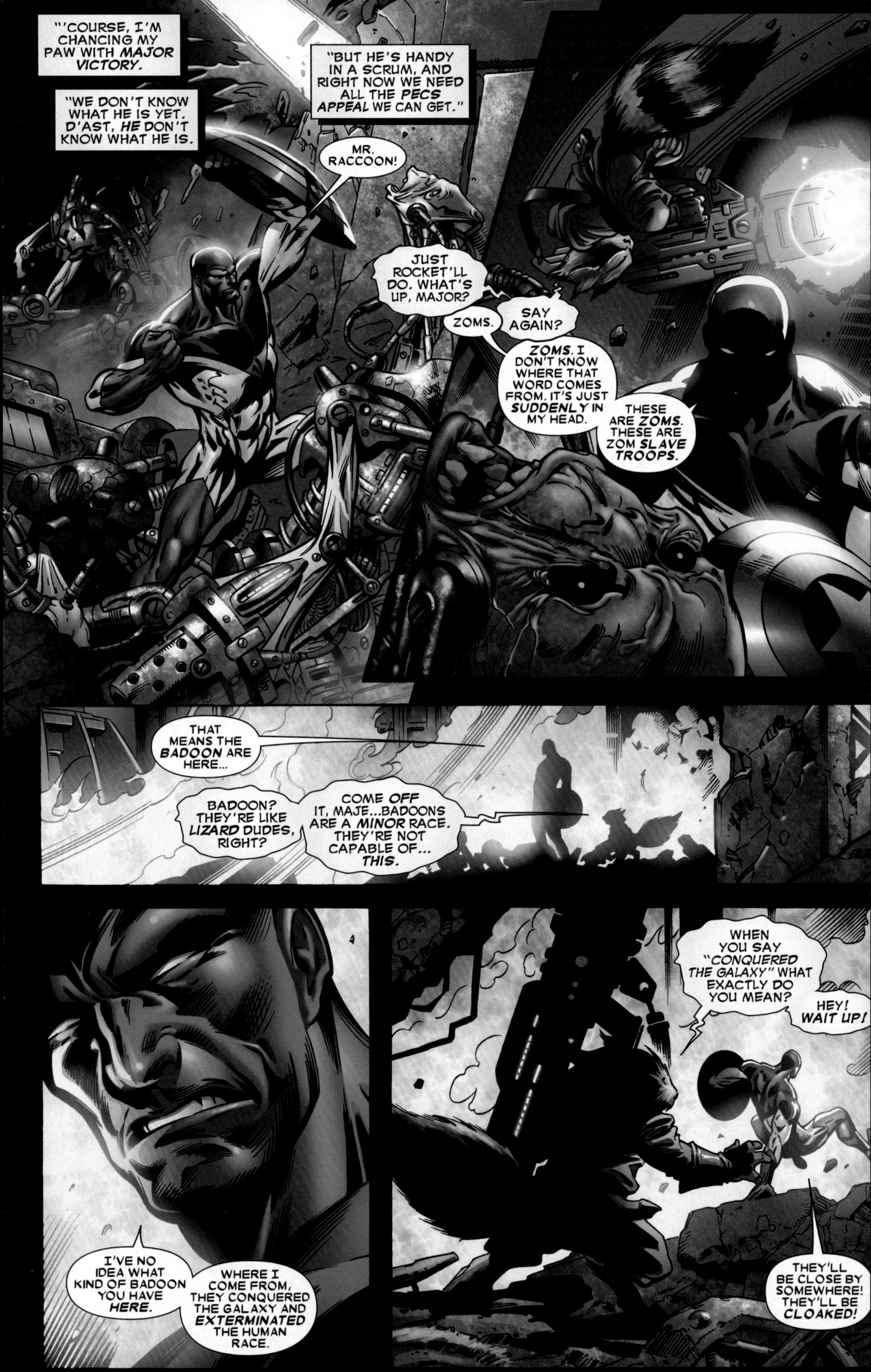
"'COURSE, I'M CHANCING MY PAW WITH MAJOR VICTORY.
"WE DON'T KNOW WHAT HE IS YET. D'AST, HE DON'T KNOW WHAT HE IS.
"BUT HE'S HANDY IN A SCRUM, AND RIGHT NOW WE NEED ALL THE PECS APPEAL WE CAN GET."
MR. RACCOON!
JUST ROCKET'LL DO. WHAT'S UP, MAJOR?
ZOMS.
SAY AGAIN?
ZOMS. I DON'T KNOW WHERE THAT WORD COMES FROM. IT'S JUST SUDDENLY IN MY HEAD.
THESE ARE ZOMS. THESE ARE ZOM SLAVE TROOPS.
THAT MEANS THE BADOON ARE HERE...
BADOON? THEY'RE LIKE LIZARD DUDES, RIGHT?
COME OFF IT, MAJE...BADOONS ARE A MINOR RACE. THEY'RE NOT CAPABLE OF... THIS.
I'VE NO IDEA WHAT KIND OF BADOON YOU HAVE HERE.
WHERE I COME FROM, THEY CONQUERED THE GALAXY AND EXTERMINATED THE HUMAN RACE.
WHEN YOU SAY "CONQUERED THE GALAXY" WHAT EXACTLY DO YOU MEAN?
HEY! WAIT UP!
THEY'LL BE CLOSE BY SOMEWHERE! THEY'LL BE CLOAKED!

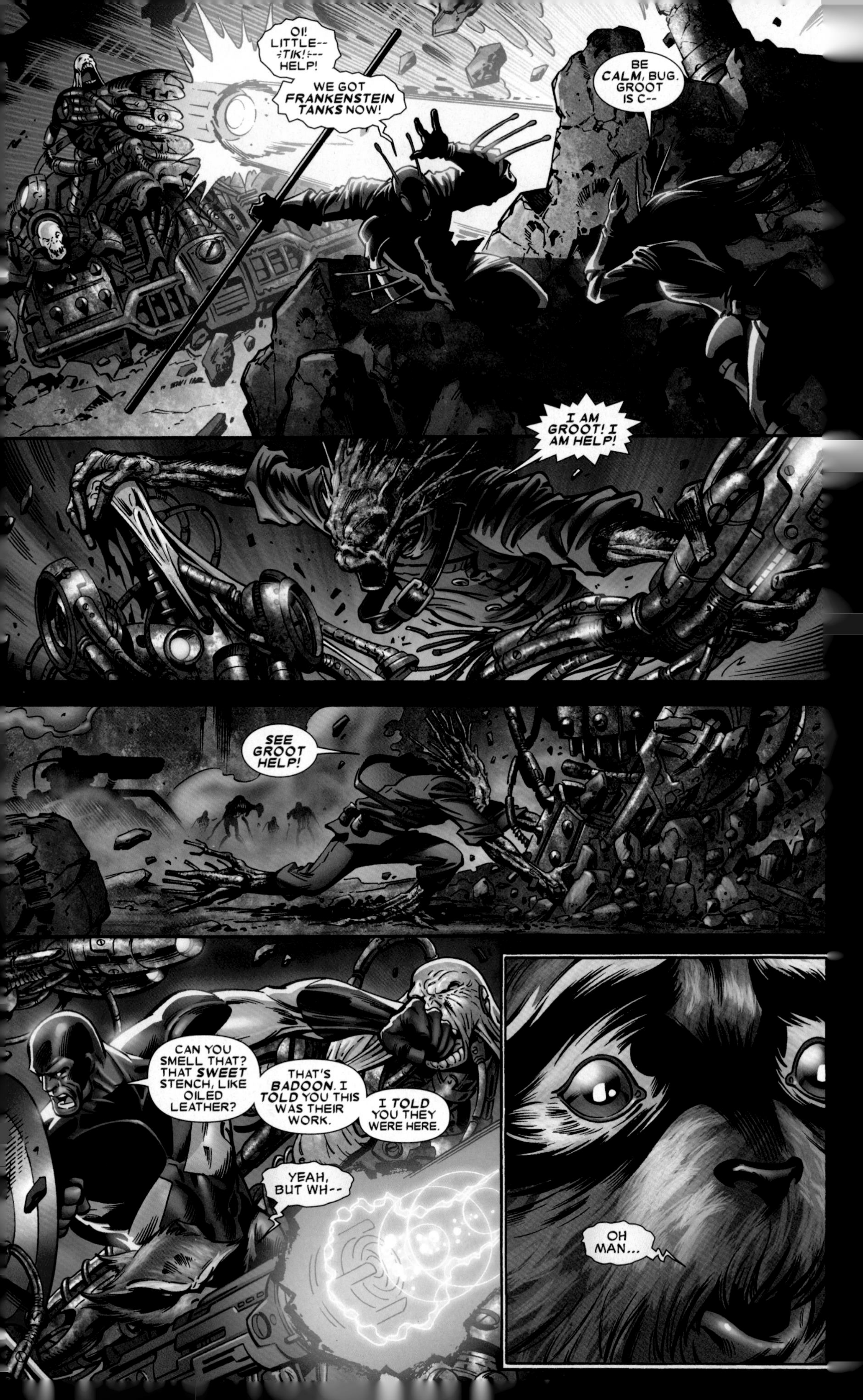
OI! LITTLE-- -TIK!-- HELP!
WE GOT FRANKENSTEIN TANKS NOW!
BE CALM, BUG. GROOT IS C--
I AM GROOT! I AM HELP!
SEE GROOT HELP!
CAN YOU SMELL THAT? THAT SWEET STENCH, LIKE OILED LEATHER?
THAT'S BADOON. I TOLD YOU THIS WAS THEIR WORK.
I TOLD YOU THEY WERE HERE.
YEAH, BUT WH--
OH MAN...

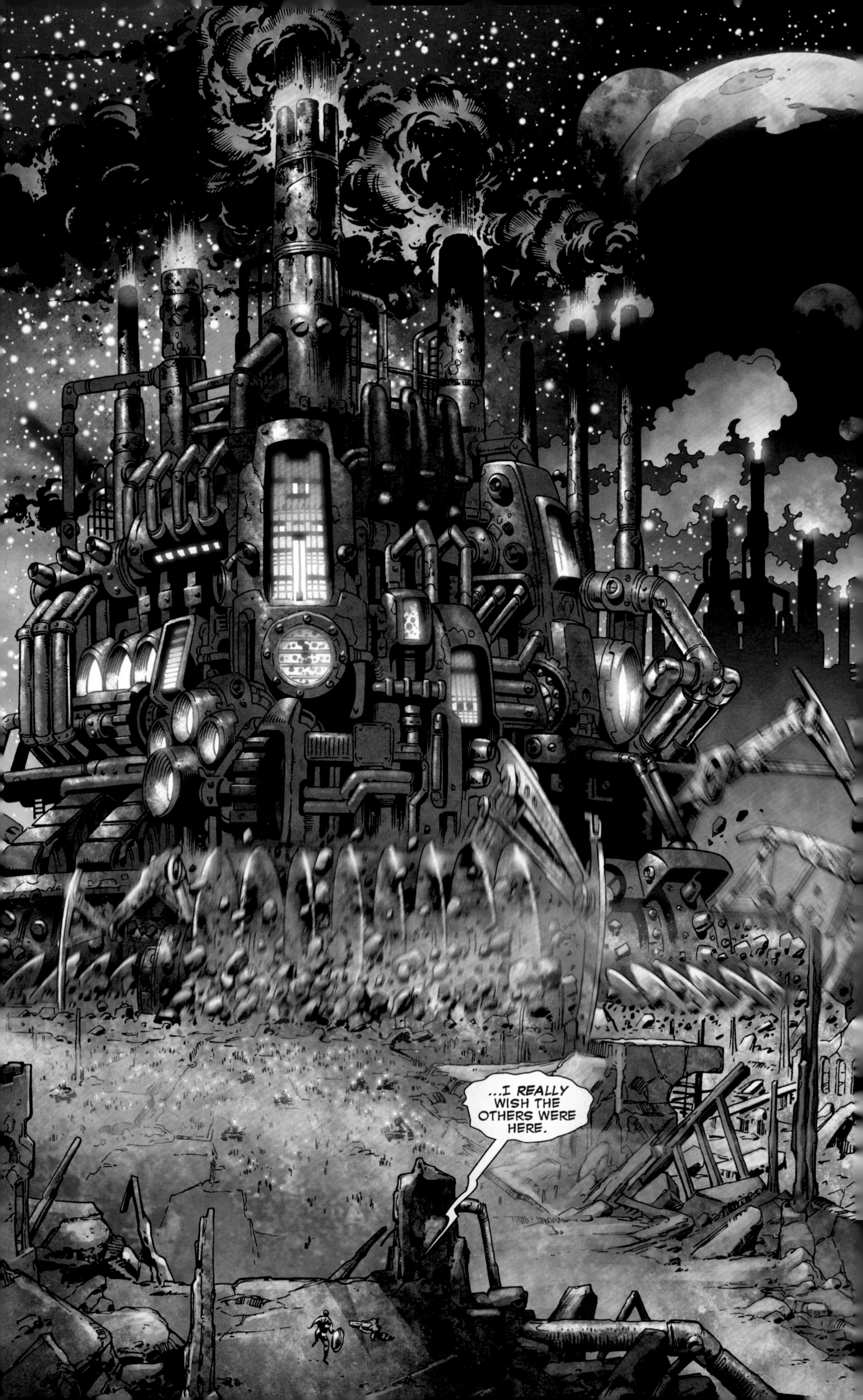
...I REALLY WISH THE OTHERS WERE HERE.

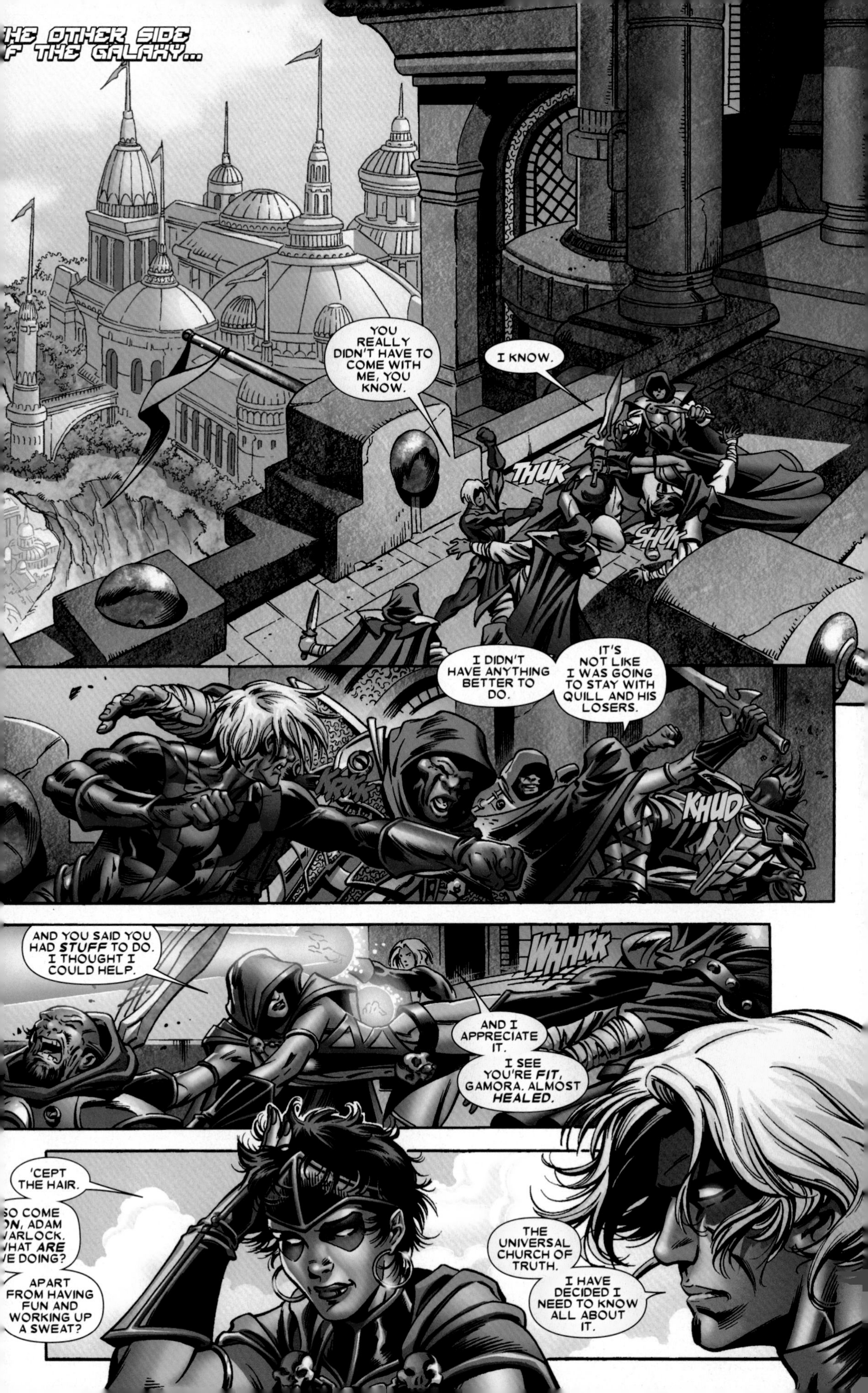
HE OTHER SIDE
F THE GALAXY...
YOU REALLY DIDN'T HAVE TO COME WITH ME, YOU KNOW.
I KNOW.
THUK
SHUK
I DIDN'T HAVE ANYTHING BETTER TO DO.
IT'S NOT LIKE I WAS GOING TO STAY WITH QUILL AND HIS LOSERS.
KHUD
AND YOU SAID YOU HAD *STUFF* TO DO. I THOUGHT I COULD HELP.
WHHKK
AND I APPRECIATE IT.
I SEE YOU'RE *FIT*, GAMORA. ALMOST *HEALED*.
'CEPT THE HAIR.
SO COME ON, ADAM WARLOCK. WHAT *ARE* WE DOING?
APART FROM HAVING FUN AND WORKING UP A SWEAT?
THE UNIVERSAL CHURCH OF TRUTH.
I HAVE DECIDED I NEED TO KNOW ALL ABOUT IT.

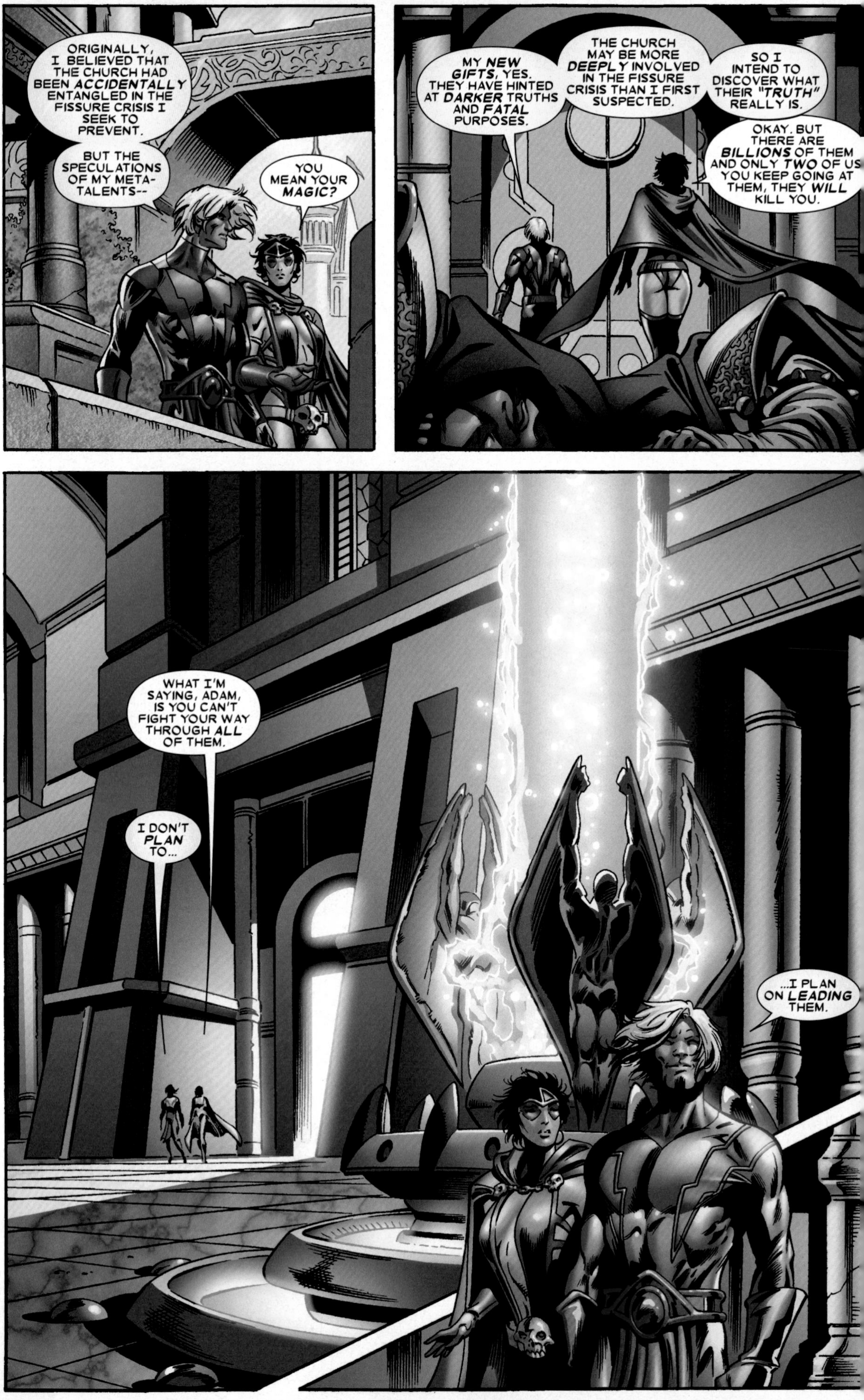
ORIGINALLY, I BELIEVED THAT THE CHURCH HAD BEEN ACCIDENTALLY ENTANGLED IN THE FISSURE CRISIS I SEEK TO PREVENT.
BUT THE SPECULATIONS OF MY META-TALENTS--
YOU MEAN YOUR MAGIC?
MY NEW GIFTS, YES. THEY HAVE HINTED AT DARKER TRUTHS AND FATAL PURPOSES.
THE CHURCH MAY BE MORE DEEPLY INVOLVED IN THE FISSURE CRISIS THAN I FIRST SUSPECTED.
SO I INTEND TO DISCOVER WHAT THEIR "TRUTH" REALLY IS.
OKAY. BUT THERE ARE BILLIONS OF THEM AND ONLY TWO OF US. YOU KEEP GOING AT THEM, THEY WILL KILL YOU.
WHAT I'M SAYING, ADAM, IS YOU CAN'T FIGHT YOUR WAY THROUGH ALL OF THEM.
I DON'T PLAN TO...
...I PLAN ON LEADING THEM.

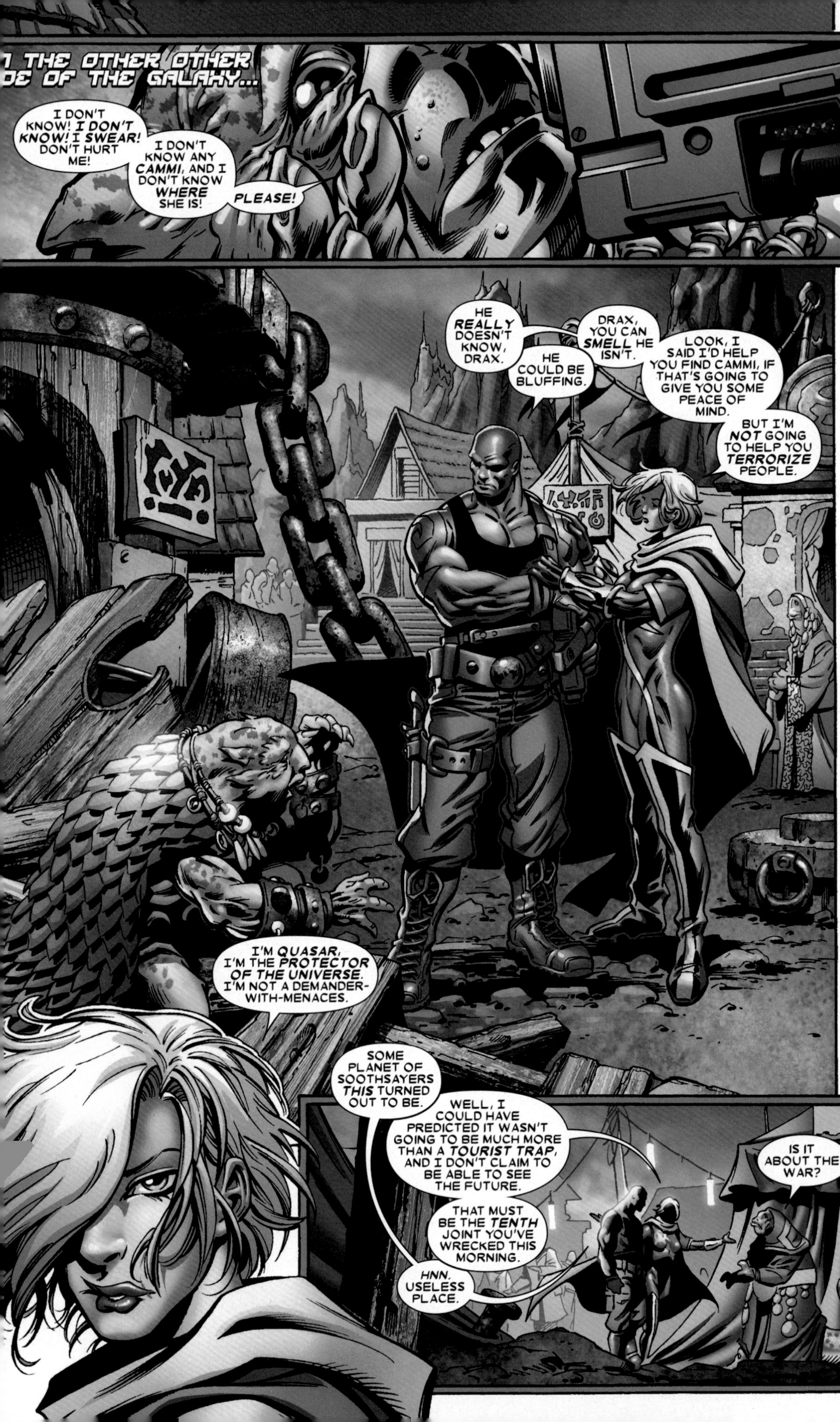

...N THE OTHER OTHER ...DE OF THE GALAXY...
I DON'T KNOW! I DON'T KNOW! I SWEAR! DON'T HURT ME!
I DON'T KNOW ANY CAMMI, AND I DON'T KNOW WHERE SHE IS!
PLEASE!
HE REALLY DOESN'T KNOW, DRAX.
HE COULD BE BLUFFING.
DRAX, YOU CAN SMELL HE ISN'T.
LOOK, I SAID I'D HELP YOU FIND CAMMI, IF THAT'S GOING TO GIVE YOU SOME PEACE OF MIND.
BUT I'M NOT GOING TO HELP YOU TERRORIZE PEOPLE.
I'M QUASAR, I'M THE PROTECTOR OF THE UNIVERSE. I'M NOT A DEMANDER-WITH-MENACES.
SOME PLANET OF SOOTHSAYERS THIS TURNED OUT TO BE.
WELL, I COULD HAVE PREDICTED IT WASN'T GOING TO BE MUCH MORE THAN A TOURIST TRAP, AND I DON'T CLAIM TO BE ABLE TO SEE THE FUTURE.
THAT MUST BE THE TENTH JOINT YOU'VE WRECKED THIS MORNING.
HNN. USELESS PLACE.
IS IT ABOUT THE WAR?

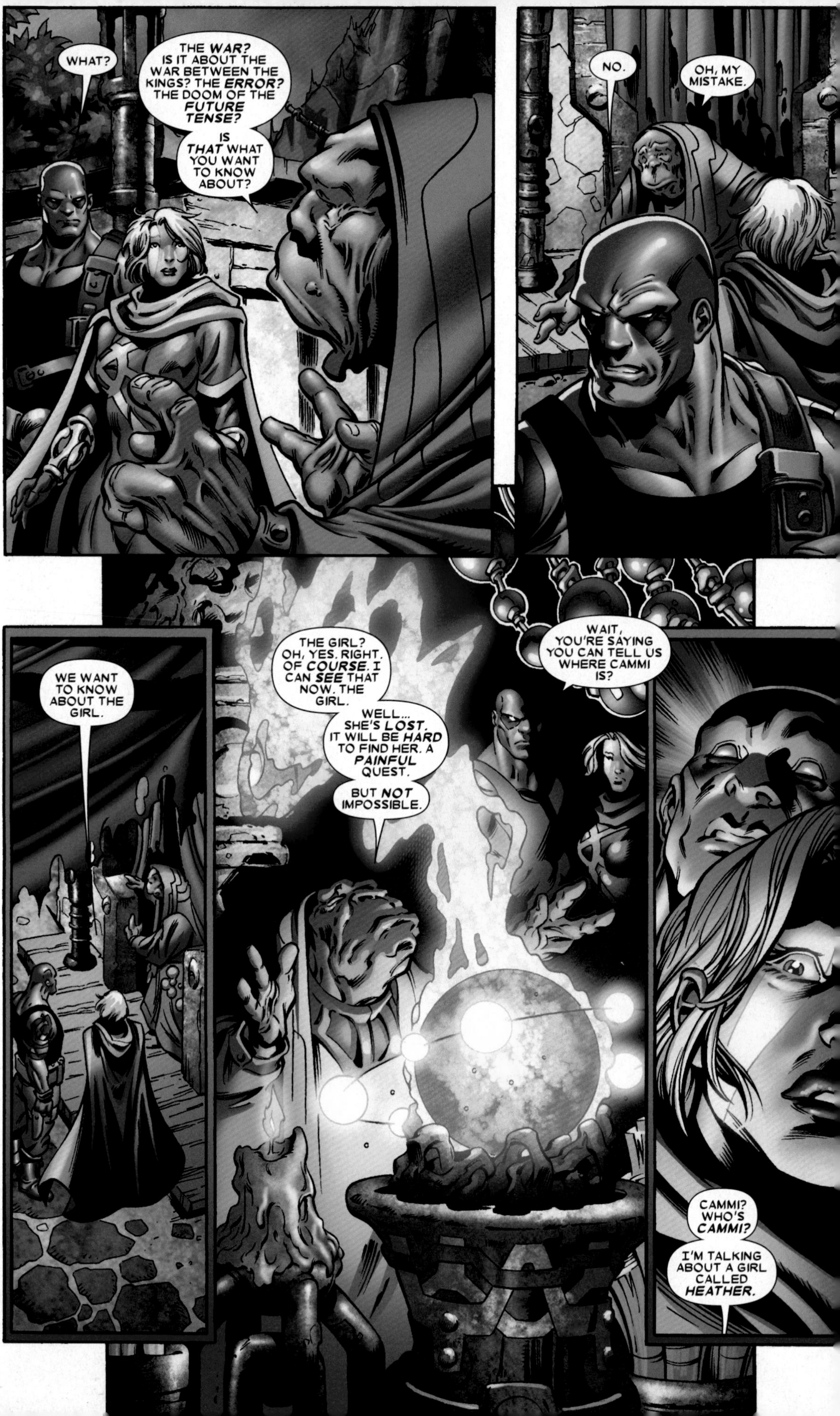
WHAT?
THE *WAR?* IS IT ABOUT THE WAR BETWEEN THE KINGS? THE *ERROR?* THE DOOM OF THE *FUTURE TENSE?*
IS *THAT* WHAT YOU WANT TO KNOW ABOUT?
NO.
OH, MY MISTAKE.
WE WANT TO KNOW ABOUT THE GIRL.
THE GIRL? OH, YES. RIGHT. OF *COURSE*. I CAN *SEE* THAT NOW. THE GIRL.
WELL... SHE'S *LOST*. IT WILL BE *HARD* TO FIND HER. A *PAINFUL* QUEST.
BUT *NOT* IMPOSSIBLE.
WAIT, YOU'RE SAYING YOU CAN TELL US WHERE CAMMI IS?
CAMMI? WHO'S *CAMMI?*
I'M TALKING ABOUT A GIRL CALLED *HEATHER*.

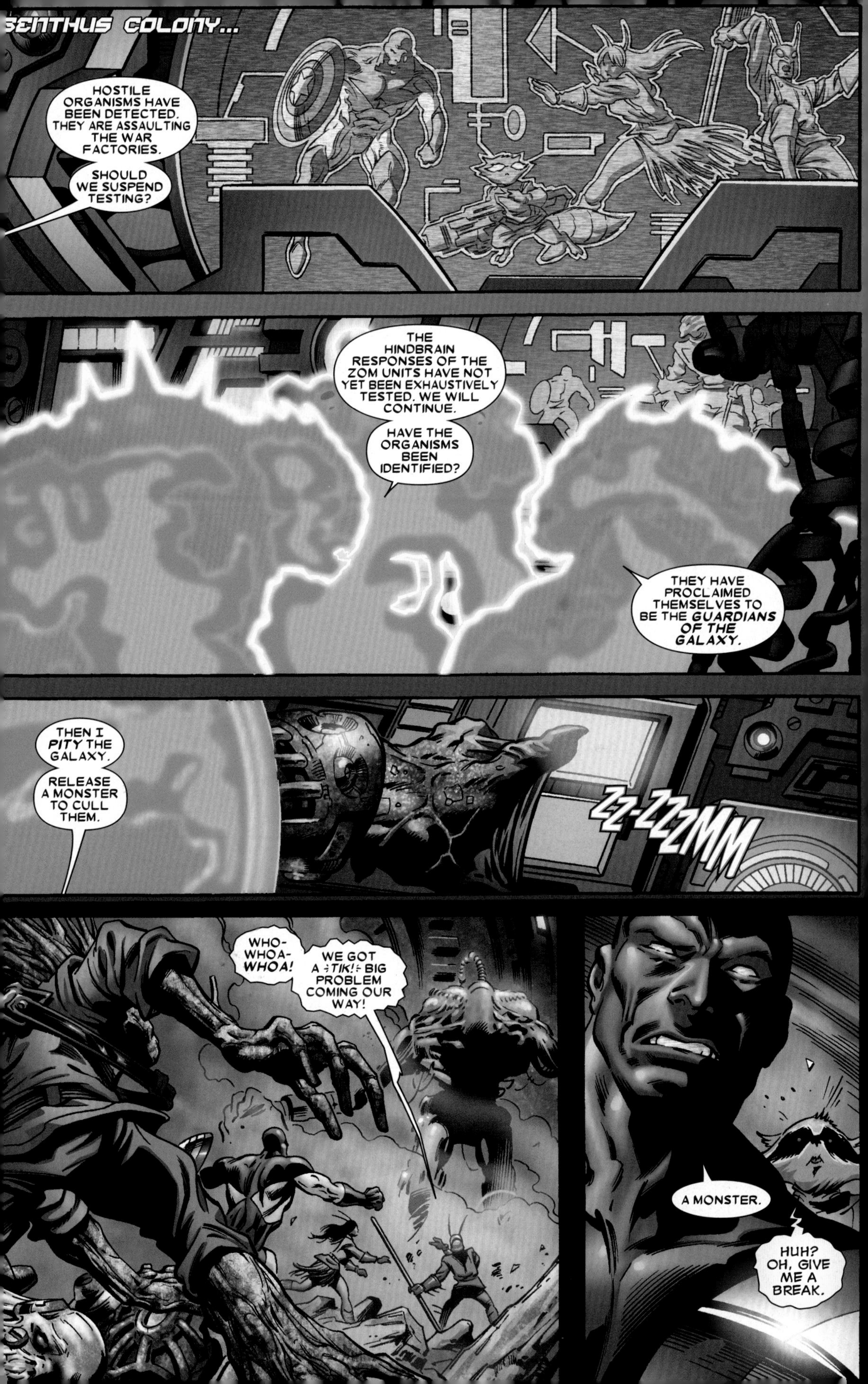

BENTHUS COLONY...
HOSTILE ORGANISMS HAVE BEEN DETECTED. THEY ARE ASSAULTING THE WAR FACTORIES.
SHOULD WE SUSPEND TESTING?
THE HINDBRAIN RESPONSES OF THE ZOM UNITS HAVE NOT YET BEEN EXHAUSTIVELY TESTED. WE WILL CONTINUE.
HAVE THE ORGANISMS BEEN IDENTIFIED?
THEY HAVE PROCLAIMED THEMSELVES TO BE THE GUARDIANS OF THE GALAXY.
THEN I PITY THE GALAXY.
RELEASE A MONSTER TO CULL THEM.
ZZ-ZZZMM
WHO-WHOA-WHOA!
WE GOT A -TIK!- BIG PROBLEM COMING OUR WAY!
A MONSTER.
HUH? OH, GIVE ME A BREAK.

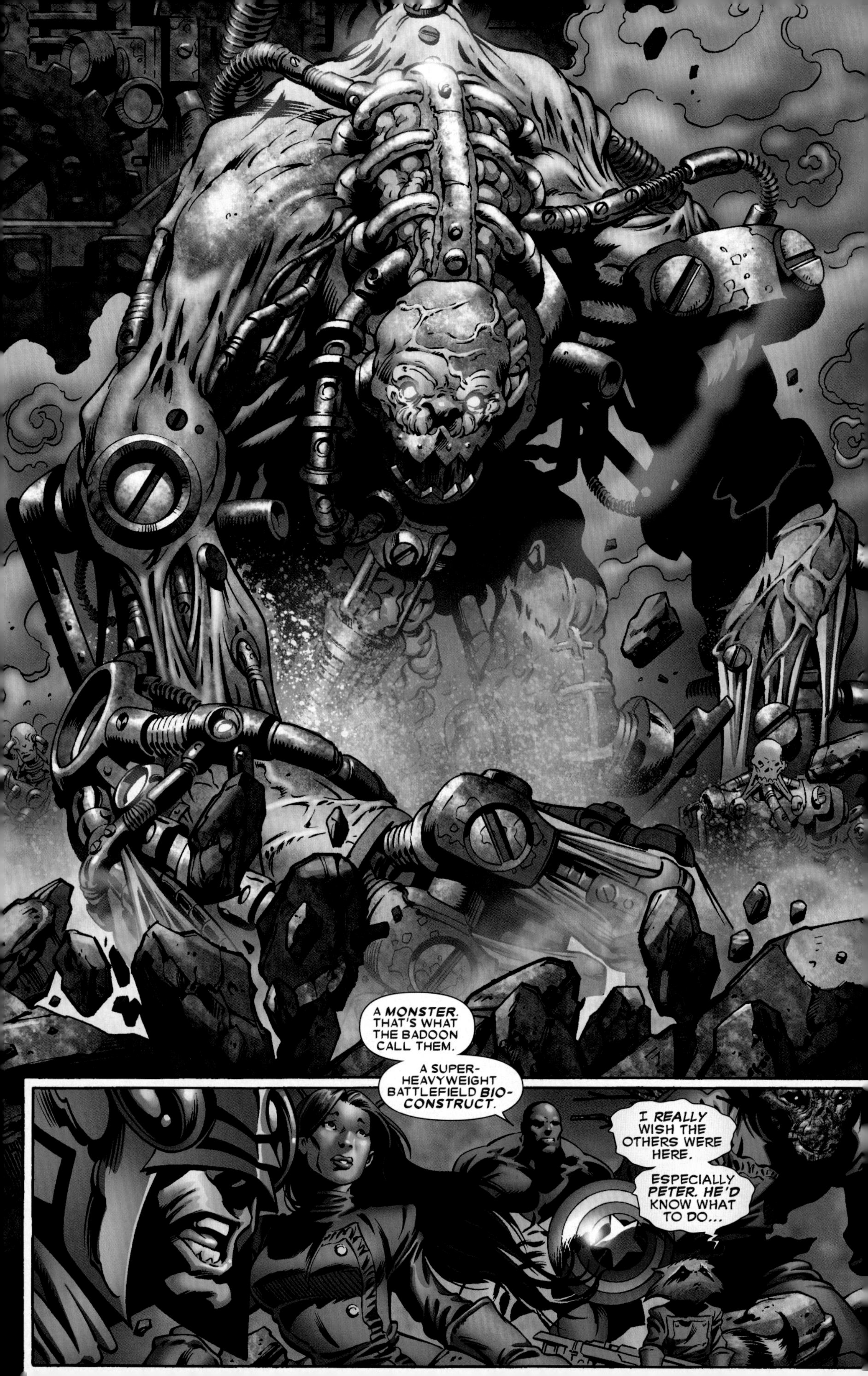

A MONSTER. THAT'S WHAT THE BADOON CALL THEM.
A SUPER-HEAVYWEIGHT BATTLEFIELD BIO-CONSTRUCT.
I REALLY WISH THE OTHERS WERE HERE.
ESPECIALLY PETER. HE'D KNOW WHAT TO DO...

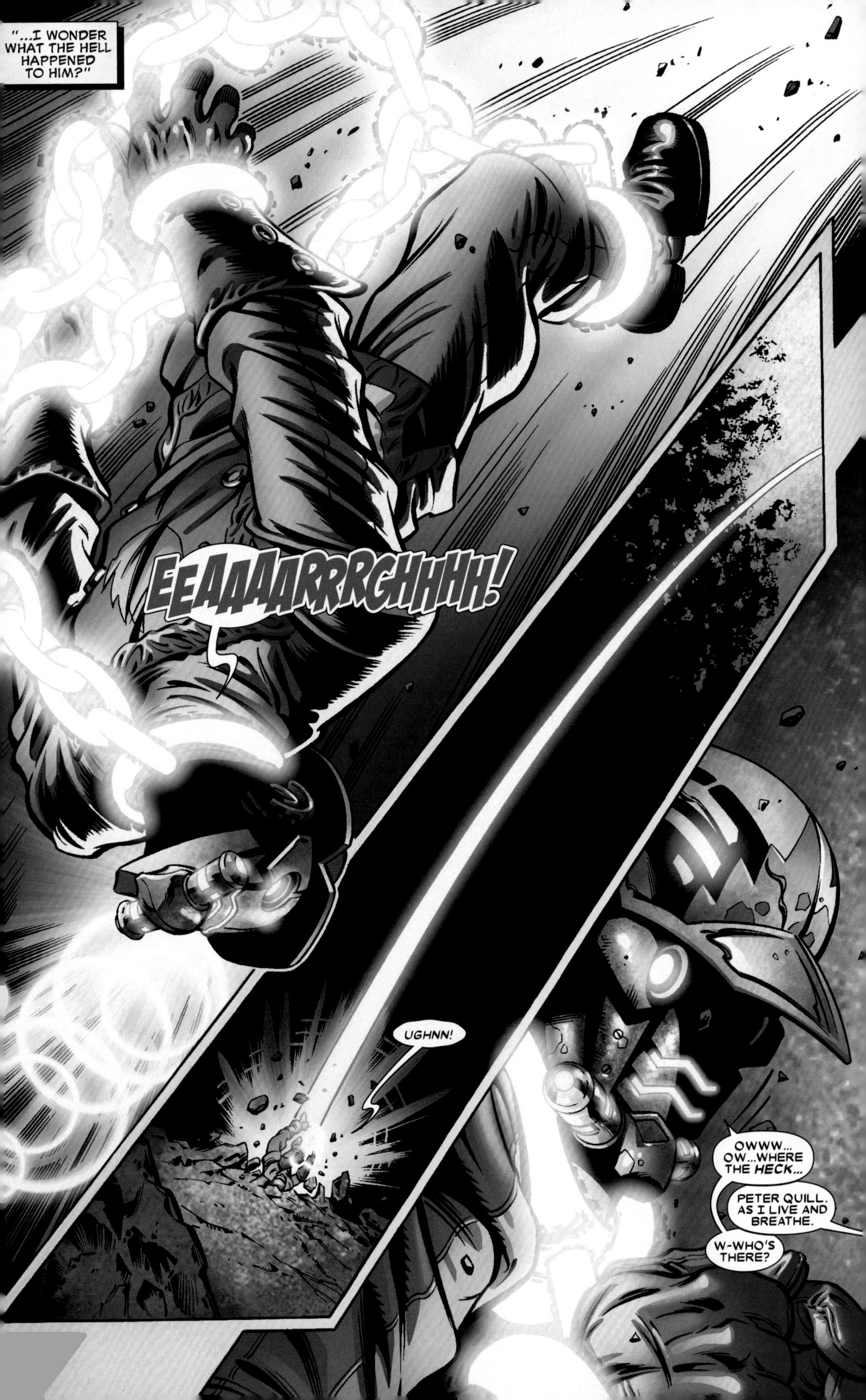
"...I WONDER WHAT THE HELL HAPPENED TO HIM?"
EEAAAARRRGHHHH!
UGHNN!
OWWW... OW...WHERE THE HECK...
PETER QUILL. AS I LIVE AND BREATHE.
W-WHO'S THERE?

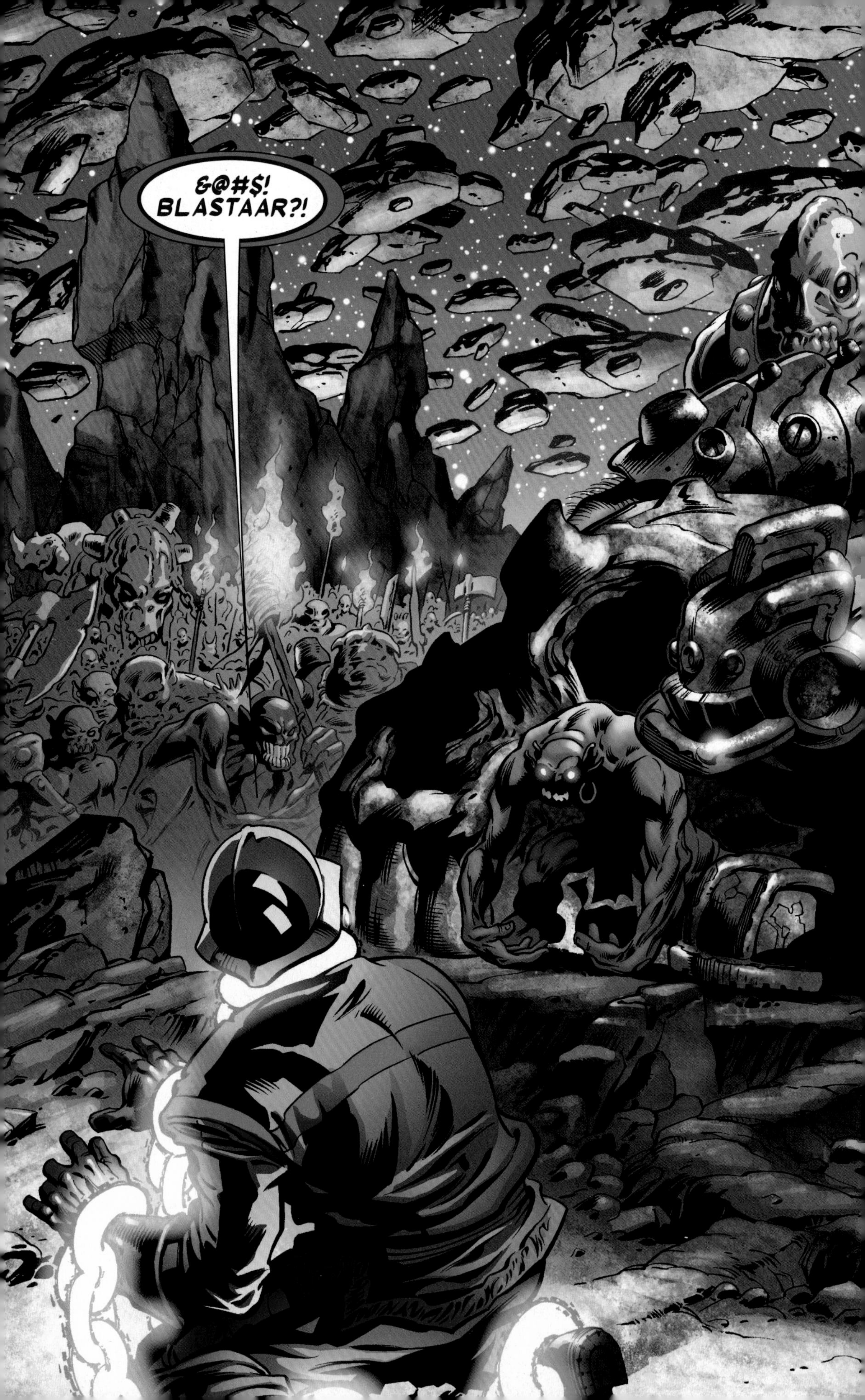
&@#$! BLASTAAR?!

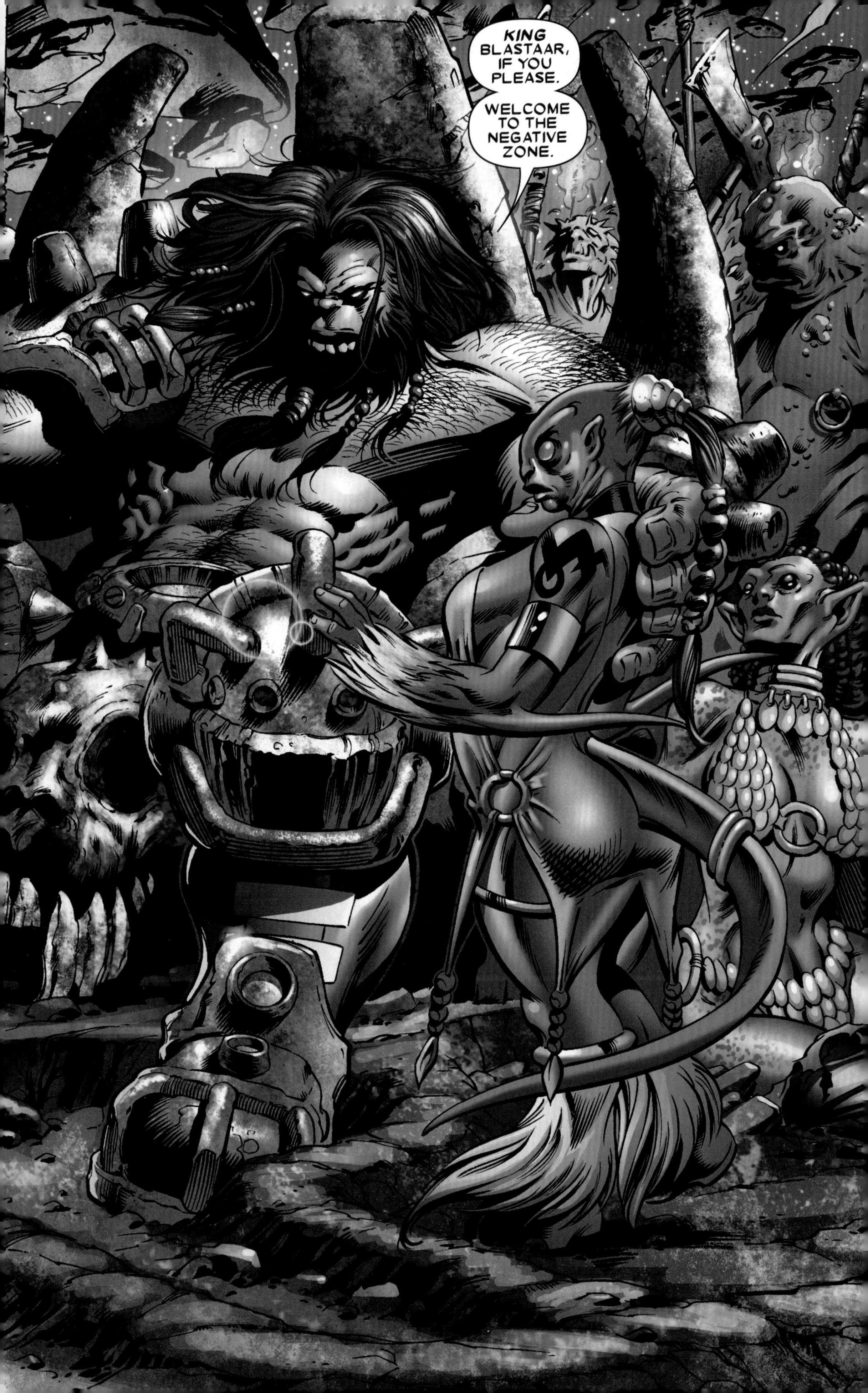
KING BLASTAAR, IF YOU PLEASE.
WELCOME TO THE NEGATIVE ZONE.

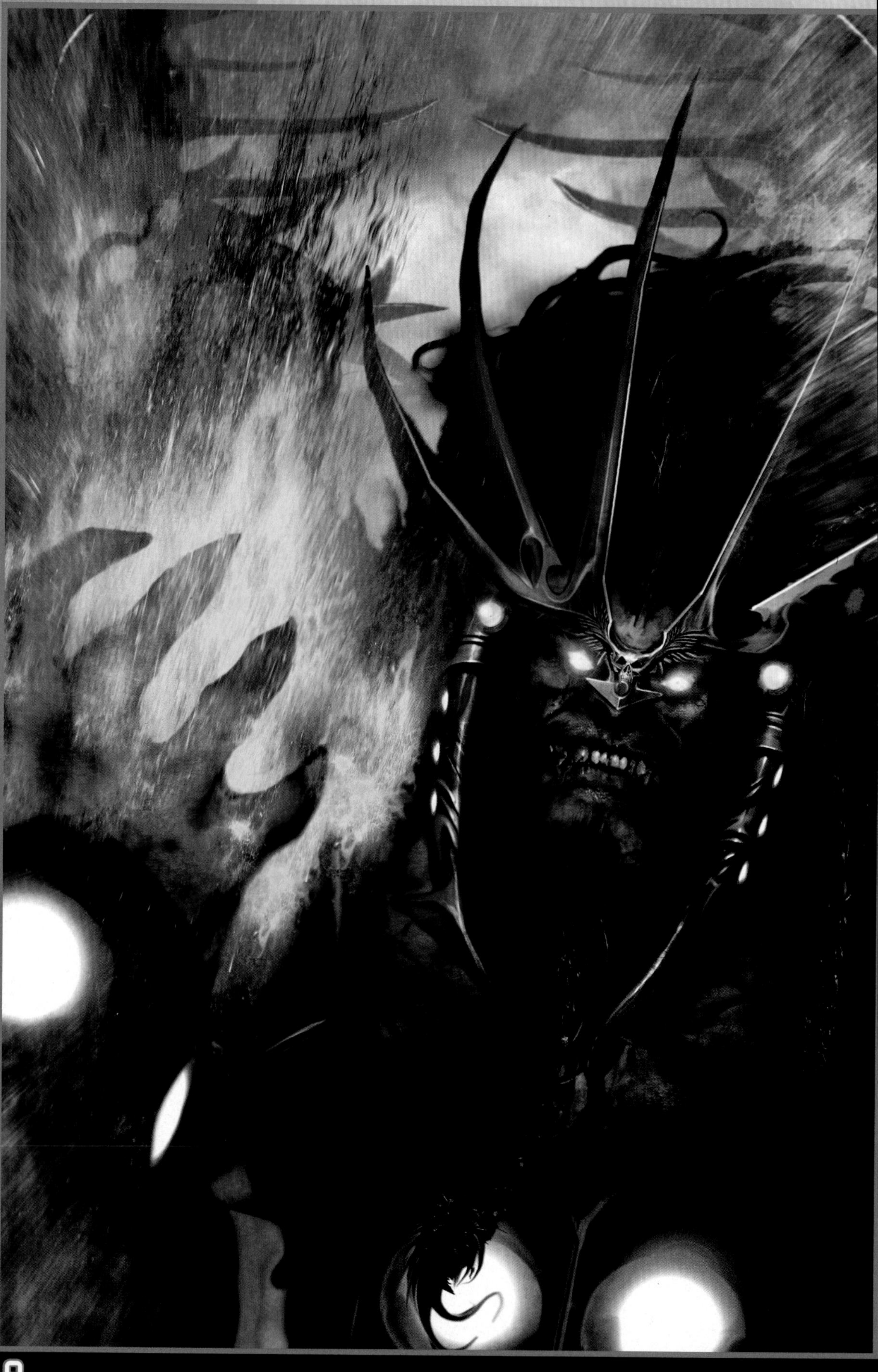

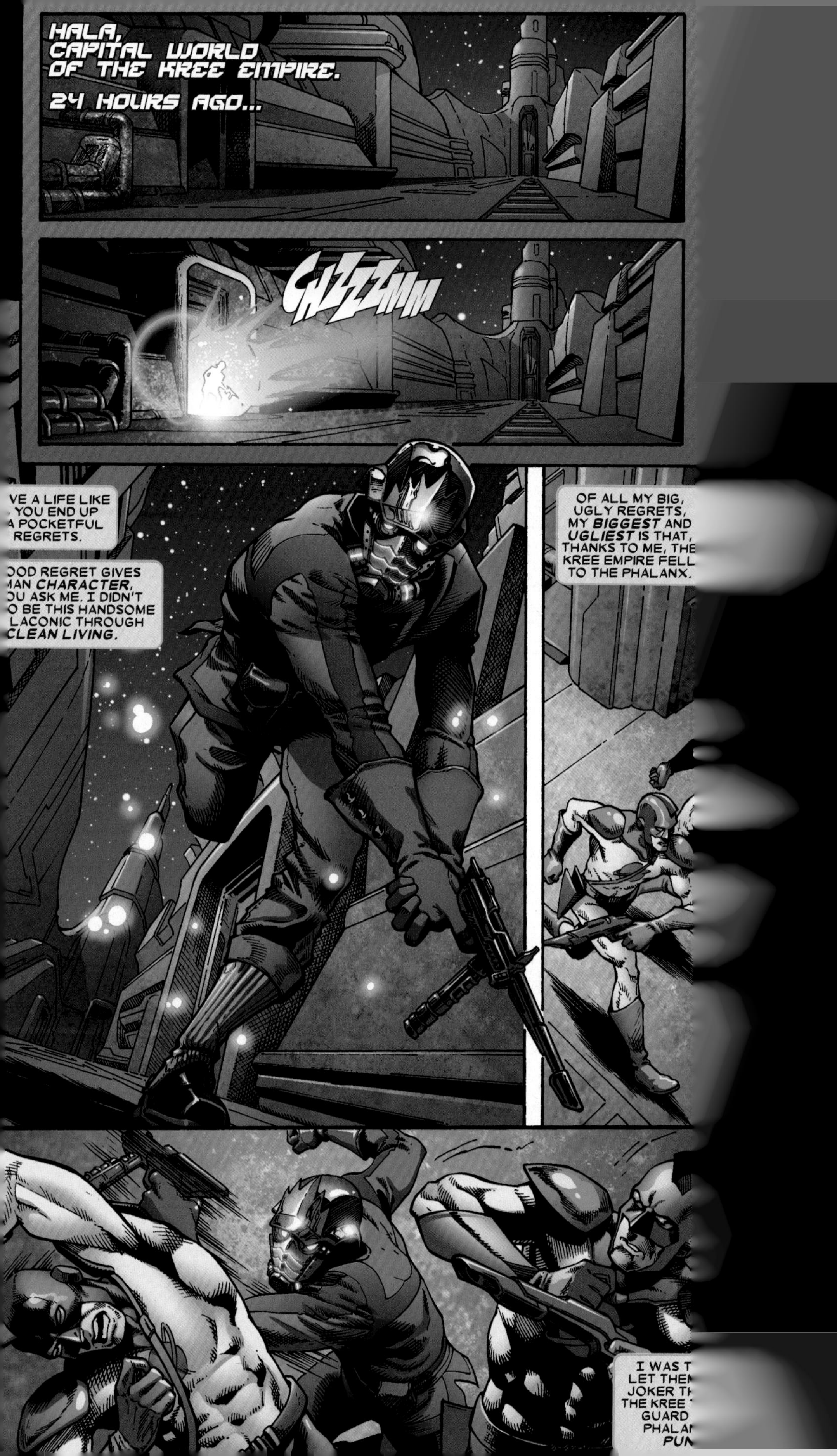
HALA, CAPITAL WORLD OF THE KREE EMPIRE.
24 HOURS AGO...
CHZZZMM
VE A LIFE LIKE YOU END UP A POCKETFUL REGRETS.
OOD REGRET GIVES MAN CHARACTER, OU ASK ME. I DIDN'T O BE THIS HANDSOME LACONIC THROUGH CLEAN LIVING.
OF ALL MY BIG, UGLY REGRETS, MY BIGGEST AND UGLIEST IS THAT, THANKS TO ME, THE KREE EMPIRE FELL TO THE PHALANX.
I WAS T LET THEM JOKER TH THE KREE GUARD PHALAN PUN

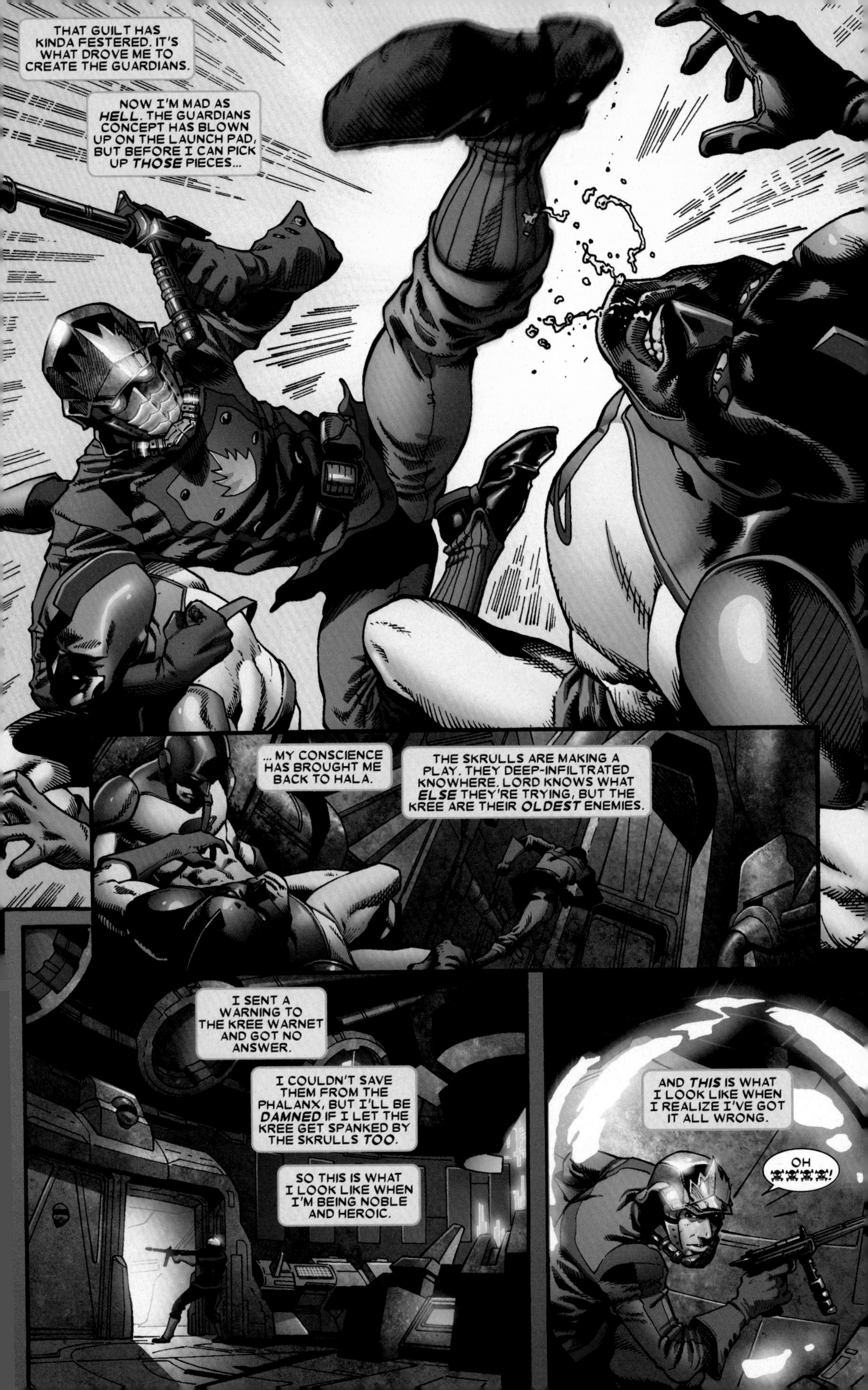

THAT GUILT HAS KINDA FESTERED. IT'S WHAT DROVE ME TO CREATE THE GUARDIANS.
NOW I'M MAD AS *HELL*. THE GUARDIANS CONCEPT HAS BLOWN UP ON THE LAUNCH PAD, BUT BEFORE I CAN PICK UP *THOSE* PIECES...
...MY CONSCIENCE HAS BROUGHT ME BACK TO HALA.
THE SKRULLS ARE MAKING A PLAY. THEY DEEP-INFILTRATED KNOWHERE. LORD KNOWS WHAT *ELSE* THEY'RE TRYING, BUT THE KREE ARE THEIR *OLDEST* ENEMIES.
I SENT A WARNING TO THE KREE WARNET AND GOT NO ANSWER.
I COULDN'T SAVE THEM FROM THE PHALANX, BUT I'LL BE *DAMNED* IF I LET THE KREE GET SPANKED BY THE SKRULLS *TOO*.
SO THIS IS WHAT I LOOK LIKE WHEN I'M BEING NOBLE AND HEROIC.
AND *THIS* IS WHAT I LOOK LIKE WHEN I REALIZE I'VE GOT IT ALL WRONG.
OH

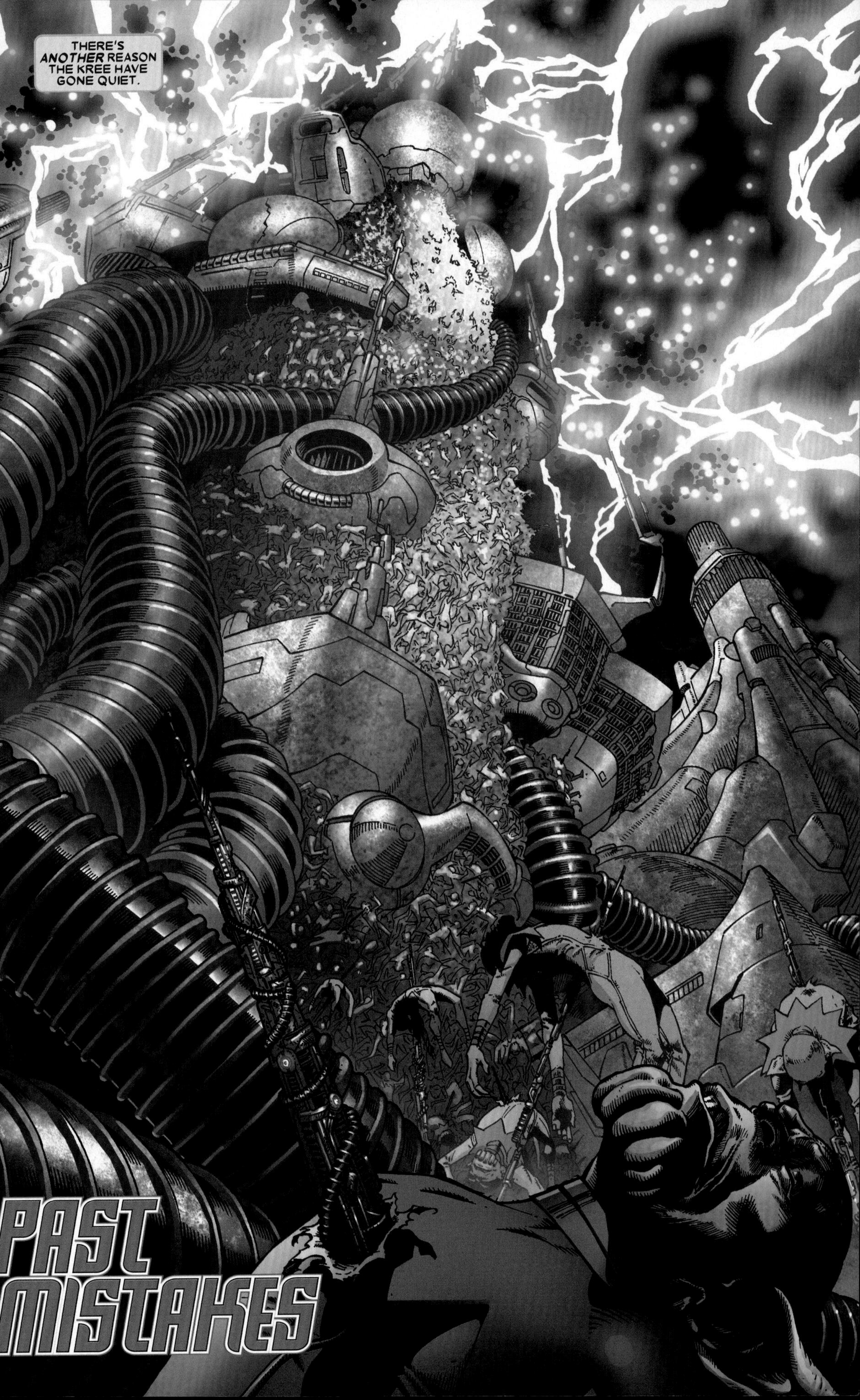
THERE'S ANOTHER REASON THE KREE HAVE GONE QUIET.
PAST MISTAKES

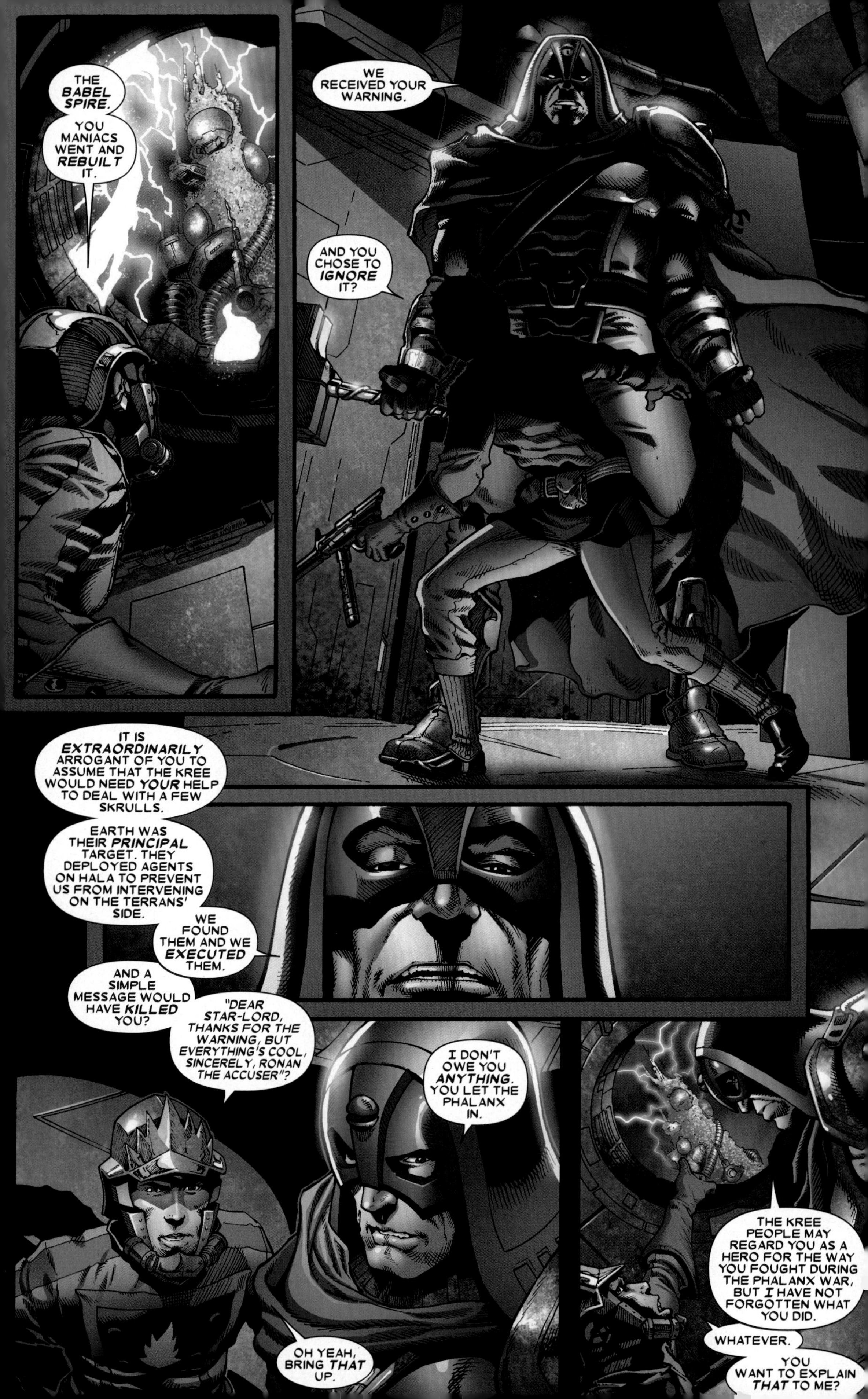
THE BABEL SPIRE.
YOU MANIACS WENT AND REBUILT IT.
WE RECEIVED YOUR WARNING.
AND YOU CHOSE TO IGNORE IT?
IT IS EXTRAORDINARILY ARROGANT OF YOU TO ASSUME THAT THE KREE WOULD NEED YOUR HELP TO DEAL WITH A FEW SKRULLS.
EARTH WAS THEIR PRINCIPAL TARGET. THEY DEPLOYED AGENTS ON HALA TO PREVENT US FROM INTERVENING ON THE TERRANS' SIDE.
WE FOUND THEM AND WE EXECUTED THEM.
AND A SIMPLE MESSAGE WOULD HAVE KILLED YOU?
"DEAR STAR-LORD, THANKS FOR THE WARNING, BUT EVERYTHING'S COOL, SINCERELY, RONAN THE ACCUSER"?
I DON'T OWE YOU ANYTHING. YOU LET THE PHALANX IN.
OH YEAH, BRING THAT UP.
THE KREE PEOPLE MAY REGARD YOU AS A HERO FOR THE WAY YOU FOUGHT DURING THE PHALANX WAR, BUT I HAVE NOT FORGOTTEN WHAT YOU DID.
WHATEVER.
YOU WANT TO EXPLAIN THAT TO ME?

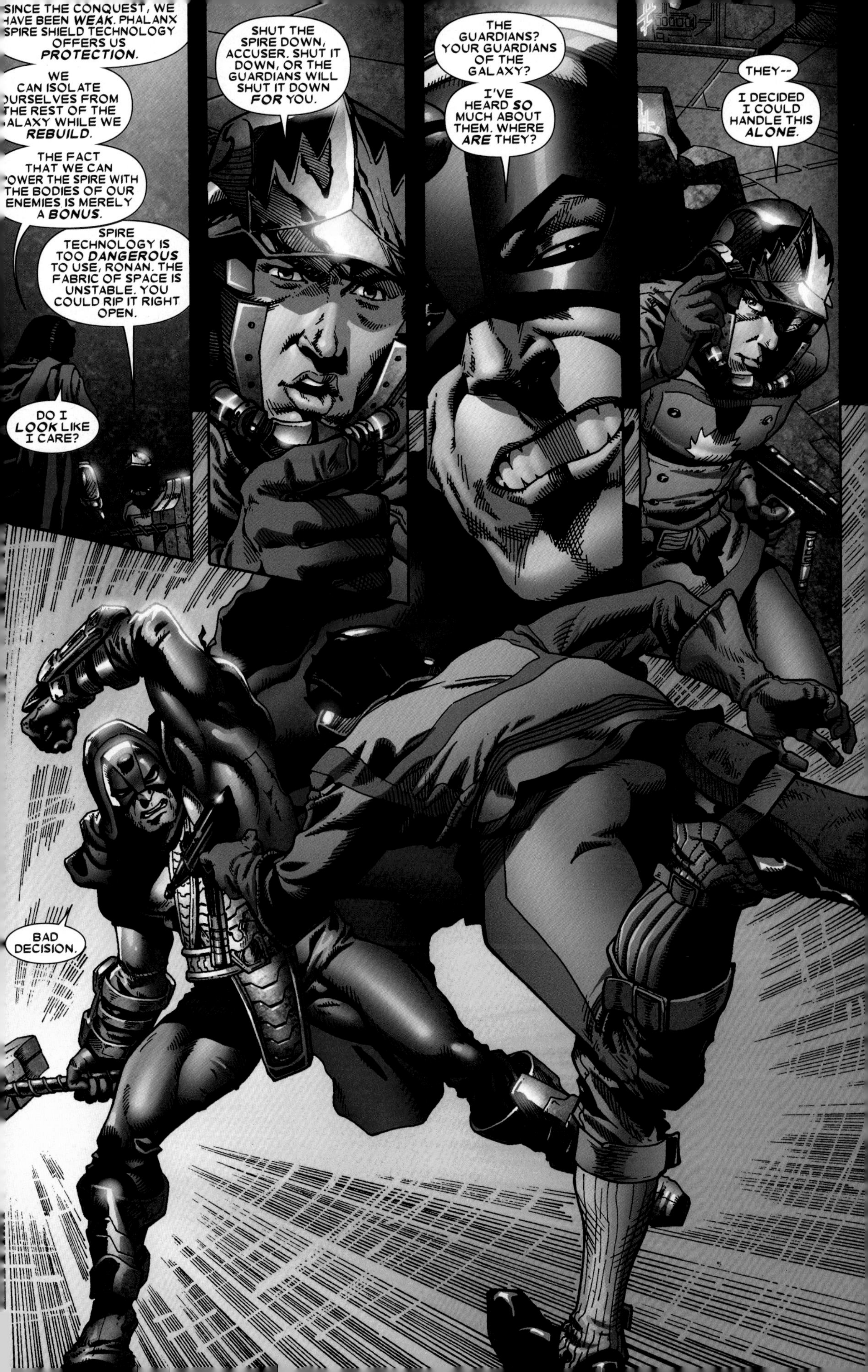
SINCE THE CONQUEST, WE HAVE BEEN WEAK. PHALANX SPIRE SHIELD TECHNOLOGY OFFERS US PROTECTION.
WE CAN ISOLATE OURSELVES FROM THE REST OF THE GALAXY WHILE WE REBUILD.
THE FACT THAT WE CAN POWER THE SPIRE WITH THE BODIES OF OUR ENEMIES IS MERELY A BONUS.
SPIRE TECHNOLOGY IS TOO DANGEROUS TO USE, RONAN. THE FABRIC OF SPACE IS UNSTABLE. YOU COULD RIP IT RIGHT OPEN.
DO I LOOK LIKE I CARE?
SHUT THE SPIRE DOWN, ACCUSER. SHUT IT DOWN, OR THE GUARDIANS WILL SHUT IT DOWN FOR YOU.
THE GUARDIANS? YOUR GUARDIANS OF THE GALAXY?
I'VE HEARD SO MUCH ABOUT THEM. WHERE ARE THEY?
THEY--
I DECIDED I COULD HANDLE THIS ALONE.
BAD DECISION.

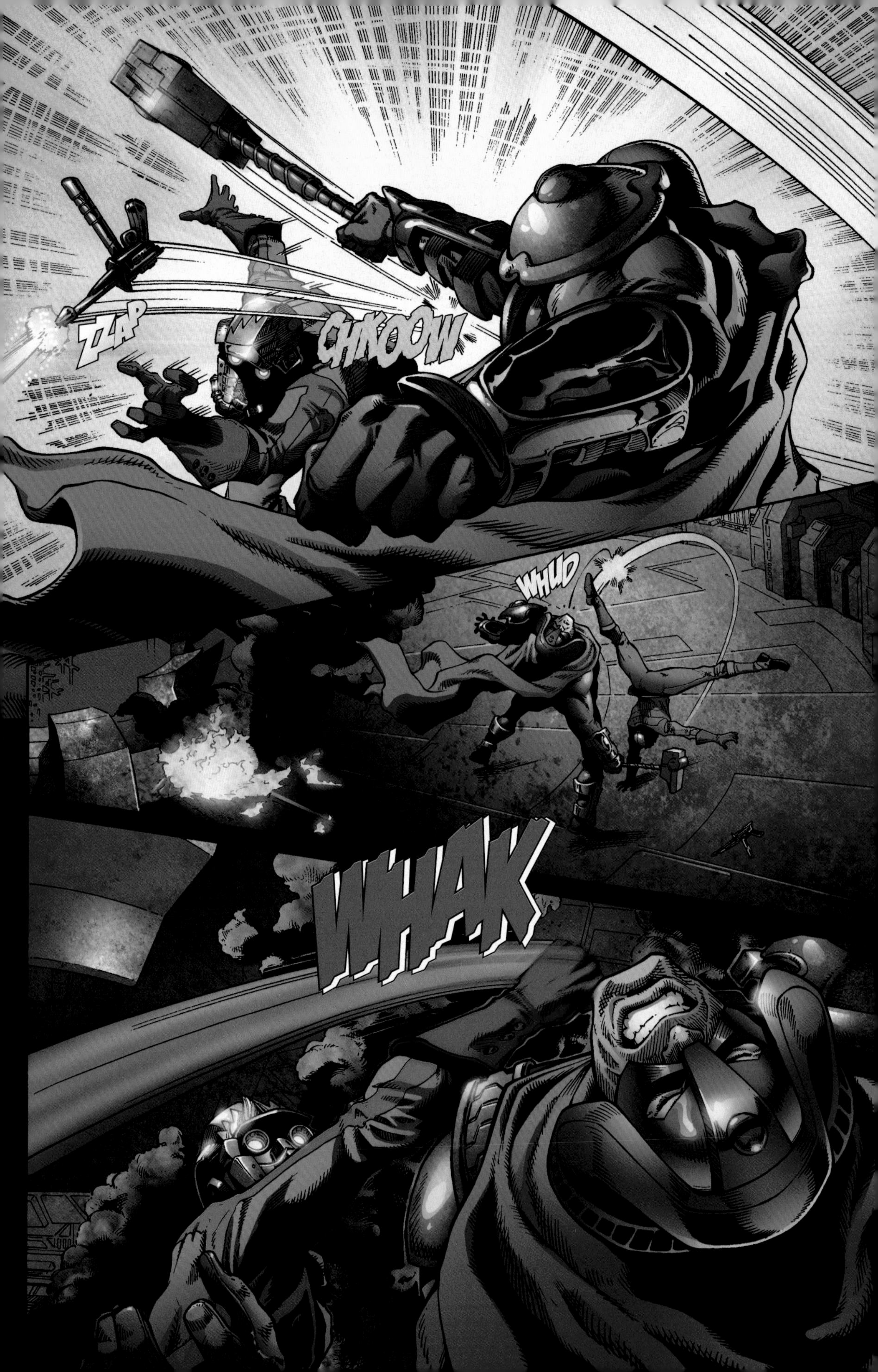
ZZAP
CHKOOW
WHUD
WHAK

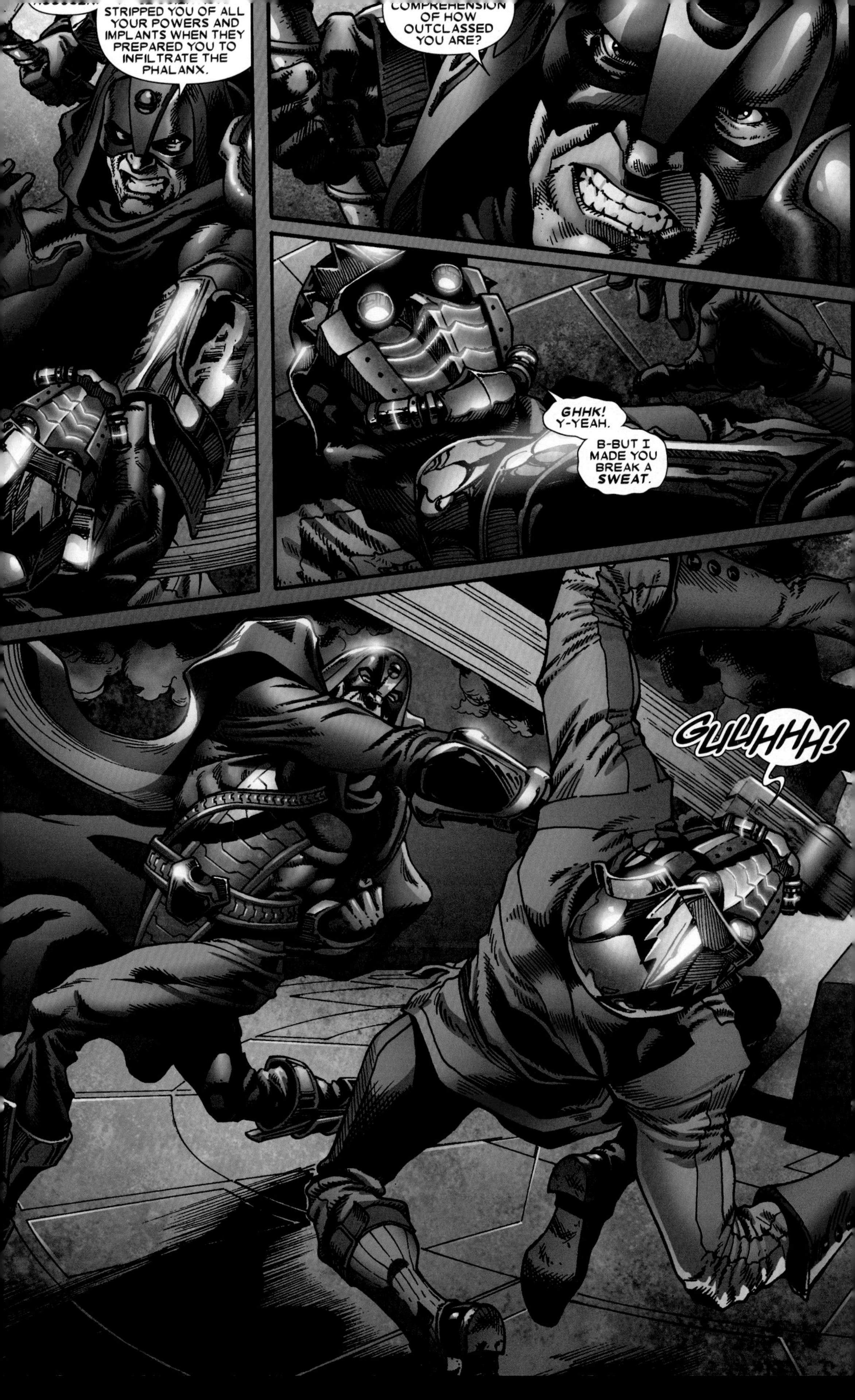
STRIPPED YOU OF ALL YOUR POWERS AND IMPLANTS WHEN THEY PREPARED YOU TO INFILTRATE THE PHALANX.
COMPREHENSION OF HOW OUTCLASSED YOU ARE?
GHHK! Y-YEAH.
B-BUT I MADE YOU BREAK A SWEAT.
GULHHH!

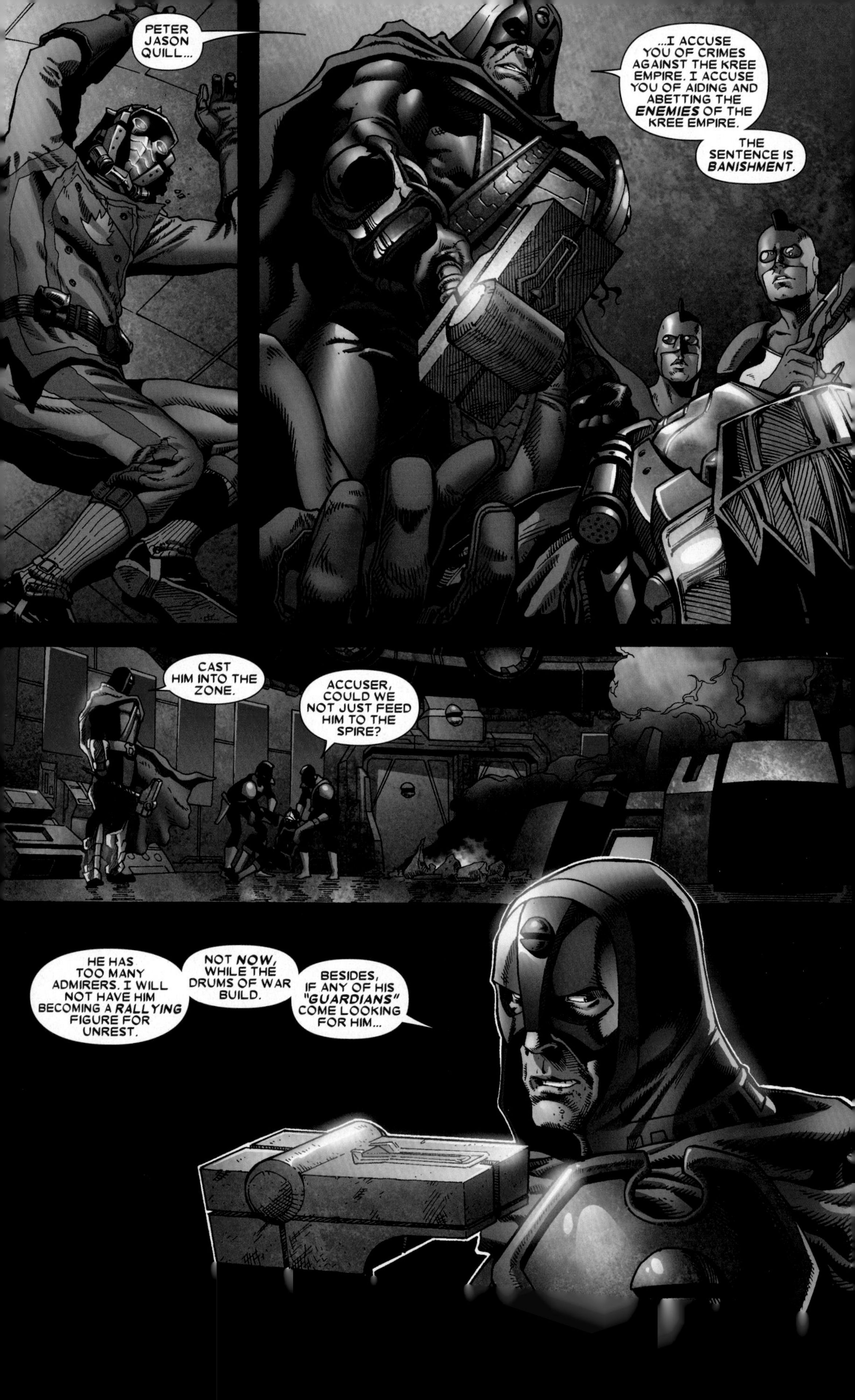
PETER JASON QUILL...
...I ACCUSE YOU OF CRIMES AGAINST THE KREE EMPIRE. I ACCUSE YOU OF AIDING AND ABETTING THE ENEMIES OF THE KREE EMPIRE.
THE SENTENCE IS BANISHMENT.
CAST HIM INTO THE ZONE.
ACCUSER, COULD WE NOT JUST FEED HIM TO THE SPIRE?
HE HAS TOO MANY ADMIRERS. I WILL NOT HAVE HIM BECOMING A RALLYING FIGURE FOR UNREST.
NOT NOW, WHILE THE DRUMS OF WAR BUILD.
BESIDES, IF ANY OF HIS "GUARDIANS" COME LOOKING FOR HIM...

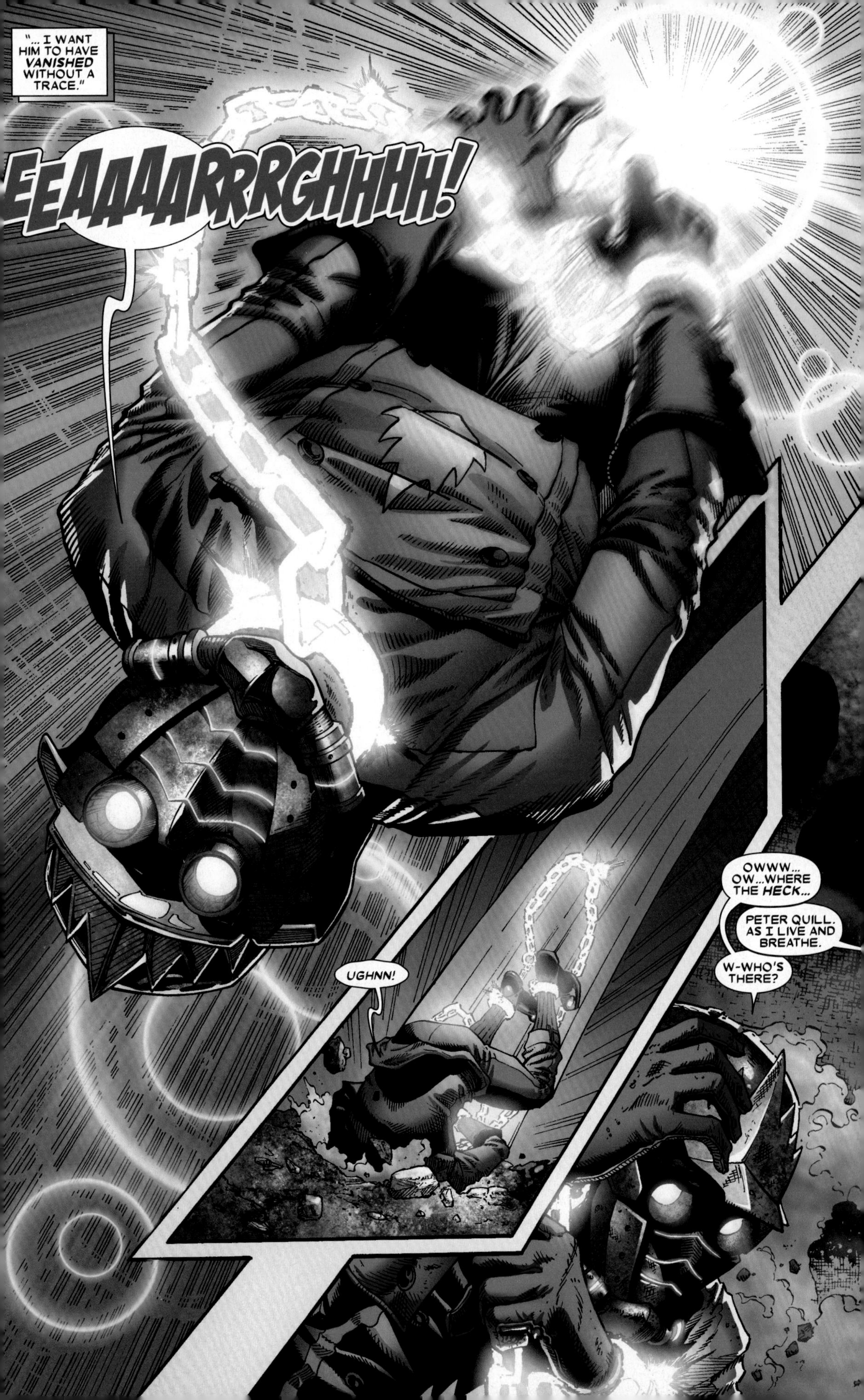
"... I WANT HIM TO HAVE VANISHED WITHOUT A TRACE."
EEAAAAARRRGHHHH!
UGHNN!
OWWW... OW...WHERE THE HECK...
PETER QUILL. AS I LIVE AND BREATHE.
W-WHO'S THERE?

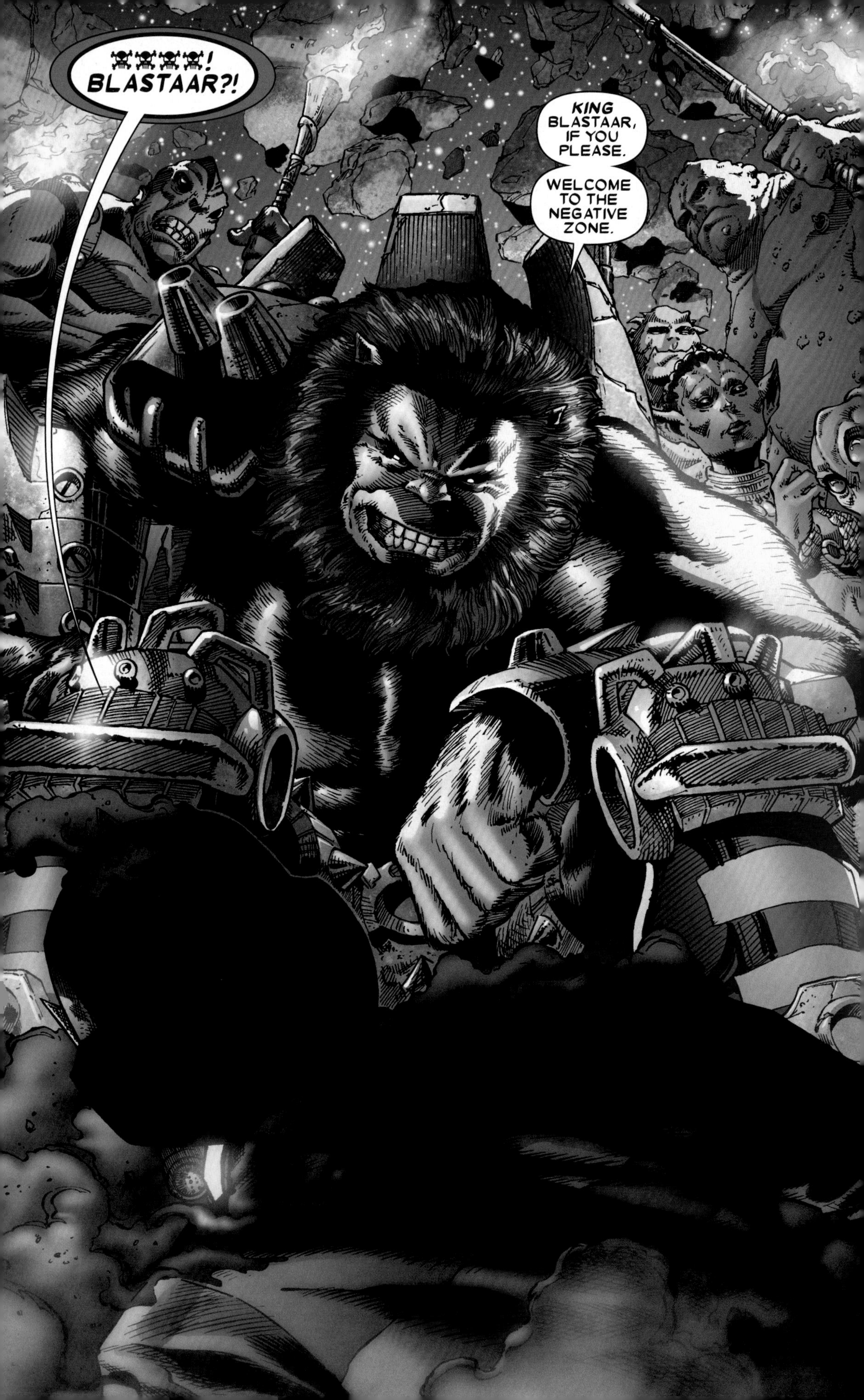
☠☠☠☠! BLASTAAR?!
KING BLASTAAR, IF YOU PLEASE.
WELCOME TO THE NEGATIVE ZONE.

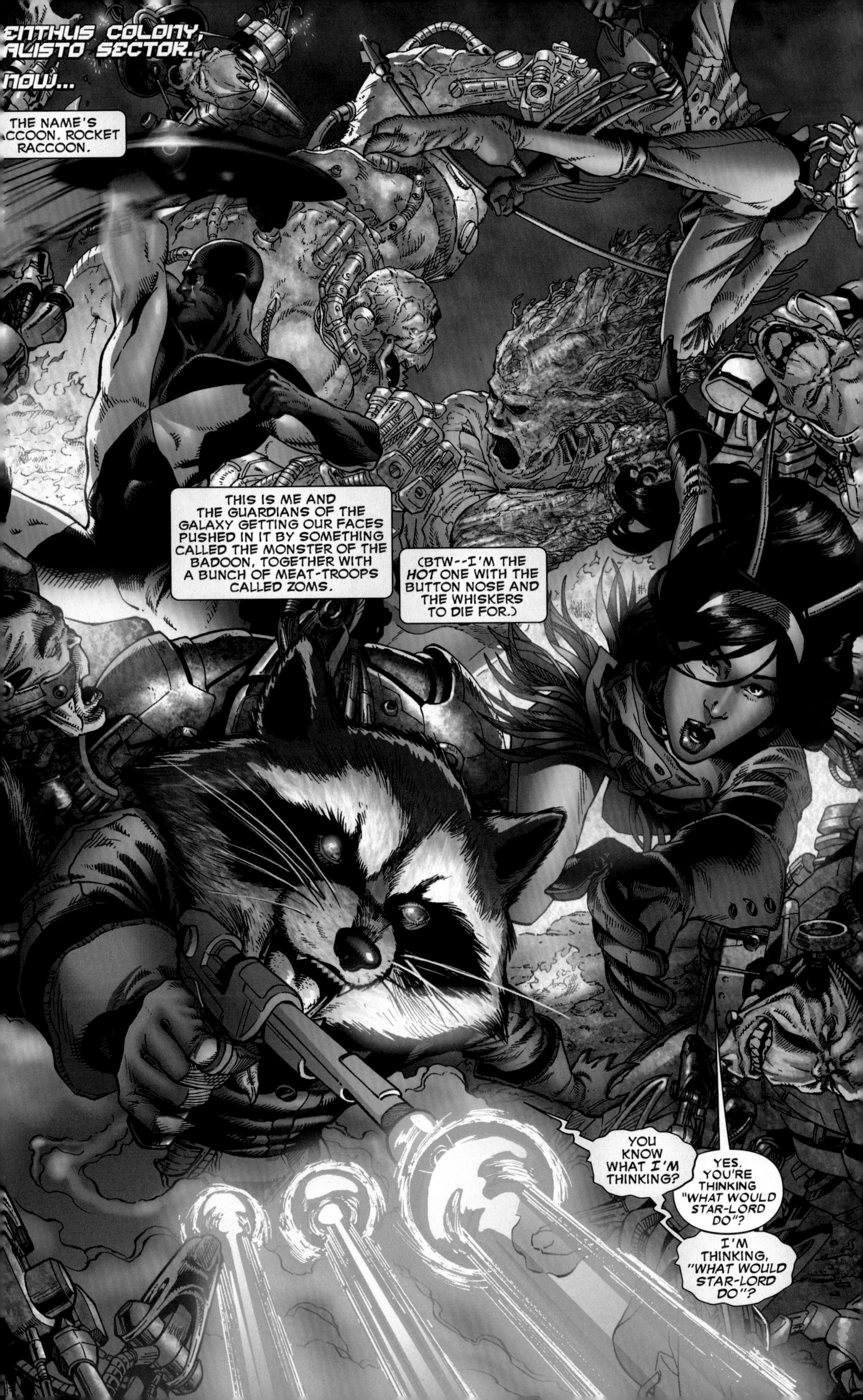

ENTHUS COLONY, ALISTO SECTOR.
NOW...
THE NAME'S ACCOON. ROCKET RACCOON.
THIS IS ME AND THE GUARDIANS OF THE GALAXY GETTING OUR FACES PUSHED IN IT BY SOMETHING CALLED THE MONSTER OF THE BADOON, TOGETHER WITH A BUNCH OF MEAT-TROOPS CALLED ZOMS.
(BTW--I'M THE *HOT* ONE WITH THE BUTTON NOSE AND THE WHISKERS TO DIE FOR.)
YOU KNOW WHAT *I'M* THINKING?
YES. YOU'RE THINKING "WHAT WOULD STAR-LORD DO"?
I'M THINKING, "WHAT WOULD STAR-LORD DO"?

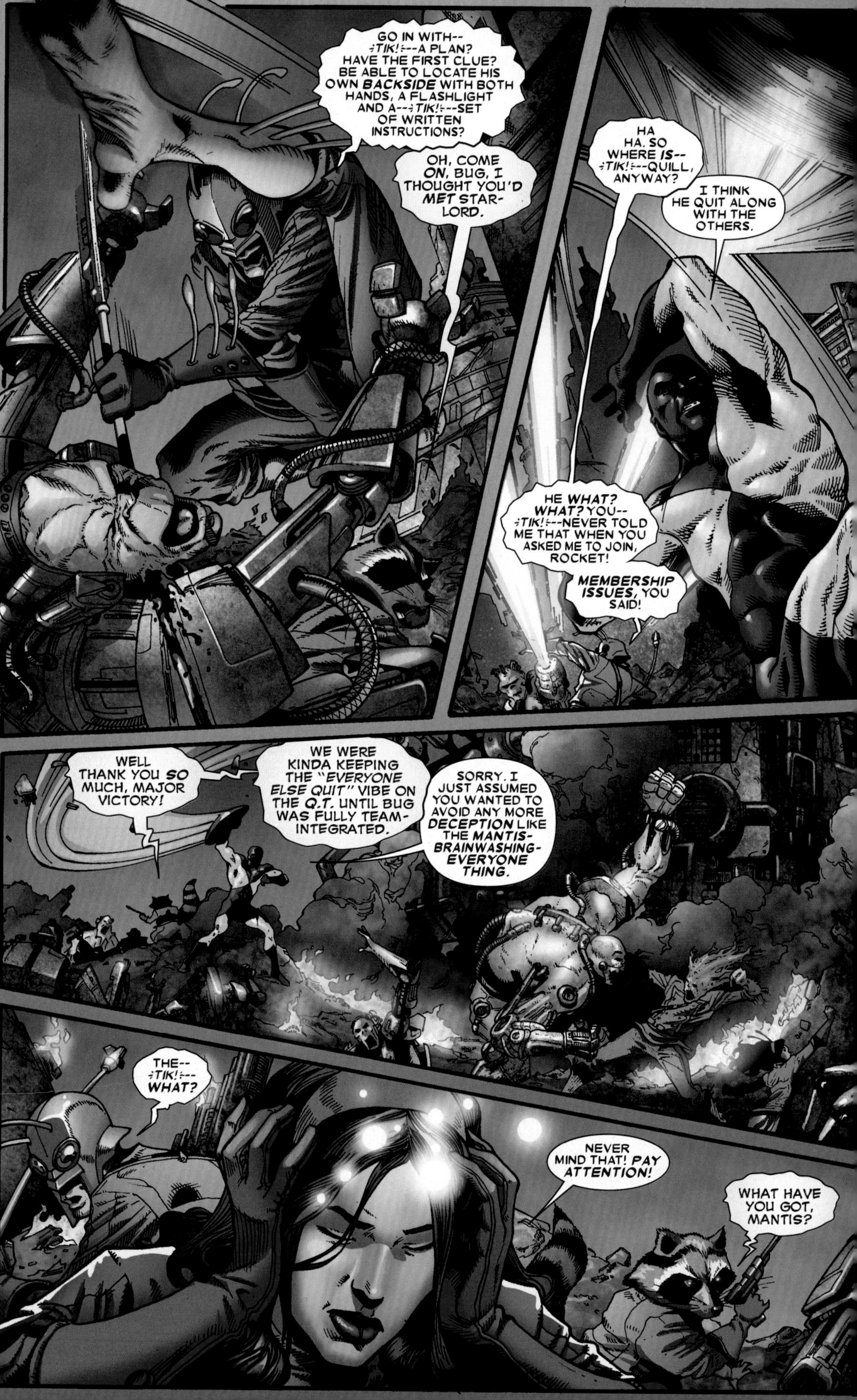
GO IN WITH-- ⸗TIK!⸗--A PLAN? HAVE THE FIRST CLUE? BE ABLE TO LOCATE HIS OWN BACKSIDE WITH BOTH HANDS, A FLASHLIGHT AND A--⸗TIK!⸗--SET OF WRITTEN INSTRUCTIONS?
OH, COME ON, BUG, I THOUGHT YOU'D MET STAR-LORD.
HA HA. SO WHERE IS-- ⸗TIK!⸗--QUILL, ANYWAY?
I THINK HE QUIT ALONG WITH THE OTHERS.
HE WHAT? WHAT? YOU-- ⸗TIK!⸗--NEVER TOLD ME THAT WHEN YOU ASKED ME TO JOIN, ROCKET!
MEMBERSHIP ISSUES, YOU SAID!
WELL THANK YOU SO MUCH, MAJOR VICTORY!
WE WERE KINDA KEEPING THE "EVERYONE ELSE QUIT" VIBE ON THE Q.T. UNTIL BUG WAS FULLY TEAM-INTEGRATED.
SORRY. I JUST ASSUMED YOU WANTED TO AVOID ANY MORE DECEPTION LIKE THE MANTIS-BRAINWASHING-EVERYONE THING.
THE-- ⸗TIK!⸗-- WHAT?
NEVER MIND THAT! PAY ATTENTION!
WHAT HAVE YOU GOT, MANTIS?

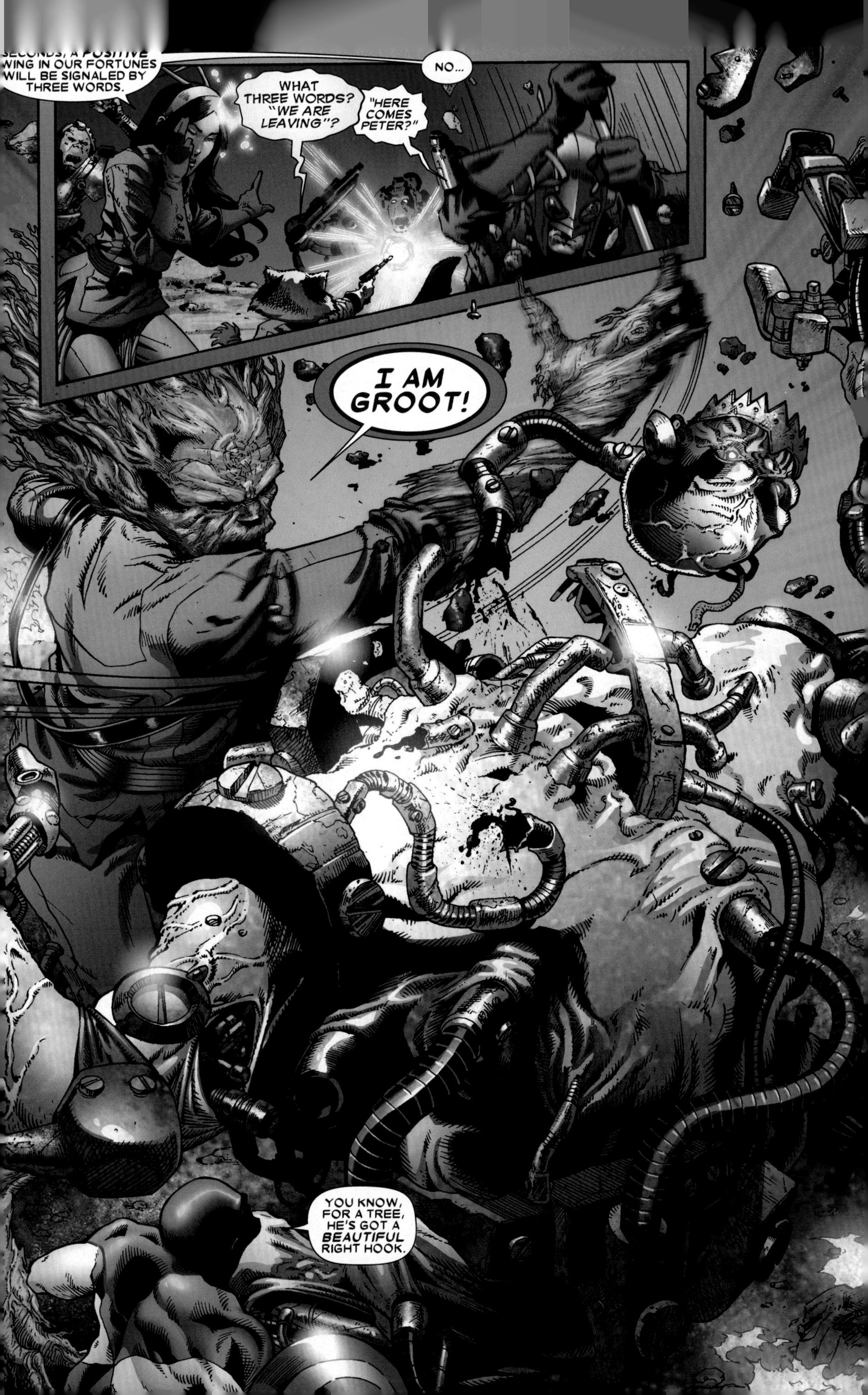
SECONDS, A POSITIVE SWING IN OUR FORTUNES WILL BE SIGNALED BY THREE WORDS.
NO...
WHAT THREE WORDS? "WE ARE LEAVING"?
"HERE COMES PETER?"
I AM GROOT!
YOU KNOW, FOR A TREE, HE'S GOT A BEAUTIFUL RIGHT HOOK.

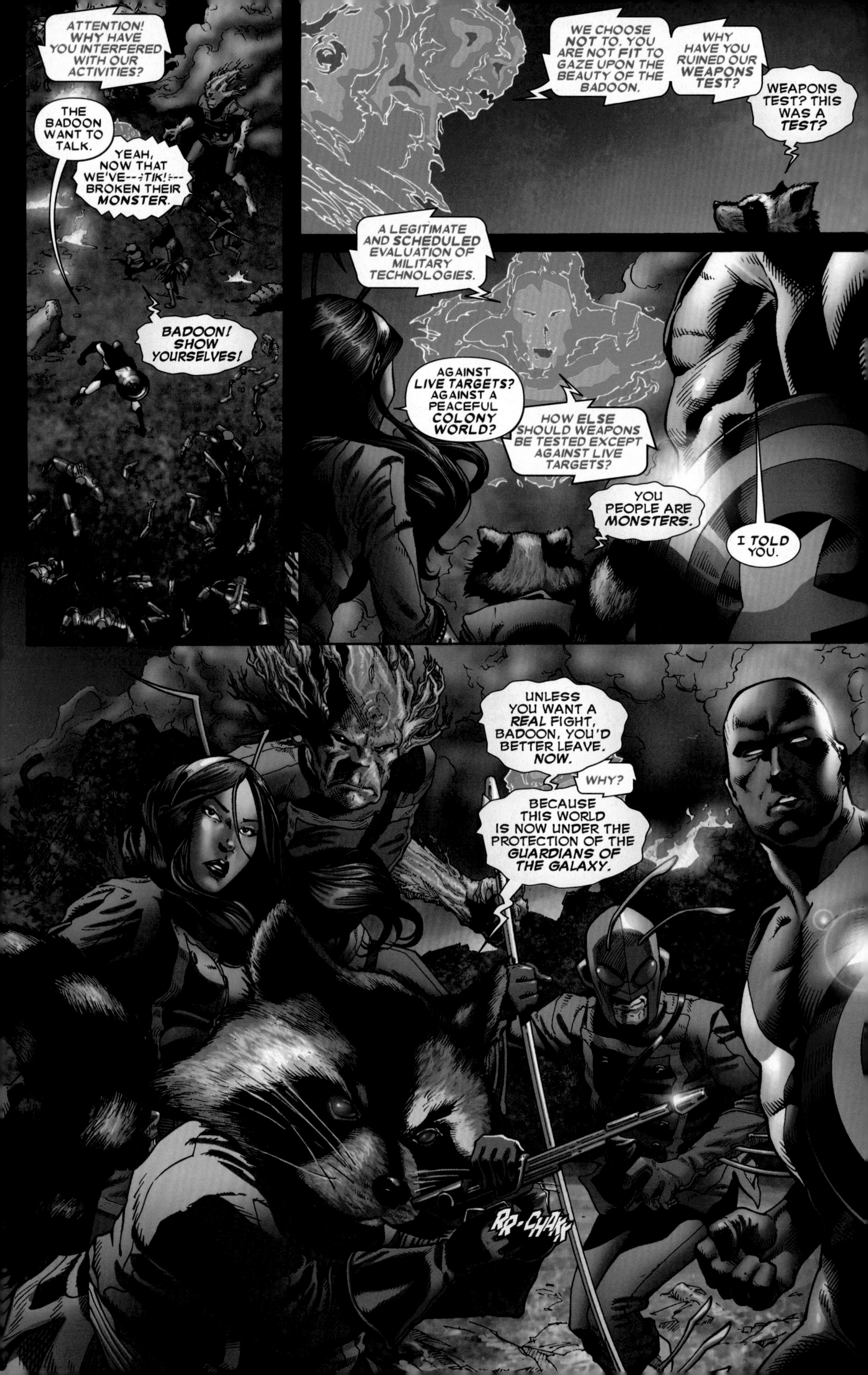
ATTENTION! WHY HAVE YOU INTERFERED WITH OUR ACTIVITIES?
THE BADOON WANT TO TALK.
YEAH, NOW THAT WE'VE--TIK!--BROKEN THEIR MONSTER.
BADOON! SHOW YOURSELVES!
WE CHOOSE NOT TO. YOU ARE NOT FIT TO GAZE UPON THE BEAUTY OF THE BADOON.
WHY HAVE YOU RUINED OUR WEAPONS TEST?
WEAPONS TEST? THIS WAS A TEST?
A LEGITIMATE AND SCHEDULED EVALUATION OF MILITARY TECHNOLOGIES.
AGAINST LIVE TARGETS? AGAINST A PEACEFUL COLONY WORLD?
HOW ELSE SHOULD WEAPONS BE TESTED EXCEPT AGAINST LIVE TARGETS?
YOU PEOPLE ARE MONSTERS.
I TOLD YOU.
UNLESS YOU WANT A REAL FIGHT, BADOON, YOU'D BETTER LEAVE. NOW.
WHY?
BECAUSE THIS WORLD IS NOW UNDER THE PROTECTION OF THE GUARDIANS OF THE GALAXY.
RR-CHAKK

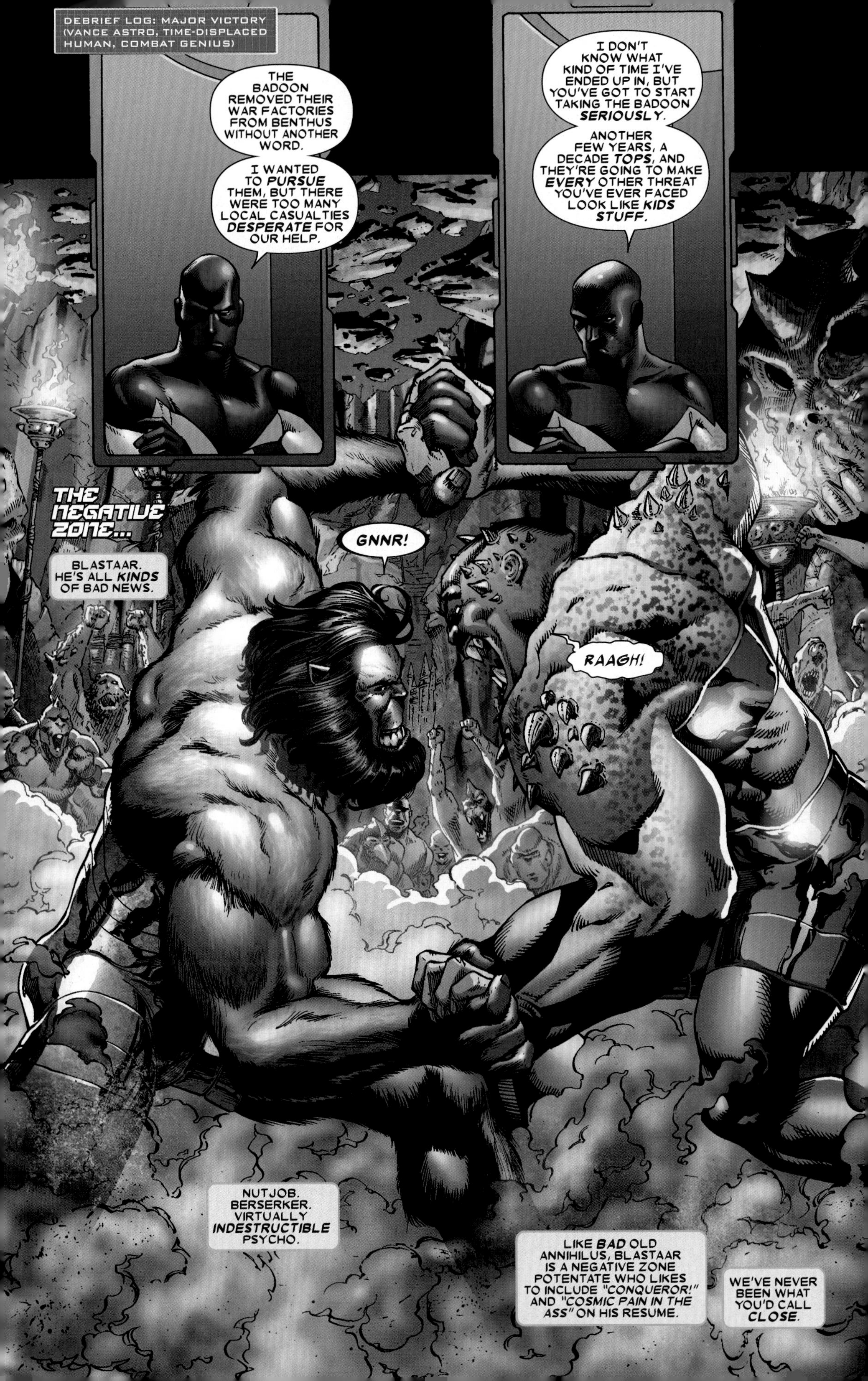
DEBRIEF LOG: MAJOR VICTORY (VANCE ASTRO, TIME-DISPLACED HUMAN, COMBAT GENIUS)
THE BADOON REMOVED THEIR WAR FACTORIES FROM BENTHUS WITHOUT ANOTHER WORD.
I WANTED TO PURSUE THEM, BUT THERE WERE TOO MANY LOCAL CASUALTIES DESPERATE FOR OUR HELP.
I DON'T KNOW WHAT KIND OF TIME I'VE ENDED UP IN, BUT YOU'VE GOT TO START TAKING THE BADOON SERIOUSLY.
ANOTHER FEW YEARS, A DECADE TOPS, AND THEY'RE GOING TO MAKE EVERY OTHER THREAT YOU'VE EVER FACED LOOK LIKE KIDS STUFF.
THE NEGATIVE ZONE...
BLASTAAR. HE'S ALL KINDS OF BAD NEWS.
GNNR!
RAAGH!
NUTJOB. BERSERKER. VIRTUALLY INDESTRUCTIBLE PSYCHO.
LIKE BAD OLD ANNIHILUS, BLASTAAR IS A NEGATIVE ZONE POTENTATE WHO LIKES TO INCLUDE "CONQUEROR!" AND "COSMIC PAIN IN THE ASS" ON HIS RESUME.
WE'VE NEVER BEEN WHAT YOU'D CALL CLOSE.

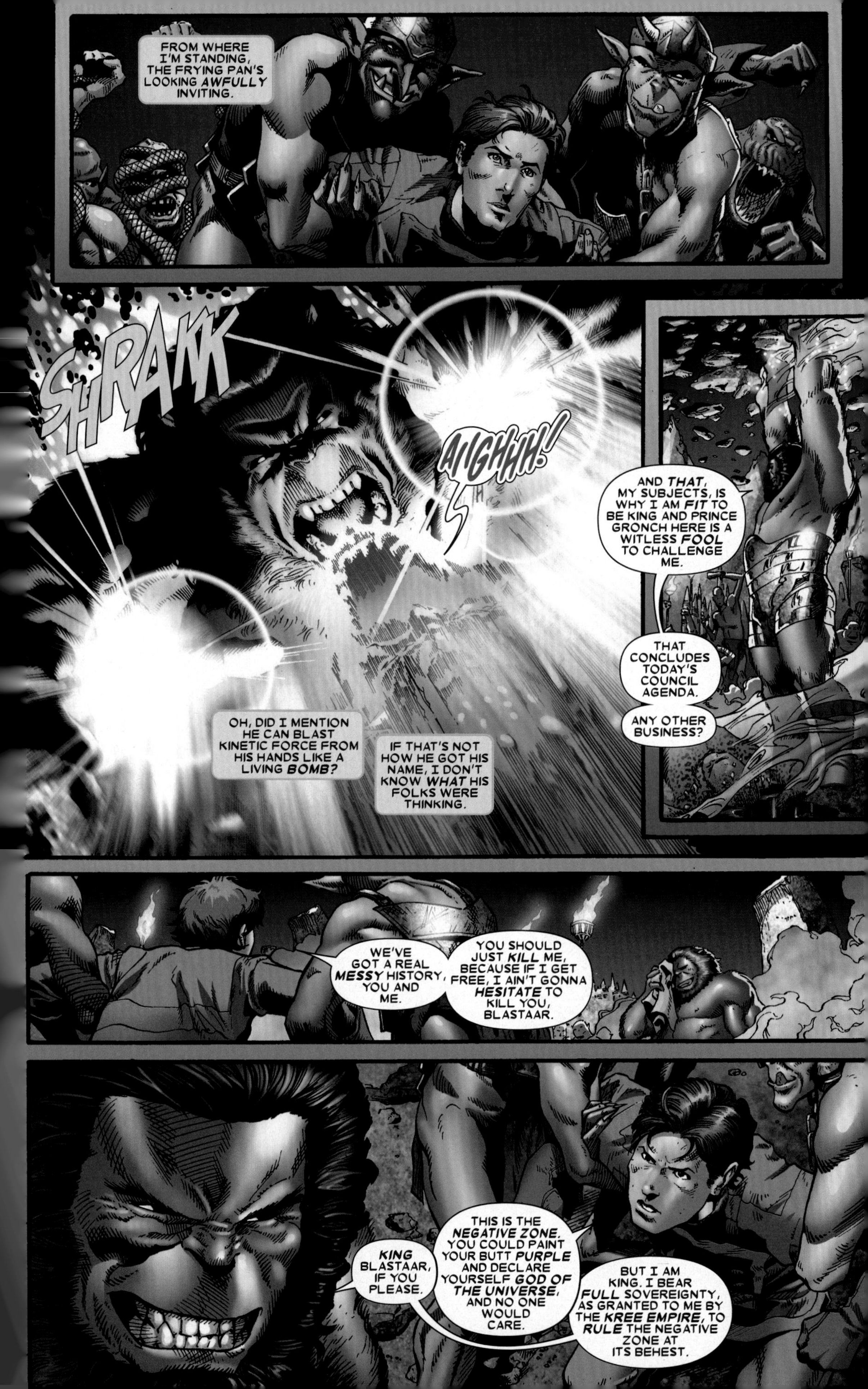
FROM WHERE I'M STANDING, THE FRYING PAN'S LOOKING AWFULLY INVITING.
SHRAKK
AIGHHH!
OH, DID I MENTION HE CAN BLAST KINETIC FORCE FROM HIS HANDS LIKE A LIVING BOMB?
IF THAT'S NOT HOW HE GOT HIS NAME, I DON'T KNOW WHAT HIS FOLKS WERE THINKING.
AND THAT, MY SUBJECTS, IS WHY I AM FIT TO BE KING AND PRINCE GRONCH HERE IS A WITLESS FOOL TO CHALLENGE ME.
THAT CONCLUDES TODAY'S COUNCIL AGENDA.
ANY OTHER BUSINESS?
WE'VE GOT A REAL MESSY HISTORY, YOU AND ME.
YOU SHOULD JUST KILL ME, BECAUSE IF I GET FREE, I AIN'T GONNA HESITATE TO KILL YOU, BLASTAAR.
KING BLASTAAR, IF YOU PLEASE.
THIS IS THE NEGATIVE ZONE. YOU COULD PAINT YOUR BUTT PURPLE AND DECLARE YOURSELF GOD OF THE UNIVERSE, AND NO ONE WOULD CARE.
BUT I AM KING. I BEAR FULL SOVEREIGNTY, AS GRANTED TO ME BY THE KREE EMPIRE, TO RULE THE NEGATIVE ZONE AT ITS BEHEST.

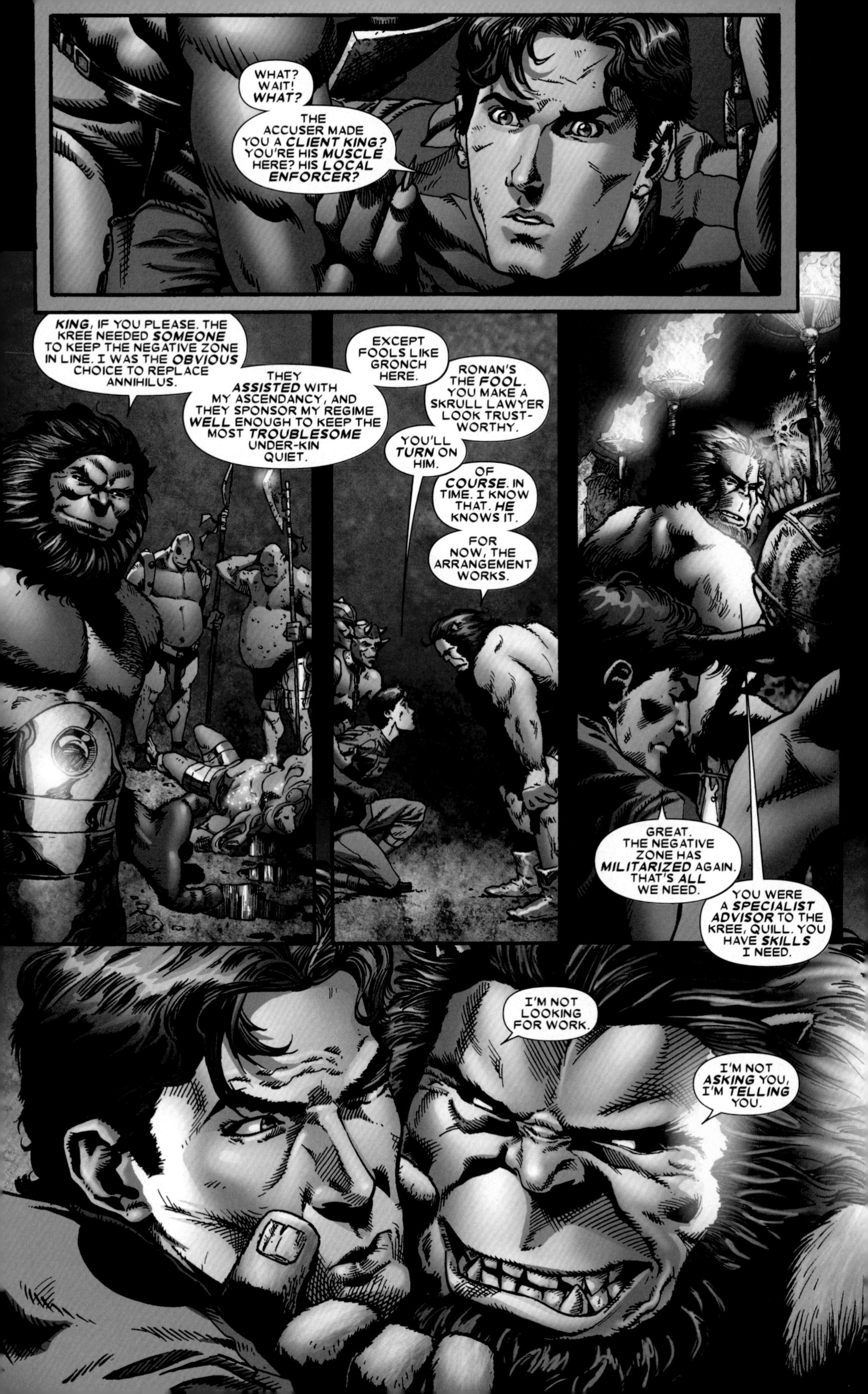
WHAT? WAIT! WHAT?
THE ACCUSER MADE YOU A CLIENT KING? YOU'RE HIS MUSCLE HERE? HIS LOCAL ENFORCER?
KING, IF YOU PLEASE. THE KREE NEEDED SOMEONE TO KEEP THE NEGATIVE ZONE IN LINE. I WAS THE OBVIOUS CHOICE TO REPLACE ANNIHILUS.
THEY ASSISTED WITH MY ASCENDANCY, AND THEY SPONSOR MY REGIME WELL ENOUGH TO KEEP THE MOST TROUBLESOME UNDER-KIN QUIET.
EXCEPT FOOLS LIKE GRONCH HERE.
RONAN'S THE FOOL. YOU MAKE A SKRULL LAWYER LOOK TRUST-WORTHY.
YOU'LL TURN ON HIM.
OF COURSE. IN TIME. I KNOW THAT. HE KNOWS IT.
FOR NOW, THE ARRANGEMENT WORKS.
GREAT. THE NEGATIVE ZONE HAS MILITARIZED AGAIN. THAT'S ALL WE NEED.
YOU WERE A SPECIALIST ADVISOR TO THE KREE, QUILL. YOU HAVE SKILLS I NEED.
I'M NOT LOOKING FOR WORK.
I'M NOT ASKING YOU, I'M TELLING YOU.

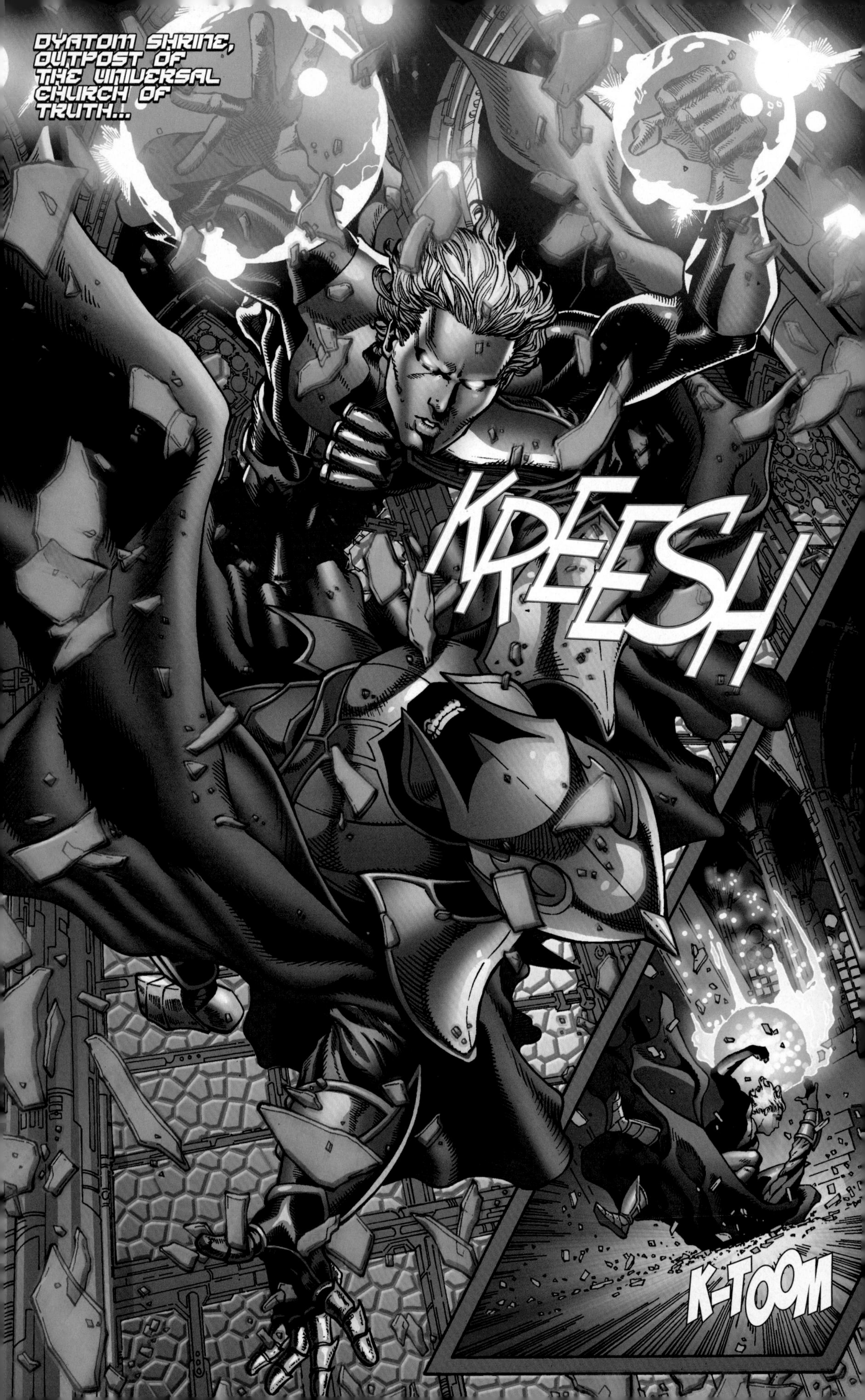
DYATOM SHRINE, OUTPOST OF THE UNIVERSAL CHURCH OF TRUTH...
KREESH
K-TOOM

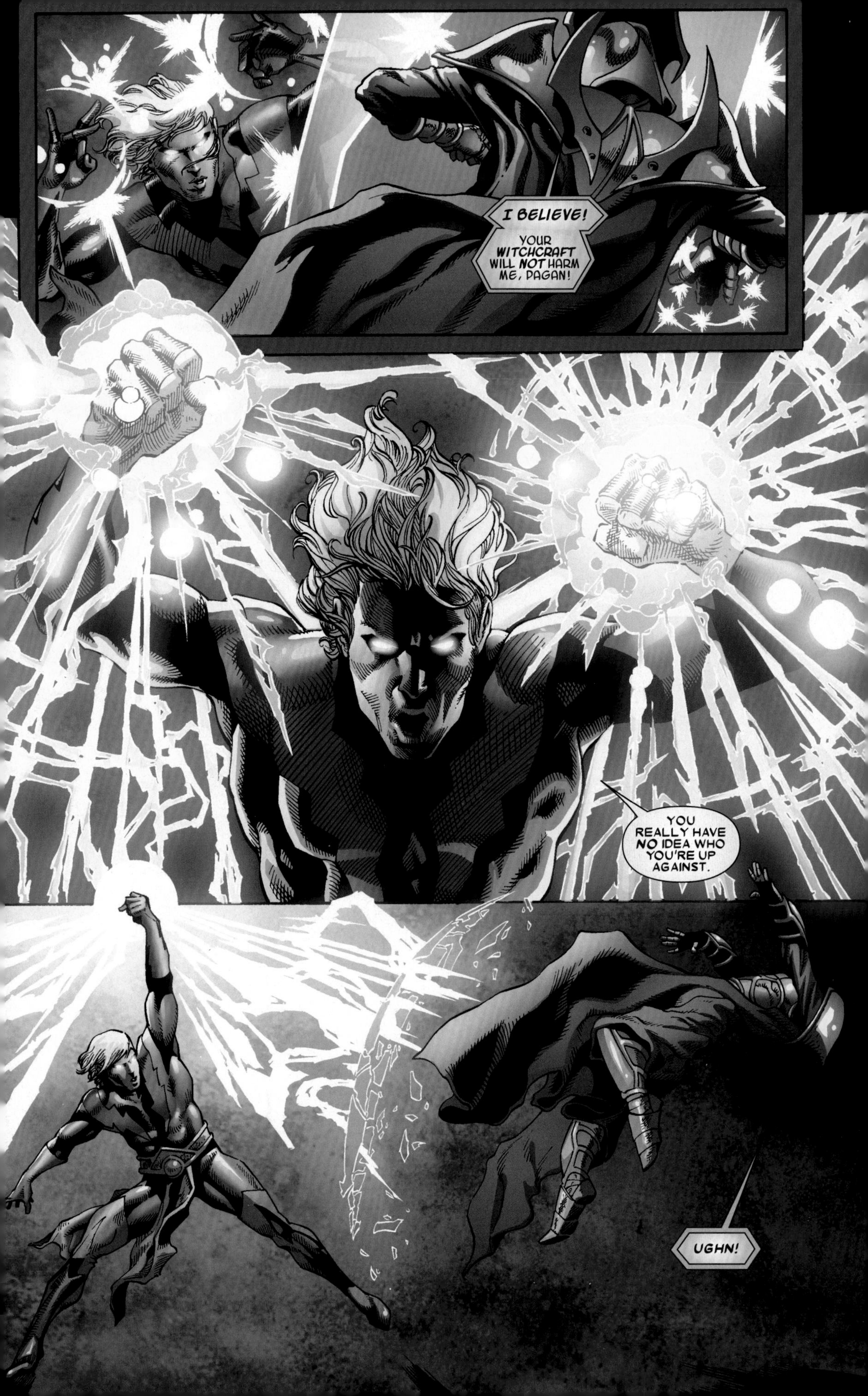
I BELIEVE!
YOUR WITCHCRAFT WILL NOT HARM ME, PAGAN!
YOU REALLY HAVE NO IDEA WHO YOU'RE UP AGAINST.
UGHN!

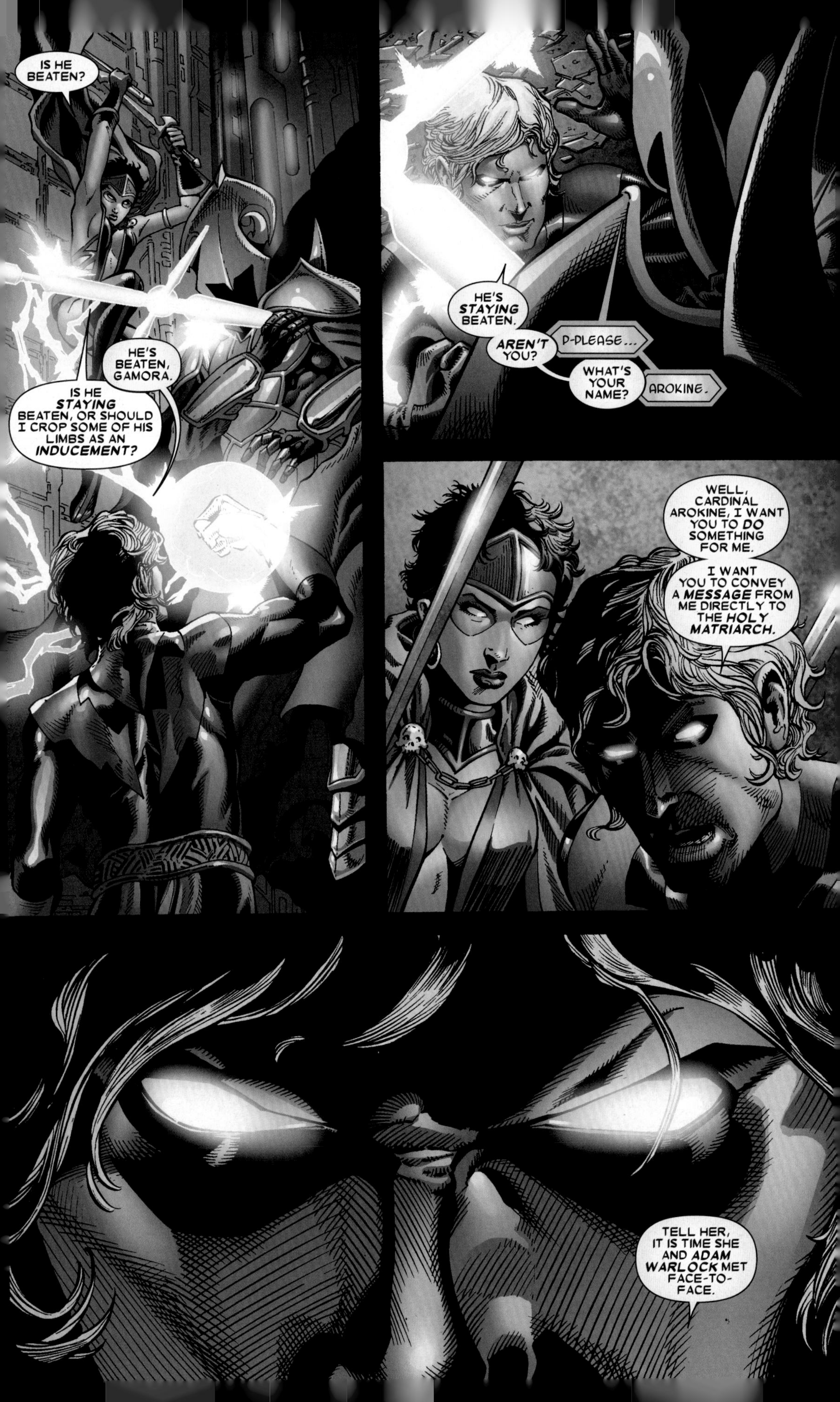

IS HE BEATEN?
HE'S BEATEN, GAMORA.
IS HE STAYING BEATEN, OR SHOULD I CROP SOME OF HIS LIMBS AS AN INDUCEMENT?
HE'S STAYING BEATEN.
AREN'T YOU?
D-PLEASE...
WHAT'S YOUR NAME?
AROKINE.
WELL, CARDINAL AROKINE, I WANT YOU TO DO SOMETHING FOR ME.
I WANT YOU TO CONVEY A MESSAGE FROM ME DIRECTLY TO THE HOLY MATRIARCH.
TELL HER, IT IS TIME SHE AND ADAM WARLOCK MET FACE-TO-FACE.

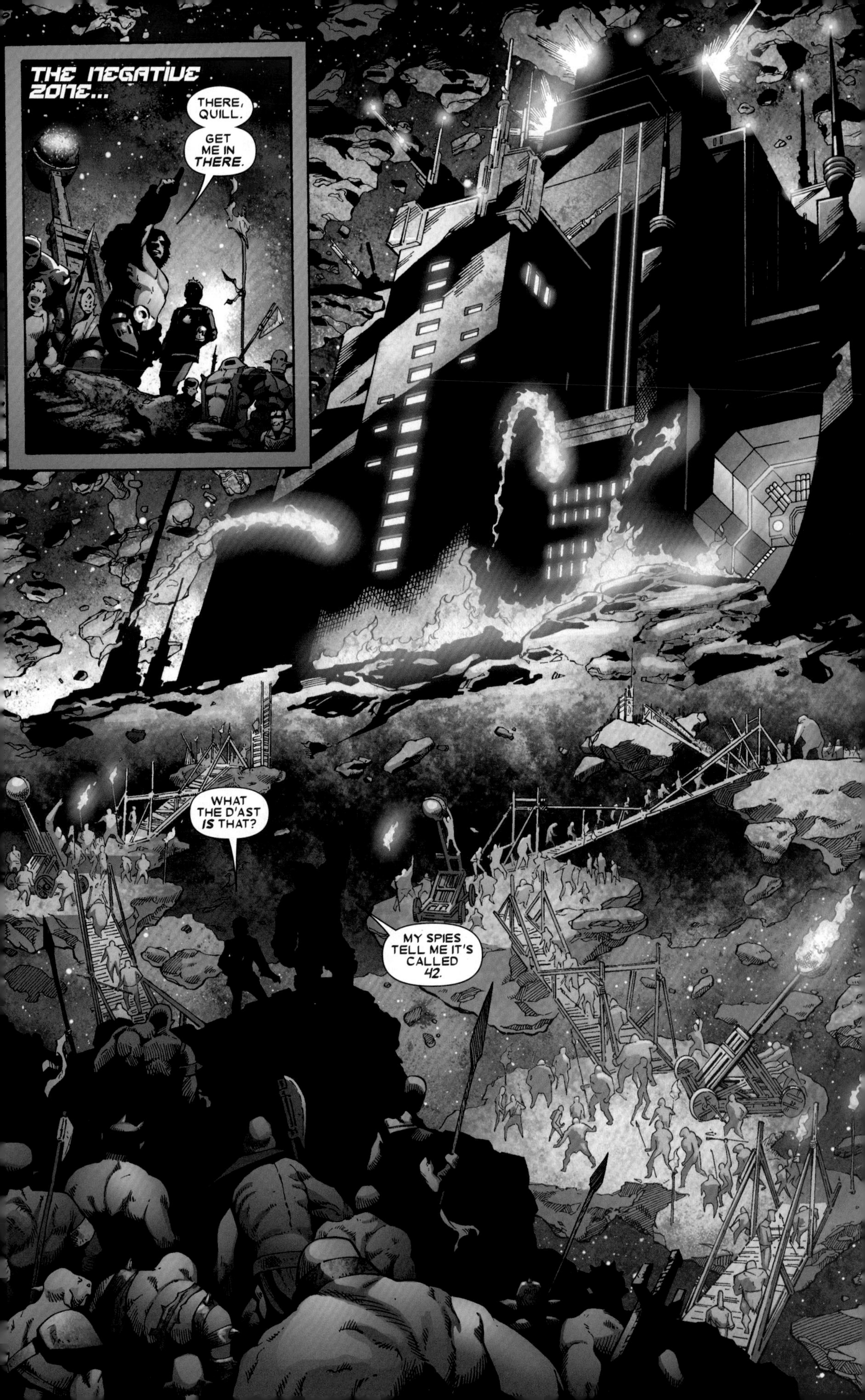
THE NEGATIVE ZONE...
THERE, QUILL.
GET ME IN THERE.
WHAT THE D'AST IS THAT?
MY SPIES TELL ME IT'S CALLED 42.

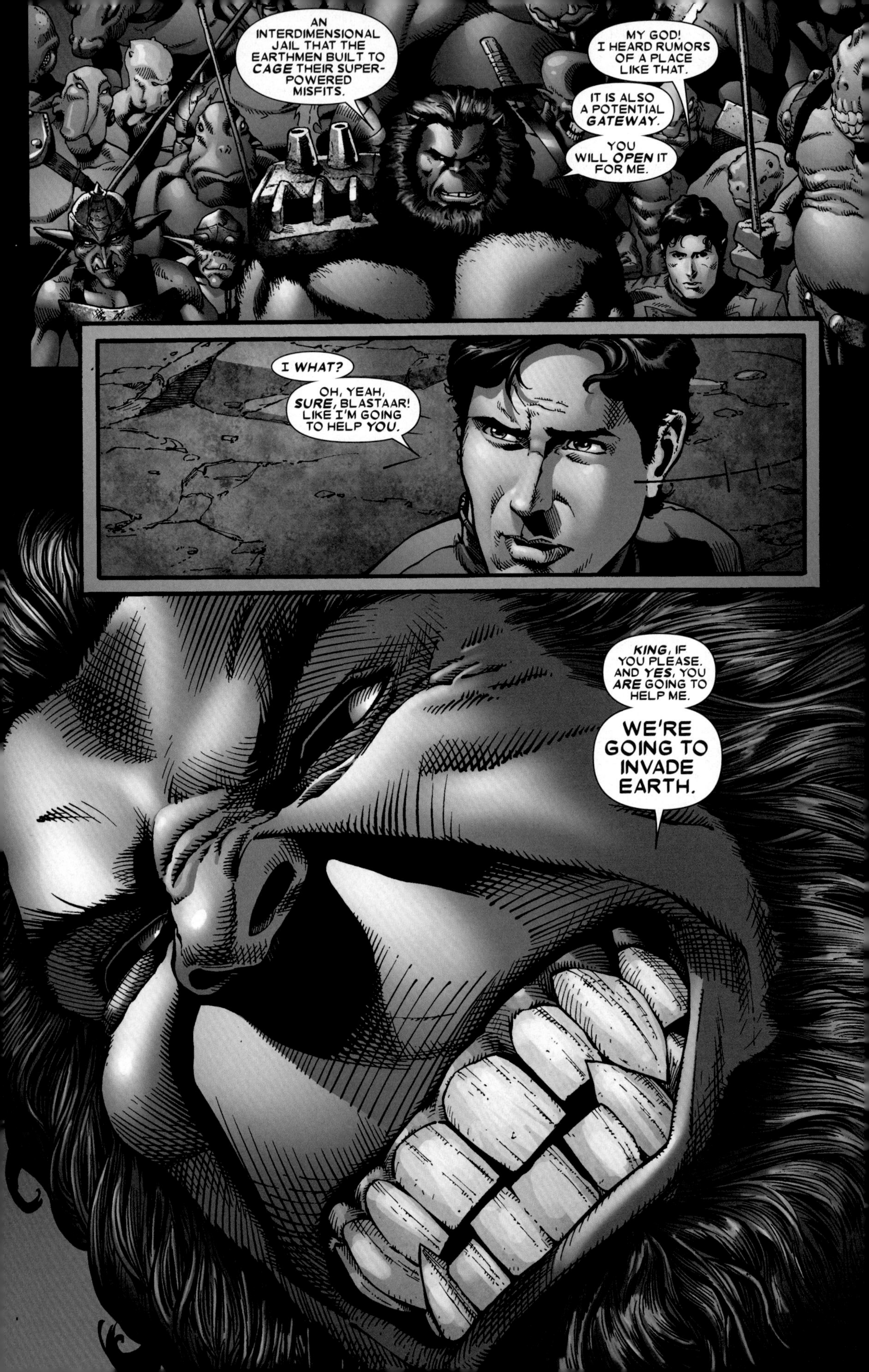
AN INTERDIMENSIONAL JAIL THAT THE EARTHMEN BUILT TO CAGE THEIR SUPER-POWERED MISFITS.
MY GOD! I HEARD RUMORS OF A PLACE LIKE THAT.
IT IS ALSO A POTENTIAL GATEWAY.
YOU WILL OPEN IT FOR ME.
I WHAT?
OH, YEAH, SURE, BLASTAAR! LIKE I'M GOING TO HELP YOU.
KING, IF YOU PLEASE. AND YES, YOU ARE GOING TO HELP ME.
WE'RE GOING TO INVADE EARTH.

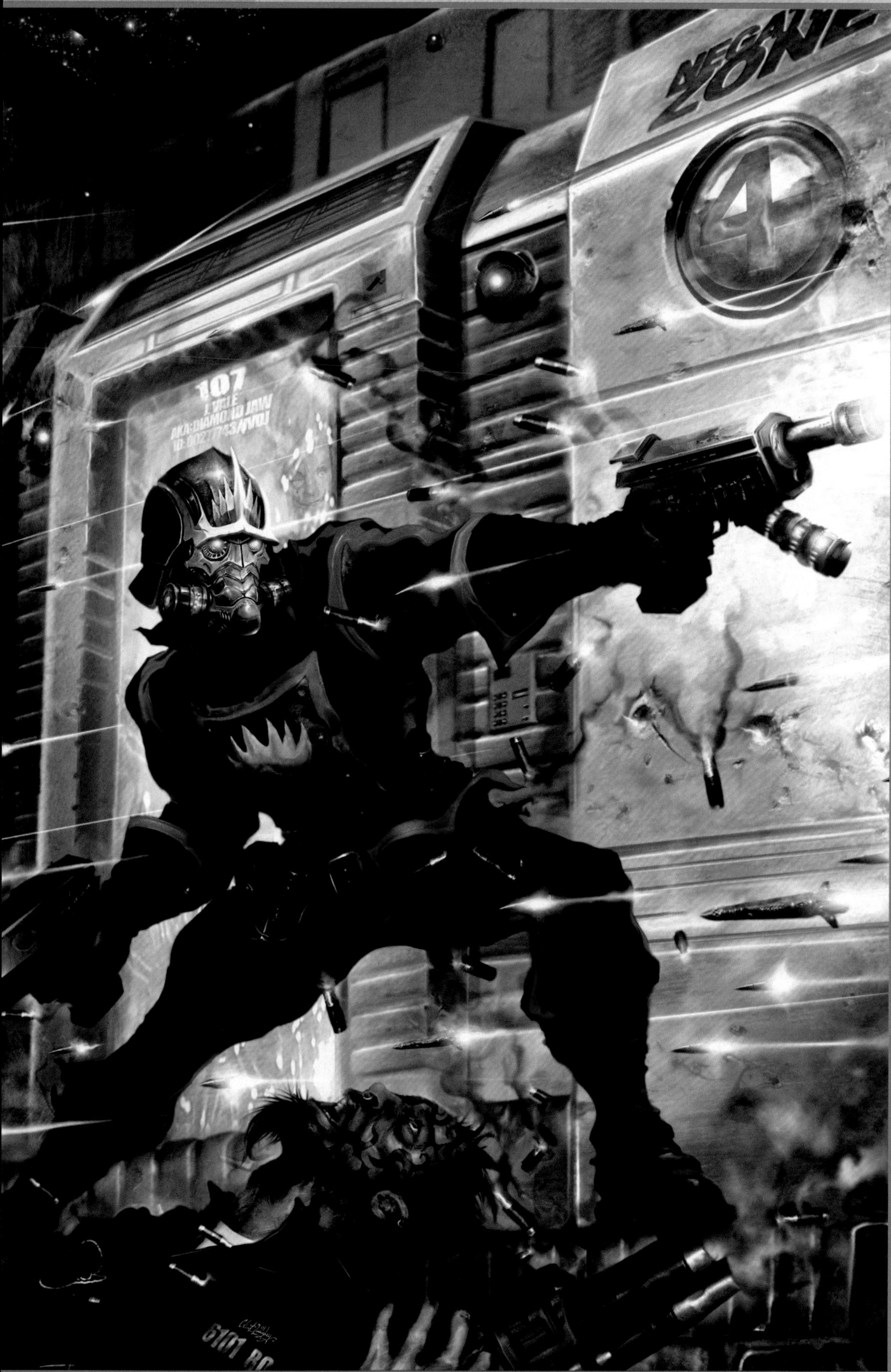
ZONE
107

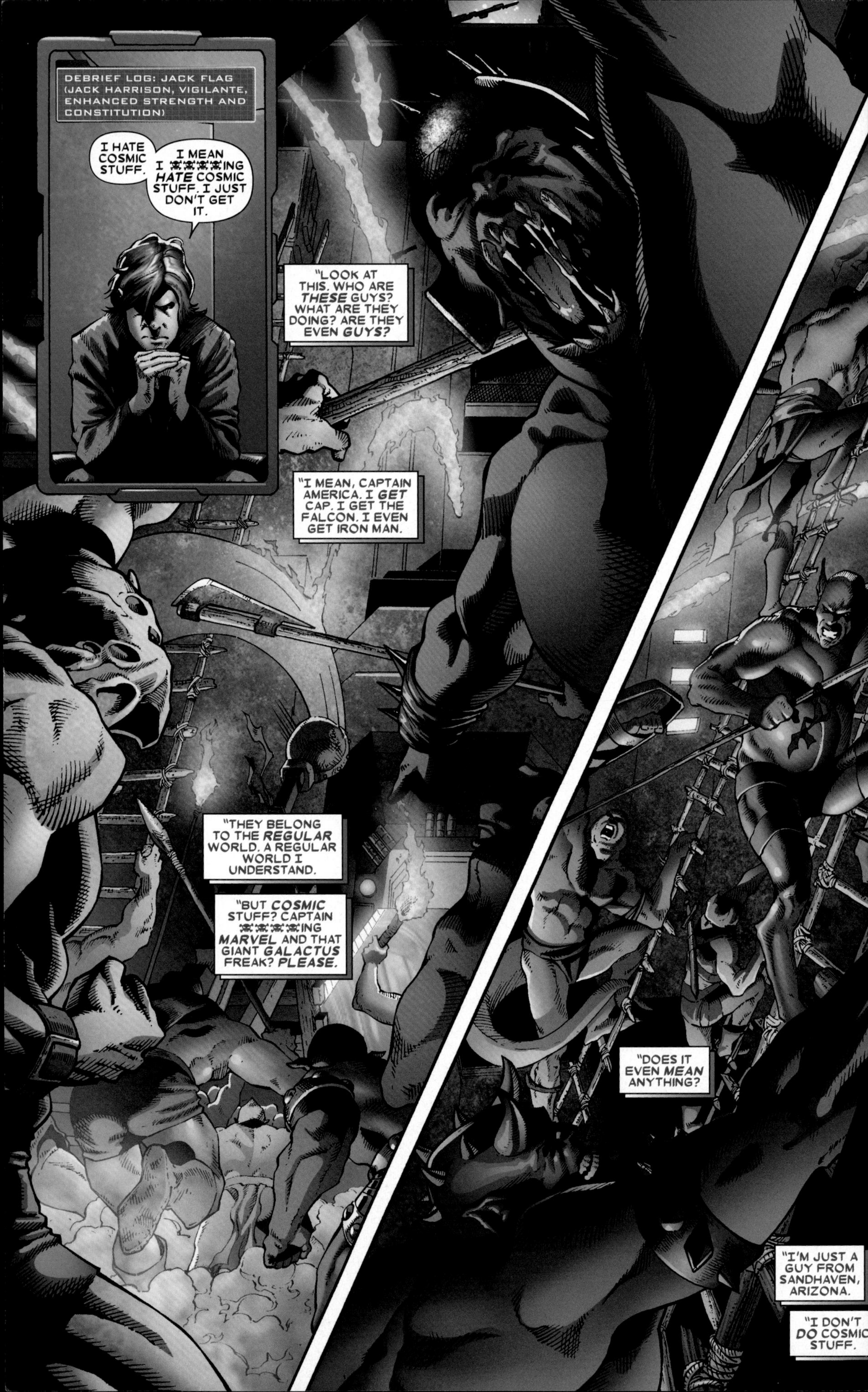
DEBRIEF LOG: JACK FLAG (JACK HARRISON, VIGILANTE, ENHANCED STRENGTH AND CONSTITUTION)
I HATE COSMIC STUFF.
I MEAN I ☠☠☠☠ING HATE COSMIC STUFF. I JUST DON'T GET IT.
"LOOK AT THIS. WHO ARE THESE GUYS? WHAT ARE THEY DOING? ARE THEY EVEN GUYS?
"I MEAN, CAPTAIN AMERICA. I GET CAP. I GET THE FALCON. I EVEN GET IRON MAN.
"THEY BELONG TO THE REGULAR WORLD. A REGULAR WORLD I UNDERSTAND.
"BUT COSMIC STUFF? CAPTAIN ☠☠☠☠ING MARVEL AND THAT GIANT GALACTUS FREAK? PLEASE.
"DOES IT EVEN MEAN ANYTHING?
"I'M JUST A GUY FROM SANDHAVEN, ARIZONA.
"I DON'T DO COSMIC STUFF.

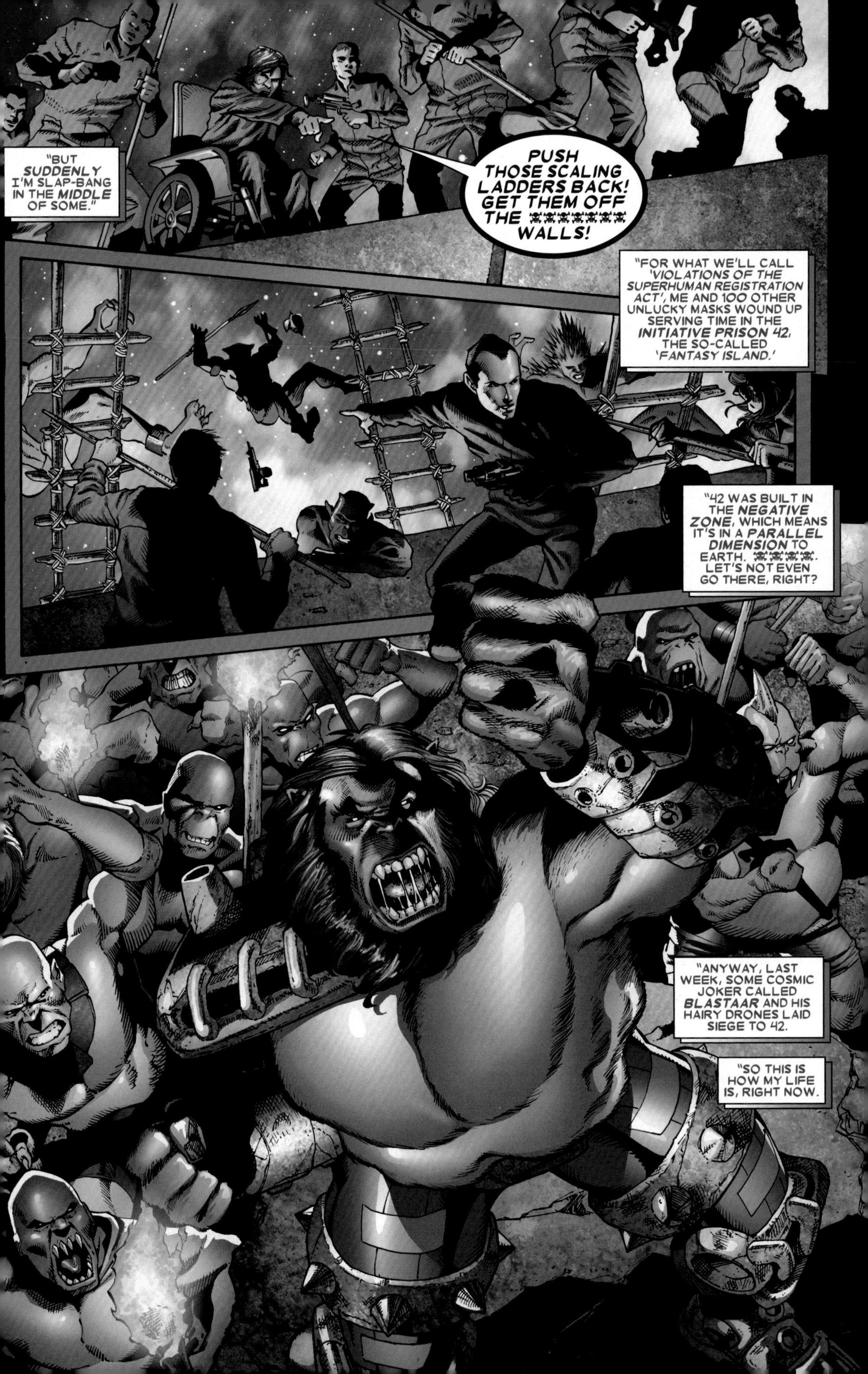
"BUT SUDDENLY I'M SLAP-BANG IN THE MIDDLE OF SOME."
PUSH THOSE SCALING LADDERS BACK! GET THEM OFF THE ☠☠☠☠☠ WALLS!
"FOR WHAT WE'LL CALL 'VIOLATIONS OF THE SUPERHUMAN REGISTRATION ACT', ME AND 100 OTHER UNLUCKY MASKS WOUND UP SERVING TIME IN THE INITIATIVE PRISON 42, THE SO-CALLED 'FANTASY ISLAND.'
"42 WAS BUILT IN THE NEGATIVE ZONE, WHICH MEANS IT'S IN A PARALLEL DIMENSION TO EARTH. ☠☠☠☠. LET'S NOT EVEN GO THERE, RIGHT?
"ANYWAY, LAST WEEK, SOME COSMIC JOKER CALLED BLASTAAR AND HIS HAIRY DRONES LAID SIEGE TO 42.
"SO THIS IS HOW MY LIFE IS, RIGHT NOW.

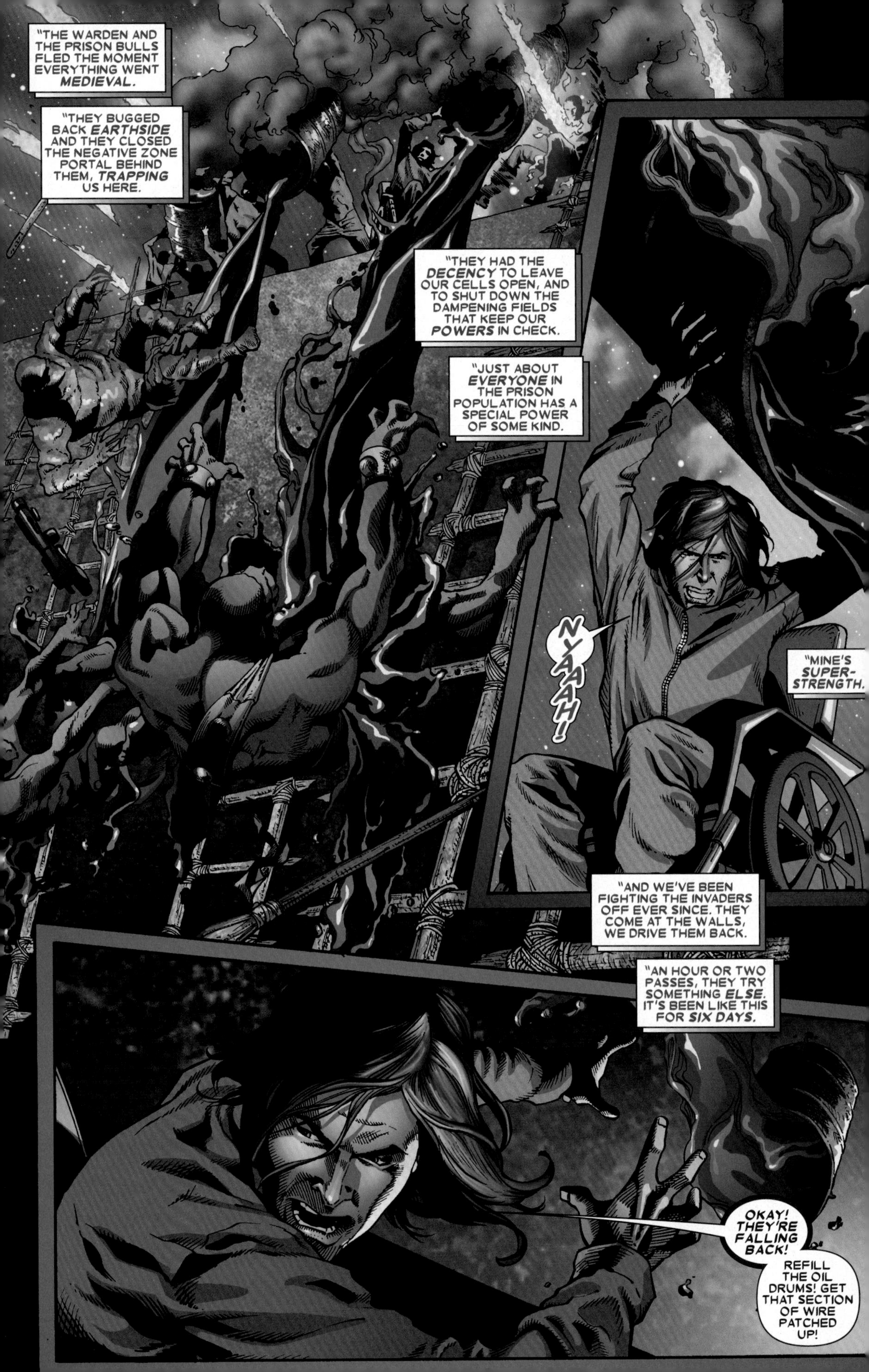
"THE WARDEN AND THE PRISON BULLS FLED THE MOMENT EVERYTHING WENT *MEDIEVAL*.
"THEY BUGGED BACK *EARTHSIDE* AND THEY CLOSED THE NEGATIVE ZONE PORTAL BEHIND THEM, *TRAPPING* US HERE.
"THEY HAD THE *DECENCY* TO LEAVE OUR CELLS OPEN, AND TO SHUT DOWN THE DAMPENING FIELDS THAT KEEP OUR *POWERS* IN CHECK.
"JUST ABOUT *EVERYONE* IN THE PRISON POPULATION HAS A SPECIAL POWER OF SOME KIND.
NYAAAH!
"MINE'S *SUPER-STRENGTH*.
"AND WE'VE BEEN FIGHTING THE INVADERS OFF EVER SINCE. THEY COME AT THE WALLS, WE DRIVE THEM BACK.
"AN HOUR OR TWO PASSES, THEY TRY SOMETHING *ELSE*. IT'S BEEN LIKE THIS FOR *SIX DAYS*.
OKAY! THEY'RE FALLING BACK!
REFILL THE OIL DRUMS! GET THAT SECTION OF WIRE PATCHED UP!

"I DON'T HONESTLY KNOW HOW MUCH *LONGER* WE'RE GOING TO HOLD."

HEY, JACK! *LOOK!*

WHAT THE ✕✕✕ IS *THIS* NOW?

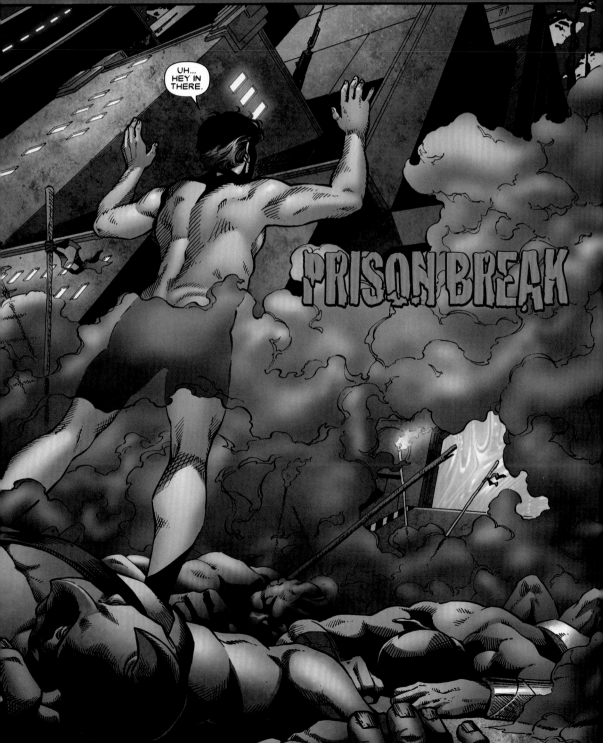

UH... HEY IN THERE.

PRISON BREAK

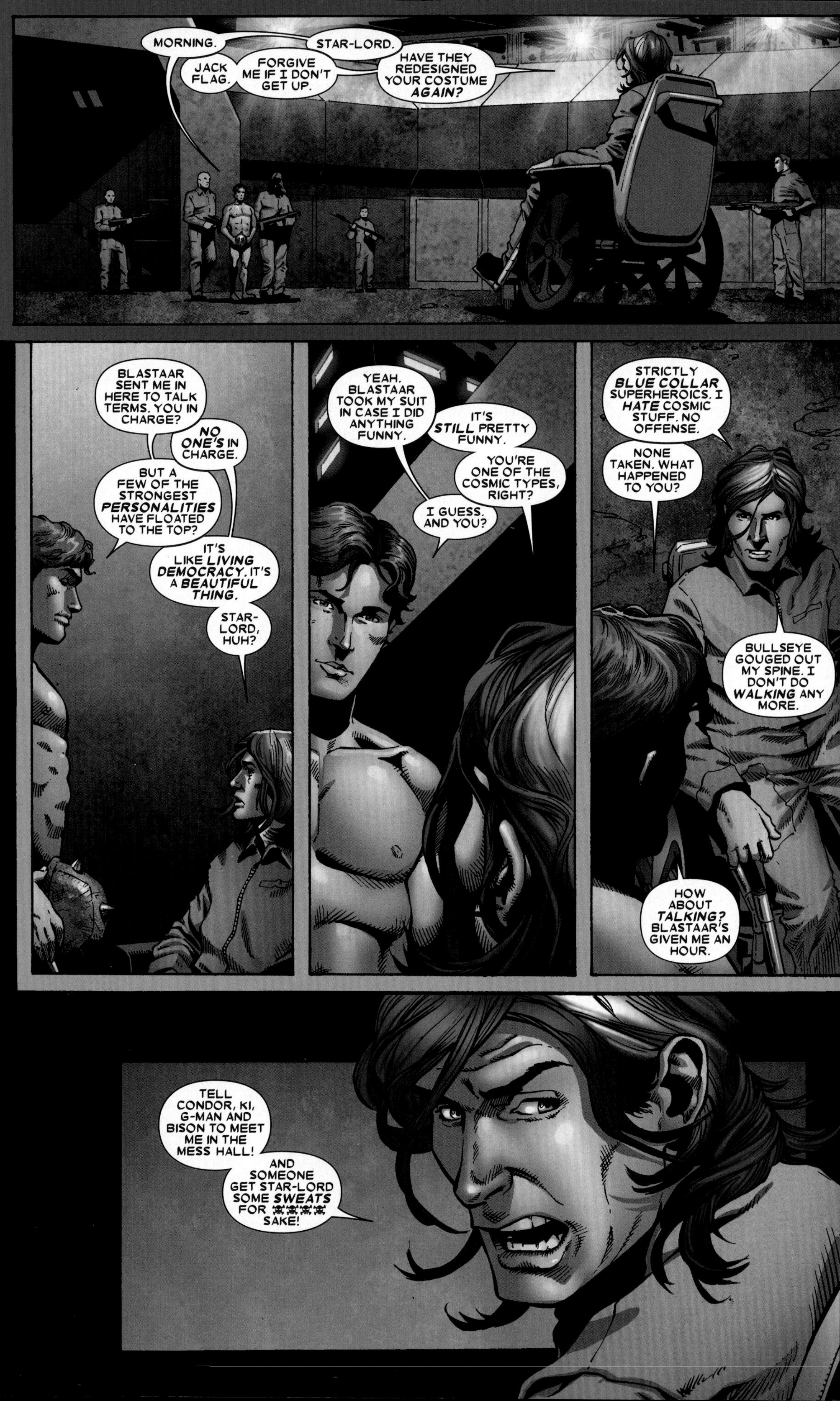

MORNING.
STAR-LORD.
JACK FLAG.
FORGIVE ME IF I DON'T GET UP.
HAVE THEY REDESIGNED YOUR COSTUME AGAIN?
BLASTAAR SENT ME IN HERE TO TALK TERMS. YOU IN CHARGE?
NO ONE'S IN CHARGE.
BUT A FEW OF THE STRONGEST PERSONALITIES HAVE FLOATED TO THE TOP?
IT'S LIKE LIVING DEMOCRACY. IT'S A BEAUTIFUL THING.
STAR-LORD, HUH?
YEAH. BLASTAAR TOOK MY SUIT IN CASE I DID ANYTHING FUNNY.
IT'S STILL PRETTY FUNNY.
YOU'RE ONE OF THE COSMIC TYPES, RIGHT?
I GUESS. AND YOU?
STRICTLY BLUE COLLAR SUPERHEROICS. I HATE COSMIC STUFF. NO OFFENSE.
NONE TAKEN. WHAT HAPPENED TO YOU?
BULLSEYE GOUGED OUT MY SPINE. I DON'T DO WALKING ANY MORE.
HOW ABOUT TALKING? BLASTAAR'S GIVEN ME AN HOUR.
TELL CONDOR, KI, G-MAN AND BISON TO MEET ME IN THE MESS HALL!
AND SOMEONE GET STAR-LORD SOME SWEATS FOR ☠☠☠ SAKE!

"I CALL THE TOP DOGS TOGETHER TO HEAR WHAT THIS STAR-LORD FELLA HAS TO SAY."

CLOSE THE DOOR. WE CAN TALK IN HERE.

WHAT THE ✕✕✕✕ IS THIS *ABOUT*, FLAG? WHO THE ✕✕✕ IS *THIS*?

I'M *STAR-LORD*. BLASTAAR SENT ME IN HERE TO TALK YOU INTO SURRENDERING.

SHOULD WE CONSIDER DOING THIS?

"CONDOR'S YOUR BASIC *GENIUS CRIMINAL INVENTOR* WITH WINGS. HE'S TOO *SMART* TO BE TRUSTWORTHY."

ABSOLUTELY *NOT*. HE'LL *KILL* YOU.

WE JUST STICK TO OUR ORIGINAL PLAN.

THIS IS HOW YOU *NEGOTIATE*, STAR-LORD?

KI *SWORE* HE COULD GET THE PORTAL OPEN.

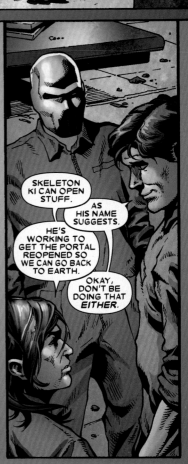

SKELETON KI CAN OPEN STUFF.

AS HIS NAME SUGGESTS.

HE'S WORKING TO GET THE PORTAL REOPENED SO WE CAN GO BACK TO EARTH.

OKAY, DON'T BE DOING THAT *EITHER*.

"GORILLA MAN IS AN OLD-SCHOOL *FREAK VILLAIN*, NOT MY PLACE TO SAY, OF COURSE, BUT I THINK HE TOOK THE WHOLE TRANSPLANT OPERATION THING *WAY* TOO FAR."

YOU GOING TO TELL US WHAT WE CAN AND CAN'T DO, SPACE-LORD?

STAR-LORD.

I'M GOING TO ADVISE YOU *AGAINST* OPENING A DIMENSIONAL GATEWAY THAT WOULD GIVE BLASTAAR AND HIS ARMIES DIRECT ACCESS TO EARTH.

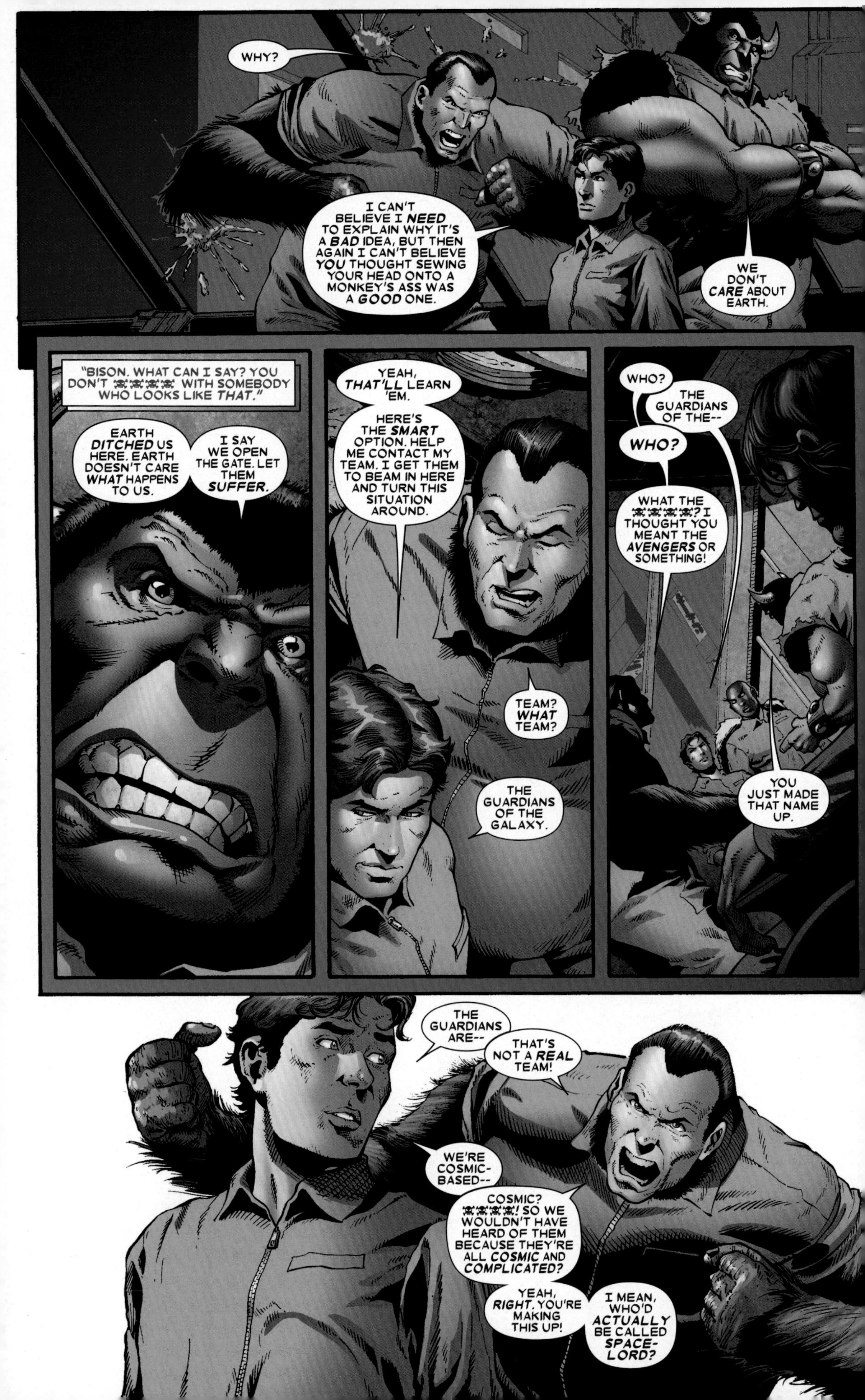
WHY?
I CAN'T BELIEVE I NEED TO EXPLAIN WHY IT'S A BAD IDEA, BUT THEN AGAIN I CAN'T BELIEVE YOU THOUGHT SEWING YOUR HEAD ONTO A MONKEY'S ASS WAS A GOOD ONE.
WE DON'T CARE ABOUT EARTH.
"BISON. WHAT CAN I SAY? YOU DON'T ☠☠☠ WITH SOMEBODY WHO LOOKS LIKE THAT."
EARTH DITCHED US HERE. EARTH DOESN'T CARE WHAT HAPPENS TO US.
I SAY WE OPEN THE GATE. LET THEM SUFFER.
YEAH, THAT'LL LEARN 'EM.
HERE'S THE SMART OPTION. HELP ME CONTACT MY TEAM. I GET THEM TO BEAM IN HERE AND TURN THIS SITUATION AROUND.
TEAM? WHAT TEAM?
THE GUARDIANS OF THE GALAXY.
WHO?
THE GUARDIANS OF THE--
WHO?
WHAT THE ☠☠☠? I THOUGHT YOU MEANT THE AVENGERS OR SOMETHING!
YOU JUST MADE THAT NAME UP.
THE GUARDIANS ARE--
THAT'S NOT A REAL TEAM!
WE'RE COSMIC-BASED--
COSMIC? ☠☠☠! SO WE WOULDN'T HAVE HEARD OF THEM BECAUSE THEY'RE ALL COSMIC AND COMPLICATED?
YEAH, RIGHT. YOU'RE MAKING THIS UP!
I MEAN, WHO'D ACTUALLY BE CALLED SPACE-LORD?

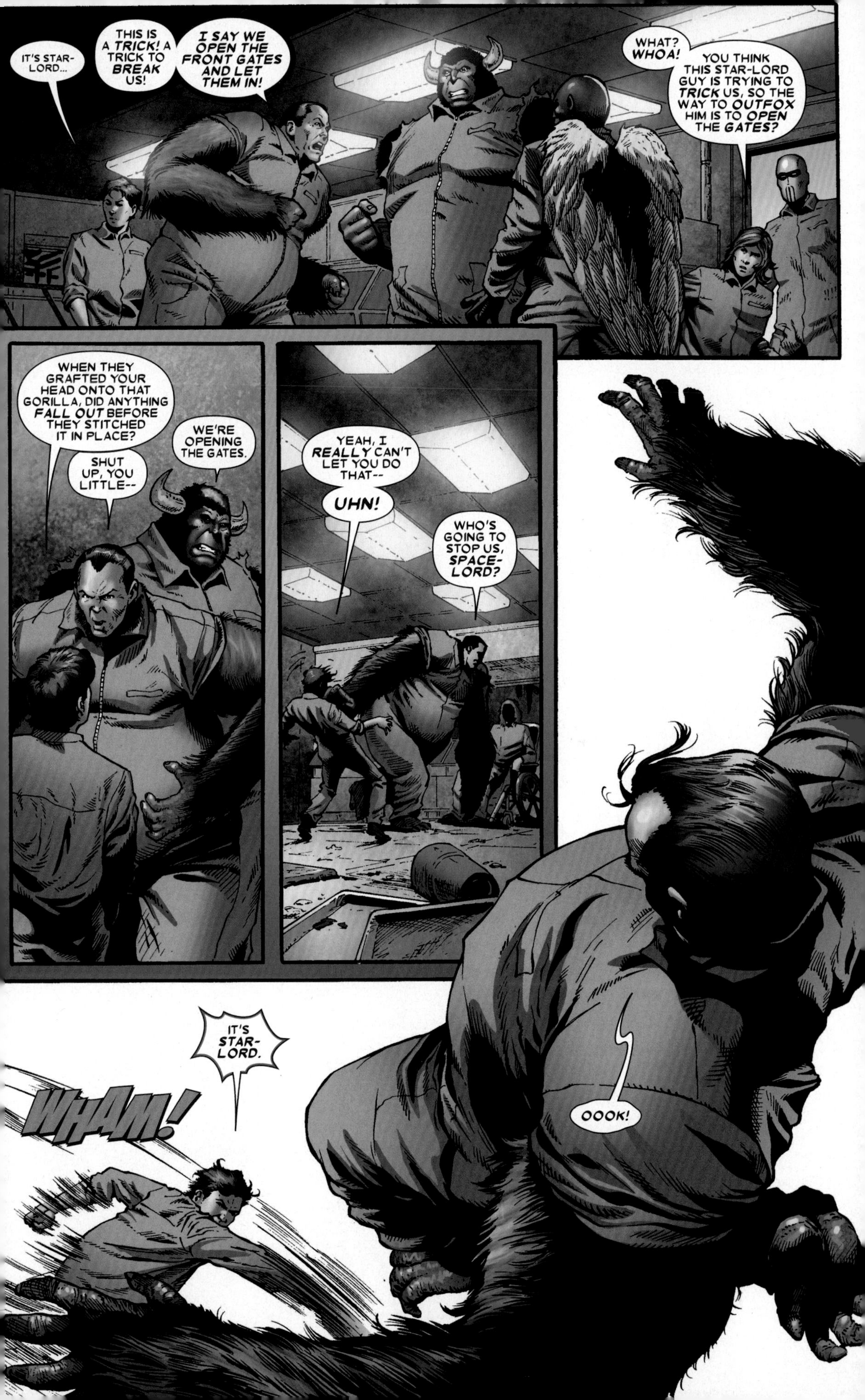
IT'S STAR-LORD...
THIS IS A TRICK! A TRICK TO BREAK US!
I SAY WE OPEN THE FRONT GATES AND LET THEM IN!
WHAT? WHOA!
YOU THINK THIS STAR-LORD GUY IS TRYING TO TRICK US, SO THE WAY TO OUTFOX HIM IS TO OPEN THE GATES?
WHEN THEY GRAFTED YOUR HEAD ONTO THAT GORILLA, DID ANYTHING FALL OUT BEFORE THEY STITCHED IT IN PLACE?
SHUT UP, YOU LITTLE--
WE'RE OPENING THE GATES.
YEAH, I REALLY CAN'T LET YOU DO THAT--
UHN!
WHO'S GOING TO STOP US, SPACE-LORD?
IT'S STAR-LORD.
WHAM!
OOOK!

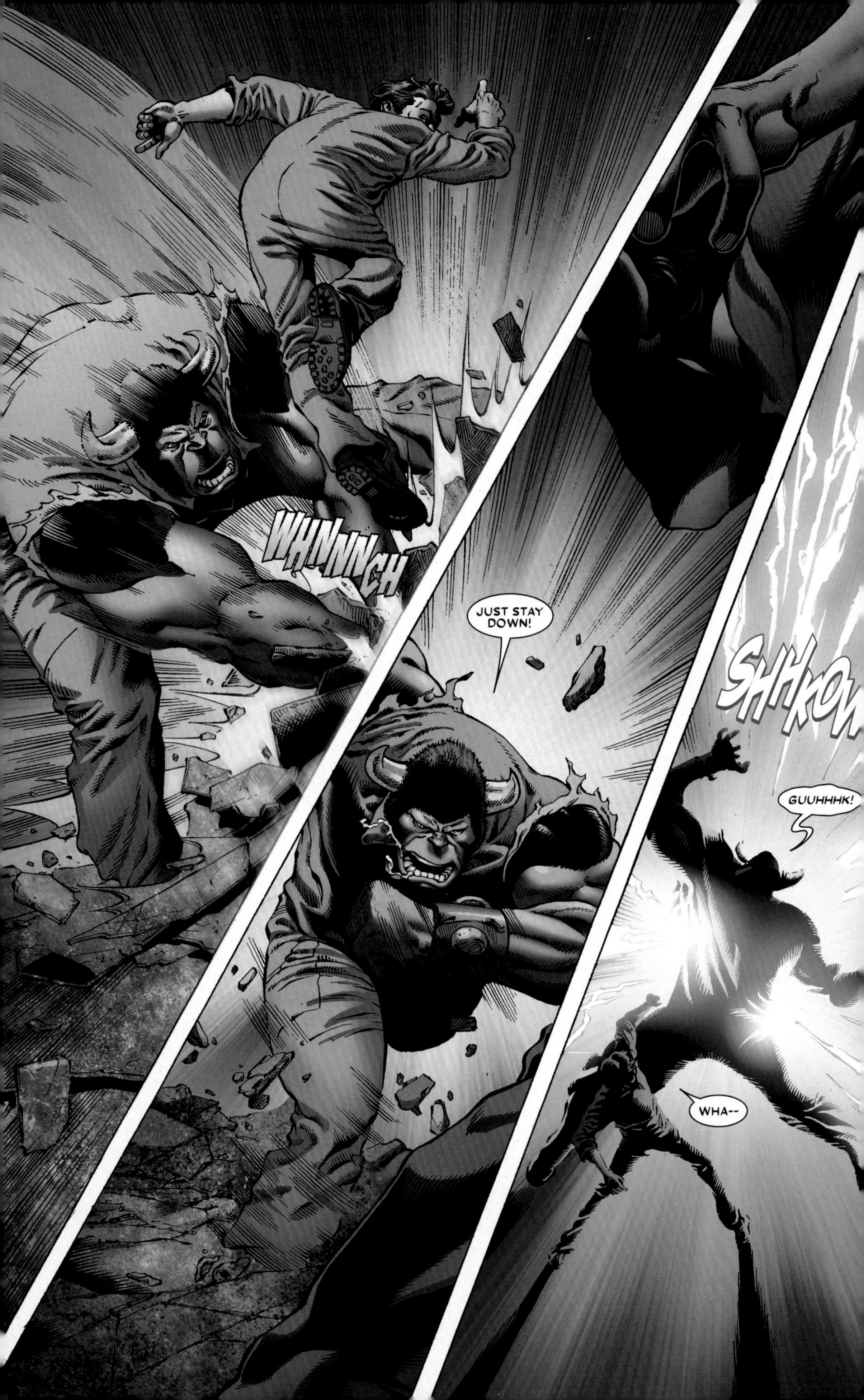
WHNNNCH
JUST STAY DOWN!
SHHKOW
GUUHHHK!
WHA--

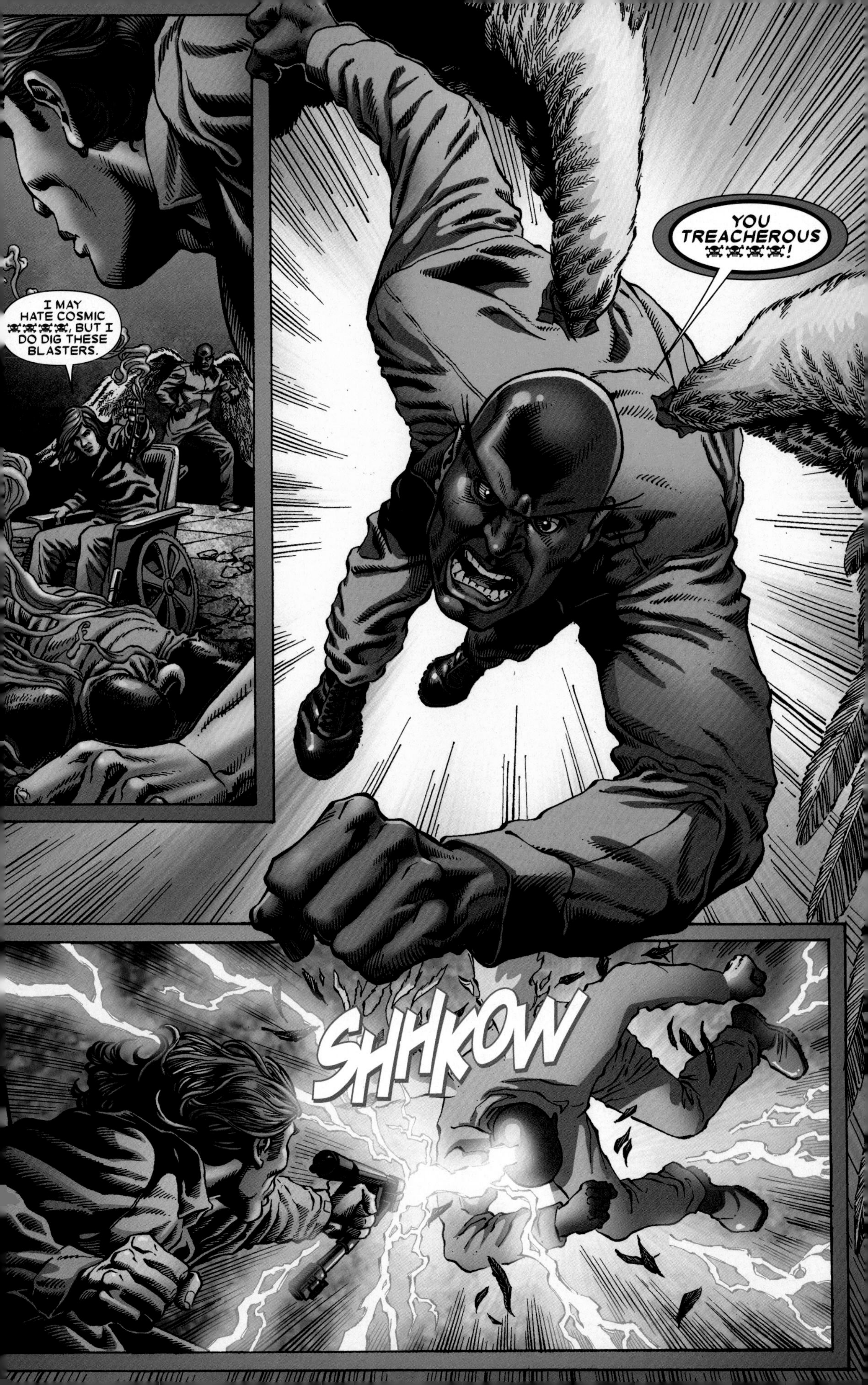
I MAY HATE COSMIC ☠☠☠☠, BUT I DO DIG THESE BLASTERS.
YOU TREACHEROUS ☠☠☠☠!
SHHKOW

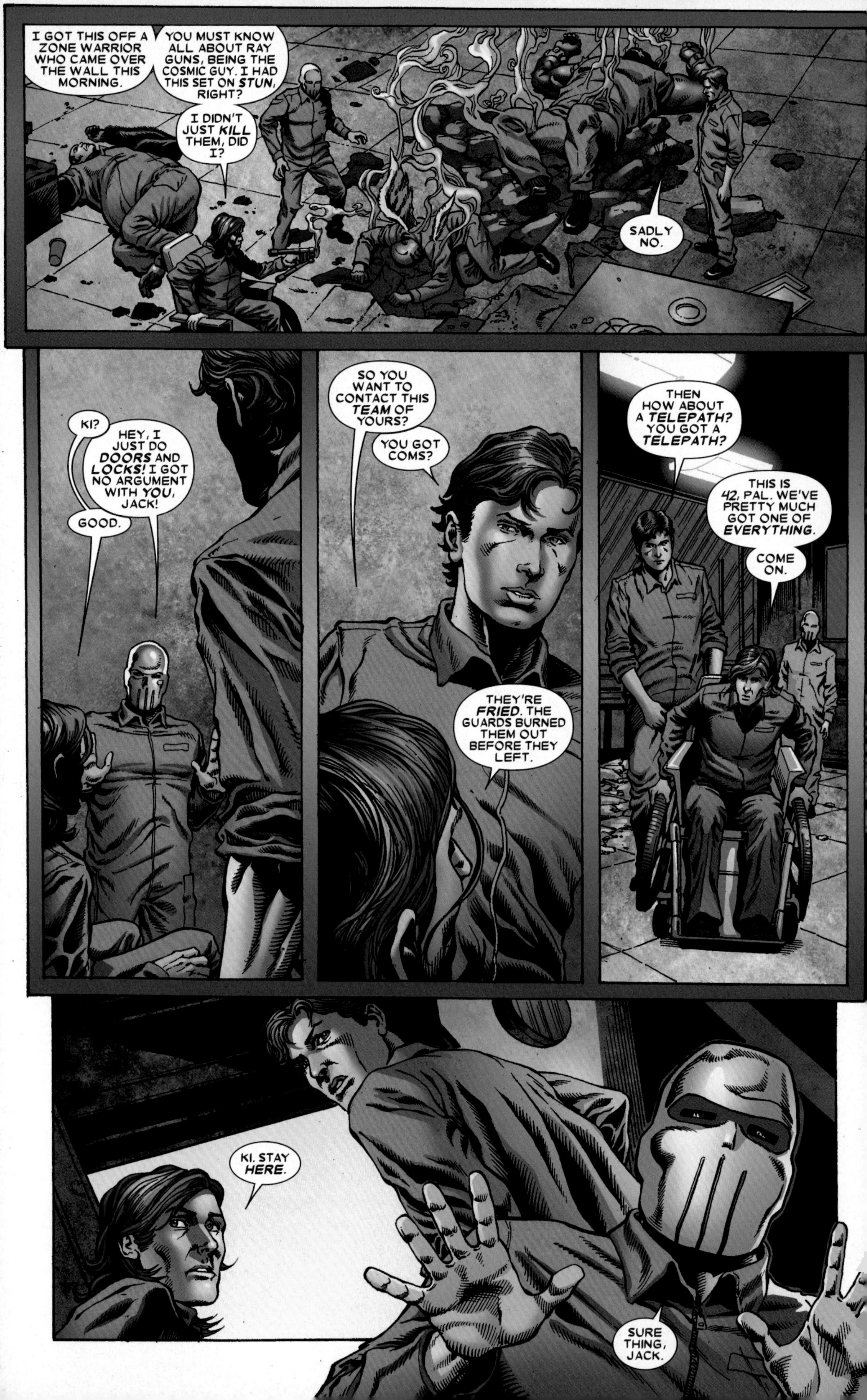
I GOT THIS OFF A ZONE WARRIOR WHO CAME OVER THE WALL THIS MORNING.
YOU MUST KNOW ALL ABOUT RAY GUNS, BEING THE COSMIC GUY. I HAD THIS SET ON STUN, RIGHT?
I DIDN'T JUST KILL THEM, DID I?
SADLY NO.
KI?
HEY, I JUST DO DOORS AND LOCKS! I GOT NO ARGUMENT WITH YOU, JACK!
GOOD.
SO YOU WANT TO CONTACT THIS TEAM OF YOURS?
YOU GOT COMS?
THEY'RE FRIED. THE GUARDS BURNED THEM OUT BEFORE THEY LEFT.
THEN HOW ABOUT A TELEPATH? YOU GOT A TELEPATH?
THIS IS 42, PAL. WE'VE PRETTY MUCH GOT ONE OF EVERYTHING.
COME ON.
KI. STAY HERE.
SURE THING, JACK.

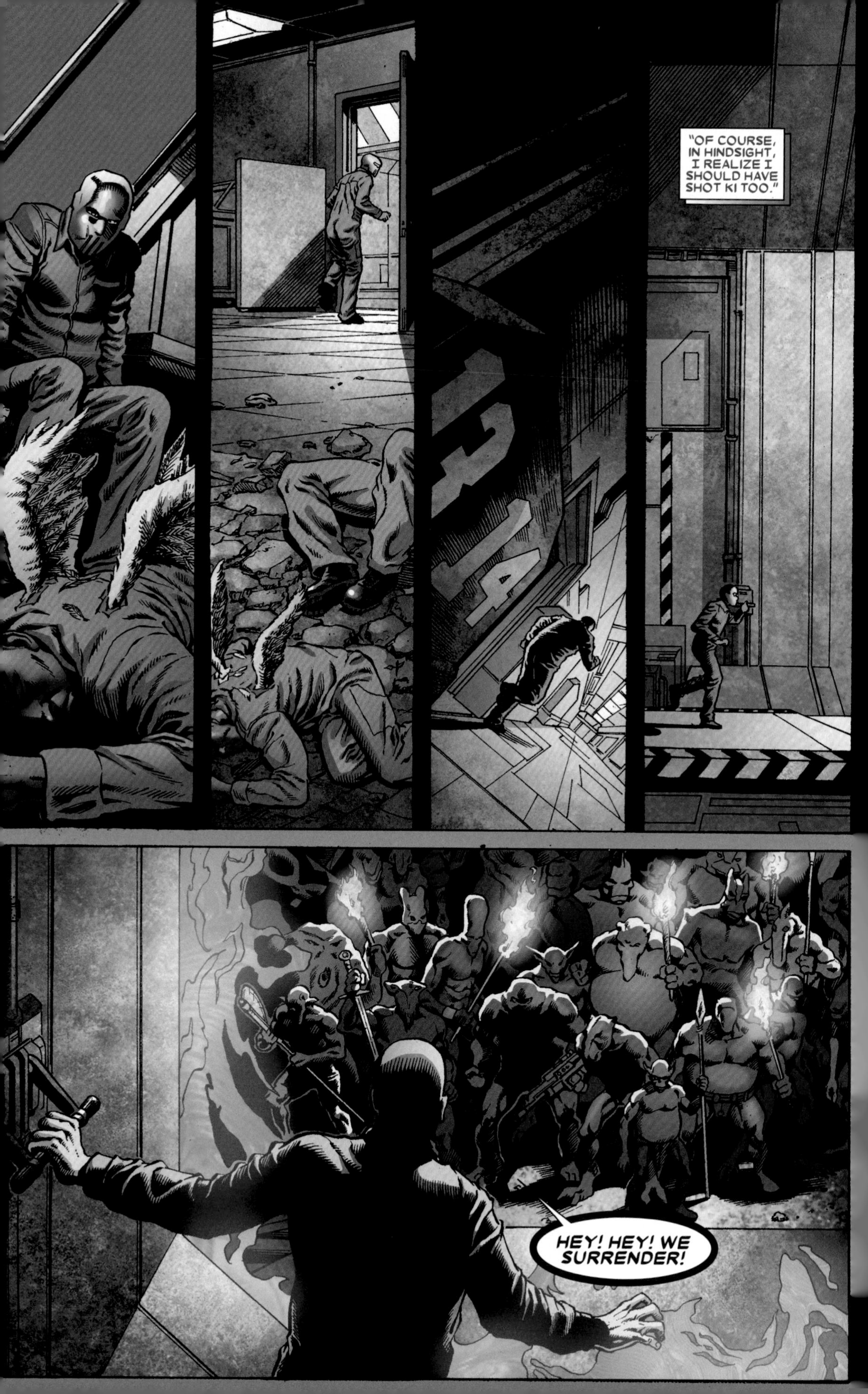
"OF COURSE, IN HINDSIGHT, I REALIZE I SHOULD HAVE SHOT KI TOO."
HEY! HEY! WE SURRENDER!

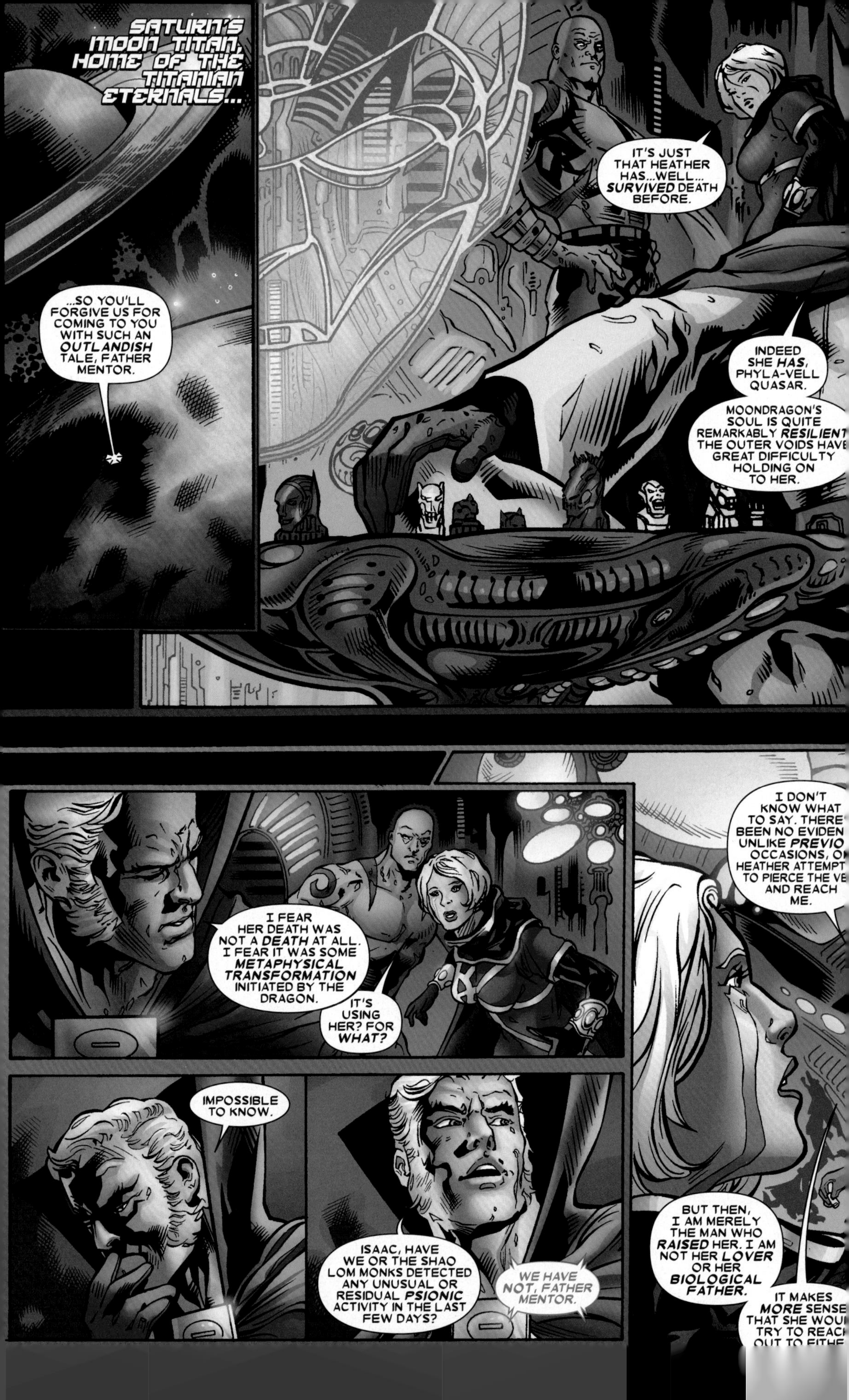
SATURN'S MOON TITAN, HOME OF THE TITANIAN ETERNALS...
...SO YOU'LL FORGIVE US FOR COMING TO YOU WITH SUCH AN OUTLANDISH TALE, FATHER MENTOR.
IT'S JUST THAT HEATHER HAS...WELL... SURVIVED DEATH BEFORE.
INDEED SHE HAS, PHYLA-VELL QUASAR.
MOONDRAGON'S SOUL IS QUITE REMARKABLY RESILIEN THE OUTER VOIDS HAVE GREAT DIFFICULTY HOLDING ON TO HER.
I FEAR HER DEATH WAS NOT A DEATH AT ALL. I FEAR IT WAS SOME METAPHYSICAL TRANSFORMATION INITIATED BY THE DRAGON.
IT'S USING HER? FOR WHAT?
IMPOSSIBLE TO KNOW.
ISAAC, HAVE WE OR THE SHAO LOM MONKS DETECTED ANY UNUSUAL OR RESIDUAL PSIONIC ACTIVITY IN THE LAST FEW DAYS?
WE HAVE NOT, FATHER MENTOR.
I DON'T KNOW WHAT TO SAY. THERE BEEN NO EVIDEN UNLIKE PREVIO OCCASIONS, O HEATHER ATTEMPT TO PIERCE THE VE AND REACH ME.
BUT THEN, I AM MERELY THE MAN WHO RAISED HER. I AM NOT HER LOVER OR HER BIOLOGICAL FATHER.
IT MAKES MORE SENSE THAT SHE WOU TRY TO REACH

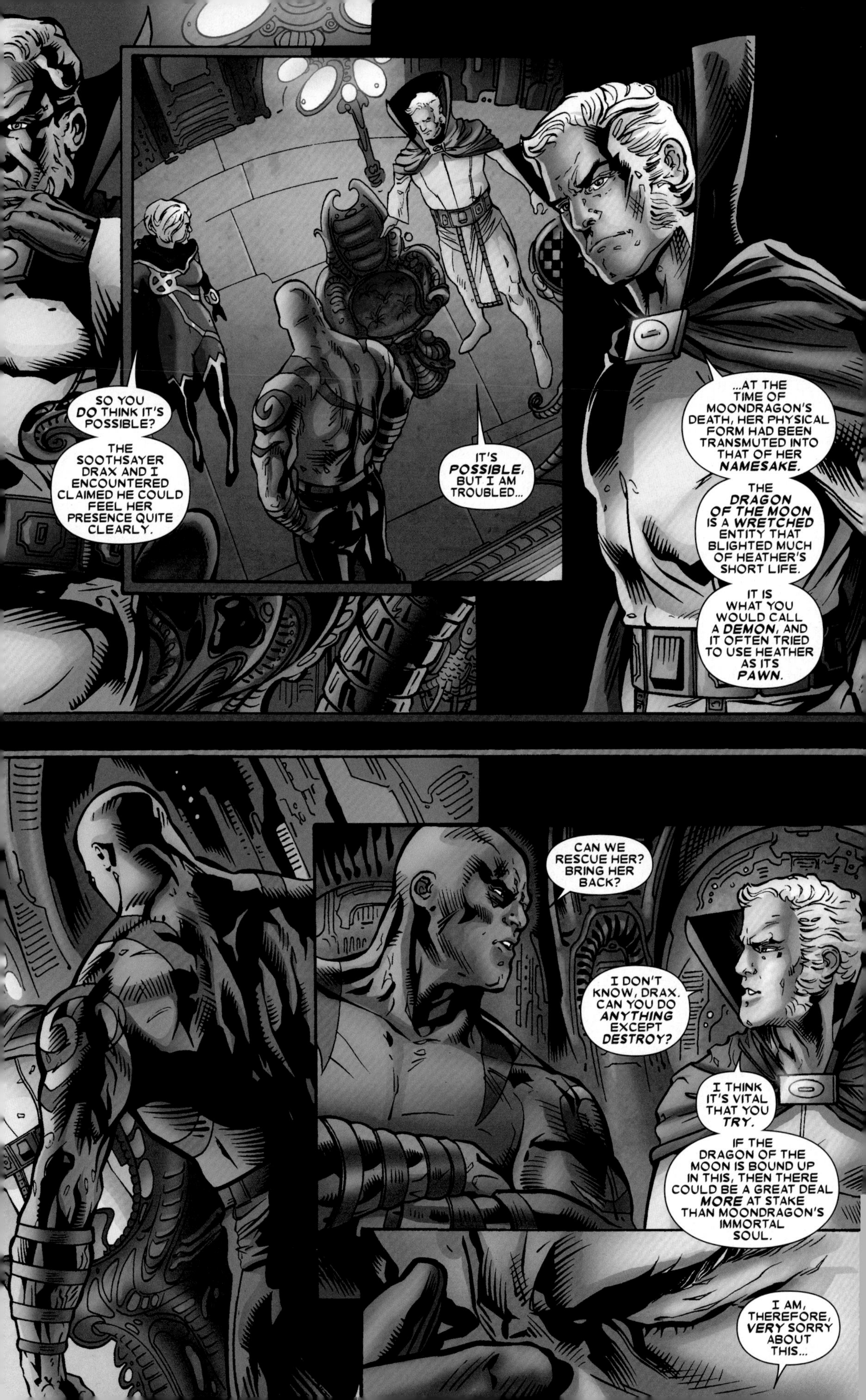
SO YOU DO THINK IT'S POSSIBLE?
THE SOOTHSAYER DRAX AND I ENCOUNTERED CLAIMED HE COULD FEEL HER PRESENCE QUITE CLEARLY.
IT'S POSSIBLE, BUT I AM TROUBLED...
...AT THE TIME OF MOONDRAGON'S DEATH, HER PHYSICAL FORM HAD BEEN TRANSMUTED INTO THAT OF HER NAMESAKE.
THE DRAGON OF THE MOON IS A WRETCHED ENTITY THAT BLIGHTED MUCH OF HEATHER'S SHORT LIFE.
IT IS WHAT YOU WOULD CALL A DEMON, AND IT OFTEN TRIED TO USE HEATHER AS ITS PAWN.
CAN WE RESCUE HER? BRING HER BACK?
I DON'T KNOW, DRAX. CAN YOU DO ANYTHING EXCEPT DESTROY?
I THINK IT'S VITAL THAT YOU TRY.
IF THE DRAGON OF THE MOON IS BOUND UP IN THIS, THEN THERE COULD BE A GREAT DEAL MORE AT STAKE THAN MOONDRAGON'S IMMORTAL SOUL.
I AM, THEREFORE, VERY SORRY ABOUT THIS...

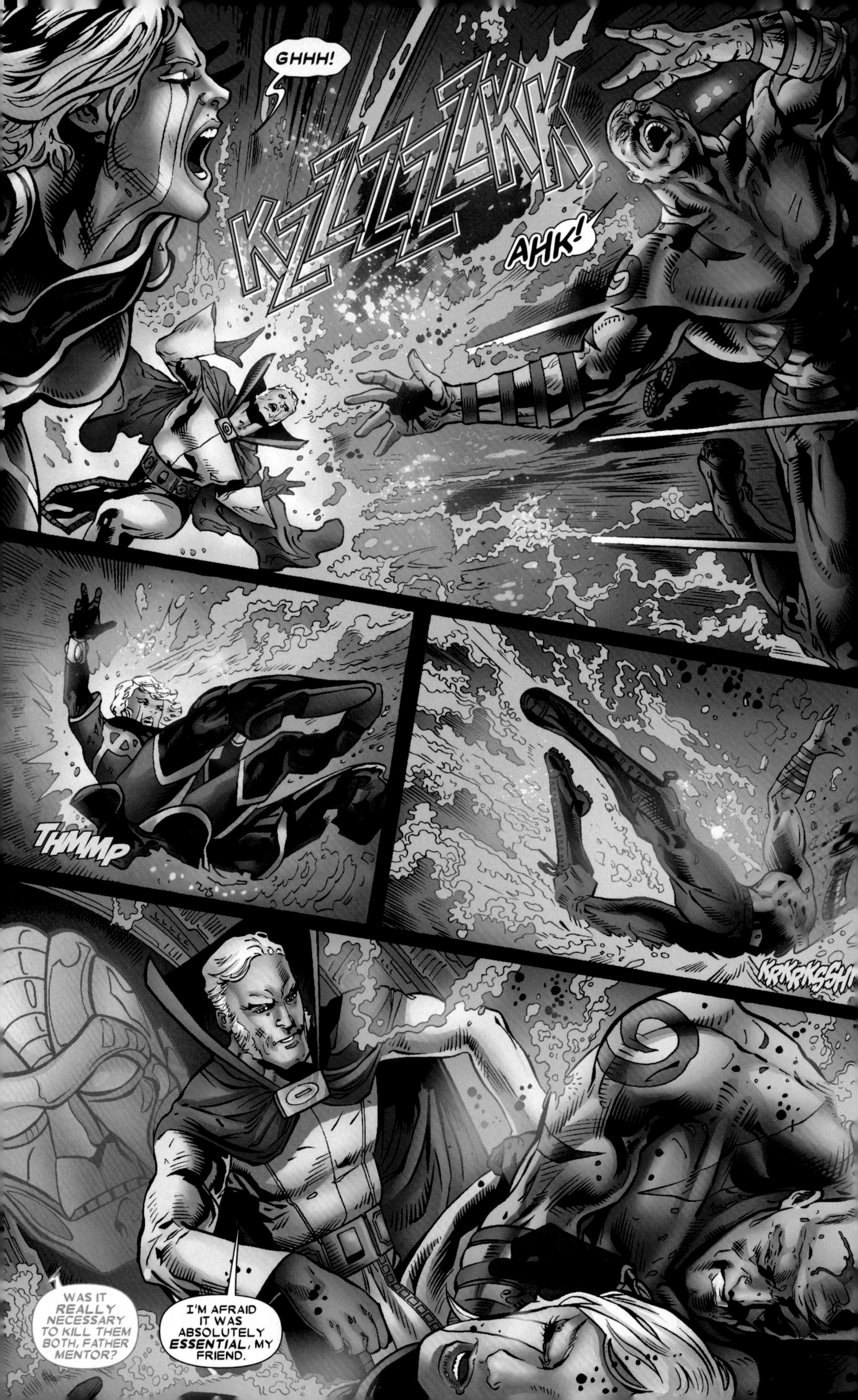
GHHH!
KZZZZZKK
AHK!
THMMP
KRKRKSH!
WAS IT REALLY NECESSARY TO KILL THEM BOTH, FATHER MENTOR?
I'M AFRAID IT WAS ABSOLUTELY ESSENTIAL, MY FRIEND.

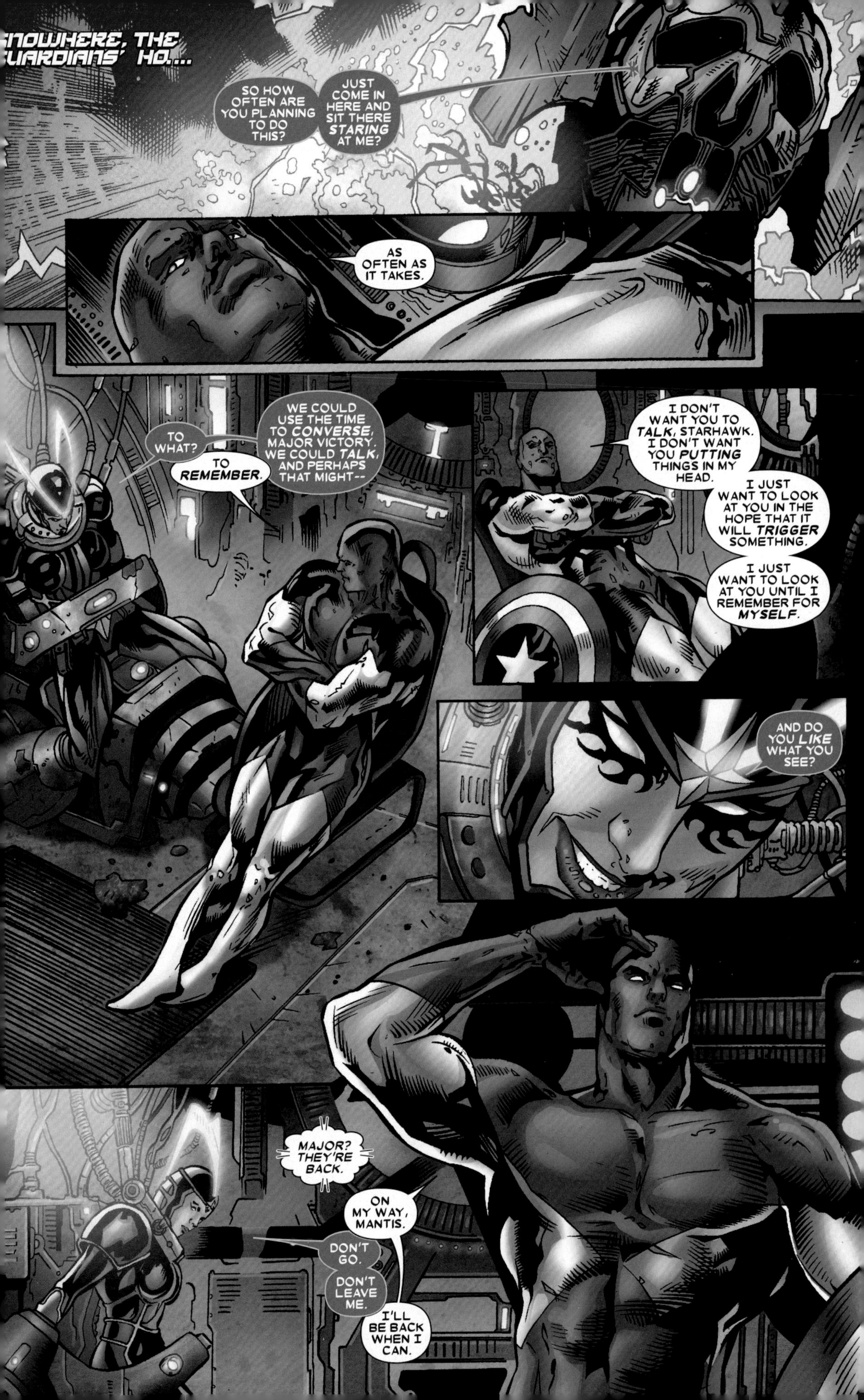
...NOWHERE, THE GUARDIANS' HQ....
SO HOW OFTEN ARE YOU PLANNING TO DO THIS?
JUST COME IN HERE AND SIT THERE STARING AT ME?
AS OFTEN AS IT TAKES.
WE COULD USE THE TIME TO CONVERSE, MAJOR VICTORY. WE COULD TALK, AND PERHAPS THAT MIGHT--
TO WHAT?
TO REMEMBER.
I DON'T WANT YOU TO TALK, STARHAWK. I DON'T WANT YOU PUTTING THINGS IN MY HEAD.
I JUST WANT TO LOOK AT YOU IN THE HOPE THAT IT WILL TRIGGER SOMETHING.
I JUST WANT TO LOOK AT YOU UNTIL I REMEMBER FOR MYSELF.
AND DO YOU LIKE WHAT YOU SEE?
MAJOR? THEY'RE BACK.
ON MY WAY, MANTIS.
DON'T GO.
DON'T LEAVE ME.
I'LL BE BACK WHEN I CAN.

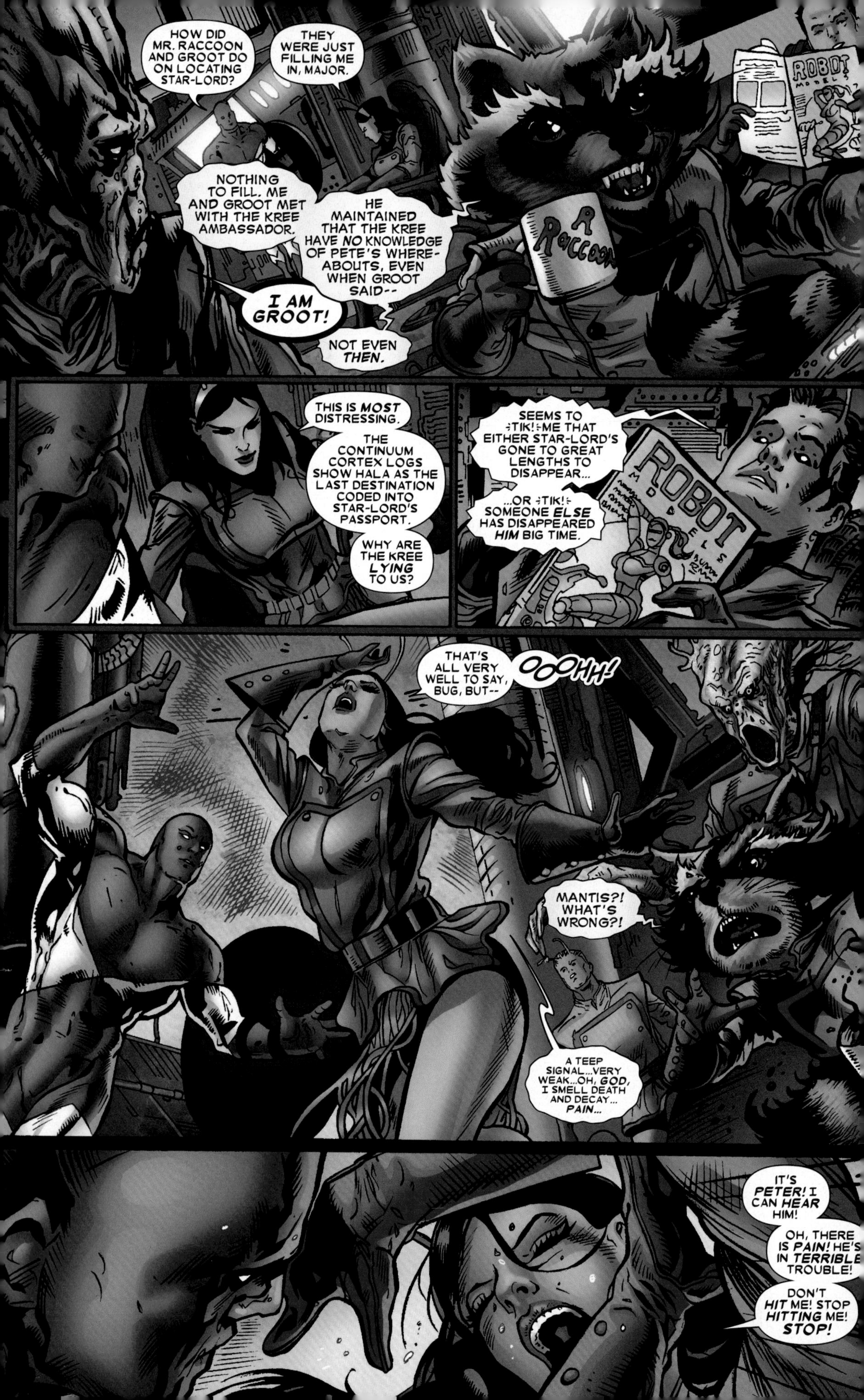

HOW DID MR. RACCOON AND GROOT DO ON LOCATING STAR-LORD?
THEY WERE JUST FILLING ME IN, MAJOR.
NOTHING TO FILL. ME AND GROOT MET WITH THE KREE AMBASSADOR.
HE MAINTAINED THAT THE KREE HAVE NO KNOWLEDGE OF PETE'S WHERE-ABOUTS, EVEN WHEN GROOT SAID--
I AM GROOT!
NOT EVEN THEN.
ROBOT MODELS
RACCOON
THIS IS MOST DISTRESSING.
THE CONTINUUM CORTEX LOGS SHOW HALA AS THE LAST DESTINATION CODED INTO STAR-LORD'S PASSPORT.
WHY ARE THE KREE LYING TO US?
SEEMS TO ÷TIK!÷ ME THAT EITHER STAR-LORD'S GONE TO GREAT LENGTHS TO DISAPPEAR...
...OR ÷TIK!÷ SOMEONE ELSE HAS DISAPPEARED HIM BIG TIME.
ROBOT MODELS
THAT'S ALL VERY WELL TO SAY, BUG, BUT--
OOOHH!
MANTIS?! WHAT'S WRONG?!
A TEEP SIGNAL...VERY WEAK...OH, GOD, I SMELL DEATH AND DECAY... PAIN...
IT'S PETER! I CAN HEAR HIM!
OH, THERE IS PAIN! HE'S IN TERRIBLE TROUBLE!
DON'T HIT ME! STOP HITTING ME! STOP!

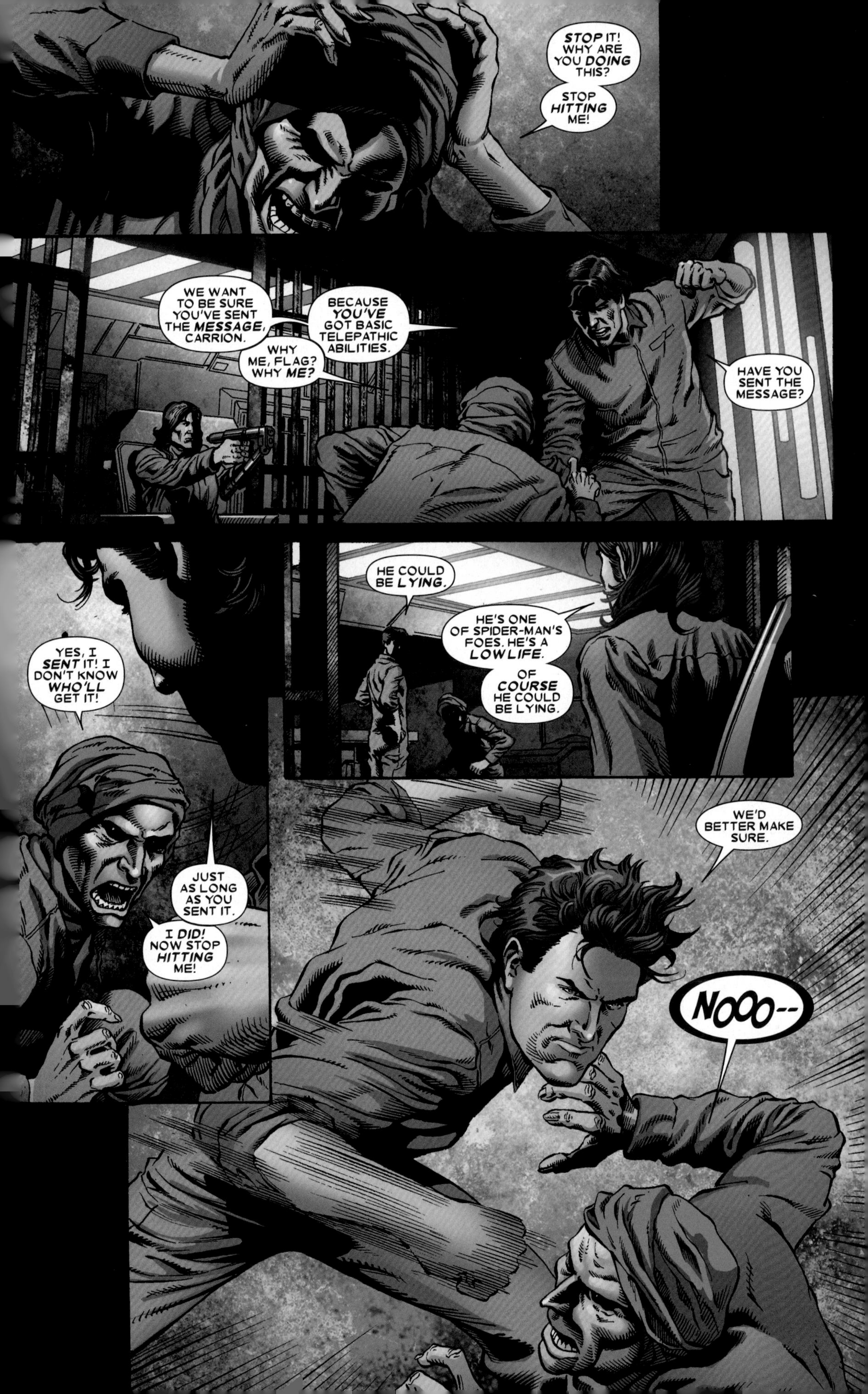
STOP IT! WHY ARE YOU DOING THIS?
STOP HITTING ME!
WE WANT TO BE SURE YOU'VE SENT THE MESSAGE, CARRION.
WHY ME, FLAG? WHY ME?
BECAUSE YOU'VE GOT BASIC TELEPATHIC ABILITIES.
HAVE YOU SENT THE MESSAGE?
YES, I SENT IT! I DON'T KNOW WHO'LL GET IT!
HE COULD BE LYING.
HE'S ONE OF SPIDER-MAN'S FOES. HE'S A LOWLIFE.
OF COURSE HE COULD BE LYING.
JUST AS LONG AS YOU SENT IT.
I DID! NOW STOP HITTING ME!
WE'D BETTER MAKE SURE.
NOOO--

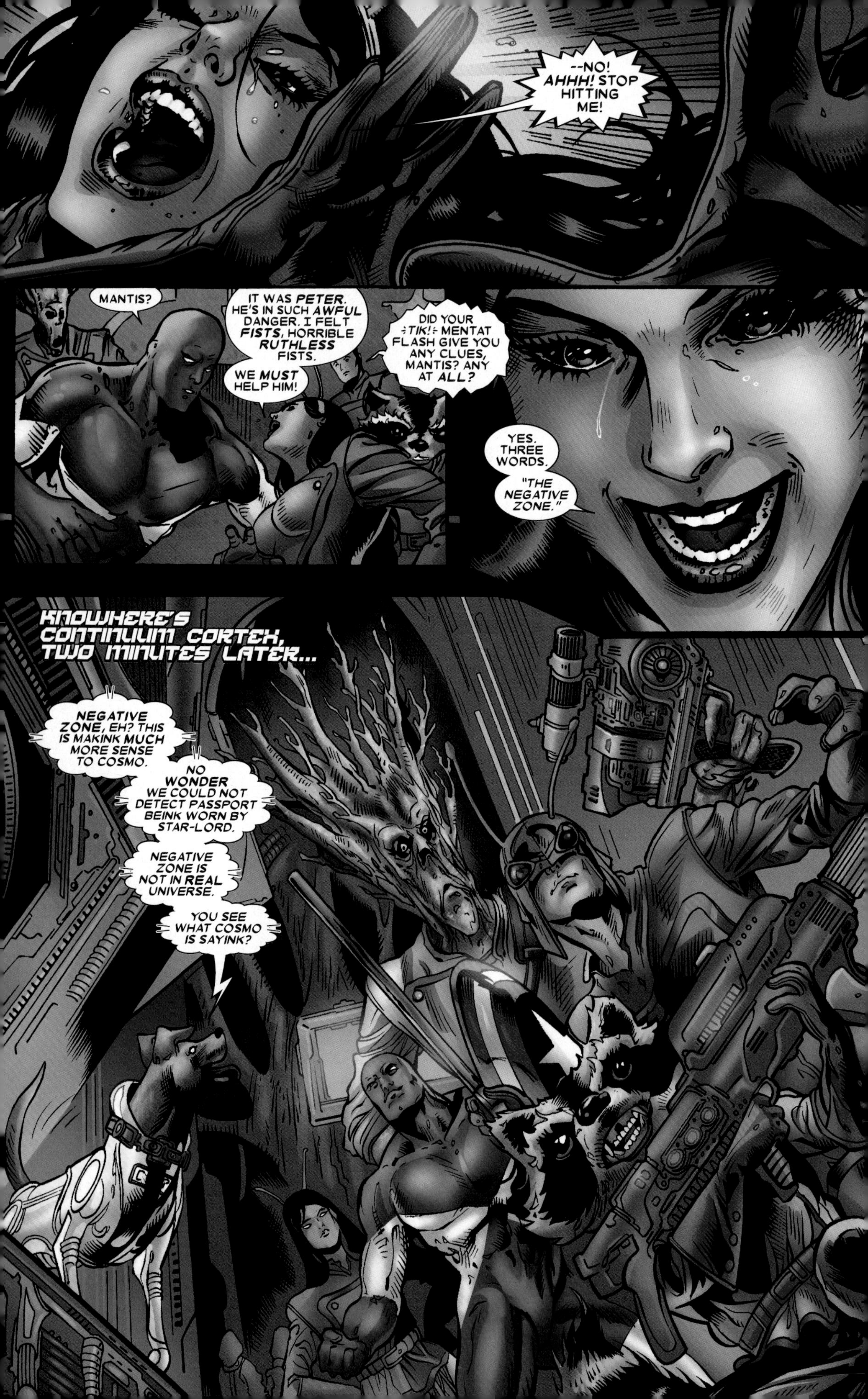
--NO! AHHH! STOP HITTING ME!
MANTIS?
IT WAS PETER. HE'S IN SUCH AWFUL DANGER. I FELT FISTS, HORRIBLE RUTHLESS FISTS.
WE MUST HELP HIM!
DID YOUR ÷TIK!÷ MENTAT FLASH GIVE YOU ANY CLUES, MANTIS? ANY AT ALL?
YES. THREE WORDS.
"THE NEGATIVE ZONE."
KNOWHERE'S CONTINUUM CORTEX, TWO MINUTES LATER...
NEGATIVE ZONE, EH? THIS IS MAKINK MUCH MORE SENSE TO COSMO.
NO WONDER WE COULD NOT DETECT PASSPORT BEINK WORN BY STAR-LORD.
NEGATIVE ZONE IS NOT IN REAL UNIVERSE.
YOU SEE WHAT COSMO IS SAYINK?

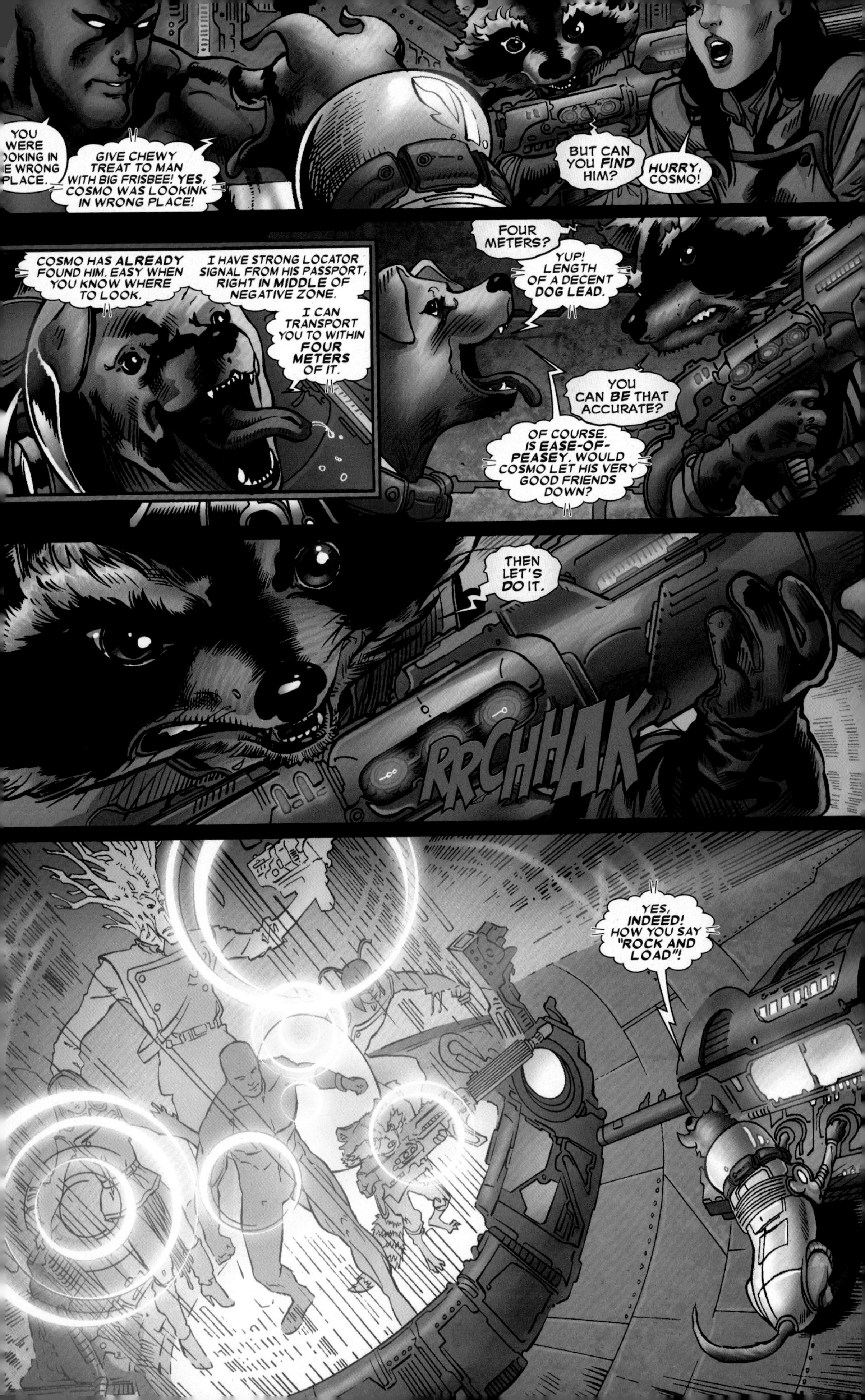
YOU WERE LOOKING IN THE WRONG PLACE.
GIVE CHEWY TREAT TO MAN WITH BIG FRISBEE! YES, COSMO WAS LOOKINK IN WRONG PLACE!
BUT CAN YOU FIND HIM?
HURRY, COSMO!
COSMO HAS ALREADY FOUND HIM. EASY WHEN YOU KNOW WHERE TO LOOK.
I HAVE STRONG LOCATOR SIGNAL FROM HIS PASSPORT, RIGHT IN MIDDLE OF NEGATIVE ZONE.
I CAN TRANSPORT YOU TO WITHIN FOUR METERS OF IT.
FOUR METERS?
YUP! LENGTH OF A DECENT DOG LEAD.
YOU CAN BE THAT ACCURATE?
OF COURSE. IS EASE-OF-PEASEY. WOULD COSMO LET HIS VERY GOOD FRIENDS DOWN?
THEN LET'S DO IT.
RRCHHAK
YES, INDEED! HOW YOU SAY "ROCK AND LOAD"!

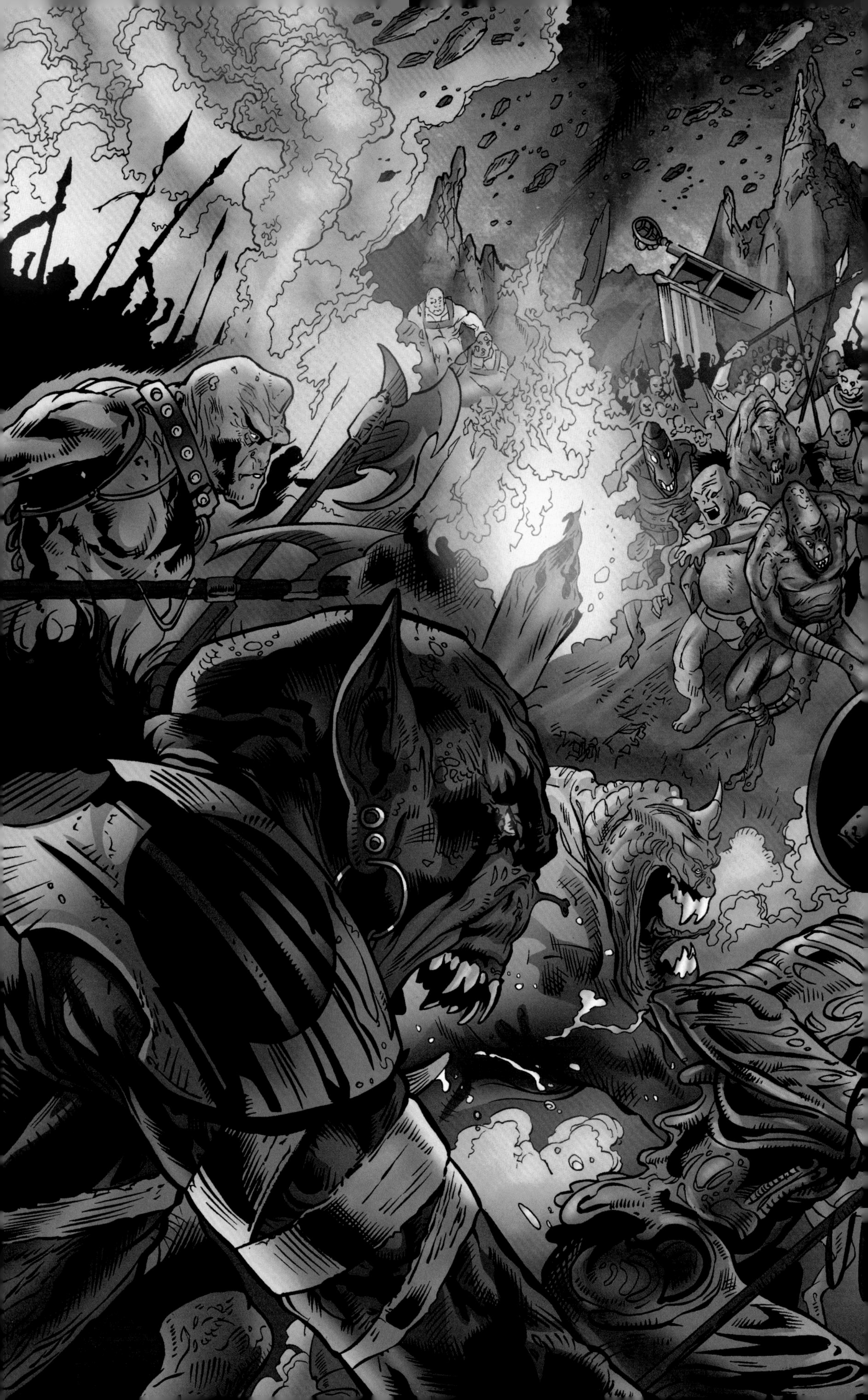

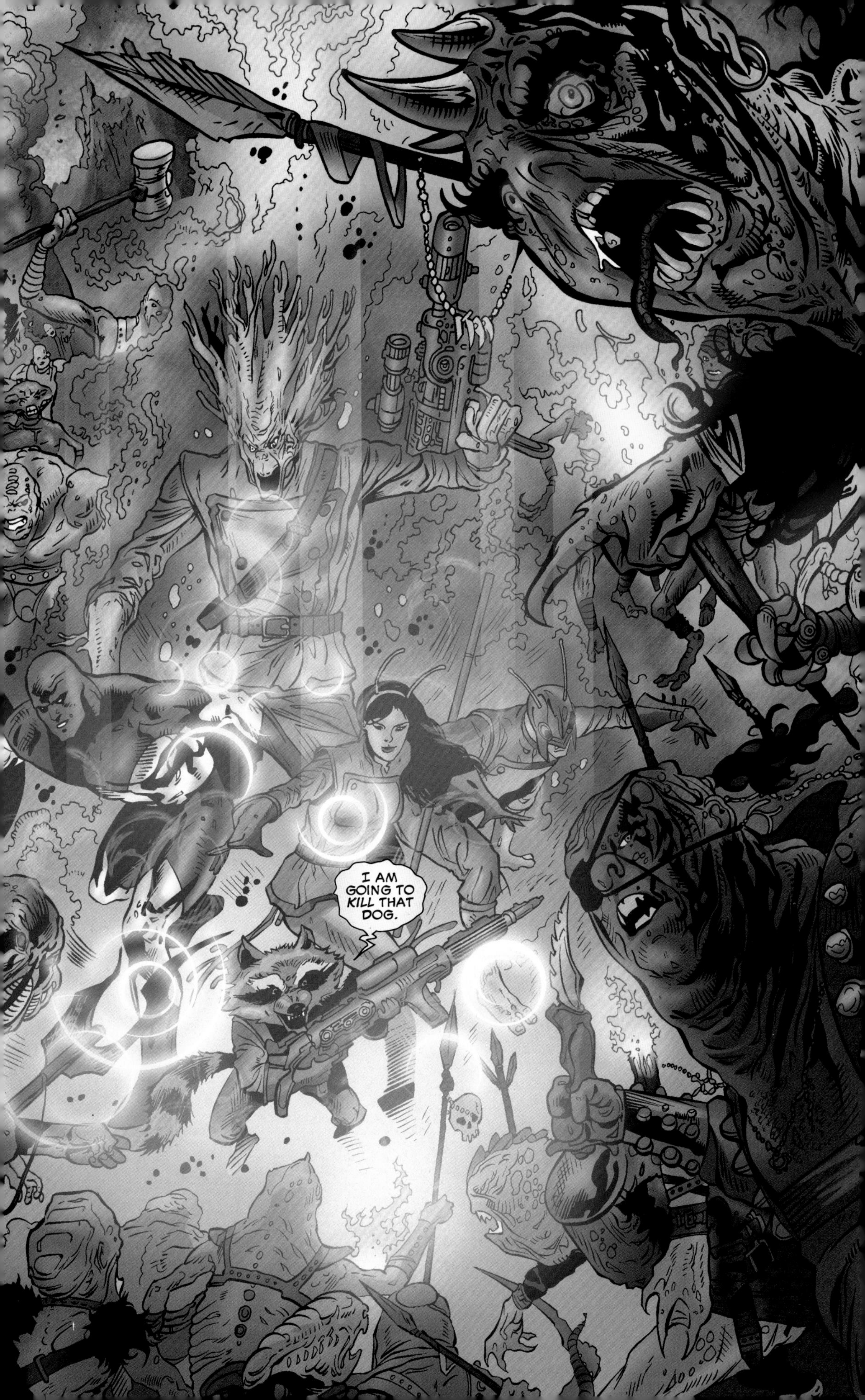
I AM GOING TO *KILL* THAT DOG.

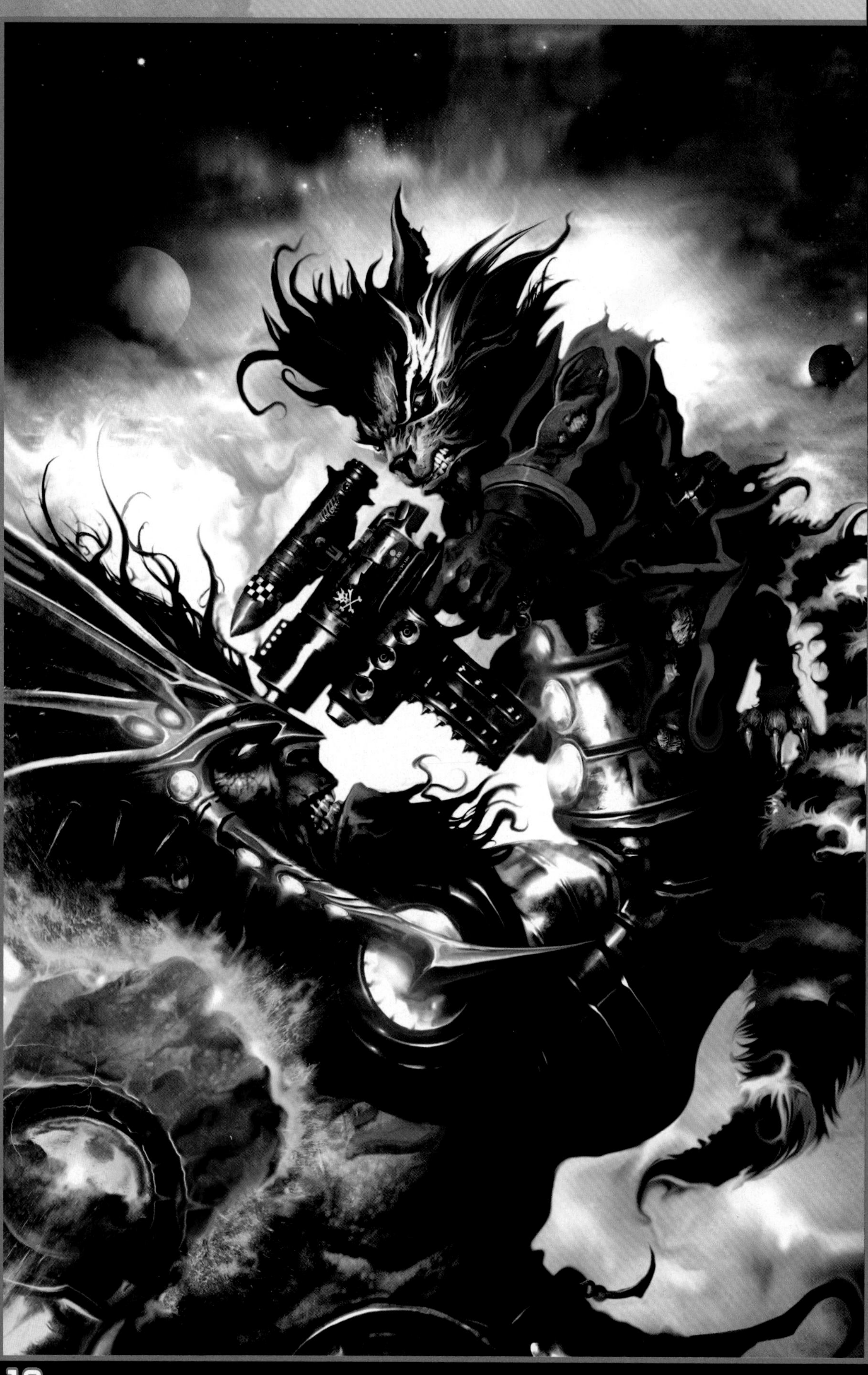

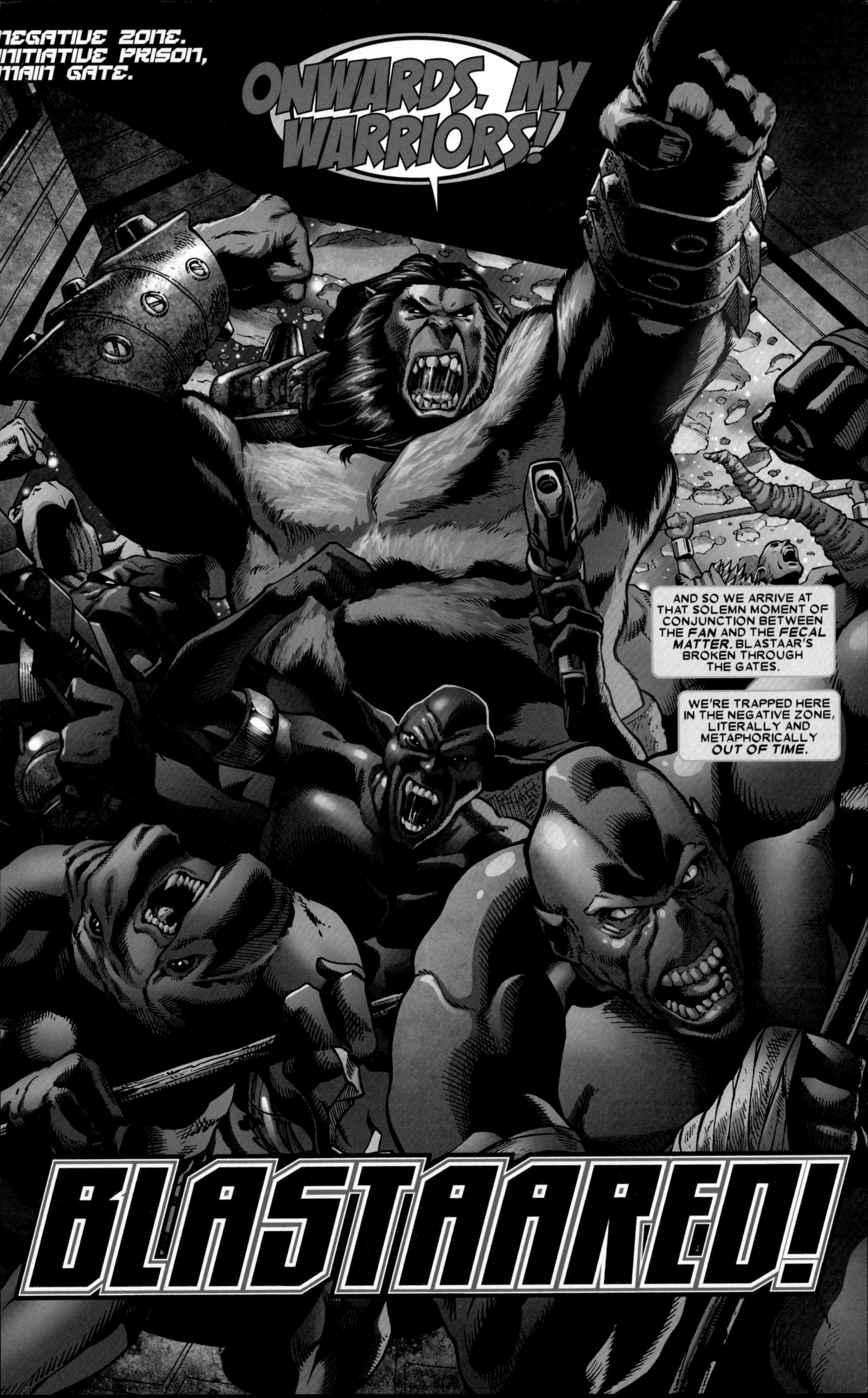
NEGATIVE ZONE. INITIATIVE PRISON, MAIN GATE.
ONWARDS, MY WARRIORS!
AND SO WE ARRIVE AT THAT SOLEMN MOMENT OF CONJUNCTION BETWEEN THE FAN AND THE FECAL MATTER. BLASTAAR'S BROKEN THROUGH THE GATES.
WE'RE TRAPPED HERE IN THE NEGATIVE ZONE, LITERALLY AND METAPHORICALLY OUT OF TIME.
BLASTAARED!

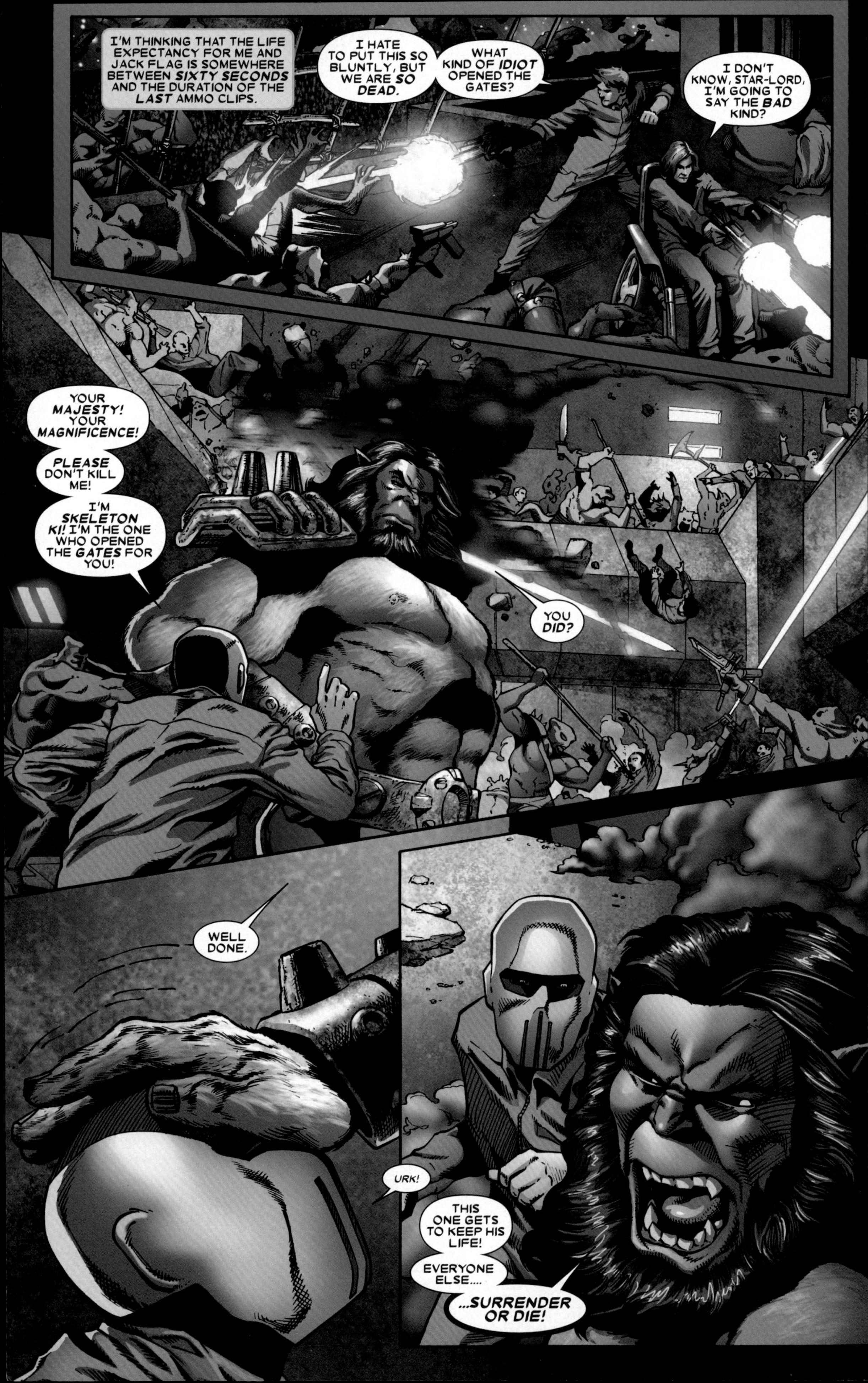
I'M THINKING THAT THE LIFE EXPECTANCY FOR ME AND JACK FLAG IS SOMEWHERE BETWEEN SIXTY SECONDS AND THE DURATION OF THE LAST AMMO CLIPS.
I HATE TO PUT THIS SO BLUNTLY, BUT WE ARE SO DEAD.
WHAT KIND OF IDIOT OPENED THE GATES?
I DON'T KNOW, STAR-LORD, I'M GOING TO SAY THE BAD KIND?
YOUR MAJESTY! YOUR MAGNIFICENCE!
PLEASE DON'T KILL ME!
I'M SKELETON KI! I'M THE ONE WHO OPENED THE GATES FOR YOU!
YOU DID?
WELL DONE.
URK!
THIS ONE GETS TO KEEP HIS LIFE!
EVERYONE ELSE....
...SURRENDER OR DIE!

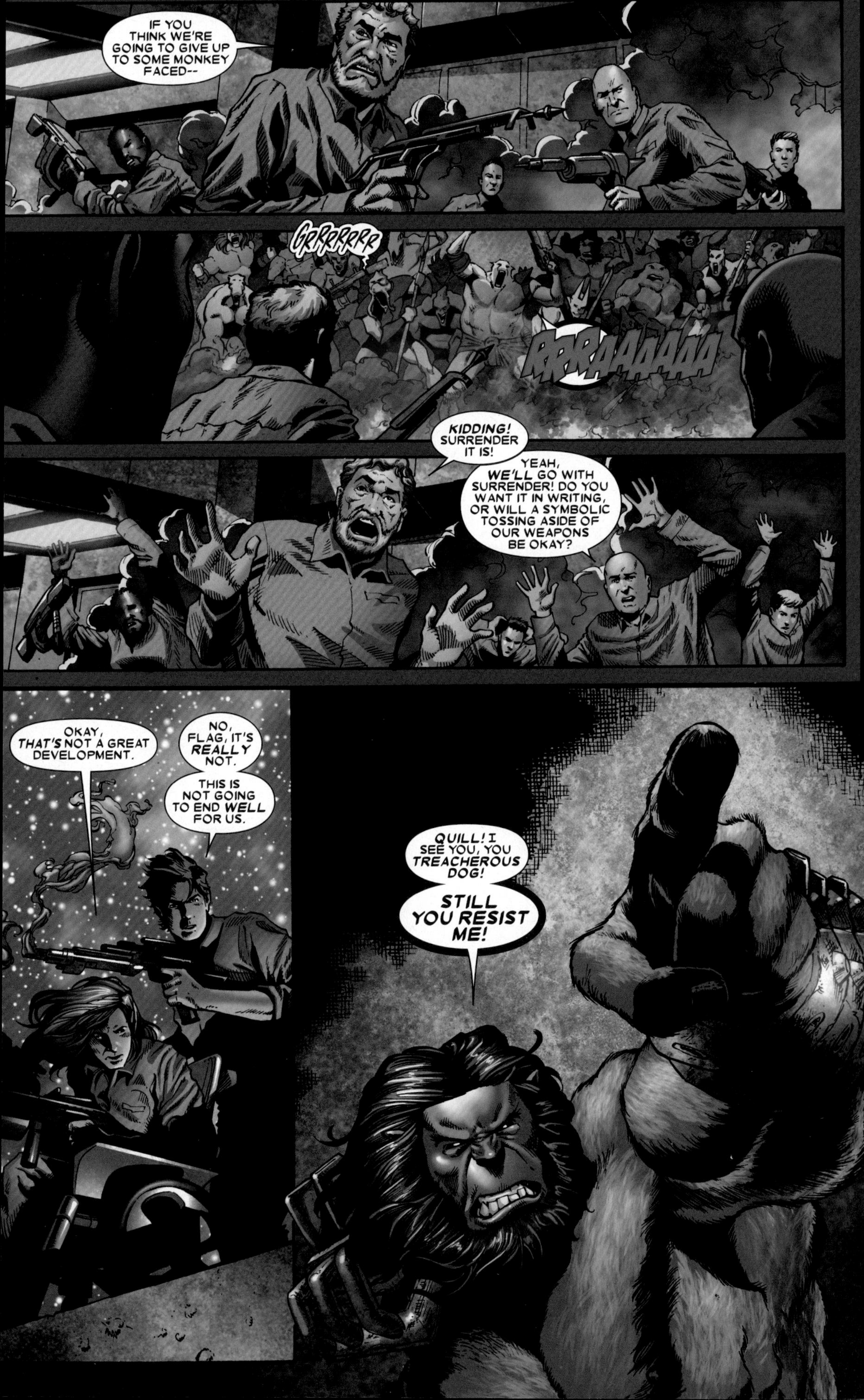
IF YOU THINK WE'RE GOING TO GIVE UP TO SOME MONKEY FACED--
GRRRRRRR
RRRAAAAAAA
KIDDING! SURRENDER IT IS!
YEAH, WE'LL GO WITH SURRENDER! DO YOU WANT IT IN WRITING, OR WILL A SYMBOLIC TOSSING ASIDE OF OUR WEAPONS BE OKAY?
OKAY, THAT'S NOT A GREAT DEVELOPMENT.
NO, FLAG, IT'S REALLY NOT.
THIS IS NOT GOING TO END WELL FOR US.
QUILL! I SEE YOU, YOU TREACHEROUS DOG!
STILL YOU RESIST ME!

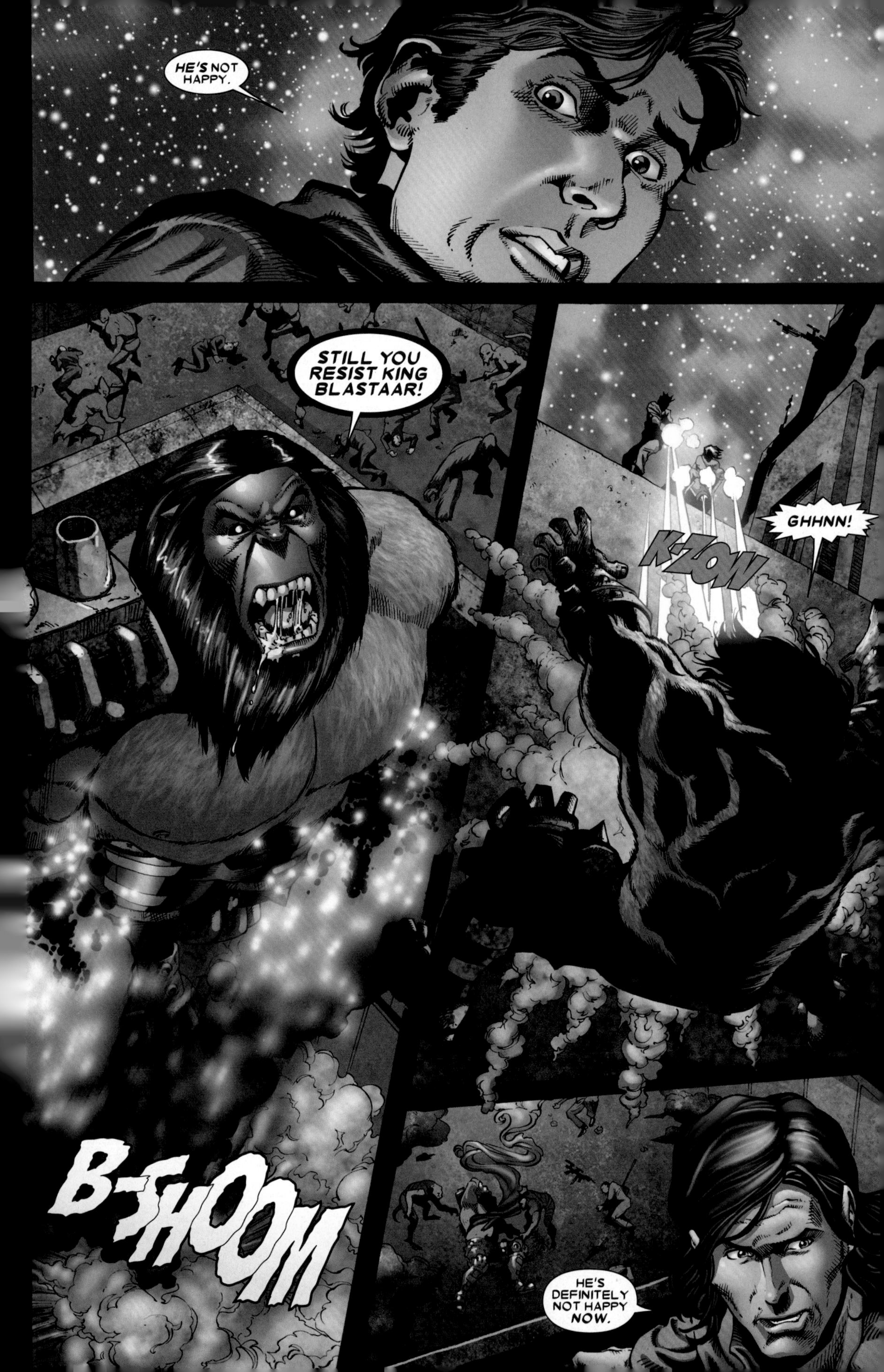
HE'S NOT HAPPY.
STILL YOU RESIST KING BLASTAAR!
K-ZOW
GHHNN!
B-THOOM
HE'S DEFINITELY NOT HAPPY NOW.

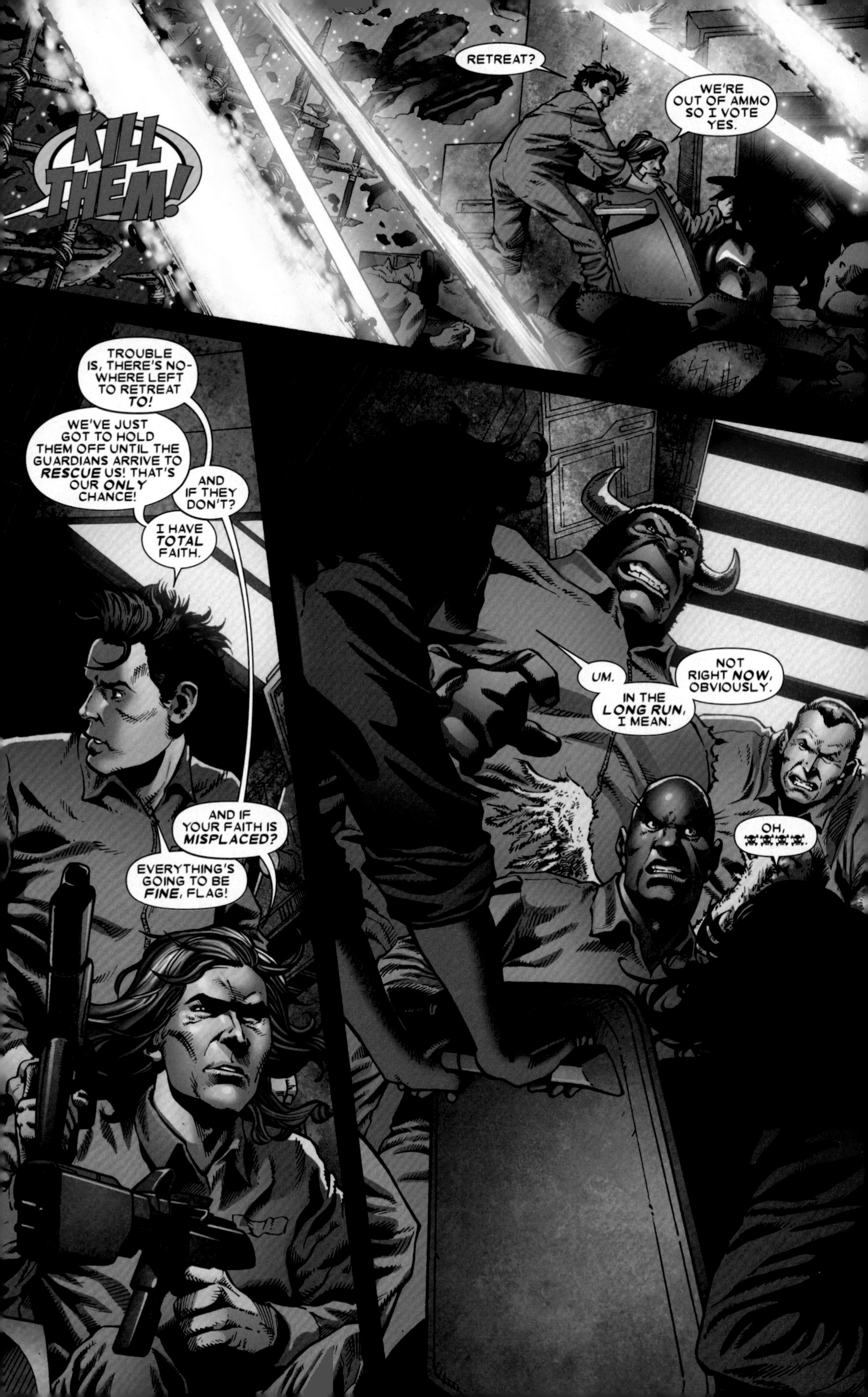
KILL THEM!
RETREAT?
WE'RE OUT OF AMMO SO I VOTE YES.
TROUBLE IS, THERE'S NOWHERE LEFT TO RETREAT TO!
WE'VE JUST GOT TO HOLD THEM OFF UNTIL THE GUARDIANS ARRIVE TO RESCUE US! THAT'S OUR ONLY CHANCE!
AND IF THEY DON'T?
I HAVE TOTAL FAITH.
AND IF YOUR FAITH IS MISPLACED?
EVERYTHING'S GOING TO BE FINE, FLAG!
UM.
NOT RIGHT NOW, OBVIOUSLY.
IN THE LONG RUN, I MEAN.
OH,

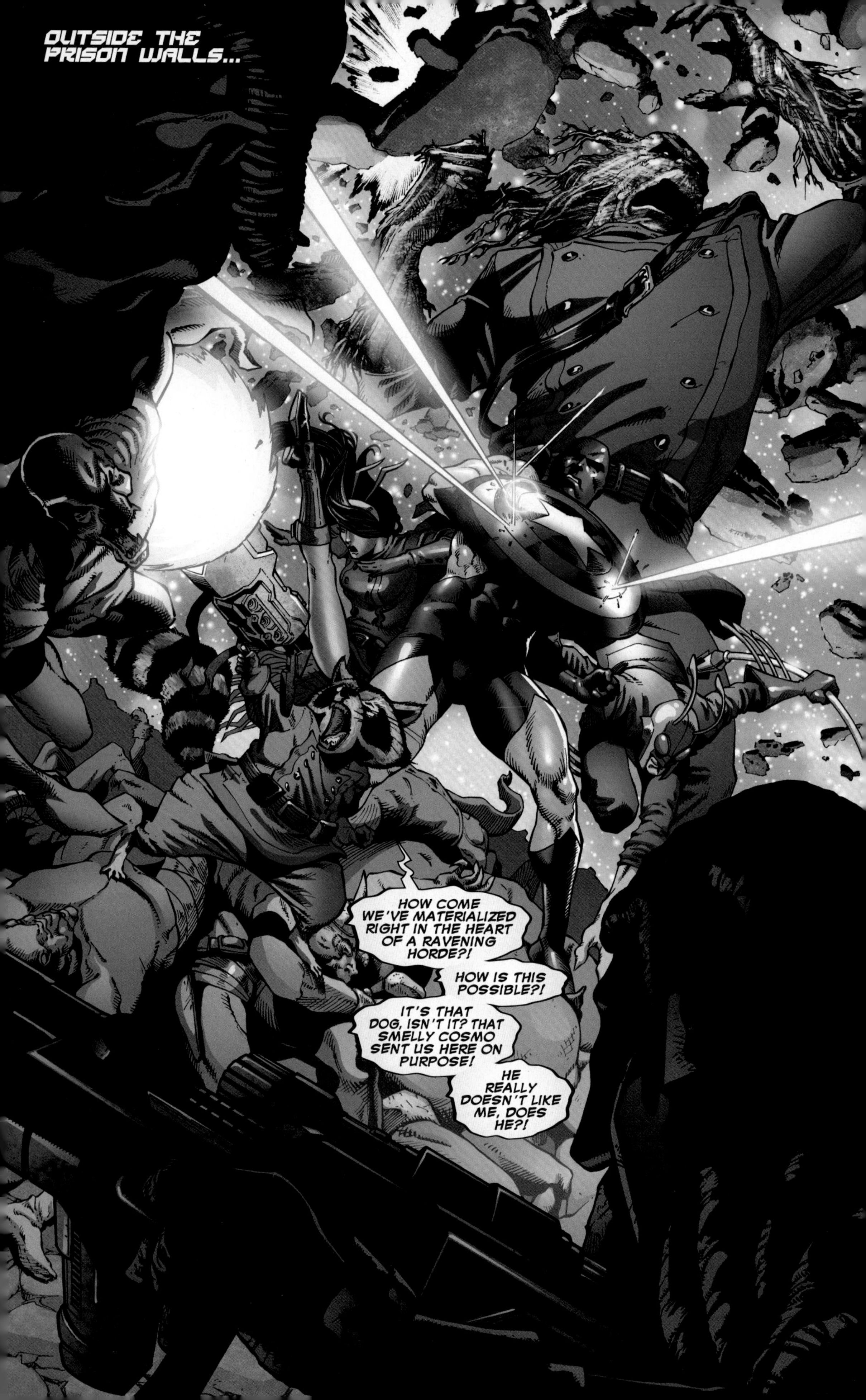
OUTSIDE THE PRISON WALLS...
HOW COME WE'VE MATERIALIZED RIGHT IN THE HEART OF A RAVENING HORDE?!
HOW IS THIS POSSIBLE?!
IT'S THAT DOG, ISN'T IT? THAT SMELLY COSMO SENT US HERE ON PURPOSE!
HE REALLY DOESN'T LIKE ME, DOES HE?!

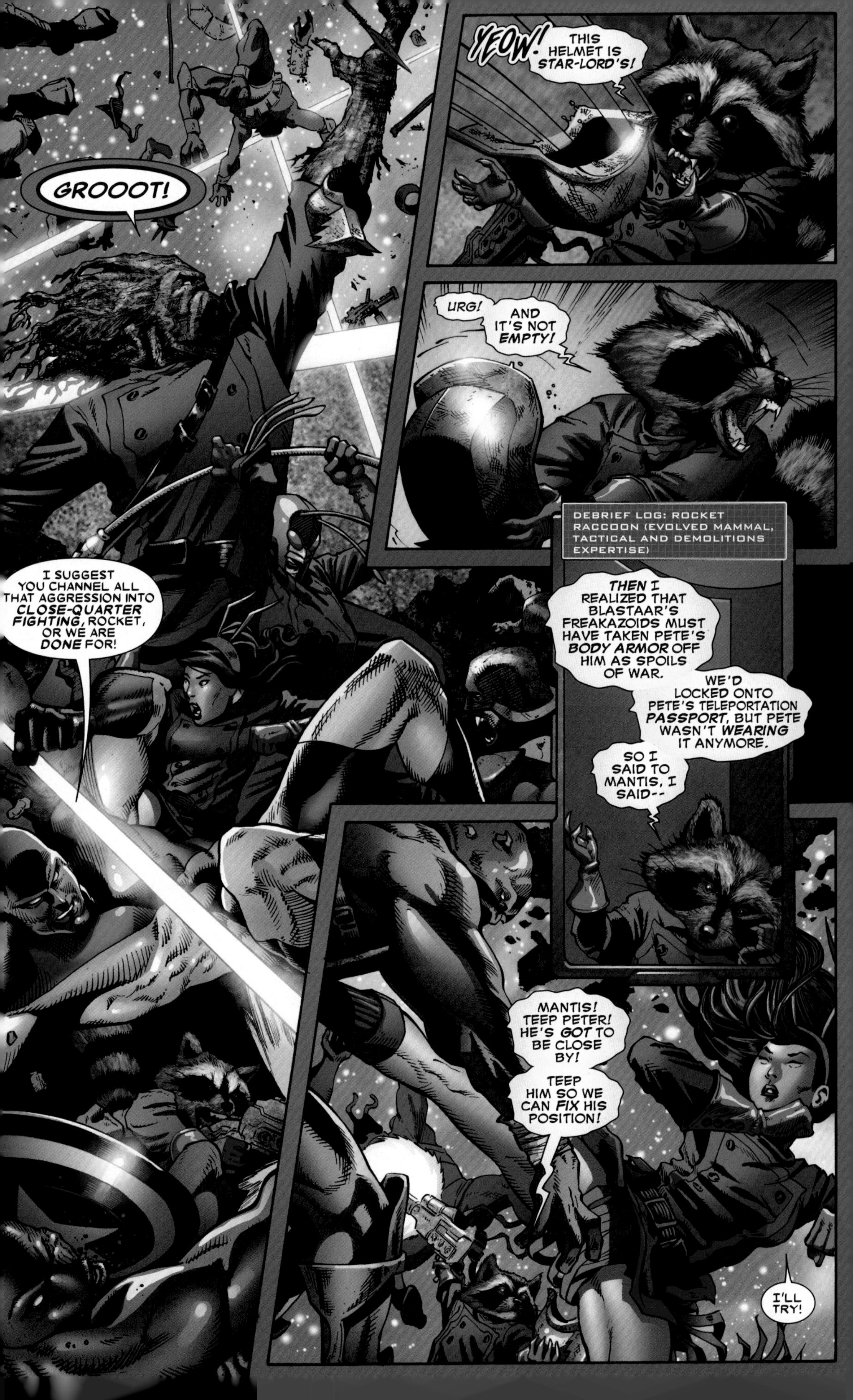
GROOOT!
YEOW!
THIS HELMET IS STAR-LORD'S!
URG!
AND IT'S NOT EMPTY!
I SUGGEST YOU CHANNEL ALL THAT AGGRESSION INTO CLOSE-QUARTER FIGHTING, ROCKET, OR WE ARE DONE FOR!
DEBRIEF LOG: ROCKET RACCOON (EVOLVED MAMMAL, TACTICAL AND DEMOLITIONS EXPERTISE)
THEN I REALIZED THAT BLASTAAR'S FREAKAZOIDS MUST HAVE TAKEN PETE'S BODY ARMOR OFF HIM AS SPOILS OF WAR.
WE'D LOCKED ONTO PETE'S TELEPORTATION PASSPORT, BUT PETE WASN'T WEARING IT ANYMORE.
SO I SAID TO MANTIS, I SAID--
MANTIS! TEEP PETER! HE'S GOT TO BE CLOSE BY!
TEEP HIM SO WE CAN FIX HIS POSITION!
I'LL TRY!

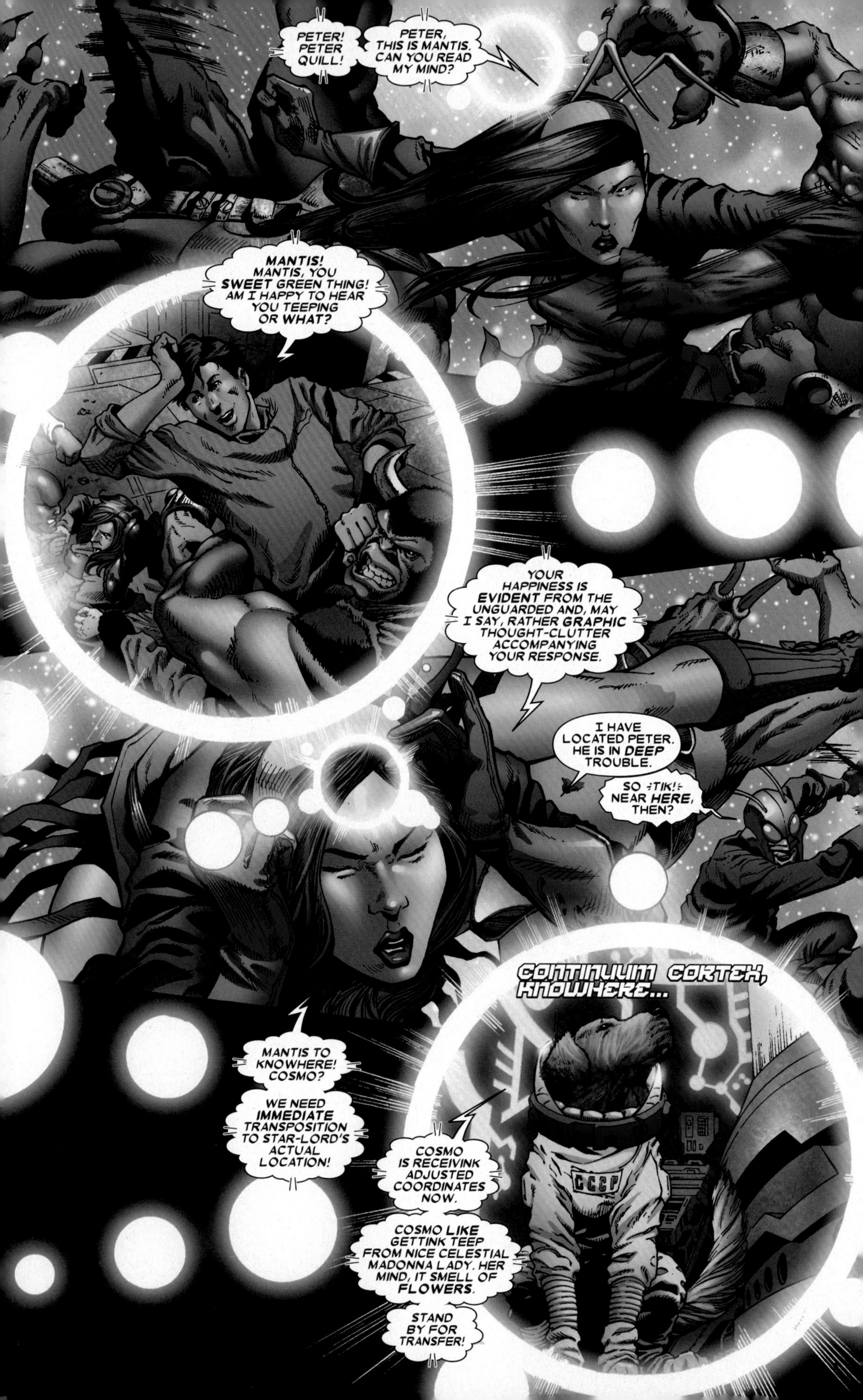
PETER! PETER QUILL!
PETER, THIS IS MANTIS. CAN YOU READ MY MIND?
MANTIS! MANTIS, YOU SWEET GREEN THING! AM I HAPPY TO HEAR YOU TEEPING OR WHAT?
YOUR HAPPINESS IS EVIDENT FROM THE UNGUARDED AND, MAY I SAY, RATHER GRAPHIC THOUGHT-CLUTTER ACCOMPANYING YOUR RESPONSE.
I HAVE LOCATED PETER. HE IS IN DEEP TROUBLE.
SO ≠TIK!≠ NEAR HERE, THEN?
CONTINUUM CORTEX, KNOWHERE...
MANTIS TO KNOWHERE! COSMO?
WE NEED IMMEDIATE TRANSPOSITION TO STAR-LORD'S ACTUAL LOCATION!
COSMO IS RECEIVINK ADJUSTED COORDINATES NOW.
COSMO LIKE GETTINK TEEP FROM NICE CELESTIAL MADONNA LADY. HER MIND, IT SMELL OF FLOWERS.
STAND BY FOR TRANSFER!
CCCP

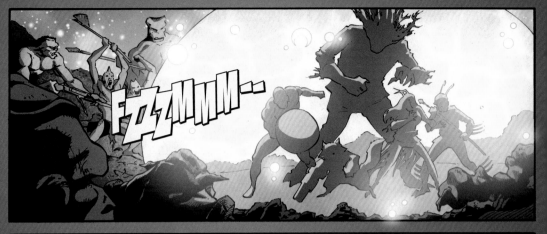

FΩZMMM--

WHAT'S--

--MMMM

GOOD TO SEE YOU ALIVE, STAR-LORD.

MAJOR VICTORY? YOU'RE ON THE TEAM?

MAN, HOW LONG HAVE I *BEEN* HERE?

K-TANG

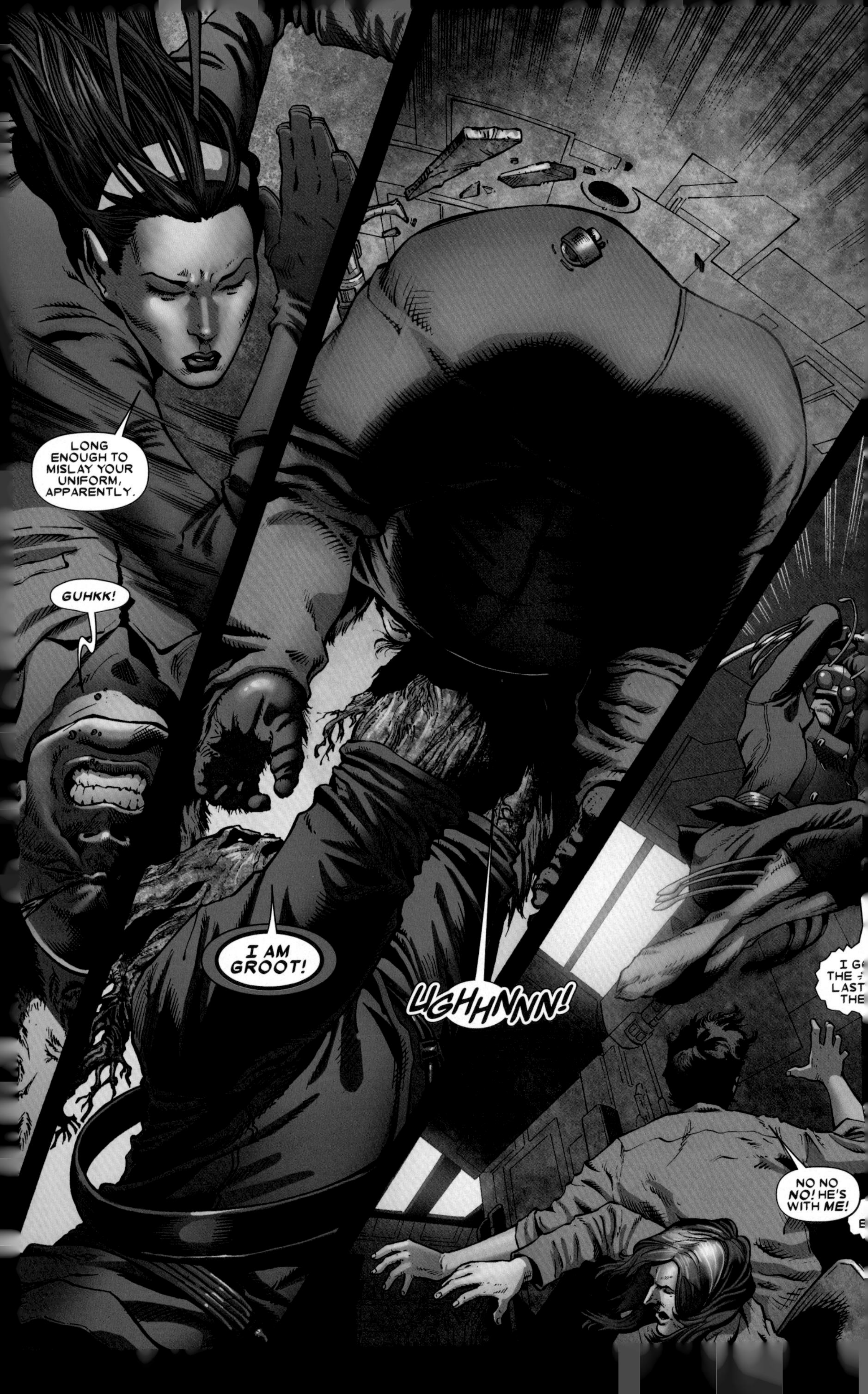
LONG ENOUGH TO MISLAY YOUR UNIFORM, APPARENTLY.
GUHKK!
I AM GROOT!
UGHHNNN!
NO NO NO! HE'S WITH ME!

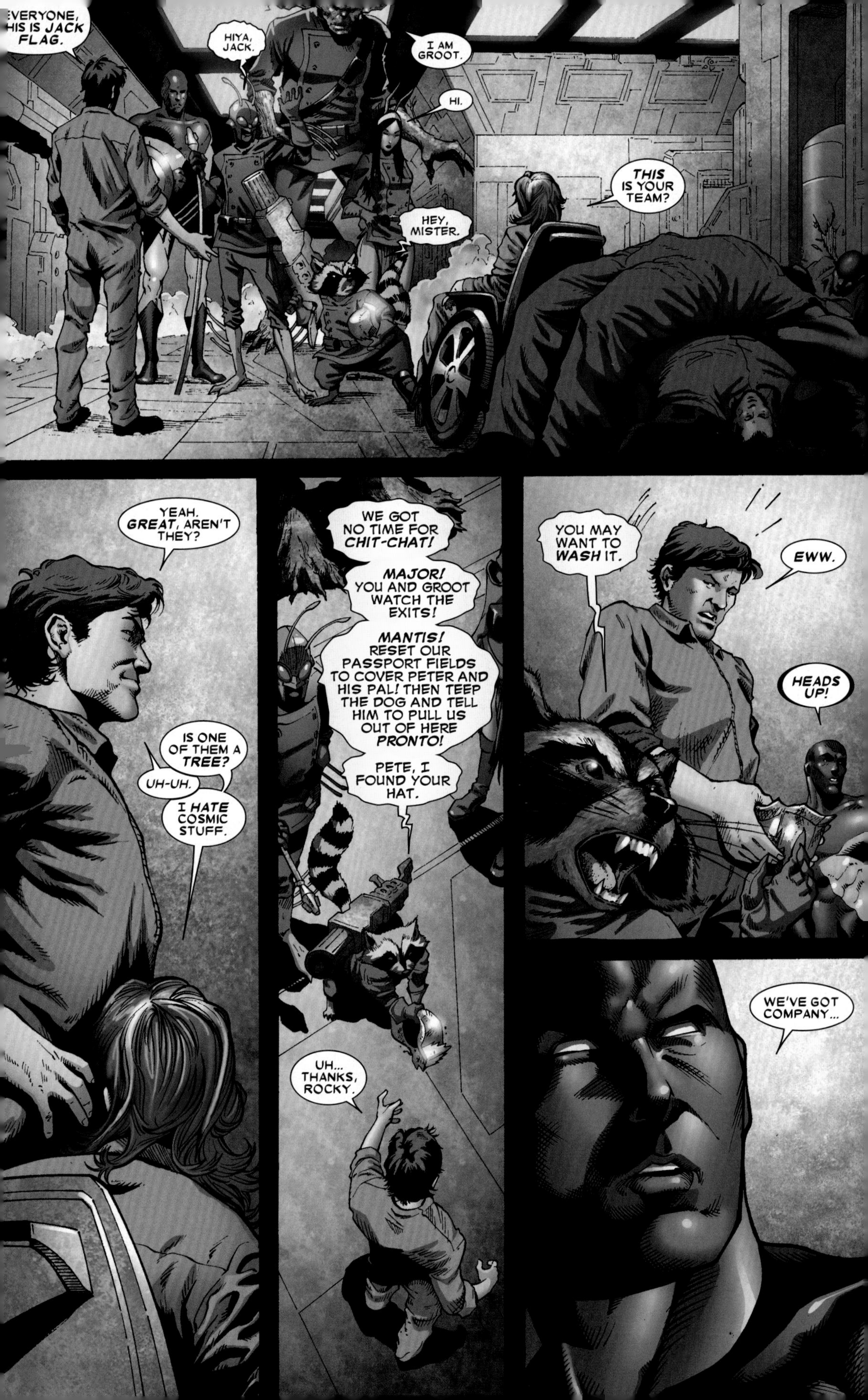
EVERYONE, THIS IS JACK FLAG.
HIYA, JACK.
I AM GROOT.
HI.
THIS IS YOUR TEAM?
HEY, MISTER.
YEAH. GREAT, AREN'T THEY?
IS ONE OF THEM A TREE?
UH-UH.
I HATE COSMIC STUFF.
WE GOT NO TIME FOR CHIT-CHAT!
MAJOR! YOU AND GROOT WATCH THE EXITS!
MANTIS! RESET OUR PASSPORT FIELDS TO COVER PETER AND HIS PAL! THEN TEEP THE DOG AND TELL HIM TO PULL US OUT OF HERE PRONTO!
PETE, I FOUND YOUR HAT.
UH... THANKS, ROCKY.
YOU MAY WANT TO WASH IT.
EWW.
HEADS UP!
WE'VE GOT COMPANY...

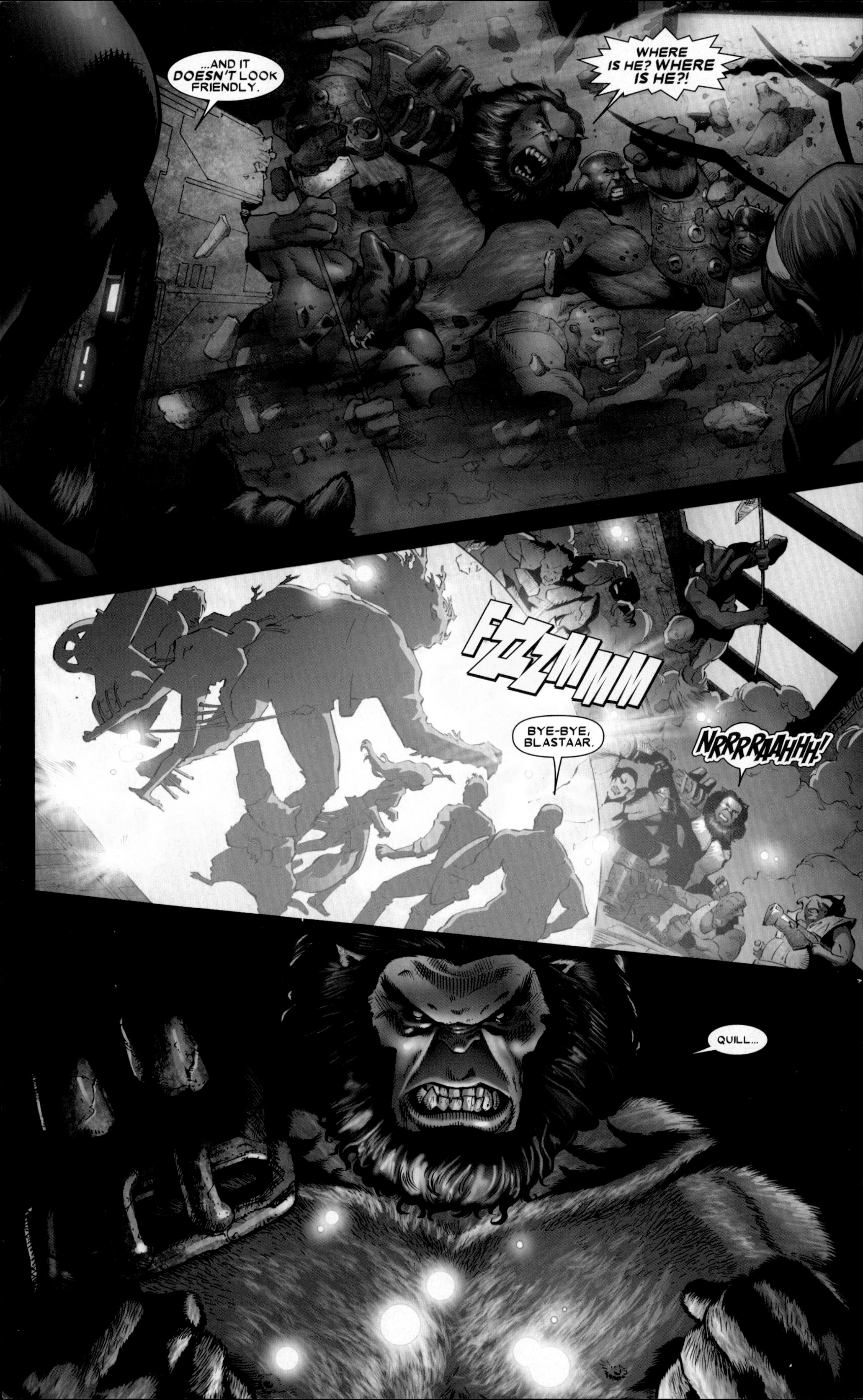
...AND IT DOESN'T LOOK FRIENDLY.
WHERE IS HE? WHERE IS HE?!
FZZZMMMM
BYE-BYE, BLASTAAR.
NRRRRAAHHH!
QUILL...

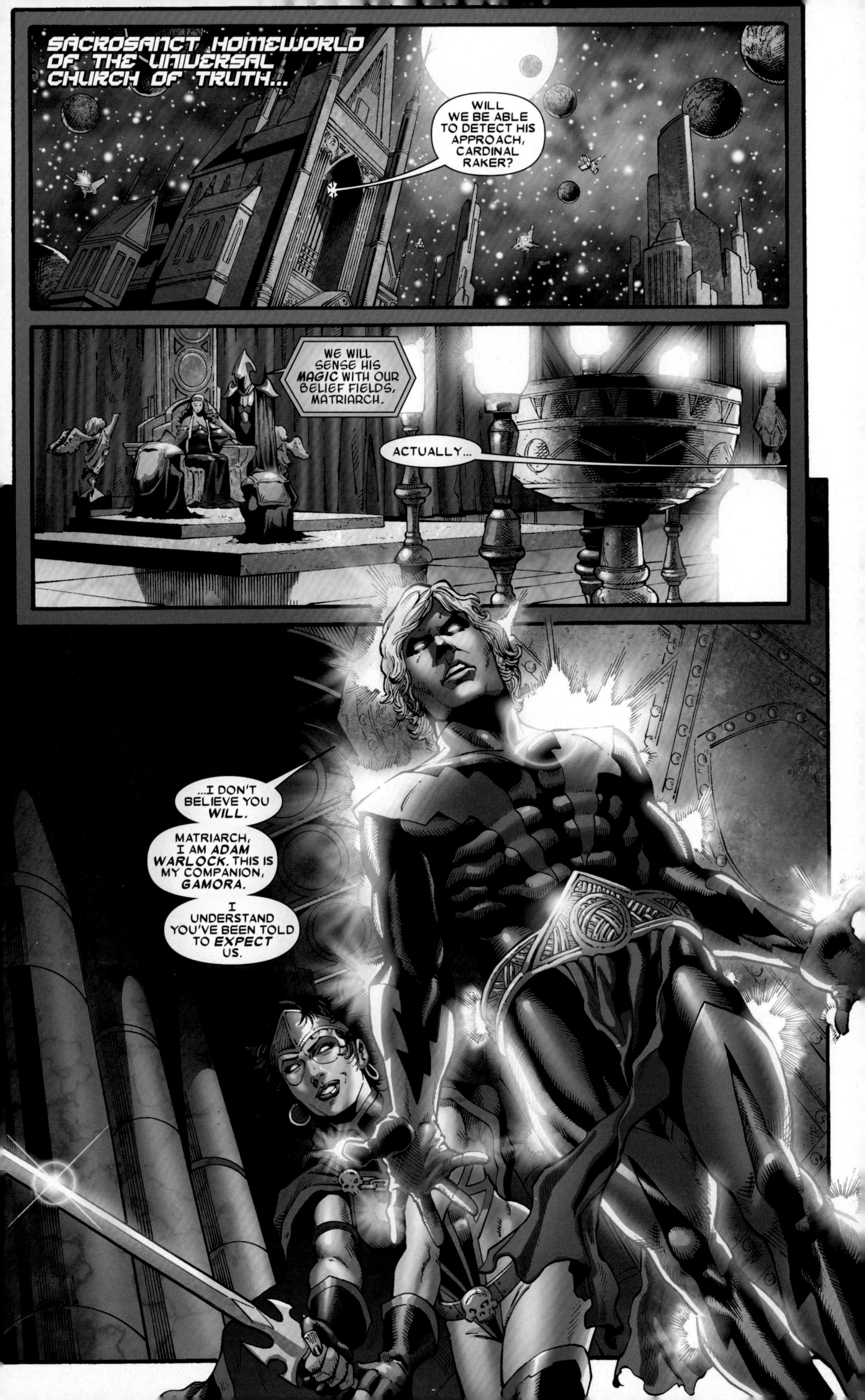
SACROSANCT HOMEWORLD OF THE UNIVERSAL CHURCH OF TRUTH...
WILL WE BE ABLE TO DETECT HIS APPROACH, CARDINAL RAKER?
WE WILL SENSE HIS MAGIC WITH OUR BELIEF FIELDS, MATRIARCH.
ACTUALLY...
...I DON'T BELIEVE YOU WILL.
MATRIARCH, I AM ADAM WARLOCK. THIS IS MY COMPANION, GAMORA.
I UNDERSTAND YOU'VE BEEN TOLD TO EXPECT US.

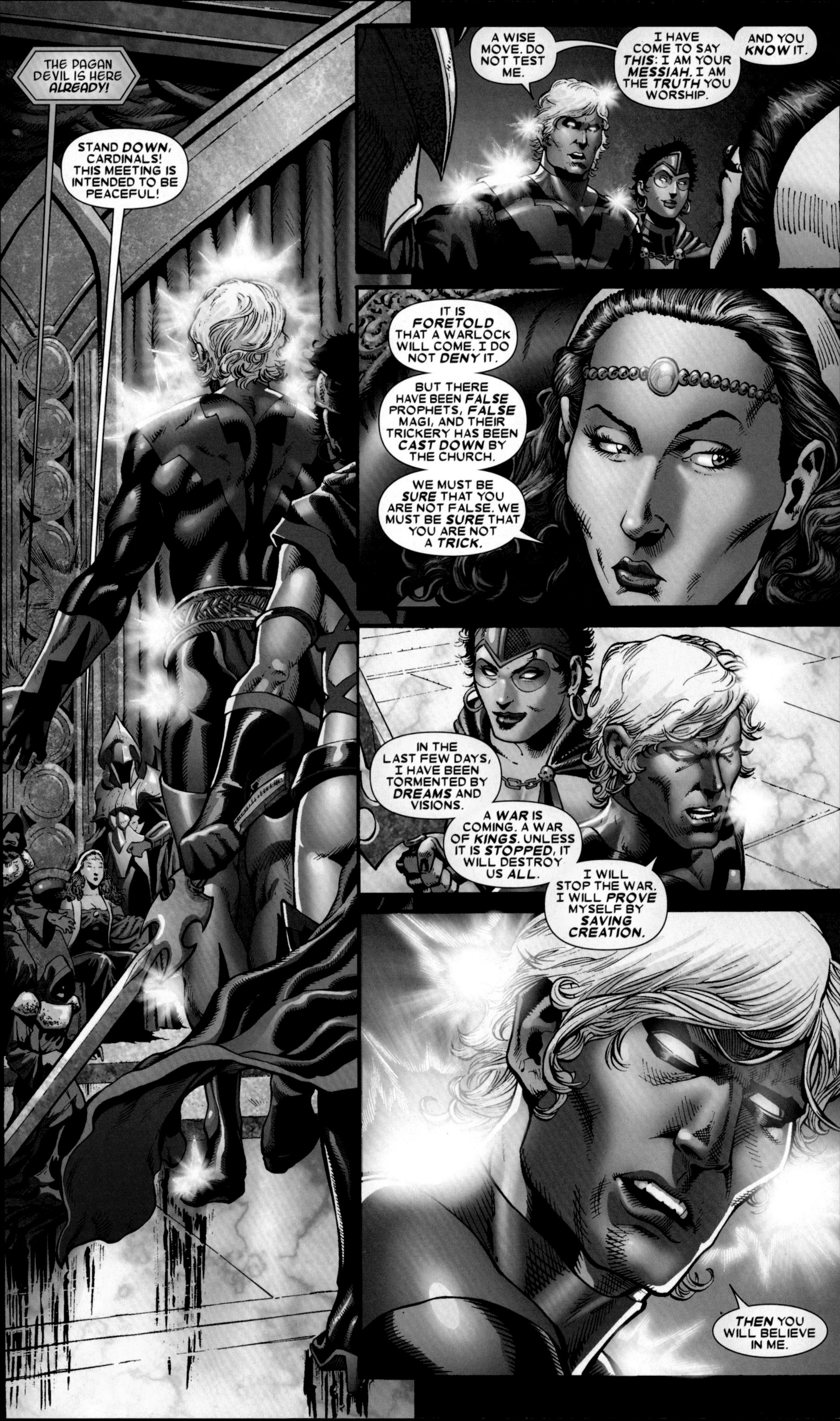
THE PAGAN DEVIL IS HERE ALREADY!
STAND DOWN, CARDINALS! THIS MEETING IS INTENDED TO BE PEACEFUL!
A WISE MOVE. DO NOT TEST ME.
I HAVE COME TO SAY THIS: I AM YOUR MESSIAH. I AM THE TRUTH YOU WORSHIP.
AND YOU KNOW IT.
IT IS FORETOLD THAT A WARLOCK WILL COME. I DO NOT DENY IT.
BUT THERE HAVE BEEN FALSE PROPHETS, FALSE MAGI, AND THEIR TRICKERY HAS BEEN CAST DOWN BY THE CHURCH.
WE MUST BE SURE THAT YOU ARE NOT FALSE. WE MUST BE SURE THAT YOU ARE NOT A TRICK.
IN THE LAST FEW DAYS, I HAVE BEEN TORMENTED BY DREAMS AND VISIONS.
A WAR IS COMING. A WAR OF KINGS. UNLESS IT IS STOPPED, IT WILL DESTROY US ALL.
I WILL STOP THE WAR. I WILL PROVE MYSELF BY SAVING CREATION.
THEN YOU WILL BELIEVE IN ME.

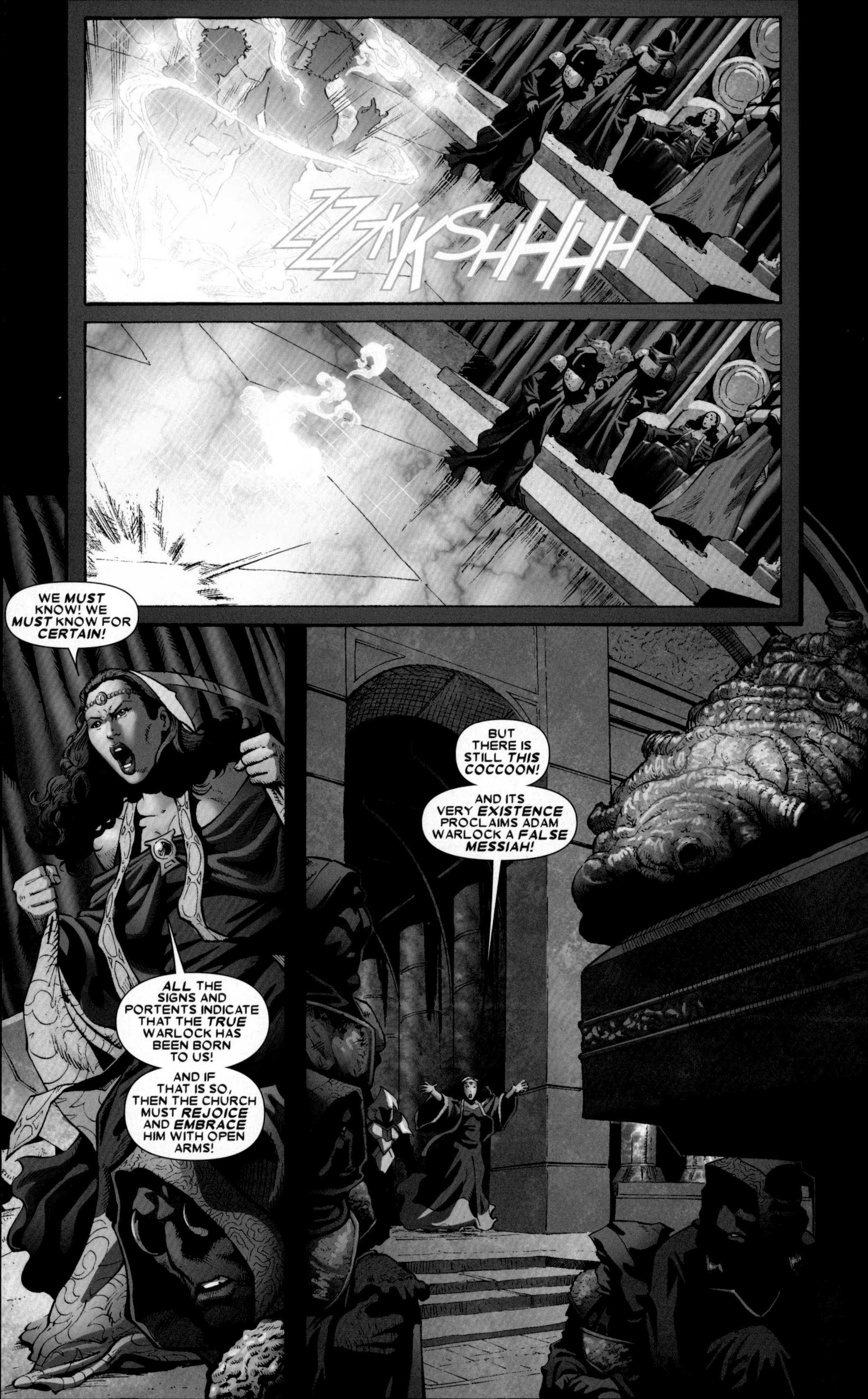
ZZZKKSHHHH
WE MUST KNOW! WE MUST KNOW FOR CERTAIN!
ALL THE SIGNS AND PORTENTS INDICATE THAT THE TRUE WARLOCK HAS BEEN BORN TO US!
AND IF THAT IS SO, THEN THE CHURCH MUST REJOICE AND EMBRACE HIM WITH OPEN ARMS!
BUT THERE IS STILL THIS COCCOON!
AND ITS VERY EXISTENCE PROCLAIMS ADAM WARLOCK A FALSE MESSIAH!

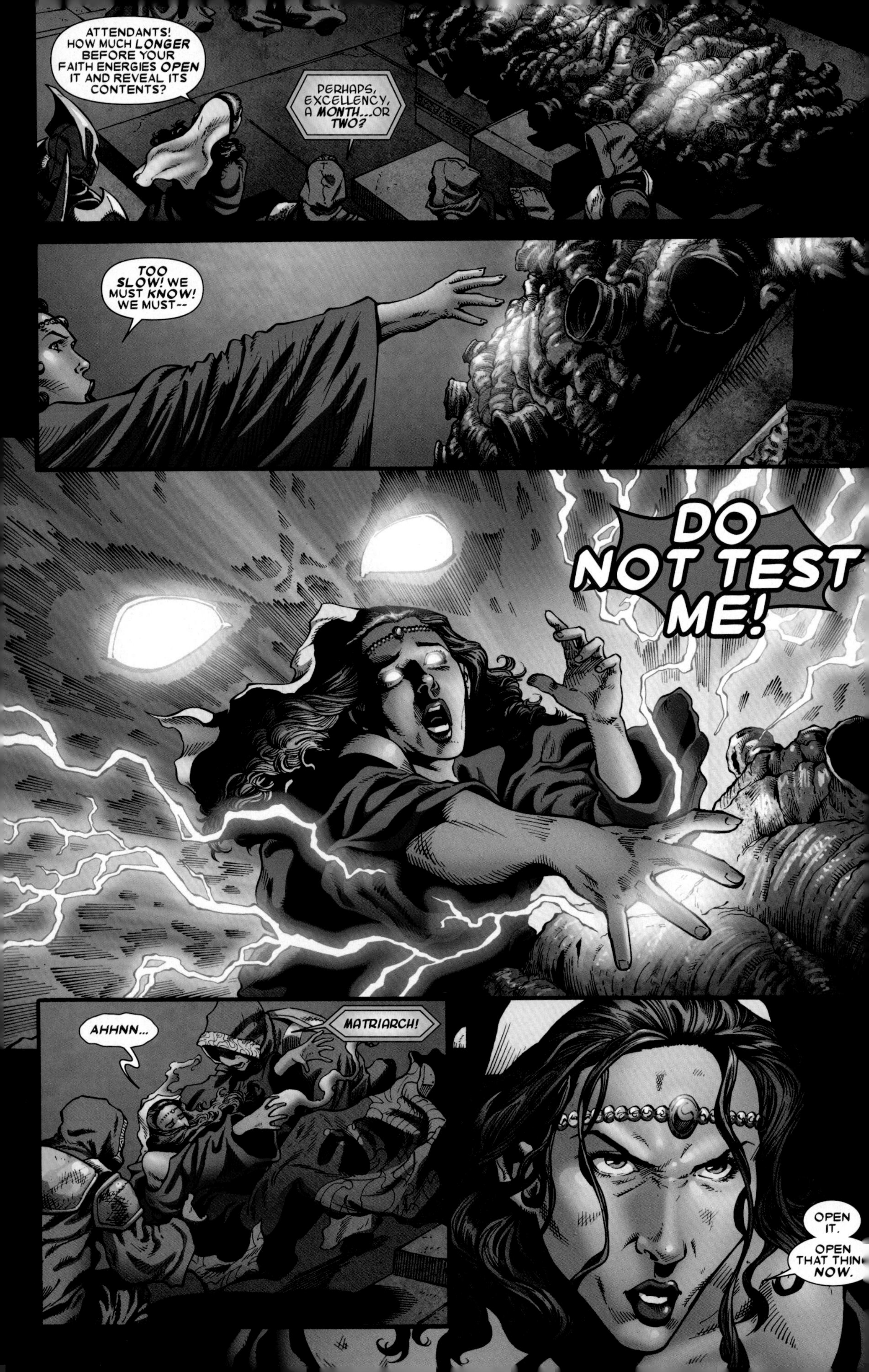
ATTENDANTS! HOW MUCH LONGER BEFORE YOUR FAITH ENERGIES OPEN IT AND REVEAL ITS CONTENTS?
PERHAPS, EXCELLENCY, A MONTH...OR TWO?
TOO SLOW! WE MUST KNOW! WE MUST--
DO NOT TEST ME!
AHHNN...
MATRIARCH!
OPEN IT.
OPEN THAT THIN
NOW.

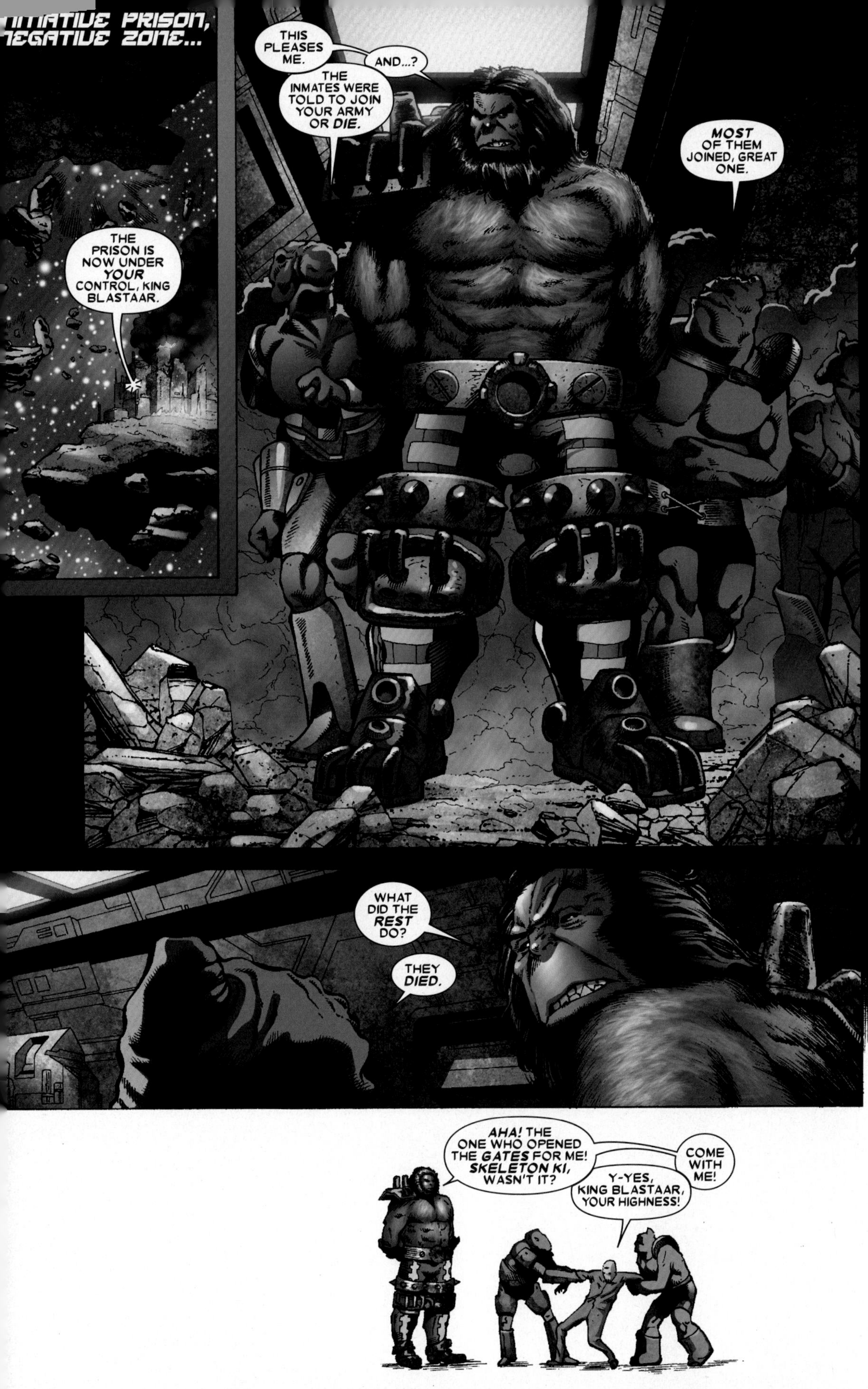
NITIATIVE PRISON,
EGATIVE ZONE...
THE PRISON IS NOW UNDER *YOUR* CONTROL, KING BLASTAAR.
THIS PLEASES ME.
AND...?
THE INMATES WERE TOLD TO JOIN YOUR ARMY OR *DIE.*
MOST OF THEM JOINED, GREAT ONE.
WHAT DID THE *REST* DO?
THEY *DIED.*
AHA! THE ONE WHO OPENED THE *GATES* FOR ME! *SKELETON KI,* WASN'T IT?
COME WITH ME!
Y-YES, KING BLASTAAR, YOUR HIGHNESS!

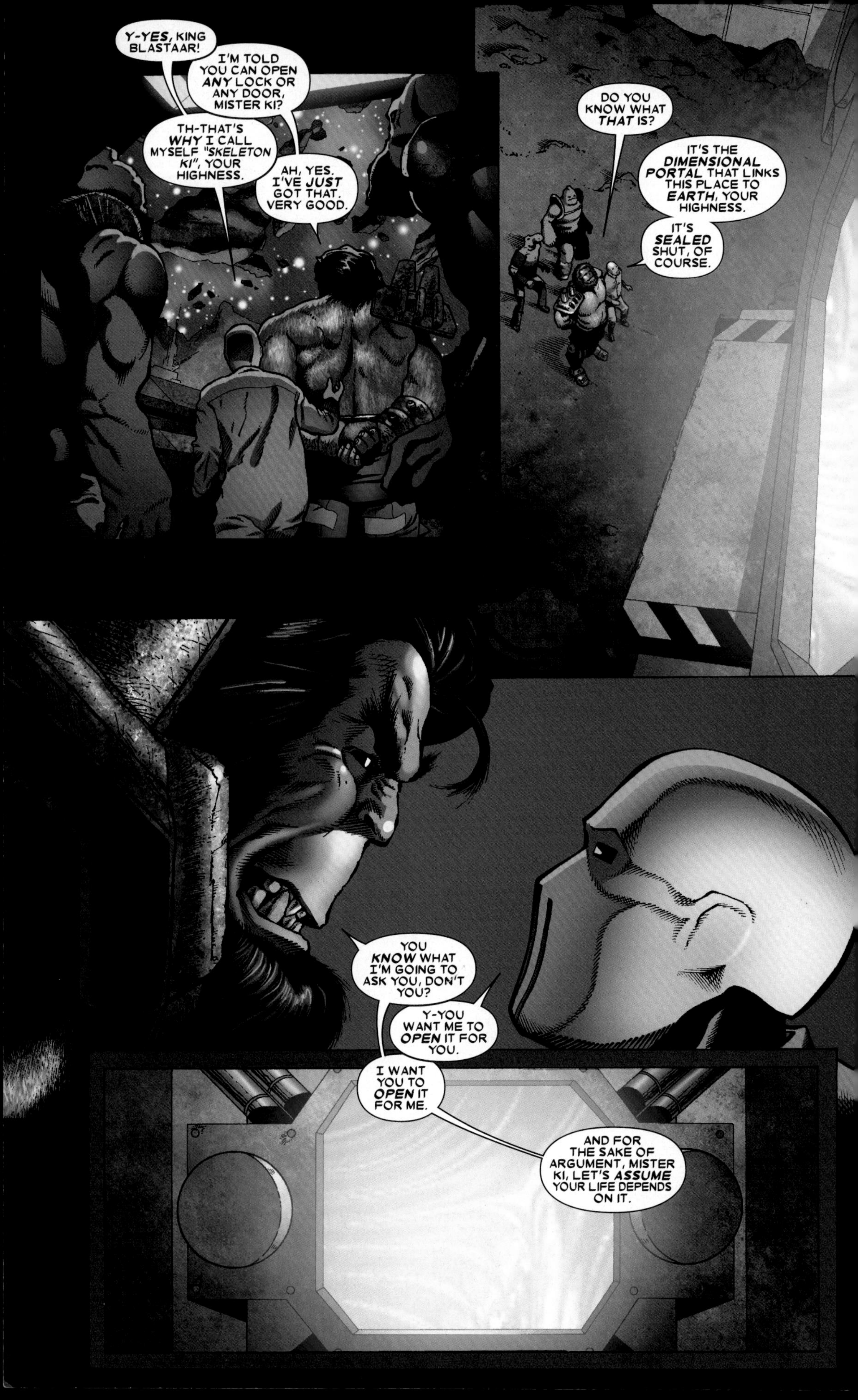
Y-YES, KING BLASTAAR!
I'M TOLD YOU CAN OPEN ANY LOCK OR ANY DOOR, MISTER KI?
TH-THAT'S WHY I CALL MYSELF "SKELETON KI", YOUR HIGHNESS.
AH, YES. I'VE JUST GOT THAT. VERY GOOD.
DO YOU KNOW WHAT THAT IS?
IT'S THE DIMENSIONAL PORTAL THAT LINKS THIS PLACE TO EARTH, YOUR HIGHNESS.
IT'S SEALED SHUT, OF COURSE.
YOU KNOW WHAT I'M GOING TO ASK YOU, DON'T YOU?
Y-YOU WANT ME TO OPEN IT FOR YOU.
I WANT YOU TO OPEN IT FOR ME.
AND FOR THE SAKE OF ARGUMENT, MISTER KI, LET'S ASSUME YOUR LIFE DEPENDS ON IT.

JUST DON'T EVER OPEN IT. EVER.
EARTHSIDE OF THE PORTAL, CAMP HAMMOND, CONNECTICUT...
I'M NOT FOOLING. THAT PORTAL STAYS SHUT OR YOU ANSWER TO ME.
AND IF YOU EVER SEE IT STARTING TO OPEN, YOU HIT EVERY PANIC BUTTON YOU'VE GOT.
ARE WE CRYSTAL?
ABSOLUTELY.
BLASTAAR'S ON THE OTHER SIDE WITH A GIGANTIC ARMY OF NEGATIVE ZONE...I BELIEVE YOU USED THE TERM... "WHACK-JOBS".
SO...DON'T OPEN THE PORTAL. GOT IT.
GREAT. THANKS, DR. RICHARDS.
OKAY, JOB DONE. WE'RE OUT OF HERE.

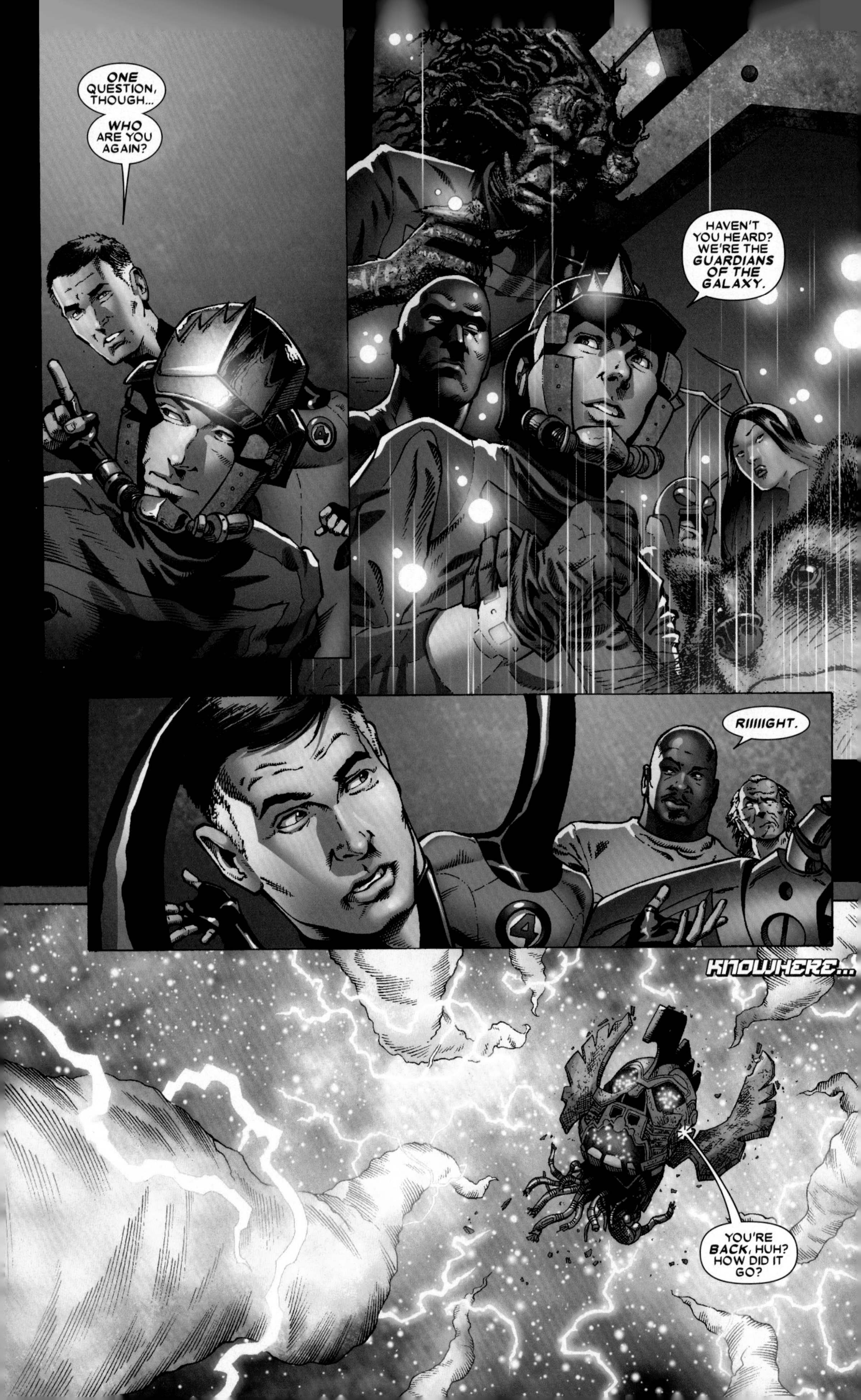
ONE QUESTION, THOUGH... WHO ARE YOU AGAIN?
HAVEN'T YOU HEARD? WE'RE THE GUARDIANS OF THE GALAXY.
RIIIIIGHT.
KNOWHERE...
YOU'RE BACK, HUH? HOW DID IT GO?

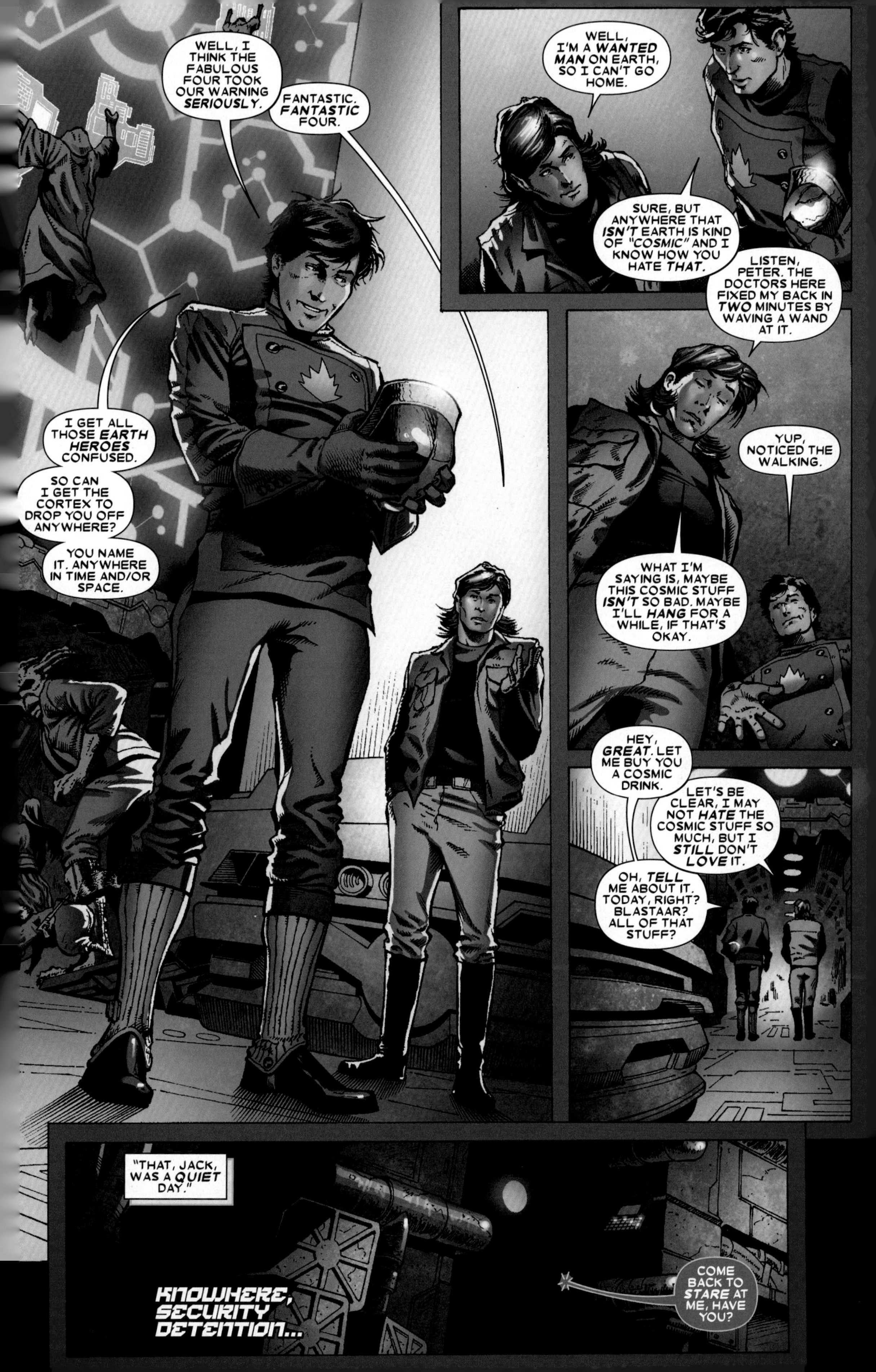

WELL, I THINK THE FABULOUS FOUR TOOK OUR WARNING SERIOUSLY.
FANTASTIC. FANTASTIC FOUR.
I GET ALL THOSE EARTH HEROES CONFUSED.
SO CAN I GET THE CORTEX TO DROP YOU OFF ANYWHERE?
YOU NAME IT. ANYWHERE IN TIME AND/OR SPACE.
WELL, I'M A WANTED MAN ON EARTH, SO I CAN'T GO HOME.
SURE, BUT ANYWHERE THAT ISN'T EARTH IS KIND OF "COSMIC" AND I KNOW HOW YOU HATE THAT.
LISTEN, PETER. THE DOCTORS HERE FIXED MY BACK IN TWO MINUTES BY WAVING A WAND AT IT.
YUP, NOTICED THE WALKING.
WHAT I'M SAYING IS, MAYBE THIS COSMIC STUFF ISN'T SO BAD. MAYBE I'LL HANG FOR A WHILE, IF THAT'S OKAY.
HEY, GREAT. LET ME BUY YOU A COSMIC DRINK.
LET'S BE CLEAR, I MAY NOT HATE THE COSMIC STUFF SO MUCH, BUT I STILL DON'T LOVE IT.
OH, TELL ME ABOUT IT. TODAY, RIGHT? BLASTAAR? ALL OF THAT STUFF?
"THAT, JACK, WAS A QUIET DAY."
KNOWHERE, SECURITY DETENTION...
COME BACK TO STARE AT ME, HAVE YOU?

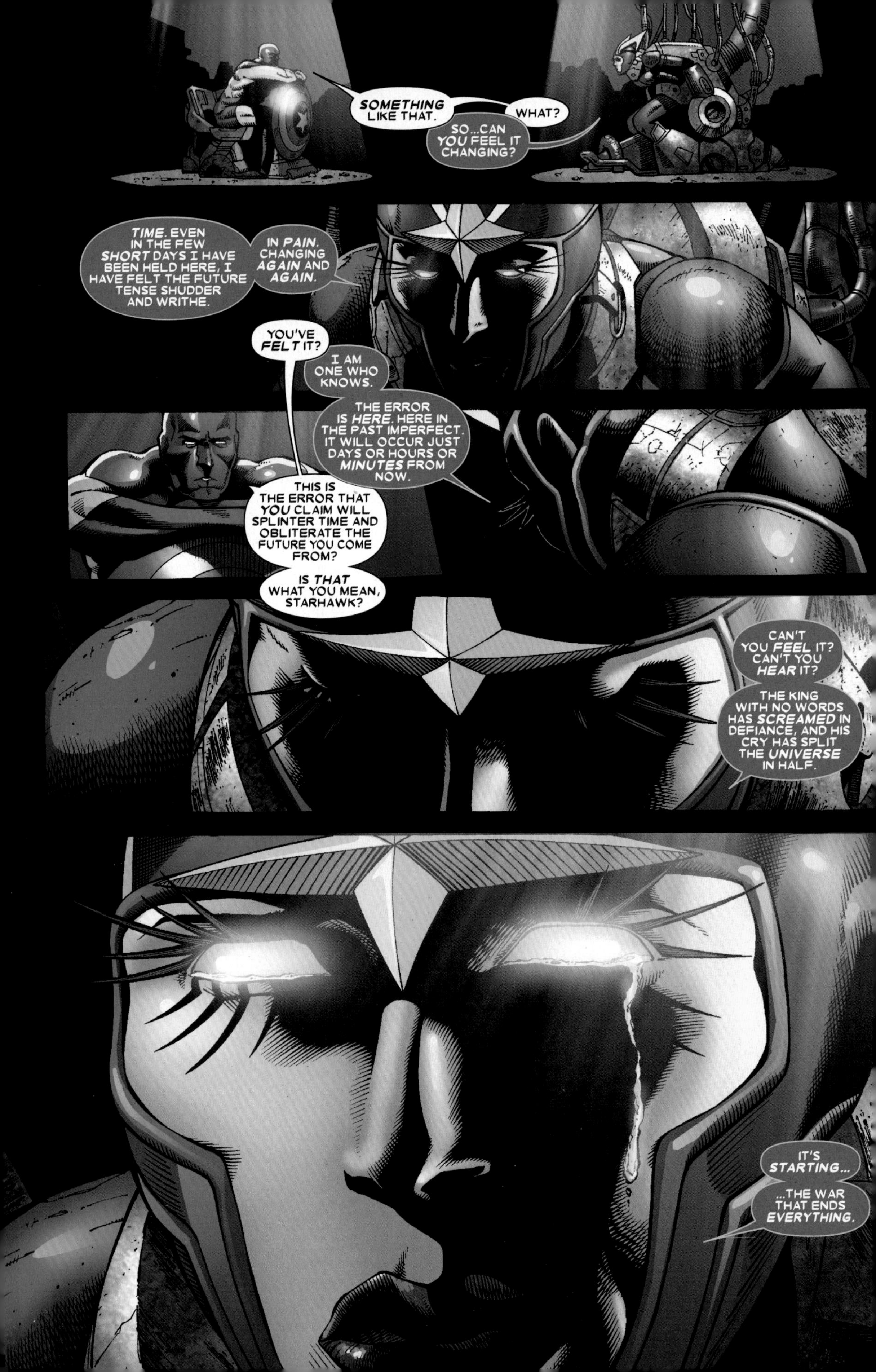
SOMETHING LIKE THAT.
WHAT?
SO...CAN YOU FEEL IT CHANGING?
TIME. EVEN IN THE FEW SHORT DAYS I HAVE BEEN HELD HERE, I HAVE FELT THE FUTURE TENSE SHUDDER AND WRITHE.
IN PAIN. CHANGING AGAIN AND AGAIN.
YOU'VE FELT IT?
I AM ONE WHO KNOWS.
THE ERROR IS HERE. HERE IN THE PAST IMPERFECT. IT WILL OCCUR JUST DAYS OR HOURS OR MINUTES FROM NOW.
THIS IS THE ERROR THAT YOU CLAIM WILL SPLINTER TIME AND OBLITERATE THE FUTURE YOU COME FROM?
IS THAT WHAT YOU MEAN, STARHAWK?
CAN'T YOU FEEL IT? CAN'T YOU HEAR IT?
THE KING WITH NO WORDS HAS SCREAMED IN DEFIANCE, AND HIS CRY HAS SPLIT THE UNIVERSE IN HALF.
IT'S STARTING...
...THE WAR THAT ENDS EVERYTHING.

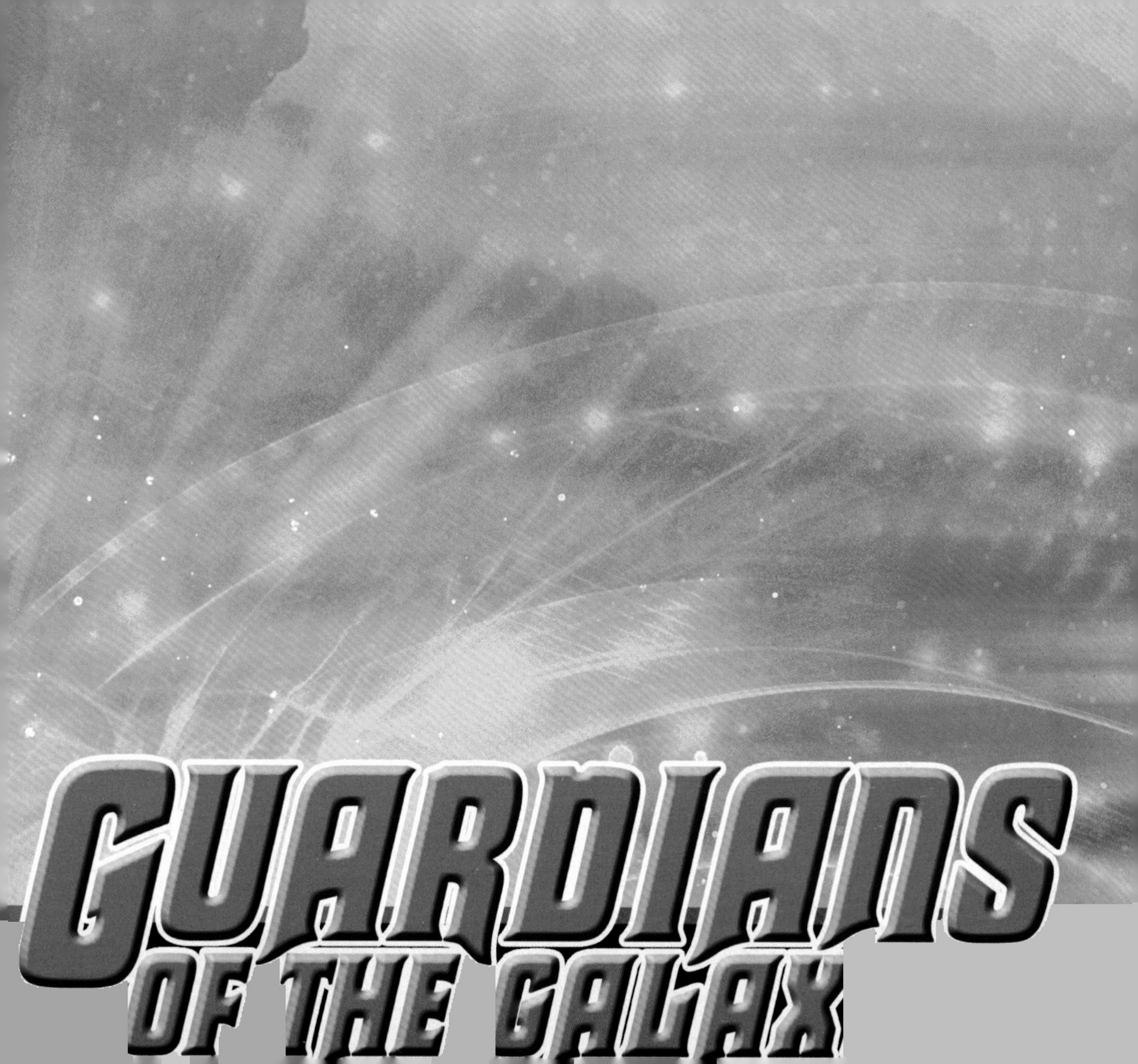
GUARDIANS
OF THE GALAX

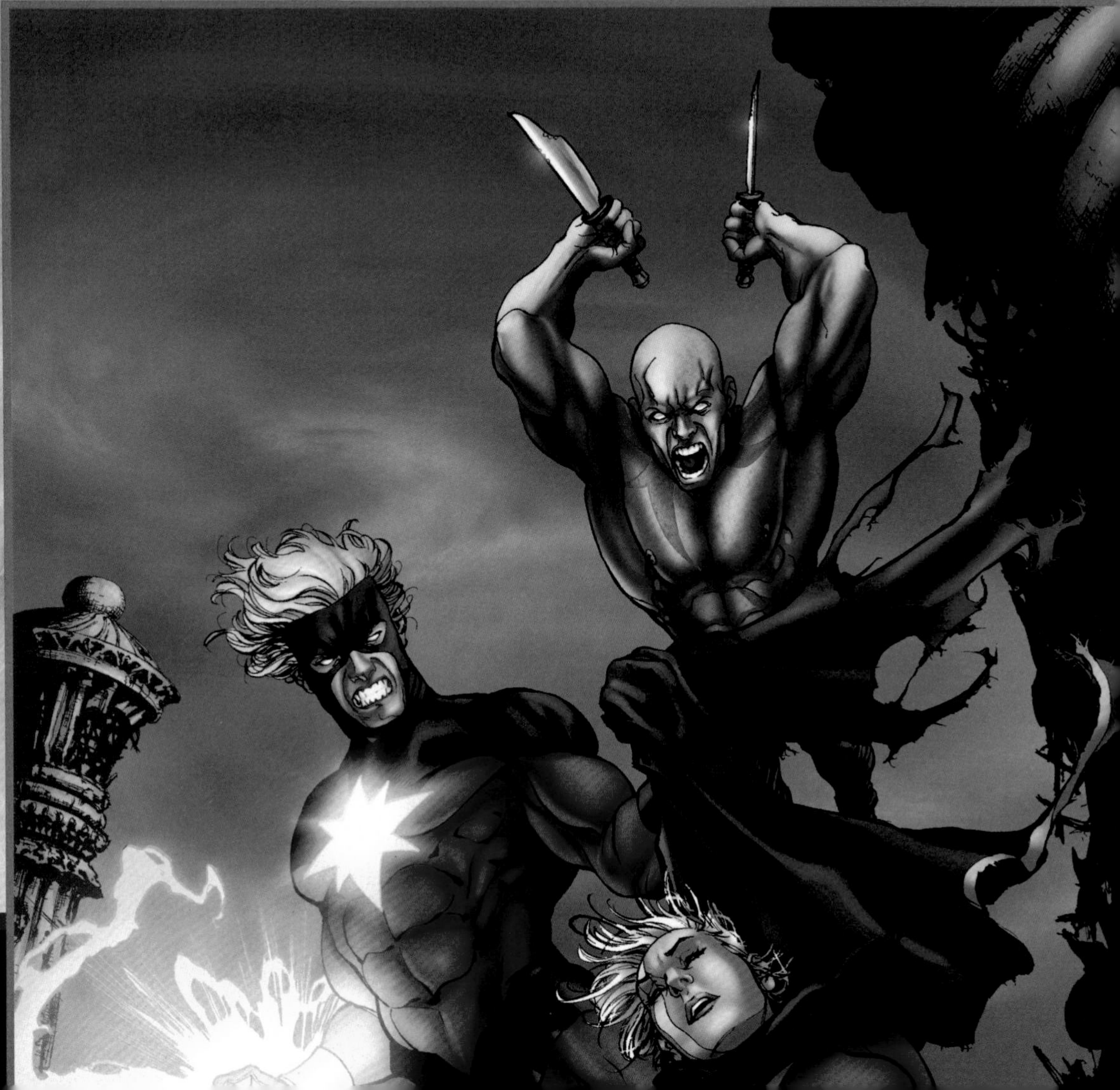

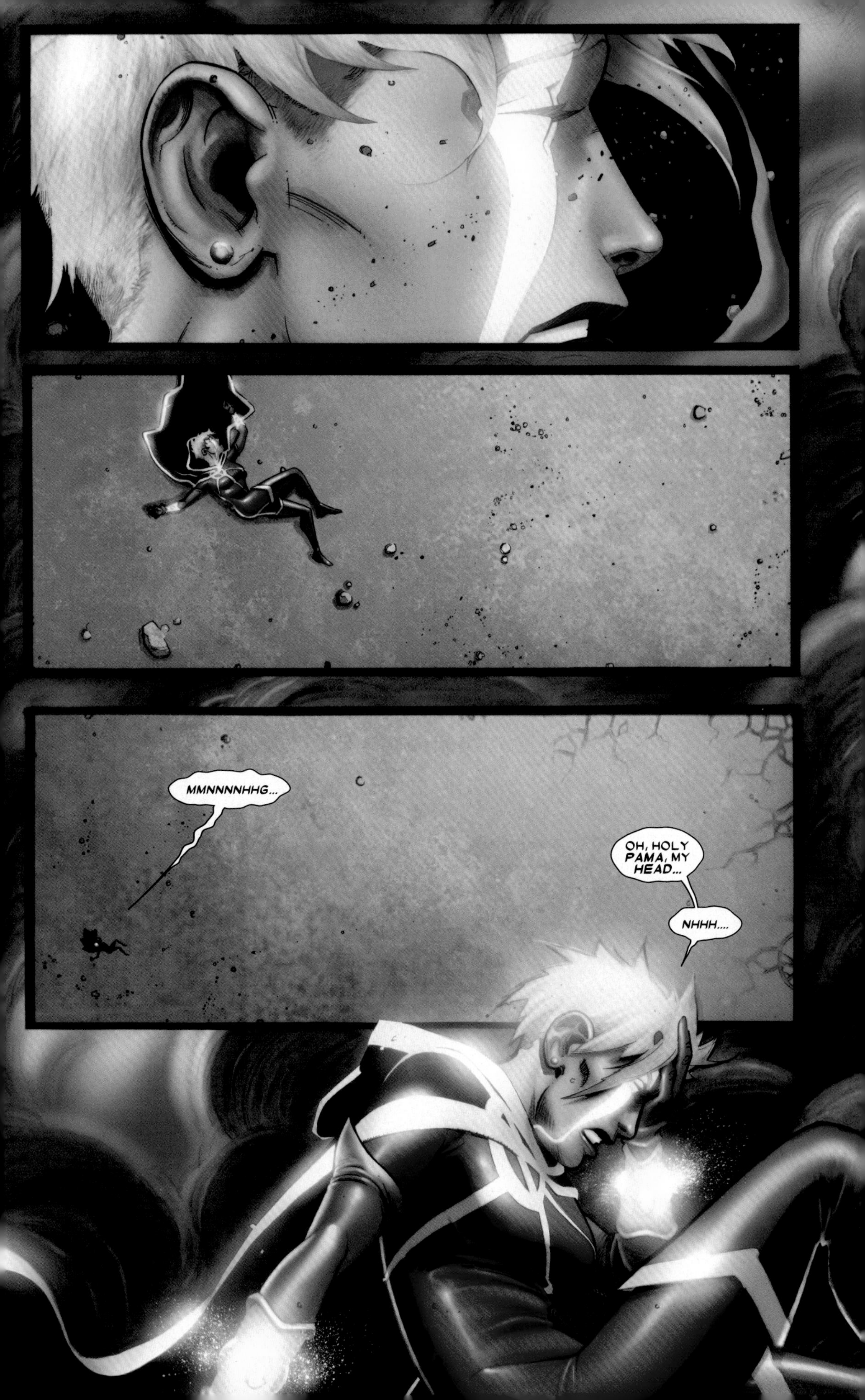
MMNNNNHHG...
OH, HOLY PAMA, MY HEAD...
NHHH....

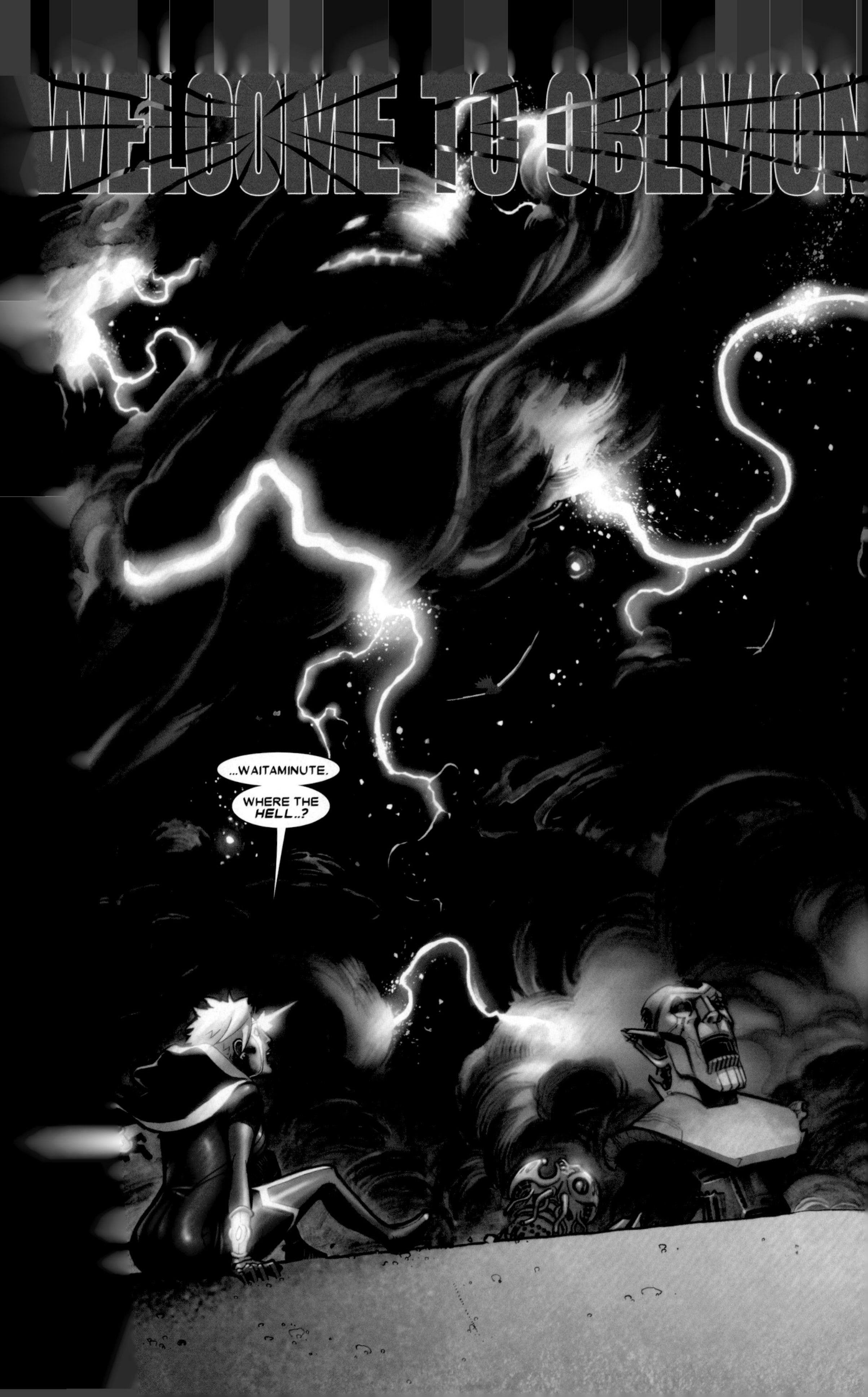
WELCOME TO OBLIVION
...WAITAMINUTE.
WHERE THE HELL..?

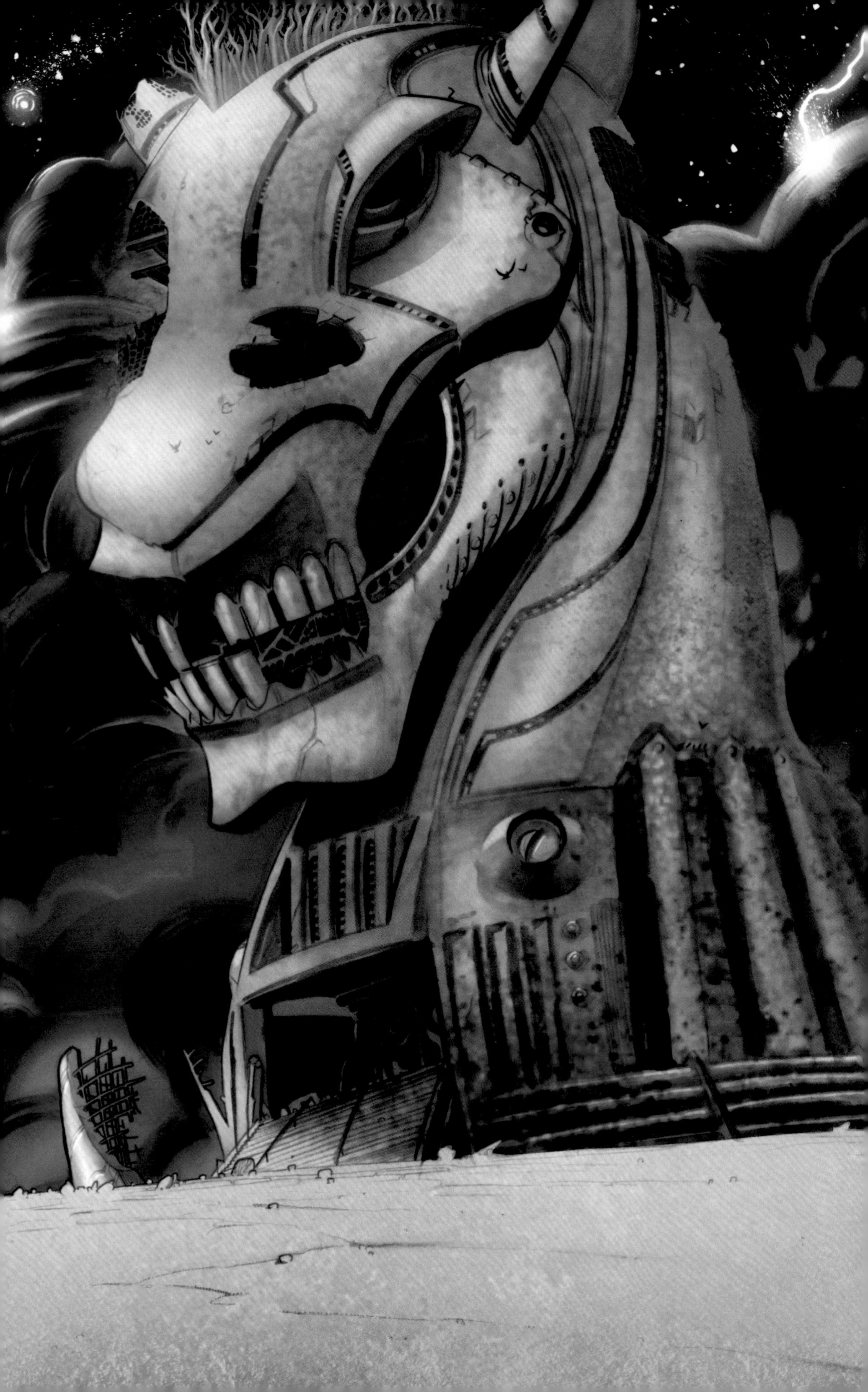

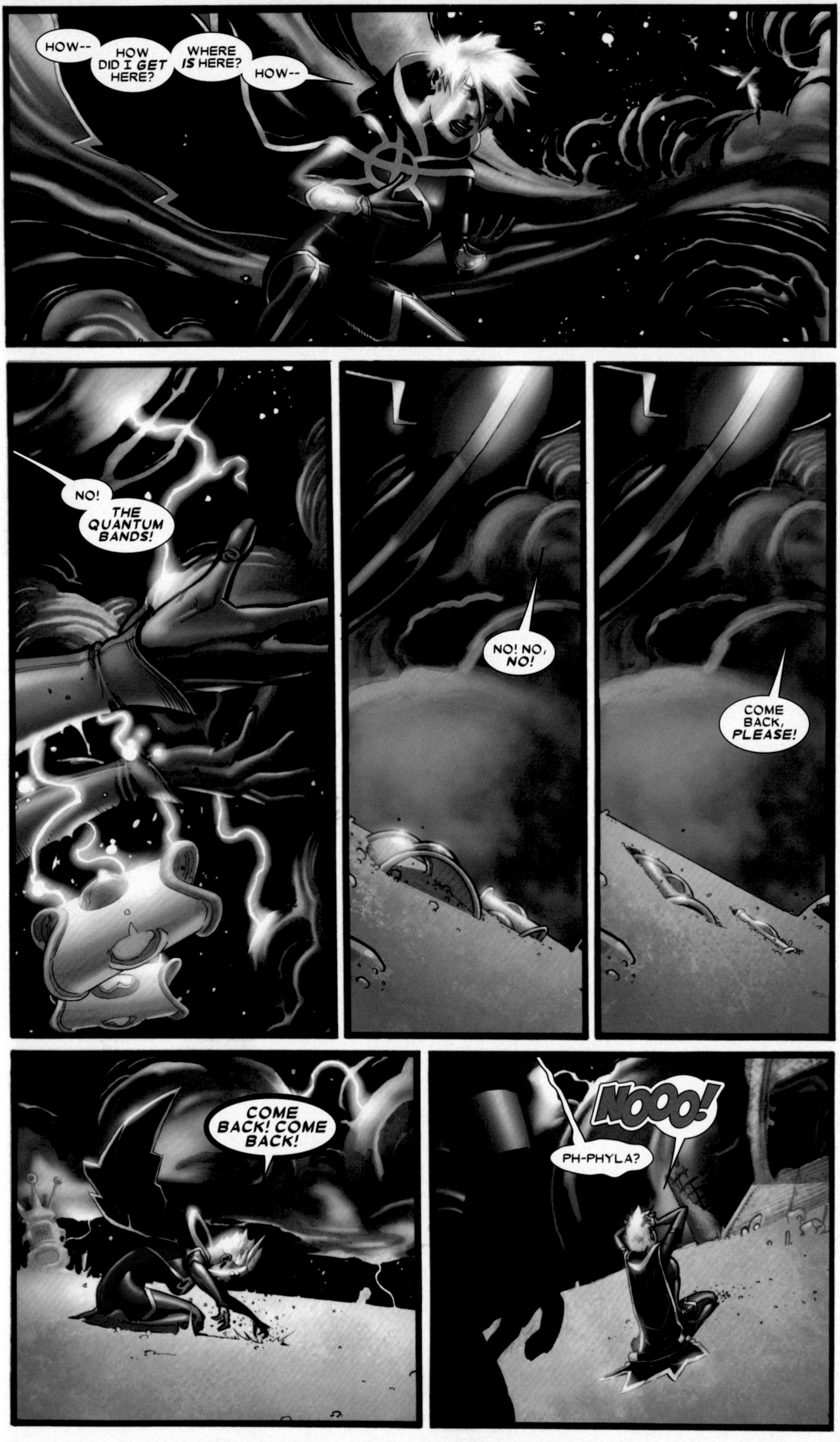
HOW--
HOW DID I GET HERE?
WHERE IS HERE?
HOW--
NO!
THE QUANTUM BANDS!
NO! NO, NO!
COME BACK, PLEASE!
COME BACK! COME BACK!
NOOO!
PH-PHYLA?

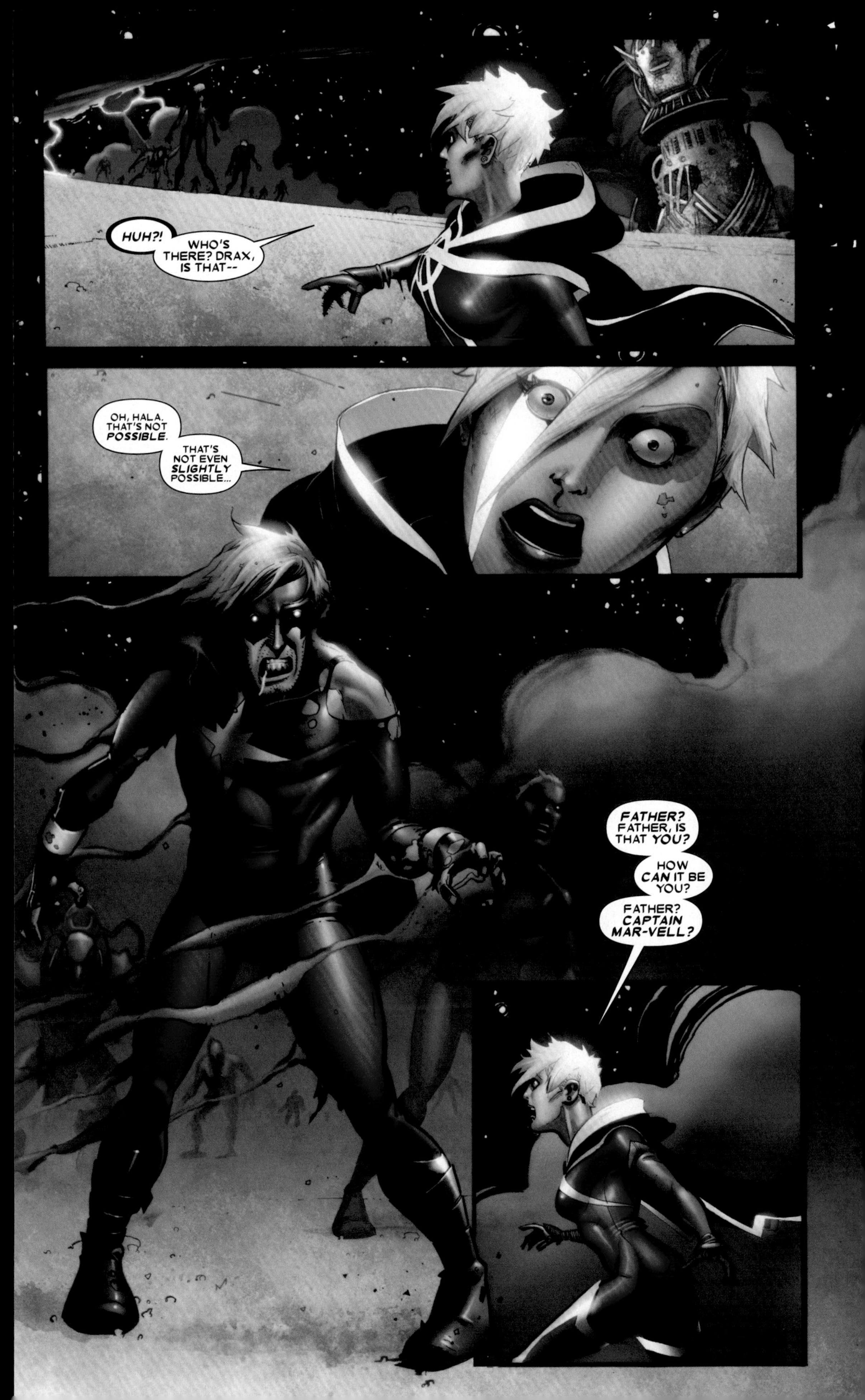
HUH?!
WHO'S THERE? DRAX, IS THAT--
OH, HALA. THAT'S NOT POSSIBLE.
THAT'S NOT EVEN SLIGHTLY POSSIBLE...
FATHER? FATHER, IS THAT YOU?
HOW CAN IT BE YOU?
FATHER? CAPTAIN MAR-VELL?

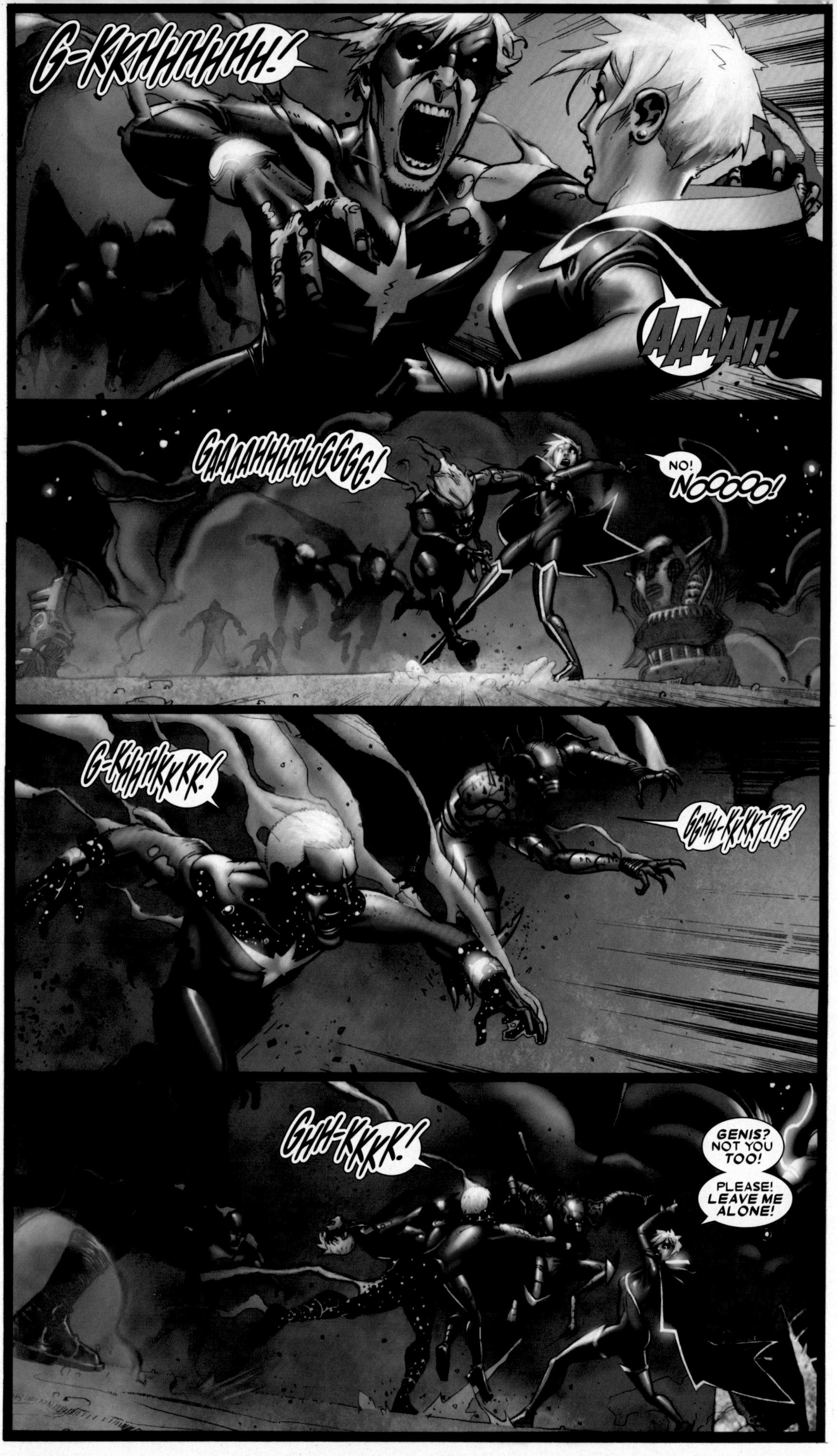
G-KKHHHHHHH!
AAAAH!
GAAAAHHHHHGGGG!
NO! NOOOOO!
G-KHHHKKKK!
GCHH-KKKKTTT!
GHH-KKKK!
GENIS? NOT YOU TOO!
PLEASE! LEAVE ME ALONE!

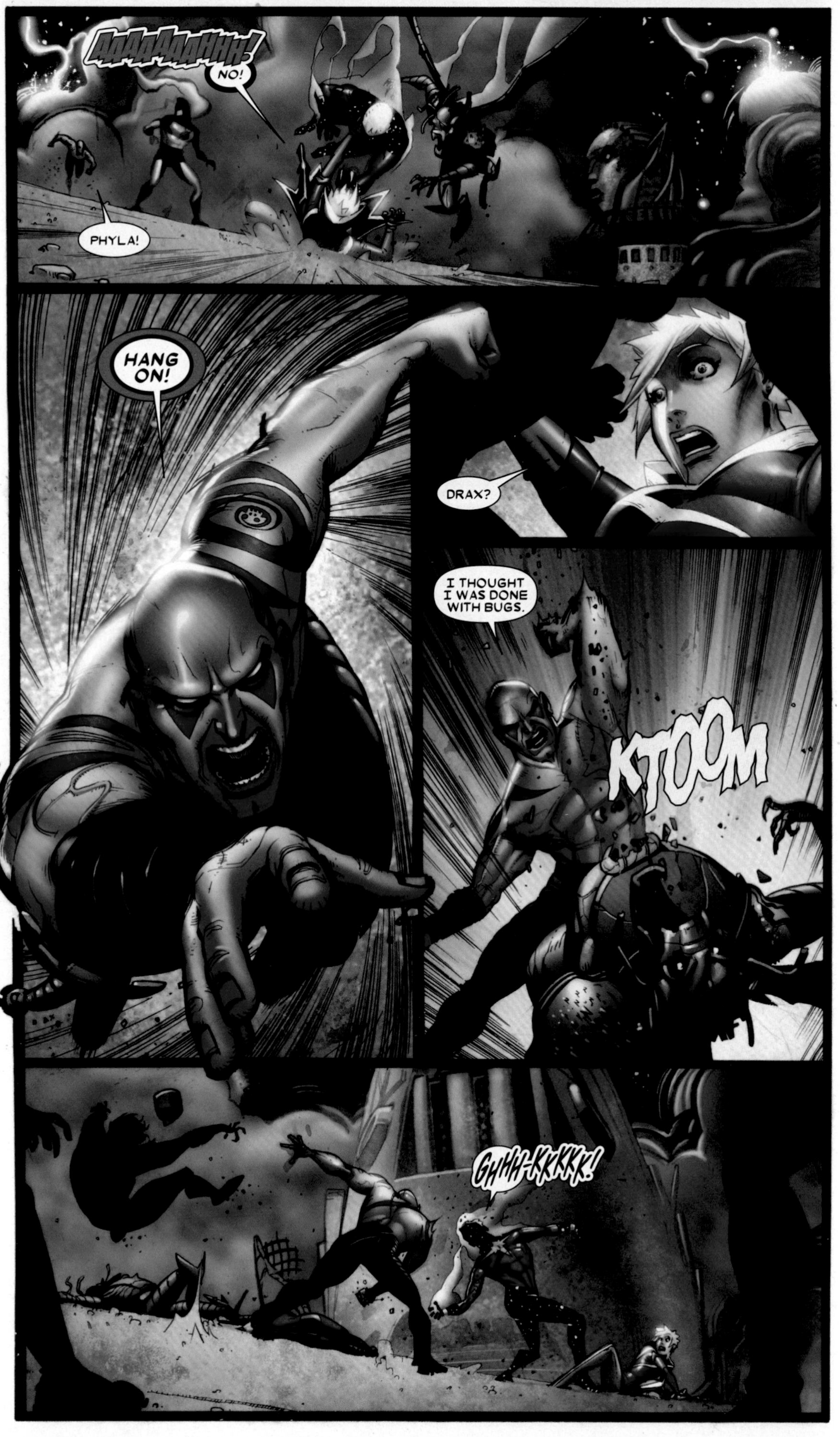

AAAAAAAHHH!
NO!
PHYLA!
HANG ON!
DRAX?
I THOUGHT I WAS DONE WITH BUGS.
KTOOM
GHHH-KKKKK!

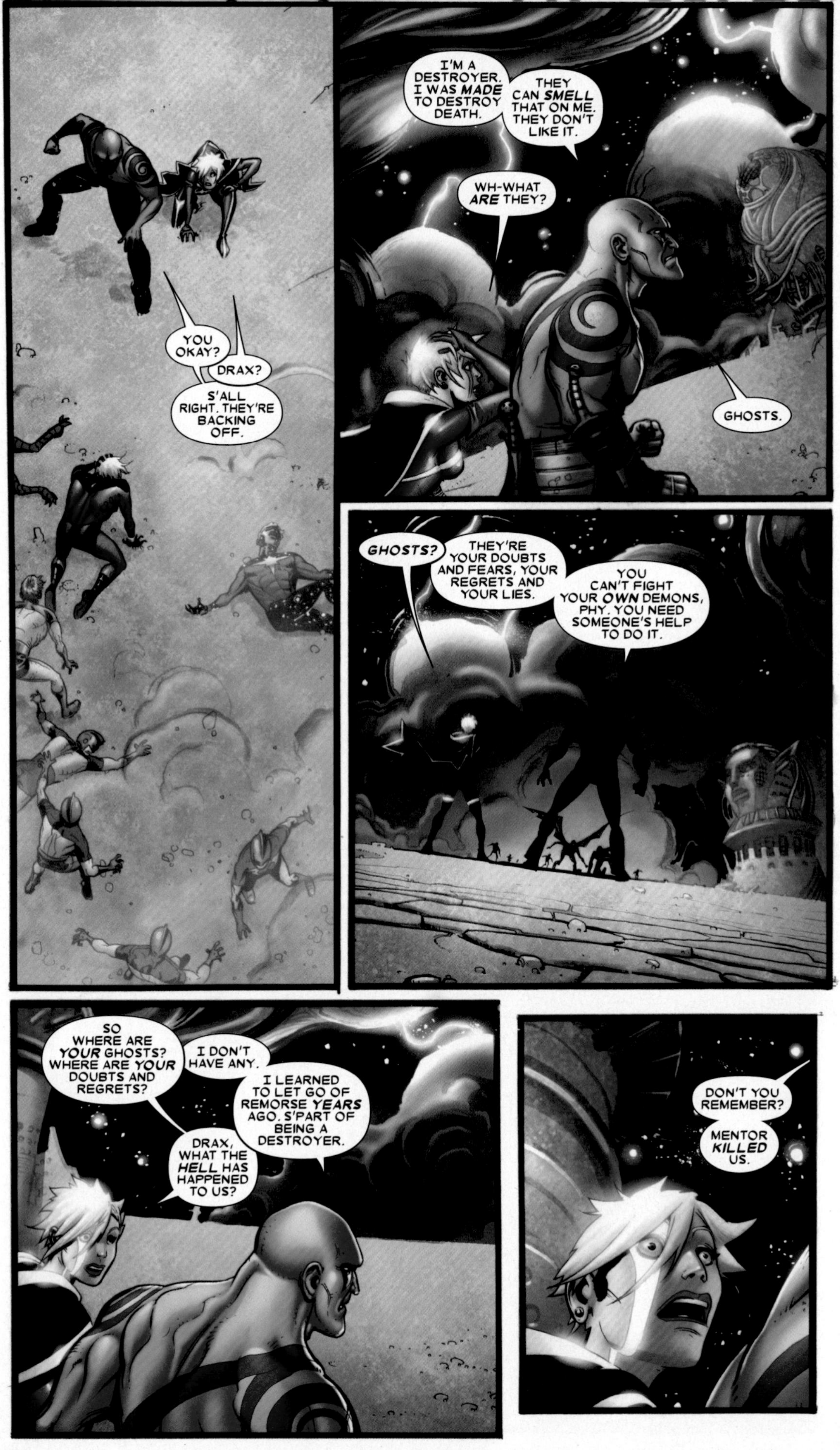
YOU OKAY?
DRAX?
S'ALL RIGHT. THEY'RE BACKING OFF.
I'M A DESTROYER. I WAS MADE TO DESTROY DEATH.
THEY CAN SMELL THAT ON ME. THEY DON'T LIKE IT.
WH-WHAT ARE THEY?
GHOSTS.
GHOSTS?
THEY'RE YOUR DOUBTS AND FEARS, YOUR REGRETS AND YOUR LIES.
YOU CAN'T FIGHT YOUR OWN DEMONS, PHY. YOU NEED SOMEONE'S HELP TO DO IT.
SO WHERE ARE YOUR GHOSTS? WHERE ARE YOUR DOUBTS AND REGRETS?
I DON'T HAVE ANY.
I LEARNED TO LET GO OF REMORSE YEARS AGO. S'PART OF BEING A DESTROYER.
DRAX, WHAT THE HELL HAS HAPPENED TO US?
DON'T YOU REMEMBER?
MENTOR KILLED US.

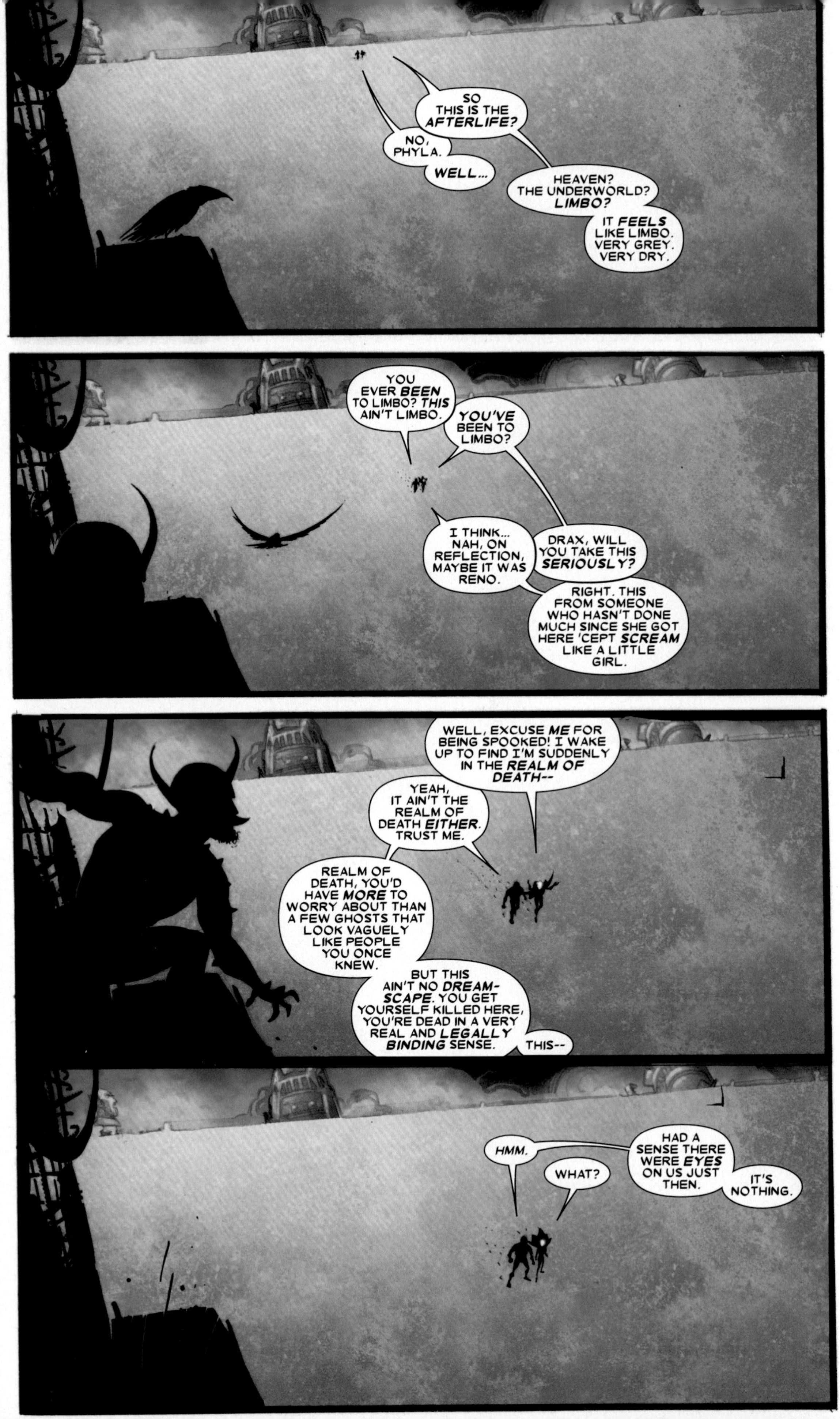
SO THIS IS THE AFTERLIFE?
NO, PHYLA.
WELL...
HEAVEN? THE UNDERWORLD? LIMBO?
IT FEELS LIKE LIMBO. VERY GREY. VERY DRY.
YOU EVER BEEN TO LIMBO? THIS AIN'T LIMBO.
YOU'VE BEEN TO LIMBO?
I THINK... NAH, ON REFLECTION, MAYBE IT WAS RENO.
DRAX, WILL YOU TAKE THIS SERIOUSLY?
RIGHT. THIS FROM SOMEONE WHO HASN'T DONE MUCH SINCE SHE GOT HERE 'CEPT SCREAM LIKE A LITTLE GIRL.
WELL, EXCUSE ME FOR BEING SPOOKED! I WAKE UP TO FIND I'M SUDDENLY IN THE REALM OF DEATH--
YEAH, IT AIN'T THE REALM OF DEATH EITHER. TRUST ME.
REALM OF DEATH, YOU'D HAVE MORE TO WORRY ABOUT THAN A FEW GHOSTS THAT LOOK VAGUELY LIKE PEOPLE YOU ONCE KNEW.
BUT THIS AIN'T NO DREAM-SCAPE. YOU GET YOURSELF KILLED HERE, YOU'RE DEAD IN A VERY REAL AND LEGALLY BINDING SENSE.
THIS--
HMM.
WHAT?
HAD A SENSE THERE WERE EYES ON US JUST THEN.
IT'S NOTHING.

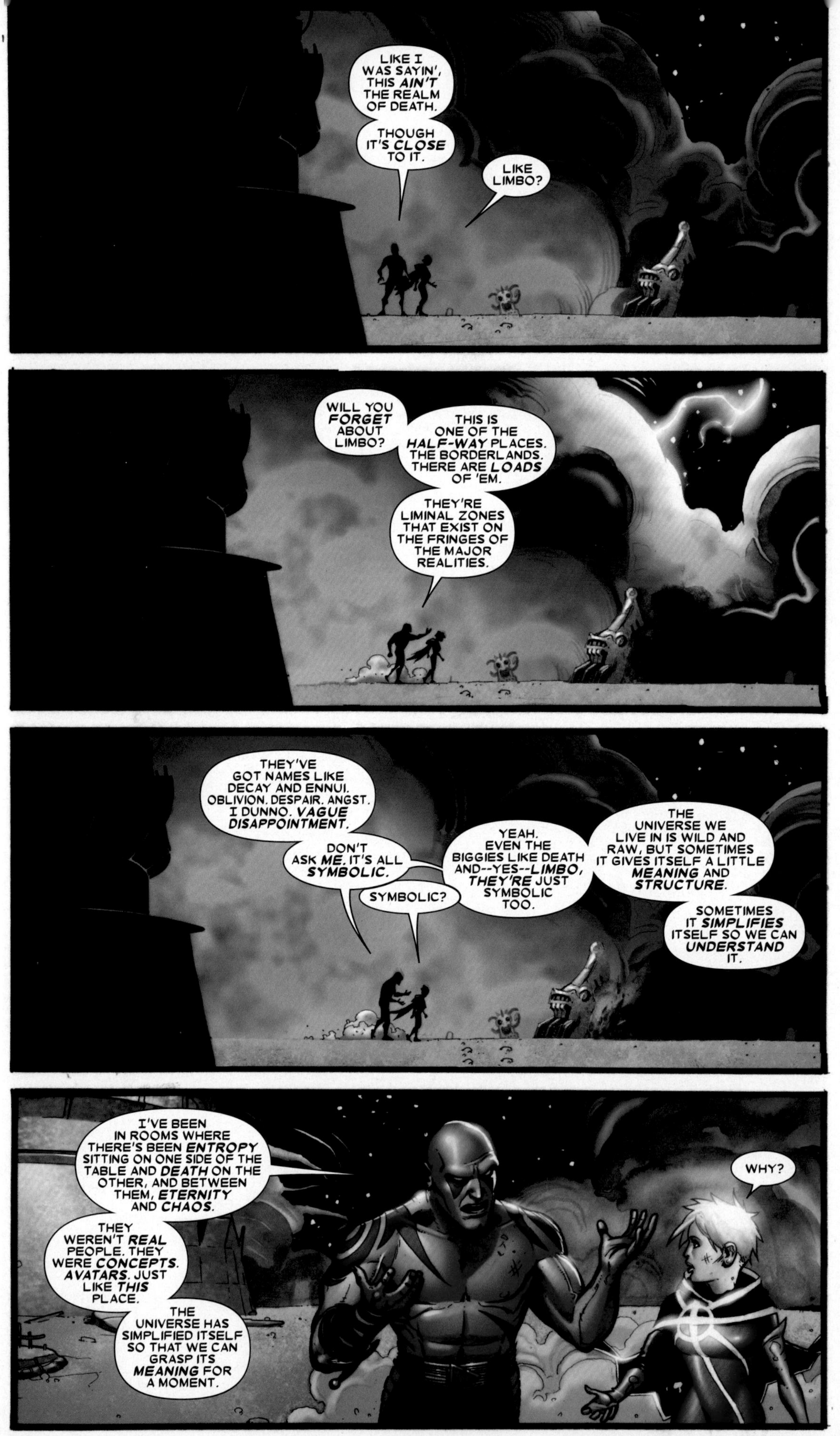

LIKE I WAS SAYIN', THIS AIN'T THE REALM OF DEATH.
THOUGH IT'S CLOSE TO IT.
LIKE LIMBO?
WILL YOU FORGET ABOUT LIMBO?
THIS IS ONE OF THE HALF-WAY PLACES. THE BORDERLANDS. THERE ARE LOADS OF 'EM.
THEY'RE LIMINAL ZONES THAT EXIST ON THE FRINGES OF THE MAJOR REALITIES.
THEY'VE GOT NAMES LIKE DECAY AND ENNUI. OBLIVION. DESPAIR. ANGST. I DUNNO. VAGUE DISAPPOINTMENT.
DON'T ASK ME. IT'S ALL SYMBOLIC.
SYMBOLIC?
YEAH. EVEN THE BIGGIES LIKE DEATH AND--YES--LIMBO, THEY'RE JUST SYMBOLIC TOO.
THE UNIVERSE WE LIVE IN IS WILD AND RAW, BUT SOMETIMES IT GIVES ITSELF A LITTLE MEANING AND STRUCTURE.
SOMETIMES IT SIMPLIFIES ITSELF SO WE CAN UNDERSTAND IT.
I'VE BEEN IN ROOMS WHERE THERE'S BEEN ENTROPY SITTING ON ONE SIDE OF THE TABLE AND DEATH ON THE OTHER, AND BETWEEN THEM, ETERNITY AND CHAOS.
THEY WEREN'T REAL PEOPLE. THEY WERE CONCEPTS. AVATARS. JUST LIKE THIS PLACE.
THE UNIVERSE HAS SIMPLIFIED ITSELF SO THAT WE CAN GRASP ITS MEANING FOR A MOMENT.
WHY?

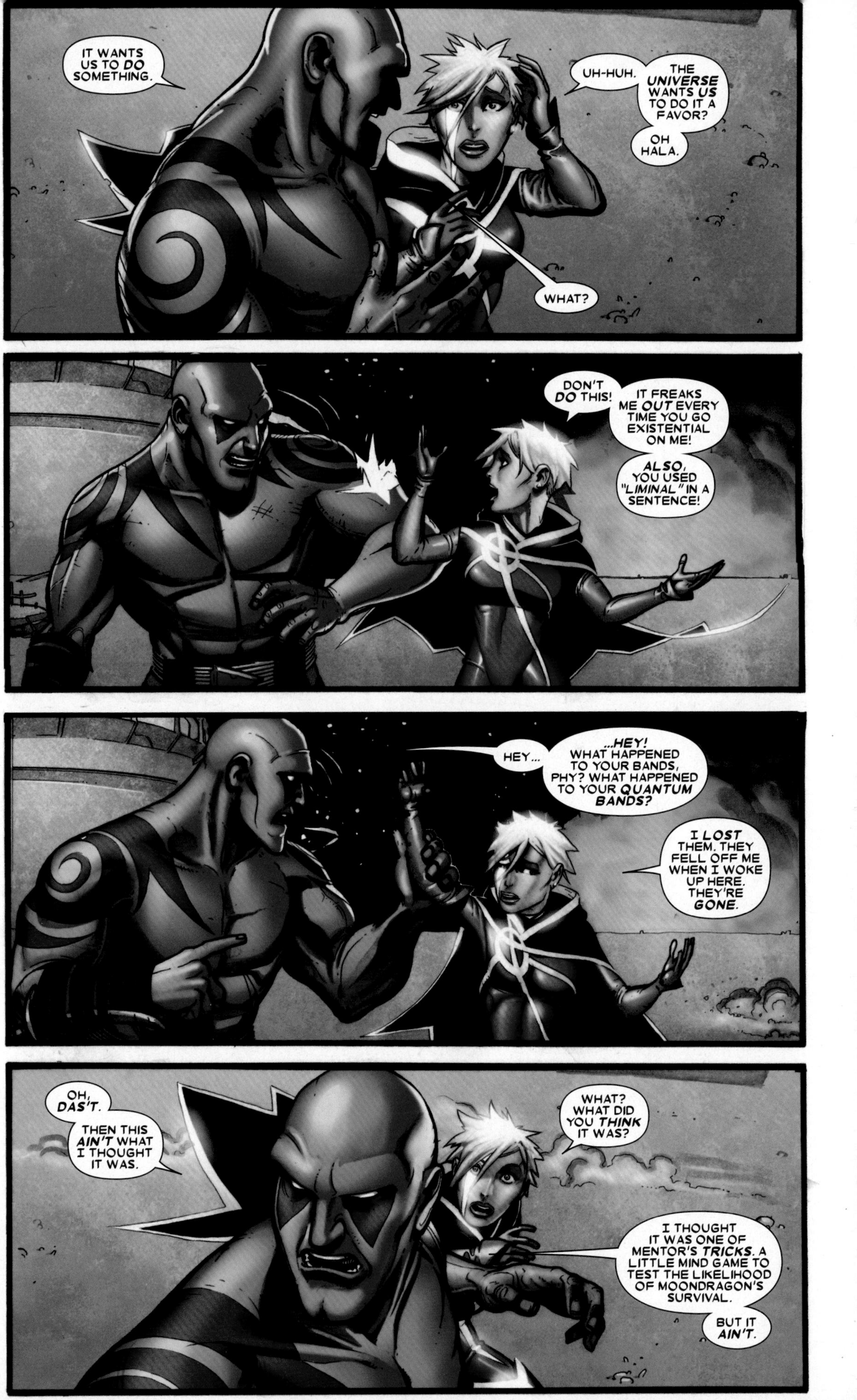
IT WANTS US TO DO SOMETHING.
UH-HUH.
THE UNIVERSE WANTS US TO DO IT A FAVOR?
OH HALA.
WHAT?
DON'T DO THIS!
IT FREAKS ME OUT EVERY TIME YOU GO EXISTENTIAL ON ME!
ALSO, YOU USED "LIMINAL" IN A SENTENCE!
HEY...
...HEY! WHAT HAPPENED TO YOUR BANDS, PHY? WHAT HAPPENED TO YOUR QUANTUM BANDS?
I LOST THEM. THEY FELL OFF ME WHEN I WOKE UP HERE. THEY'RE GONE.
OH, DAS'T.
THEN THIS AIN'T WHAT I THOUGHT IT WAS.
WHAT? WHAT DID YOU THINK IT WAS?
I THOUGHT IT WAS ONE OF MENTOR'S TRICKS. A LITTLE MIND GAME TO TEST THE LIKELIHOOD OF MOONDRAGON'S SURVIVAL.
BUT IT AIN'T.

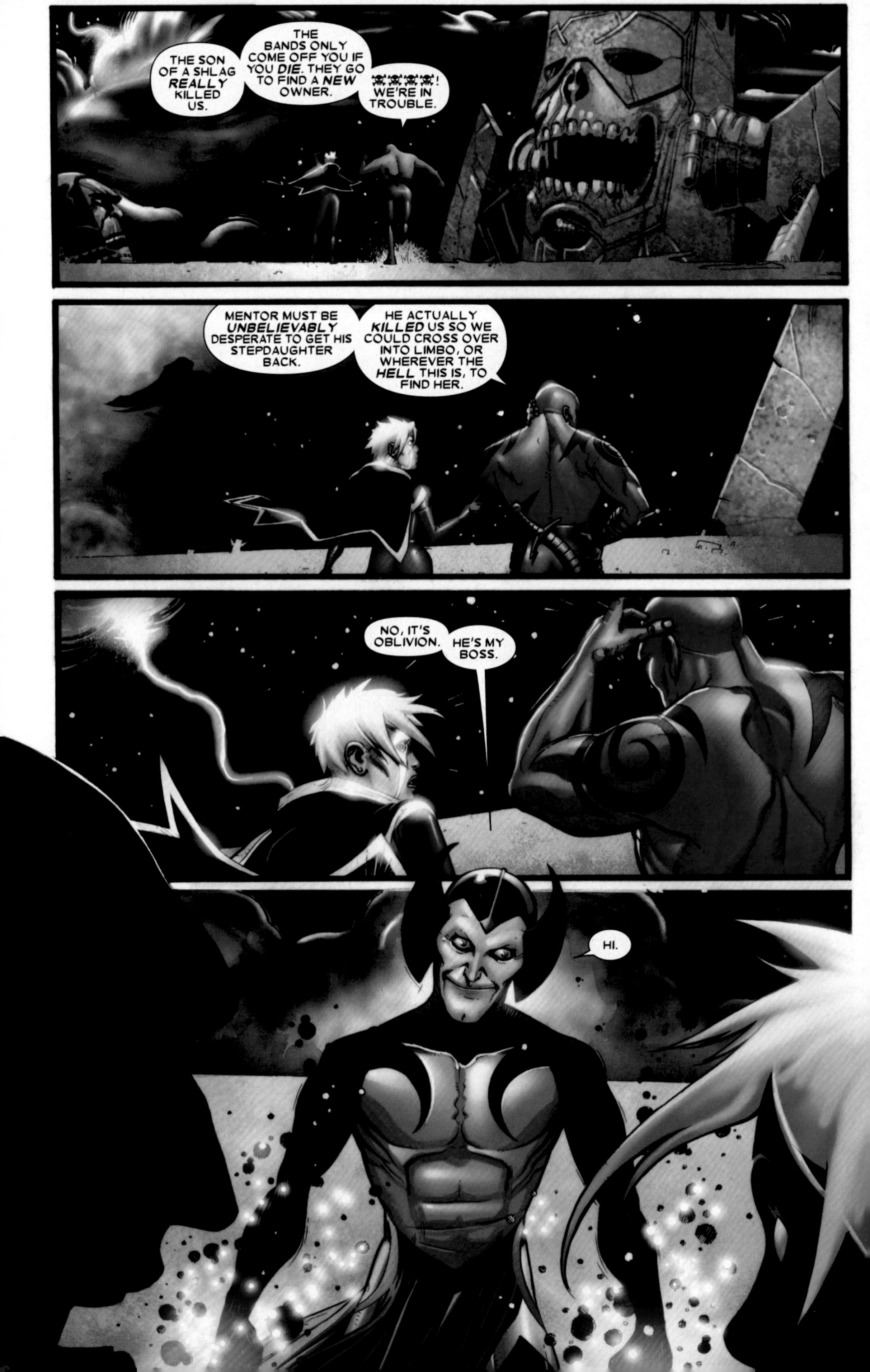
THE SON OF A SHLAG *REALLY* KILLED US.
THE BANDS ONLY COME OFF YOU IF YOU *DIE*. THEY GO TO FIND A *NEW* OWNER.
☠☠☠☠! WE'RE IN TROUBLE.
MENTOR MUST BE *UNBELIEVABLY* DESPERATE TO GET HIS STEPDAUGHTER BACK.
HE ACTUALLY *KILLED* US SO WE COULD CROSS OVER INTO LIMBO, OR WHEREVER THE *HELL* THIS IS, TO FIND HER.
NO, IT'S OBLIVION.
HE'S MY BOSS.
HI.

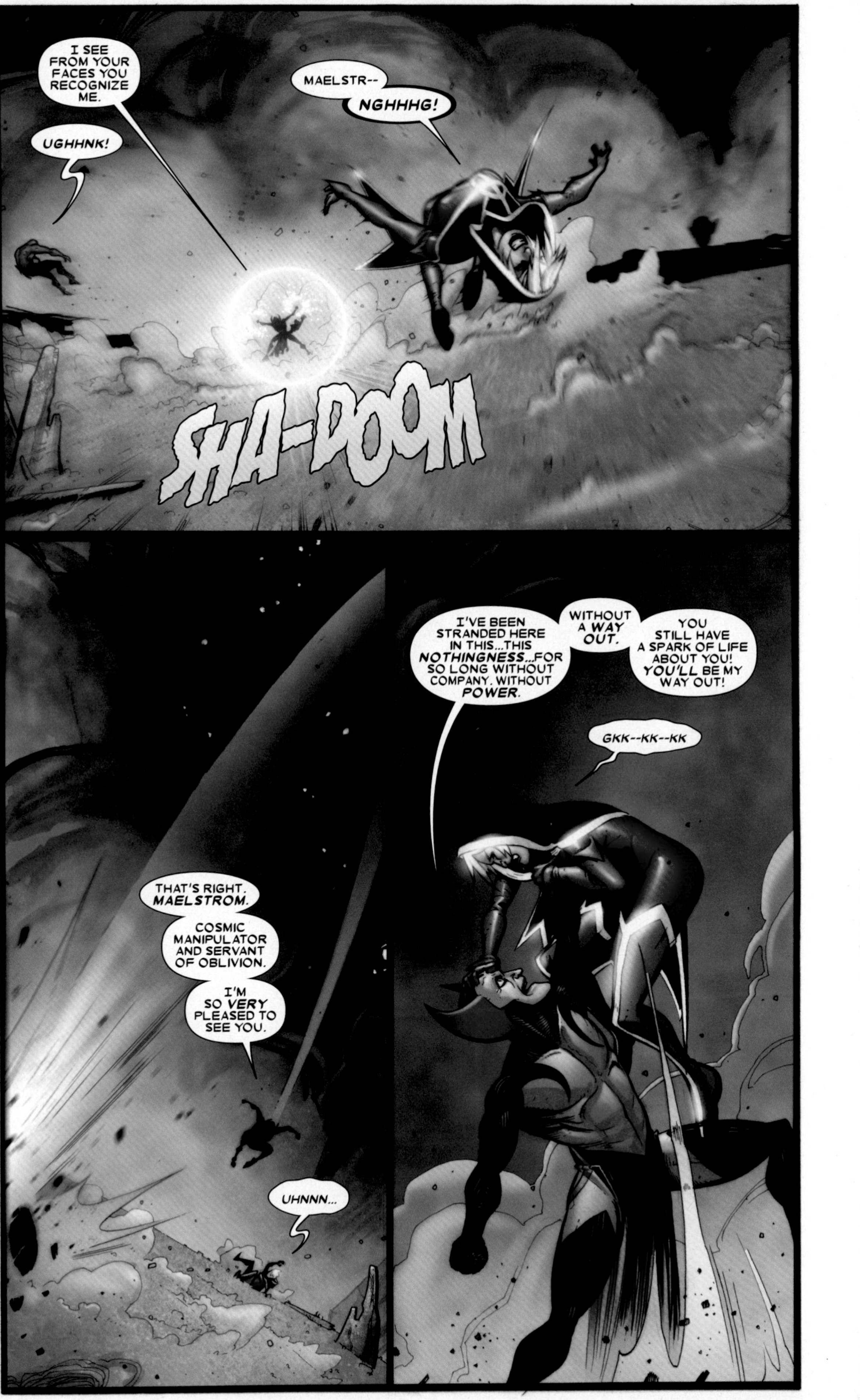
I SEE FROM YOUR FACES YOU RECOGNIZE ME.
UGHHNK!
MAELSTR--
NGHHHG!
SHA-DOOM
THAT'S RIGHT. MAELSTROM.
COSMIC MANIPULATOR AND SERVANT OF OBLIVION.
I'M SO VERY PLEASED TO SEE YOU.
UHNNN...
I'VE BEEN STRANDED HERE IN THIS...THIS NOTHINGNESS...FOR SO LONG WITHOUT COMPANY. WITHOUT POWER.
WITHOUT A WAY OUT.
YOU STILL HAVE A SPARK OF LIFE ABOUT YOU! YOU'LL BE MY WAY OUT!
GKK--KK--KK

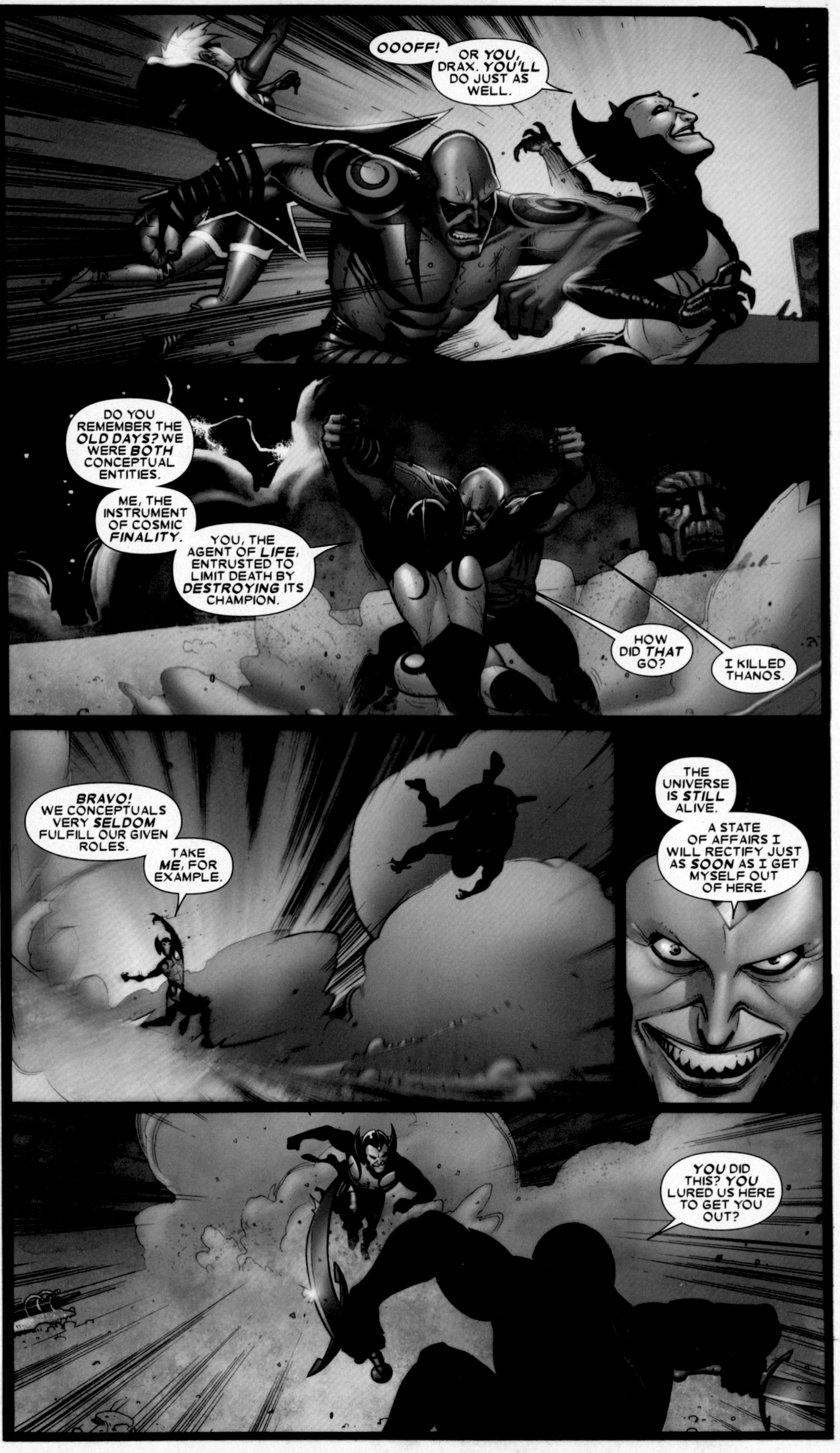
OOOFF!
OR YOU, DRAX. YOU'LL DO JUST AS WELL.
DO YOU REMEMBER THE OLD DAYS? WE WERE BOTH CONCEPTUAL ENTITIES.
ME, THE INSTRUMENT OF COSMIC FINALITY.
YOU, THE AGENT OF LIFE, ENTRUSTED TO LIMIT DEATH BY DESTROYING ITS CHAMPION.
HOW DID THAT GO?
I KILLED THANOS.
BRAVO! WE CONCEPTUALS VERY SELDOM FULFILL OUR GIVEN ROLES.
TAKE ME, FOR EXAMPLE.
THE UNIVERSE IS STILL ALIVE.
A STATE OF AFFAIRS I WILL RECTIFY JUST AS SOON AS I GET MYSELF OUT OF HERE.
YOU DID THIS? YOU LURED US HERE TO GET YOU OUT?

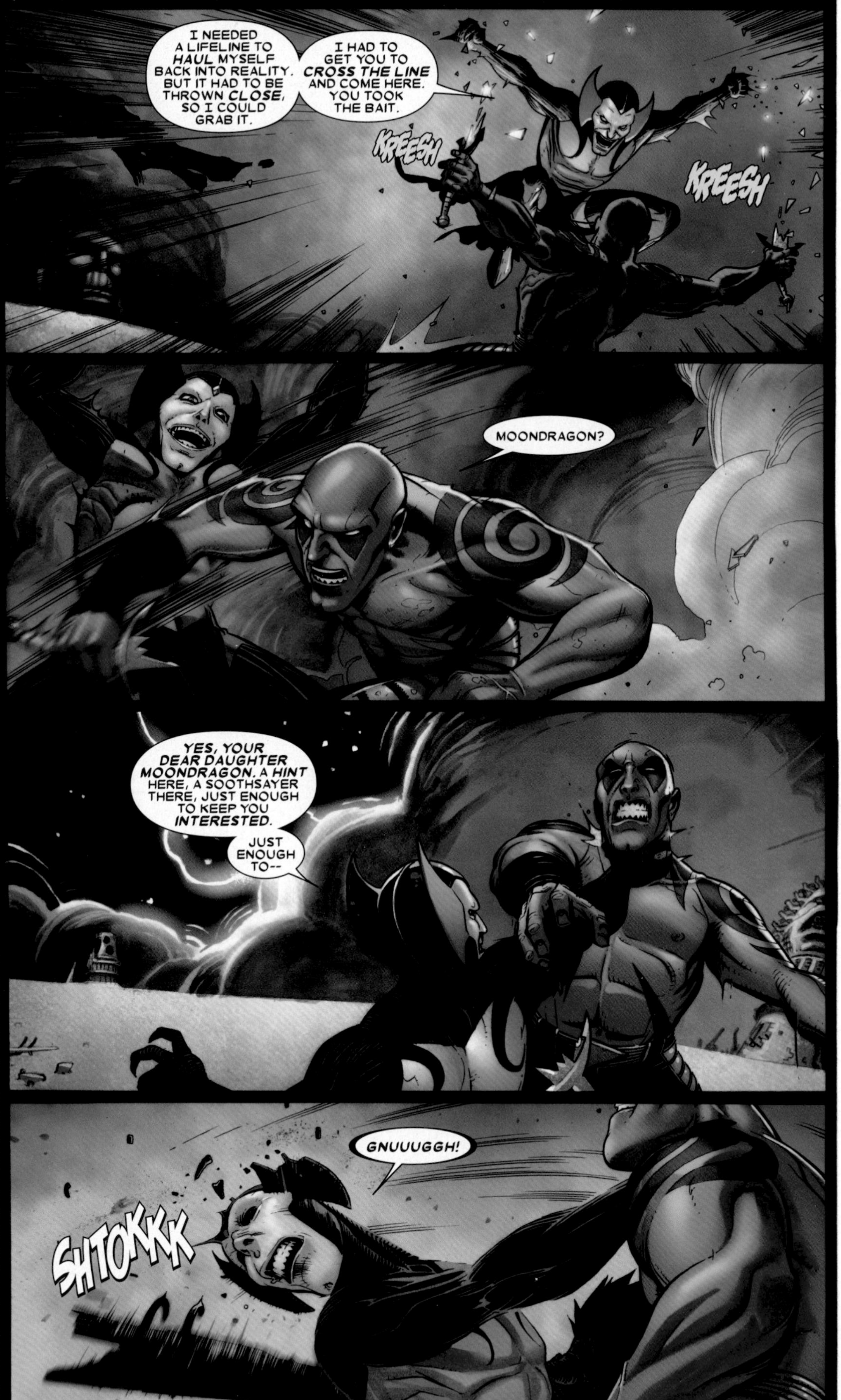

I NEEDED A LIFELINE TO HAUL MYSELF BACK INTO REALITY. BUT IT HAD TO BE THROWN CLOSE, SO I COULD GRAB IT.
I HAD TO GET YOU TO CROSS THE LINE AND COME HERE. YOU TOOK THE BAIT.
KREESH
KREESH
MOONDRAGON?
YES, YOUR DEAR DAUGHTER MOONDRAGON. A HINT HERE, A SOOTHSAYER THERE, JUST ENOUGH TO KEEP YOU INTERESTED.
JUST ENOUGH TO--
GNUUUGGH!
SHTOKKK

I THOUGHT SHE WAS *ALIVE!*

I THOUGHT I COULD STILL *SAVE* HER, YOU ✦✦✦☠✦✦✦!

WHKK WHKK

WHKK

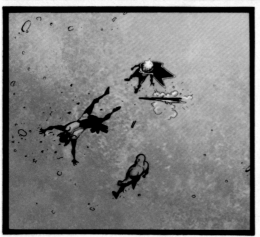

OKAY, WE'RE DONE HERE. LET'S FIND A WAY OUT.

IT WAS A *TRICK.*

YEAH, I'M SORRY. IT WAS *HIS* TRICK. THERE WASN'T *EVER* A HEATHER WE COULD RESCUE.

COME ON... OF *COURSE* THERE WAS. I COULDN'T FOOL *YOU.* THE BAIT HAD TO *SMELL* RIGHT.

I CAN TAKE YOU TO HER, IF YOU LIKE.

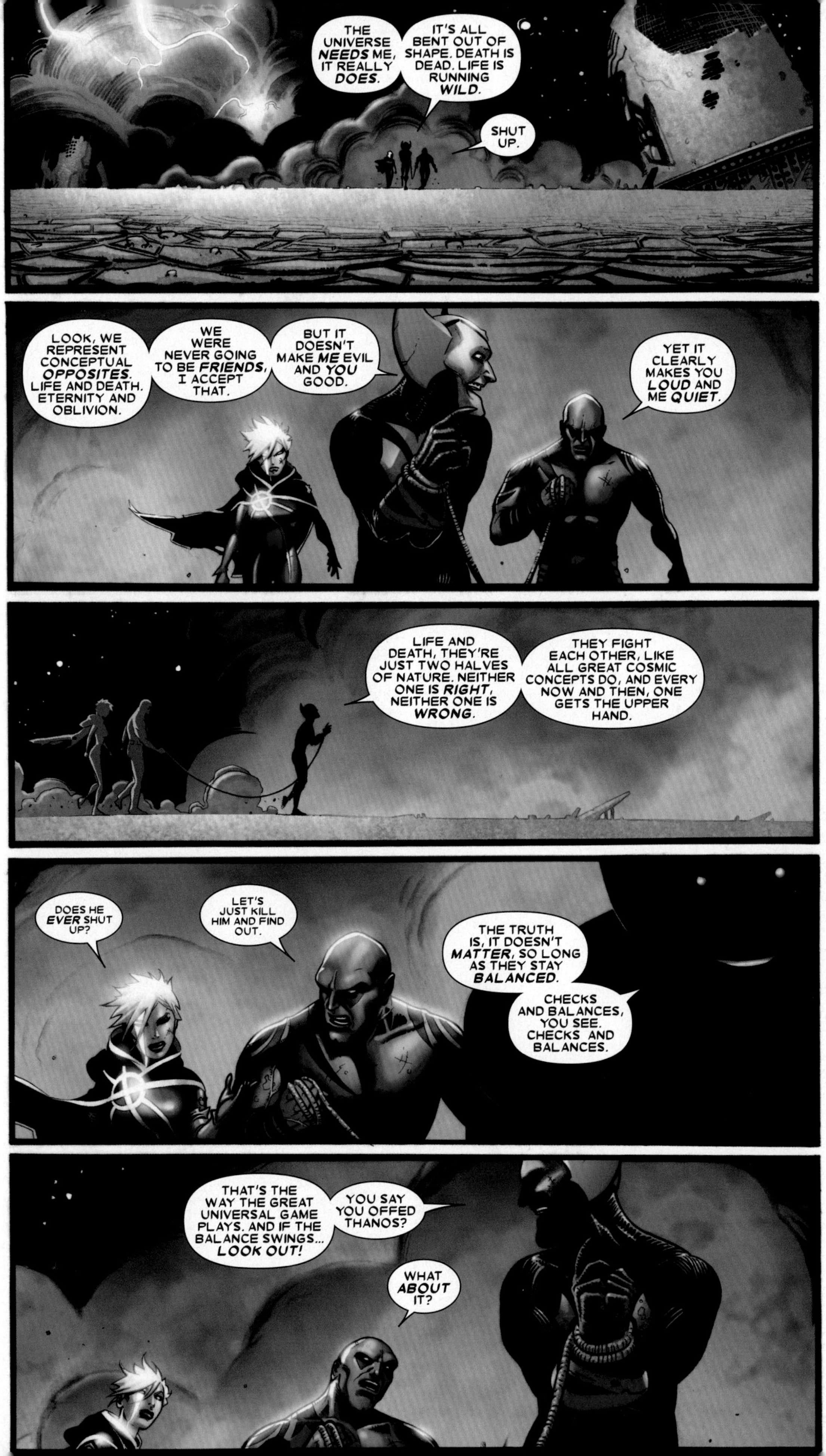
THE UNIVERSE NEEDS ME, IT REALLY DOES.
IT'S ALL BENT OUT OF SHAPE. DEATH IS DEAD. LIFE IS RUNNING WILD.
SHUT UP.
LOOK, WE REPRESENT CONCEPTUAL OPPOSITES. LIFE AND DEATH. ETERNITY AND OBLIVION.
WE WERE NEVER GOING TO BE FRIENDS, I ACCEPT THAT.
BUT IT DOESN'T MAKE ME EVIL AND YOU GOOD.
YET IT CLEARLY MAKES YOU LOUD AND ME QUIET.
LIFE AND DEATH, THEY'RE JUST TWO HALVES OF NATURE. NEITHER ONE IS RIGHT, NEITHER ONE IS WRONG.
THEY FIGHT EACH OTHER, LIKE ALL GREAT COSMIC CONCEPTS DO, AND EVERY NOW AND THEN, ONE GETS THE UPPER HAND.
DOES HE EVER SHUT UP?
LET'S JUST KILL HIM AND FIND OUT.
THE TRUTH IS, IT DOESN'T MATTER, SO LONG AS THEY STAY BALANCED.
CHECKS AND BALANCES, YOU SEE. CHECKS AND BALANCES.
THAT'S THE WAY THE GREAT UNIVERSAL GAME PLAYS. AND IF THE BALANCE SWINGS... LOOK OUT!
YOU SAY YOU OFFED THANOS?
WHAT ABOUT IT?

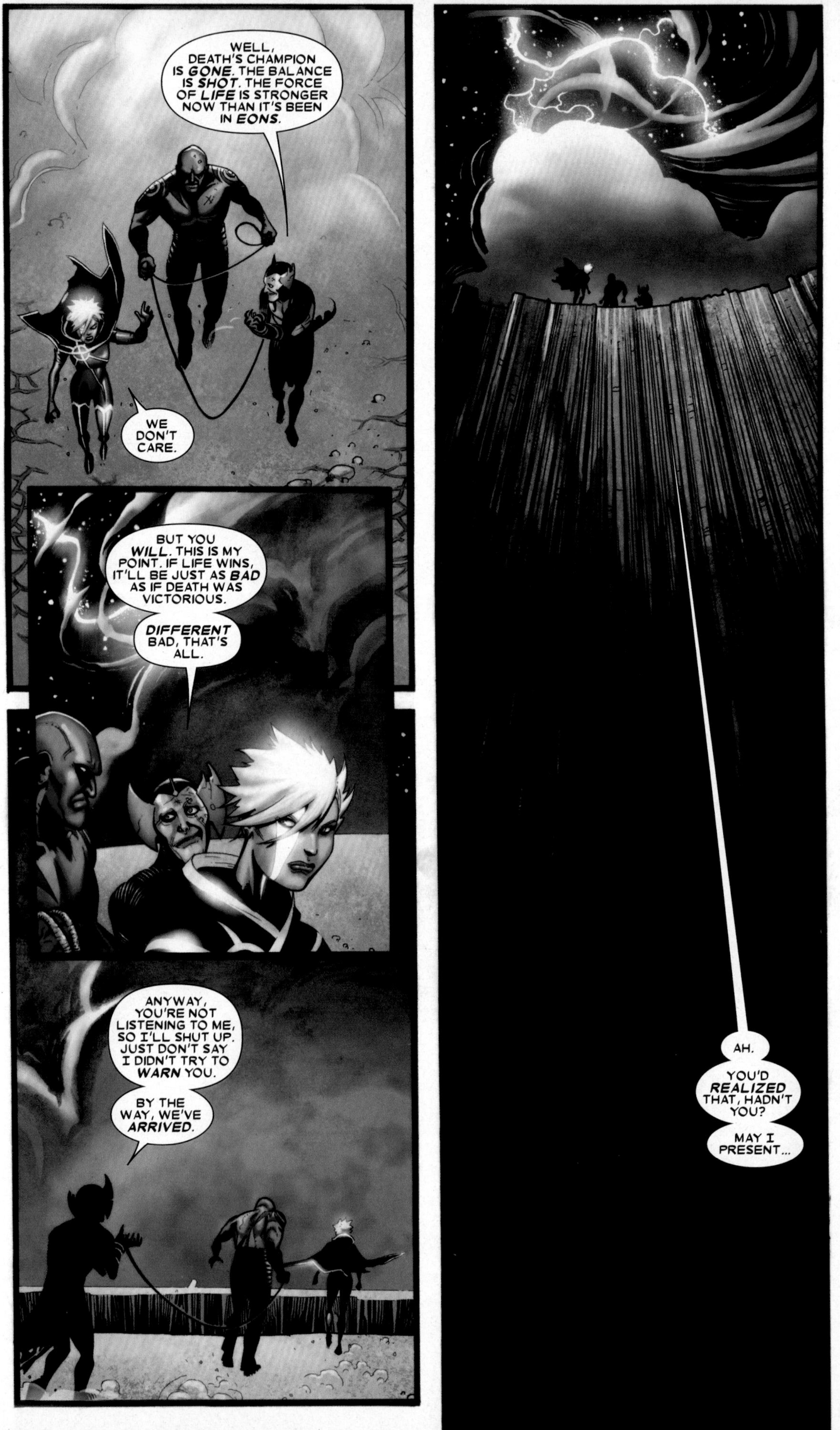
WELL, DEATH'S CHAMPION IS GONE. THE BALANCE IS SHOT. THE FORCE OF LIFE IS STRONGER NOW THAN IT'S BEEN IN EONS.
WE DON'T CARE.
BUT YOU WILL. THIS IS MY POINT. IF LIFE WINS, IT'LL BE JUST AS BAD AS IF DEATH WAS VICTORIOUS.
DIFFERENT BAD, THAT'S ALL.
ANYWAY, YOU'RE NOT LISTENING TO ME, SO I'LL SHUT UP. JUST DON'T SAY I DIDN'T TRY TO WARN YOU.
BY THE WAY, WE'VE ARRIVED.
AH.
YOU'D REALIZED THAT, HADN'T YOU?
MAY I PRESENT...

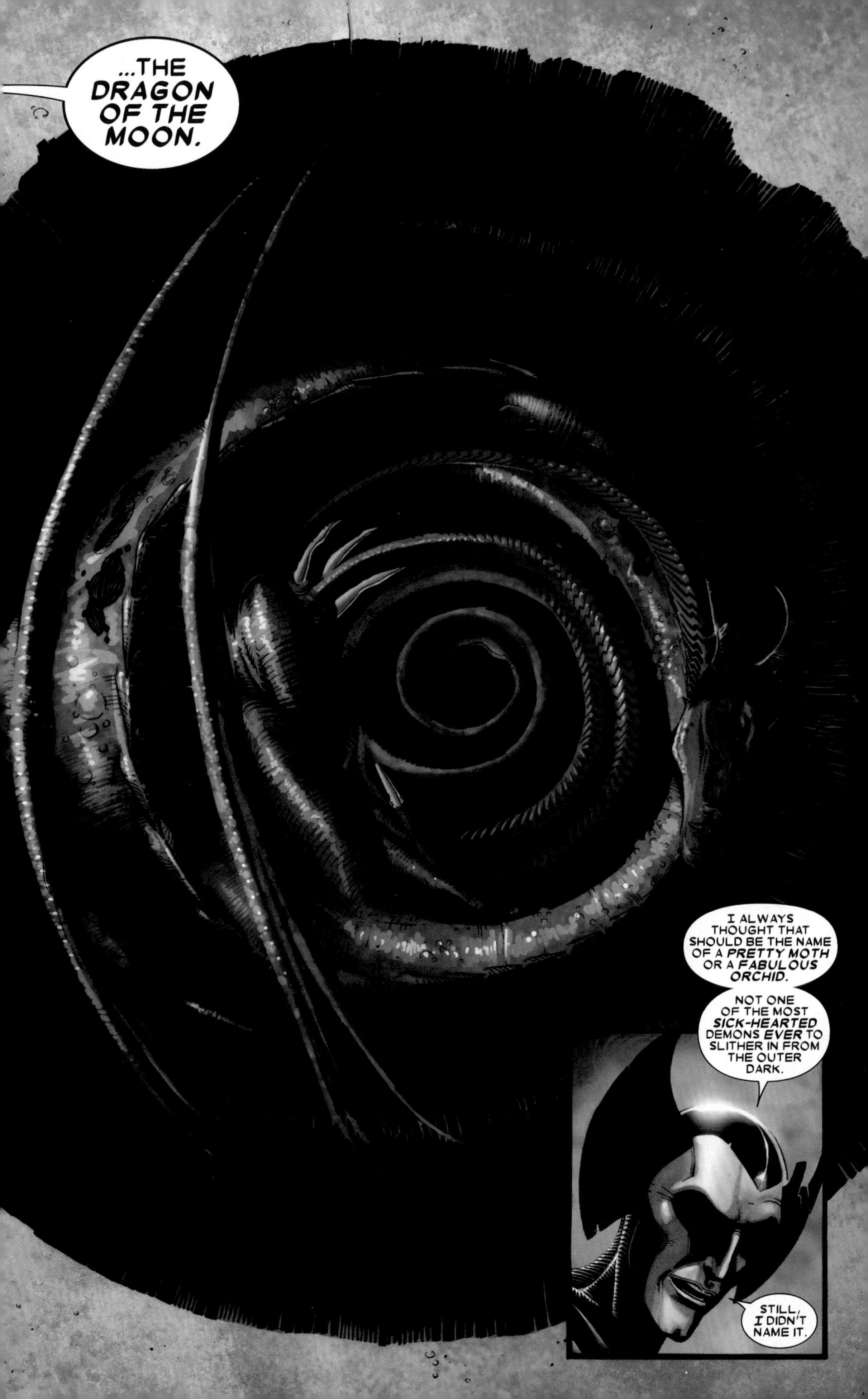
...THE DRAGON OF THE MOON.
I ALWAYS THOUGHT THAT SHOULD BE THE NAME OF A *PRETTY MOTH* OR A *FABULOUS ORCHID.*
NOT ONE OF THE MOST *SICK-HEARTED* DEMONS *EVER* TO SLITHER IN FROM THE OUTER DARK.
STILL, *I* DIDN'T NAME IT.

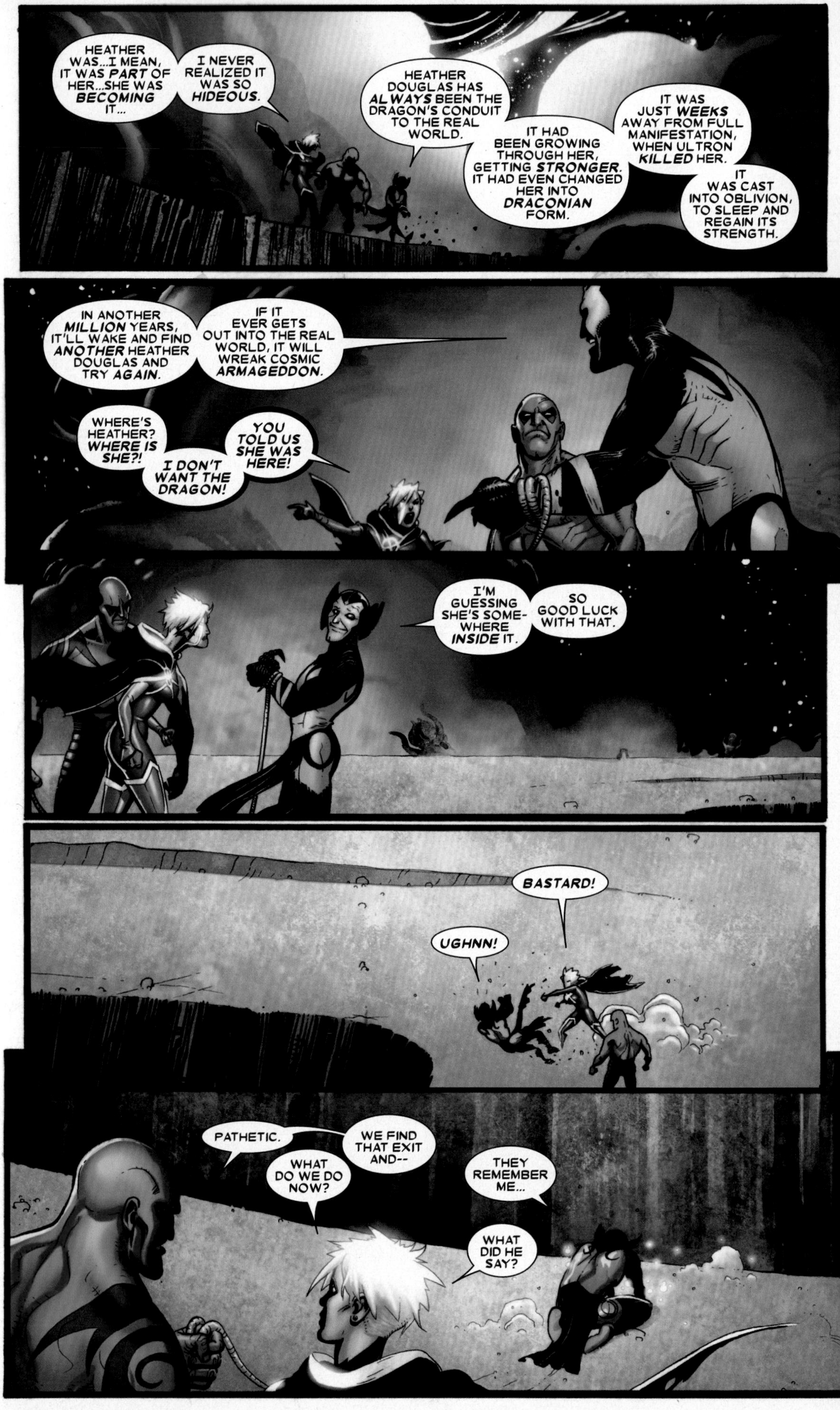
HEATHER WAS...I MEAN, IT WAS PART OF HER...SHE WAS BECOMING IT...
I NEVER REALIZED IT WAS SO HIDEOUS.
HEATHER DOUGLAS HAS ALWAYS BEEN THE DRAGON'S CONDUIT TO THE REAL WORLD.
IT HAD BEEN GROWING THROUGH HER, GETTING STRONGER. IT HAD EVEN CHANGED HER INTO DRACONIAN FORM.
IT WAS JUST WEEKS AWAY FROM FULL MANIFESTATION, WHEN ULTRON KILLED HER.
IT WAS CAST INTO OBLIVION, TO SLEEP AND REGAIN ITS STRENGTH.
IN ANOTHER MILLION YEARS, IT'LL WAKE AND FIND ANOTHER HEATHER DOUGLAS AND TRY AGAIN.
IF IT EVER GETS OUT INTO THE REAL WORLD, IT WILL WREAK COSMIC ARMAGEDDON.
WHERE'S HEATHER? WHERE IS SHE?!
I DON'T WANT THE DRAGON!
YOU TOLD US SHE WAS HERE!
I'M GUESSING SHE'S SOME-WHERE INSIDE IT.
SO GOOD LUCK WITH THAT.
BASTARD!
UGHNN!
PATHETIC.
WE FIND THAT EXIT AND--
WHAT DO WE DO NOW?
THEY REMEMBER ME...
WHAT DID HE SAY?

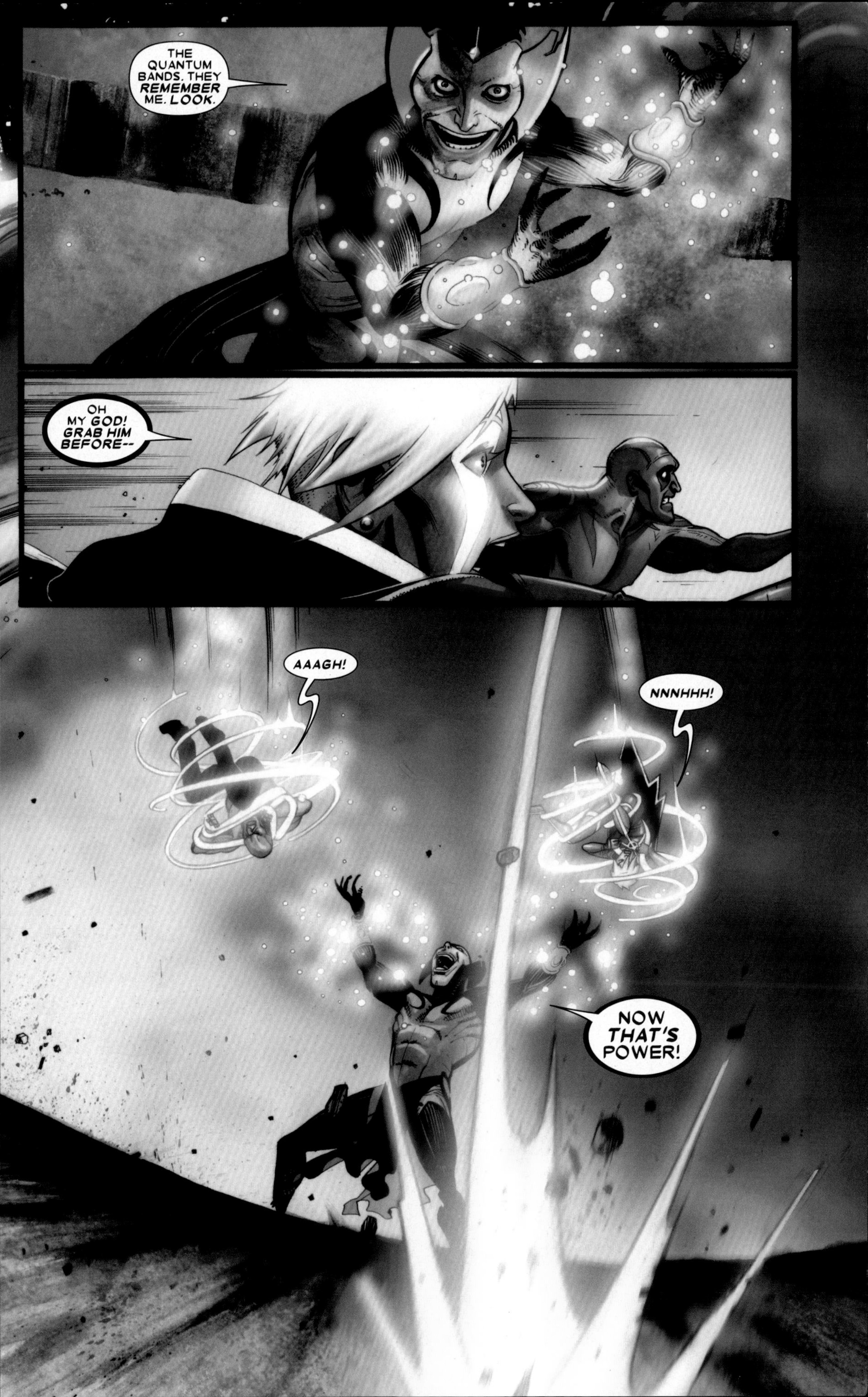
THE QUANTUM BANDS. THEY REMEMBER ME. LOOK.
OH MY GOD! GRAB HIM BEFORE--
AAAGH!
NNNHHH!
NOW THAT'S POWER!

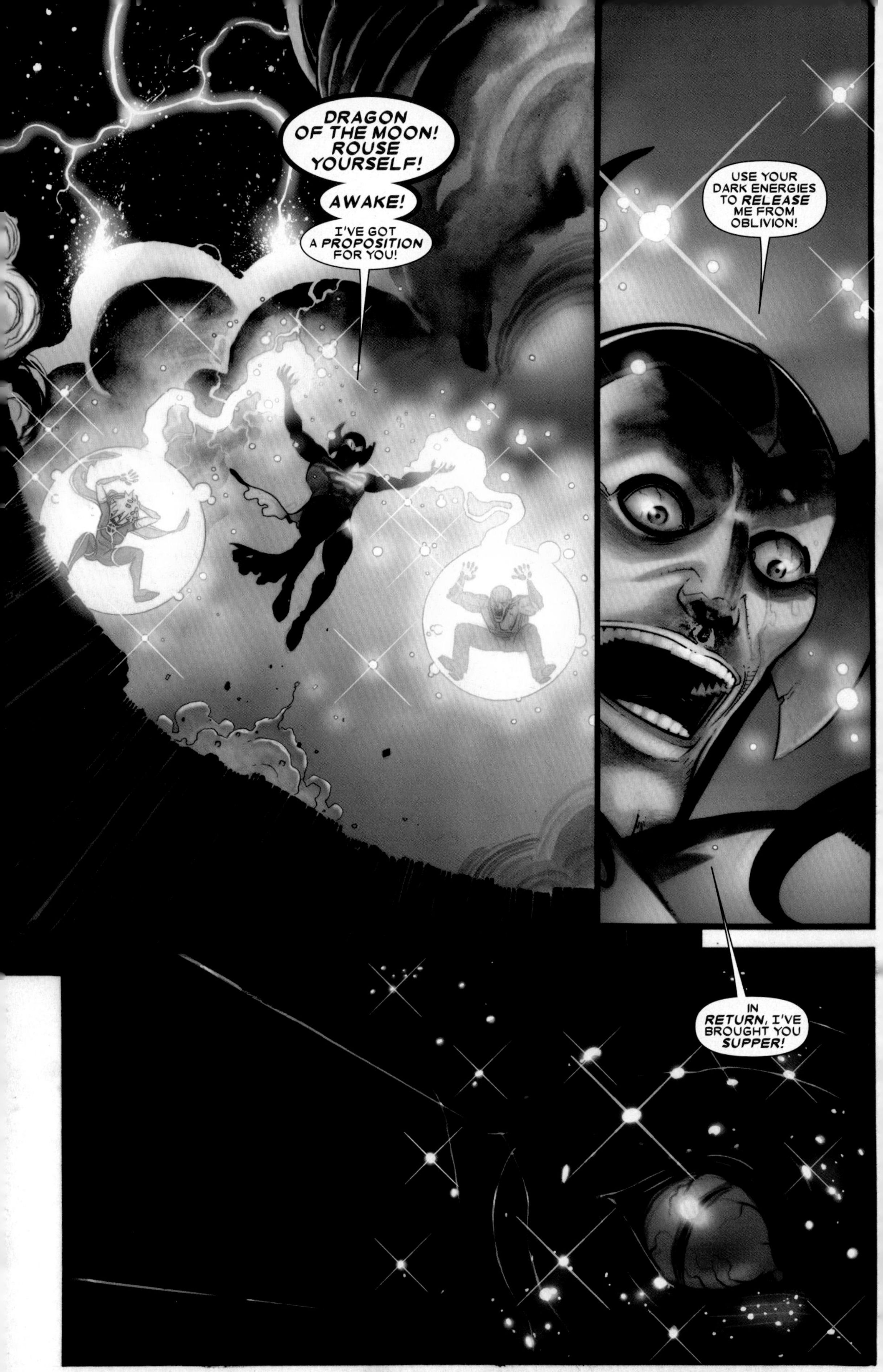
DRAGON OF THE MOON! ROUSE YOURSELF!
AWAKE!
I'VE GOT A PROPOSITION FOR YOU!
USE YOUR DARK ENERGIES TO RELEASE ME FROM OBLIVION!
IN RETURN, I'VE BROUGHT YOU SUPPER!

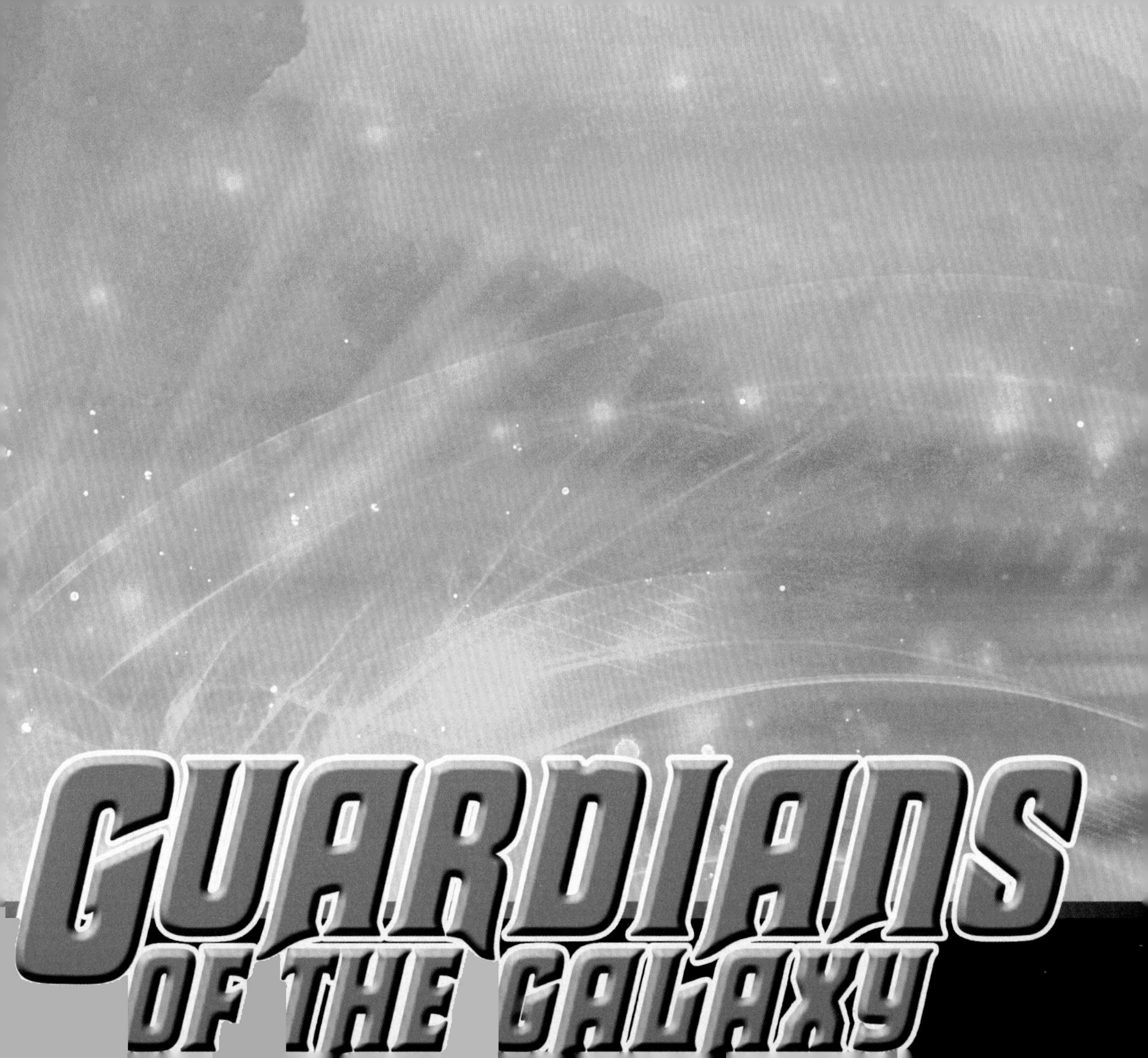
GUARDIANS
OF THE GALAXY

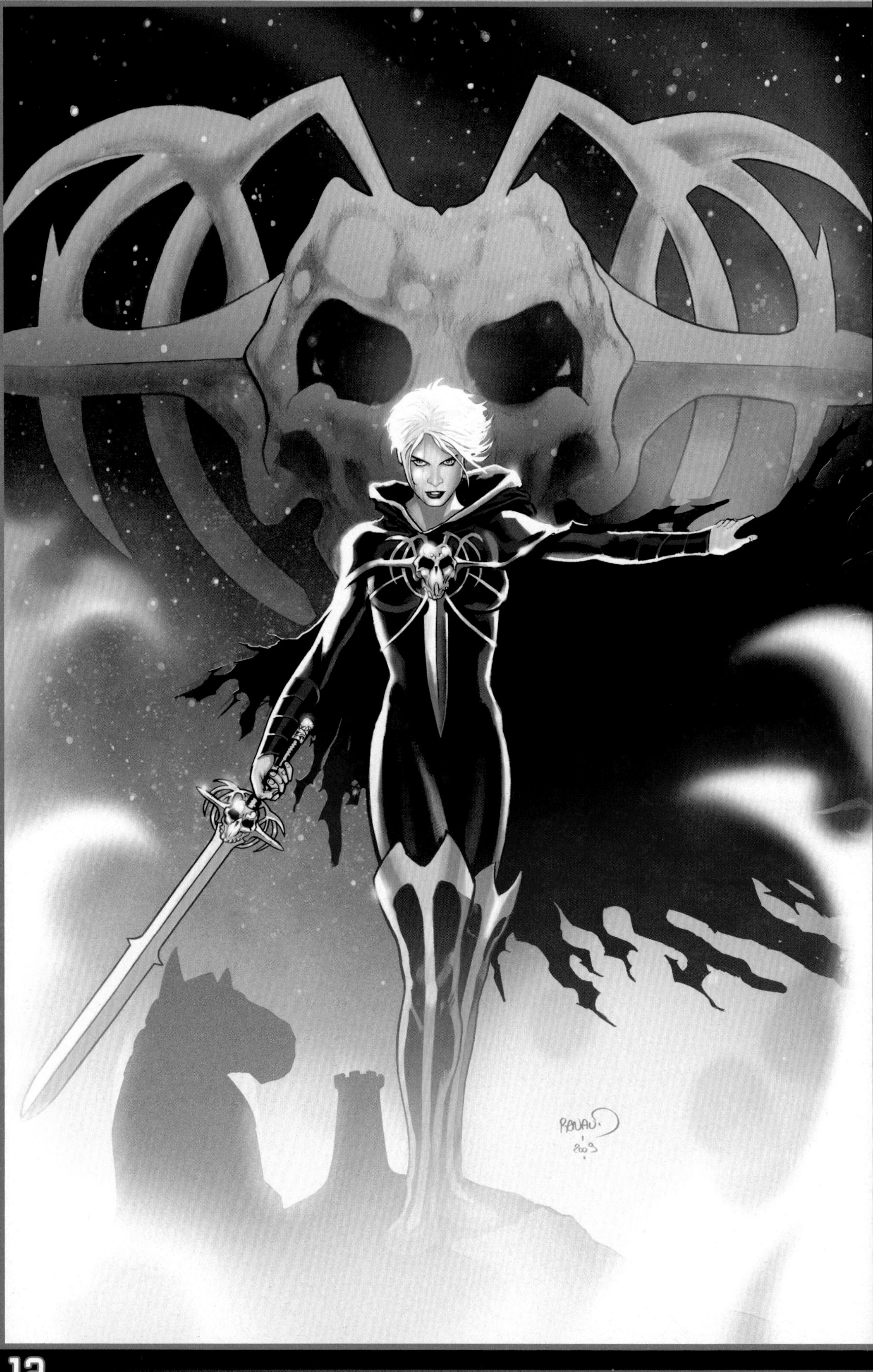

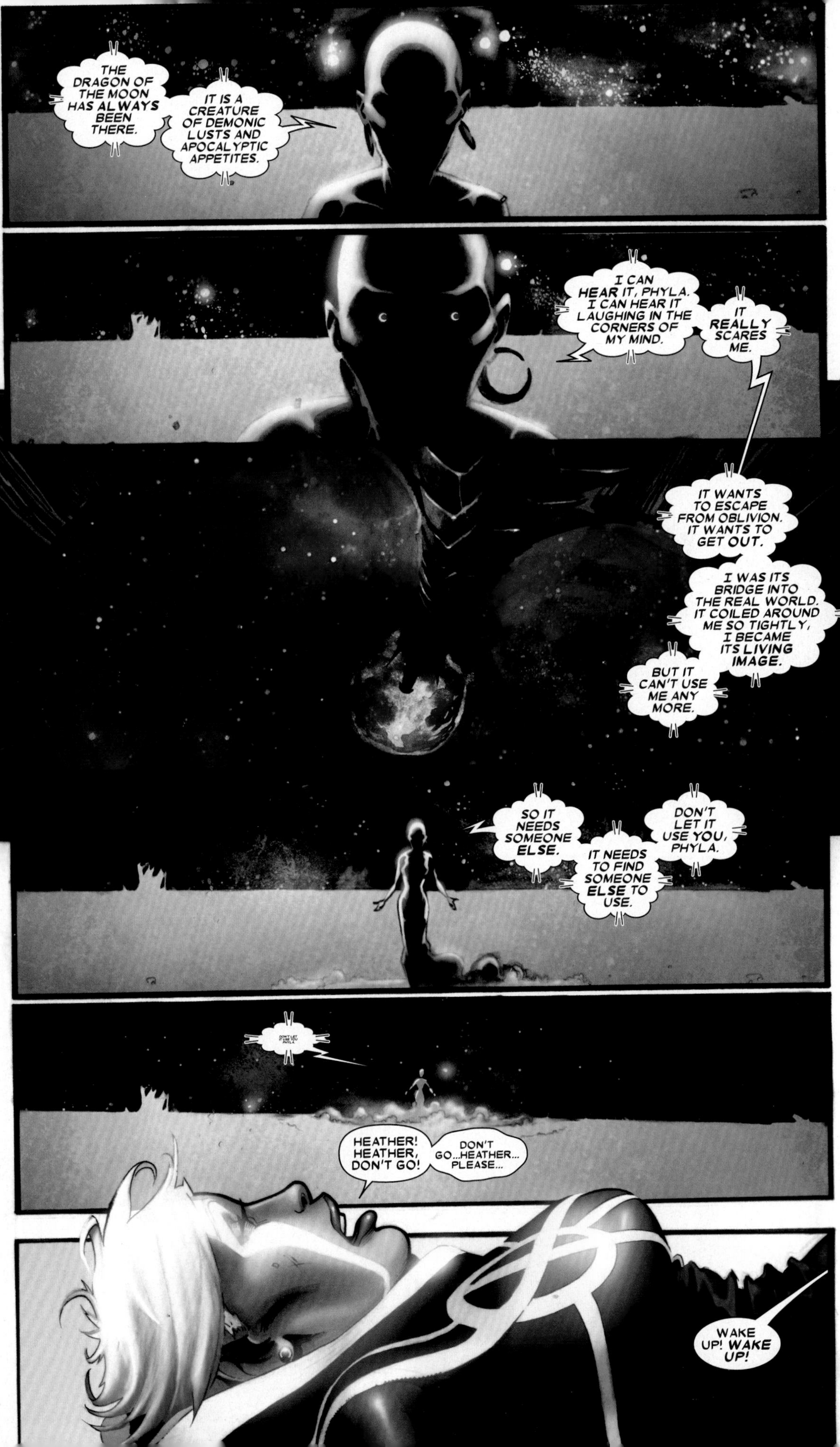
THE DRAGON OF THE MOON HAS ALWAYS BEEN THERE.
IT IS A CREATURE OF DEMONIC LUSTS AND APOCALYPTIC APPETITES.
I CAN HEAR IT, PHYLA. I CAN HEAR IT LAUGHING IN THE CORNERS OF MY MIND.
IT REALLY SCARES ME.
IT WANTS TO ESCAPE FROM OBLIVION. IT WANTS TO GET OUT.
I WAS ITS BRIDGE INTO THE REAL WORLD. IT COILED AROUND ME SO TIGHTLY, I BECAME ITS LIVING IMAGE.
BUT IT CAN'T USE ME ANY MORE.
SO IT NEEDS SOMEONE ELSE.
IT NEEDS TO FIND SOMEONE ELSE TO USE.
DON'T LET IT USE YOU, PHYLA.
HEATHER! HEATHER, DON'T GO!
DON'T GO...HEATHER... PLEASE...
WAKE UP! WAKE UP!

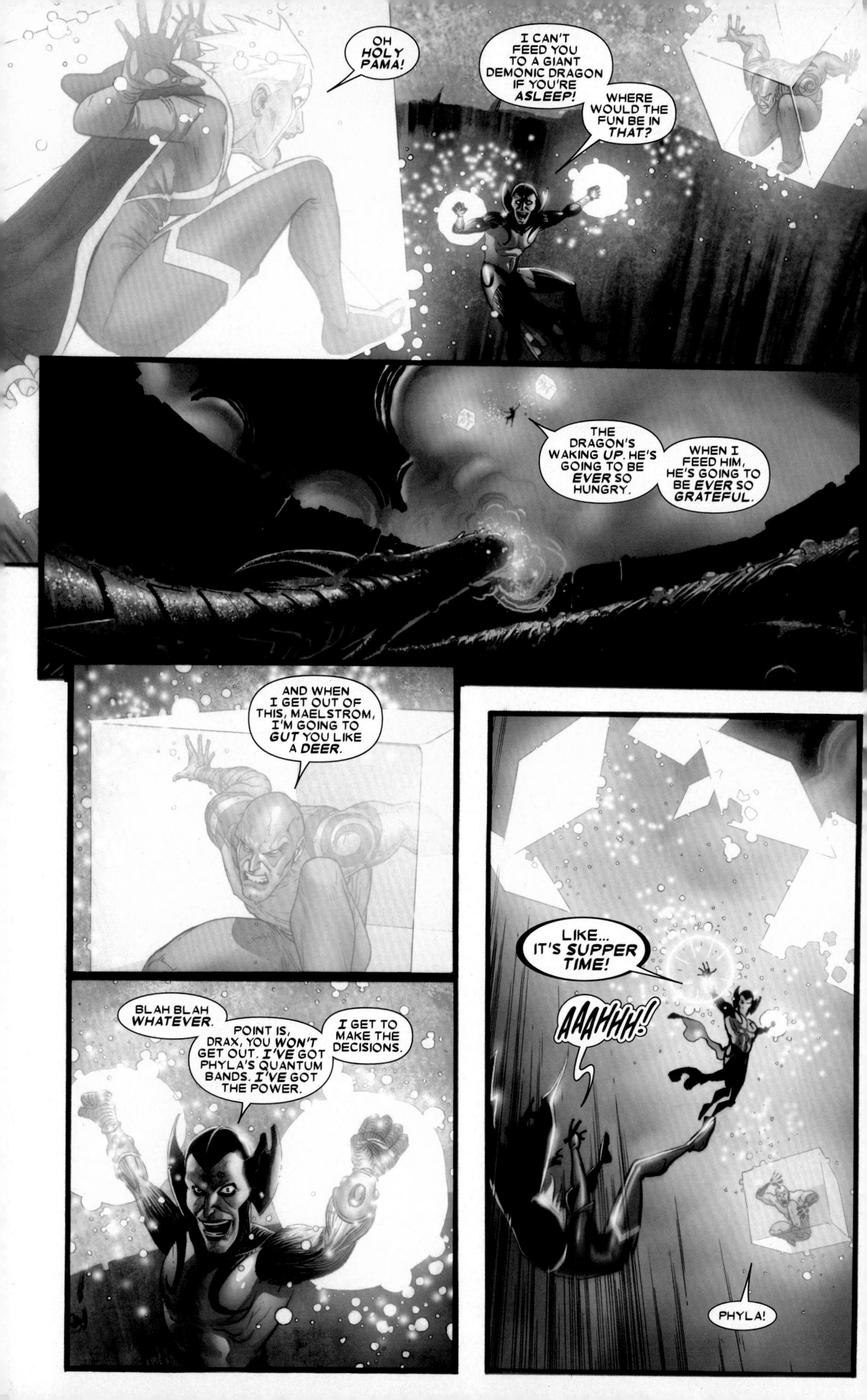
OH HOLY PAMA!
I CAN'T FEED YOU TO A GIANT DEMONIC DRAGON IF YOU'RE ASLEEP!
WHERE WOULD THE FUN BE IN THAT?
THE DRAGON'S WAKING UP. HE'S GOING TO BE EVER SO HUNGRY.
WHEN I FEED HIM, HE'S GOING TO BE EVER SO GRATEFUL.
AND WHEN I GET OUT OF THIS, MAELSTROM, I'M GOING TO GUT YOU LIKE A DEER.
BLAH BLAH WHATEVER.
POINT IS, DRAX, YOU WON'T GET OUT. I'VE GOT PHYLA'S QUANTUM BANDS. I'VE GOT THE POWER.
I GET TO MAKE THE DECISIONS.
LIKE... IT'S SUPPER TIME!
AAAHHH!
PHYLA!

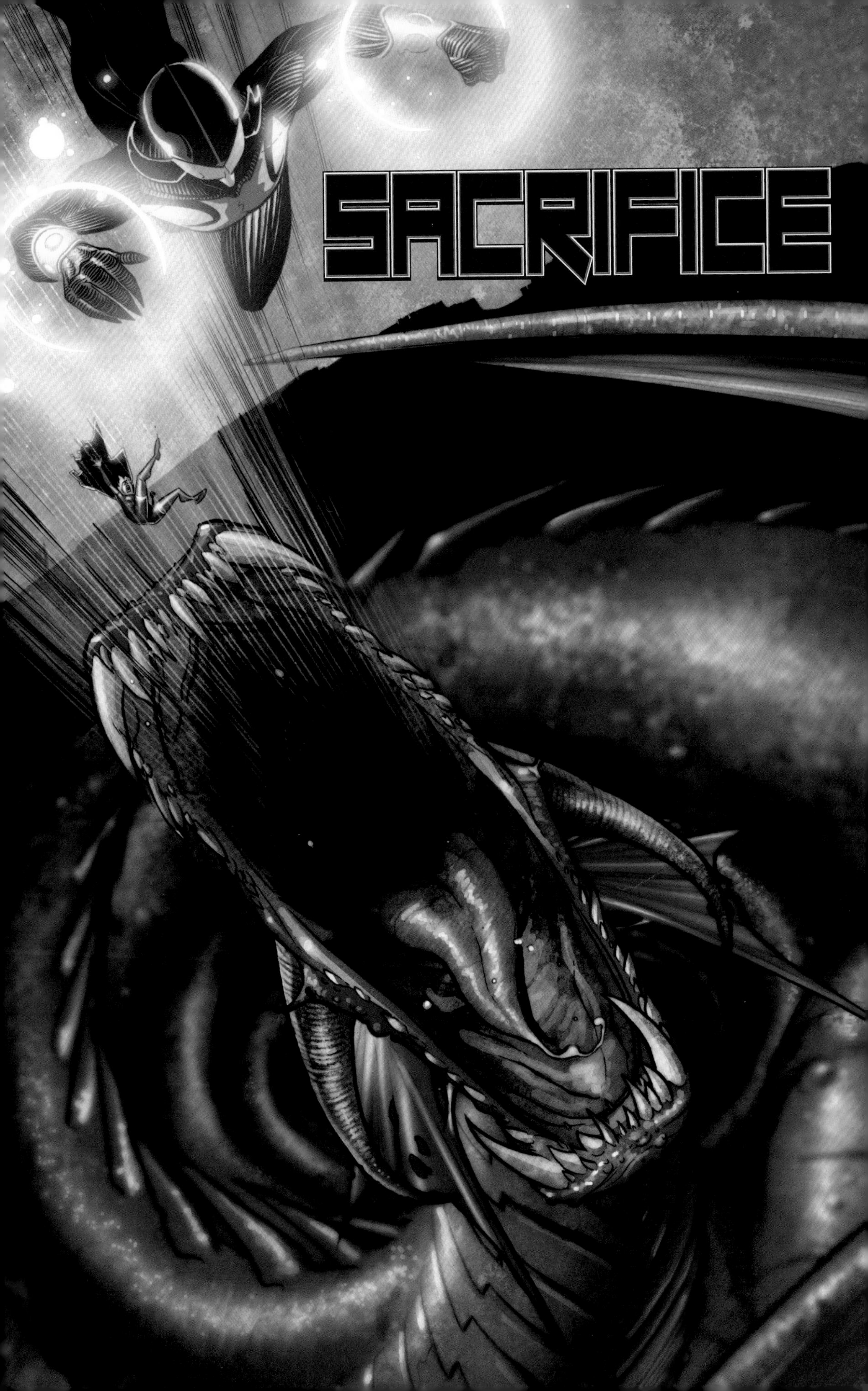
SACRIFICE

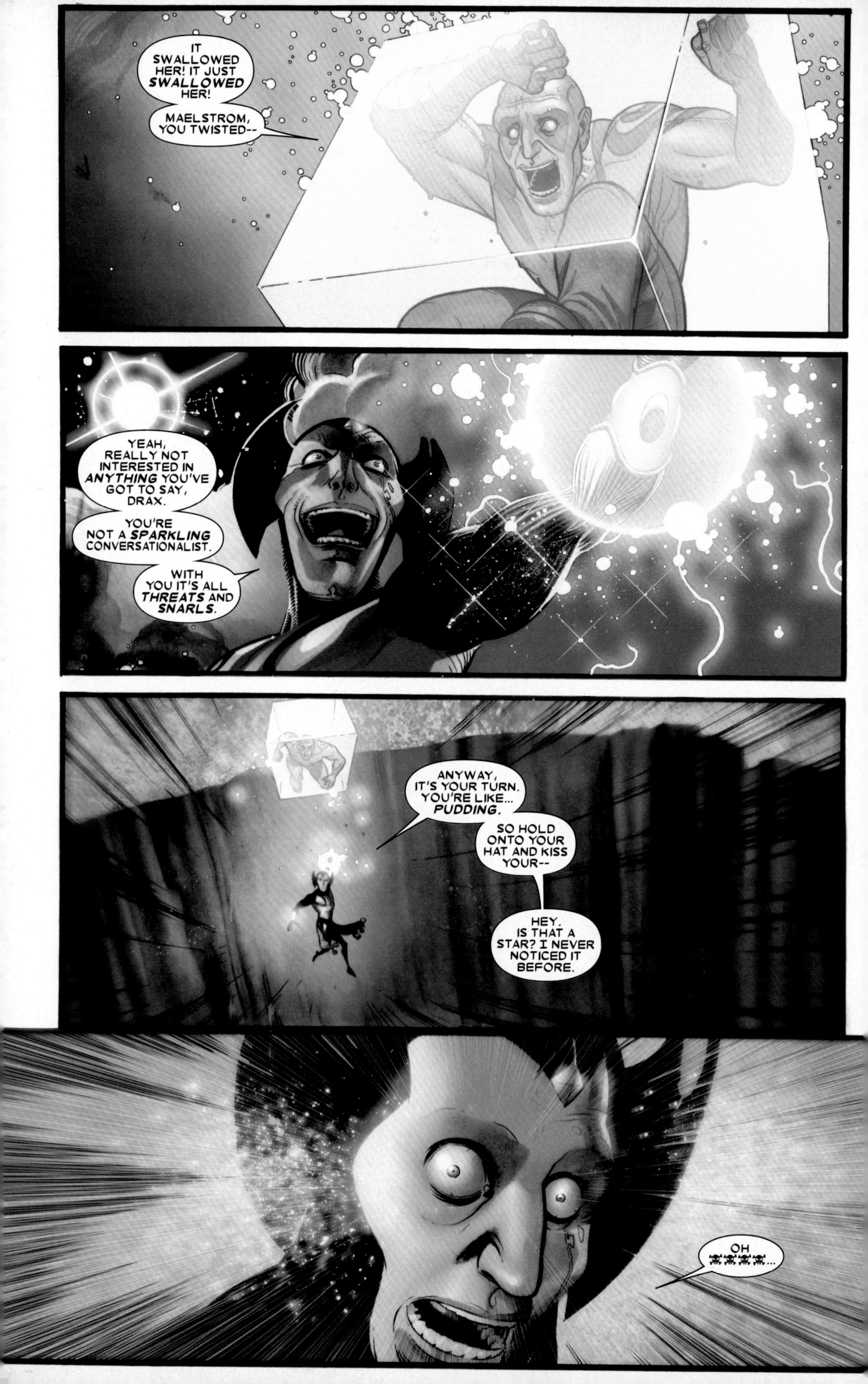
IT SWALLOWED HER! IT JUST SWALLOWED HER!
MAELSTROM, YOU TWISTED--
YEAH, REALLY NOT INTERESTED IN ANYTHING YOU'VE GOT TO SAY, DRAX.
YOU'RE NOT A SPARKLING CONVERSATIONALIST.
WITH YOU IT'S ALL THREATS AND SNARLS.
ANYWAY, IT'S YOUR TURN. YOU'RE LIKE... PUDDING.
SO HOLD ONTO YOUR HAT AND KISS YOUR--
HEY. IS THAT A STAR? I NEVER NOTICED IT BEFORE.
OH

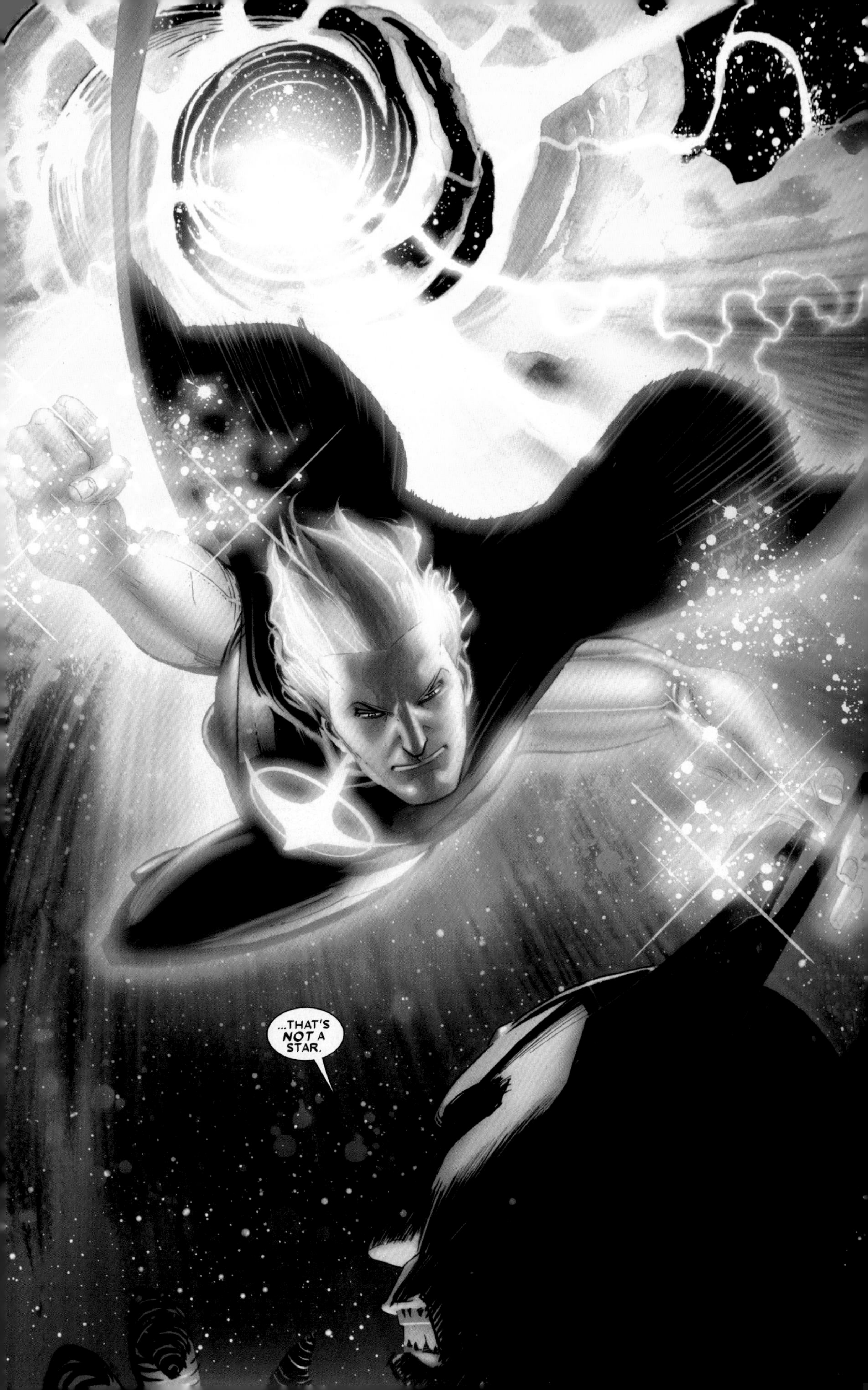
...THAT'S NOT A STAR.

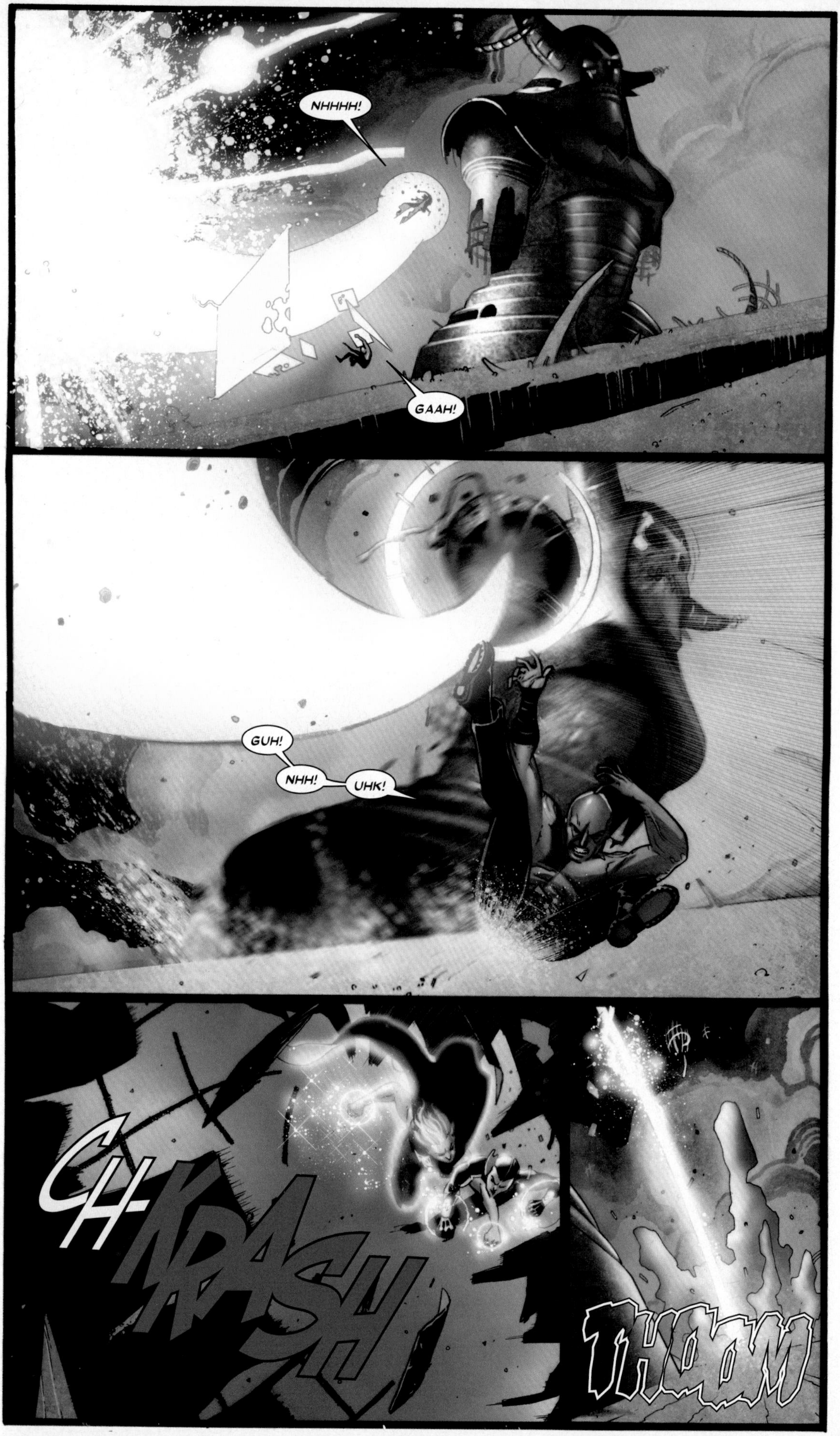
NHHHH!
GAAH!
GUH!
NHH!
UHK!
CH-KRASH
THOOM

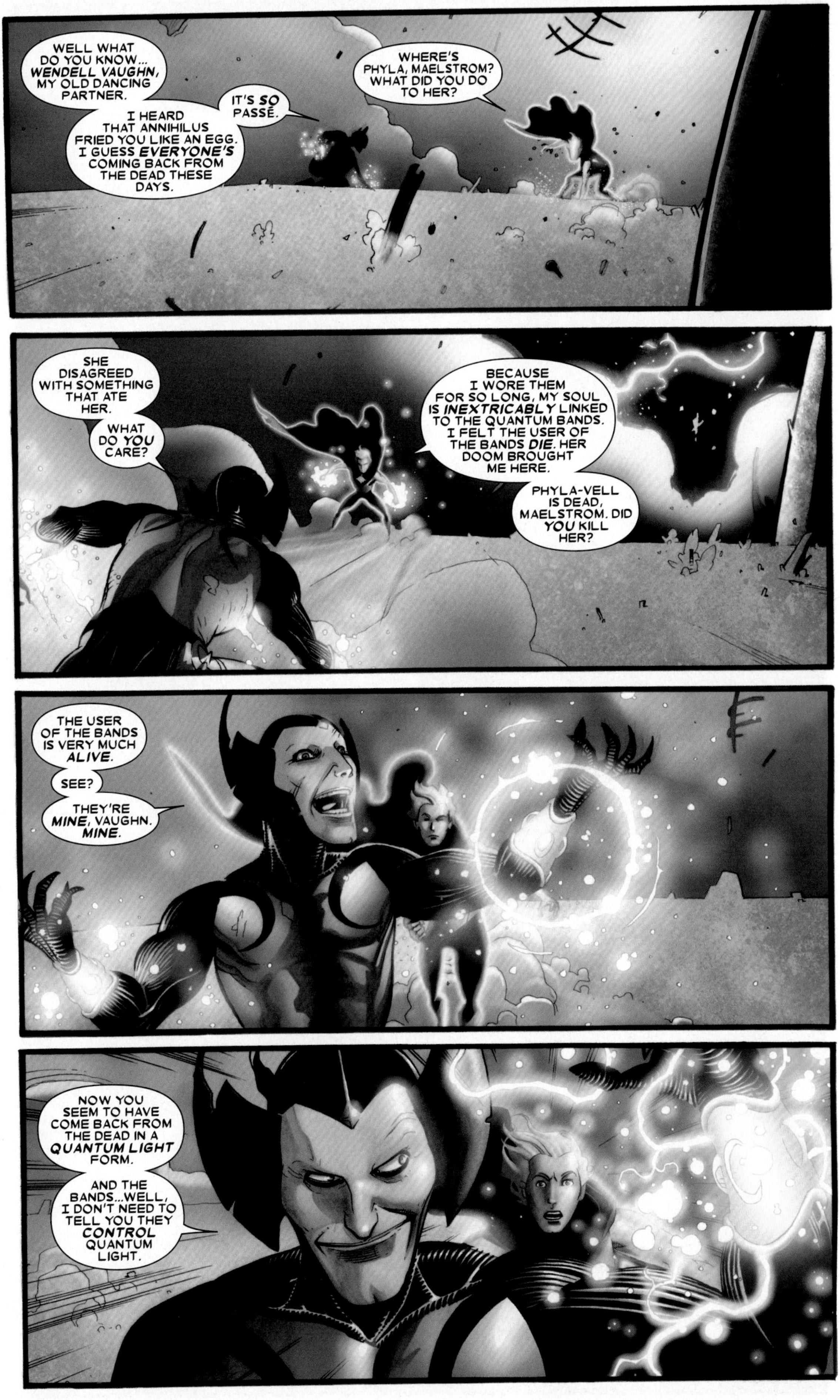
WELL WHAT DO YOU KNOW... WENDELL VAUGHN, MY OLD DANCING PARTNER.
I HEARD THAT ANNIHILUS FRIED YOU LIKE AN EGG. I GUESS EVERYONE'S COMING BACK FROM THE DEAD THESE DAYS.
IT'S SO PASSÉ.
WHERE'S PHYLA, MAELSTROM? WHAT DID YOU DO TO HER?
SHE DISAGREED WITH SOMETHING THAT ATE HER.
WHAT DO YOU CARE?
BECAUSE I WORE THEM FOR SO LONG, MY SOUL IS INEXTRICABLY LINKED TO THE QUANTUM BANDS. I FELT THE USER OF THE BANDS DIE. HER DOOM BROUGHT ME HERE.
PHYLA-VELL IS DEAD, MAELSTROM. DID YOU KILL HER?
THE USER OF THE BANDS IS VERY MUCH ALIVE.
SEE?
THEY'RE MINE, VAUGHN. MINE.
NOW YOU SEEM TO HAVE COME BACK FROM THE DEAD IN A QUANTUM LIGHT FORM.
AND THE BANDS...WELL, I DON'T NEED TO TELL YOU THEY CONTROL QUANTUM LIGHT.

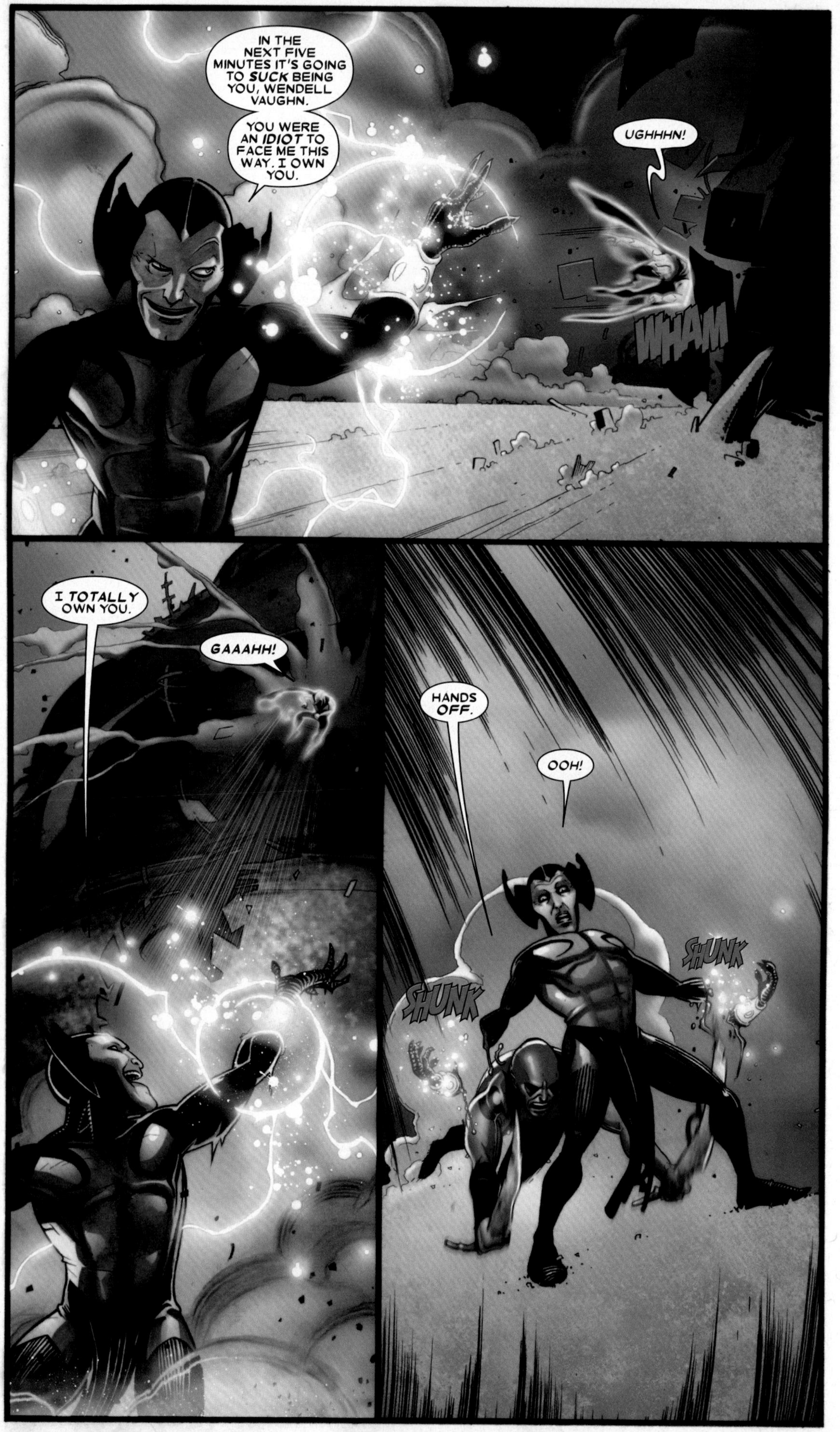
IN THE NEXT FIVE MINUTES IT'S GOING TO SUCK BEING YOU, WENDELL VAUGHN.
YOU WERE AN IDIOT TO FACE ME THIS WAY. I OWN YOU.
UGHHHN!
WHAM
I TOTALLY OWN YOU.
GAAAHH!
HANDS OFF.
OOH!
SHUNK
SHUNK

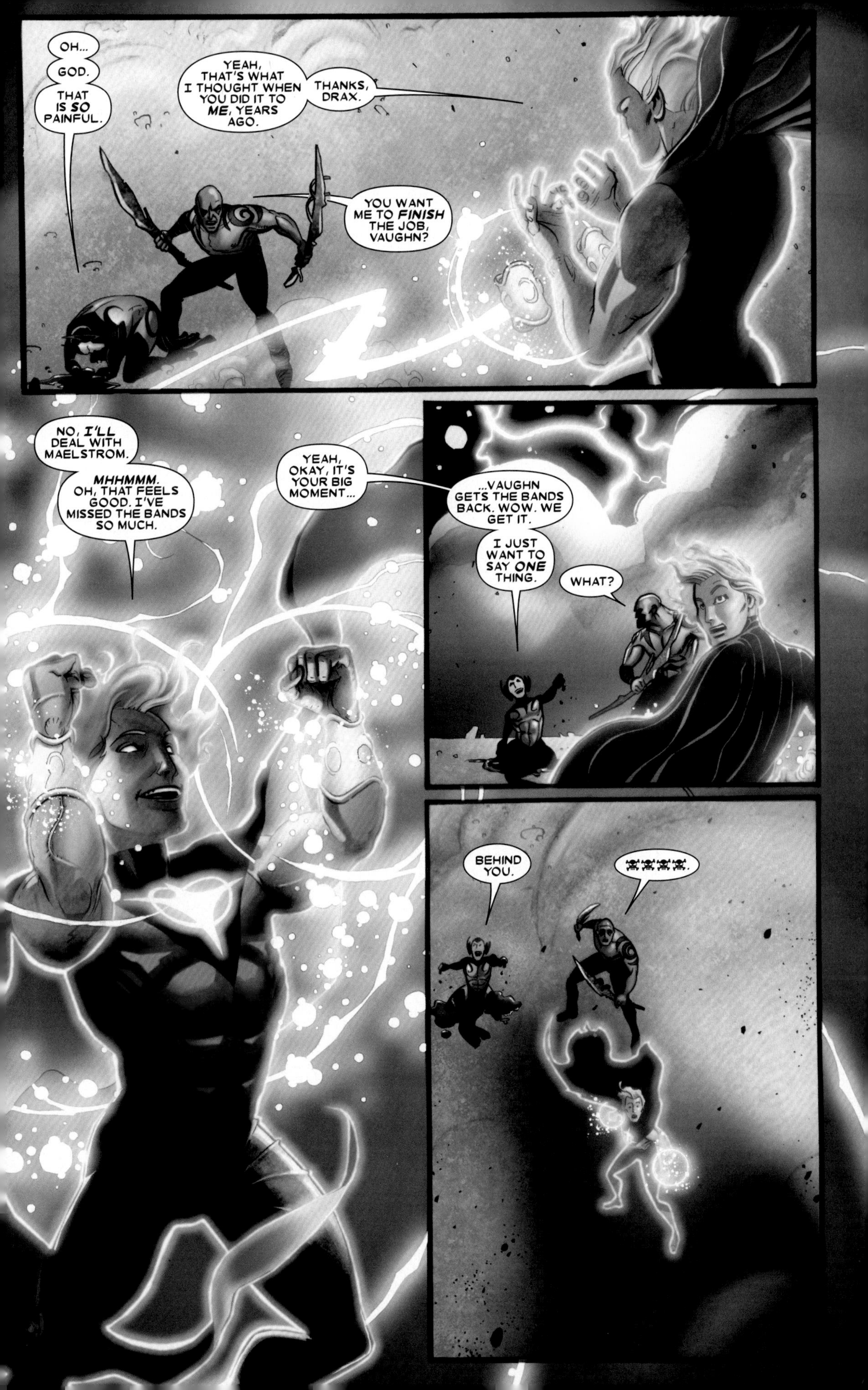
OH...
GOD.
THAT IS SO PAINFUL.
YEAH, THAT'S WHAT I THOUGHT WHEN YOU DID IT TO ME, YEARS AGO.
THANKS, DRAX.
YOU WANT ME TO FINISH THE JOB, VAUGHN?
NO, I'LL DEAL WITH MAELSTROM.
MHHMMM. OH, THAT FEELS GOOD. I'VE MISSED THE BANDS SO MUCH.
YEAH, OKAY, IT'S YOUR BIG MOMENT...
...VAUGHN GETS THE BANDS BACK. WOW. WE GET IT.
I JUST WANT TO SAY ONE THING.
WHAT?
BEHIND YOU.

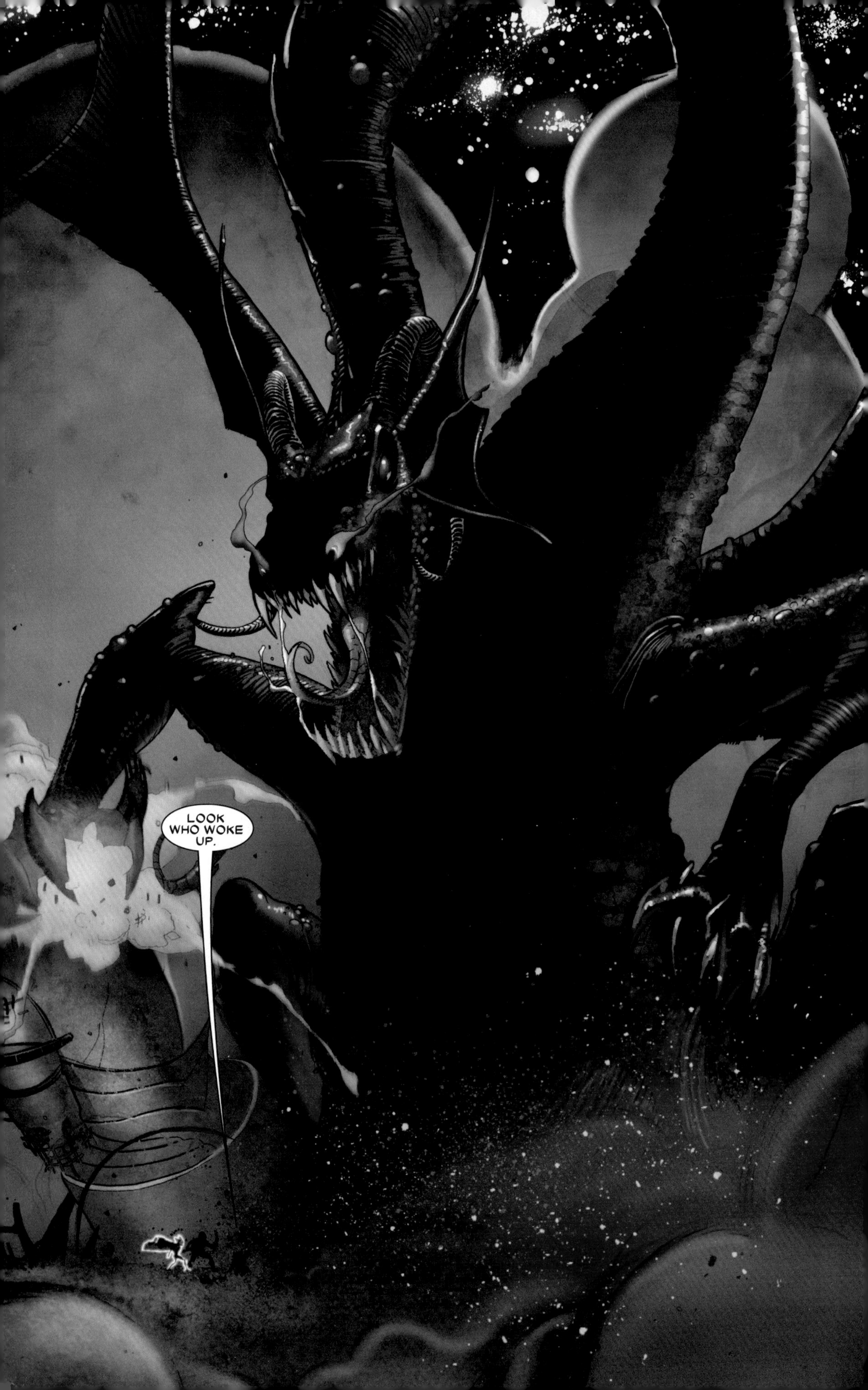
LOOK WHO WOKE UP.

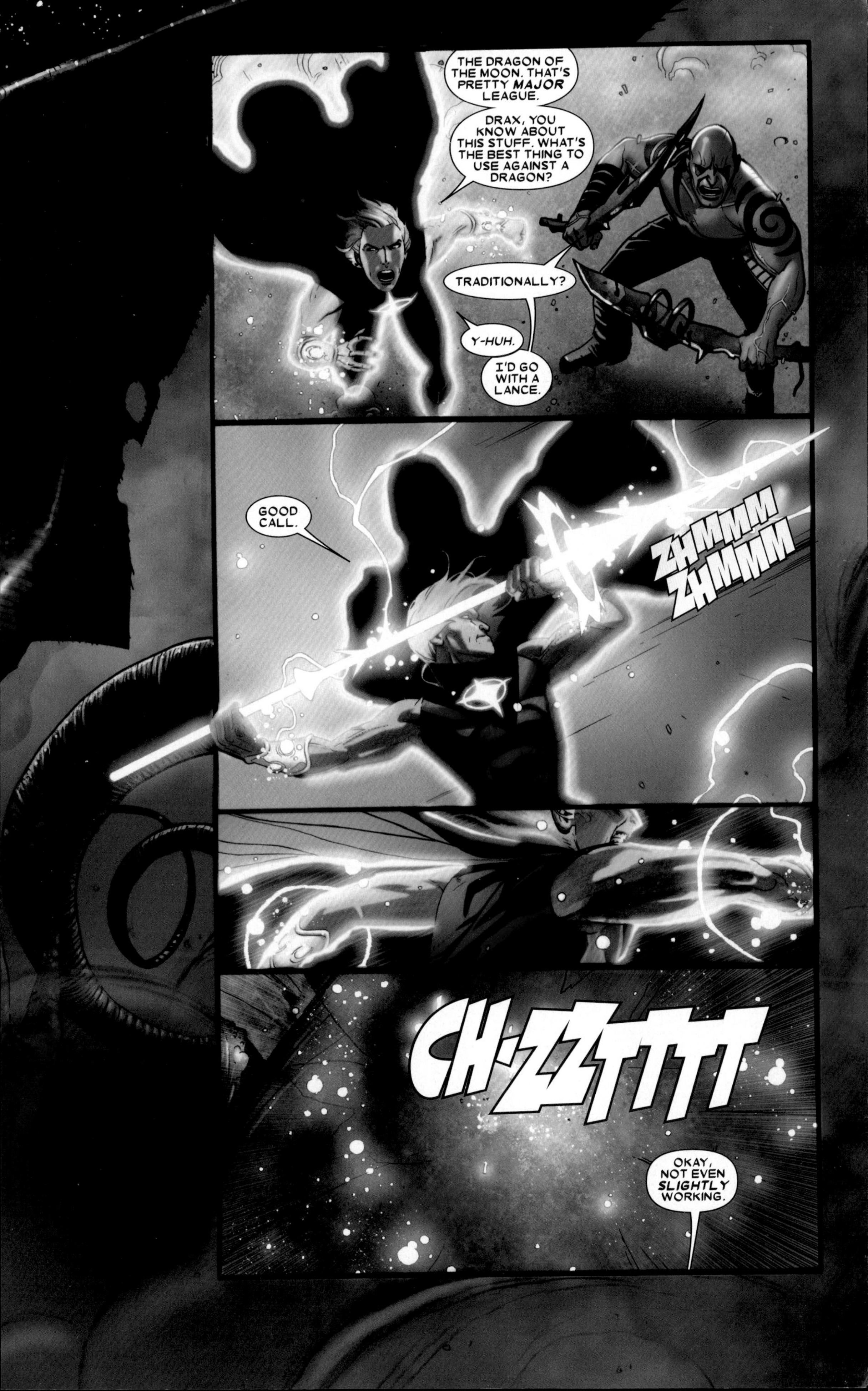
THE DRAGON OF THE MOON. THAT'S PRETTY MAJOR LEAGUE.
DRAX, YOU KNOW ABOUT THIS STUFF. WHAT'S THE BEST THING TO USE AGAINST A DRAGON?
TRADITIONALLY?
Y-HUH.
I'D GO WITH A LANCE.
GOOD CALL.
ZHMMM ZHMMM
CH-ZZTTTT
OKAY, NOT EVEN SLIGHTLY WORKING.

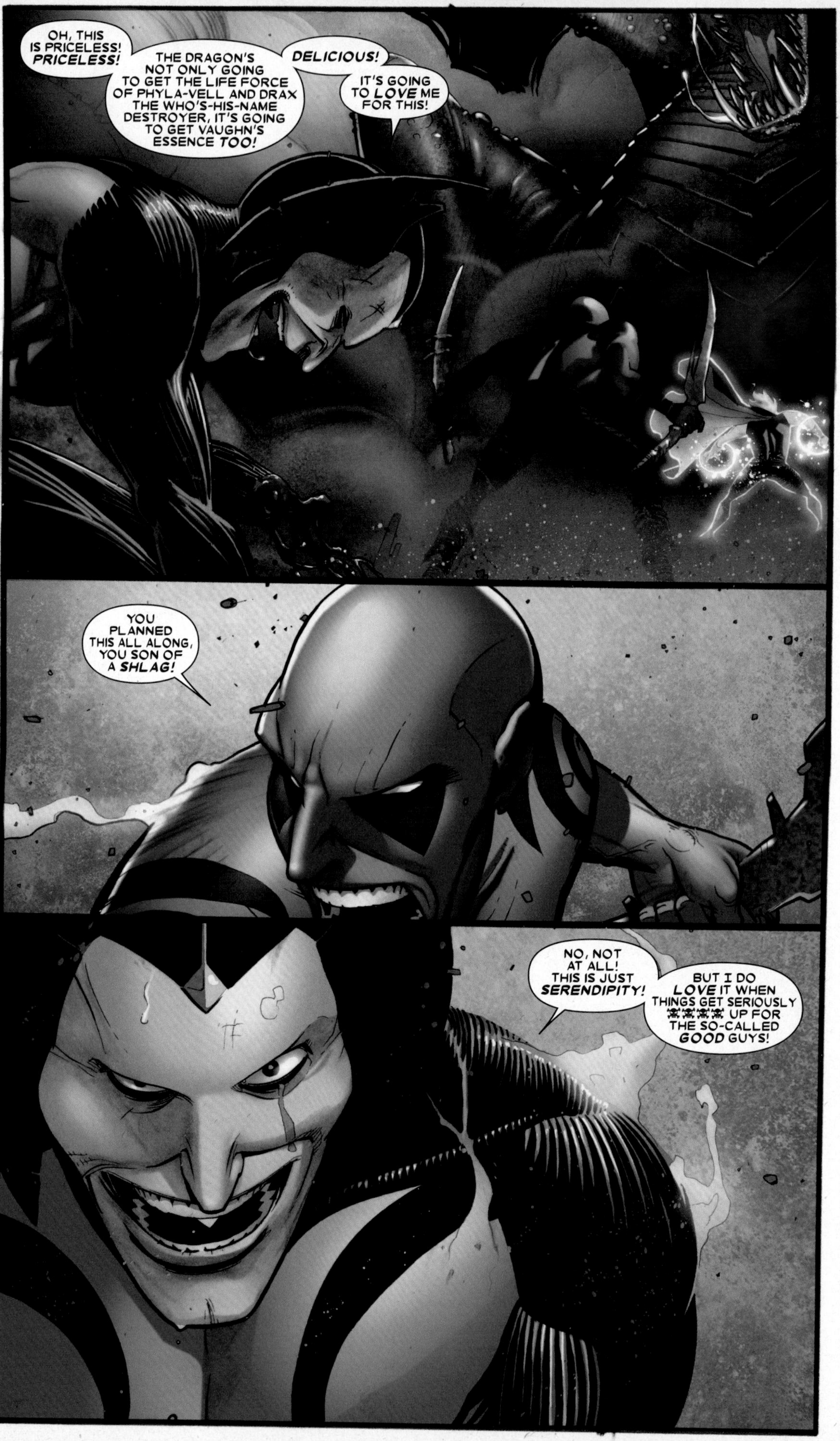
OH, THIS IS PRICELESS! *PRICELESS!*
THE DRAGON'S NOT ONLY GOING TO GET THE LIFE FORCE OF PHYLA-VELL AND DRAX THE WHO'S-HIS-NAME DESTROYER, IT'S GOING TO GET VAUGHN'S ESSENCE *TOO!*
DELICIOUS!
IT'S GOING TO *LOVE* ME FOR THIS!
YOU PLANNED THIS ALL ALONG, YOU SON OF A *SHLAG!*
NO, NOT AT ALL! THIS IS JUST *SERENDIPITY!*
BUT I DO *LOVE* IT WHEN THINGS GET SERIOUSLY ☠☠☠☠ UP FOR THE SO-CALLED *GOOD* GUYS!

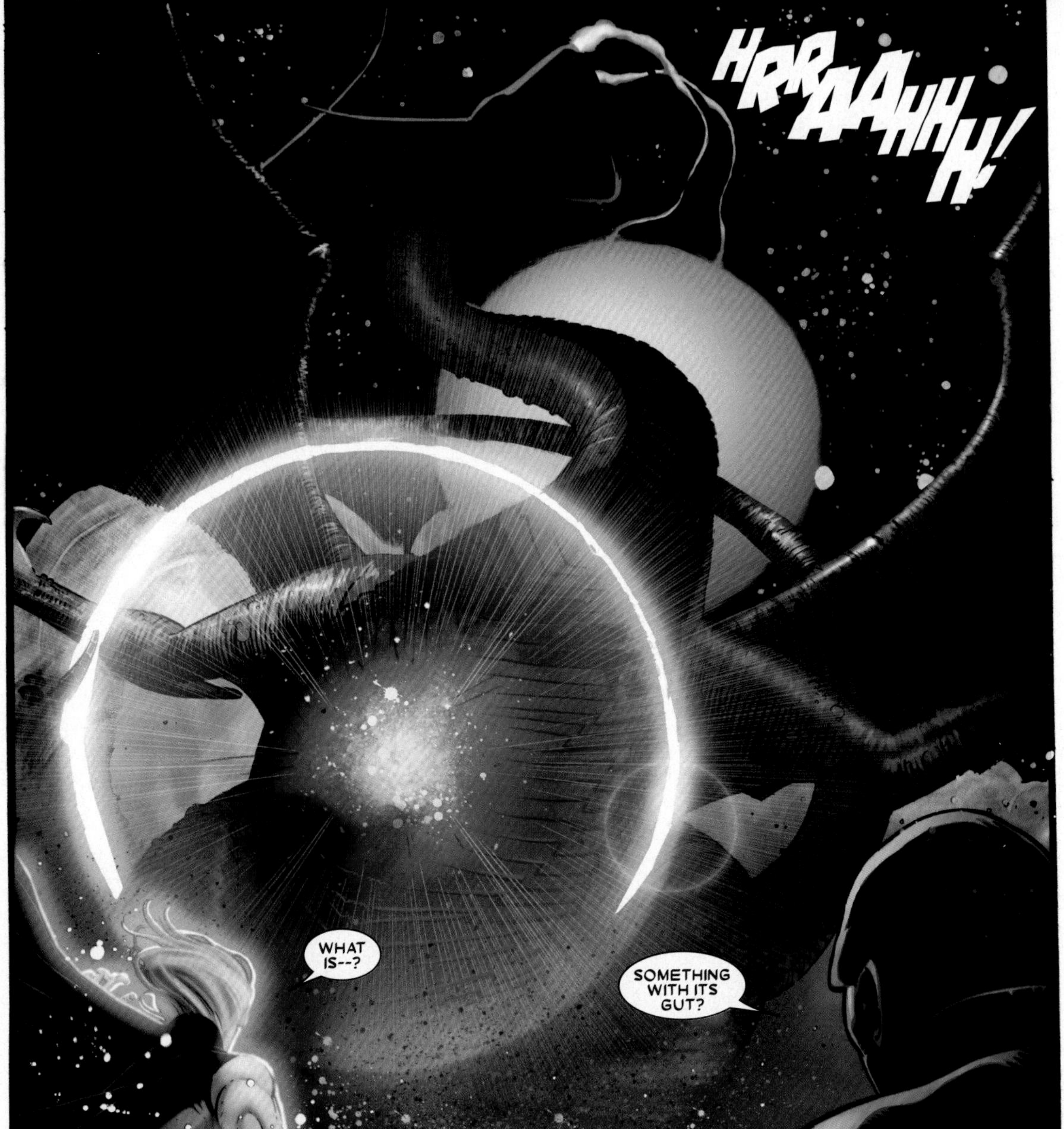
HRRAAHHH!
WHAT IS--?
SOMETHING WITH ITS GUT?
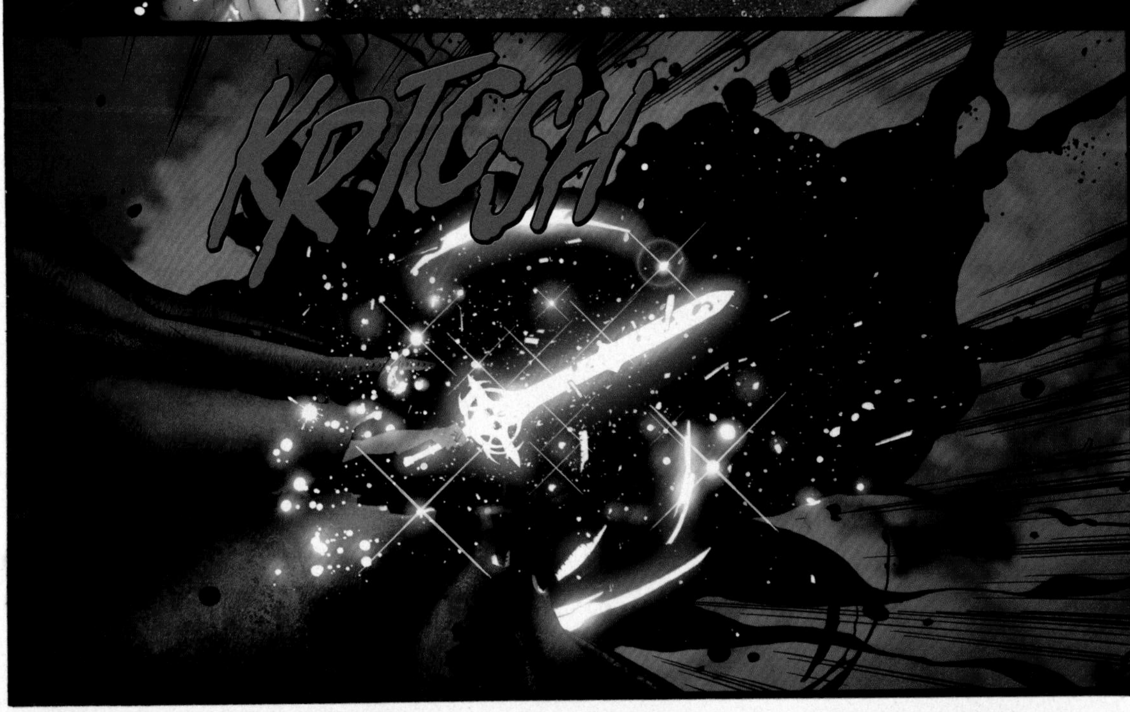
KRTCSH

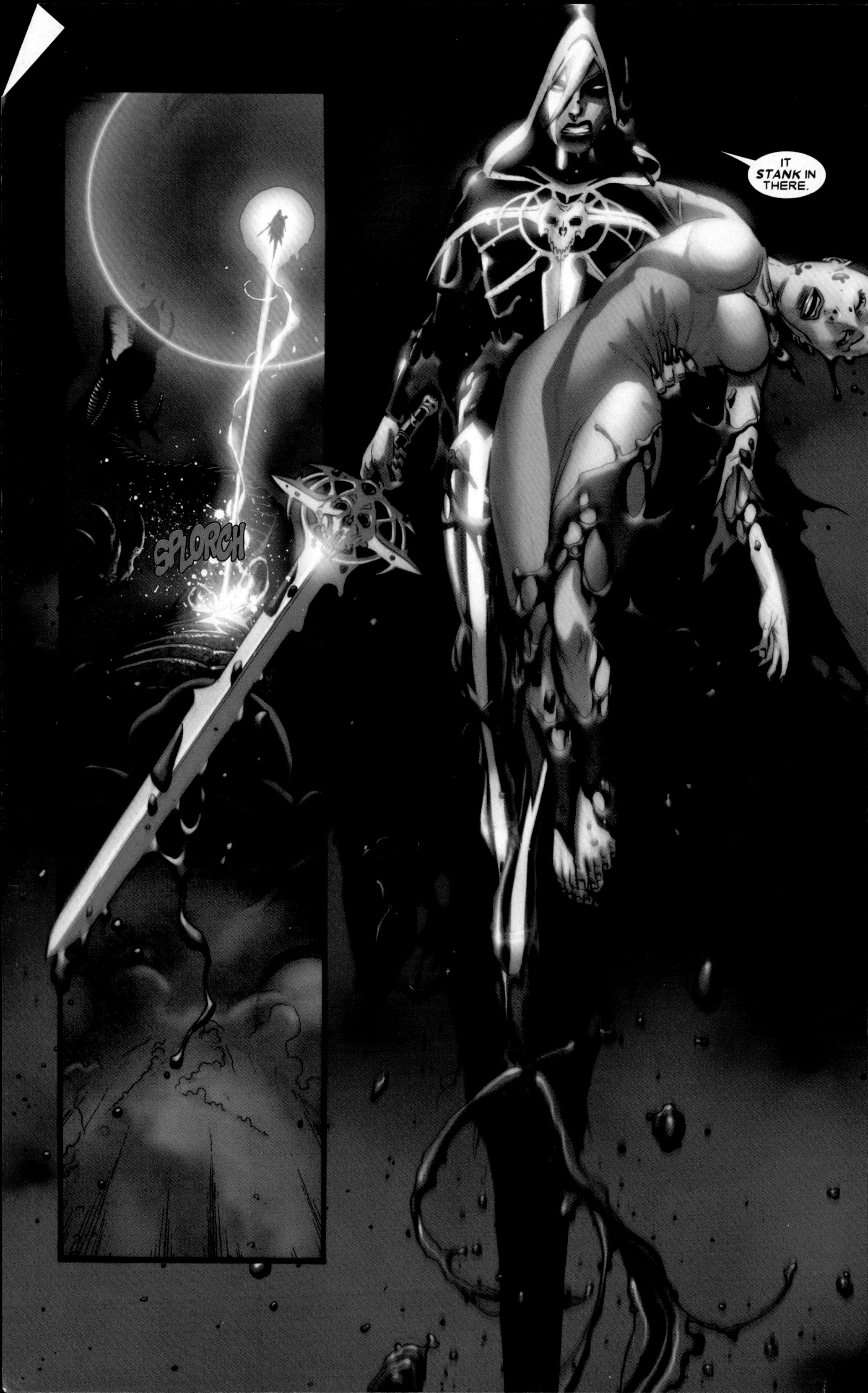
SPLORCH
IT STANK IN THERE.

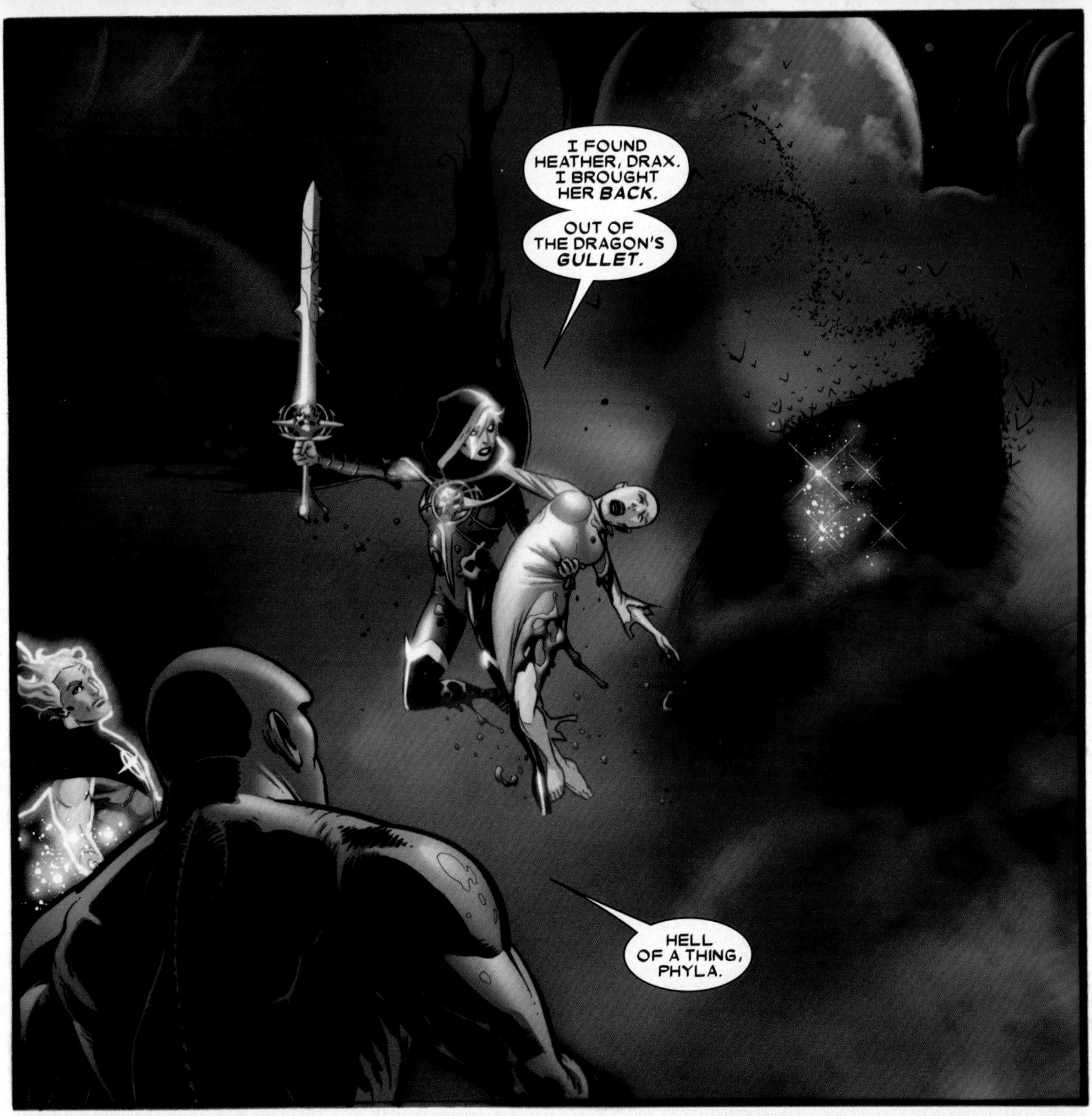
I FOUND HEATHER, DRAX. I BROUGHT HER BACK.
OUT OF THE DRAGON'S GULLET.
HELL OF A THING, PHYLA.

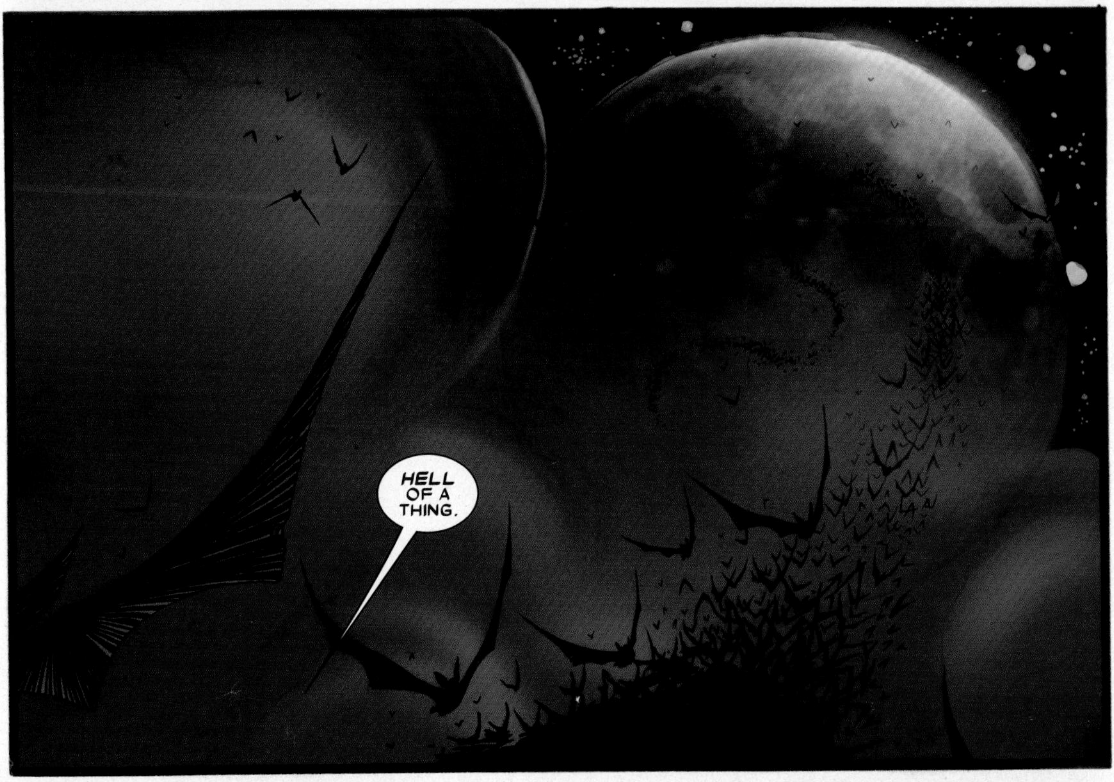
HELL OF A THING.

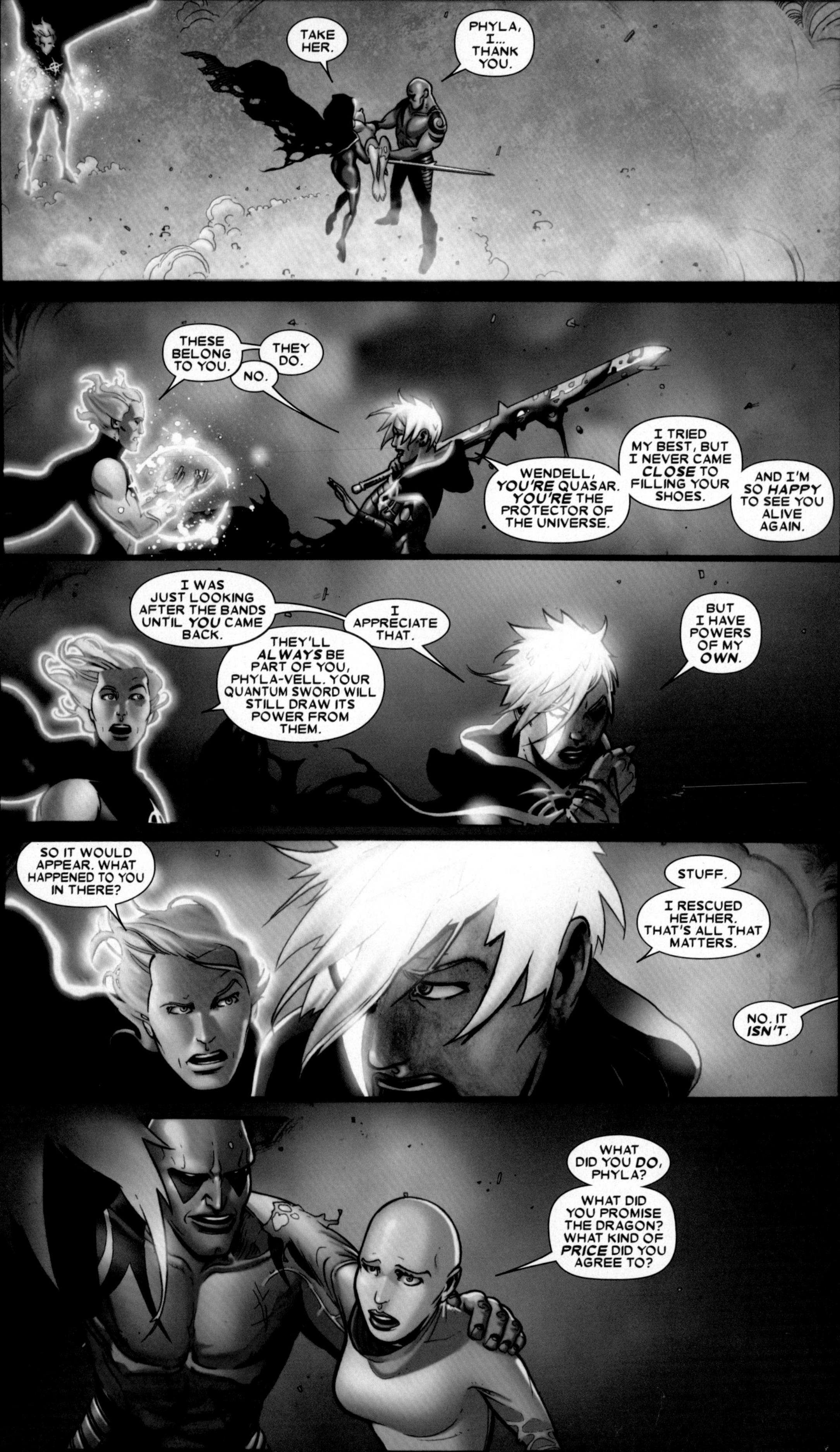
TAKE HER.
PHYLA, I... THANK YOU.
THESE BELONG TO YOU.
THEY DO.
NO.
WENDELL, YOU'RE QUASAR. YOU'RE THE PROTECTOR OF THE UNIVERSE.
I TRIED MY BEST, BUT I NEVER CAME CLOSE TO FILLING YOUR SHOES.
AND I'M SO HAPPY TO SEE YOU ALIVE AGAIN.
I WAS JUST LOOKING AFTER THE BANDS UNTIL YOU CAME BACK.
I APPRECIATE THAT.
THEY'LL ALWAYS BE PART OF YOU, PHYLA-VELL. YOUR QUANTUM SWORD WILL STILL DRAW ITS POWER FROM THEM.
BUT I HAVE POWERS OF MY OWN.
SO IT WOULD APPEAR. WHAT HAPPENED TO YOU IN THERE?
STUFF.
I RESCUED HEATHER. THAT'S ALL THAT MATTERS.
NO. IT ISN'T.
WHAT DID YOU DO, PHYLA?
WHAT DID YOU PROMISE THE DRAGON? WHAT KIND OF PRICE DID YOU AGREE TO?

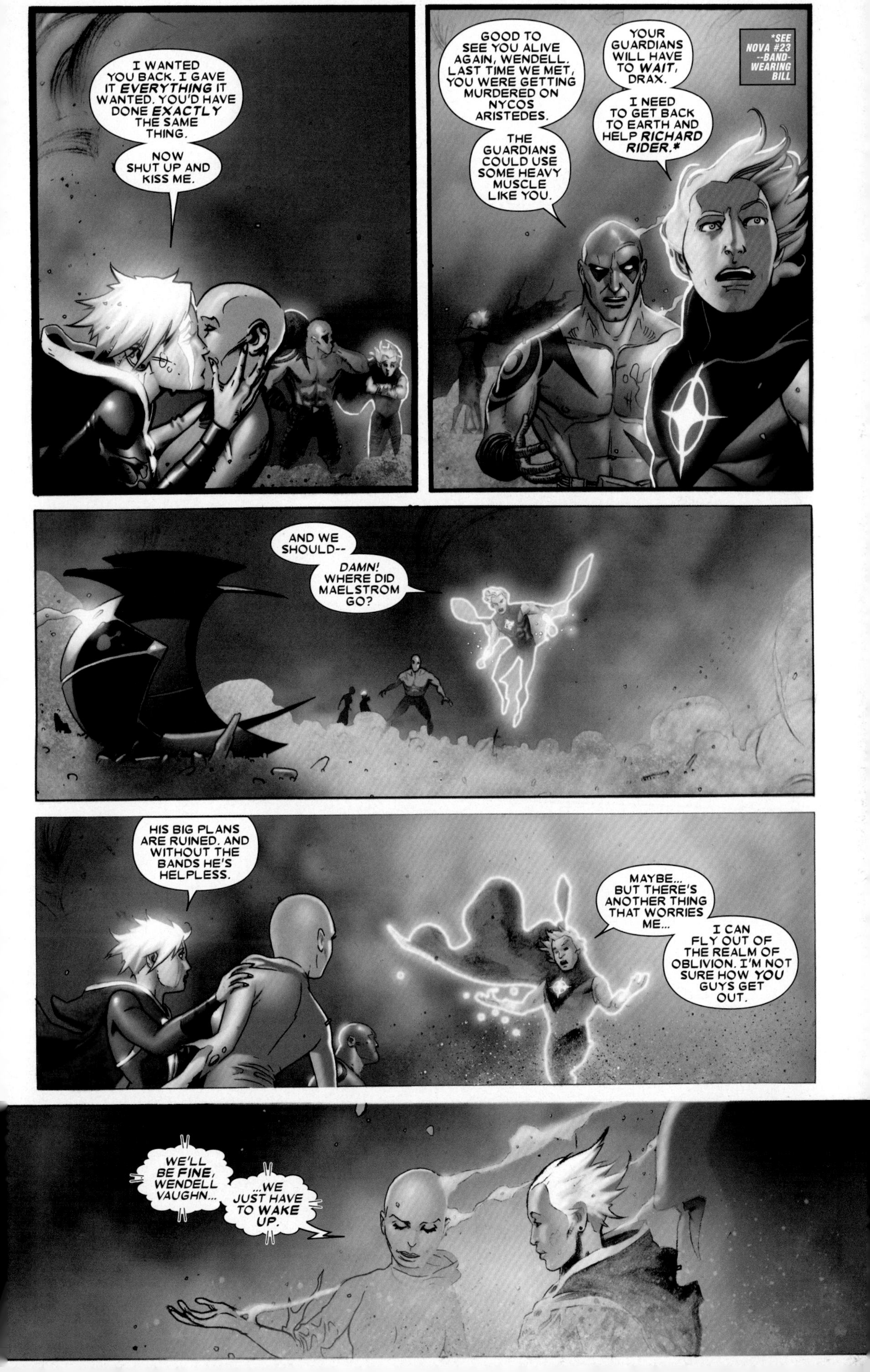
I WANTED YOU BACK. I GAVE IT EVERYTHING IT WANTED. YOU'D HAVE DONE EXACTLY THE SAME THING.
NOW SHUT UP AND KISS ME.
GOOD TO SEE YOU ALIVE AGAIN, WENDELL. LAST TIME WE MET, YOU WERE GETTING MURDERED ON NYCOS ARISTEDES.
THE GUARDIANS COULD USE SOME HEAVY MUSCLE LIKE YOU.
YOUR GUARDIANS WILL HAVE TO WAIT, DRAX.
I NEED TO GET BACK TO EARTH AND HELP RICHARD RIDER.*
*SEE NOVA #23 --BAND-WEARING BILL
AND WE SHOULD--
DAMN! WHERE DID MAELSTROM GO?
HIS BIG PLANS ARE RUINED. AND WITHOUT THE BANDS HE'S HELPLESS.
MAYBE... BUT THERE'S ANOTHER THING THAT WORRIES ME...
I CAN FLY OUT OF THE REALM OF OBLIVION. I'M NOT SURE HOW YOU GUYS GET OUT.
WE'LL BE FINE, WENDELL VAUGHN...
...WE JUST HAVE TO WAKE UP.

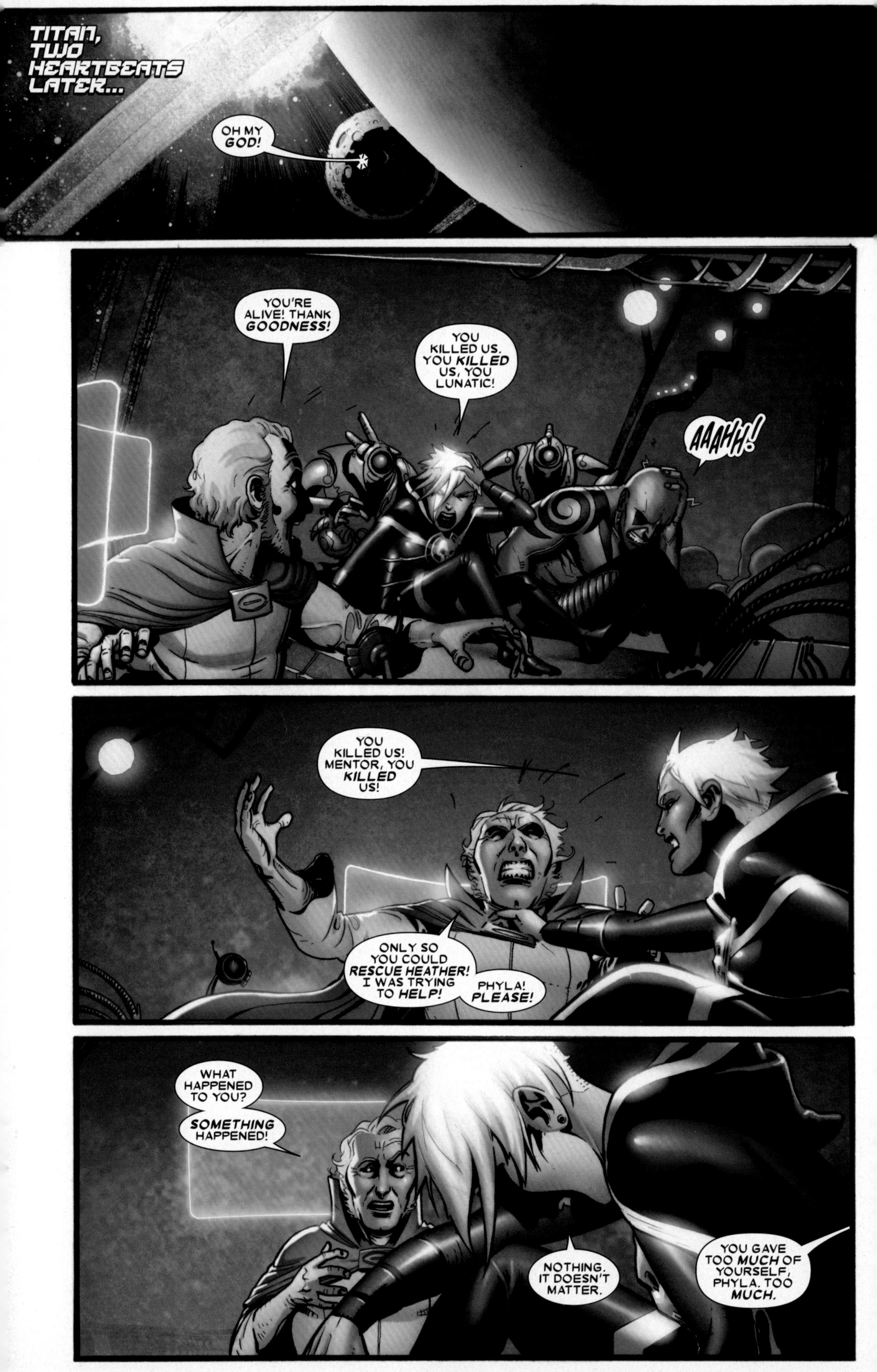
TITAN, TWO HEARTBEATS LATER...
OH MY GOD!
YOU'RE ALIVE! THANK GOODNESS!
YOU KILLED US. YOU KILLED US, YOU LUNATIC!
AAAHH!
YOU KILLED US! MENTOR, YOU KILLED US!
ONLY SO YOU COULD RESCUE HEATHER! I WAS TRYING TO HELP!
PHYLA! PLEASE!
WHAT HAPPENED TO YOU?
SOMETHING HAPPENED!
NOTHING. IT DOESN'T MATTER.
YOU GAVE TOO MUCH OF YOURSELF, PHYLA. TOO MUCH.

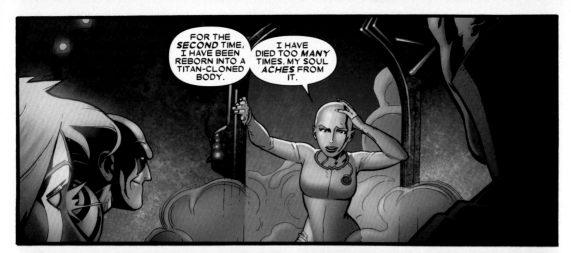

FOR THE *SECOND* TIME, I HAVE BEEN REBORN INTO A *TITAN-CLONED* BODY.

I HAVE DIED TOO *MANY* TIMES. MY SOUL *ACHES* FROM IT.

FATHER. YOU CAME FOR ME.

YOU'RE *MY* KID. WHAT *ELSE* WOULD I DO?

MENTOR.

I LOVE YOU, PHYLA-VELL.

AND I LOVE *YOU,* HEATHER DOUGLAS.

I'VE *MISSED* YOU.

I KNOW.

BUT WHAT DID YOU DO, PHYLA? WHAT DID YOU DO?

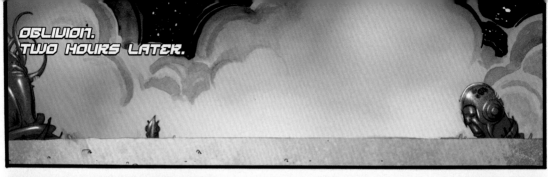

OBLIVION.
TWO HOURS LATER.

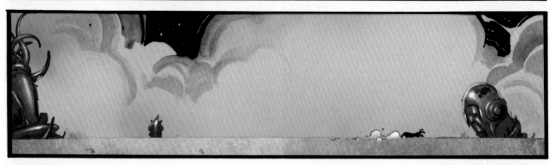

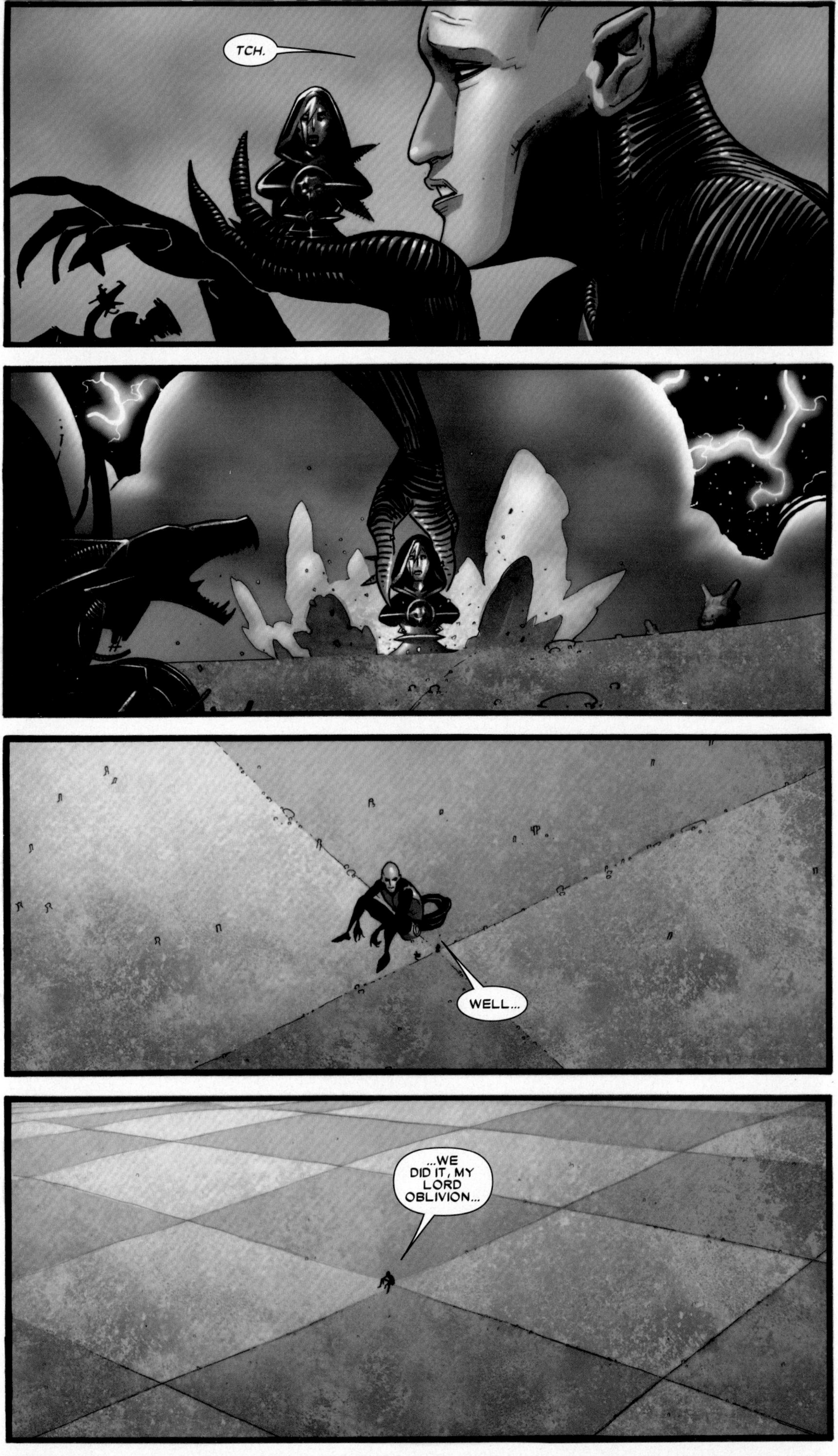
TCH.
WELL...
...WE DID IT, MY LORD OBLIVION...

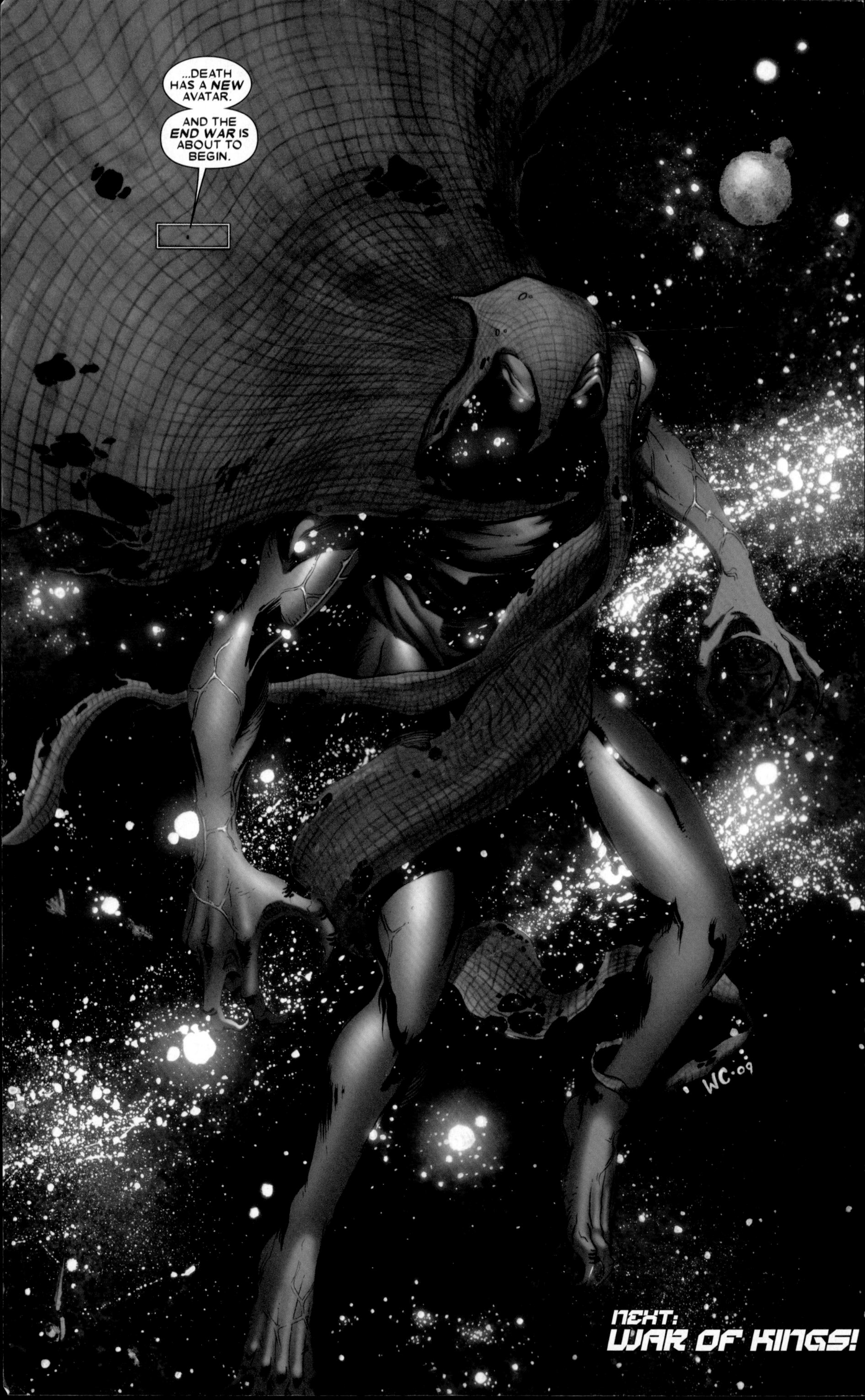
...DEATH HAS A NEW AVATAR.
AND THE END WAR IS ABOUT TO BEGIN.
WC·09
NEXT: WAR OF KINGS!

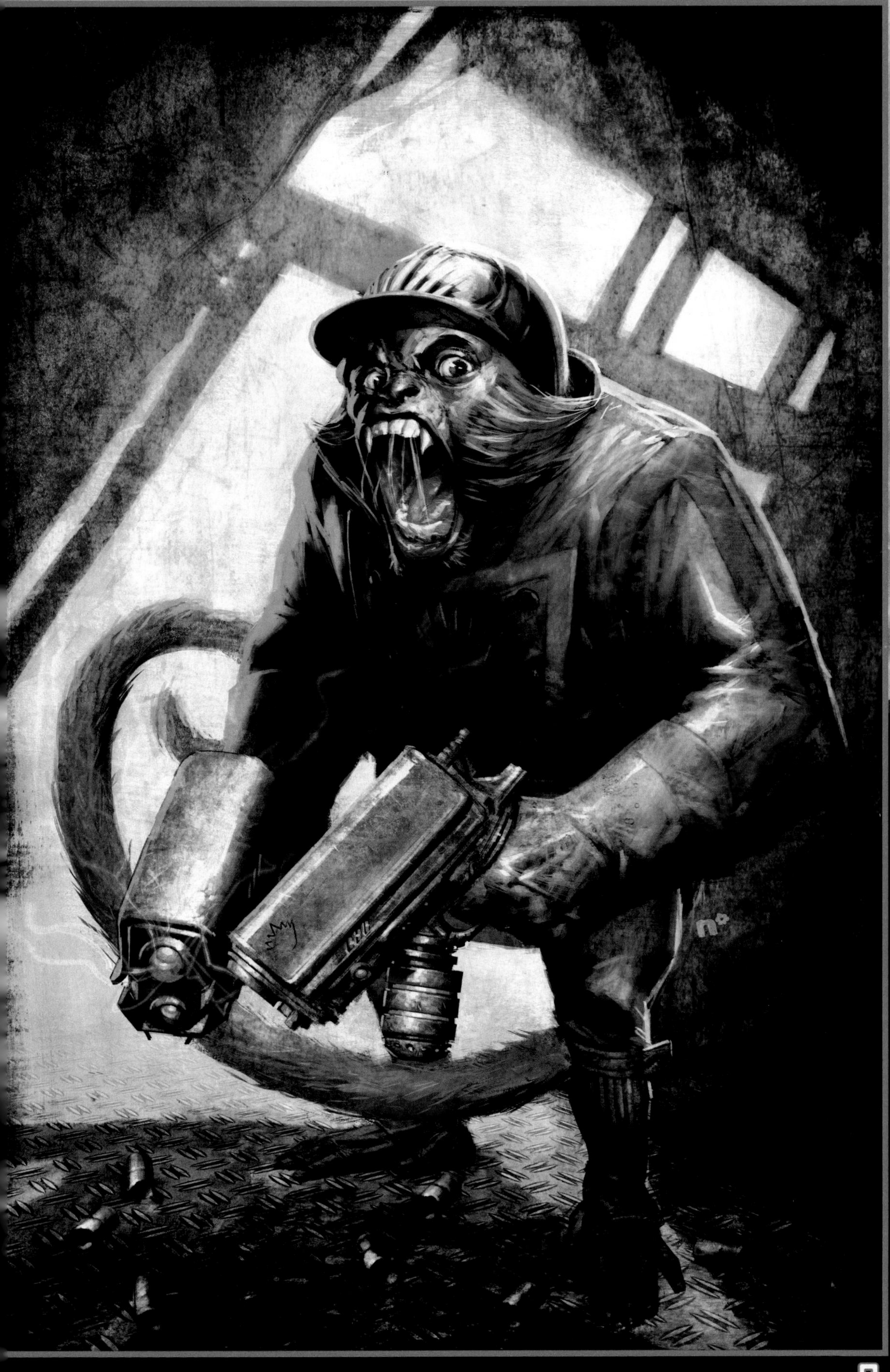

APES VARIANT BY NIC KLEIN 5

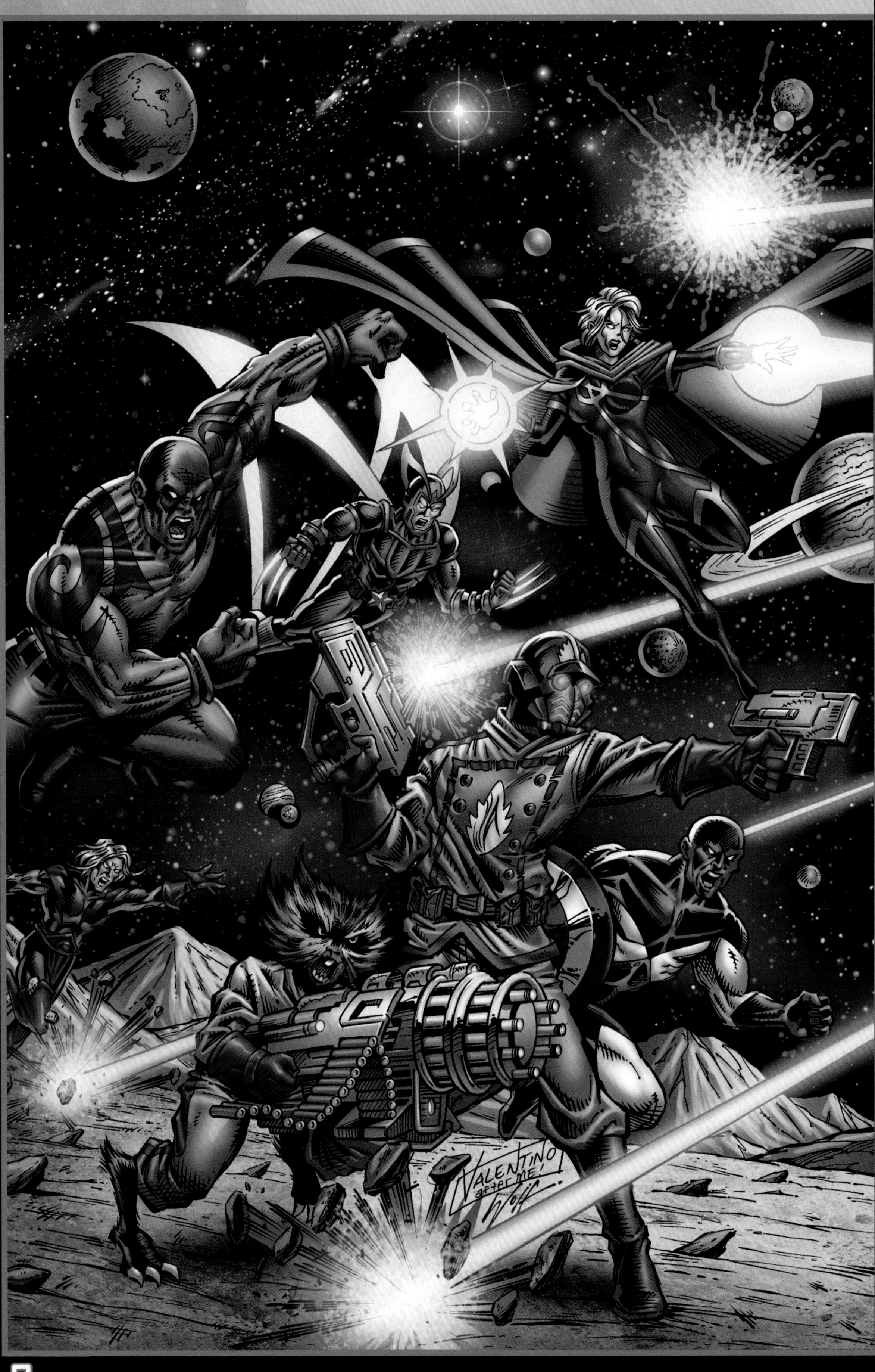
VALENTINO

7 VARIANT BY JIM VALENTINO & CHANCE WOLF

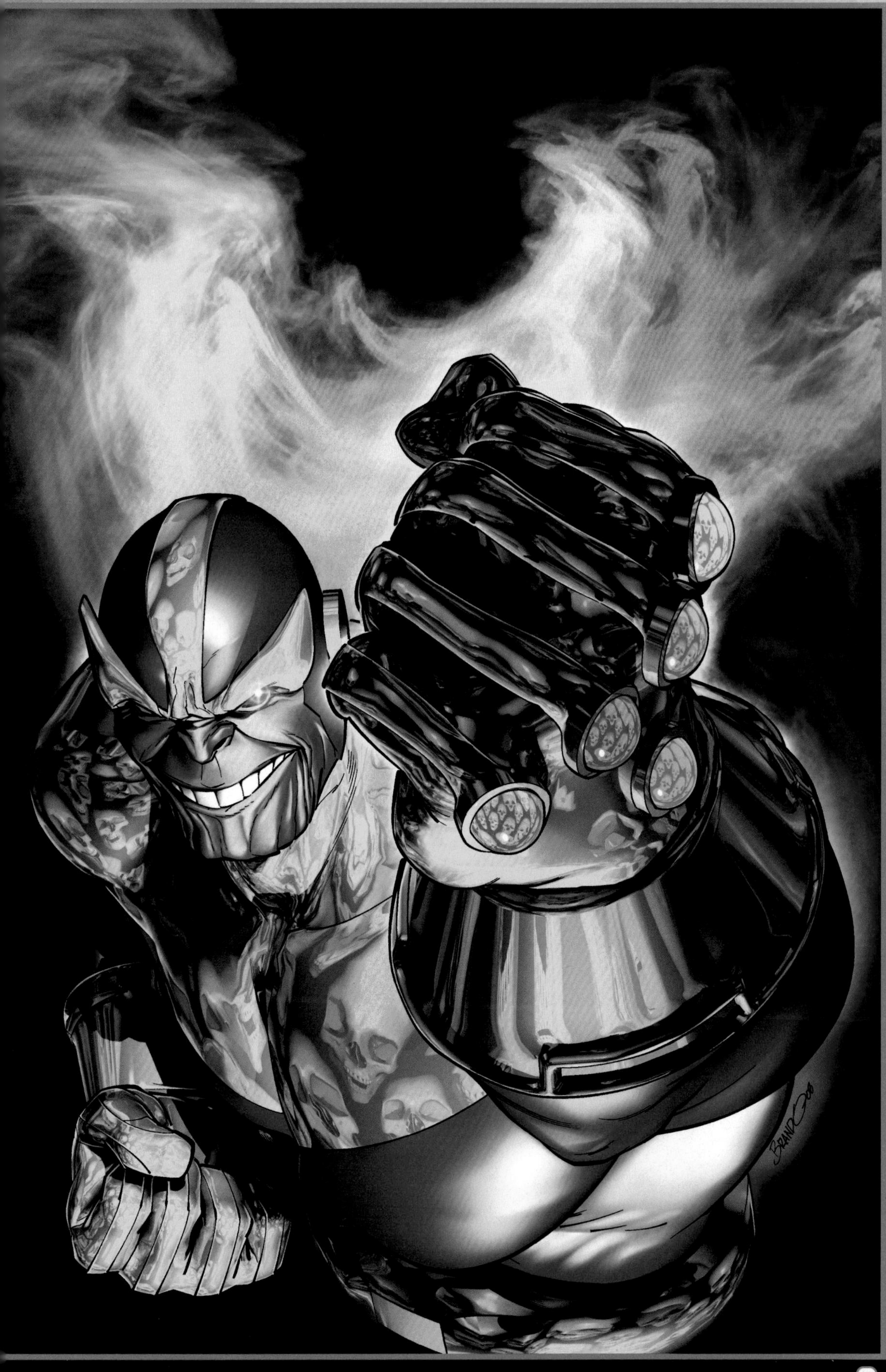

VARIANT BY BRANDON PETERSON 8

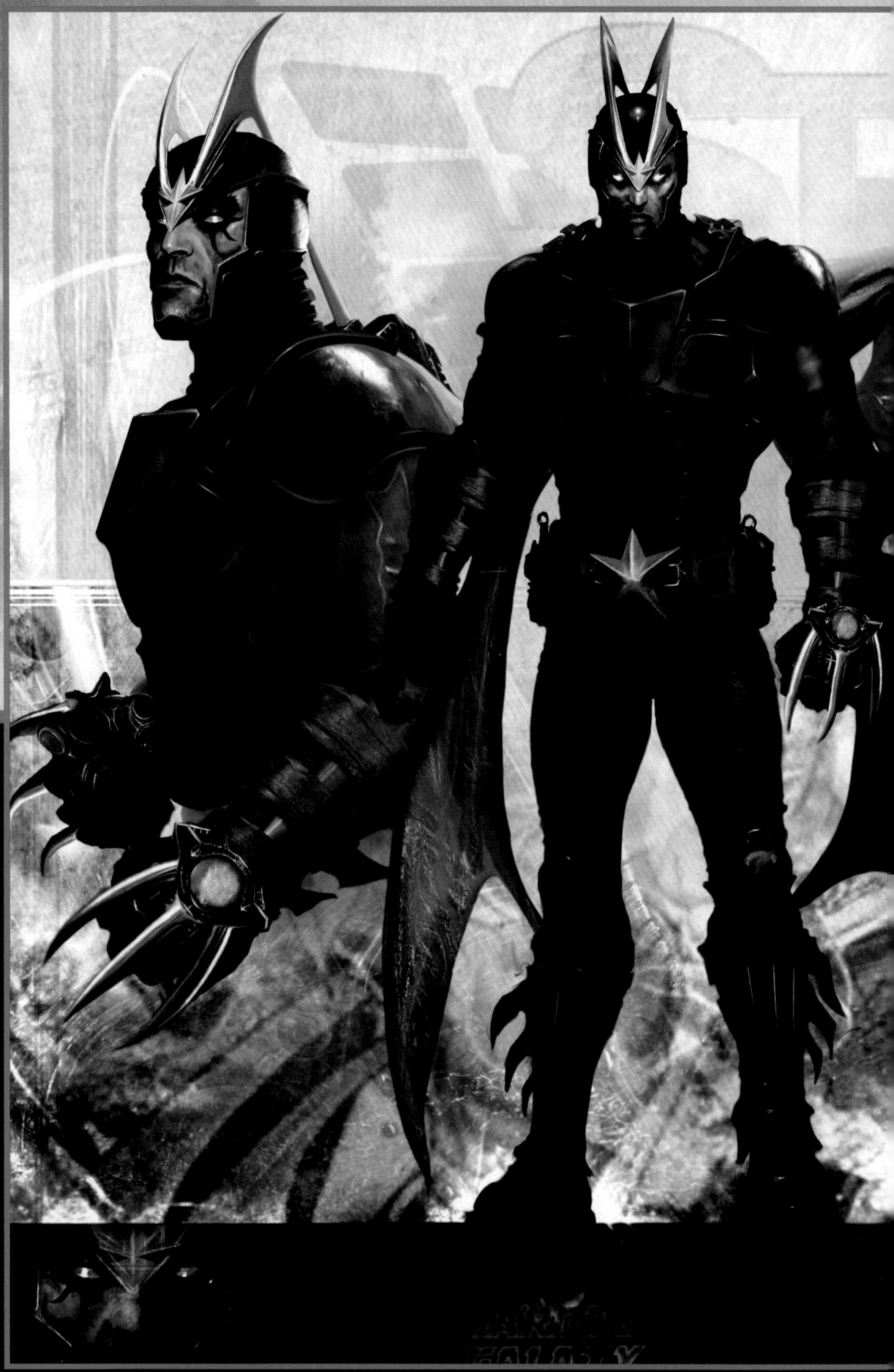

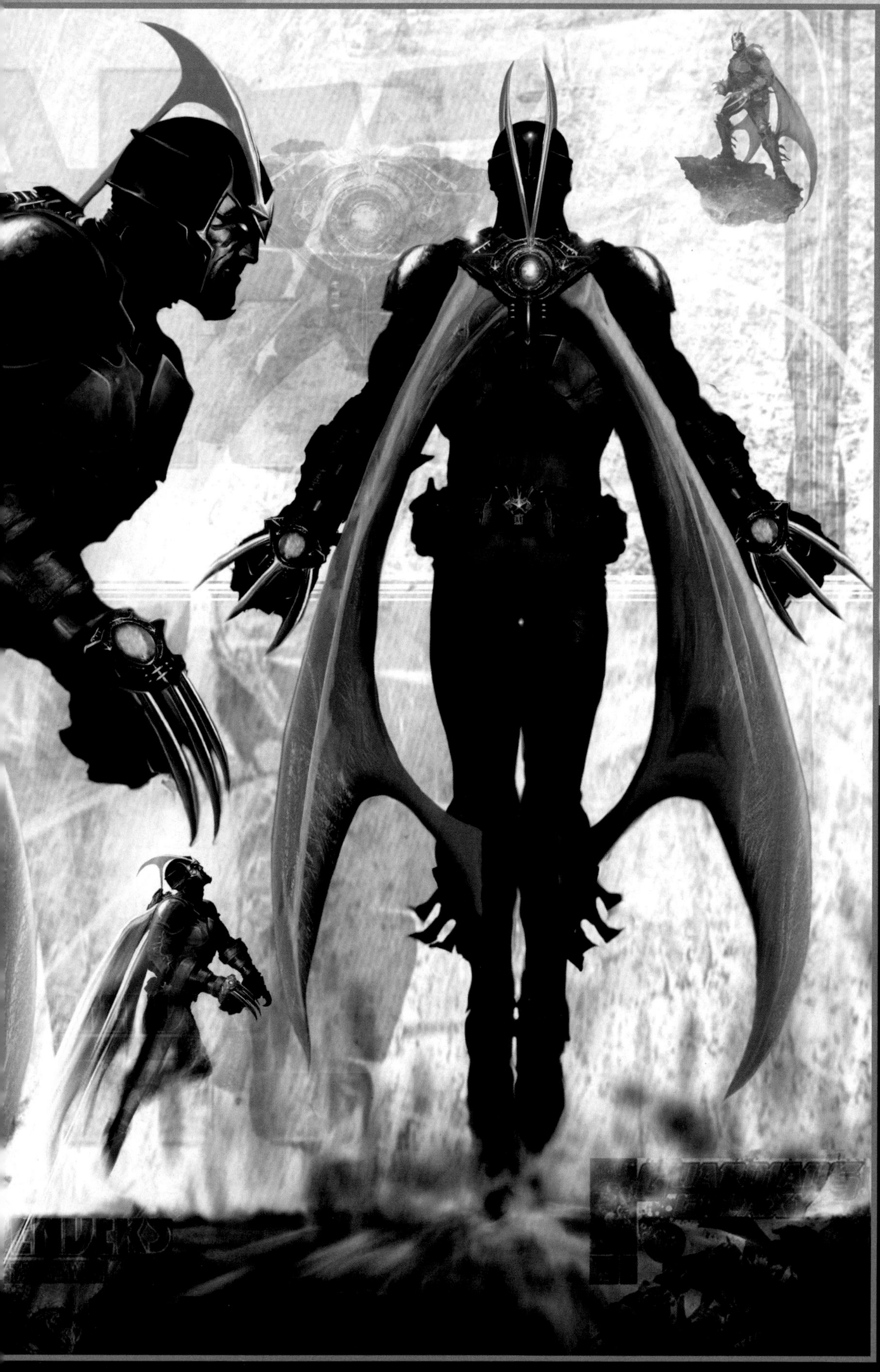

STARHAWK CONCEPT ART BY CLINT LANGLEY

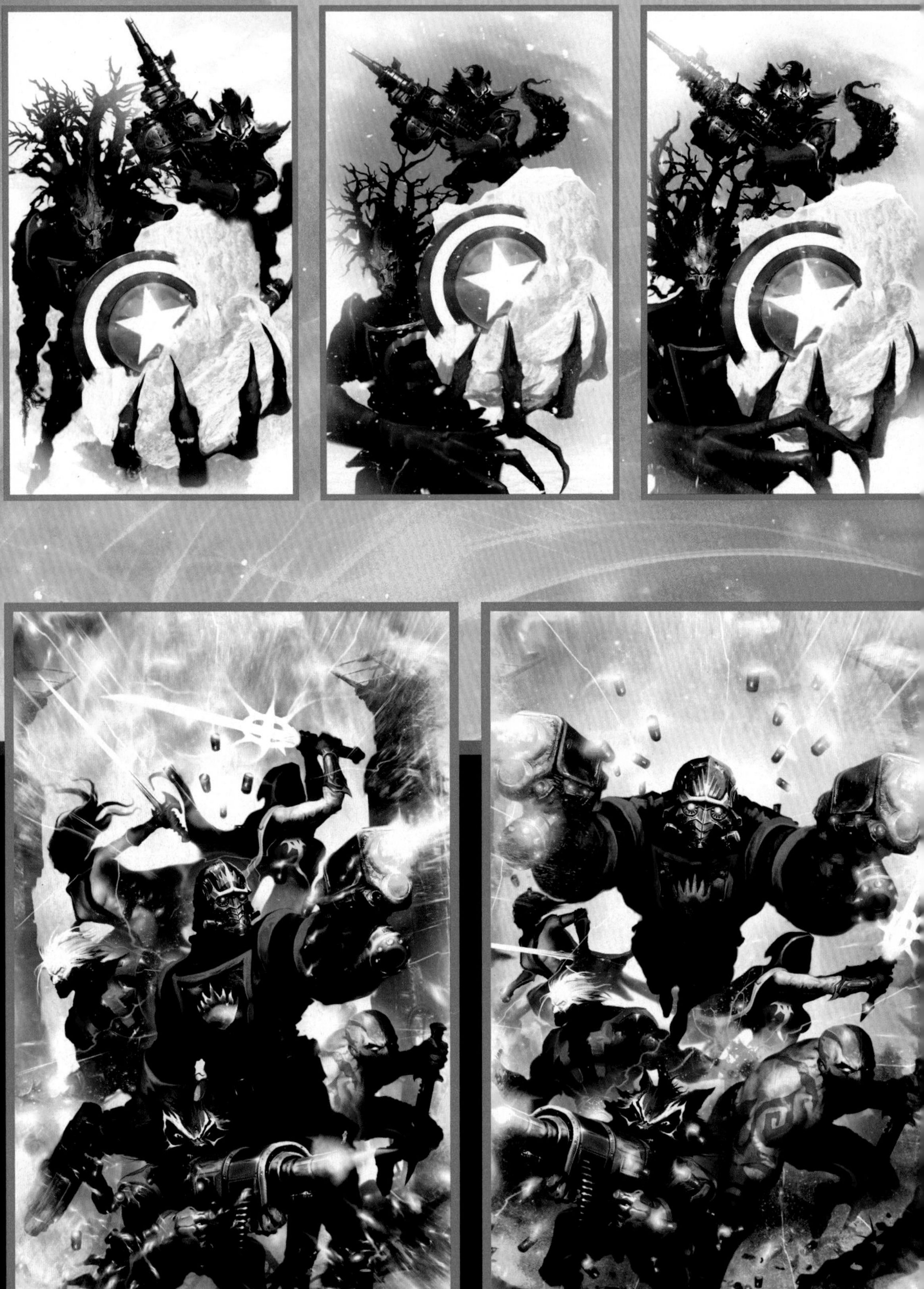

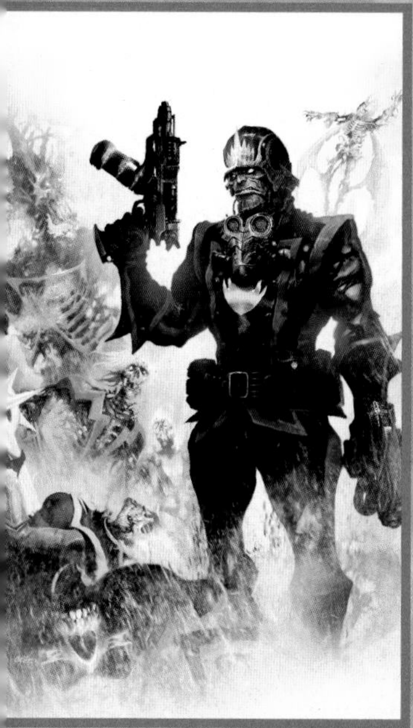

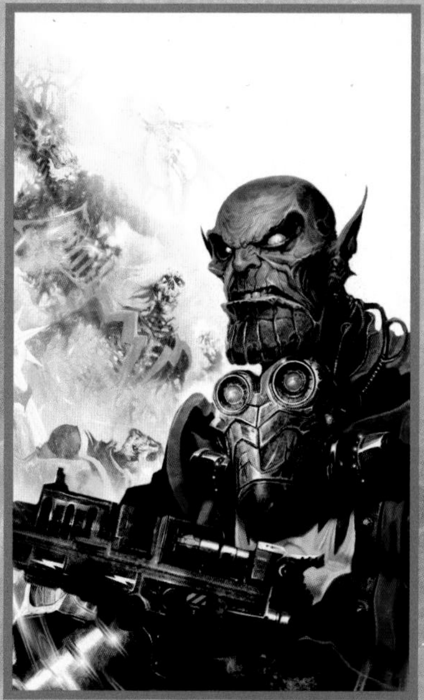

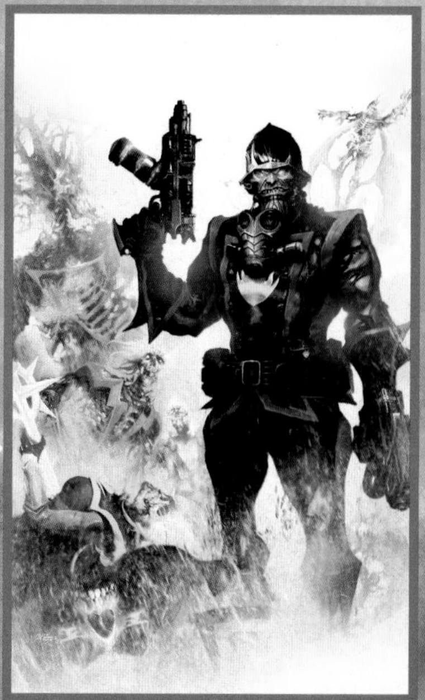

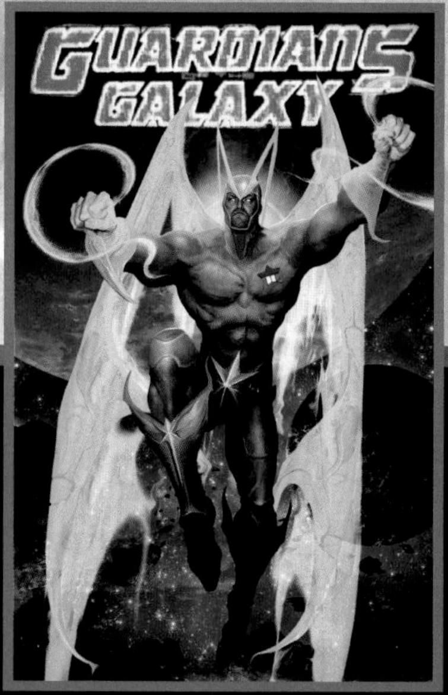
GUARDIANS
GALAXY

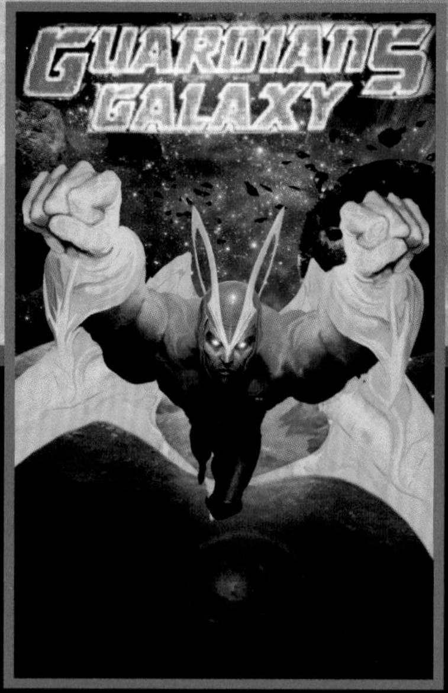
GUARDIANS
GALAXY

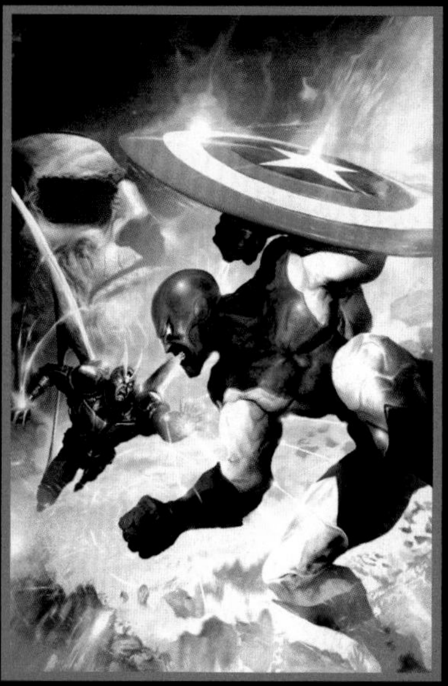

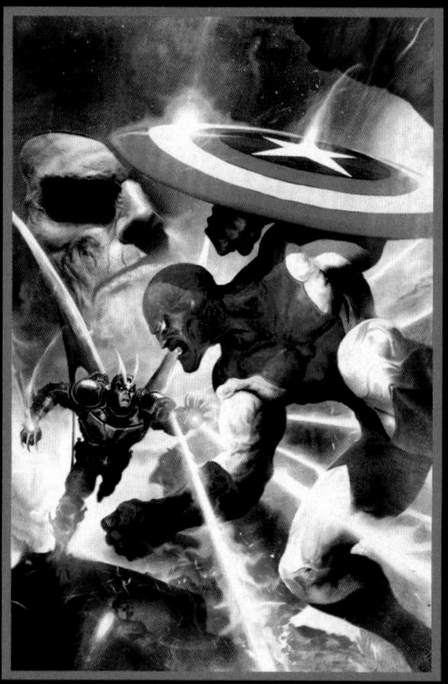

UNUSED COVER OPTIONS BY CLINT LANGLEY

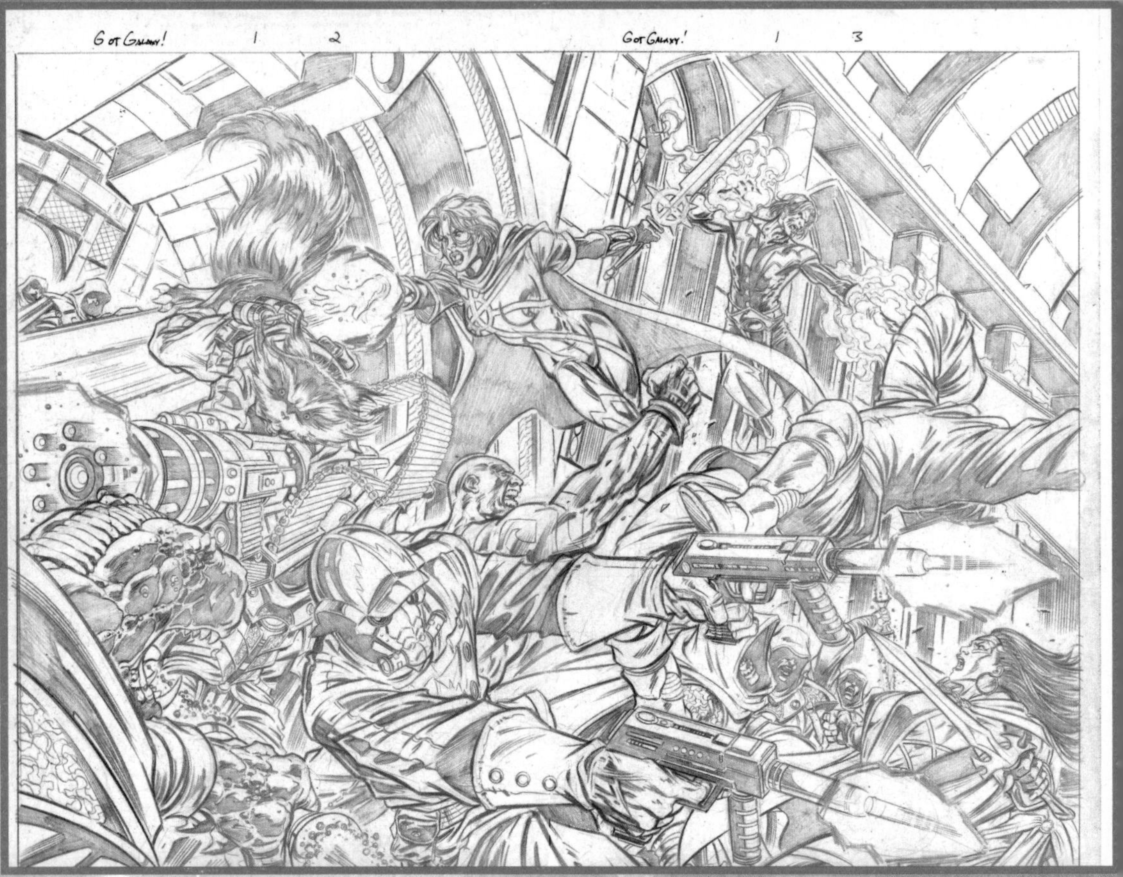

Got Galaxy! 1 2
Got Galaxy! 1 3

ISSUE #1, PAGES 2-3 PENCILS BY PAUL PELLETIER

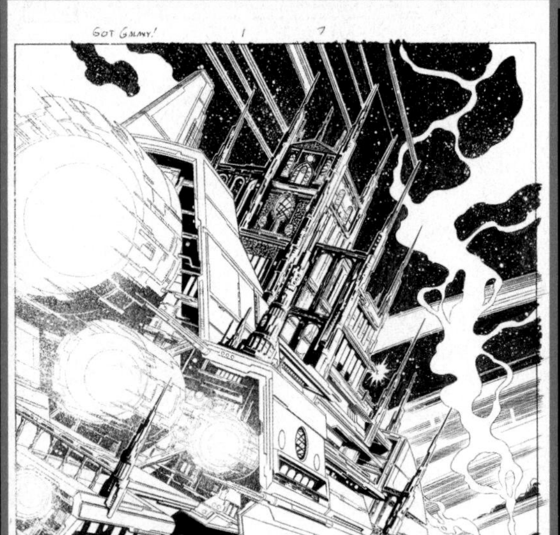

Got Galaxy! 1 7

ISSUE #1, PAGE 7 ART BY PAUL PELLETIER & RICK MAGYAR

IMAGES COURTESY OF HERITAGEAUCTIONS.COM